Abstracts of

Karl Rahner's

Theological Investigations 1–23

by

Daniel T. Pekarske, SDS

MARQUETTE
UNIVERSITY

PRESS

Marquette Studies in Theology
No. 31
Andrew Tallon, Series Editor

Library of Congress Cataloging-in-Publication Data

Pekarske, Daniel T.
  Abstracts of Karl Rahner's Theological investigations 1-23 / by Daniel
Thomas Pekarske.
      p. cm. — (Marquette studies in theology ; no. 31)
  Includes bibliographical references and index.
    ISBN 0-87462-683-8 (pbk. : alk. paper)
    1. Rahner, Karl, 1904- Schriften zur Theologie. 2. Catholic
Church—Doctrines. 3. Theology, Doctrinal. I. Title. II. Marquette
studies in theology ; #31.
    BX1751.3.R347P47 2003
    230'.2—dc21
                                            2002154292

© Marquette University Press 2002

Association of American
University Presses

MARQUETTE UNIVERSITY PRESS
MILWAUKEE

The Association of Jesuit University Presses

Contents

Abstracts of Karl Rahner's
Theological Investigations
Volumes 1–23

Daniel T. Pekarske, SDS

Introduction

Whenever my efforts to explain this unusual project succeeded, I would invariably hear, "Oh I get it. You're writing Cliffs Notes for Karl Rahner!" I'm sure the writers of Cliffs Notes would say the same thing about their work as I do about mine. It is not intended to substitute for reading Rahner's *Theological Investigations.* On the contrary I sincerely hope this reference book will open his treasure trove of essays both to the scholar as well as to other serious readers of theology.

Everyone familiar with Rahner's great 23-volume *Theological Investigations* knows the series is hard to use because it lacks a key. The titles often fail to describe the contents of the essays accurately; there is no cumulative index in English; the existing indices at the end of each volume are tedious and failed to distinguish significant discussions of a topic from casual references; and short of wading through an entire essay there is no way to know quickly whether it contains the material one is looking for. This book attempts to address these problems by providing:

- a common numbering system for the essays whose current English titles and original German titles are given;
- a bibliographical reference to the earliest appearance of the essay;
- a cumulative index of major topics;
- a cumulative index of subsidiary discussions;
- a very brief abstract of each essay;
- a precis of the entire essay.

A word about the abstracts, topics, subsidiary discussions, and precise. The **Abstract** is intended to convey the content of the essay in a nutshell. Wherever possible in less than four lines I attempt to identify the topic Rahner covers, the steps in which he addresses it, and his main conclusion/s.

Under the heading **Topics** one can find the main contents of any particular Investigation. These answer the question, What is this essay basically about? At the back of the book these topic headings are collected in the **Index of Topics**. This resource directs interested readers to all the Investigations which offer substantial treatments of those particular theological areas.

Subsidiary Discussions is a further refinement of Topics. Everyone passingly familiar with Rahner's style knows how often he sets the stage for discussing one topic by briefly surveying other topics which one might never connect with the title of the essay. At other times he simply digresses. Since even these seeming digressions often contain very insightful material this second sifting of topics is meant to insure they are not lost. When readers use the **Index of Subsidiary Discussions** at the end of the book in conjunction with the Index of Topics they can be confident of having been directed to all the salient material on any topic discussed at any length in Theological Investigations. Because blending the two indices presented more problems than it solved, they appear separately at the back of the book. The two indices are not cross referenced to one another. Hence, the user must consult both.

To further assist the reader I have followed closely the systems of headings and sub-headings found in the original texts. I have made no attempt to harmonize them.

The **Precis** comprises the longest section and is the most difficult element to describe adequately. In no way does it pretend to replace or even improve on Rahner's original essay. Brief as it is, it cannot hope to match the richness of his work. But it does have the dual advantages of brevity and clarity. These precis follow the twists and turns of Rahner's theological and philosophical arguments, reducing the intellectual terrain to simple lines in much the same way road maps simplify and reduce actual geography to a simple series of colored lines. The precis should clarify for serious researchers whether a particular essay will be useful. First-time readers armed with this book should keep from losing themselves in the thickets of Rahner's prose.

As much as possible I have attempted to avoid commentary, both because the book is already very long and also because the reader is justifiably more interested in what Rahner says than in what I think about what Rahner says. The few critical comments I do make appear in brackets [ ].

The only other evaluative material is the very unscientific rating system I use to indicate each essay's **Level of Difficulty.** This number is found at the head of each article just below the Investigation number enclosed in braces{ }. An essay rated 0.5, the lowest score, could be read and completely comprehended by any intelligent reader with no specialized training in theology or philosophy. An essay rated 4—the highest score—can present challenges even to a theological expert either because of the content of the essay or because of difficulties with Rahner's style.

I wish to thank Dr. Robert Masson of Marquette University for introducing me to the work of Karl Rahner, and for his encouragement over the almost fifteen-year gestation of this project. I am also grateful to my religious community, the Society of the Divine Savior, for affording me a sabbatical to complete the manuscript; and to my dear friends, the Benedictine Sisters at the Monastery of St. Gertrude in Cottonwood, Idaho, for sheltering, sustaining, and suffering me while I wrote.

Dr. Daniel T. Pekarske, SDS
July, 2002

I. God, Christ, Mary, and Grace
I. *Gott, Christus, Maria, Gnade*

German edition: Einsiedeln, Benziger, 1954
U.S. edition: Baltimore, MD, Helicon Press, 1961
Cornelius Ernst, O.P., translator

1.01 The Prospects for Dogmatic Theology

Über den Versuch eines Aufrisses einer Dogmatik (includes 1.02)
{2.0} Previously unpublished.
Abstract: This schema (cf., 1.02) attempts to revivify theology by rehabilitating dogmatic theology within textbook, moral, and historical theology.
Topics: THEOLOGY, dogmatic.
Subsidiary Discussions: Theology, textbook (2ff); Faith, deposit of (3ff); Sin, mortal/venial (5); Dogma, history of (7ff); Dogma, special questions in (10ff); Theology, moral (16f); Theology, fundamental (17f).
Precis: Rahner finds the first fifty years of twentieth century theology (textbook, history of dogma, and specialized topics) sorely wanting. Textbooks are mechanically repetitive; historical treatments are not forward-looking; specialized studies lack scope and courage. No appeal to the immutability of the deposit of faith can justify stagnant textbook theology since current textbooks contain even less material than classic Thomistic texts, and have not yet responded to the flowering of biblical studies. In addition, every age needs to appropriate for itself the truths of the past by creating new technical terminology which is missing today (e.g., the treatment of mortal/venial sin, angels, etc.). Textbooks today not only fail to proclaim and witness the truth to a new age they even fail to preserve the treasures of the past in their purity.

Historical dogmatic treatments because either they fail to treat relevant themes or lack the courage to extend their insights to present circumstances, remain largely insignificant. Studies of specialized topics (e.g., Mariology) remain largely peripheral leaving the impression dogmatic theology is substantially complete except for a few edifying details. Arguing to the contrary Rahner lists large areas of theology in desperate need of study: christology, theology of death, of heaven, of eschatology, of time and history. Rahner suggests possible reasons why certain subjects are developed and others languish (13).

A common feature of the three divisions of theology analyzed here is its orthodoxy. However, this orthodoxy is achieved at the expense of vitality. Scientific theology must devote itself "to the reality in question with that passionate sympathy which this unique reality can demand more than any other, and without which it does not become truly accessible" (13f). He prescribes including more dogmatic theology in every area of theological study. His sketch of dogmatic theology (01.02) suggests how this might look.

Rahner's schema entails three major presuppositions which he discusses here: 1) Theology is always necessarily and validly a theology of essence and existence, i.e., it must simultaneously address the facts of salvation history and the intrinsic theoretical structures which connect them (logically or metaphysically) with general human experience and the history of the world. 2) Dogmatic theology must reassert its preeminence over moral theology in setting the authentic foundation of the Christian can, ought, and may. 3) *Theologia fundamentalis* must be recognized as an independent discipline even where this necessarily leads to some overlapping of individual themes, e.g., Eucharist.

1.02 A Scheme for a Treatise of Dogmatic Theology
Aufriss einer Dogmatik

{0.5 Previously unpublished. Appears in the German edition as one essay with 1.01, *Über den Versuch eines Aufrisses einer Dogmatik.*

Abstract: This schema of the whole of dogmatic theology provides a place for all particular questions in the field and provides a formal outline of Rahner's organizational categories.

Topics: THEOLOGY, dogmatic; THEOLOGY, formal; THEOLOGY, fundamental; THEOLOGY, special dogmatic.
Subsidiary Discussions: God "as ever greater" (19 ftn1); Mysticism (34 ftn2).

1.03 The Development of Dogma
Zur Frage der Dogmenentwicklung

{2.5} *Wissenschaft und Weltbild* 7 (1954) 1-14, 94-106.

Abstract: An analysis of propositional knowledge and apostolic succession argues that development of dogma is not a novelty. It is true and necessary. "New" doctrines are recognized by the church and held on divine authority.

Topics: DOGMA, development of; REVELATION; KNOWLEDGE, propositional.

Subsidiary Discussions: Spirit (41, 43, 50ff, 68f, 74); Church (45, 49ff, 59, 75ff); Jesus Christ (48ff, 65f); Scripture, inspiration (62f); Love (63f, 71f); Apostolic succession (66ff); Theological method (46, 74); Magisterium (42, 54, 61, 75).

Precis: Many Catholic doctrines have not always been present in the conscious faith of the church in an expressly apprehensible form. They have in a certain sense "developed." What are the meaning, possibilities, and limits of such development of dogma? (Bibliography, 39 ftn1.) These cannot be deduced but only discovered inductively from the actual facts of such development. Difficulty arises because the Spirit-directed development of dogma in the church is *sui generis* and any perfected law of development can only be known at the end of time. So how can one guard against the rankest enthusiasms? 1) Certain laws of development are known by the church a priori; 2) the more a doctrine develops the less room there is for new developments; 3) nothing can completely remove the risk. Only the promise of the Spirit keeps dogmatic development true.

What are some essential features of Catholic doctrinal development? Since revealed truth always remains true, complete historical relativism is false. Yet all human statements, even those relating divine truth, are finite but true adequations and as such surpassable. Any new formulation is not an empty curiosity. It can have an essential significance for us and our salvation because as historical beings we must continually translate salvific truth into the current categorial idiom. Failure either to preserve or to change leads to betraying the truth either by falling into error or by failing to appropriate the truth in a really existential way (45).

It first seems Rahner is talking about changes in theology rather than development within revealed faith. Rahner offers two reasons to maintain the latter: 1) the church understands its dogmatic statements as faith and not merely as theology; 2) the dogmatic word can only be understood broadly since developments are often not identical with previous statements (e.g., Trinity, 46). Thus, *quoad nos,* a development of dogma does in fact exist as shown in the actual practice of the church when it proclaims a new doctrine. Such development is necessary because of the very historicity of existence (47).

Rahner next considers the nature of development from the seemingly contrary proposition that revelation was closed with the death of the last apostle. Revelation is never simply the communication of propositions. It is an historical dialogue between us and God—a continuous "saving happening" that reaches its unsurpassable climax in Jesus Christ (49). In this sense it is closed: Jesus has forever answered the question of God's attitude toward us as being one of love. But it remains open in the sense that we now plumb the inexhaustible but concealed divine plentitude manifested in Christ. God is revealed to a believing church already in possession of the revealed reality.

Sure knowledge of dogma comes from hearing true propositions about the God who is present in the church and is yet to come. The Word and reflection on it are a reflection on propositions heard in living contact with the Word. This leads to new faith propositions and not just to new theology both in word and in reflection. Just as common experience yields more true knowledge than we can consciously express (knowledge which expands with reflection), so the work of the Spirit guides reflection on the truths and on the experience of God in faith to new dogmatic truths. The work of the Spirit is more than a negative promise to keep doctrine free from error. It develops and unfolds the original treasure of faith under a positive influence of the light of faith bestowed upon the church. The same is true for theological knowledge (55).

How does logic further or limit the development of doctrine? Though doctrine can develop with stringent logic this is not necessary. Logic can also simply yield proximate reasons (*convenientia*). In any case true development does not rest on logic but on the faith of the church proper (not on theologians) which sometimes anticipates or outstrips the logic of theologians.

How are new formulations "contained" in earlier dogmatic propositions since revelation closed with the death of the apostles? After a summary (56), Rahner argues that old and new knowledge must be connected. Formerly theologians spoke of explicating implicit cognition (70 ftn2). What is the nature of this explication? Traditionally theologians began with the revealed proposition from which they drew consequences, much as a mathematician does. This led to one thought that previously existed in one proposition being truly expressed in two. Alongside this was the theory that explication made explicit what was "virtually implicit" in a proposition.

But can knowledge arrived at by deduction properly be said to be revealed by God and thus be believed on the authority of God, or does it yield ecclesial faith believed on the authority of the church (59)? Rahner holds the former. In any case it is quite difficult to distinguish between formally and explicitly implicit explanations. But arguing from their existence to their possibility Rahner maintains the legitimacy of the latter. These can bear divine revelation held on God's authority because God can speak in such a way that elements which are only implicitly deducible by us are already consequences intended by God. This insight is not a *carte blanche* for canonizing every possible deduction because: 1) not every proposition is actually connected to the original revealed proposition; 2) any connection worthy of belief needs church approval; 3) God already knows what implications will be explicated. One might object that since inspiration in scripture does not extend to the propositions themselves it would be illegitimate to believe propositions developed from them on the authority of God (62). Rahner counters that

since the object of the written propositions is the oral preaching of the
apostles, they can quite legitimately contain an excess of what the writers
themselves had explicitly appropriated and set out in propositional form
(summary, 63).
  Rahner refutes the idea dogmatic explication always starts with propositions. He links doctrinal development to an analogous kind of knowledge
in the natural order (e.g., the experience of love) wherein reflecting on
oneself in propositions is part of one's progressive self-realization of love
itself. Such "original, non-propositional, unreflexive yet conscious possession of a reality on the one hand, and reflexive (propositional), articulated
consciousness of this original consciousness on the other—these are not
competing opposites but reciprocally interacting factors of a single experience necessarily unfolding in historical succession" (64f).
  In the case of the apostles themselves the original revelation, the global
experience behind the propositions they preached and wrote about, was
Christ—the living link between God and the world. Doctrinal explications
are based on this relationship with Christ and not simply on logical
deduction. Such new, developed propositions are both more and less than
their implicit source. More because they formulate a true dimension of the
original experience, less because they never capture the whole. (Generally
greater reflexive articulation of a spiritual possession is gained at the expense
of an unhampered (naive) connection with the reality given in faith. In any
case we must deal with the consciousness of our age. Any desire to return to
the times and mind set of the apostles is romantic nonsense.)
  Some object that the apostles are an exceptional case whose experience
cannot be applied to the way we explain doctrine. This leaves us with only
the tools of logical deduction. Rahner counters that in fact what the apostles
bequeath us (*successio apostolica*) is not a set of propositions "but their Spirit,
the Holy Spirit of God, the very reality, then, of what they experienced in
Christ" (68). Recourse to this reality validly connects original revelation,
scriptural propositions, and the new knowledge of developed dogma.
  To appreciate this more Rahner returns to an analysis of propositions.
There are two kinds: 1) those modeled on mathematics whose content can
be exhaustively and unambiguously known; 2) human propositions whose
content comes up against an intrinsic and irreducible marginal indistinct-
ness—an overflow. The first are like packages containing a reality (e.g., the
definition of a circle); the second are like windows on reality (e.g., She is my
mother.). With the latter it is possible to communicate an important but
implicit element of the reality which remains implicit to both speaker and
hearer perhaps over generations. This is the appropriate model for propositions of revealed truth (e.g., Christ died for us.).
  Rahner is not postulating a new method for theology (74). He is simply
arguing that applying existing theological methods "need not necessarily
lead to a result outside the sphere of what has been really stated and

communicated formally by God (as though its discovery must necessarily be a piece of merely human wit)" (74), e.g., Mary's Assumption. The true and binding status of any proposition arising from the development of doctrine is for the church and its magisterium to decide. It lies beyond the purview of any particular theologian. Conclusion (75ff).

1.04 *THEOS* in the New Testament

THEOS im Neuen Testament
{4.0} *Bijdragen* 11 (1950) 211-236; 12 (1951) 24-52.

Abstract: The New Testament use of *theos* to refer to the first person of the Trinity has implications for Christology and argues that Greek rather than Latin trinitarian theology is closer to the biblical and patristic witness.
Topics: GOD in the New Testament; THEOLOGY, biblical; TRINITY.
Subsidiary Discussions: God in Greek/Roman thought (80f, 90ff); God, natural knowledge of (81ff, 132ff); Revelation (81ff); Revelation history (86ff); God in Old Testament (88f, 92ff, 118ff); God as person (84ff, 104ff); God, attributes of (112ff); God as love (117f); God-talk (130ff, 125ff); Jesus Christ (88, 99, 123, ff, 135ff, 144ff).

OUTLINE

Part One: Introduction.
  I. Preliminary remarks.
    1. Method.
    2. Matter. [non-Christian conceptions]
    3. Matter. [within the history of revelation]
  II. The Greek and Old Testament conceptions of God.
    1. The Greek conception of God.
      a) [Fundamentally polytheistic]
      b) [A monotheisitic note]
    2. The Conception of God in the Old Testament.
      a) [Preliminary remark]
      b) [Yahweh is unique]
Part Two: *Theos* in the New Testament.
  I. The point of departure.
    1. The unquestioning assurance.
    2. The inner reason.
  II. The content of the New Testament conception of God.
    1. The uniqueness of God.
      a) significance.
      b) meaning.
    2. God as person.
      a) as the one who acts.
      b) as the one who acts freely.
      c) as the one who acts in an historical dialogue with men.

    d) the attributes of God.
3. The Love of God.
    a) God's love in the Old Testament.
    b) The nature of God's relationship to man in New Testament.
       1) that God is love.
       2) that God has bestowed himself upon us in Christ.
4. God as the first person of the Trinity in the New Testament.
    a) the question formulated.
    b) questions of method.
    c) arguments against the thesis.
    d) positive demonstrations of the thesis.
       1) *Theos* almost always refers to the Father.
       2) *Theos* is used in critical instances.

Precis: PART ONE: Introduction
I. Preliminary Remarks:
   1. Method: This brief study necessarily omits detailed exegesis and takes the form of a study in philosophy of religion and speculative theology.
   2. Matter [non-Christian conceptions]: Because this is theology and not history of religion, Rahner approaches it as one who reads scripture in the church, with a faith instructed by the church and the whole prior knowledge of theology. In asking how a Christian notion of God differs from pagan or purely philosophical notions he focuses on the classical Greco-Roman milieu in which Christianity arose. Christians maintain even the pagan world is supernatural, i.e., ordered as a whole to the personal, Trinitarian God beyond the world. Thus, nature and the whole development of religion and philosophy are always embedded in a supernatural context (81). There are no "natural religions." Christianity owes nothing to non-Christian religion or speculation. Similarities are a posteriori matters of fact. Christ did not bring God into the world for the first time. He clarified and completed God's intra-mundane presence.
   How does this apply to the knowledge of God? Vatican I taught that the one God as *principium et finis* of the world can be known with intrinsic certainty "by the light of natural reason" from the objective world. For all the problems this raises (82f) Rahner argues the theological meaning of the term "natural man" simply points to the person as a potentially receptive subject of revelation and theology. For revelation to be grace, humans must have something to do with God from a locus that is not already grace (83).
   The content of this natural knowledge of God is two-sided. God's transcendence and existence is revealed as personal; we in turn are revealed as inescapably responsible. Non-Christian religions and philosophy know God: 1) from below, through the world; 2) in a deteriorated way due to original sin; 3) through the existence of grace and primitive revelation. Insofar as they are deeply influenced by sin non-Christian religions are

polytheistic. They interpret God's infinity as an infinity of powers and forces active in the world. In their search for unity among these forces such religions will necessarily be pantheistic. Each will become devoted to this world instead of obeying the unique and living God. Inversely, Christianity will always: 1) confirm what is true of God in other religions and strive to free them from the encumbrance of sin; 2) stand against every polytheistic and pantheistic deification of the world; 3) witness to God's free self-communication to the world which inevitably results in a judgment of salvation or damnation.

3. Matter [in the history of revelation]: Should we expect in advance to see a fundamental difference between Old and New Testament conceptions of God? What might this be? God's revelation has a real history. As free persons our acts can never be worked out in advance. We do not establish a religion, we can only obey the revelation God freely bestows. Whether God freely bestows or denies himself is the central question of serious religion. We cannot know the answer through metaphysics but only if God freely acts. Any such act is connected to all others in saving history and its meaning is discerned only from the meaning of the whole. God's central saving act is the incarnation, death, and resurrection of Christ. Insofar as Christ gives final clarity to what had been obscure prophetic anticipation in the Old Testament it can be said that God is the same in both testaments. The whole of saving history is a progressive revelation of the way the one free God has entered into relationship with the world.

II. The Greek and Old Testament conceptions of God.

1. The Greek conception of God: These summary remarks on the Greek religious milieu in which Christianity arose show why the call to monotheism is not based on a metaphysical Christian assumption but comes from the very heart of its message. **a)** Pantheistic and Polytheistic: By *theos* the Greeks meant not one unified personality but the unity of the religious world. Greek polytheism is an ordered totality of gods conceived of mythically, ideally, or as an ultimate principle (*arche*). These forces confront people with conflicting demands. While people search for the meaning or intelligibility of this world, *theos* remains an adjective describing the cosmos. **b)** Monotheistic: Greek religion contains a genuine, unrealized knowledge of a truly personal transcendent God whom it approached in prayer and in the search for the One.

2. The conception of God in the Old Testament: a) Preliminary remark on method: This inquiry does not focus on what concept of God actually prevailed in the minds of Old Testament people but on the true and binding portrait of God offered in their scripture. **b)** Monotheism is not some static metaphysical monism comparable to deism. It is not based on the rational considerations of one seeking unity. It derives from Israel's experience of Yahweh's free saving activities directed toward them. Cosmological metaphysics ascends from cause to higher cause. Old Testament theology developed in the reverse: from an historical experience of a person to the realization of Yahweh's absolute transcendence. Summary (94).

PART TWO: *Theos* in the New Testament
I. The point of departure.
   1. Unquestioning assurance: a) New Testament authors never question the existence of God who is simply really there. They want to know how God behaves so they will know how to act. Assurance is not derived from metaphysical reflection nor is such knowledge discussed or invoked. History, however, is. **b)** Their assurance is never disturbed by their pagan neighbors' ignorance of God. They view failure to apprehend God as a moral fault or punishment. To them the pagans' idolatrous worship of the world as an absolute is demonic. It is a culpable refusal to acknowledge a God whom they knew even before hearing Christian preaching.
   2. The inner reason: New Testament people were assured by God's saving intervention in human history, both in Israel's history and now in their personal experience of Jesus. God spoke to them through his only Son. They associate Christ and God. One can know God prior to knowing Christ, but once having heard of Christ one faces the crisis of decision.
II. The content of the New Testament conception of God.
   1. The uniqueness of God: a) Significance: New Testament monotheism is not a leftover Old Testament tradition. It is a new, essential part of the Christian confession: eternal life is to know the one true God. **b)** Meaning: This confession is not primarily metaphysical. It is an instance of prophetic monotheism—the proclamation of a God who is revealed in his actions. In the New Testament this means the Father of Jesus Christ. This monotheism is not static but slowly unfolding. This confession entails accepting the task of building the Kingdom of God. This answers the question how God can be both known and believed. We know the existence of a first cause of the world, but we can only believe by faith in a person living and active in history.
   2. God as person: The God of the New Testament is addressed as Thou. This is only possible towards a person: **a)** Who acts: God can be known somewhat through his activity within the world. Although scripture never deifies the cosmos it does celebrate God's sovereign, free acts within human history. Such free action illuminates the meaning of creation; **b)** Who acts freely: God manifests himself as person precisely by the fact that his acts are voluntary and free, not the result of an inevitable world-process. There is an ultimate meaning and purpose to creation revealed finally in Christ. Nonetheless, since the existential concreteness of this future remains a mystery, God never falls under the sway of human calculation; **c)** Who acts in an historical dialogue with people: In this dialogue God allows us to be persons too. We have the freedom to say no to God's plan and thus alter its outcome for ourselves without, however, derailing it completely; **d)** Who revels his attributes to us through his acts: Our metaphysical judgements about God's essence manifest his attributes. These are often contradictory. Theological reflection on God's historical actions, especially the incarnation, death and glorification of Jesus, reveals God's real attitude towards us. Summary (117).

3. The love of God: The decisive revelation in God's saving acts is that God is love: the Father has graciously called us in his Son to the most intimate communion. This is God's definitive word by which God has bound himself irrevocably. It marks the beginning of the final time. Rahner asks (a) how this new situation differs from God's previous modes of behavior; what is peculiar to it (b). a) God's Love in the Old Testament: What Christ reveals draws all earlier revelation into a unified order as its fullness and goal. It differs from love in the Old Testament much as a metaphysical notion of love differs from a personal I-Thou relationship. In the Old Testament, God enters into personal relationship with a people he promises never to abandon. It remains oriented to something obscure yet to come (summary, 122). In the New Testament we are drawn into the depth of God's inner life. **b)** The nature of God's relationship to man in the New Testament: Characterizing God's free historical behavior in the fullness of time as love means two things: **1.** this love is the free act of God in Christ, an event not an attribute or emanation of a world process; **2.** this love is a communication of God's inmost life to us (summary, 125).

4. God as the first person of the Trinity in the New Testament:
a) The question formulated: Who, Father, Son, or Holy Spirit, is meant when the New Testament speaks of 'ο θεός? In scholastic terms Rahner maintains, "in the New Testament 'ο θεός *signifies* the First Person of the Trinity, and does not merely stand for him often, this applies to every case in which another meaning of 'ο θεός does not become clearly evident from the context. These few exceptions in no way support the opinion that 'ο θεός merely stands for the Father without actually signifying him" (126f). [Cf. 127 ftn1 to distinguish designation from signification.] Rahner insists on the importance of this distinction in matters of theology and kerygma (cf., 146) claiming that "the Trinitarian structure of our whole religious life will become more vital, and our consciousness of Christ's mediation with regard to the Father become more sharp, than if the word 'God' merely calls to mind in our prayer to God the God of natural theology and the trinity in general (and hence indistinctly)" (129f).

b) Questions of method: Rahner further distinguishes "designate" and "signify" (cf., 136 d). He also sets out **c)** Arguments against the thesis: **1.** θεός must signify the Trinity when applied in the New Testament to the object of natural theology or to the creator. But since natural theology knows God as necessarily subsisting, unoriginated, and personal, it speaks of the Father. The same applies to knowledge of God as creator. **2.** θεός is used to speak of the Son. The six attributions are used in a predicative sense (summary, 138). **d)** Positive demonstrations of the thesis: Rahner reiterates and applies his method: **1)** θεός is nearly/always used to speak of one thing: the Father. After an exhaustive look at citations Rahner summarizes his argument (143f). **2.** θεός is used in critical instances even when another clearer word is available (summary, 146). Rahner concludes that Régnon's "Greek" trinitarian theology is closer to the biblical witness than the "Latin" scholastic approach. His study also clarifies the term "children of God" to mean "we are children of the Father of Christ by participation in the eternal sonship of the only begotten Son" (147). Rahner suggests his insight is helpful when applied to questions of uncreated grace and other aspects of trinitarian theology.

1.05 Current Problems in Christology
Probleme der Christologie von heute
{3.5} A. von Grillmeier, H. Bacht, eds., *Das Konzil von Chalkedon*, III, Würzburg, 1954, 3-49, as, *Chalkedon—End oder Anfang?*

Abstract: No one formula exhausts christological speculation. The inexhaustible riches of scripture which challenge the adequacy of the Chalcedonian formula addresses some of its problems and opens new avenues of study.

Topics: CHRISTOLOGY; HYPOSTATIC UNION; CHRISTOLOGY, Chalcedonean.

Subsidiary Discussions: Dogma, formula (149ff); Theology (151ff, 199f); Theology, biblical (154f); Jesus Christ as mediator (155ff); Creation (162ff, 176 ftn1); Salvation history (166f); Jesus Christ, self-awareness (168ff); Redemption/Salvation (178f, 192ff); Theological Anthropology (183ff); Jesus Christ, faith in (185ff); Jesus Christ and world religions (189); Jesus Christ, mysteries in the human life of (190ff); Death (192ff); *Sarx* (196f); Incarnation (165, 197ff).

Precis: Introduction: (139-154). Reflection on revealed truth yields precise formulas which are never ends but always beginnings. Every formula transcends itself not because it is partly false but because the reality it expresses is always greater. We neither abandon old formulations nor preserve them in petrified form. This is equally true of the Chalcedonian formula expressing the mystery of Jesus. It is our duty to understand it, to investigate its incompleteness. There is always a tendency to disparage those who criticize ancient formulations. But theology must seek what it has always known and also what it has forgotten. Dogmas must be appropriated anew by every generation. We do not have to measure them against theological novelties. It is enough to honestly investigate them with the mind and heart we actually possess.

Part I. Transcendental hermeneutic for biblical christology (154-174). Rahner argues that since the church's christological dogma never claims to be an adequate condensation of biblical teaching and since dogma grows sterile without living contact with scripture, there remains even from the viewpoint of dogmatic theology a place for further christological biblical theology. To those who say nothing more is possible beyond the Chalcedonian formula he cites *Humani generis'* description of the inexhaustible riches of scripture. He illustrates the inadequacy of the Chalcedonian formula to explain sufficiently the messiahship and mediatorship of Christ (155-166); saving history (166-168); Christ's self-consciousness (168-174).

Regarding messiahship and mediatorship Rahner focuses on the two-nature formula and its failure to allow for Christ to mediate salvation to anyone besides himself. He suggests applying to christology in an analogous fashion a truly theological, biblical doctrine of creation which stresses the direct proportionality between independence and radical proximity (162). Just as God is known from the world, and yet we start from God in order to say what the world is, it is legitimate to propose that Christ is known from humanity, and yet we can start from Christ in order to say what humanity is. Summary (166).

Classical christology fails to locate Christ in saving history. Even his human nature comes across as being completely provisional, having no further role once Christ is glorified. A deeper more biblical theology of time and history than Chalcedon's is needed to address Christ's inaugurating and actually being the fullness of all time, past and future.

Classical scholasticism approaches the self-consciousness of Christ relying on a handful of biblical citations. Isn't a fuller use of scripture a better ground for a theology of Christ's self-consciousness? After a detailed review of the problem Rahner maintains that if there is an ontic christology which relies on universal categories of being, there can also be an existential one which relies on categories appropriate to the description of consciousness (172). Such an ontological christology could, he suggests, be derived from Christ's own statements in scripture about his relationship with the Father. Rahner sets out three parameters any statement must meet which refers to Christ's self-consciousness (172), and concludes this section with an example of how biblical theology fills out ontic christological categories.

Part II. Investigating the Chalcedonian formula (174-185).

This formula speaks of two natures united in one person. Rahner focuses on how difficult it is to understand this unity. These difficulties are compounded by the doctrine of the unchangeableness of the divine nature. But on such a reading how can Christ be said to have suffered? What is the meaning of his *kenosis*? In what sense is his death redemptive? What is the abiding meaning of his physical resurrection or ascension? How can we avoid an incipient monophysitism or a slide into myth? For Rahner the answer lies in rethinking the concept of unity. Rahner concludes that just as the human nature of Christ can only be known by its relation with the Logos (not by its separated existence), so the real meaning of human nature can only be known by reference to Christ. Hence, "Christology is at once beginning and end of anthropology, and that for all eternity such an anthropology is really theo–logy" (185).

Part III. Problems of modern christology beyond Chalcedon's formula (185-200).

1) The question why we are capable of faith in the Christ of Christian dogma might be answered by developing a "transcendental deduction." Christ is too unique, too mysterious, too existentially significant to be

known simply in the same way other contingent objects are known. In addition, any a priori sketch of the idea of Christ must still remain open to the actual, a posteriori event of revelation—God's free epiphany in history. Such an approach would help to keep christology from being dismissed as mythology.

2) A new theological phenomenology of religious attitudes toward Christ might retard the latent monophysitism in today's piety and spur theology to reappraise the abiding value of the glorified humanity of Christ.

3) Viewing Christ from the standpoint of world religions might highlight the essentials of human nature and broaden the sense of our dialogue with God.

4) Retreating from an abstract, formal christology might increase interest in the mysteries of Christ's human life and illuminate the meaning and interpretation of our own lives which are first and last the life of God.

5) The standard satisfaction theory of a purely formal and juridical kind does not exhaust the biblical truth of redemption. Revisiting soteriology would have to connect the hypostatic union with the satisfaction theory; it would require a new theology of death and a reappraisal of the *sarx* of Christ.

6a) Why only one incarnation? Why as a human? How is it meaningful for the redemption of the whole cosmos (including angels) that God became man? 6b) Why and how is Christ's incarnation the unsurpassable fullness of all time?

7) Christology should be more closely related to other branches of theology: dogmatics, morals, sacraments, ecclesiology, theology of history.

8) Someone should survey the existing state of Christian belief in Christ to guide future theological research, catechetics, preaching, liturgy.

1.06 The Immaculate Conception
Die Unbefleckte Empfängnis
{3.0}   *Stimmen der Zeit* 153 (1954) 241-251.
Abstract: Mary's Immaculate Conception belongs to the doctrine of redemption. It is unique as the perfect form of redemption not as an event out of time.
Topics: BVM, Immaculate Conception of; REDEMPTION.
Subsidiary Discussions: Christology (202ff); Church, office and holiness in (204ff, 209); Baptism of infants (207f, 212); Predestination (209ff).
Precis: Catholics cannot remain indifferent to the doctrine of the Immaculate Conception. Rahner highlights the intelligibility of this dogma by viewing it in the context of the whole Christian faith, most especially from the doctrine of the redemption. He shows, "how it derives its life from this whole and how its meaning and content can be clarified by reference to the whole" (202).

"Mary is only intelligible in terms of Christ" (202). Hence, all Marian reflection must begin with the Catholic belief that the Word of God became man in Adam's flesh so that the world might be taken up redemptively into the life of God. Because Jesus is true God and true man, Mary is in truth the Mother of God. This divine motherhood is not simply a biological fact. It is Mary's free act of faith. It is an event of public saving history. Her motherhood is personal, the result of free consent. Her obedience in faith is no less free because it is also a pure grace of God.

Catholics are often reproached for valuing the institutional over the charismatic. Even though institution and holiness never completely coincide, neither is there an absolute discrepancy between them. That would belie the definitive nature of Christ's victory and its ongoing presence in the church. In short, "Office...and personal holiness coincide at the decisive points of saving history, so that each supports the other and makes it possible" (205). The eschatological and decisive event of public saving history inaugurated by Mary's personal act of faith represents the consummate unity of office and holiness. Thus, Mary is the *holy* Mother of God. (Rahner discusses further how this free act is nonetheless God's grace.)

In sum, "Mary is she who is most perfectly Redeemed" (206); "the example and exemplar of redemption" (207) because redemption consists in accepting Christ in the act of faith, something Mary did par excellence in conceiving him in her own body. To those who say this undervalues the redemptive death of Christ, Rahner responds that his death actually begins the moment he assumes the flesh of Adam, the flesh of death, when he is conceived in Mary's womb.

Two points complete the preliminaries: 1) Even unbaptized infants are objects of God's infinite mercy with a remote claim on divine sonship through Christ. Their originally sinful status is already comprehended within God's grace and love. This points to a "supra-temporal region" wherein these children exist. Thus, what is distinctive about Mary's immaculate conception is something deeper than its seeming retrojected temporality. 2) God's causal relation to our morally good, free acts can be called predestination so long as one excludes from it everything fatalistic, unfree, and deterministic. If the incarnation was predestined by God as his first, original plan, then so too was an earthly mother (holy and fully redeemed) for the Son predestined along with her free consent.

What does this imply for Mary's immaculate conception? (recap, 210). Mary's predestination to salvation through Christ differs from anyone else's in that ours is hidden from us. The very existence of Christ and his predestined, saving mission depend on none of us except Mary. It is in the mystery of her special predestination that the meaning of her immaculate conception is found. But does it follow from God's unique predestining purpose for salvation towards her that Mary was also "preserved from original sin, redeemed by being preserved and not just by being freed from original sin?" (211).

Mary's preservation from original sin is a consequence of her predestination and not an addition to it for two reasons: 1) Redemption does not necessitate a previous state of being unredeemed, i.e., of sin and alienation from God. Though the person delivered from sin to grace and the person preserved in grace both owe their redemption equally to God, the latter form of redemption is more perfect. Insofar as we know Mary was the most holy and perfectly redeemed, she must enjoy the most perfect form of redemption, i.e., preservation from sin. 2) Why are not all people graced with preservation from sin from the moment of their conception? The interval between the beginning of our existence and our justification manifests historically the fact that we cannot in general be regarded as redeemed and predestined simply by the fact of Christ's irrevocable victory. Mary is the exception not because she does not require redemption but because "she is the one member of the redeemed without whom it is impossible to think of the Redemption as victorious" (213).

1.07 The Interpretation of the Dogma of the Assumption
Zum Sinn des Assumpta-Dogmas
{3.0} *Schweizer Rundschau* 50 (1951) 585-596.
Abstract: The true content of the doctrine of Mary's Assumption is found in the fusion of three articles of the creed: "born of the Virgin Mary"; "descended into the kingdom of the dead"; "the resurrection of the flesh."
Topics: BVM, Assumption of; RESURRECTION.
Subsidiary Discussions: Creed: Born of the Virgin Mary (216ff, 224); Creed: He descended into hell (218-224): Creed: Resurrection of the flesh (218-224); Redemption (218, 224f); Eschatology, heaven (221ff); Time and space (221-224).
Precis: Explicating the content of the doctrine of Mary's Assumption will help overcome epistemological and psychological misunderstandings that surround its reception. Like any datum of faith this doctrine is only understood in the context of faith enunciated in the Apostles' Creed. The central but by no means the only tenet involved here is "Born of the Virgin Mary."

This article of the creed has always meant more than simply the physical motherhood of Mary, a personal link between her and Jesus. It points to a public, saving, graced, eschatological event for the whole world, irrevocable and unsurpassable. This event took place in Mary, *in her flesh* insofar as Christ became a son of Adam in the flesh through her; and *through her faith* insofar as this event was her free assent. Thus, "Her objective service, by means of which her bodily reality is delivered to the Word, is her subjective action, one in the other" (217). In this way she cooperates in the redemption of the world and enjoys the most perfect redemption herself, preservation from sin from the moment of her conception. Summary (217f).

Other articles of the creed (i.e., the descent into the kingdom of the dead, the resurrection of the flesh, 218-224) are also immediately and essentially related to the doctrine of the Assumption. Rahner treats them together since Christ's death makes resurrection possible, and we profess to being saved by his death and resurrection. In addition, Matt. 25:53f indicates Christ did not rise alone. This does not surprise Rahner given the impact of Jesus' definitive salvific act on all humanity.

This leads to two related questions: the nature of the resurrected body, and its location in space and time. On the first issue, since each being perceives reality according to its proper mode of reception, only those already glorified can experience and grasp the true nature of the resurrected body. It is an experience we are not privy to now. Regarding its location Rahner shows why the view of the ancients is not acceptable to us, nor is the contemporary description of heaven as a "state," since both of these locate the resurrected body in a segment of a homogeneous world space. He suggests that instead of thinking of time as a function of space, space should be thought of as a function of time and history. Christ, having ushered in the new age, eschatological time has redeemed a new space (summary, 223). Moreover, if the world itself shares in his resurrection then this present earth already participates in the new heaven, although this redeemed reality is not immediately present to every redeemed person or event to the same degree as it is to Mary whose redemption is most perfect.

Recapping his comments on the article "Born of the Virgin Mary" (224) Rahner admits the concept "perfect redemption" is open to the objection that it can arbitrarily accommodate any content. Nevertheless, scripture attests to the fact that bodily glorification is not an arbitrary invention. Nor can one deny that Mary's unique role in redemption would dignify her with a claim to the fruits of perfect redemption (225). Thus, these articles of the creed fuse to reveal the content of the doctrine of Mary's Assumption. Her privilege is not unique in itself. It is unique in that no time for bodily corruption elapsed between her death and glorification, as seems to have been the case with other saints scripture claims rose from the dead (Matt. 27:5f).

The church in Mary is already redeemed totally, though not in all its members. The flesh too has already begun its final form. Perhaps Protestants who focus on a theology of the cross find it hard to embrace the doctrine of the Assumption. For them glory remains a promise whereas for Catholics it has already begun despite all appearances. The doctrine of Mary's Assumption clarifies this truth.

1.08   Theological Reflections on Monogenism
Theologisches zum Monogenismus
{4.0}   *Zeitschrift für katholische Theologie* 76 (1954) 1-18, 171-184.

Abstract: Magisterial teaching and exegesis of *textus classicus* on original sin do not settle definitively the question of monogenism. Rahner defends monogenism by tying it to redemption and offers a metaphysical defense.

Topics: THEOLOGICAL ANTHROPOLOGY, mono-/polygenism; SIN, original.

Subsidiary Discussions: Certainty (233ff, 245f, 249ff); *Humani generis* (231ff, 248ff); Trent (240ff, 268ff); Assent, degrees of (234ff, 242f); Definition, implicit (241ff); Scripture, exegesis (252ff, 263, 264ff); Redemption (274ff, 284f); *Sarx* of death (275ff); God, attributes of (290f); Evolution (249f).

Precis: To avoid discussions of great generality and the question of authentic tradition, this essay restricts itself to a few questions about monogenism in the strictly theological sense (bibliography, 229 ftn1).

I. Monogenism and the official teaching of the church (231-251).

1) The encyclical, *Humani generis*. Rahner begins his analysis of magisterial teaching on monogenism with the most recent teaching (1950) because truth unfolds ever more fully over time. He interprets the document in its most restricted sense. Polygenism, "the doctrine which either leaves room for the existence, after the Adam of theology, of other men who do not belong to his bodily posterity; or which holds that 'Adam' is a collective concept which combines into one the totality of human progenitors" (232f) is condemned as a *coniecturalis opinio*, i.e., a hypothesis. Leaving open the question of "Pre-Adamites," it teaches that polygenism is impermissible (not heretical) on theological grounds, whereas monogenism is "theologically certain" and must be held by the faithful with inner (not irreformable) assent. This theological certainty rests principally on the doctrine of original sin reenforced by scripture's idea of the one Adam.

2) The Decree of the Biblical Commission in 1909 (Denz. 2123). This decree's insistence that monogenism belongs to the historical content of Genesis 2-3 adds nothing to *Humani generis* since it leaves open whether monogenistic unity can be strictly deduced from this text with modern exegetical tools.

3) The Council of Trent. Here Rahner responds to those who maintain monogenism was "implicitly defined" in Trent's teachings on original sin. It is possible for a teaching to have true implications for a controversy which appears centuries later and about which the church at that time had no inkling. It is also possible that certain propositions can attach themselves to church teaching which even though held by the people of the day are actually false and were never taught as such by the church. A proposition can be said to be "co-defined" if: i) it was present in the mind of the definer; ii) it is indissolubly connected to the doctrine being defined. From a close reading

of Trent, Rahner concludes its doctrine of original sin does not imply monogenism "with that immediacy which would be necessary for an implicit definition" (246). It maintains that the force of hereditary sin necessitates an individual without thereby defining the unique individuality of Adam (247).

4) The Vatican Council [I]. Insofar as the schema mentioning monogenism was never promulgated by this abbreviated council, its problematic positions bear only the weight of contemporary theologians. Section I summary (249ff).

II. Monogenism and the scriptures (251-285). Rahner begins with a preview and some comments on method: He analyzes: 1) whether it can be said with certainty that scripture testifies directly to monogenism; 2) whether other scriptural doctrines postulate monogenism as a necessary presupposition.

A. The direct proof, its possibility and limits.

1) The Old Testament. a) Genesis 2-3. Although Genesis presents Adam as an individual, is it the author's intention to present him as such *eo ipso*? After discussing genre and historical content in scripture (253ff) and the difference between inspiration and revelation (255f) Rahner concludes that one is hard pressed to assert that monogenism can be shown by purely exegetical method to be contained in Genesis 1-3 as a direct statement (256). Not only does this not refute monogenism, it shows Genesis 1-3 is positively open to its possibility (summaries, 261, 262). b) Wisdom 10:1. Since whenever a later text takes over an earlier text without commentary, as here Wisdom does Genesis, nothing further can be deduced from it than from the earlier text. Hence, Wisdom 10:1 adds nothing to this discussion.

2) The New Testament. Acts 17:24-26. Within a discussion of how to regard Old Testament passages quoted in the New Testament (266f) Rahner maintains that nothing more is being stated by Paul in this passage than is found in Genesis: the historical unity of the human family. What is said of Genesis 1-3 both positively and negatively he applies to Acts 17: 24-26.

B. The indirect proof (from scripture and the church's magisterium).

1) The usual form of the indirect proof. After recapping Trent's view on monogenism based on the universality of original sin, Rahner's analysis of its terms (*origine, unum, propagatione*) leads him to doubt the conclusiveness of the indirect argument (summary, 273). He intends to present a binding argument for monogenism based on scripture's view of salvation/damnation history.

2) The community of a stock as the basis of the community of salvation and damnation. After an aside on the relation of scientific and theological objects, Rahner builds a case for monogenism based on redemption. Christ is able to redeem all people because he shares with us a common stock. At the incarnation he assumed the flesh of death. To the objection that such

thinking is archaic Rahner asks what's wrong with archaic concepts? Summary (279).

3) The institution of the community of salvation and damnation by the act of an individual. That the act of one individual can have an effect on the entire community is clearly true in the case of Christ and also of Adam. This Rahner proves by showing the minimum content of Trent's doctrine of original sin can only be upheld: i) if the universal situation of damnation based on a community of stock was established at the origin of this community; ii) if this historical origin proceeds from an individual. Either one Adam has made us all into sinners (Rm. 5:12f) or we must reject the notion of original sin as myth. But then the redemption of all by the one would be superfluous. Thus, monogenism is definitively proven by an appeal to a central doctrine: redemption. Summary (285).

III. The possibilities of a metaphysical proof for monogenism (286-296).

1) Rahner assumes that to science monogenism and polygenism are equally plausible. Science cannot definitively prove one or the other.

2) Monogenism could be proven philosophically.

3) Notes for a metaphysics of generation: Rahner sketches a possible ontology of human generation: a) Man is a bodily spirit; b) Man needs human community; c) Man is codetermined by the totality of material reality; d) Man is determined by the essential form of life in which he participates; e) This life form reaches its completion and concrete manifestation in generation; f) Man lives as a spirit in human community; g) Thus, monogenism and the unity of species, though conceptually distinct, are inseparable in reality.

4) Monogenism and the transcendence of the divine creation of man. To the objection that we limit God's power when we insist God could not have created many people on this earth independently of one another, Rahner says:

a) Because we are distinguished metaphysically from everything below, we are not the bare product of terrestrial forces but God's original institution.

b) In treating of God one must distinguish an abstract from a concrete possibility. Insofar as God's free creative act reveals God's will, certain abstract possibilities would be contrary to the revealed meaning of God's action and thus be concretely impossible.

c) Assuming a) and b), polygenism is impossible since: 1. No effect (i.e., no person) can have two different causes. 2. Repeated institution of a terrestrial cause would make God's intervention a terrestrial event, i.e., a miracle. This calls into question the meaningfulness of such actions as well as the metaphysical principle of economy. In the end any theory of polygenism necessarily reduces either to biological materialism or to a naive anthropomorphism of God's relationship to the world.

d) To the objection that such a divine institution would need to be invoked to explain the rise of any new species, Rahner counters that we alone are world-transcending, metaphysically new beings. Rahner concludes that his approach to monogenism is also compatible with a moderate theory of evolution.

1.09   Concerning the Relationship between Nature and Grace

Über das Verhältnis von Natur und Gnade
{3.5}   *Orientierung* 14 (1950) 141-145.

Abstract: While agreeing with *la nouvelle Théologie*'s critique of an extrinsic view of nature/grace, Rahner demonstrates the inability of that approach to insure the unexactedness of grace. Rahner concludes with his own theory.
Topics: NATURE and grace; GRACE and nature; THEOLOGICAL ANTHROPOLOGY; SUPERNATURAL EXISTENTIAL.
Subsidiary Discussions: *Conversio ad phantasma* (301 ftn1); Love (305f); *Potentia obedientialis* (303f, 309, 315f).

Precis: *La nouvelle Théologie* was justified in challenging the prevailing textbook approach to nature/grace for being too extrinsic—a problematic and dangerous position on many counts (summary, 298ff) but most especially because it maintains that our self-experience here and now is the same as it would have been in an order of pure nature. This makes it seem as if God's offer of grace is forced upon us as something foreign. It also assumes we can clearly separate in our experience what is nature and what is grace (whereas Rahner insists we need only distinguish the possibility of experiencing grace from the possibility of experiencing grace *as* grace). It also contains the ontologically untenable position that we could be completely unaware of or indifferent to our binding ordination to our proper supernatural end.

The key theological problem is how to avoid an extrinsic view of nature/grace while maintaining its unexactedness. In light of *Humani generis*, Rahner distances himself from *la nouvelle Théologie* because based on its presuppositions "grace and beatific vision can no longer be said to be unexacted" (304). At this point Rahner presents a critique of *la nouvelle Théologie* (304-310) as it is described in an article by the anonymous D. (cf., 303 ftn3). [Without this article the gist of Rahner's critique is difficult to grasp.] According to Rahner, D. is unable to distinguish between the unexactedness of God's self-communication in creation and in itself (305); D.'s analogy to the unexactedness of human love fails to show how one can resist God's self-communication (306); 3) D. misinterprets Trent on grace and merit (306f); D.'s appeal to mystery is theologically premature (307); D. cannot show how our disposition to or desire for grace does not demand its fulfillment (307ff).

The essay now turns to Rahner's position (310-317) beginning with a brief kerygmatic statement (310f) from which he draws 4 theological points.

1) We should be *able* to receive this love which is God's very self. We must *always* have a real potency for it. This capacity is our central abiding existential as we really are.

2) We should be able to receive this love as a free gift, unexacted, not simply because we are a creatures or because this existential is simply identical with our nature, since either case would make God's love necessary.

3) Thus "nature" in the theological sense is a remainder concept: what is left once the central existential openness to God is subtracted. This is why one is unable to achieve a chemically pure idea of nature. Summary (315).

4) Thus, the relationship between nature and supernature remains a theologically valid consideration. Our spiritual nature can remain open and dynamic in an unlimited way without demanding grace providing only that it is not taken as an unconditional ordination or dynamism. It can be meaningful even in those without the explicit experience of grace as the condition for the possibility of their spiritual life. The article concludes with a list of questions on nature/grace with remain open and deserve serious study (316f).

1.10   Some Implications of the Scholastic Concept of Uncreated Grace

Zur scholastichen Begrifflichkeit der ungeschaffenen Gnade
{4.0}   *Zeitschrift für katholische Theologie* 63 (1939) 137-157.
Abstract: Rahner defines the essence of created grace more sharply with elements drawn from scholastic theology's treatment of human cognition.
Topics: GRACE; THEOLOGICAL ANTHROPOLOGY, cognition; (326ff); SACRAMENTS, quasi-formal causality (328ff).
Subsidiary Discussions: Grace, uncreated (320ff); Grace, created (324f); Beatific vision (326ff); Hypostatic union (330f); God, *lumen gloriae* (332f, 341, 343); Trinity (343ff).
Precis: 1) The problem: a) Grace in the primary sources of revelation: In scripture, especially in St. Paul, "man's inner sanctification is first and foremost a communication of the personal Spirit of God" (322)—what the scholastics called uncreated grace. This is also true of St. John and also of Patristic thought, especially the Greek Fathers.

b) Grace in scholastic speculation: However they explain it, scholastic theologians see "the indwelling of the Spirit...merely as a *consequence* of the bestowal of created grace, as the end-term of a (categorial) relationship of man to God given with created grace" (325).

c) The precise point at issue (summary). How can one do justice to and harmonize these two ways of looking at things using scholastic terms?
2) The presuppositions of the solution offered: a) The relation of the state of grace to the beatific vision of God. The future life of glory (the beatific vision) is not simply a reward for our present life of grace. It is the full

flowering of a life we already possess. Hence, Rahner finds it acceptable to apply to an ontology of grace the same scholastic concepts which have proven to be valid in discussing the ontology of the immediate vision of God.

b) On the ontology of the *visio beatifica*. Fundamental conceptions of the nature of knowledge in general hold the answer to the essence and presuppositions concerning the immediate vision of God. An outline of Aquinas' metaphysics of knowledge (327f) highlights the role of species in human knowledge. When we know an object we become entitatively one with it by assimilating its species. The problem arises when in the beatific vision God's own essence comprises the species.

This real relationship between God and knower cannot be due to a real, accidental modification in either one, i.e., by efficient causality. One must turn for an explanation to formal causality which can only be known through revelation. Such causality cannot be doubted as rationally possible because of the existence of the hypostatic union, and because God's relationship to creation is formal (it cannot simply be efficient). Rahner attaches the prefix "quasi" to "draw attention to the meta-categorial character of God's abidingly transcendent formal causality" (330) and to reenforce the analogical nature of these causal concepts as applied to God (331). What scholastic theology teaches about quasi-formal causality, found under the heading hypostatic union, can rightly be applied here. Rahner summarizes and concludes that "the reality of the mind in the beatific vision...is the very Being of God" (332). This self-communication of God also extends to the will of the knower.

3) **The proposed solution: a)** The statement of the solution. Rahner summarizes his entire argument (334). Anything further that could be said of God's self-communication by way of quasi-formal causality can only be determined negatively in terms of the beatific vision: i) that this union is not the consequence of created grace; ii) this union is posited independently of an actually exercised apprehension of God; iii) this union is not a vague unity of natures, but is "the ontological aspect of the unity of the created spirit with God in the act of immediate loving contemplation" (336). At this point one can return to traditional scholastic discussions of the divine indwelling.

b) Hints of this view in the theologians. Rahner names as precursors of his theory Alexander of Hales, St. Bonaventure, Aquinas, Lessius, Scheeben, Franzelin, and Galtier.

c) Difficulties. Some might object that this approach endangers Trent's view of hte significance of created grace for justification, adoption, etc. Rahner counters that in his theory one cannot even begin to think of created grace apart from uncreated grace. To conceive of created grace as the disposition for uncreated grace in no way deprives the former of its theological attributes.

d) A consequence of the proposed solution. A question disputed by the scholastics was whether the justified person was appropriated to each divine person or only to the triune Godhead in an undifferentiated way (cf. 335 ftn1). Rahner argues that his theory at least proves the question is still an open one.He leans to the possibility that each person of the Trinity could communicate "itself to the knowing mind in quasi-formal causality after the fashion of a *species impressa*, otologically prior to knowledge as such" (344). Rahner contends this solution seems closer to scripture and reverses the present attenuation of the Trinity into a kind of pre-Christian monotheism.

1.11 The Theological Concept of *Concupiscencia*
Zum theologischen Begriff der Konkupiszenz
{3.5} *Zeitschrift für katholische Theologie* 65 (1941) 61-80.

Abstract: This analysis of concupiscence presumes all prerequisites of free decision are present in human nature both now and in Adam before the fall.

Topics: CONCUPISCENCE; THEOLOGICAL ANTHROPOLOGY, mono-/polygenism; HUMAN NATURE, gift of integrity; FREEDOM and decision (360-369); NATURE and person (362-368); SUPERNATURAL EXISTENTIAL (376-382).

Subsidiary Discussions: Sin in biblical theology, (347 ftn1); *Sarx* (354 ftn2); Theology, dogmatic (proofs in) (349); Grace, grades of (356 ftn1); Appetite, structure of (358-359); Cognition in scholastic anthropology (359-360); Matter (363 ftn1); Repentance (366 ftn2); Concupiscence, Christ's freedom from (364 ftn1, 367-368); Sin, venial (370-371); *Apatheia* (374); "Heart," German mysticism of (374).

Precis: An adequate Catholic dogmatic understanding of concupiscence must hold: 1) concupiscence is a power weighing us down and driving us to moral transgression; 2) freedom from concupiscence even in Adam before the fall remains an unexacted preternatural gift. But if concupiscence necessarily involves sin, it would seem to be oppressive; and if concupiscence is found in Adam then it would seem to be a part of human nature and thus be innocuous (347-348). Dogmatic clarity is further hampered because we know concupiscence in two ways: through explicit revelation and concrete experience (348-350).

I. Critical approach to the current conception of concupiscence. Current formulations fail in two respects:

1) Envisioning concupiscence as a disorderly appetite rather than as neutral or bivalent confuses the dogmatic and ascetico-moral dimensions of concupiscence. This would make freedom from concupiscence a total domination of spontaneous appetites, and the gift of integrity would become a series of discontinuous, divine interventions.

2) Envisioning concupiscence as a purely sensitive power pitted against a spiritual will posits an initially self-contradicted nature. This would make it impossible to uphold the unexactedness of the gift of integrity.

II. The theological concept of concupiscence.

1) The concept of concupiscence. Rahner distinguishes three sense of concupiscence: a) broadest sense as desire: any witting reactive attitude adapted to a value or a good vs. mere receptive awareness; b) narrower sense as the necessary presupposition of a free, personal decision; c) narrowest (theological) sense as the unbridgeable gap in any creature between nature and person, essence and existence, matter and spirit. This gap is most often expressed in the dualism of sensitivity and spirituality but is not identical with it. A long discussion of free decisions concludes that concupiscence does not consist i) in the givenness of a spontaneous act prior to a free act; ii) in the ability to freely expunge spontaneous acts; or iii) in the orientation of a spontaneous act to evil vs. free decision.

2) The significance of concupiscence. a) Concupiscence and moral action: theological concupiscence is not open to moral qualification in the strict sense. Concupiscence is not evil or sin in itself but only as it is present existentially in virtue of the fall and can lead to sin. b) Naturalness of concupiscence: because concupiscence is bivalent, and since it is a consequence of our metaphysical nature as material essences, the absence of concupiscence cannot be conceived of in purely natural terms, and its absence cannot be thought of as our due. c) The gift of integrity: preternatural integrity applies only to concupiscence in the theological sense. Such freedom is freedom *for* wholly disposing of ourselves through personal decision in a sovereign way.

3) Concupiscence and the present order of salvation: Does this make concupiscence innocuous? Rahner presupposes: a) we are endowed with a real, ontological, existential, unexacted ordination to God; b) such a supernatural, existential, being a priori actually enters into consciousness and alters the reception of experience. Thus, though in a "pure nature" concupiscence would be innocuous, in our already freely elevated natures it is not. The very fact that concupiscence expresses itself as a profound feeling of "what ought not to be" which stands in need of explanation argues against our being "pure natures."

II. Man in the Church
II. *Kirche und Mensch*

German edition: Einsiedeln, Benziger, 1954
Dedicated to his mother on her eightieth birthday
U.S. edition: Baltimore, MD, Helicon Press, 1963
Karl-H. Kruger, O.F.M., translator

2.01 Membership of the Church according to the Teaching of Pius XII's Encyclical, *Mystici Corporis Christi*

Die Gleidschaft in der Kirche nach der Lehre der Enzyklika Pius'
XII. "Mystici Corporis Christi"

{3.5} *Zeitschrift für katholische Theologie* 69 (1947) 129-188.

Abstract: Attempting to determine who belongs to the church in the fullest sense clarifies the meaning of baptism and salvation as well as the church's sacramental nature. It illuminates theological anthropology and ecumenism.

Topics: CHURCH, theology of; CHURCH, membership; BAPTISM; SALVATION.

Subsidiary Discussions: Ecumenism (2, 24ff, 62ff, 69); Definition (4ff); *Potestas ordinis/jurisdictionis* (6ff); Heresy/schism (9ff, 27ff); Church as *Ursakrament* (15ff); Sacraments (15ff, 55, 71ff); Church, excommunication (17, 30ff); Mystical body (33, 65ff); Baptism of infants (43f, 49); Spirit (60ff, 67f); God, hiddenness of (76); Theological anthropology (79ff); Incarnation (81ff): Church as People of God (82ff).

OUTLINE

I. What the encyclical says about the conditions for membership of the church.
    1) The church's previous teaching on conditions for church membership.
      a) A posteriori collection of doctrinal statements.
      b) Systematic argument for membership based on a posteriori statements.
      c) Membership and the canonistic literature.
      d) Concluding remarks.
    2) The teaching of the encyclical about membership of the church.
      a) The teaching of the encyclical.
      b) Indications for a more detailed explanation of the principles laid down by the encyclical.
      c) Evaluation of the doctrinal significance of this teaching.

II. What does the encyclical say about the possibility of union with Christ through grace for those who, in a sense of the reply to our first question, are not members of the church?
    1) The necessity of membership of the church for salvation, as found in the church's teaching before the encyclical.
      a) Dogmatic sitations.
      b) Scripture.
      c) Salvation outside the church (*votum baptismi*).
      d) How can baptism be necessary yet unbaptized can be saved?
      e) Church membership *voto ecclesiae*.
      f) Problems.
    2) The teaching of the encyclical on the possibility of grace and salvation for those who are not members of the visible church.
      a) The texts themselves.
      b) Some general considerations about interpretating these texts.
      c) About the particular interpretation of three statements.
    3) Summary and supplementary remarks to Part II (a-e).

III. With regard to the church's nature itself, what further facts, and what further indications for lines of inquiry can be gathered from the answer to the first two questions?
    1) The unseparated and unmixed divine and human natures of the church.
    2) Stratification within the nature of the church as sacramental sign.

Precis: This is a difficult and important question (bibliography, 1 ftn1) because: 1) some see it as a new teaching detrimental to the vital issue of Christian unity; 2) much about the question is obscure. [Methodologically, Rahner begins with the unsystematic doctrinal statements of the church hoping to find a logical order.]; 3) clarifying issues of membership in the church promises to add much to ecclesiology in general. Preview (3f).

I. What does the encyclical say about the conditions for membership of the church? Neither "church" nor "membership" is unequivocal. Clarification must proceed from the church's own doctrinal pronouncements: "Church means Roman Catholic Church which knows itself to be founded by Christ, even as an external, visibly organized society with the Bishop of Rome at its head, and which as such declares itself to be basically necessary for salvation" (5). The church has the right to determine the correct usage of theological terms.

1) The church's previous teaching on the conditions of membership of the church [before *Mystici corporis*]. The powers of the visible church are divided into: *potestas jurisdictionis* (the absolute power to enact binding decisions on faith and morals); *potestas ordinis* (sacramental power). It is always possible for either one to outstrip the other. Baptism, the act by which one becomes a church member, is a matter of sacramental power not jurisdiction.

a) A posteriori collection of doctrinal statements. "Baptism is a necessary condition for belonging in any way to the Church" (8). There can be members of the church who are not in the state of grace. Those baptized persons are no longer members of the church who have publicly sided against the church through schism or heresy, and that by a morally sinful act (9). Heretics and schismatics in good faith do not belong as members to the visible church (10). Rahner leaves aside the *excommunicati vitandi* and the putatively baptized, but raises the issue of those who inwardly abandoned the true faith without revealing this fact in the external forum (these remain members since they cannot be differentiated from sinners). Those who argue the contrary confuse two ecclesial spheres (the external and the graced realm) either of which can be present without the other. Hence, baptism can be conferred validly without sacramental grace being bestowed and vice versa (15).

b) Systematic argument for membership based on a posteriori statements. The church conforms to the hypostatic union with its visible and invisible structure. This is generally spoken of by dogmatic theologians under the heading of the relationship between sacramental sign and its graced effect. Whenever the church speaks of membership it is referring directly to the external, visible, and legally structured community of believers, and only indirectly to one's inner faith and union with Christ by grace. From this follows all that has been said above about membership. Summary (17).

c) Membership and the canonistic literature. One theory among canon lawyers argues that all baptized persons (even heretics) always remain members of the church. Only their rights largely fall into abeyance. They distinguish constitutional from operative membership. Rahner disagrees with this position because it obscures what is needed for salvation; it exaggerates the confusion on the topic in fundamental theology; it is refuted by the recent encyclical; it jumps to conclusions. Baptism is only one condition for membership, but this approach would argue that all the remaining conditions are always co-present. In the end canonists obscure rather than clarify the borderline between membership and non-membership (24).

d) Concluding remarks. The church's teaching on membership before the encyclical does not maintain there is nothing Christian outside the Catholic Church. For even outside the church there is faith, baptism, scriptures, tradition, and even valid apostolic succession and *potestas ordinis* in the case of the Orthodox. While insisting to be the only Church of Christ, Catholics never claim to always and everywhere manifest the whole of truth, grace, or love. Only a fully reunited church could approximate this.

2) The teaching of the encyclical about membership of the church.

a) The teaching of the encyclical: Rahner quotes the encyclical on the three elements which comprise church membership (and conversely non-membership).

b) Indications for a more detailed explanation of the [three] principles laid down by the encyclical. Rahner's analysis of the three elements necessary for membership show only a minor shift on the issue of *excommunicatio vitandi* (30ff). Two further notes underscore this position: i) the encyclical discusses membership in the church and not in the *corpus Christi mystici*: ii) there is no discussion of types of membership (constitutive, operative, etc.) thus indicating the church knows of only one type.

c) Evaluation of the doctrinal significance of this teaching. Although the encyclical proposes no new teaching on church membership, the non-infallible doctrine must now be held with inner assent. It does not, however, open the door to Christian unity as a purely inward, pneumatic community of love. This would contradict the incarnational principle of Christianity.

II. What does the encyclical say about the possibility of union with Christ through grace for those who, in a sense of the reply to our first question, are not members of the church? This question is vital insofar as the church teaches that full membership is needed for salvation. Since salvation requires possessing the spirit of Christ it must be shown that outside the church it is impossible to possess this grace of the Holy Spirit. Thus, Part II divides into two: 1) the church as necessary for salvation; 2) the possibility of justification for non-members. Rahner continues the same method.

1) The necessity of church membership for salvation, as found in the church's teaching before the encyclical. Historically this question was first posed in the context of the necessity of baptism for salvation. What is valid and true of the necessity for baptism is by extension true of the church. Hence, what follows applies first to the necessity of baptism.

a) On the necessity of membership in the church for salvation, there are many dogmatic citations synonymous with "*extra ecclesiam nulla salus.*"

b) The necessity of baptism for salvation is emphasized as strongly as church membership. In addition, baptism has even clearer scriptural warrant.

c) The church also teaches that those outside the church living in invincible ignorance can be saved. Trent teaches the legitimacy of *votum baptismi*. This encourages Rahner to give a wider interpretation of the possibility of salvation even to those who never enter the church because: i) this position is increasingly maintained by Catholic theologians; ii) it has never been refuted by the magisterium. Traces of this position from earlier times argue there never was a complete dogmatic consensus, although earlier positions on unbaptized children indicate more is necessary for salvation than the absence of subjective guilt. This raises two question (d and e below).

d) In what more precise way is external membership of the visible church necessary for salvation? The church holds as theologically certain that baptism (and by extension full membership in the visible church) is a necessary means and not just a necessary precept for salvation. But how does this square with the church's teaching that some of the unbaptized can be saved?

e) How can one reconcile the requirement for membership in the visible church for salvation with the fact some unbaptized can actually be saved? It is relatively simple to give a purely formal solution to this problem. Just as there is a *baptismus in voto*, so there is full membership in the church by desire (*voto ecclesiae*). Such desire can either be explicit (a catechumen) or implicit (one with a serious moral outlook who intends what is needed for salvation). Thus, actual full membership is only conditionally necessary.

f) There lie hidden within this formal solution a number of theological problems. One cannot assume that everyone after Christ was prevented from embracing the church without personal fault. Nor can they be regarded as the equivalent of moral infants. Desired full membership is plainly speaking not the same as actual full membership, and it is illegitimate to introduce some concept of church other than the visible church. Furthermore the discussion of actual and desired baptism/membership confuses two orders within the church: the inner realm of grace and the outer realm of visibility. If the inner state can bring about membership in the visible order one would have to argue that sin would effectively revoke church membership. It would also seem to reduce visible membership to a precept rather than a necessary means. To insist on the need for an inner attitude of faith for valid baptism/membership raises the question of how God could demand from infants what they are constitutively incapable of manifesting for salvation. Summary (50).

2) The teaching of the encyclical on the possibility of grace and salvation for those who are not members of the visible church. a) The texts themselves. Rahner cites three magisterial statements and discusses each in turn below.

b) Some general considerations about the interpretations of these texts. Once again Rahner maintains *Mystici corporis* adds nothing new to the church's teaching on the necessity for salvation of church membership, baptism, and subjection to the Roman pontiff (summary, 51f). This arises not from the fact that the issue of salvation outside the church is not important or already settled but because this topic is not the concern of the encyclical. Reasons for not discussing membership *in voto* are: i) its objectively inferior status to visible membership; ii) its continuing historical development; iii) it concerns the sovereign freedom of God more than one's existential state.

c) About the particular interpretation of each of the three statements. *Membra a corpore omnio abscissa* can be interpreted: i) all those who are not members (through no fault of their own); ii) those not fully members who are utterly and in every respect separated from the church. If the latter is the correct interpretation there must "be some way of belonging to the church which is to be distinguished from the notion of full and proper membership and yet is not purely fictitious" (55). To Rahner both positions ultimately reduce to the same thing. Summary (27f).

Pius IX's statement on the uncertainty of salvation for Protestants does not infer we know definitively the salvation status of Catholics. It concerns the lack of objective presuppositions for salvation, not one's inner state before God. Although the salvation of a person not a member of the church in the fullest sense is objectively more uncertain, salvation is not ruled out.

Rahner responds to the third statement by recapping his first two arguments and concluding "anyone who is divided from the Church by faith or government, cannot possess its divine Spirit, unless he be in good faith and has the *votum Ecclesiae*" (62). He summarizes with two long quotes (62ff).

3) Summary and supplementary remarks to Part II.

a) Even terminologically *Mystici corporis* adds nothing on the need for church membership for salvation.

b) The encyclical takes a new turn when it speaks synonymously of the church and the mystical body of Christ to emphasize that for salvation one needs a relationship with the visible church.

c) On the other hand the encyclical concerns the church and not the mystical body, a notion predicated of the church. Though the visible church is formally the mystical body the two notions are not materially identical.

d) Since the Holy Spirit is the soul of the visible church and can properly speaking only be found there, there must be some relationship between the visible church and justified persons who are not members (cf., Part III).

e) Progress toward Christian union is never well served by obscuring real differences. Insistence on the uniqueness of the visible Catholic Church for salvation does not impute the good faith of others, denigrate their gifts, or deny how much Catholics would be enriched by our reunion.

III. **With regard to the church's nature itself, what further facts, and what further indications for lines of inquiry can be gathered from the answer to the first two questions?** 1) The unseparated and unmixed divine and human natures of the church. To those who see the church's nature exclusively in visible, juridically verifiable terms it would seems theologically certain there is no salvation outside the visible church in the strictest sense. But the encyclical and the magisterium declare the nature of the church is more than this: "She is the body of Christ" (71). This presents a dilemma to which applying the notion of sacrament to the church is fruitful. A sacrament has a visible dimension and an invisible effect and can be validly administered without achieving its effect (and vice versa). Sacraments are just one instance of this general structure of Christian reality which is also seen in the church, the *Ur-Sakrament*. Hence, there is a legitimate two-fold notion of church as grace and sign. When the encyclical speaks of the church it proceeds from this second notion. What is says in this sphere remains fully valid without denying the full validity of the divine interiority of the church. This distinction insures the valid physical conferral of grace without thereby restricting God's sovereign freedom or reducing sacraments to magic.

2) Stratification within the nature of the church as sacramental sign. The formal solution to the problem of salvation outside visible membership in the church by way of desire left unanswered how the necessity of member-ship in the visible church remains sufficiently concrete (77). Rahner first offers a metaphysical response (77-82) based on the unity of the human race grounded in the universality of original sin and salvation in Christ. After reviewing the two-foldedness of human existence (i.e., body/spirit, person/ nature) Rahner maintains that our free personal acts necessarily conditioned by the givenness of nature (physical and historical) must also be conditioned by the reality of the incarnation. Hence, our total decision about ourselves includes a definitive stance toward God.

To clarify the objective content of the above Rahner begins with the incarnation which already sanctifies all individuals. Nowhere do people exist as "mere people" but always and only as "People of God which extends as far as humanity itself" (83). The real unity of humanity is based on its natural unity (cf., *Humani generis*) and the fact of the incarnation. Though the existence of this "People of God" precedes Christ's foundation of the church it does not make the latter inconsequential since the visible church is the vehicle God has willed to make grace more concrete. Hence, accepting the concrete reality of one's nature totally in the free act of supernatural justification by faith and love constitutes membership in the People of God. Membership becomes the expression of this justifying act. This is the *votum ecclesiae* revealed in its concreteness. Summary (86f).

2.02 Freedom in the Church
Die Freiheit in der Kirche
{1.5} Previously unpublished.

Abstract: Freedom without a theological end starves or exhausts itself. God, the freedom of freedom, is the inner reality of the church, God's sacramental sign. To respect freedom the church must temper its impulse to legislate.

Topics: CHURCH and freedom; FREEDOM and church; LAW.

Subsidiary Discussions: God (93f); Community (94ff); Incarnation (95f); Society, totalitarianism (99f); Ethics, existential (103ff); Church, subsidiarity in (105f).

Precis: A brief review of the topic freedom and church shows a much greater interest in gaining freedom *for* or *from* the church than freedom *in* the church.

I. The church as sacramental sign of freedom. There is such a thing as inescapable psychological freedom. It is at the core of our humanness and makes us responsible. What the Greeks saw as freedom from coercion became in time an inner freedom of detachment or indifference. But everything depends on the object of freedom. If it remains completely on the finite level freedom either exhausts itself in the pursuit of endless possibilities or starves itself by complete withdrawal from the choices the world presents.

It might seem that if we must totally dispose of ourselves for salvation or damnation through our free choices, then salvation must be part of our nature from the start—something we can attain or achieve by our own power. In short, it would seem that we must be our own salvation. But this is the great falsehood (93). God, the One we do not have but need to have to be free, remains a grace. God freely chooses to communicate himself to us as a choice. Only because we have this choice is our freedom liberated from the bondage of finitude. God is the freedom of our freedom. Summary (94).

God's free offer of self-communication is the decisive factor of the human situation. This alone makes humanity one community—a community of freedom lost in Adam (original sin) and of freedom regained in Christ (redemption). The redemption of human freedom is accomplished for the human community in the incarnation. This freedom of freedom has its source, is made accessible, and is applied to us in Jesus. "Now the Church is nothing other than the visible, socially composed communion of men with Jesus, the source of sanctifying grace...[it] is the continuation of the historically tangible reality of Christ" (96). Scripture explicitly connects this liberation of freedom with the church (96f). Because the church possesses the *Pneuma* it is the locus of spiritual freedom, its historical quasi-sacramental sign (97). The church renders this freedom effective by proclaiming it and through its administration of the sacraments. The life of the church is a sign of this freedom insofar as it is a life of love. Summary (98).

II. Freedom in the church. As a visible society on earth the church has a right and duty to limit the freedom of its members so long as this is done in love. How does it balance these bonds and human freedom? The church differs essentially from a totalitarian regime because the latter refuses to recognize individual freedom whereas this freedom is the essence of the church (99f). It looks totalitarian when it extends ultimately basic but very general principles with increasing exactitude and certainty. After arguing the church's right and duty to set general norms and concrete binding norms, Rahner squares this with the Pauline view of Christian freedom from the law (100f).

Three points must be kept in mind: a) It cannot be the business of any person or society to deprive anyone of the scope for making even morally wrong decisions. The church does not curtail a genuine right to freedom but only keeps people from objects which cannot be the true objects of free choice; b) these church laws oblige only its own members; c) church members are bound by church law even if they do not understand why these laws are binding. This does not mean they can justifiably surrender all subsequent freedom in the one act of surrendering to the church. Nor does it mean that wherever the church has not spoken definitively its members are free to take any course of action. Everything is not right which simply avoids conflicting with general norms.

Rahner argues the relevance of "existential ethics" based on the fact that the most essential choices effecting one's salvation/damnation (the choice of vocation, marriage partner, God's holy will for me here and now, etc.) are too particular to be known by the church. They constitute a "zone of freedom" in which decision is left to the individual, one's conscience, one's own charisms, and the guidance of the Holy Spirit. This same principle applies organizationally to the church in the principle of subsidiarity.

The church might make more room for freedom within itself: a) in allowing freer expression of public opinion; b) in theological research; c) in greater freedom of association; d) in its charismatic/prophetic dimension.

2.03 Personal and Sacramental Piety

Personale und sakramentale Frömmigkeit

{2.0}   Previously unpublished.

Abstract: Applying Aquinas' notion of the incarnational nature of grace to the question of sacramental efficacy harmonizes otherwise dualistic theories and clarifies the relationship between sacraments and their subjects.

Topics: GRACE; SACRAMENTS, *ex opere operato/operantis*; CHURCH.

Subsidiary Discussions: Incarnational principle (119ff); Causality, sacramental (122ff); Love (129f).

Precis: **I. Introduction to the problem.**

1) The question of how frequently to receive sacraments has long been discussed in many forms. Here Rahner asks whether pious acts (e.g., spiritual communion, examination of conscience with perfect contrition) can substitute for the reception of the sacraments without loss of benefits, and whether these pious acts have the same value and effects. Can one receive the *res sacramenti* independent of the sacrament?

2) Insufficient answers. It is not enough to say sacraments always and only give grace (*ex opere operato*) because: a) grace does not increase arithmetically with frequency of reception but in proportion to one's disposition; b)

though certain effects can only be had sacramentally (e.g., public position in the visible church through Orders) sanctifying grace is increased by living the Christian life. Also, though reception of sacraments is seldom required by canon law, it is wrong to neglect them. But what constitutes neglect?

II. A positive attempt at a solution: the inner unity of faith and sacrament. Rahner hopes to show personal piety and sacramental acts are not "two ways" to the same goal but two moments/phases of one event.

1) The teaching of current sacramental theology about the "two ways" of justification and of the increase of grace. Some theologians use infant baptism as their formal model of sacraments because it minimizes personal activity. Others hold to a subjective way of justification with little visible connection to Christ, the church, or the sacraments, and point to baptism of desire. This debate makes it seem as if there are two different causes which lead to one effect.

2) Critique of the doctrine of the "two ways of salvation" by showing the inner unity of faith and sacrament. Though metaphysically two causes can produce the same effect, methodologically a simpler explanation should always be preferred. Scripture stresses the need for both faith and sacrament without ever speculating on or solving our question. For Rahner the answer lies in correctly understanding the relation between *opus operatum* and *opus operantis* which receives its deepest treatment by Aquinas who leaves no room for contradiction between the two. A brief history of the relationship follows (116ff).

3) Theologico-speculative clarification: a brief, synthetic and speculative outline of a basic theory. Due to its incarnational character grace is simultaneously directed to the inner life of God and towards the world. It is meant to transform the world and always becomes externalized. Thus, no human act is ever purely internal or external (121). Every grace is essentially God's action in a saving dialogue with humanity. Because this dialogue is radically communal God insists it become visible as the church (122). The church is not static. It progressively unfolds in its teaching, and commandments "as the sanctification of men in her sacraments" (123).

The sacraments are constitutive signs. They are sign of grace not only because they are its cause but essentially because as causes they are signs. This causality, *per modum signi*, must not be confused with any other causality, though by analogy it is much like the visible church being the expression of grace in time and space of the actions of Christ. Insofar as Christ acts on us by giving his grace the form of constitutive signs it is Christ who renders the sacraments efficacious and not the minister or the recipient. This is the real meaning of *opere operatum* (summary, 124). Though the recipient of grace in the sacrament must provide a disposition, even this is already borne by the grace of Christ and the church, for disposition is never purely interior. In accepting the sacrament we take our place in the historical dialogue between Christ and the church and us, and this dialogue is the constitutive effective sign at that moment. "A sacrament takes place, therefore...as a dialogic unity of the personal acts of God and of man in the visible sphere of the Church's essential...sanctifying ministration" (125) with a certain variability. The more significant an act is for the community the greater is its public explicitness; the more mundane it is the less noted. Conclusion Part II (126).

III. Conclusion: One way of salvation by faith and the sacraments.

1) The quasi-sacramental visible appearance of the workings of God's grace in faith and love. "*God's* action on man occurs even in the 'subjective' way, and even the 'subjective' way occurs in the Church. Here, too, there is a dialogue of grace between God and man..." (127).

2) Grace and love inspired and embodied in the visibleness of the sacraments. Receiving sacraments even when not obliged to do so allows one's internal faith to grow. The divine cooperation is more tangible and hence more intense in the public, sacramental sign, although in both faith and sacrament the same powers are at work: "Christ, the Church, and the human person as the recipient of grace" (129). Hence, there is no competition between *opus operatum* and *opus operantis* (summary, 130f).

3) Consequences of the foregoing for determining the frequency of the reception of the sacraments. Constantly repeating sacraments is senseless because one's dispositions is the measure of sacramental effect, and "two kisses of love are not always more than one."

4) The inner unity of personal and sacramental piety. Finally, the sacraments are superior to pious devotions because in the incarnational order of Christ and our flesh everyday pious acts only attain their proper essential climax in sacraments.

2.04 Forgotten Truths Concerning the Sacrament of Penance

Vergessene Warheiten über das Bußsakrament

{1.0}   Previously unpublished.

Abstract: Attending to some neglected truths about penance gleaned from the tradition can deepen our understanding and participation in the sacrament.

Topics: PENANCE, sacrament of: SIN; CHURCH, restoring peace with.

Subsidiary Discussions: *Caritas* (150); Sacraments, *res et sacramentum* (153ff, 170ff); Baptism (157f, 171ff); Liturgy (160f).

Precis: Certain truths of tradition regarding penance are not "forgotten" as much as overlooked by theologians today. Though not the most theologically certain or the most important, the following truths "penetrate more and more, in ever new ways, into the infinite breadth and depth of divine truth" (136).

1) Consideration of sin as sin against the church. Offense against God is the essence of sin. It is additionally an offense against one's nature and

supernatural calling, against growth in holiness, and also against the church. Sin denies the holiness of the church and renders it sinful. This is borne out in scripture and the penitential practice of the early church. It is true of both mortal and venial sin. Would sinners not approach penance differently if they recalled the church too has something for which to forgive them?

2) "Binding." Matt 16:18; 18:18 points to the distance that arises between the sinner and the church on account of sin—a moral not a juridical effect as is excommunication. In matters of grave guilt the church simply makes visible the fact that sinners by their own actions are now excluded from the innermost life of the church. Binding and loosing are not two acts, but two phases of one act. The church binds in order to loose. The second phase depends on the repentance of the sinner. Rahner counters the objections: 1) such binding (apart from excommunication) no longer exists today (144-149); 2) there is no possibility of binding in the case of confession of devotion (149-152). He insists venial sin is never innocuous.

3) The "matter" of the sacrament of penance. Far from being an empty verbal wrangle the debate over the matter and form of penance contains an important forgotten truth (cf., 153-159 for history of development). Because acts of the penitent are an essential part of the sacramental sign we are not mere passive recipients but subordinate/associate causes of the sacramental grace. We actively celebrate the sacred mystery. This is possible because penance is always an ecclesial act and we come to it as members of the church in which divine grace always actively anticipates and facilitates our return.

4) The prayer of the church. Prior to Vatican II's renewal of penance the rite contained two brief aspirations, the *Misereatur* and *Indulgentiam*. These vestigial formulations pointed to a forgotten truth: "Because the Church prays and does penance in her Saints and justified members, God anticipates the sinner with his grace and leads him to the conversion without which no absolution is of any avail" (165). Hence, the interior conversion which brings one to the sacrament is already the work of the praying church.

5) Loosing on earth and in heaven. Forgiveness of sin does not exhaust the meaning of "loosing." The forgotten truth is sin is forgiven and guilt remitted in heaven precisely because it is loosed on earth in sacramental penance. The church grants sinners peace with God by restoring peace and communion with itself. After showing how this insight is consonant with scripture and the Fathers, Rahner explains it in scholastic concepts (170-172) and ends with random remarks on the nature of penances; the connection of penance and baptism; and between this and all the sacraments to Christ's pascal mystery.

2.05 Remarks on the Theology of Indulgences
Bemerkungen zur Theologie des Ablasses
{1.5}   *Zeitschrift für katholische Theologie* 71 (1949) 481-490, as, "*Über den Ablaß.*"

Abstract: A less juridic or extrinsic notion of "punishment due to sin" contributes significantly to an existentially compelling theology of indulgences.
Topics: INDULGENCES; PENANCE, sacrament of; SIN, punishment due to.
Subsidiary Discussions: Church, treasury of (183ff, 193f); Eschatology, intermediate state (198).

Precis: Indulgences are among those theological truths "silenced to death" by neglect—theologically true by existentially uncompelling. The reason lies in the inability or unwillingness of theologians to translate the doctrine into meaningful concepts for today. Rahner regrets this neglect and welcomes B. Poschmann's recent [1948] work on indulgences. After detailing Poschmann's historical thesis (179-186) Rahner analyses its dogmatic ramifications (186-194). [Since the present article concludes with Rahner's brief summary of Poschmann's position (200f), and since the first part of the essay represents the *status questionis* of 50 years ago that article is not abstracted here.]

Rahner's original contribution is found in the second part of the essay (194-200). It concerns punishment due to sin. Rahner maintains this concept holds the key to addressing Protestant and Orthodox objections to the Catholic position on satisfaction and indulgences. Current theology sees punishment due to sin too exclusively as vindictive, extrinsically imposed on us by God's justice. With an eye to the Fathers, Rahner explores the "living basis" which gave rise to the Catholic theory of temporal punishment: the longer time needed to scrutinize lapsed believers as opposed to catechumens. Its historical genesis sets the stage for moving the theory of punishment out of the realm of the juridical.

Citing Aquinas, Rahner contends God does not distinguish between vindictive and medicinal punishment. Sin punishes itself with co-natural consequences. How and why can only be understood against the backdrop of the ontology of spiritual (human) persons and their surroundings. Because of the unity of body and spirit every human act of spiritual freedom is always embodied. The incarnate consequences of sin are not simply canceled out by interior changes of heart. Hence, in our physical surroundings the sinful consequences of our sinful acts can outlast our contrition even beyond our earthy existence.

Although such suffering arises from guilt it is external to guilt. "Payment" for this kind of debt is not simply juridical. It can be thought of as the fruit of personal maturity, though Rahner is quick to add that no post-mortem maturing process ever changes one's "*option fondamentale*" finalized in this life. The afterlife is never true growth in grace. Thus, purgatory need not be thought of as mere passive endurance of vindictive punishment which leaves us essentially unchanged. It could be an integration of the whole stratified human reality into that free decision and grace which, having been made and won in this life, is in itself definitive. Although in this view remission is less juridical or extrinsic, it remains possible for God's indulgence to complete this process more or less quickly and intensely and therefore less painfully, however hard it may be for us to picture this. The article concludes with some unresolved questions which would need to be answered to develop a completely satisfying theology of indulgences.

2.06 The Resurrection of the Body
Auferstehung des Fleisches
{2.0} *Stimmen der Zeit* 153 (1953) 81-91.

Abstract: The reasonableness of bodily resurrection rests on Jesus' irrevocable victory extending to material reality however difficult it is to imagine.
Topics: RESURRECTION of the body; DEMYTHOLOGY; ESCHATOLOGY.
Subsidiary Discussions: BVM, Assumption of (205); Theological anthropology (211-216); Creed, "Resurrection of the flesh" (213f).

Precis: This essay divides into three unequal parts: the neglected state of the doctrine today (204-208); a note on demythologizing (207-210); Rahner's approach to the doctrine (210-216). Despite it's inclusion in the creed, its attestation in scripture, and its perennial mention in theology, resurrection of the body is in danger of being marginalized or replaced by more acceptable concepts like the immortality of the soul. The doctrine undeniably presents many serious theological and scientific difficulties (207).

Many say the doctrine needs to be demythologized. Rahner disagrees. For him the core task of theology is to bridge the poles of human knowledge (i.e., the conceptual and intuitional) to re-present theological concepts in new and more existentially compelling images. This never ending task is most difficult with theological notions of proto-history and eschatology including the consummation of the world, resurrection of the body, and second coming of Christ. Rahner admits it is impossible to combine scripture's descriptions of these realities into a unified picture however much they mean the same thing objectively. Asking what reality these images are meant to convey is an unavoidable and justified task of theology. It is not strictly speaking demythology.

Belief in the resurrection of the body means we at least profess: "the termination and perfection of the *whole* man before God, which gives him 'eternal life'" (211). But the multi-dimensional nature of man makes it possible to say that a person may achieve union with God after death in the beatific vision and still remain united with the world. Spiritual union with God and relation to the material world do not grow in inverse proportion.

However difficult it is to imagine (and it is less difficult for us than for earlier generations) the self-propagating history of the world will end. This will not be a sheer cessation, but participation in the perfection of the spirit, since personal spirit is the meaning of the whole reality of the world. The meaning of the material world is further revealed in its history. Jesus Christ, who possessed simultaneously the life of God and the history of human reality, is the perfect, total, and irreversible achievement of human history. His second coming takes place at the consummation of his victory in power and glory which reveals that the world as a whole flows into his resurrection and transfigured body. The resurrection of our bodies completes our perfection begun in death. Though we cannot imagine the how, we believe that since matter is not an illusion but part of true reality, the material world enters and participates in the state of finality and completion revealed in Christ. Ours becomes a spiritual body (I Cor. 15:44) completely one with the *Pneuma* of God. Thus, heaven remains a place and not merely a state, although with a time and space essentially different and incommensurable with the what we experience now (215). Complete, all-embracing solutions are the most difficult. But Christians can hold that the end of existence brings either our complete spiritualization or our complete demise along with the corruption of our bodies. We believe we are children of earth and spirits as well, and that both dimensions once reconciled can come to the one completion God intended.

2.07 On the Question of a Formal Existential Ethics

Über die Frage einer formalen Existentialethik

{1.5}   Previously unpublished.

Abstract: Rahner's critique of universal essentialist ethics on which traditional Catholic morality is based makes existentialist ethics more promising.

Topics: ETHICS, existential; ETHICS, essentialist.

Subsidiary Discussions: Ethics, situational (217ff); Particularity (225ff).

Precis: This essay divides into four parts: distinguishing extreme situation ethics from existential ethics (217-220); describing essentialist ethics (220-223): its critique (223-230); potential applications of existential ethics (231-234). (Bibliography of Rahner's work on situation ethics, cf., 217 ftn1.)

   Even allowing the persuasiveness of the theoretical foundations of situation ethics, no Catholic can ascribe to such a massive nominalism which denies the possibility of any universal knowledge with objective significance and true application to concrete reality. Although its absolute elevation of individuality conflicts with both scripture and the magisterium, it is here that existential ethics finds its core truth.

   In addition, essentialist ethics contains serious often overlooked problems (list, 219f). The basic question Rahner poses for essentialist ethics is how it produces a concrete, materially determined imperative for the individual in a particular determined situation. How does it apply universal norms to concrete individuals? What is the moral meaning of the range of acceptable possibilities (permissiveness) which arise from applying its procedure? Essentialist ethics is fundamentally a syllogistic, deductive ethics. It runs into serious problems formulating an acceptable minor premise from which to deduce a binding imperative. This approach also has difficulties dealing with a divine imperative addressed to an individual (e.g., religious vocation). This does not dispute the legitimacy or value of this approach in many cases but it certainly leaves much unanswered on the relationship between the universal and the individual. All Rahner hopes to do here is elaborate.

Instead of attacking the claim that a concrete situation can be adequately analyzed into a finite series of general propositions (223f), Rahner chooses a different approach. Even supposing one could completely render the individual under a universal norm, Rahner argues it remains an open question whether the imperative so deduced is identical with what we are obliged to do here and now. This is because "The concrete moral act is more than just the realization of a universal idea happening here and now in the form of a case. The act is a reality which has a positive and substantial property which is basically and absolutely unique" (225). Rahner holds this practically self-evident notion is not unthomistic. Summary (226).

At least two points argue the importance of the individuality of such spiritual acts in the real world: 1) regardless of the results of deduction one must still make crucial moral choices among the field of possibilities it leaves open; 2) one performs an act with an attitude which has moral consequences. In addition, the positively individual element in the moral action is absolutely the object of the binding will of God. This is true despite the fact it cannot be reduced to universal propositions and does not come about in the same way as the perception of universal law. Summary (229).

As to why there can and must be a "formal" existential ethics Rahner offers the analogy that just as there cannot be any true science of the singular individual and yet there is a formal ontology of individual reality, so there can and must be a formal doctrine of existential concretion. The urgent problem is, of course, how to perceive the individual moral reality and its obligation. Rahner suggests this is an underappreciated function of conscience, one of many important topics he cannot discuss in detail here (list, 229ff).

To underscore its practical importance Rahner concludes with nine concrete applications of existential ethics: 1) to postpone the recourse to probabilism so often invoked by casuists; 2) to clarify the Ignatian notion of choice in spiritual discernment; 3) to heighten appreciation for the fact that all sin is a failure of the personal-individual love of God; 4) to expand and safeguard the legitimate zone of individual decision in the church; 5) to balance the notion of religious obedience; 6) to clarify the relationship between the pastoral and teaching offices of the church; 7) to develop a theology of vocation; 8) to clarify our duty to strive for perfection; 9) to clarify the hierarchic and charismatic dimensions in the church.

2.08 The Dignity and Freedom of Man
Würde und Freiheit des Menschen.
{1.5} Previously unpublished 1952 lecture to *Katholikentag* in Austria.

Abstract: These reflections on human dignity and freedom, with notes on freedom and the state and in the church, were meant to stimulate discussion.
Topics: THEOLOGICAL ANTHROPOLOGY, dignity; FREEDOM.
Subsidiary Discussions: Human nature (238ff); Supernatural existential (240f); Redemption/salvation (243f); Power, coercion (248ff); Conscientious objection (251f); Society and freedom (255ff); Church, subsidiarity in (256f, 259f); Church, freedom in (258ff); Religious liberty (262f).
Precis: I. The dignity of man.
   1. Dignity in general is objectively identical with the essential structure (i.e., nature) and task of an entity.
   2. The nature of human dignity is found by appeal to reason and revelation. **a)** Since revealed knowledge is superior to knowledge gained by rational metaphysics, Rahner begins with revelation and then determines the natural remainder of human dignity. **b)** The methods of natural science cannot reveal human nature. Knowledge of essences relies on a twofold method: i) transcendental method; ii) reflection on our historical experience of self. Since this is always unfinished, self-understanding is always *in via*. Hence, knowledge of essence is never a-historical or a priori. It relies on tradition and risk.
   3. Human dignity consists in the capacity and task to open oneself to God's self-communication. This pre-established dignity can never be lost although it can be denied. We only come to know our nature and God slowly.
   4. Achieving our nature is the goal of our freedom and our salvation.
   5. The dignity of human nature contains these mutually determining moments: **a)** Our natural (personal) being which is: i) Spirit, always dependent on God, the total unity of reality; ii) Freedom; iii) Individual, unique, undeduced, immortal subject of an eternal destiny; iv) Community-building: perfect to the extent we open ourselves in love to serve others; v) Incarnate and mundane: self-realization comes only in extending oneself in space and time. **b)** The supernatural existential: each person is called to direct personal communication with God. **c)** God's gift unites our natures with the supernatural existential to form our elevated "supernatures."
   6. With this essence and dignity is given a plurality of human existential dimensions: **a)** corporeal-material; **b)** spiritual-personal; **c)** religious, God-centered; **d)** Christ-centered.

7. a) These existential dimensions are mutually dependent. It is illegitimate to make any one of them independent or self sufficient (e.g., ethics, economics, law, etc.). b) This permanent plurality must be respected. c) In cases of conflict the higher dimensions take precedence over the lower.

8. Our nature and dignity are threatened a) from without (material forces and other persons); b) from within (failure to find oneself). c) These internal and external factors determine each other. Guilt and fate intertwine.

9. Every person, precisely as a free subject, either takes control or denies control and responsibility for his/her concrete reality. How much control one actually has, how free one is, is fully known only to God.

10. Where one embraces one's nature and dignity there is redemption by the grace of Christ. This means: a) the call of the supernatural existential is realized. b) This presupposes God's free self-communication of the divine nature. c) This is accomplished by God's grace. d) This is true even if it is merely the fulfillment of our natural essence by the laws of nature since: i) a sufficient grasp of our nature is only possible with the help of revelation; ii) even such a natural attainment is oriented toward salvation. All this does not depend on our being conscious of the source of our redemption as such. Who Christ saves remains his secret. We cannot judge.

11. We should aim to reach a common understanding of the nature of human dignity and the natural law that flows from it even with non-Christians, recalling: a) when it is achieved revelation is at work in the non-believer; b) one must expect only modest practical consequences from such an understanding.

12. A formal definition of human dignity and its consequences: a) the person is an end possessing absolute (unconditional) dignity (summary, 245); b) human dignity is enhanced because God calls us into direct partnership.

II. The freedom of the person in general. Because human freedom is threatened today we must examine its nature and proper exercise.

1. Freedom is self-achievement of the person using finite material before the infinite God. It is, therefore, a datum of theology.

2. Human freedom is finite. Its governing conditions give rise to its ontological and ethical basis for a legitimate limitation of freedom. Equal rights is a matter of having each person's rights respected rather than attaining a material equality of rights for everyone by rationing them out.

3. Freedom is not simply a formal capacity, it is a good in itself which should not be frustrated even if the same results were attainable without it.

4. Human dignity demands that people be free even if this means allowing them to abuse that freedom. This is not to say people have a right to moral evil but only that coercing them to do good is wrong.

5. There is a legitimate zone of personal freedom in every human sphere.

6. The moral law as such is not a limit to freedom since it orients freedom to its proper goal.

7. The flight from responsible freedom into a merely secure life is immoral. Human freedom should never be sacrificed for mere material goods.

8. It is sometimes justified to limit freedom.

9. E.g.,: a) imprisoning dangerous people; b) compelling children to go to school; c) necessity can demand an objective action (rationing); d) conscientious objectors present special problems. e) Acts which demand a free consent cannot be coerced (e.g., marriage or religion). Coercion should never be applied in dubious cases.

10. This makes it difficult to demarcate when to allow freedom and when to apply coercion. a) Demarcation must respect both principles; b) there is no a priori demarcation line; c) the church has no revealed knowledge where to demarcate; d) Christians are bound to work to restore the proper proportion; e) since the demarcation line varies i) one must tolerate what is wrong when its removal would cause even greater harm. Such toleration is better seen as "active esteem and respectful deference before the conscience of others" (253); ii) decisions in this area will always be historically unique; f) Hence, Christians must often act in the dark. This calls for humility and prudence, and a capacity to live with irreducible pluralism. g) Though the balance of freedom and coercion should evolve, social revolution can become necessary; h) Each dimension of human life has its own balance. Material dimensions are generally more restricted, spiritual dimensions are more free.

III. The state and freedom.

1. The state exists for the person, not the person for the state. It must serve personal dignity and freedom with the degree of subsidiarity consistent with its nature as one institution among many.

2. Yet the state is a natural institution whose rights are not arbitrarily given by its citizens.

3. The state guarantees and harmonizes human rights and freedom. It is not their source.

4. Even a legitimately established democracy is no better than a dictatorship if the majority tyrannizes the minority.

5. The state must allow constitutional redress against itself.

6. Universal suffrage is not a natural right, nor does it guarantee natural rights. Much more is demanded of a good state than universal suffrage (list, 257).

7. Christians must work to insure that states embody social principles akin to natural law. We are handicapped today because Christians share no common vision of the good state.

IV. The church and freedom (cf., "Freedom in the Church" 2.02).

1. The church by its nature is an indispensable shelter and champion of human freedom.

2. Today the church must guard against seeming totalitarian. The past excesses perpetuated in her name stand out as aberrations.

3. Subsidiarity must determine the extent of freedom within the church.

4. The church can never replace the believer's personal responsibility.
    5. Concretely there should be more freedom in the church today: a) in the
expression of public opinion; b) in theological research; c) in freedom of
association; d) in the exercise of legitimate charisms.
    6. To those who fear the church would become totalitarian and oppress
others where circumstances should allow, Rahner points out: a) the church
cannot by its very nature coerce membership; b) the church is not bound by
old ideals even if they were once valid. Though there is no right to a false cult
as such, neither is there a right to suppress such cults forcibly. Where the state
allows its citizens their natural rights, where it does not engage in culture
politics or anti-religious bigotry, Christians would not need nor would they
seek state patronage.

2.09   Guilt and its Remission: the Borderland between
         Theology and Psychotherapy

{3.0}   *Schuld und Schuldvergebung als Grenzgebiet zwischen Theologie und*
        Psychotherapie
   Anima 8 (1953) 258-272, as, *Schuld und Schuldvergebung.*

Abstract: The roles of priest and physician in remitting guilt are distinguished by object and procedure based on the nature of sin and suffering.
Topics: SIN and guilt; CHRISTIAN LIFE, suffering; PSYCHOTHERAPY;
THEOLOGICAL ANTHROPOLOGY, guilt.
Subsidiary Discussions: Sin, original (267ff); Protology, fall (268); Becoming (271f); Heart (277).
Precis: An attempt to demarcate the border between the role of the church
and psychotherapy in sin/guilt and its remission is complicated because
schuld means both sin and guilt (cf., 265 ftn1).
    1. The theological premise that to God man is both sinner and redeemed
implies: a) Guilt is an irreducible phenomenon. It is not the same as illness.
Since guilt is an intentional happening with an intrinsic constitutive
moment of truth/falsehood it can only be repaired by attaining to objective
good, not by alleviating physical suffering that comes from sin. b) Whether
one understands it clearly or not, all sin is an offense against God. c) Guilt
has different degrees based on the sinner's degree of knowledge and freedom.
God can never put us into the tragic situation where sin is our only choice.
    2. Sins are principally acts, not states, although sins create a sinful mind
set which begets more sin. Genesis 3 reenforces the insight that we are
responsible for our sinful acts and guilty state. Sin and guilt have such a
diffuse existence in human history that we can never adequately resolve
through reflection the conjunction of act and state, habitual disposition and
original decision, sin and sinfulness.
    3. We attain self-consciousness only by being conscious of something
other than ourselves. Freedom (and ultimately our relationship with God)

is necessarily achieved in material embodiments of our real spiritual core. Our relationship to ourselves and to God is inevitably mediated. The culpable desire-to-be-God and be free from all constraint (sinfulness) leads to, but differs from, particular material acts of defiance (sin). Such acts are the constitutive sign of our revolt against finite nature. These are merely signs of underlying guilt because not all material acts are personally sinful. This does not rule out the possibility of sinning in thought or sinning directly and explicitly against God.

4. We have a spiritual-personal core, a "seminal person," which gives us an intentional transcendental relation to "Being as such" and hence to God. But we must always achieve ourselves *qua* "transcending person" in a relationship with something which is neither us nor God. This "intermediate reality" is at the same time different yet unseparated from the seminal person. There is no fixed boundary between these two human spheres. "Only by passing out of the depth of his being into the world, can man enter into the depth of the person where he stands before God" (273). Finally there is the "achieved person" freely self-fulfilled via his/her intermediary reality. The intermediary world, the realm of constitutive signs, the outer world, has a life relatively independent of the seminal person. It is also the realm where other physical influences affect the seminal person. Because the seminal person and the Other find their realization on the same intermediary plane they manifest here a complex interpenetration.

5. Sin occurs when in a free act of the seminal person one absolutizes some aspect of one's intermediate reality. The constitutive sign of sin is suffering—the painful resistance generated by the structures in the intermediate realm against which we offend. Of course not all suffering is occasioned by sin. Yet all suffering raises the question of whether it is to be accepted in faith as a share in the passion of Christ or denied in a guilty manner which then becomes the tinder of sin and the source of its own guilt. Sinfulness is the state of the seminal person which was achieved via one's intermediary reality but which now persists even after the constitutive sign has ceased.

6. Because we can never assess our freedom objectively but only through its constitutive signs, we are left in an essentially ambiguous situation regarding knowledge of our guilt. This inability to deal definitively with oneself is an essential aspect of the creature and should lead to unconditional surrender to God. Analysis reveals only the constitutive sign of sin. The heart remains hidden until it is fully revealed when stopped by death.

7. Though ontologically different, sin and suffering are connected. Suffering is the constitutive sign of guilt (though not all suffering is caused by guilt). No suffering is neutral. Since one cannot remain personally indifferent to any suffering one must either embrace or deny it.

8. Only God can deliver us from guilt in the strict sense. This demands a free, personal act of conversion on our part to re-enter the dialogue with

God. This converted heart must, however also be met with God's willingness to dialogue. In short, we are incapable of delivering ourselves from sin.

9. Suffering, insofar as it manifests itself in the intermediate realm can be combated and remediated by outside interventions whether or not this suffering is caused by sin. Similarly, guilty suffering can remain even after sin has been remitted. In addition to the medical model of combating suffering there is the Christian approach of accepting suffering in faith. The ambiguous nature of suffering will always make questionable our attempts to alleviate it. Saying "no" to the suffering of this world is a Christian duty which poses the greatest danger: seeking to steal past the cross. Our "no" must consist in helping others shoulder the cross without bitterness or despair.

10. Like sin and suffering, the proper tasks of priest and physician are mutually related yet different. Each has its own object and procedure. The priest remits sin and restores a right relationship with God without necessarily alleviating suffering, even when it is directly due to sin. Physicians aim to alleviate suffering. They must not simply bypass the question of real theological guilt even though they cannot relieve it. Relief demands a sinner's conversion and faith in God's willingness to remit one's guilt.

2.10 Peaceful Reflections on the Parochial Principle

Friedliche Erwägungen über das Pfarrprinzip
{1.0} *Zeitschrift für katholische Theologie* 70 (1948) 169-198.
Abstract: In the post-war debate over the competence of pastors vs. extra-parochial ministers Rahner denies the hegemony of the parochial principle.
Topics: CHURCH, pastoral ministry in; PARISH.
Subsidiary Discussions: Freedom of association (302ff); Parish, history of (307ff); Religious life (310ff).
Precis: I. Rahner begins with distinctions (283-286): There are two kinds of principles, those which are always and only correct and valid, and those whose validity is shared with others. The parochial principle is among the latter. Two principles are contained within it: the parish-priest principle which governs who supplies ministry, and the parish principle which governs the geographical boundaries of ministry (definitions, 286). Rahner also distinguishes between ordinary and extraordinary care of souls.

Changes in the spiritual field and subsequent theoretical concerns generally led to the re-emphasis of the parochial principle. Such changes in post-war Germany included increased competence of secular clergy, a greater desire of parishioners for community, a greater secularization of society. These support imposing the parochial principle. Theoretical arguments include the similarities between the pastor-to-parish and bishop-to-diocese model of administration; the geographical rootedness of those to whom the church ministers; the venerable antiquity of the principle. Pastoral argu-

ments include the need to center ministry on the local altar community. Although the parochial principle is recognized by canon law (291-292) it never binds the faithful to discharge their religious obligations in their local parish.
II. However, the parochial principle is not the only one governing pastoral activity. Parishes are human not divine institutions whose organization is up to the local bishop. The overriding concern should never be how ministry is organized but how well it attains its goal. Having a geographical home is only one (and not necessarily the most important) dimension of the modern urban dweller who requires more association-minded-ministry. Increasingly large parishes challenge the exclusive application of the parochial principle. Pastors themselves cannot be expected to have all the gifts needed to minister effectively to an increasingly diverse parish. To insist on a strict application of the parochial principle limits Catholics' right of association. Summary (306).
Rahner's brief history of pastoral ministry indicates that the parochial principle has never been the exclusive or even always the preferred means of organizing pastoral care (307-310). His concluding discussion of the role of religious orders in pastoral care (310-314) indicates the principle of "extra-parochial" care of souls shares equal canonical and pastoral legitimacy.
III. Conclusions: 1) Since it is impossible to fix concrete boundaries between these two principles, good will is required to maintain harmony among pastoral ministers and the institutions they represent. Love demands that friction be met first with self-examination. 2) This situation calls for cooperation and compromise. 3) Competition in pastoral ministry is not always a bad thing.

2.11 Notes on the Lay Apostolate
Über das Laienapostolat
{1.5} Previously unpublished.
Abstract: Lay apostolate differs from the apostolate of the hierarchy insofar as laity stay in their places in the world to transform them by their example.
Topics: LAITY; CHURCH, hierarchy.
Subsidiary Discussions: *Potestas ordinis/jurisdictionis* (319ff, 331f); Women (321); Religious life (322); Charism/s (325f, 334); Catholic Action (328, 346ff).
Precis: I. The layman.
1. The lay state does not demarcate sacred and secular. It refers to a definite position within the one consecrated church.
2. This can be described negatively and positively.
3. Negative description: a) A lay person is distinguished from those with proper hierarchical powers in the church (*potestas ordinis, potestas jurisdictionis*) although this distinction is quite fluid, especially regarding women (321)

and those in "minor orders." b) A lay person does not publicly profess the evangelical counsels in a permanent way of life in the church.

4. Positive description: a) From the point of view of the world: Unlike clerics or religious, lay people retain their original place and task in the world. b) From the point of view of the church: What are laity as such in the church? What do they take into the world? What do they realize there as church members? i) Concise definition. ii) They are sacramentally empowered and commissioned, and contribute to the holiness of the church by their personal holiness. iii) They can possess and manifest proper spiritual charisms. iv) They actively participate in the mission and responsibilities of the church. v) If they freely consent they can be invested with specific non-clerical tasks *de jure humano* (e.g., catechist, parish trustee) so long as they are not removed from their proper station in the world.

5. Summary.

II. The apostolate in general.

1. By virtue of divine right Christ instituted hierarchical and non-hierarchical roles in the church. The hierarchy represents Christ to the church. Their powers come from him not from the members of the church.

2. Although the church can and has divided its hierarchical powers in various ways, whoever shares in these powers thereby ceases to be a lay person. It follows there is an "apostolate in the church." Participation in this apostolate by lay people is legitimate if and when the lay apostolate meets the church apostolate in the same object or goal. But this does not alter the fact there is a non-transferrable apostolate of the hierarchy which must not be confused with the apostolate of the laity.

3. This hierarchic "office of apostolic mission" is best distinguished by apostolic succession. Those called to this office are taken out of their original place in the world for the purpose of uniting their entire lives with the mission of the church. They are sent out to the world aggressively to preach not themselves but Christ. Summary (335).

4. Negatively, wherever this "sending out" is not part of an apostolate it is most likely an example of lay apostolate.

5. This distinction is difficult to apply in practice. After listing particular difficult cases (e.g., Legion of Mary, Sodality of St. Peter Claver) which he does not see as examples of lay apostolates, Rahner alludes to the restored married diaconate, his model for expanded ministry brought under the apostolate of the hierarchy.

6. Consequences: simply because organizations like Catholic Action are predominantly staffed by the non-ordained, they are not thereby lay organizations. In fact Rahner sees such full-time staffers as part of the hierarchy.

III. The lay apostolate.

1. Lay apostolate is the concern for the salvation of others incumbent on all baptized Christians—their duty to love their neighbors in that place in the

world which belong to them, without participating in the hierarchial ministry or its apostolates. Through baptism and confirmation they are empowered to witness their own Christian faith. Their ministry is from below. They do not "go out" but work on the spot. They are missionaries by the example of their Christian living.

2. Such a lay apostolate is obligatory for all the baptized. Though it embraces all, it begins at home. This is both its limitation and strength.

3. This apostolate is exercised essentially by example in all the fields of human endeavor: science, art, medicine, politics, economics, etc.

4. This apostolate must be exercised in marriage, and secondly in public life strengthened by the sacraments of marriage and confirmation respectively. Lay apostolate differs from that of the hierarchy not by goal or object but by its way of achieving them. Simply because it does not propagandize or recruit does not mean the lay apostolate is limited to the private realm.

5. Thus, the goal of formation of the laity should be education for a holy interior Christian life, not techniques for organizing social action.

6. The laity also has tasks oriented to the church itself: to worship there, to support it financially, to serve on committees, etc.

7. The laity is also endowed with authentic charisms by the Holy Spirit.

8. Rahner further identifies two types of ecclesiastical organizations: a) church organizations properly so-called, set up by the church to enlist the aid of the laity in furthering the hierarchial mission (e.g., Third Orders, mission support groups); b) organizations of the laity meant to further their Christian lives as such (e.g., student associations, benevolent societies) and whose goals are often temporal or "profane." These often exhibit true independence from priests and from diocesan control.

9. Rahner draws some specific conclusions for Catholic Action.

IV. The importance of the lay apostolate and final summarizing remarks.

1. a) In the Middle Ages the church and theological concerns were the only game in town. Today innumerable factors vie for interest and attention. Hence, the laity must work to prevent the Christian element in these new areas from being ignored or crushed. If this new world is to be Christianized it will happen through lay efforts. They are not in competition with the clergy. b) Whatever organizations in the Church are not geared to aid the laity in this task must be seriously re-examined, and if found superfluous, jettisoned.

2. a) Serious thought should be given to protecting the real autonomy of lay organizations with positive law. Clerical attitudes also must change. If the laity are given responsibility they should be free to fulfill it as they see fit. The church must avoid totalitarianism and manipulation. b) Rahner hopes this essay will insure that the laity are not enlisted in works not properly theirs, however heroic or necessary these may seem. Instead the laity should be helped to perform their proper mission in their place in the world.

III. THE THEOLOGY OF THE SPIRITUAL LIFE
III. *Zur Theologie des geistlichen Lebens*

German edition: Einsiedeln, Benziger, 1956
U.S. edition: Baltimore, MD, Helicon Press, 1967
Karl-H. and Boniface Kruger, O.F.M., translators

3.01 Reflections on the Problem of the Gradual Ascent to Christian Perfection

{1.5}   *Über das Problem des Stufenweges zur christlichen Vollendung*
        Zeitschrift für Aszese und Mystik 19 (1944) 65-78.

Abstract: The commonly accepted notion of gradual growth in holiness is problematic. Rahner suggests an approach based on the intensity of moral acts.

Topics: SPIRITUALITY; CHRISTIAN LIFE, holiness.
Subsidiary Discussions: Gnosis (5f); Virtue (17f); Mysticism (9f, 22f).

Precis: Conventional wisdom affirms the possibility of a gradual assent to perfection in the spiritual life. Classically this assent is divided into stages. Rahner finds these notions problematic. Without questioning the reality of growth in holiness Rahner asks whether there is in fact "a way" to Christian perfection; whether this way is gradual; whether such growth really is analogous to building a savings account of graces.

On this point scripture remains vague. It speaks of *metanoia* without ever alluding to a particular path or stages. Although one is said to mature, advance, and increases in holiness, scripture never says this state becomes final, absolute, or unchanging. In scripture this assent is always oriented toward *gnosis*—ever greater knowledge and experience of the secrets of God.

This gnostic characteristic tends to endure in the history of doctrine. Rahner briefly tours this history through Clement of Alexandria, Origen and Evagrius, Gregory of Nyssa, Pseudo-Denis, Augustine, Bonaventure, the Spanish mystics. He concludes that the two traditional sets of stages are problematic: one assumes the goal of spiritual growth is a heavily gnostic mysticism; the stages of the other are so formal as to be empty. Summary (10).

Problems begin as soon as one asks concretely about growth in holiness. The common notion that it coincides with the increase in sanctifying grace not only fails to connect ontic with moral holiness, it also fails to move growth in holiness into the realm of personal experience. Hence, ontically a quite imperfect, embittered, loveless old religious could have stored up many years worth of sanctifying grace with no personal experience of growth in holiness. Some approach this problem by identifying the stages of growth in holiness with different objective values of the classes of moral acts (i.e., one begins by avoiding mortal sin and ends in infused contemplation). But Rahner finds such divisions too artificial for it seems possible to skip or miss certain stages altogether (e.g., juvenile saints).

Rahner suggests thinking about one's changing life "situations" conditioned as they are by internal factors (age, health), external factors like culture, and past experiences and decisions. What is necessary to get a clearer picture of growth in holiness is a schema of such situations based on an empirical, differential psychology of different age groups.

Discussing growth in terms of attaining virtuous habits (17) seems to explain how one can acquire perfection as a possession. But it is problematic since habitual actions become sub-human, instinctual reactions. How can these be the proper goal of holiness, especially since the effects of some such habits can be brought about by drugs? This leads to intractable problems (19).

Rahner's way out begins by asking whether moral acts can increase in intensity. Can the perfectly moral person perform the same moral act differently from the way a beginner performs it? If so, one could develop a law of stages in which this intensity grows. This approach would demand clarifying types of intensity and numerous other questions (21). Nevertheless this seems to be a fruitful point of departure for taking a new look at the subject of holiness.

Rahner concludes with a note on mysticism (22f) arguing that although traditional mysticism cannot be seen as the goal of the spiritual life, perhaps the intensification of moral actions would ground a new understanding and connect both mysticism and growth in holiness. Summary (23).

3.02 Thoughts on the Theology of Christmas
Zur Theologie der Weihnachtsfeier
{1.0}   *Wort und Wahrheit* 10 (1955) 887-893.

Abstract: Silent self-reflection prepares the heart to experience, understand, accept, and celebrate the mystery of Christ's incarnation.

Topics: LITURGICAL YEAR, Christmas; GOD incarnate; LITURGICAL YEAR, Advent.

Subsidiary Discussions: Heart (25f, 33f); Creation (31ff).

Precis: The best way to prepare to celebrate Christmas is not by thinking about the incarnation but by experiencing how the incarnation answers our deepest, most fundamental stirrings. Begin with the courage to be alone, to withdraw into silence, and there to wait and listen, doing nothing. The self-awareness of the heart may initially be horrifying or uncomfortable. Endure yourself, and you will experience an all-encompassing, nameless remoteness which at first appears as emptiness. It cannot be left alone. It demands a response. Do not call it God. But if you let the silence speak to you of God then this loudly calling silence will become strangely ambiguous. In revealing your world as finite does this silence judge it? Or does it wait for you to open to its promised beatitude? Is it salvation or judgment? Life or death? Does the silence announce the one who is to come? The heart alone, burdened by all its fears cannot discern. Still, this silence says something quite exact: the message of Christmas told from within. Without the silence of the heart the message of Christ's birth remains external. It could never enter or be celebrated in the heart. Here experience from within meets the message from without and celebration begins. Summary (28f).

This experience of the heart must be augmented with a conceptual explanation of the message of Christmas. That "God became man" is too often taken in a Monophysite or Nestorian sense. Rahner prefers the formula "God is man" for it tells something about God's very self: that this human nature is God's very reality. When God manifests his humanity, there we meet God. It is a mistake to place the human and divine natures side by side since they arise from a common ground. This is revealed in the experience of the heart: that God is present as one who is silent; God is present in a nearness of distance; God is the absent one we need in order to be fully ourselves; we are a mystery always referred beyond ourselves into the mystery of God. When we imagine this absolute remote and transcendent mystery coming intimately close to us and accepting us completely, then we are imagining the incarnation.

Rahner re-imagines this mystery from the viewpoint of creation (32f). Very often one thinks of creation as a self-evident act, and God's becoming a creature as a subsequent act. But if one imagines God's creating the world out of a desire to share prodigal love, then the free creation of a being completely open to receive such love is the mystery at the center of creation. Christ is that point in creation at which our full openness to God is answered by God's full self-communication. This is the dimension of creation we glimpse in our encounter with silence.

Rahner returns to his theme that one prepares to celebrate Christmas by listening to the heart (33). Admittedly one can not deduce the actual truth of the incarnation by reflecting on experience. But plumbing the heart's depth does prepare us to receive and celebrate the Christmas message. Summary (34).

3.03 The Eternal Significance of the Humanity of Jesus for Our Relationship with God

Die ewige Bedeutung der Menschheit Jesu für unser Gottesverhältnis
{1.5}   *Geist und Leben* 26 (1953) 279-288.

Abstract: Warns against the dangers of an absolute monotheism which envelops and annuls the adoration of the Sacred Heart and the veneration of the saints.

Topics: GOD incarnate; JESUS CHRIST, Sacred Heart of; SAINTS, veneration of; ESCHATOLOGY.

Precis: **I.** Do adoring the Sacred Heart or venerating saints reach their purported objects of devotion or are they swallowed up in the infinity of God? We deal with only two things: the world which impinges from the outside, and God whose incomprehensibility is known in silence and through revelation. Angels, saints and the glorified humanity of Christ fall in the realm of God. Without questioning their existence, Rahner wonders whether for us they don't all meld into the one over-arching reality of God.

In previous ages the danger was polytheism. Today it is an absolute monotheism which swallows up every particular thing, indeed the whole world, in the beatific vision, the blazing abyss of God. As to the Sacred Heart in particular, Rahner questions whether it is for us just one more colorful word for God and the incomprehensibility of God's unbounded love. But he insists this Heart exists now as a real human heart. How can the religious act attain to such a heart and not be swallowed into the abstract immensity of God?

II. Rahner leaves aside the subjective question: how to overcome the shrinking existential potency of realizing genuinely numinous powers and realities distinct from God. He contributes two reflections: 1) the relationship between God and created numinous realities; 2) the relationship between God and the humanity of Christ and his Sacred Heart in particular. The problem starts with our notion of a God who obscures our individuality the closer we approach. It is just the opposite: the nearer we come to God the more real we become. We do not feel this way because we hate the finitude that is revealed as we approach God. We hate created reality because we long for the absolute on our own terms. But to love God means to love the created world as valid and eternal precisely because it exists through the love of God.

"A pluralistic world of the numinous finds its meaning and its justification in the sight of the God of Christianity. The effort of holding on to this truth is the effort of overcoming our unchristian outlook and solving the *sinful* dilemma into which original sin throws us" (41). Theology must do more to distinguish *laetria* from *dulia* and to counteract a misguided mysticism. This is an important first order question in Christian thought which affects Christians as they mature in their relationship with God. The three stages of this maturing process (leaving creatures, serving creatures, rediscovering the creature in God) provide the framework for learning how to honor Christ's humanity in general and his heart in particular. For the God-man is the basis and climax of God's relationship to creation. Christ not only *was* but *is* the gate and door to any personal relationship with God. Any other relationship is a mystical flight into the infinity of dissatisfied finitude. Thus, Christ's glorified humanity is never provisional. That this reality is difficult to express and raises many new questions does not make it false. Summary (46).

3.04 Reflections on the Theology of Renunciation
Zur Theologie der Entsagung
{1.5} *Orientierung* 17 (1953) 252-255.
Abstract: Christian renunciation is legitimate because only it can embody a way to love God in hope (eschatologically) and in the church (ecclesially). It relocates one's center of action beyond the realm of intra-mundane values.
Topics: CHRISTIAN LIFE, renunciation; RELIGIOUS LIFE, evangelical counsels; ESCHATOLOGY and evangelical counsels.

Subsidiary Discussions: Love (47ff); Natural order (49f, 52f); Death (54); Church (55); Sacraments, *res et sacramentum* (56).

Precis: Renunciation is not merely the self-control demanded by any ethics. It is the particular radical renunciation expressed in all three evangelical counsels as a permanent form of life in the church. A detailed examination of its essence clarifies this common connection.

I. 1) Christian perfection consists simply and solely in the perfection of the love given us in Christ by the Spirit of God who is communicated to us in justification and sanctification. This love embraces all spiritual creatures and has a theological, ecclesial, and eschatological character insofar as it is directed towards a transcendent, supra-mundane goal. Thus, human relationships formed and elevated by this divine love become themselves a part of that love.

2) All acts of virtue make this love concrete while retaining their proper fullness or perfection. All people are called to realized this love in Christ in their own irreducibly individual and personal way.

II. 1) Christian renunciation cannot be explained from the standpoint of purely natural ethics. Natural law can never demand it, nor can it be explained as a preemptive strike against concupiscence. For most it is not the "better way" to perfection. Before Christ it never existed as an option.

2) Renunciation finds its ultimate meaning in love.

3) The essence of Christian renunciation is the sacrifice of positive intra-mundane goods and values—not mere instrumental goods, but things good in themselves. In a purely natural order there would be no other values for the sake of which these could be sacrificed. To base renunciation on a resentful devaluation these goods is objectively false and raises psychological suspicions.

4) The evangelical counsels comprise only one among many legitimate paths to Christian perfection.

III. 1) Positive intra-mundane values can only be sacrificed out of love which is supernatural, eschatological, and ecclesial. This tangibility of the church can only be expressed through renunciation of intra-mundane values. **a)** Expressing eschatological love in pure renunciation is either senseless (from the natural viewpoint) or the realized combined expression of faith, hope, and love which reaches out to God's very self without any worldly mediation. Renouncing an intra-mundane value for a higher value is a characteristic proper to Christian renunciation. But how is it a means of love? One cannot appeal simply to its difficulty, or to the example of Christ, or to a calculus of lessened moral dangers in the intra-mundane realm since such appeals merely beg the question.

Why is such a life even justified? Because only renunciation embodies that believing love which reaches out to God in hope. Loving God in hope moves our existential center beyond the realm of the empirical, whereas any concrete embodiment of love leaves open the question of its intra-mundane moral value. Summary (54). One needs to be called to this life by God. Renunciation parallels the dynamic of Christian death. **b)** Why does God will such a sign? Because such renunciation (along with the sacraments) makes visible the inner nature of the eschatological love of the church. The evangelical counsels are an inalienable and essential part of the church just as attachment to the church is essential to the evangelical counsels.

2) The relationship of renunciation to love can also be expressed in terms of the relationship of *res et sacramentum.*

3) Evangelical renunciation is objectively a "better" or "happier" way of life only in the special sense that it is the best/only way to embody the church's eschatological love of God. And for those who are called to it, it is the happier life.

3.05 The Passion and Asceticism: Thoughts on the Philosophical-theological Basis of Christian Asceticism

Passion und Aszese
{3.0}   *Geist und Leben* 22 (1949) 15-36.

Abstract: Rahner answers those who revile Christian asceticism as world-hating by showing that only Christians in a spirit of eschatological faith can love the world afresh with a powerful, intimate love which renounces freely what they are not required to give up in hopes of an extra-mundane fulfillment.

Topics: CHRISTIAN LIFE, asceticism; CHRISTIAN LIFE, suffering; CHRISTIAN LIFE, renunciation.
Subsidiary Discussions: Death (67f, 72ff ftn1); Mysticism (66ff, 80); Nature and person (69ff, 82f); Jesus Christ (68f, 81f); God (76f).
Precis: In answer to the charge that Christianity is a world-hating religion Rahner recalls that the first article of the creed proclaims a God who created and loves the world. This is not simply obvious (e.g., gnosticism). Christianity by contrast maintains that fulfilling our worldly tasks has fundamental significance for salvation. Christian asceticism never minimizes the goodness of whatever it renounces. Defining three different varieties of mysticism sets the stage for discovering the starting-point to explain the essential nature of Christian asceticism.
I. The three types of mysticism outlined below are not pure types. Because they participate in another to a confusing extent they are defined here only roughly. **1. Moral asceticism:** Many people, including Christians, labor under a "bourgeois" conception of asceticism (cites Ries, 60) and regard it as "a pure means for a moral self-discipline with a view to attaining an undisturbed harmony between the different forces in man" (61). The sacrifices of worldly goods entailed by this self-discipline are simply means to attain greater goods, and thus no real sacrifice at all. But this is not at the heart of Christian asceticism. It fails to make sense of the actual history of the

asceticism of the saints and fails to do justice to the revealed and mysterious nature of Christian asceticism. Moral asceticism misidentifies the dangerous condition facing us as the loss of this worldly goods rather than as the loss of our other worldly calling.

2. Ritual asceticism: There is a kind of asceticism often associated with worship where one forgoes certain acts (e.g., sex, food) to remain ritually pure, or sacrifices certain things to enter into contact with the godhead. This is superior to moral asceticism insofar as its inter-mundane renunciations have an other-worldly orientation. If through such acts of believing readiness one remains open to divine action it is similar to Christian asceticism. If it is a means to contact God purely though one's own initiative it is a variety of mystical asceticism.

3. Mystical asceticism: Despite its long history and varied manifestations this type of mysticism is a direct preparation of the subject for a mysterious experience of the divine. Here asceticism already establishes the possibility of mysticism by the very psychological conditions it calls for (e.g., trances, emptiness). Though it is a liberation of the divine in us it differs from Christian asceticism when it claims "an autonomous overcoming of true death and the intentional dissolution of the Passion" (67) as if God must fill with a mystical presence the space one has made inside oneself.

II. Rahner approaches Christian asceticism by way of the concept of death and passion, metaphysically and theologically related concepts insofar as renunciation achieves what passion and death also demand of us (preview, 69).

1. The nature of "passion" touches every human life insofar as we know pain, suffering, anxiety, fear, diminution, death, etc. These sensible experiences only become passion when experienced by a free *person* with control over one's own person and who shapes an internal life by free decisions within the confines of one's *nature*. Neither pure nature nor pure person can suffer. Suffering is only possible where both exist together (71). What attitude should we adopt toward the fate involving suffering coming from the outside? Stoic withdrawal and eradicating spirit are unsuccessful in practice since every moment of existence is affected by the fate which befalls our nature. Hence, passion is an essentially personal phenomenon—a problem we cannot solve from below. How, therefore, can the one human being combine an absolute, active power over oneself and one's absolutely subject condition at death (the climax of passion)? Only by saying yes to the death-reality of human existence "can a free person turn a necessary fate externally imposed on him into a free act of the person itself" (73). (A "no" would only be successful if it could make death a purely biological, non-personal event.) "Asceticism, therefore, is nothing other than the personal, free grasping-of-his-own-accord of his necessary being-onto-death" (73). Thus, passion and asceticism are two sides of one coin: "Passion expresses the necessity of death in man taken as nature, whereas asceticism expresses the freedom of death in man taken as person" (73).

2. The Christian meaning of passion and death. All this leaves open two questions: what is this death we embrace, and how do we embrace it? Death puts the meaning of the whole of human life into question. There are three possible responses: life is meaningless; its meaning is beyond this world; faith transmutes death into the grace of eternal life (which as a hoped-for-reality still does not make suffering innocuous). Christian asceticism is precisely "an existential faith exercised in a Passion which can no longer be given any complete and positive this-worldly meaning" (75). Although one can come to know God by creation, human metaphysics cannot reveal God's absolute attitude towards us.

The proper response to this impasse is to listen for a word from God. Once God addressed the world through Jesus Christ it was no longer possible to maintain an internally closed, intra-mundane harmony of human existence. Jesus revealed our transcendent destiny and the new danger in the temptation to find absolute meaning in the world of nature which is now revealed as something temporary, second-rate, subject to a standard beyond itself. The act of faith in God's offer of new life beyond this world and the act of embracing death daily are the same. This opens the possibility of renouncing the world (*fuga saeculi*)—the existential confession that God has shifted the center of our existence beyond this world does not deny death but embraces it. Christian asceticism is the anticipating grasp of Christian death understood as the most radical act of faith (79). It is more than moral asceticism and less than mystical asceticism. God remains greater than asceticism and can make both flight from the world and embrace of the world the means for drawing nearer to God. Since God is revealed not in a decree but in a person, Jesus Christ, every act of asceticism which responds to this revelation is a response to Christ and to his passion and death.

3. Conclusions. a) The voluntary/imposed characteristic of Christian asceticism can never be separated. **b)** Voluntary Christian asceticism demands a vocation in some sense which is rightfully regulated by the church. **c)** Asceticism is an eschatological reality. **d)** Christian asceticism as *fuga saeculi* can never be considered the sole legitimate or the best approach to God.

3.06 Reflections on the Experience of Grace
Über die Erfahrung der Gnade

{0.5} *Geist und Leben* 27 (1954) 460-462.

Abstract: Acts which have no pay off in this life reveal the infinite depths of our spirit where we glimpse the supernatural and begin to experience grace.
Topics: GRACE, experience of; SPIRITUALITY.

Precis: Rahner asks whether the reader has ever experienced grace—"that visitation by the Holy Spirit of the triune God which has become a reality in Christ through his becoming man and through his sacrifice on the Cross" (86). Is it even possible in this life, and if so, is it perhaps accessible only in stages? Have we ever experienced the spiritual? Most would say yes, and point to experiences of love, happiness, enjoyment, mental engagement, etc. But are these experiences of the spirit in its proper transcendence? Where do we look inside ourselves to discover the experience of grace?

Rahner asks the reader to consider selfless, unrewarded acts—even acts positively detrimental to us (e.g., not defending ourselves when maligned, having our forgiveness taken for granted, loving God when God seems silent and far off, continuing to do good in the face of ingratitude). Precisely because no intra-mundane value accompanies them, these acts are spiritual experiences, experiences of eternity. They show that our meaning is not confined to this world. These kinds of experiences are the secret and (from the natural point of view) seemingly perverse joy of the saints.

By experiencing the spirit in this way Christians who live their faith experience the supernatural. When we let ourselves go in this experience, when our actions lose their relish, *this* is the hour of grace when we move out of this world and into the world of God. It is the hour of grace and of eternal life. This chalice of the Holy Spirit is identical with the chalice of Christ which liberates the spirit by grace. At the same time we must avoid claiming such grace as a possession. For we only find it in losing ourselves. The value of periodically asking where we experience this destructive yet vivifying grace helps us estimate how far we have yet to go in our spiritual journeys.

3.07 The Church of the Saints
Die Kirche der Heiligen
{1.0} *Stimmen der Zeit* 157 (1955) 81-91.

Abstract: Canonized saints constitute an essential dimension of the church by proving that its holiness is actual and not merely hypothetical. Saints offer historically unique and original models of holiness to their contemporaries.

Topics: SAINTS; CHURCH, holiness of; CHRISTIAN LIFE, holiness.
Subsidiary Discussions: Saints, canonization (92f, 101ff); Grace (93f); Charism/s (103f); Creed, "I believe in the holy church" (passim).
Precis: There is no developed treatise on the doctrine of "the finally redeemed, holy members of the holy Church." Generally any discussion of saints centers on their meaning for us along with the rationale for venerating them.

The theology of the church of the saints. Rahner beginning by asking why the church has the right to canonize a person. Even the presence of miracles adds only a relative degree of certainty whereas the church's judgment is absolute. How does the church know to venerate the saints? Rahner insists canonization is a necessary element for the church to realize its own being. Its confidence in canonization has the quality of faith. Why is this so?

In praise of grace. Because of God's grace the church must humbly professes herself to be holy. In this it praises not only God's grace in itself but also the effects of that grace: that it is holy and has holy members (along with sinners). Its holiness is not only potential it is actual. **Eschatological testimony of faith.** The visible church declares itself holy. Although this is a profession of faith, its reality is not entirely beyond the realm of experience for those who seek it with humble, open minds. While remaining a free act of the individual, the church's proclaimed holiness is first and foremost a gift from God. Hence, the church must proclaim its holiness. It is an eschatological statement of faith not merely a kind judgment of history. But because this holiness must be more than merely possible there must be saints whom the church can call by name. "The prize of her actual Saints belongs to her innermost being and is not something which she 'also' achieves 'on the side', something which has been inspired by a purely human need for hero worship" (96). Summary.

The saints: creators of new Christian modes of life. What is the exact function of saints in the church? They are more than its successful products. They belong to its essence. The saints are the church, the people of God. This is true of saints in the biblical sense (97) no less than of canonized saints. Together they form "the holy Church as the historical witness of the holy and sanctifying God and his grace which has already and finally begun its reign" (98).

However, the special task of the saints cannot be explained completely in term of their greater, even heroic virtue. Theirs is a historical task of making holiness real in new circumstances. They do not simply instantiate an essential, unchanging concept of holiness. Saints "are the initiators and the creative models of the holiness which happens to be right for, and is the task of their particular age. They create a new style; they prove that a certain form of life and activity is a really genuine possibility" (100). This significance does not simply begin once they die. Their deaths seal their lives. Their canonizations give their lives a permanent form which represents a real development in the history of Christian holiness. No single model of holiness, past or present, can ever claim ultimate validity.

The adventure of the saints. Canonization declares a particular way of life is genuinely Christian, even when this is not self-evident. The life of the saints is an adventure. It is original. It is lived as a risk. To the claim that any unique life situation might be equally saintly, Rahner objects that although holiness is always an individual achievement it is never atomic. It is only achieved in the context of a community—the church. Public recognition (canonization) separates the saint from everyday saints.

The charismatic order. As much as we desire to see holiness always coincide with office in the church, this is never necessarily the case. The characteristic of the church as a church of sinners extends at times even to its leaders. Holiness exists in the charismatic order not in the institutional order, although at decisive points in the history of salvation (e.g., in Mary) office and holiness have fused perfectly.

3.08 Some Thoughts on "A Good Intention"
Über die gute Meinung
{2.0}   *Geist und Leben* 28 (1955) 281-298.

Abstract: By applying the body/soul paradigm to actions and intentions, Rahner concludes that even in this psychological age if we do what can reasonably be expected we need not be overly concerned with the purity of our motives.

Topics: THEOLOGICAL ANTHROPOLOGY, action and intention; CHRISTIAN LIFE, morality; THEOLOGICAL ANTHROPOLOGY, hylomorphism.
Subsidiary Discussions: Freedom (106ff, 113); Heart (107ff, 114f ftn4); Consciousness, reflex (108 ftn2); *Pneuma* (110); Church (111); Duty (112, 115, 128); Salvation/Damnation status (108 ftn2).
Precis: I. Internal and external activity in general.
   1. The twofold unity of intention and action. Human life consists of external actions and internal thoughts, feelings, and attitudes. We never reduce to pure spirit; even internal states are achieved though material conditions. There are for us no purely internal processes. The spiritual life has both internal and external facets. Internal and external is a matter of degree. Inner freedom is achieved through external actions. Interior and exterior are related as soul to body.
   2. The ambiguity of the external action. Still, external action is not identical with internal act. One may be weak and the other strong. A single act may have a host of different motives. An action can as easily obscure as reveal its motive. This is much like the relation of body and soul. Hence, nothing definite can be said about the value of people or their deeds based solely on the correctness of their external actions. Whatever is of eternal value springs from the heart. Everything depends on intention—an area which only God sees and into which scientific psychology cannot peer. [Excursus on inability to know for certain one's salvation/damnation status, 108 ftn2.]
   3. The ultimate source of the moral act. Internal and external acts are not simply related as cause and effect. They are related as soul to body—the soul animating the body and achieving its own being in return. Neither act nor intention can be unconcerned with the other. "True Christian morality is therefore a balance between the internal intention of the heart and the external act" (109). It rests neither in internal nor in external acts.
II. Good intention.
   1. Task and goal. This brief section summarizes Part I with a Christian definition of good intention: one which animates the external act and realizes itself in it, if it is directed to the good or the perfect.

2. Christian motivation. What are the presuppositions for the super-natural meritoriousness of an act? Do they include a faith motive? Theologians generally say yes. Internal intentions can only be good intentions when they give saving significance to our actions, when they answer the Word communicated in faith (leaving aside the status of those who never heard the Word).

3. Actual and virtual intention. How explicit and reflex does this intention need to be? Moral theologians distinguish actual from virtual intention. The former are held clearly in consciousness and are known and willed to cause the action; the latter are real causes even though they subsist at the edge of conscious reflection. It is sufficient for a supernaturally meritorious action to be caused by a virtually good intention. Thus, in practice, whenever Christians do their duty in the external activity of life these are truly Christian actions so long as one would say on reflection that one would not have acted in this way had s/he not been formed as a Christian.

III. The problem of good intention.

1. The simultaneous occurrence of different motives. In reality motives are never "chemically pure." They are often numerous and conflicting. Just as we are many layered so are our motives.

2. The "unknown" nature of many motives. Many of our motives are unconscious or subconscious. Yet even these can be motives for which we are morally responsible. Thus, we have a moral duty to purify our motives.

3. The necessity of purifying motives. Summary (115). Although the necessity to purify one's motives cannot be denied, the degree to which this duty obliges us is open to discussion. Conclusion (116f).

IV. Good intentions in practice.

1. Choice of motives. a) False attempts. Some intentions only appear good. Such apparent good intentions only accompany an action without really causing it. To allow that a basic Christian attitude *can* virtually influence our daily actions is different from saying that it actually *does*. Intending a good intention does not in itself create such a good intention. b) Objective motivation: Rahner is skeptical about attempts to cultivate explicitly "spiritual" motives, except perhaps where one's work is complete drudgery. He suggests instead locating explicit Christian motives in the activity itself by attending to its real Christian meaning (e.g., cleaning a room because it aids the community rather than "for the greater glory of God").

2. The purification of motives. a) Distinction between motive and impulse. Purifying motives can seem difficult, virtually impossible because: i) it is often impossible to suppress an undesired motivation; ii) it is not recommendable to cut off any motive simply because it is not the highest. After all, inclination and desire count for something. God has instilled them in us and they may lead to social ends larger than we can grasp. Rahner distinguishes motives from urges. The former are morally proposed in a free manner whereas the latter belong to the still indifferent stratum of psycho-

physical vitality. Hence, the morality of an act can only be determined by motive. But what is the real motive in any particular case? **b)** Education through life. We should do what we can to alter the real state of our motives and impulses by directing our attention. In addition we should try to strengthen our true and desired motives by prayer and contemplation so as to be prepared to act on these higher motives when lesser impulses fail. Life itself has a way of purifying our complex motives and impulses. **c)** Orientation towards things instead of unmasking of self. Rahner concludes it is "superfluous and harmful for a normal person to devote great efforts to an exaggerated reflection and 'depth psychology' with regard to the world of his motives" (127). Unbridled unmasking of motives leads to moral cynicism which sees everything as hollow and base sensuality. One forgets that even authentic spiritual motives very often require other urges to assert themselves. "It is better to try to purify and refine one's motives by looking away from oneself to things and by letting oneself be occupied by life, others and their needs" (128). If we attend honestly and humbly to our duty we need not worry ourselves sick about the ultimate motives for our actions.

3.09 The Dogma of the Immaculate Conception in Our Spiritual Life

Das Dogma von der Unbefleckten Empfägnis Mariens und unsere Frömmigkeit

{2.0}   *Geist und Leben* 27 (1954) 100-108.

Abstract: For Rahner the Immaculate Conception is the concrete realization of the fundamental truth of the undialectical preeminence of grace over guilt.

Topics: BVM, Immaculate Conception of; GUILT and forgiveness; SALVATION.

Subsidiary Discussions: Love (130f); Sin, original (131ff); Baptism (133); Concupiscence (134f); Evil (138f); Ideal, substantial (138f).

Precis: On the centenary of the promulgation of the Immaculate Conception, Rahner asks what this dogma means for our salvation over and above the fact directly proclaimed in it. Most simply it tells us more about Mary so we might love her more. But this truth about a privilege reserved for Mary hardly satisfies this impoverished age which must pray simply to love Mary more.

Certain facts and structures of salvation are also revealed by this mystery. It shows the universality of original sin: that even though one human being, not the Mediator, was by God's grace free from sin, no life, not even Mary's, can be thought of as simply free from original sin. This should lead us to glorify Mary, being glad that her love of God never became ordinary. This, however, raises two questions. First, "is the difference caused by the

Immaculate Conception between us sinners and Mary really as great as has been made out? … Are we not also in the realm of Christ's redemption even from the first moment of our existence?" (132). Is not original sin permitted insofar as God willed it, knowing it would not be the last word? "[A]re we not *always* and from the beginning *redeemed* sinners?" (133). Some theologians reply that our redemption begins with baptism which still leaves us (unlike Mary) with a divided, concupiscent heart.

This leads to the second question—the heart of this essay: does Mary's undivided state point by way of exception to our eternally divided state? "Or does the Christian understanding of existence lie precisely in the fact that the bottomless perdition, which exists, is *completely* overcome by the immeasurable mercy of God?" (134). Without treating guilt as innocuous or necessary Rahner asks about *forgiven* guilt. Can we wish that guilt had never been? After cautioning against equating guilt as we forgive it with guilt as forgiven by God, Rahner insists that sacred optimism allows us to call guilt a *felix culpa* since otherwise we would be making ourselves out as worthy of forgiveness.

Since he cannot countenance the idea the *Immauculata* represents for us simply a fulfillment we will never achieve, Rahner insists she points to the fact that "God has two very different ways to the same happy perfection, viz., the preservation from guilt and the forgiveness of guilt" (136). Without discussing why God permits sin and guilt, Rahner suggests the reason for the difference between Mary's state and ours lies not only in her position in salvation history but also in God's desire to make forgiveness visible in our history.

Admittedly, this does not explain why there are two ways to the same blessed perfection. For Rahner the answer lies in the fact that by forgiving our guilt God desires to tell us God alone is the origin of our perfection; whereas Mary's Immaculate Conception tells us even our perfection "is light and not darkness, the pure and not the tragically torn asunder, the whole and not what has just managed to get saved" (138). Only by viewing both ways to perfection together do we get the whole picture.

Whoever, in spite of the experience of one's own sinfulness really believes and hopes in an undivided perfection has, without knowing it, loved Mary's Immaculate Conception (139). We who know the Immaculate Conception in a reflex way love the created, unambiguous realization of what is essential for the exercise of Christian piety: the yes to God's grace which alone overcomes our original condition. Christian theology must always fight the temptation to regard guilt and grace, light and darkness, as polar and inseparably mutual conditioning opposites of the one human existence. The dogma of the Immaculate Conception helps with just this.

3.10 The Comfort of Time
Trost der Zeit
{2.0} *Stimmen der Zeit* 157 (1955) 241-255.

Abstract: "Revivification of merit" leads Rahner to speculate that in eternity nothing in our previous lives is lost. All our acts subsist in our decision for or against God. A state of total happiness necessitates total perfection.

Topics: ETERNAL LIFE; MERIT, revivification of; TIME/ETERNITY; SALVATION.

Subsidiary Discussions: Love of God (142f); Fundamental option (145f, 154); Eschatology, intermediate state (149, 152f); Renunciation (150, 154); Sin (154ff).

Precis: To Christians time is comforting. Where others see the past swept into oblivion and regret, Christians see eternal life initiating something entirely new. Time itself passes away. Rahner approaches time and eternity through the seemingly unpromising question of the revivification of merit: whether and how merit won by someone in a state of grace but lost by sin is regained.

Merit is never our claim on God. It is always God's gift. Merit means eternity in time: our actions elevated to the possibility of acts of eternal life. We can increase in supernatural merit. We can be increasingly seized by God's life and its claims. Far from considering these merits our own we forget ourselves in loving God and neighbor. Instead of being a juridical concept, merit reveals something about our lives and the free persons we become in the process of living. Permanent merit, a sign the past is never lost, underpins Christian hope in eternal life in which *becoming* and not *what has become* passes away. When life ends the perfect arrives: what we have finally become by the use of our freedom. (This despite the fact that so long as we live our final status before God remains an open question). Our final decision not only determines our final disposition it is a result of our previous decisions. "In every moment of the free, personal achievement of existence, the past becomes an inner, essential principle of the present and its acts" (146).

At this point Rahner returns to problems in the standard treatments of revivification of merit. He concludes one can assume a full revivification of merit because conversion results from all the person had become in the past. Hence, all of life remains preserved for us whether or not we remember it in detail. Since everything can be retrieved and transformed by love we need not be anxious even about our past sins. Repentance is not escape but transformation. This hope is not cheap optimism but stems from the fact that in life we are not about many things, just one thing: saying yes to God. Summary (149).

Rahner says something more explicit and far reaching: if our lives are saved into God's grace then they are saved completely. This not only means nothing of what has been realized is lost, but not even those possibilities offered to us by God are lost or unrealized. The saved person, the one we have become, is the full realization of the one we were able to be. There are no regrets in saved eternity, for in attaining God we attain our full potential. To the objection that our experience of falling short is so pervasive in life we are justified to imagine the same of eternal life (150), Rahner counters that eternity is pure actuality with no shadow of possibility (the condition for the possibility of regrets). In arriving at God we reach our true end however imperfectly we may have arrived. To find perfect happiness is to achieve complete perfection even though it may take some time for all our many dimensions to catch up with our yes. Hence, purgatory (153).

Finally, Rahner considers the status of our evil acts and the acts we performed while in open rebellion toward God. Without disputing the reality of serious sin and its effects, and without making sin necessary for one's self-actualization, Rahner insists that "sin can exist only because it is something more and better than sin ..." (155). Even sin is a moment of partial self-realization (the more radical the sin, the deeper the level of self-realization). It may take tremendous courage to steal, for example. Hence, sin is not completely and forever a deficit. When one experiences conversion, sinful times and acts are not killed but redeemed, purified, and saved.

Rahner summarizes (156) that understood from the Christian perspective time is very comforting since nothing is lost and all is gained. In eternity there is not only resurrection of the body but also resurrection of time. Then it will be revealed that in every particular thing we did only one thing: attempted to attain ourselves completely and to transfer this completely into the reality of loving God. If we succeed, even if our success seems piecemeal from the perspective of time, in eternity all is conserved and perfected.

3.11 The Eucharist and Suffering
Eucharistie und Leiden
{1.5}   *Zeitschrift für Aszese und Mystik* 11 (1936) 224-236.
Abstract: Faith reveals that by sharing in the Eucharist we share Christ's sufferings since: **I.** It is the renewal of the sacrifice of Calvary; **II.** It communicates Christ's life; **III.** It unites us with Christ's body, the church.
Topics: EUCHARIST; CHRISTIAN LIFE, suffering; CROSS.
Subsidiary Discussions: Jesus Christ, sacrifice of (161ff); Renunciation (163); Grace (163ff); Mystical Body (168ff).
Precis: The mysterious but essential relationship between sharing in the Eucharist and in the cross of Christ relies heavily on the letters of St. Paul.
I. "The Holy Eucharist is a sacrifice; in it we receive the body and blood of Jesus Christ given and poured out for us" (161). It is a true, visible sacrifice which renders present the bloody sacrifice of Christ offered once and for all on the cross and preserves the memory of this event forever. Christ offers both sacrifices with the same sacrificial outlook which gives them their propitiatory value. All Jesus did had value insofar as it was incorporated into

the sacrifice of the cross. This includes his Last Supper and his command that the apostles continue to reenact it. A closer look at Jesus' sacrificial dispositions shows his willingness to suffer out of obedience, since it was through suffering, active renunciation, that God willed to save the world.

Though the manner of sacrifice differs from the cross to the table, both are offered by the same priest with the same intention. "The sacrificial intention and sacrificial offering of the sacrifice of the Mass are thus submerged in the mystery of the Cross; they announce this mystery and speak of the death of the Son of God for our salvation" (164). This mystery suffuses the Mass and takes hold of all who celebrate it, subjecting us to its unfathomable laws. We cannot help but take on the sacrificial outlook of Christ, his resignation and willingness to suffer. This happens to us not simply as co-celebrants, but as recipients of Christ's body and blood which change us into what we receive.

II. Since Eucharist is also the sacrament of our daily growth in grace, this growth too is subject to the vital laws of this divine life of grace which Rahner sees in the writings of St. Paul. Chief among these laws is that participation in the life of Christ means participation in his cross. Thus, for the Christian, suffering is never merely natural misfortune. It is a consequence and expression of our Christian existence and our union with Christ by grace. Suffering and death no longer have the character of punishment but participation in the fate of Christ begun with our baptism. Eucharist renews the memory of our incorporation with Christ's sufferings.

III. The Eucharist is also the sacrament of the Mystical Body of Christ. Participating in it unites each with the sufferings of all the members. This is the law of life of the Mystical Body: that together we make up in our sufferings whatever was lacking in Christ's sufferings for his church. The essay closes with a summary (170) urging us not to fear the suffering that accompanies communion with Christ since in God's wisdom the suffering we endure is always apportioned to the degree we can bear it.

3.12 The Renewal of Priestly Ordination
Priesterweihe-Erneuerung
{2.0}   *Geist und Leben* 25 (1952) 231-234.
Abstract: This highly rhetorical essay insists that renewing one's priestly ordination (like renewing baptismal vows) is no mere pious remembrance of the past but is actually God's sacramental grace again at work in us.
Topics: PRIESTHOOD; SACRAMENTS, renewal of.
Subsidiary Discussions: Spirit (174f).
Precis: I. Rahner explores the dogmatic meaning of renewing one's ordination. Every sacrament is a moment in the process of encountering God by grace. What happens within the sacrament should continue in the intimacy of the heart. Extending what Trent teaches about spiritual communion, Rahner concludes that renewing the three unrepeatable sacraments (bap-

tism, confirmation, orders) is no less efficacious. What happens in them is no less a grace-filled happening than when we originally assumed a particular role in the visible church. This self-communication of God's life and love is not of its nature a once and only event but a process. Hence, even these unrepeatable sacraments can be renewed despite their indelible character.

This renewal is no sentimental remembrance or exercise in wishful thinking. It is a true encounter with God by grace—the same grace as was active in the original reception of the sacrament. Even though the sacramental sign may be missing, renewing our yes to this merciful deed of God in our lives may be even more fruitful today than it was many years ago. "The renewal of ordination is not indeed an *opus operatum*, but it is truly an *opus operantis Dei et hominis ex opere operato*" (173).

II. Renewal of ordination is God's work in us not merely our good resolution "in spite of everything." On the day of our ordination God foreknew all that would befall us. He has freely given his Spirit to help with everything so that each one of us should become the very one whom God conceived and loved. Section II ends with a paean to how the Spirit wraps even our failures and shortcomings in grace if only we say, "do *thou* ordain us anew today" (175).

III. Renewal of ordination is the yes of our good will. If God's grace ordains anew then we find the courage for a new yes. Believing in God's loving action thus becomes a time for new resolutions. We summon the whole of our past lives together with the dark future and once again entrust it to God, saying yes so that God may shape all of it into our priestly existence. Summary (176).

3.13 The Meaning of Frequent Confessions of Devotion

Vom Sinn der häufigen Andachtsbeichte

{1.5} *Zeitschrift für Aszese und Mystik* 9 (1934) 323-336.

Abstract: The intrinsic reason for frequent "confessions of devotion" lies in its ability to renew our confidence in the law of sacramentality: God actually draws near us in such humble, concrete, historical moments as these.

Topics: SACRAMENTS, theology of; PENANCE of devotion.

Subsidiary Discussions: Spiritual direction (180f): Sin, mortal and venial (181f); Eucharist (182f).

Precis: Without questioning the value or efficacy of frequent confessions of devotion, Rahner asks, "which among the ultimate structural laws of the spiritual life can allow us to trace frequent confession back till it is seen as a normal manifestation of that [spiritual] life" (179). What essential characteristic establishes its particular validity? One must not deduce from the fact that frequent confessions of devotions did not exist for centuries that it has no value for the spiritual life in our times. Insofar as the spiritual life is always a battle against sin for which Christ died, every means to conquer sin is important and valuable to us. Nor must this practice be seen as a false development since it has been approved and encouraged by the church.

Rahner suggests, analyses, and dismisses three often invoked defenses for the practice of frequent confessions of devotion: it aids in spiritual direction; it remits sin; it increases grace. None of these outcomes is peculiar to the sacrament. In fact Rahner makes the case that frequent participation in the Eucharist is second to no other sacrament in remitting venial sin and increasing grace.

To identify the special significance of the sacrament of penance Rahner looks at sacraments in general. Since every sacrament is an inbreaking of God's activity in the world every supernatural act is unique, independent, historical "and not merely an individual case of a clear general rule" (184). Thus, the supernatural life seems supported by human, worldly things. To many this represents the "scandal" of the sacraments: that they should be so incarnate, so mundane (examples, 184f).

In the sacrament of penance in particular, God's forgiving grace comes to us by the effective juridical verdict of the church through her priestly representative. The penitent does not cause the remission of sin, it is God's free mercy most generally and most visibly mediated by the church. Approaching the sacrament and receiving this supernatural forgiveness from human hands is of decisive importance to the formation of the Christian in the sacramental principle. Hence, frequent confession of devotion is a most useful development for the spiritual life (187). Two further facts are organically associated with this: i) audible contrition leaves the last word concerning forgiveness up to God; ii) since even venial sin is a spiritual injury to the whole Mystical Body, visibly confessing to a priest, the representative of the church, is the most fitting way to make reparation.

Rahner cautions that one must not object that this insight is too lofty even for simple believers since they seem most comfortable with the notion of God acting through the visible world. This insight does not settle the question of the appropriate frequency of confession (nor can it ever be settled with mathematical precision). That remains up to the individual.

3.14 Problems Concerning Confession
   Beichtprobleme
{1.0} *Geist und Leben* 27 (1954) 435-446.
Abstract: This 1956 essay proposes that the future theory and practice of the Sacrament of Penance will be theologically fuller and more personal.
Topics: PENANCE, Sacrament of.
Subsidiary Discussions: Sacraments, *opus operatum/operantis* (197); Conversion (198); Punishment (202ff); Eschatology, intermediate state (203f); Psychotherapy (205).
Precis: Without calling into question any of the accepted dogmatic or pastoral teachings on Penance, Rahner concentrates on posing questions for which there are not yet clear solutions or liberating, exhaustive answers.

I. Changes in the institution of confession. Rahner first recalls that the sacrament of penance has undergone considerable changes over the centuries without, however, jeopardizing its essence. The many examples of change (192f) prove one thing: the sacrament is alive and will change again. Regarding what directions such changes may take Rahner suggests looking carefully at the current status of the sacrament, especially at its outstanding questions.

II. Legalistic and magical tendencies in the practice of confession. In the past and even today there is a great deal of legalistic and magical thinking surrounding penance (examples, 194f). These bring both penance and religion into disrepute. In this climate penance is reduced to absolution from sins given by the priest, and becomes an objectively mechanical process. These tendencies must be challenged and reversed.

III. New tendencies in the current practice of confession. Putting penance on theologically fuller and more personal footing means:

1. The sacrament is an *opus operatum*. Without disputing this truth Rahner calls for revaluating the role of the penitent's disposition. Without inner growth the mechanical repetition of the sacrament is of little use since no sin is forgiven unless it is already blotted out *ex opere operantis*. Simply receiving the sacrament never negates the need to repent (Rahner prefers the expression "to change one's life"). [The section closes with practical suggestions for celebrating the sacrament many of which are used today.]

2. The sacrament must be experienced in a theologically fuller fashion. Penance must be seen as more than absolution. It is one of Christ's mysteries; a liturgy; a dialogue with God; a confession of guilt for sins against the church for which one should feel responsibility. All this is made more clear when penance is celebrated in a fuller liturgy. In this connection penances imposed should also reflect the communal nature of sin and its remission.

3. The confession of sin. Although allowing the priest to know what he is being asked to absolve is an essential factor in the sacrament, the confessor must never act as an examining magistrate and thus inadvertently humiliate or shame the penitent. The confession of the penitent is never the object for examination. When penitents have confessed what they regard as their guilt they have sufficiently confessed their guilt.

4. The imposition of penance. This facet of the sacrament is often obscured because we conflate the burden of guilt which is able to be absolved with the burden of punishment. The latter is never a purely juridical or external matter. Rahner weaves an interesting approach to the doctrine of purgatory into his suggestion that the burden of punishment is precisely one's own self with its egoism, hardheartedness, cowardice, etc. All this is the result of sin and must be worked through either here on earth or "on the other side." In any case it cannot simply be absolved away. Forgiveness of sin is only the beginning. Complete conversion is the goal. Looking at things this way reveals the need to reassess the practice of imposing penances as well as the frequency of approaching the sacrament.

5. Penance vs. psychotherapy. The priest has nothing to fear from the psychotherapist so long as he clearly recalls his own role—not so much to counsel or even relieve sickness as to speak the word of God to the penitent and thus to lift the death and despair which accompany guilt.

6. Penance unnecessary as a preparation for communion. Much has been done to uncouple these two sacraments, and to overcome the notion that Eucharist is a reward for confessing one's sins. Rahner suggest that relative to the frequency of receiving the Eucharist, penance should be "rare."

3.15 The Apostolate of Prayer
Sendung zum Gebet
{0.5}   *Stimmen der Zeit* 152 (1953) 161-170.

Abstract: This spirited promotion of the movement known as The Apostleship of Prayer stresses the validity and value of intercessory prayer and the need for every member of the church to pray for the church and for the whole world.

Topics: PRAYER, intercessory.

Precis: Do we live at a time when prayers of petition are the sole concern of very primitive even naive believers? After the incarnation who can claim God is not concerned with world events? Why is the most perfect prayer, the Our Father, made up primarily of petitions if intercessory prayer has no effect? Intercessory prayer in fusing the greatest boldness with the deepest humility is the highest form of prayer. Rahner concludes his introduction with a somewhat sketchy transcendental deduction of the truth of prayer (212). He imagines how transformed the world would be if everyone took intercessory prayer more seriously. People would pray for the whole church and for those in pain anywhere in the world. "Such prayer would generate a power sufficient to transform their lives: their piety would become less egoistic and introverted" (213). This would lead to the transformation of the world.

Though there are many paths to the kingdom of heaven, prayer is especially important, even more important than the sacraments (214). The highest form of prayer is steeped in the love of God and neighbor and inspired by the care of souls. Such prayer which enfolds all others with oneself in the community of sin and salvation is essential to Christianity. The apostleship of prayer deliberately fosters such prayer among ever greater numbers of the faithful (brief history, 215).

Yet to be honest this apostolate of prayer poses difficulties for the modern intellectual on two fronts: the need to enroll publicly in a particular movement; the need to pray using particular forms. But these objections are not decisive since only two things are actually demanded: i) externally, though the very act of enrolling can be a valuable form if witness, it is not essential; ii) interiorly, praying verbally at the start of each day is essential, though not necessarily with a fixed formula. This format is due to our nature whose intentions do not survive unless shorn up with concrete acts of discipline. One who begins with this simple program will slowly begin to find greater value in the Eucharist, the rosary, devotion to Mary, etc.

The final two pages form a kind of summary (218f) in which Rahner reiterates the necessity for the continual practice of prayer (the essential attitude of a genuine Christianity) and for a community of mutual support and encouragement. Intercessory prayer for the whole world is doubly necessary given the challenges we face in this tumultuous time.

3.16 A Spiritual Dialogue at Evening: On Sleep, Prayer, and Other Subjects

> *Geistliches Abendgespräch über den Schlaf, das Gebet und andere Dinge*

{1.0}   *Wort und Wahrheit* 2 (1947) 449-462.

Abstract: This essay in dialogue form considers those dangers of sleep which necessitate an especially intense prayer which relies heavily on imagination.
Topics: THEOLOGICAL ANTHROPOLOGY, sleep; THEOLOGICAL ANTHROPOLOGY, imagination.
Subsidiary Discussions: Adam (222f); Devil (224, 227ff); Prayer, imaginal (230ff).

Precis: After two pages of stage setting Rahner examines the anxiety which often accompanies falling asleep. Granting we must sleep, he asks whether Adam before the fall slept as we do. He thinks not. Free of concupiscence, "Adam did not sleep in a stupefied state as we do, but opened the innermost chamber of his spirit in some other way to the silent entry of those fairies which bring the nocturnal blessings of the kingdom of a thousand names to the spirit" (223). In short, Adam slept with a waking heart.

Without worrying about proper nomenclature, Rahner returns to the question of why we often dread falling into sleep and concludes, "the wellspring of our personal waking thinking and acting, to which we can never penetrate completely, is altered during sleep, and this in an uncontrollable way" (225). Sleep is not wholly trustworthy. During the day we can pick and choose among the many fantasies that occur to us. Sleepers have no such control. In sleep a "dangerous Something" has a much freer hand over our material natures. Rahner summarizes, "there is danger in sleep. For it is into that kingdom where the evil spirits have their abode that man allows himself to sink—in sleep" (228). To this Rahner's "dialogue partner" objects that insofar as sleep is necessary we need not take these dangers too seriously.

Rahner deduces from all this that one ought to pray really well before sleep (229). Real prayer is based on faith, "an unconditional commitment of the whole man to...that one truth which is genuine reality" (230). In addition to all the regular qualities of prayer (surrender to God as an act of trust in his goodness, submitting our acts to the judgment of eternity, etc.) night prayer must be particularly fitted to the character of that kingdom into which we descend in sleep, to arm one against this region, to exorcise and bless it. Since neither the sleeping self nor whatever might assail it are ever free from the laws of our nature, Rahner identifies the image as peculiar to the realm of sleep. With C.G. Jung, Rahner agrees "the spirit of man draws its life also from this kingdom" [the kingdom of images and archetypes] (231). Thus, in the best evening prayer one submerses oneself in "good, genuine, holy images...archetypes blessed and redeemed, pure and radiant" (232). Through some "secret sympathy" these images protect the sleeper making it more difficult for other images to take root.

To the objection this is a mere play of fantasies Rahner counters that certain images in fact embody a kind of semi-sacramental reality. To the objection this realm of imagination is "unreal" Rahner counters it is indeed often more real than the tangible world. The very word "imagination" stands in need of retrieval today. This leads to the question of primordial religious images which Rahner chooses not to address. The dialogue concludes with Rahner's suggestion that such an approach as he has outlined finds support in tradition, citing Prudentius, Ambrose, and Ignatius.

3.17 Priestly Existence
Priesterliche Existenz
{2.0} *Zeitschrift für Aszese und Mystik* 17 (1942) 155-171.
Abstract: By locating the essential character of Catholic priesthood in its apostolic/prophetic rather than its cultic dimension, this essay lays the foundation for understanding the nature of priestly existence.
Topics: PRIESTHOOD; CHRISTIAN LIFE, vocation.
Subsidiary Discussions: Jesus Christ, one priesthood of (246ff); Word, theology of (244ff, 250f); Church (247ff); Religious life, profession (255f); Theology, kerygmatic (248ff); Truth, propositional (259f); Laity, vocation of (260f).
Precis: I. Preliminary Note. Does the Catholic priesthood essentially influence the existential condition of the one possessing it? Does it "penetrate deeply enough into the 'core' of man's existence to give this as a whole a definite character" (239)? After posing this question Rahner provides a preview of the territory to be covered in this essay: determining whether the concrete essence of priesthood resides in its cultic or prophetic dimension.
II. The essential structure of the priesthood.
1. The concepts of priest and prophet in general. History and philosophy of religion distinguish priest and prophet. The former attempts to establish a relationship with God from below. It can be visibly organized and passed on. The latter originates from God's inspiration and cannot be handed down without diminution. Summary (243).

2. The transformation of the concepts priest and prophet in the context of Christianity. These two concepts undergo fundamental changes within the revealed religion of Christianity (preview, 243).

a) The mutual conditioning and essentially complementary relationship of (cultic) priesthood and prophetism in the Catholic priesthood. "Christianity is firstly and fundamentally Christ himself" (243) an historical, salvation reality wherein the incarnate Son of God redeemed humanity with the absolute and final sacrifice. This reality: i) is posited by God as an unmerited gift; ii) is sacramental in the sense that "among the intrinsic constitutive elements of the presence of the fact of salvation within *human* history … must be numbered the *word* as sign" (245); iii) is essentially constituted by the Word. A brief theology of the Word concludes that the cultic and prophetic elements of priesthood are essentially combined just as the priesthood of Christ combines these two realities in an interior reality. The sacrifice of Christ founds its cultic dimension. Its claim on the hearer of its message establishes its prophetic, apostolic dimension. "The same is now true of the *official priesthood* in the Church" (246) but its subservience to the unique priesthood of Christ enfeebles both dimensions of priesthood in the church, transforming them into ministry.

b) The enfeeblement of (cultic) priesthood and prophetism in the official priesthood of the church. Rahner first asserts the absolutely unique character of Christ's sacrifice. Its eschatological finality is equally true of the sacramental word which manifests it. Even the visible church is secondary in the sense that the "social accessibility of the historico-sacramental permanent presence of the salvation-reality of Christ" (248) is always prior. Thus, office holders in the visible church do not first create it, nor do they ever mediate between God and us. They are analogous to sacramental signs pointing to the harmony achieved between us and God by Christ alone.

i) Cultic priesthood in Christianity is enfeebled insofar as the sacrifice offered is not a priest's own but only makes Christ's sacrifice present. In addition this is the church's sacrifice and in an anterior way belongs to the universal priesthood of the faithful above which the cultic priest has no advantage. Still he remains a cultic priest insofar as he is authorized to posit the cultic action and thereby make the invisible visible. Summary (250).

ii) Prophetism in Christianity is enfeebled since no new prophecy is possible except insofar as it gives continuing witness to Christ. At the same time prophetism remains a necessary character of the church since otherwise all it would have to offer is talk about Christ rather than Christ present in the proclamation. Catholic prophetism is further weakened by the fact that it contains no new information about things in this or any other world. At best it can convey greater self-understanding. Summary of Part II (253).

III. Priestly existence. Rahner now tackles the question whether and how being a priest affects one's total existence as such in a way that lends it a specific character. After rejecting a claim that an appeal to the sacramental "character" of orders answers this question (253f), he argues that one can assert that priesthood has existential significance even before establishing what it is. The fact that orders is a sacrament which confers both the power of office and grace in an inseparable union can only be explained if we assume the content of the official power affects the existential kernel of one's being. Otherwise every professional calling would have an equal right to a sacramental sign. But since there are specific vocational sacraments (marriage and orders) the vocational sacraments of the ordinary believer are limited to baptism and confirmation. Even the monastic vocation is a development of this baptismal life and not the subject of a special sacrament. Summary (256).

Which of the two essential characteristics of priesthood provides its distinguishing existential condition? Rahner rules out the cultic since the priest is not constantly taken up in cultic activities. And even when he is so occupied the validity of his cultic acts do not depend on his personal worthiness. Insofar as he becomes worthy by identifying himself with the attitude proper to the universal priesthood, his cultic power is a new obligation to develop the old vocation given at baptism, not a new obligation to a new vocation of existential import not previously possessed. Hence, Rahner concludes the prophetic/apostolic dimension of priesthood supplies its existential character. He offers two reasons:

1) Prophetic element of priesthood lays claim to the *whole* existence of the person. The work of evangelization imposes limitless demands on priests. More importantly preaching the gospel demands the personal commitment of the apostle to his innermost core. Here Rahner launches into a theology of kerygma and an excursus on propositional truth which concludes that, "the proclamation of the revelation of God, by reason of the specific concentration of truth in its content, demands as an intrinsic element the existential commitment of the proclaimer" (260).

2) The prophetic element of priesthood lays claim to the existence of the person in a quite *new* way. Because the apostle is authorized to act as a cultic priest as well as proclaimer his mission is new. In fulfilling it he does not bear witness to his own Christian faith and life as such (as is the obligation of all the baptized) but speaks the very word of Christ (summary, 262). Rahner concludes with New Testament references confirming his views.

3.18 The Consecration of the Layman to the Care of Souls
Weihe des Laien zur Seelsorge
{1.5} *Zeitschrift für Aszese und Mystik* 11 (1936) 21-34.
Abstract: Baptism and confirmation empower/commission us to work for the care of others' souls. Yet the inviolability of personal freedom makes this impossible if approached directly. It can only be accomplished through love of God.

Topics: LAITY; CHRISTIAN LIFE, care of souls; LOVE of God and neighbor.
Subsidiary Discussions: Community (263ff, 272ff); Death (264f); Freedom (265); God (265ff, 269f); Knowledge vs. love (267ff); Sin (269); Prayer (271); *Caritas* (272); Miracles (273); Baptism and Confirmation (274f); Matrimony (275f).
Precis: This is an analysis of the seeming a priori impossibility that one could be empowered or commissioned to care for the souls of others.
I. Humans necessarily live in community: communities of work where efforts are pooled for some greater end; communities of spirit where spiritual goods (art, science, law, etc.) are communicated through speech; communities of love in which one hopes to offer and have accepted by others one's most intimate personal mystery. But can this deepest mystery be offered and received, or are there spheres within us that can never be reached even by love? Rahner says yes to the latter. He points to the unsharable reality of death and to the mystery of human liberty which are essentially solitary. Here there is no intermediary before God. This God is not some reality alongside us like a second being. In God we live and move and have our being. God is what is deepest within us. Hence, "the realm of free decision reveals that the impossibility of the direct care of [others'] souls is so radical that the attempt does not merely fail in practice, but becomes evidently self-contradictory" (266). One must save oneself. No one can save another for two reasons. First, we lack the capacity insofar as the personal liberty of the one for whom we care is unbreachable unless that person freely accepts help. At best we are left with the duty to care for our own souls. Secondly, we lack the call since no one can be bound to an impossible task.

Is there then no such thing as care for souls? Have we no responsibility to others except the duty to work out our own salvation? Rahner disagrees. What to us is deepest and most inaccessible in others is not so to God. We enter that sanctuary through God by first finding our own way to God and then finding the way from God to the other. This is done through love. There follows a long discussion on the relationship between love and knowledge leading to the insurmountable problem of the limits of our ability to love the other especially when sin is part of the picture (their sin or ours). Only God's love can overcome this impasse. Thus, we love the other "for God's sake." It is demeaning among us to be loved for the sake of loving another. But in reference to God who is not simply one person among others but the intimate depth of the one whose soul we care for, this difficulty is overcome. Whoever loves God with one's whole being "is by that very fact in the innermost kernel of the loved man. He has penetrated behind the ultimate mystery of that man, because he has reached where God is. He can now truly exercise the care of souls, in union with God who alone can care for souls, for he has become one spirit with him; …. And because pastoral care takes place in an act of love for God, it bears all the characteristics marks of that love" (271). Such care of souls is essentially prayer (summary, 271f). Rahner is now able to locate the origin of the consecration to the care of souls in baptism. "Everyone who is baptized is consecrated a pastor" (272). II. This pastoral love is not hidden in whispered prayers. It manifests itself in activities accessible to all in each of the earthly communities in which we live. It manifests itself in the community of work through acts of charity. When Christians assist others it is not mere philanthropy but a participation in the ongoing miracle of Christ's unquenchable love for the world. In communities of spirit it manifests itself in discourses which attempt to introduce and realize in the communal search for knowledge of all that is eternally true and good. This is nothing less than transmitting to others the living Word of God: Jesus Christ. We are empowered and commissioned to do this though the sacraments of baptism and confirmation (summaries, 274, 275). It manifests itself in the community of love most clearly in the sacrament of marriage where two people are empowered and commissioned to see to one another's salvation. Although even for the two spouses this is never possible directly but only in the love of God. Summary (276).

3.19 The Ignatian Mysticism of Joy in the World
Die ignatianische Mystik der Weltfreudigkeit
{1.0}   *Zeitschrift für Aszese und Mystik* 12 (1937) 121-137.
Abstract: For St. Ignatius a mystic's joy in the world is not found in falsely harmonizing God and the world but in doing God's will. It makes no difference to that joy whether God wills one to flee or to embrace the world.
Topics: MYSTICISM; CHRISTIAN LIFE, renunciation; MYSTICISM, Ignatian.
Subsidiary Discussions: Monasticism (281f); Cross (281ff); God and nature (283ff); Ignatius Loyola, Exercises (287f); Ignatius Loyola, *indifferençia* (290f); Life, active/contemplative (290, 292).
Precis: It seems mysticism and joy in the world are not only obscure but contradictory. If mysticism demands flight from the world how can one delight in it? Rahner suggests the need to reexamine these terms and recast the question. Beginning with Ignatian mysticism he hopes to arrive at Ignatian joy.
I. The mysticism of Ignatius. Mysticism is a word with such a rich tradition it says so much it risks saying nothing. Without attempting a complete definition of Christian mysticism Rahner is content with the vague empirical concept found in the experience of the saints, especially the mystics of whom Ignatius was one. Of the many facets of Ignatian mysticism (280) Rahner concentrates on Ignatian joy in the world. Its characteristic piety has two notes:
1. Ignatian piety is a piety of the cross. In being a piety of the cross it is like every form of Christian piety. In addition it tends to be monastic in the sense

that it seeks God single-mindedly, often by fleeing the world, by dying with Christ and renouncing the world. Whatever Ignatian joy might be, it is never an embrace of the world as if the world were in complete harmony with God. Thus, it would seem the mystic can find no joy in the world but must flee it, except that for Ignatius accepting the world is the basis for fleeing it.

2. Ignatian piety is directed to God who: a) is beyond the whole world. The ultimate reason for Ignatian flight from the world is the fact that since God has spoken to the world in the person of Jesus Christ it is no longer a closed world. We can no longer accept "Nature" and its processes as God. The world becomes provisional. Now sacrificing the world (renunciation) becomes both possible and necessary, not in the world's eyes but in the eyes of faith for only in this way does one find real joy (summary, 287). b) God deals with us freely, personally, and historically. This insight grounds Ignatius' Exercises where we do not discern the impulses of our own hearts but listen for, seek, and find a command addressed to us by God. Because he finds this command in Christ, Ignatius commits himself to his cross and finds joy in the world.

II. The joy in the world of Ignatius. (Review, 288.) Christian mysticism is a grace from God not a personal accomplishment. Christian flight from the world means neither annihilating the world nor forcing God's hand. Renunciation is a gesture responding to God's voluntary love. It can legitimately take the form of fleeing the world or serving it (*vita contemplativa* or *vita activa*). Since God can be found in all things an Ignatian mystic is characteristically "indifferent" to the means. All seeming dichotomies are resolved in "the perpetual readiness to hear a new call from God ... and to serve him" (291). Summary (291ff).

3.20 Priest and Poet

Priester und Dichter

{1.0} Previously unpublished foreword to *La hora sin tiempo*, poems by Jorge Blajot, S.J.

Abstract: Priests and poets are entrusted with the word. Poets powerfully concentrate primordial words. Priests proclaim Gods' word. Poetry longs for the infinite which only the word of God entrusted to priests can answer.

Topics: WORD, primordial; WORD, theology of; ARTS, poetry; PRIEST-HOOD; SACRAMENTS, *ex opera operatum*.

Subsidiary Discussions: Incarnation (303f); Church, holiness of (312f); Scripture as poetry (314f); Theology as poetry (315f).

Precis: Rahner attempts to explain why even though we do not experience it now, "the perfect priest and the perfect poet are one and the same" (294).

I. The poet is entrusted with the word. Rahner rhapsodizes on the theology of the word. Word is related to thought as body to soul. It is more original even than thought. "Words bring light to us, not we to them. They have power over us because they are gifts from God, not creations of men" (296). Shallow, technical words are clear. Deep words, because they convey mystery, are necessarily obscure. These are "primordial words" (*Urworte*) whose status can change over the course of their history. Primordial words cannot be precisely defined without being killed (e.g., H_2O can never really substitute for water). Their very simplicity conceals all mysteries. Such words form the basis of spiritual existence. Deep knowledge relies on primordial words (examples, 298). Such knowledge is always indistinct and obscure like reality itself—deeper and more clear than our so-called "clear ideas" not because the user is muddle-headed but because these words convey so much complex reality. Primordial words always have both a literal and an intellectual-spiritual meaning.

"The primordial word is in the proper sense the presentation of the thing itself" (299). It is not merely a sign; it does not simply speak about a thing. When it is pronounced something happens: the advent of the thing itself to the listener. Not only does one take possession of reality by knowing such words, the reality known itself takes possession of the knower—and lover— through the word. This is because all realities sigh for their own unveiling which happens precisely when they are grasped, expressed, and received as primordial words. "Everything is redeemed by the word. It is the perfection of things" (300). "Invariably the word [particularly the primordial word] is the sacrament by means of which realities communicate themselves to man, in order to achieve their own destiny" (301).

Poets do not obscure clear speech in rhymes. They speak primordial words in powerful concentration. Their beauty comes from the transcendence of the reality they convey. After comparing the word with other forms of art Rahner summarizes, "For this reason the primordial word...is the primordial sacrament of all realities. And the poet is the minister of this sacrament" (302).

II. What is a priest? Essentially he is a minister of the word. He is entrusted with the efficacious word of God as a gift and mission. It is not his own word which leads others from darkness to salvation but God's word— the eternal logos who was made flesh and thus became the word of man. This word, spoken freely by God is a word of grace, of faith, of love. It is a sacramental word whose fullness will not be revealed until the end time. Till then it is spoken by others to whom Christ has entrusted it: to the priest. This word is efficacious. It is not discourse about Jesus, rather it makes God's love truly present and calls for a response. Though the efficacy of the spoken word has degrees depending on who speaks and with what skill, in the words of consecration a priest pronounces *the* efficacious word.

III. Is the priest then simply *the* poet *tout court?* Yes, although no priest is a poet simply by dint of the great word entrusted to him. For it is possible for this word to be efficacious even when spoken by a distracted, blasé, or even unworthy priest. The grace of the poet is that he fully experiences himself in his poetry. Even when the priest speaks from the heart he never reaches the terrible remoteness of the transcendent God. Thus, the priest "is always more but mostly less than a poet" (310). But what a happy and meaningful marriage it would be if the priest were also a poet!

IV. The priest calls upon the poet. Although it is true that a priest does not proclaim himself but proclaims God's word, Rahner argues that the quality of the priest's life makes a real difference. The holiness of the church which is based on the infallibility of God's grace is not simply transferrable to its priests whose very salvation is never assured. Priests must express the word of God with their Christian existence because that word wants to be manifested in them. But who can adequately utter oneself; who can speak to the center of the heart of another if not the poet? This is not to say that all scripture is poetry, although some surely is (314f), as is the greatest theology (315f). "This remains true: wherever the word of God utters the sublime and pours it into the depths of the human heart, there too a human poetic word is to be found. And the priest calls upon the poet, that the poet's primordial words may become consecrated vessels of the divine word, in which the *priest* effectively proclaims the word of God" (316).

V. The poet calls upon the priest. The poet's words are words of longing—longing for the infinite, the incomprehensible, the nameless. They are acts of faith, hope, and love. This is true of all art and therein lies its power to move the heart. In just this way the poetic word calls upon the word of God; the poet calls upon the priest. One generally thinks of the interplay between poet and priest as question to answer. But imagine what happens when priest and poet are one and the same person who can with full passion articulate God's word in the concentrated power of primordial words. How great! How rare!

3.21 "Behold This Heart!": Preliminaries to a Theology of Devotion to the Sacred Heart

"Siehe dieses Herz." Prolegomena zu einer Theologie der Herz-Jesu-Verehrung

{0.5} *Geist und Leben* 26 (1953) 32-38.

Abstract: Appreciating the Sacred Heart demands understanding the human heart. This for Rahner is a primordial word, an archetypic symbol expressing the original unity of human experience, the mysterious point of contact with God.

Topics: THEOLOGICAL ANTHROPOLOGY, heart; JESUS CHRIST, Sacred Heart of; WORD, primordial.

Subsidiary Discussions: Arts, poetry (326f, 329); Symbol (327f).

Precis: Rahner hopes an analysis of the word "heart" will "open up for us the way into the Heart of the Lord which pours itself out in streams of blood" (321). He speaks of the "word" heart and not of the concept because for him the word is prior. Next he introduces his notion of primordial words (*Urworte*) of which "heart" is one. It has its origin not in anatomy but in experience. It is prior to the dichotomy between body and soul, thought and action, internal and external. It speaks of one's original unity. "It is the point where man borders on the mystery of God" (323). It is distinctly human (not angelic or animal) because only we must go out of ourselves to meet ourselves in the other. In doing this we come to know we have a heart.

For all these reasons it is wrong to ask whether heart is first corporeal or spiritual precisely because it lies across any possible distinction between body and soul. In concrete life we are never either matter or spirit. We are always a unity. The word "heart" refers to this unified experience which is in some sense sacramental. To the objection that this is all too obscure, Rahner replies that knowledge conveyed by this primordial word necessarily evokes mystery, the incomprehensible depth of reality to which poets draw most closely. We must not be blinded by the surface of reality.

Rahner appends two observations: 1) "Heart" does not immediately imply love. A heart can also be hollow or filled with hate. That the heart of the Lord is filled with love is the greatest revelation; 2) Using the physical heart to represent this original unity is not completely arbitrary. It is a primordial symbol (*Ursymbol*). Rahner equates it to the sacramental sign which belongs to sacramental grace: "one is never without the other, one is present in the other, is first fully itself in the other, and yet the two are not simply the same" (328).

Rahner eschews the idea that someday we might be able to speak directly about the original unity we experience and avoid completely the word "heart." Such words are ever young, inexhaustible like the mystery they point to. Such words make present the reality they announce. They are archetypic. "They ought to be used sparingly, with discipline and reticence.... So long as man has a heart, he will have to speak of it with this precise word 'heart'" (329). To speak of the Sacred Heart we must first know the full import of the primordial word "heart." Only then can we know what it means that the eternal Logos has a human heart.

3.22 Some Theses for a Theology of Devotion to the Sacred Heart
Einige Thesen zur Theologie der Herz-Jesu-Verehrung
{1.5} J. Stierli, *Cor Salvatoris*, 2nd printing (Freiburg 1956) 166-199.
Abstract: Rahner defends devotion to the Sacred Heart by arguing that everything essential to it is also found in dogmatic theology, and everything questionable within it is not an essential part of such devotion.
Topics: JESUS CHRIST, Sacred Heart of.
Subsidiary Discussions: Word, primordial (331f); Theological anthropology, heart (332, 335, 343f); Symbol, real (333); Revelation, private (338f,

351f); Ignatius Loyola, spirituality of (342f); Reparation (344ff); Consoling the Lord (347ff).

Precis: I. Preliminary questions.

1) On the theological method: a) What does devotion to the Sacred Heart mean according to the doctrine and practice of the church? b) No one can impose one particular style of this devotion as the only correct one.

2) On the general concept of "heart": a) To understand heart one needs a proper frame of reference (in this case not physiology). b) Heart is a cross-cultural, primordial word (*Urwort*) incapable for being defined in simpler concepts. It describes realities arising from our original unity and spans the distinction between body and soul. The physical heart is a symbol of a deeper reality. c) Heart denotes the core of a person—the point at which one relates to others and to God. d) Heart does not immediately connote love. e) The physical (albeit stylized) heart is a natural symbol of this heart. f) Heart functions as an archetype in depth psychology.

3) On the phenomenology of the Sacred Heart devotion: a) Actual devotion can be vital and profound even when reflex theological thinking is imprecise or lacking. b) Where devotion is based on private revelation it is subject to interpretation by the laws governing private revelation. c) The critic must distinguish among the many forms of devotion, some of which contain existentially false elements. d) Different forms of devotion will be appropriate to different people based on age, education, etc.

4) Some preliminary propositions from the existential-ontological sphere: a) There is a particular type of honor given to a person. It is determined by the essence of the honoree. b) Of decisive importance is the fact the honoree has not only attributes (natural capacities) but attitudes (freely developed, personal elements of character). These merge in one structured, meaningful whole. c) This whole is the heart, unique to human beings. d) Honor paid to the person is paid to the heart—to the original, inmost, formative center of one's attitudes. e) The proper object of devotion to the Sacred Heart is the person of the Lord. It takes the form of adoration. All prayers addressed to the heart are actually addressed to the person. f) Summary (336). The ultimate discovery is that the center of this heart is love, the inmost essence of God bestowed on us as grace. g) In this particular devotion there is no need dogmatically or didactically to distinguish between the formal object in itself and in relation to the material object.

II. On the question of theological foundations for the Sacred Heart devotion.

1) It is theologically possible and necessary to establish the material content of this devotion from scripture and tradition.

2) This would not, however, sufficiently ground today's devotion because so much extra has evolved with the influence of Paray-le-Monial without severing continuity. The extra does demand justification even though it cannot be derived from scripture and tradition alone.

3) A private revelation does not reveal something new so much as it insists that some aspect of Christianity be given new emphasis.

4) Private revelation must be interpreted according to the historical situation in which it appears.

5) The message of Paray-le-Monial appeared against a background of growing secularization marked by the end of 'Christendom," the rise of the individual, and "the absence of God."

6) The message of Paray-le-Monial (inwardness, belief in the presence of God's love, and reparation) becomes understandable against this historical background.

7) This insight answers several time-dependent questions about this devotion: a) Certain 17th Century deficits which often accompany this devotion are not essential and can easily be overcome. b) Individual material points of this devotion are elements of dogma and thus valid for all periods of Christian history. c) The expanded devotion promulgated by Pius XI is closely related to historical circumstances which will continue for the foreseeable future. d) No one can say whether this devotion will last to the end of time. Humility in this regard will guard against fanaticism.

III. On the integration of the Sacred Heart Devotion into the whole of Ignatian spirituality.

1) This devotion is rightly called "*totius religionis summa.*" It is not simply one practice among many others.

2) The devotion must not be identified with one of its particular forms. It must always blossom in works of love and service. It would be dangerous to conflate this devotion with the whole of Christianity.

3) Ignatian spirituality allows the most diverse kinds, degrees, and dosages of this devotion.

IV. On the "object" of the Sacred Heart devotion.

1) What was said about the heart as a primordial word applies to the Sacred Heart.

2) The object of this devotion is the Lord with respect to his heart. This supplies the criteria to judge the appropriateness of any particular prayer or practice.

3) This heart becomes visible love of God manifested in the redemptive suffering and death of the Lord.

4) The love of the Lord's heart is not only human but also divine, revealing that love and not the just anger is the first and ultimate word of God to the world.

V. On the theology of "reparation" in the Sacred Heart devotion.

1) Insofar as this devotion adores the redemptive love of the Lord it also shares in the accomplishment of that love: reparation.

2) Reparation for the sin of the world consists in lovingly accepting a share in the Lord's suffering.

3) Thus, all reparation remains "in Christ."

4) Because love and not even reparation is the form of all virtues, this devotion must not swallow up the whole of the spiritual life.

5) After touching on which person of the Trinity offers reparation to which, Rahner concludes that prayers which confuse these theological distinctions are not essential to the devotion. Summary of the theology of reparation (346f).

VI. On "consoling" the Lord.

1) The concept of wanting our co-suffering to console the Lord in his human suffering needs careful interpretation.

2) It is useful to meditate intensely on the sufferings of the Lord. Sometimes, however, this involves eliminating psychologically the time differential between then and now.

3) To imagine ourselves actually affecting the suffering Christ in the garden would be mere fiction. This meditation puts us in touch with what made Jesus who he is now: the Lord in glory.

4) An active consoling of the suffering Lord can be construed from the divine foreknowledge of the then suffering Lord who saw the love with which others would freely participate in his great act of reparation. a) It would still have to be proven that the Lord was in fact consoled by this foreknowledge. b) It must be recalled that all acts of love would console the Lord and not only those performed with explicit reference to this devotion. c) Might it be too much to expect simple believers to understand and make such fine theological distinctions?

5) For all these reasons Rahner does not include "consoling the Lord" among the constitutive elements of this devotion. He concludes with a summary of what is essential in the Holy Hour (351).

VII. The promises of Paray-le-Monial.

1) These are subject to the rules of interpretation for private revelation. Errors and inaccuracies are always possible.

2) Nothing new is promised which is not already found in the gospels. What is new are the circumstances under which the promises are obtained.

3) These promises must be interpreted in the same light as the promises of scripture. None of our actions ever gives us power over God. God's gifts are given to those who love.

4) The "Great Promise" of the nine First Fridays can be preached by those who believe it does not contradict dogmatic principles, but only in such a way that it does not lead others to the sin of presumption.

3.23 The Christian among Unbelieving Relations
Der Christ und seine ungläubigen Verwandten
{1.0} *Geist und Leben* 27 (1954) 171-184.

Abstract: Although Rahner argues hope is justified for family members who have fallen away from the church, this is never a reason not to do our duty to work assiduously for our own salvation and for that of our lapsed family members.
Topics: ANONYMOUS CHRISTIAN; SALVATION/DAMNATION.
Subsidiary Discussions: Church, diaspora (358ff); Ignorance, invincible (362f); Fundamental option (365f); Eschatology, *apokatastasis* (371f).
Precis: Christians today live in a diaspora which penetrates deep into the circle of our relatives. This is especially painful because of the doubt it casts on the eternal salvation of those we love. For is not the church "necessary for salvation" and do we not have a duty toward them in charity? Rahner makes three points. 1) Although we must work for the religious unity of our families, scripture foresees this diaspora situation as something normal "if viewed in the light of the essence of Christianity .... [diaspora] Christianity is more personal, less dependent upon the institutional, the traditional, less conditioned by its surroundings" (359). Hence, authentic Christianity today is not so much a cultural given as a type of martyrdom. 2) Even though family relations can be looser today, Rahner warns against letting the offering of one's faith to God "become the pretext for refusing to parents and relatives what is by nature their due according to God's will" (360). 3) Many are anxious about the eternal salvation of their loved ones.

Rahner replies to these concerns recalling that the status of anyone's salvation or damnation is never known with certainty save by God alone. We all work out our salvation "in fear and trembling." In addition no one deserves damnation who is living in invincible ignorance. Rahner extends this category beyond missionary lands to those in our own families who in good faith cannot embrace our religion for any number of good reasons. Although theologians may dispute precisely what is necessary for the salvation of non-believers it remains a fact that everyone who is saved is saved through the grace of Christ, whether or not one expressly knows this. Rahner further appeals to the notion of fundamental option, arguing that even though one may transgress certain important moral laws, one is judged on the final disposition of one's heart.

Rahner adds a word about the salvation/damnation status of fallen away Catholics. Here there are grounds for hope because: 1) many who seem to have fallen away never actually possessed a definite and precisely understood faith. In addition, those who fell away may have actually returned to the faith but not in that form in which it was lost. Summary (369).

Rahner admits that for many who want a clear answer his comments may seem round about. But this is because God takes pains to make our own duty clear to us and leaves obscure the things concerning the status of others. We know our duty towards God and must fulfill it. Yet to those who are morally uncomfortable doing nothing for unbelieving relations Rahner reminds us it is possible that in answer to our prayers God may have opened a door to them about which we know nothing. It is arrogant to excuse ourselves from working for the salvation of others based on a cavalier belief that in the end all will be saved. Nothing excuses us from working out our salvation and working for the salvation of those we love. Summary (372).

3.24 On Conversion to the Church
Über Konversionen
{0.5}   *Hochland* 46 (1953) 119-126.

Abstract: The new historical situation among Christian confessions affects our contemporary attitudes towards conversion.
Topics: CHURCH and the churches; ECUMENISM; CONVERSIONS.
Precis: Ever since there were divisions in Christendom there have been conversions, and these for many reasons. Each camp used conversions to underscore its correctness or the insidious nature of the other. But no camp has the right to judge the actions of any convert. The phenomenon of conversion has changed greatly since the time of the reformers. Rahner hopes to analyze these changes to see what conclusions can be drawn.

I. In earlier times the various camps in Christendom were utterly hostile. Convinced of the correctness of their own positions they believed others were steeped in bad will. Today's situation is different. Many accept the divisions of Christendom and see all camps as relatively equal. Catholics on the contrary maintain these divisions are over essential matters. This very different situation forces the realization that our faith is different from our forbearers'. All converts bring this history into their adopted community. The long religious history of Protestantism cannot be dismissed as completely negative. Since the time of divisions these communities have legitimately developed genuine Christian potentialities missing in the Catholic Church. "[T]hey belong of themselves to the actual fullness of the historical realization of what is Christian" (376f). Rahner mentions in particular their reverence for scripture and their valuable exegesis.

II. From this new situation and what has been said it is not possible to conclude that individual conversions to the Catholic Church are a mistake and that everyone ought simply to wait for the reunion of divided communions. Those who hold the relativist position that the Catholic Church is one legitimate church among others but prefer it for its discipline or liturgy should be actively dissuaded from converting. But for those who have come to see that the one true church of Christ subsists in the Catholic Church, for those who hold that the church is not divided although Christendom is, there can be no question of desertion. "If the Church of Christ is to be found in the concrete in the Catholic Church and if according to the will of Christ it is necessary for salvation to belong concretely to this concrete Church...then there is no longer any room for asking what consequences follow from this" (380). Summary (381).

III. What is the significance of the new relationship among Christian confessions for conversion? Since converts are heirs to a past which has many positive Christian elements, they have a mission to bring these into their adopted church. This includes especially their reverence for and daily use of scripture. Unfortunately converts may find themselves in local Catholic churches whose faith is tepid, whose preaching is poor, whose music and liturgy are anemic, and whose symbols are foreign. Converts may feel homeless in their new home. Such converts will have to content themselves with the knowledge they have done what Christ has demanded of them.

3.25 Science as a "Confession"?
Wissenschaft als "Konfession"?
{2.0} *Wort und Wahrheit* 9 (1954) 809-819.

Abstract: The right relationship between science and religion is rooted in the historico-metaphysical insight that religious knowledge and experience is more original than science. Scientists grounded in faith resist self-idolization.

Topics: SCIENCE and religion; RELIGION and science.
Subsidiary Discussions: God (388ff); Atheism (390ff); God-talk (394f); Demythology (396f).
Precis: Ours is a world of pre-given facts and spirit. These spiritual datum are of two kinds: metaphysical (presupposed a priori structures of unity and meaning) and historical (whose starting-points we can never escape or get behind). They "constitute in the limited and conditioned singularity of their combination the immediate context of his existence" (387). The truth of religion is a priori to a scientific worldview since it springs from a source higher and more original than science—from a more original act of existence. Rahner locates this origin in the background against which particular things are apprehended. "This ultimate ground of all reality, which is present only by precisely *not* being part of our world-image, and which is the end-goal of our movement to acquire a view of the world, a goal essentially beyond the reach of our own power, we call God" (388). Summary (388f).

Though Christianity has always known this, it has lived this truth too little. This is due in large part to the fact that the worldview of the past was so small God seemed to be part of it. Today's deeper worldview no longer sees God this way. Rahner finds the roots of modern atheism in this discovery that the world is not God and cannot contain God. Rahner is not interested in militant atheism but in "troubled atheism"—a spirit kindred to belief. Academics must not suppress this realization about God but must learn to proclaim God in a new way: a God beyond analogies who often seems far away, even silent. Only then do we discover the truth which is incomprehensible, immense, and worthy of adoration.

Needless to say Christianity is more than the silent honoring of a nameless God. It is tidings from God, history, institution, authority, propositions about God, etc. Here is where science is likely to find scandal for God always speaks in representations drawn from our worldview (e.g., Son of God, divine anger, reparation, etc.). How are we to understand such God-talk? Rahner notes first that our age is less apt to interpret analogies literally. Still, theologians must use analogical language for in the last analysis the object of their interest remains mystery. Complete clarity about God would reveal only how wide of the truth they have strayed. A second limitation which seems to make God-talk unacceptable is its reliance on naive mythological language. Rahner sees no need to demythologize such expressions because they retain their original meaning in spite of their outmoded expression. One can argue that it has always been possible to distinguish between the form and content of these expressions. In addition no church definitions stand or fall on the truth of these ancient worldviews. When religion moves away from such picture thinking to think more abstractly it is doing what science does. This increase in abstraction is not mere loss. One gains appreciation for the inexpressible greatness of God.

From the priority of religious knowledge over the scientific worldview, and from the situation of concrete historico-metaphysical existence beyond the reach of scientific reflection, Rahner concludes it is wrong to embrace science as a confession, as if it contained everything necessary and important to human life and whatever was outside science held no interest. Rahner sees this arrogant attitude in its death-throes. Science avoids poisoning human existence only when it emanates from the original, unreflective understanding of existence (i.e., from God). This conclusion makes it incumbent on the scientist to be a person of prayer, silence, faith, sturdy religious practice, and moral effort. This combats any tendency for self-idolization.

IV. MORE RECENT WRITINGS
IV. *Neuere Schriften*

German Edition: Einsiedeln, Benziger, 1960
U.S. edition: Baltimore, MD, Helicon Press, 1966
Kevin Smyth, translator

4.01 Considerations on the Development of Dogma
Überlegungen zur Dogmenentwicklung
{3.0}   October 1957 lecture at Innsbruck.
Zeitschrift für katholische Theologie 80 (1958) 1-16.

Abstract: To reconcile the authentic identity between revelation and really genuine development of dogma Rahner considers five constitutive elements of any truth of faith. These reveal the dynamism of dogmatic development.
Topics: DOGMA, development of; MAGISTERIUM and development of dogma; REVELATION and development of dogma; FAITH.

Subsidiary Discussions: Scripture, development of (6f); History (8, 24); Revelation, close of (8ff); Spirit (11f, 18f); Knowledge (13ff); Infallibility (16f, 31ff); BVM, Assumption of (17); Rationality (19ff); Congruity, argument from (22f); Tradition (24ff).

Precis: Since the church is never a source of new revelation, dogmatic theologians must show how dogmas are contained in original revelation. Though church magisterium guarantees these connections, theologians must show what they are. Although such reflection has always been part of theology, since the 1800s the issue is controverted on two fronts: "how namely authentic identity on the one hand and really genuine development on the other can be reconciled" (5).

I. The development of dogma within the scriptures. A real development of dogma and not merely of theology can already be seen in scripture, especially in the relationship between the Old and New Testaments (examples, 7).

II. A priori rules for the framework of development of dogma.

a) Since development of dogma is not a single process which can be adequately comprehended by formal rules it cannot be predicted. It is a human, historical process unique in each instance. Still, this does not mean development has no formal principles which can at least indicate false developments.

b) "The revelation in Christ is the final, unsurpassable revelation, which was closed with the end of the apostolic generation" (8). That is to say: 1) revelation is closed not because God arbitrarily ends some series of statements, but because after having uttered himself, there is no more left to communicate. Final revelation implies the existence of a believing church. 2) Because the human word and finite concepts together constitute this final revelation, an element of unfolding is possible.

c) If dogma develops, all the essential constituent elements of such a dogma (those carried along in an ultimate indissoluble unity) also develop. Since each element must have the innate capacity to develop, any attempt to explain the development of dogma solely in reference to one element (however prominent) must be rejected.

III. Constitutive elements of the dynamism of dogmatic development. In this section Rahner identifies the five elements of a truth of faith and hence of dogmatic development.

a) The Spirit and grace. God's self-disclosure in revelation presupposes grace in the hearer. The Holy Spirit is in the word of revelation, hence, the infinite openness of the closed revelation and the dynamism of self-development. Spirit and word are possessed in an indissoluble unity. Rahner bases this on the nature of human knowledge, insisting that in addition to knowledge based on the experience of things themselves, and knowledge based on testimony, there is a third kind of knowledge wherein the thing itself (Spirit) is given in the word. Thus, the Spirit is an intrinsic although not an isolated element in development by means of the believing consciousness of the church. Rahner alludes to the transcendental deduction of experience (background/horizon of consciousness) to indicate how the Spirit is present as a process of consciousness.

b) The magisterium of the church. The word is always delivered by the authorized bearer of doctrine and tradition in the hierarchically-constituted church. Hence, insofar as the magisterium itself is in a process of ongoing dialogue with other thinking elements of the church, dogma is able to develop. The magisterium alone is never an adequate cause for development. Authentic development rests on the Spirit and on developments in theology.

c) Concepts and words. Divine revelation is always given in human words and concepts. For all our guarantees that the Spirit speaks the truth and the church passes it on, words and concepts remain human and subject to reflex theological unfolding. Rahner rejects the notion of development by authority or mystical insight. Even without knowing its exact mode theologians must affirm a connection between any new dogma and original revelation. One must not demand too high a standard for proving this connection (20) or insist the connection be shown in terms of scholastic, syllogistic rationalism (21). Rahner ends this section with a discussion of the argument from congruity.

d) Tradition. Every revelation is handed on as communication between persons. Its developmental dynamism resides in the fact that this happens through events in time. It is an historical process apprehended in faith. As such it is impossible to deduce in advance how development will occur. In fact two tendencies are possible: an ever greater multiplication of distinct particulars about God's self-communication, or a mysticism in which everything converges on the one great mystery.

e) The acknowledged presence of dogma, *as* dogma, *and as* revealed by God. Here is the real problematic point: that with the definition of a dogma the church explicitly articulates a divine revelation it was not always consciously aware it possessed. How does this new realization take place? To say it happens because the pope articulates it merely raises the question of how he came to know it. To say he knows it through tradition begs the question of how it became clear over time. To say the answer rests on the rationality of the argument never leads to the certainty of faith (27ff).

Rahner sees this ancient question as analogous to the problem of belief: how one comes from a position of non-belief to faith. All that can be said is that the process is rational even thought there is a qualitative difference between faith and unbelief. Rahner insists on two points: there is a mental clarity which does not precede the decision but which can only be found in the decision; this is a decision and a movement of the whole church without thereby impugning the power of the pope to define a dogma or insisting that every Catholic must actually believe an article of faith prior to its being defined. Because the development of dogma is an action of the whole church it is easier to understand than an individual's coming to faith. For among other things it is a matter of the church moving from faith to faith rather than of an individual moving from unbelief to belief. Summary (34f).

4.02 The Concept of Mystery in Catholic Theology

Über den Begriff des Geheimnisses in der katholischen Theologie
{3.0}   Siegfried Behn, ed., *Beständiger Aufbruch. Przywara-Festschrift* (Nürnberg 1959) 181-216.

Abstract: Using a more primordial notion of mystery than the scholastics, Rahner distills the Christian mysteries strictly speaking to three: Trinity, incarnation, human divinization in grace and glory. He comments on each. **Topics:** MYSTERY; GOD as mystery. **Subsidiary Discussions:** Reason, *ratio* (38ff); Revelation (38ff); Beatific Vision (40f, 66); Virtues, *perichoresis* (42ff); Spirit, transcendence (42, 49ff); Propositions (44ff); Incarnation (65ff); Hypostatic union (67ff); Trinity (69ff).

Precis: I. First lecture. The question of mystery is important in apologetic and dogmatic theology. Whether Christian doctrine is a labyrinth of mysteries or one mysteriously simple thing of infinite fullness is an existential problem. It holds the promise of freeing us from diluting religion and of revealing us as beings already facing the nameless mystery we adore.

Lecture I finds fault with the conventional scholastic notion of mystery in three particulars: it regards mystery as the property of statements; it allows for a multiplicity of mysteries; this multiplicity is comprised of truths which are only provisionally incomprehensible. Casting mystery in terms of *ratio* seems to equate mystery with a mysterious truth. Not only does mystery then merge with the notion of revelation, it becomes provisional when one recalls that all mysterious truths will be cleared up in the vision of glory. Summary (40).

What happens if one thinks differently? Following this lead Rahner shows first that the scholastic notion of mystery fails when brought into dialogue with the doctrine of God's abiding incomprehensibility (41f). It also fails when brought into dialogue with the nature of spirit which according to Rahner is always oriented to the primordial and fundamental—the ultimate transcendental condition for the possibility of knowledge (42). The scholastic notion also fails when measured against the *perichoresis* of knowledge and love. Since love and not knowledge is the ultimate word which conjures up our essence and finally saves us, mystery must lead to the self-surrender of love by which it accepts mystery and so attains its proper perfection (42ff).

Rahner returns to the inadequacy of framing mystery in terms of propositions (44f) particularly the inability of this approach to distinguish between natural and supernatural mysteries. Not only does it leave no room for the numinous, it fails to explain why some truths can only be known by revelation and why these are mysteries in the strict sense. It is not enough to say these mysteries surpass even angelic reason or to say that grace is required to receive them. Finally, identifying mysteries with propositions leaves open the assumption there can be an infinite number of mysteries since there can be an infinite number of propositions. After developing this problem in some detail Rahner leaves its solution for future lectures.

II. Second lecture. The first part of this lecture is philosophical (48ff) the second theological (54ff). They share one aim: to clarify the essence of mystery. Rahner begins by looking at the subject of mystery, i.e., its recipient: the finite human person (preview, 49). Rahner states three obvious presuppositions of human transcendence: its limitless openness whose act and finality form a unity; its pre-reflexive nature; its co-present, primordial, implicit knowledge of God. Before answering how transcendence is accorded its "Wither," Rahner gives his reasons for steering clear of identifying this as God or as an object (50). Next he argues the "Wither" of transcendence is always nameless, indefinable, and unattainable (immeasurable). He concludes that we possess the "Wither" of transcendence "only in the form of the condition of possibility of the grasp of the finite" (52). This "Wither" of transcendence is most properly called holy (53).

Thus, Rahner comes to the limits of philosophy's contribution to this problem. Since mystery is a transcendent concept one cannot expect to find a clear definition here. We do, however, now possess a clearer view of the human person as spirit, as transcendence, as the being of holy mystery, even if one remains only unreflexively conscious of the fact. "If man himself is therefore to be understood as the being of the holy mystery, it also follows that *God* is present to man *as* the holy mystery" (54).

Rahner now takes a theological turn. He discusses the subject of mystery precisely as elevated by grace—"the spiritual being which is ontologically directed to the beatific vision" (54). It is precisely this graced elevation that, without promising to eliminate mystery, introduces the radical possibility of the absolute proximity of mystery. Our experience of transcendence reveals mystery as distant and aloof. Our experience of grace reveals the abiding nearness of mystery without thereby making it fully comprehensible.

A few closing remarks on the subject of the mystery in itself. Insofar as it cannot be reduced to any simpler principles or concepts Rahner describes the "Wither" of transcendence as "self-evident" (57). He claims nothing is more familiar or obvious to the alerted spirit than the silent question which hovers over it: the question of one's relation to the "Wither" of transcendence. Christianity must exploit the self-evident quality of mystery to speak to a new generation suspicious of religion which appeals to numerous mysteries at every turn. Finally this mystery is "the sole peace of him who trusts himself to it, loves it humbly, and surrenders to it fearlessly in knowledge and love" (58). The last paragraph of this essay sets up the question whether there is a multiplicity of mysteries in Christianity or whether in relation to the primordial mystery discussed above these are only derivative.

III. Third lecture. After a lengthy review of the first two lectures (60-63) which rules out the notion of natural mysteries, strictly speaking, Rahner asks whether there are Christian mysteries, strictly speaking, in the plural, and if so what they are (63). He identifies three: Trinity, incarnation, and human divinization in grace and glory. All other contenders (original sin, Eucharist, etc.) can be seen as subsets of these three. To understand why these qualify as mysteries strictly speaking, Rahner divides the Trinity from the other two insofar as these latter deal with God's dealings with the non-divine. Their common element is their relation to God through quasi-formal (rather than efficient) causality wherein God accomplishes self-communication immediately to something distinct from God. These qualify as mysteries strictly speaking because "it is only through revelation ... that we can know that such a thing is actual and possible" (67).

At this juncture Rahner sees the need for an additional and quite dense word about the hypostatic union—how God's self-communication to the creature which happens uniquely in the Logos is related to Christ's beatific vision and to ours (68f). Rahner then returns to the mystery of the Trinity (69ff) where he argues that the Trinity we experience in the history of salvation is the immanent Trinity. Thus we should have no misgivings about starting our reflection on God with Jesus and the life of the Spirit within us. This presupposes: 1) each person in the Trinity has its own proper relationship to humanity; 2) only the Logos "can assume hypostatically a created reality and hence be the essential and irreplaceable revealer of the Father" (71). After a brief summary (71f) Rahner concludes that the three mysteries strictly speaking are not intermediate or provisional, nor do they lie behind or beyond what we experience of God. They signify and articulate the one mystery of God revealed in Jesus. Christian mysteries in the plural are the concrete form of the one holy mystery. Hence, we cannot deduce the Trinity beginning from some abstract principle. All that Christians know about God can only be known a posteriori from the experience of the incarnation and of grace.

4.03 Remarks on the Dogmatic Treatise *De Trinitate*
Bemerkungen zum dogmatischen Traktat "De Trinitate"
{3.5} *Universitas. Festschrift für Bischof A. Stohr*, Vol. I, (Mainz 1960) 130-150.

Abstract: Rahner seeks to overcome the seeming isolation and irrelevence of trinitarian dogma by arguing the ecomonic Trinity is the immanent Trinity: i.e., the God available to our experience is also God's very self.
Topics: TRINITY; GOD.
Subsidiary Discussions: Incarnation (79f, 87ff); Augustine, psychology of (84ff); Grace, trinitarian (94ff); Trinity in Old Testament (99ff); Person, divine (101f).

Precis: I. After a brief review of major writers on the Trinity (bibliography ftns1-5) Rahner concludes most Christians despite their orthodox professions of faith are actually monotheists. Little would change for them if the doctrine of the Trinity were rescinded. Few can distinguish who they pray to in the Our Father, why the second person of the Trinity became flesh, or to whom satisfaction was made. The same monotheism pervades the doctrine of grace. This anti-trinitarian timidity affects theologians as well when they write of eschatology, sacraments, or creation. They justify their silence on the supposition that divine acts *ad extra* are performed so communally that one cannot distinguish in them any significant signs of inner-trinitarian life.

II. The doctrine of the Trinity remains isolated in the structure of dogmatic theology. Once dealt with it seldom recurs, as if it had little or nothing to do with our salvation, nothing to teach us about ourselves. This may shed some light on why the treatise *De Deo Uno* is often divided from and placed before the doctrine of the Trinity in dogmatic manuals. Although no case can be made for this approach from scripture, the Greek Fathers, or even up to the time of Aquinas, Rahner wonders if it is not foreshadowed in Augustine's psychological approach to the Trinity (84f). In any case Rahner insists that beginning with concepts of knowledge and love taken from natural philosophy and applying them to the Trinity just doesn't work. These "essential" concepts never become personal and thus never reach the heart of the Trinity. His point is that in our day the unity and interconnection between the two treatises *De Deo Uno* and *De Trinitate* are not well enough worked out. Rahner adds that a certain embarrassment about finding presentiments of the Trinity in the Old Testament or in secular philosophy also contributes to modern theologians' desire to treat the doctrine of the Trinity briefly and in isolation.

III. Something is wrong when treatises on the Trinity fail to show its intrinsic connection to salvation. The basic thesis which links the two is the fact that the Trinity of the economy of salvation *is* the immanent Trinity and vice versa. Rahner attempts to explain (85ff) and prove this thesis (94ff) and in the process apply it to christology. Section III ends with Rahner drawing some conclusions from this thesis.

The core of this thesis is in the fact that precisely the second person of the Trinity became flesh. From this Rahner concludes that in at least this case one reality in the economy of salvation is not merely appropriated to a certain divine person. Rahner raises and disposes of three objections to this conclusion: 1) that because the hypostatic union is a unique event no generalizations can be made from it to other persons of the Trinity (88ff); that incarnation only reveals the second person as he is to us and not as he is in himself (90ff); 3) although the Logos is formally active and present in the Word, Jesus' unmixed nature argues that his words and actions betray nothing of the Logos as such (93f). Summary (94).

Rahner next attempts to prove his trinitarian thesis based on the doctrine of grace. This argument too rests on the controverted notion of the non-appropriated relationships of the divine person to the justified. Briefly, "each of the three divine persons communicates himself as such to man, each in his own special and different way of personal being, in the free gift of grace" (95). To reveal oneself otherwise would make that person of the Trinity absolute rather than one in relation to the others. As it is each self-communication of the one God is accomplished in the relative way in which God actually subsists. This communication is not an image or analogy but the very Trinity itself.

Rahner offers a further proof beginning not from grace but from the nature of God's self-communication in which, through quasi-formal causality God gives us not merely a share in himself but gives himself in the strictest sense. According to scripture this self-communication has a threefold aspect (97) each of which is properly identified with a different person of the Trinity: Father, Word, Spirit. Rahner goes on to show how this understanding avoids Sabellianism, Arianism, and modalism.

Rahner concludes: 1) we need not hesitate to appeal to the experience of Jesus and the Spirit when approaching the doctrine of the Trinity because the God experienced in salvation history is the immanent Trinity; 2) the Trinity has living, existential importance to us prior to its dogmatic formulation; 3) we should always formulate trinitarian dogma in light of our experience and align it with the economy of salvation; 4) we should not be shy to explore the history of the Trinity even in the Old Testament, especially in terms of Word and Spirit; 5) although when applied to the Trinity the word "person" is inadequate in many ways, it should not be jettisoned as Barth suggests; 6) this thesis allows for the relationship between *De Deo Uno* and *De Trinitate* to be completely rethought.

4.04 On the Theology of the Incarnation
Zur Theologie der Menschwerdung
{3.5}   *Catholica* 12 (1958) 1-16.
Abstract: Rahner's meditation on incarnation begins by analyzing what man is and what it means for God to become man by emptying himself. He concludes that anthropology is first and last christology. It remains forever theology.
Topics: THEOLOGICAL ANTHROPOLOGY; MYSTERY; CHRISTO-LOGY, incarnation.
Subsidiary Discussions: *Potentia obedientialis* (110); Becoming (112ff); God, immutability of (112f); Trinity (115); Anonymous Christian (118f).
Precis: This analysis of incarnation, the inexhaustible center of Christian life, presupposes the truth of the ancient dogmatic formulae. But it sees them as merely starting-points. Each generation must plumb this incomprehen-

sible mystery for itself. As fruitful as it might be to begin this examination of "The Word of God becoming man" with the subject, Rahner instead spends Part I considering the predicate "man," and Part II considering the verb, "becomes."

I. The Word of God has become *man*. What is man? What is his essential nature assumed by the Word of God? Unlike objects understandable in themselves, man is "an indefinability come to consciousness of itself" (107). To call us rational animals begs the question, what is rationality? We are essentially mystery insofar as we are referred to the incomprehensible God. We only understand ourselves to the degree we allow ourselves freely to be grasped by God. This mystery is always present; it is not provisional, not even in the beatific vision. Our bliss consists in lovingly accepting the vision of incomprehensible mystery.

When the Word of God assumes as his reality this indefinable nature he has simply arrived at the point to which this nature always strives by virtue of its essence (109). When it surrenders itself to the mystery, it belongs so little to itself that it becomes the very nature of God. The incarnation is therefore, "the unique, *supreme* case of the total actualization of human reality, which consists of the fact that man *is* insofar as he gives up himself" (110). This does not mean: 1) the possibility of the incarnation can be deduced a priori from the nature of man without revelation; 2) that such a possibility must be realized in every person who possesses this nature.

Since this is man's nature, "he attains his supreme fulfillment...only when he adoringly believes that somewhere there is a being whose existence steps so much out of itself into God, that it *is* just the question about the mystery utterly given over to the mystery" (111). This occurs fully in Jesus of Nazareth. This christology based on metaphysical insights into the nature of spirit avoids the appearance that the incarnation is a divine disguise. It also does justice to the fact that the humanity of God possesses nothing essentially more or less in the line of closeness to and encounter with God than what is provided for each of us in grace.

II. The Word of God *has become* man. God's "becoming" anything seemingly contradicts the notion of God's unchangeability. Yet when faced with the incarnation we must say God can become subject to change in something else. Although this might never appear to a purely rational ontology, revelation discloses that the infinite can become finite. It does this through self-emptying. Hence, this self-emptying and not the assumption of our nature is the ruling paradigm for the incarnation. This comes as no surprise since it is precisely this self-emptying love (God's self-utterance in his eternal fullness) that distinguishes the second person of the Trinity, that is revealed in the incarnation, and in relation to which creation (God's self-utterance outside himself) is secondary.

To say the Logos *becomes* man indicates that in the incarnation "the Logos creates by taking on, and takes on my emptying himself" (117). The difference between the Logos and us is that the "what" he utters is his self-expression. For he is love. "If God wills to become non-God, man comes to be, that and nothing else" (116). Hence, all theology is eternally an anthropology with christology as its beginning and end. This in turn is eternally theology. God becoming man through a process of self-emptying reveals that our personal independence grows in direct not inverse proportion to our submission to God.

Rahner rejects as heretical any christology which leaves the impression that Jesus merely dons the guise of humanity to signal his presence. That, and not the orthodox faith in the God-man, is mythology. At the same time many who reject the admittedly complex and difficult orthodox formulae are not thereby rejecting the reality of the incarnation. "Anyone who accepts his own humanity in full...has accepted the Son of Man, because God has accepted man in him" (119). Rahner concludes with a summary (119f).

4.05 Dogmatic Questions on Easter
Dogmatiche Fragen zur Osterfrömmigkeit
{2.5}   B. Fischer, J. Wagner, eds., *Paschatis Solemnia. Jungmann-Festschrift* (Freiburg 1959) 1-12.

Abstract: If we see Jesus' death as his ultimate act of freedom then Good Friday and Easter are two aspects of the same reality. This sheds light on the incarnation and on the enduring salvific meaning of Jesus' glorified life.

Topics: LITURGICAL YEAR, Easter; RESURRECTION; JESUS CHRIST, death/ resurrection of.

Subsidiary Discussions: Redemption, satisfaction theory (123f); Christology, neo-Chalcedonian (125ff); Death (127f); Sacrifice (129); Incarnation (130f); Immediacy, mediated (131f); God, *lumen gloriae* (132f); Eschatology (133).

Precis: This essay asks more questions than it answers. It is occasioned by the sad fact so little is said today about Easter, the central mystery of salvation history, especially compared to the attention given Good Friday. Rahner hopes to disclose here more of what there is to say about Easter.

Why has theology of the resurrection shrunk so astonishingly? Perhaps because after the 18th Century when apologetic and fundamental theology split, each branch left it to the other to develop the treatise (122f). More likely it stems from the fact that post-Tridentine theology concentrated almost exclusively on the incarnation and crucifixion because of the West's fixation on Jesus' paying the debt for sin. In this context the only possible meaning for Easter lies in the private realm of Jesus' life. It has no real significance for salvation despite an obscure Thomistic doctrine that argues the opposite (124ff). These historical questions surrounding Easter end with a inconclusive discussion of the effects of Arian and neo-Chalcedonian christology (125f).

The remainder of the essay raises questions about the content of the Easter dogma. For Rahner the key question is the meaning of Jesus' death (127f). A brief sketch of his theology of death argues that death is not simply one in a line of human actions. It is the supreme act in which the whole of one's life is gathered up in a final decision of freedom and is mastered, so that one ripens for his eternity. This being so, the resurrection is best thought of as the manifestation of what happened in the death of Christ. Thus, "Good Friday and Easter can be seen as two aspects of a strictly unitary event of the existence of Christ which are essentially related" (128). Because God has fully accepted a real piece of the world, the resurrection makes an ontological and not merely a juridical change in our condition. It marks the inauguration of an eschatological age. Rahner further illuminates this argument by showing its relation to the notion of sacrifice (129f).

From this vantage point we can look backwards and review the essence of the incarnation in light of the saving meaning of the resurrection, and forward to see the permanent meaning for us of the mediation of the glorified Lord. If the death/resurrection of Jesus accomplishes our redemption as the summit of his freedom, then the incarnation is not so much about his assuming flesh, a medium in which to suffer, as it is the beginning of the unique history of his freedom (130f). His resurrected life continues to have salvific meaning insofar as he continuously mediates to us the immediacy of God (131f). Rahner concludes with remarks on eschatology noting that Easter is not so much an event as an effect which continues eternally in time. We participate in the Easter reality through *anamnesis* each time we celebrate the Eucharist (132f).

4.06 *Virginitas in Partu*. A Contribution to the Problem of the Development of Dogma and of Tradition
Virginitas in partu. Ein Beitrag zum Problem der Dogmen-entwicklung und Überlieferung
{3.0} J. Betz, H. Fries, eds, *Kirche und Überlieferung. Geiselmann-Festschrift* (Freiburg 1960) 52-80.

Abstract: In submitting the tradition of Mary's status *"virginitas in partu"* to the norms of doctrinal development, Rahner affirms the substance of the tradition without insisting that its concrete details are universally binding.
Topics: BVM, *virginitas in partu*; DOGMA, development of.
Subsidiary Discussions: Revelation, two source theory (143ff); BVM, Mariology (154ff); Pain (159f).
Precis: This essay contributes to a discussion of the binding nature of belief in the notion and details of Mary's *virginitas in partu*, i.e., her perpetual, physically intact virginity, her freedom from the pangs of childbirth and its attendant physical aspects (bibliography, 134 ftn1). Using a method more critically speculative and concerned with the history of dogma than in years

past, A. Mitterer proposes that *virginitas in partu* is not a separate process but simply the application of the doctrine of the perpetual virginity of Mary to her childbearing. Rahner offers these reflections as "marginal notes."

I. This *status questionis* reveals why modern theology can demand reserve in determining the content of this *de fide* doctrine even though 1500 years of theological tradition on the whole gives little sign of such reserve. Rahner concludes it is quite proper to assert that the doctrine can be justifiable even if the exact content of the doctrine remains undetermined.

II. This doctrine is a perfect example of the complex and problematic nature of the history of development of dogma. It throws into relief two essentially different meanings of the argument from tradition and the Fathers: **a)** the dogmatic meaning: that something taught and believed by the church at any time in the past is for that reason binding today; **b)** the meaning in the history of dogma: that all dogma must stem from apostolic preaching and can and must be traced back to it historically. Failure of textbooks to distinguish these two meanings can give the impression a doctrine has apostolic origins even if it can only be traced back to the beginning of the third century. (Rahner launches into an excursus on the two source theory of revelation: scripture and tradition (143-147). He concludes that even this theory leaves theologians with the problem of tracing tradition back to the apostolic witness.)

In tracing *virginitas in partu* to the apostolic witness Rahner cites as a minority opinion Clement of Alexandria (2nd Century) the first to testify to the concrete details of the doctrine. **a)** Origen and Tertullian see no problem dismissing these concrete details. **b)** The apocryphal reference are dismissed even by Jerome as clearly docetic. **c)** Since a really explicit apostolic tradition in this matter is most unlikely, Rahner concludes the doctrine must be contained only implicitly in apostolic teaching. Since later preaching does not provide sure dogmatic proof of the details they need not be held *de fide*. Theologians are free to interpret them.

III. Where in the apostolic witness might the doctrine of *virginitas in partu* be implicitly found?

a) Mary is a real theological theme in the apostolic preaching. After a synopsis of her place in salvation history (154f) Rahner concludes that her act of giving birth is no mere biological event. It is an act involving the whole person—the whole of Mary's nature. All this can be true even if it conveys no concrete details of how Mary's nature affects her act of giving birth.

b) To the objection that the above merely indicates her giving birth was "Marian" but skirts the question of what makes it "virginal," Rahner insists *virginitas in partu* is not a concept anterior to the virgin birth. Concrete details of Mary's post partum condition cannot be drawn from prior definitions of particular physical parameters of virginity. In Mary's case virginity stands for Mary "in her whole reality" (157). Immaculately conceived and free of concupiscence (though in an infralapsarian context) all we can say about her childbearing is that Mary was able to experience and appropriate it in a very different way than other mortals "who always experience what the life-forces of the world inflict on them as something alien and restrictive, which works upon them to the detriment of their freedom" (159). But this insight does not allow us to conclude that she experienced no pain in childbirth. After all, who can say what pain would be to someone free of concupiscence?

c) After considering other details which tradition associates with Mary's childbearing, Rahner concludes that her childbirth, like the conception of her son, is in its total reality an act of the virgin which corresponds fully with her nature, and is hence, unique, miraculous, and "virginal." But this does not thereby offer the possibility of deducing concrete details of the process which would be certain and universally binding (summary, 162).

4.07 Nature and Grace
Natur und Gnade. Nach der Lehre der katholischen Kirche
{3.5}   L. Reinisch, ed., *Theologie heute,* 2nd printing (Munich 1960) 89-
102.

Abstract: This theoretical analysis of nature and grace necessitated by advances in philosophy and history improves on the scholastics' theory and makes significant contributions when combined with metaphysical anthropology.

Topics: GRACE and nature; NATURE and supernature; THEOLOGICAL ANTHROPOLOGY.
Subsidiary Discussions: *Potentia obedientialis* (167f, 186f); Thomism, transcendental (169f); Sin, *simul justus et pecator* (173); Trinity (175ff); Incarnation (176f); God as horizon (178); *Pneuma* (179); Anonymous Christian (179ff); Dialogue (185).
Precis: Since the Reformation controversies cooled, nature and grace has seemed to all but a few specialists a closed topic. Rahner begins this essay with an "average" concept of nature and grace in post-Tridentine and neoscholastic theology (166-169). His starting-point is the seemingly marginal notion that supernatural, justifying grace by which one is able to perform salutary acts is beyond the realm of consciousness, even though it is our most sublime and divine element. Once this is accepted "nature" becomes what we know about ourselves without the word of revelation. Nature and grace appear as two layers so carefully placed they penetrate each other as little as possible. Nature is seen quite negatively, as if it could find its perfection as readily in its own proper realm as in the intuition of God in the beatific vision. We do not find grace where we find ourselves. Many characterize this scholastic view of nature and grace as extrinsic. They see in it practical dangers. For if whatever is grace is impossible to experience, it is easy to see why no one would be particularly interested in it.

The correctness or adequacy of this standard view is now a matter of theological debate for four reasons (169-174): 1) Philosophically, Rahner points to Maréchal and his school which argue that in our intellectual and transcendental dynamism, in the innermost heart of our being, we are *desiderium naturale visionis beatificae.* This real longing for the absolute being is the motive for every spiritual act even when this is not consciously grasped (summary, 170). 2) Historically it now appears the neo-scholastic concept of nature and grace developed slowly over time. In the process gains came at the expense of older insights. The history of dogma may help recover some of these forgotten truths. 3) Renewed dialogue with Reformed theologians especially over the notion *"simul justus et pecator"* has revived interest in the nature/ grace debate. 4) Today's existentialist mentality also helped renew this debate as people desire to experience the workings of God in their own lives. More conscious effort has also been made in recent times to reflect on the ecclesial aspects of grace, on the history of grace outside the walls of the Catholic Church, and even among non-Christian religions.

Rahner sketches seven unofficial results of this new approach to nature and grace (175-188).

1) The notion of uncreated grace, the true center of grace, has been applied far more extensively. As God's own self-communication it not only explains the mysterious character of grace it also serves to link the two doctrines Trinity and incarnation.

2) This view of grace allows one to rethink the relationship between the economic and immanent Trinity. In this way Trinity is not only known but experienced.

3) This new approach questions whether we must think of grace and incarnation as two different acts. Why not embrace the Scotist position and consider God's primal act as the self-exteriorization of God who is love which gives itself in the incarnation? Such an approach also has consequences for understanding the Trinity along pre-Nicene, Greek lines.

4) This approach also goes "beyond the notion of *merely* entitative, creative state and the merely 'ontic' and non-existential element of a 'physical accident'" (177). God's work is God's very self since it is God who is imparted. Grace is no longer a thing at our disposal. It is a gift disposing of us in the miracle of love, whatever concepts we must use to express it.

5) This grace affects our conscious life not just our being and existence. By presenting the a priori formal object of the act of reflection, and not a formal object clearly distinguishable in reflection, it reveals God as the a priori horizon of consciousness, the metaphysical condition of the possibility of any cognition.

6) This approach to grace is also more grounded in scripture which speaks of giving the Spirit, *Pneuma.*

7) It also opens new ways to consider the graced status of the acts of those who are not justified. God offers himself even to those outside the church

and her sacraments as the "Wither" of the dynamism of all spiritual and moral life which is in fact elevated by God.

Rahner suggests "we are now in a position to face the real problem of 'nature and grace'" (181f), the point at which it combines with metaphysical anthropology. The first conclusion Rahner draws from this combination is that our nature is never a "pure nature" not even in the sinner or unbeliever. Furthermore the existentials of our concrete, historical natures are not purely states beyond consciousness. Through metaphysical reflection we can discern our natures; but with revelation we become more cautious, not knowing which elements are unmerited gifts of grace. The natural and supernatural freely mix. It is often impossible to tell when our natural openness to the fullness of reality is at play or when it is our supernatural openness to absolute reality in general. We experience both forms of openness in our infinite longings, our radical optimism, our protest against death, etc. (184).

In short, Rahner maintains that wherever we experience our essence grace is experienced and vice versa. Thus, when we ask specific question about human destiny it becomes clear there is no such thing as purely natural beatitude nor is there a pure philosophy of the essence of natural man. "Pure nature" remains a legitimate concept insofar as it points to the necessary background against which one recognizes the beatific vision as a gratuitous grace. For human nature is ordained to grace as a *potentia obedientialis*. A brief discussion of this concept (186f) leads Rahner to conclude that we need not think it a loss if this analysis does not yield a "chemically pure" human nature with no trace of the supernatural. Though much more could be said, Rahner ends here with an comment on the power of such seemingly theoretical theology to yield significant practical effects.

4.08 Questions of Controversial Theology on Justification

Fragen der Kontroverstheologie über die Rechtfertigung
{4.0}   *Tübinge Theologische Quartalschrift* 138 (1958) 40-77.
Abstract: Küng's book, "Justification," is the occasion for Rahner to clarify the relationship of faith and love, to banish the notion of meriting grace by faith, and to show how christology conserves a graced creation after the fall.
Topics: THEOLOGY, controversial; GRACE and justification; CREATION.
Subsidiary Discussions: Justification/sanctification (199ff); Virtues, *perichoresis* (faith and love) (199ff); Love and faith (199ff); Faith and love (199ff); Creation, Christ in (210ff); Sin (210, 214); Covenant (211, 214).
Precis: I. Barth's agreement with the Catholic doctrine of justification. Küng successfully argues that those truths the great Protestant theologian Karl Barth finds lacking in the Catholic position on justification are actually held by the church. Barth admits as much in the book's introductory letter, provided the position set out by Küng is the Catholic position. Rahner maintains Küng presents the Catholic position faithfully even if he uses

arguments different from those employed by the magisterium. This is unavoidable and even laudable in the realm of controversial theology. Rahner finds Barth's agreement an astonishing sign of hope and chides skeptics who characterize it as mere "verbal" agreement. For one can never get behind verbal assent without indulging that neurotic fear which devises increasingly subtle formulations to prove the existence of mutual dissent. Against those who criticize Küng's accomplishment as lacking formal (i.e., magisterial) authority Rahner argues: 1) the existence of formal authority does not insure agreement; 2) Catholics and Protestants share a source of formal authority: scripture. Summary (198).

II. Minor points of criticism. Without questioning the orthodoxy of Küng's presentation Rahner raises certain questions and objections of a minor nature concerning Catholic doctrine and not Barth's position.

a) Justification and signification: faith and love. This very dense section objects to the way Küng seems to push love completely to the side when speaking of the one process of justification-sanctification (205). Rahner grants scripture distinguishes (formally) between justification and sanctification and also between faith and love such that we speak of being justified by faith and not by love. Nonetheless, Rahner asks whether faith and love are best seen as two sides of one and the same process or two stages one following the other. He argues that Trent and Catholic theology embrace the first option. Küng, however, leaves himself open to misunderstanding when he speaks at times as if love, in the faith which justifies, is present merely in embryo and only appears later as works. Love, according to Rahner is no more a work than faith (202). As such it belongs to the side of faith and not to works, for it is the quality that makes faith a living, justifying faith.

b) Faith as an act inspired by grace. Both Protestant and Catholic theology insist the grace of justification is absolutely beyond all meriting. Küng insures this by distinguishing along with Barth between "an act of faith which man makes as the condition of justification, and a faith which *God* brings about" (205). Rahner finds this way of speaking both infelicitous and unhelpful. He prefers the ordinary Catholic textbook presentation which he suggests does justice to Barth's purposes. The remainder of this section is a very compact, technical discussion of the Catholic theology of faith and grace. Faith should not be parsed as Küng suggests since the very possibility of our act of faith is itself a gift and thus cannot claim to merit anything.

c) Other themes. Rahner simply mentions the many other topics which Küng touches on in his book which Rahner suggests makes it a fine reference work.

III. Creation and Christ. Küng strongly links creation and christology using scriptural arguments seldom used in magisterial teaching: even as a natural order the actual order of creation is founded on Christ and reposes on him. Due to this link nature is conserved in grace even after sin and the fall. Rahner summarizes Küng's views (210f) and maintains that one can hold them and remain within the limits of Catholic teaching. Rahner does, however, question whether Küng's statements (i.e., that God could have created a world without Christ had he willed to, and could have created spiritual being without the grace of his self-communication and divine sonship) are simply innocuous, abstract, hypothetical and of no theological consequence, or whether they contain something significant for our actual situation. Rahner holds the latter.

Rahner fears the return of the errors of *nouvelle Théologie* which went so far in saying "all is grace" that they could not safeguard the completely gratuitous nature of supernatural grace. They could not conceive of a world without a right to an incarnation. Rahner spends the remainder of this essay distinguishing the grace of creation in Christ from the God's actual self-communication in Christ. These graced moments differ not only in degree but in kind (e.g., 216). Rahner insists that while it is quite impossible for God to create a world which is not open to his self-communication, no such world can compel God's self-communication. It remains always a gift. Here Rahner suggests using the scholastic distinction between modally and entitatively supernatural grace (217). [He does not, however, introduce the distinctions he generally uses when speaking of uncreated grace: efficient and quasi-formal causality.] Thus, Rahner concurs with Barth and Küng that it is possible to consider the existence, conservation, and activity of fallen humanity as it now exists as grace in the actual order of things.

4.09 The Theology of the Symbol
Zur Theologie des Symbols
{4.0}   A. Bea, *et al.*, eds., *Cor Jesu*, Vol. I (Rome 1959) 461-505.
Abstract: The basic structure of Christian reality is symbol. These are not arbitrary, extrinsic signs but ontological structures. Rahner applies 6 principles of symbol to Trinity, christology, church, anthropology, eschatology.
Topics: SYMBOL.
Subsidiary Discussions: Sacred Heart devotion (221f, 249ff); Ontology (224ff); Trinity (226f, 235ff); Cognition (229ff); Causality (231f); Resultance (232f); Incarnation (236ff); Church as symbol (240f); Sacraments as symbol (241f); Image, sacred (243); Eschatology (244f); Hylomorphism (245ff).
Precis: This is a prolegomena to a theology of devotion to the Sacred Heart. This theology rests inescapably on symbol, a concept that becomes more complex and ambiguous the more closely one examines it (bibliography, 222 ftn3).
I. The ontology of symbolic reality in general. After apologizing for the lack of philosophical and historical preparatory work, Rahner enunciates the basic principle of an ontology of symbolism: 1) "all beings are by their nature symbolic, because they necessarily 'express' themselves in order to attain their own nature" (224). If all that were necessary for one thing to symbolize

another were some vague "agreement" then anything could symbolize anything and symbols would vary among themselves only in their degree of adequacy. Though such "signs" do exists they are not symbols. Rahner's task is to look for the highest and most primordial manner in which one reality can represent another from the formal ontological point of view—the symbol, the reality which renders another present.

All beings are really (not merely conceptually) multiple. This is what makes symbolization possible. Each finite being bears the stigma of the finite in its not being absolutely simple. But not all multiple beings are finite, (e.g., Trinity). Hence, multiplicity is not strictly negative. It also mirrors the strength of the divinity which created it. These plural moments must also have an inner agreement among themselves on account of the unity of being. Rahner understands this plurality in a superior unity in light of the Trinity (227ff). Each being in its own way fulfills itself by forming something distinct from itself yet one with itself. It does so in such a way that what is originated and different is in agreement with its origin and hence has the character of expression or symbol. This dynamism of self-expression is the condition for the possibility of self-possession in knowledge and love (229). Hence, the symbol is not a secondary relationship between two different beings imposed by an observer who sees agreement between them. Beings are symbolic in themselves and hence knowable (summary, 230). Rahner fills out this section by translating these insights in Thomistic terms. He discusses in turn, knowledge as leaving and returning to the self, causality, and resultance. He concludes with his second principle: 2) "the symbol... is the self-realization of a being in the other, which is constitutive of its essence" (234f).

II. On the theology of symbolic reality. Rahner insists the whole of theology is incomprehensible if it is not essentially a theology of symbols. This section illustrates the prevalent structure of Christian reality as a unity of reality and its symbolic reality by applying this insight to six themes.

-Trinity: Rahner focuses on Logos, the symbol of the Father, as Rahner understands symbol. Setting aside Augustine's approach to Trinity which reserves no unique character to the Logos due to him as symbol such that any of the divine persons could equally well be incarnate, then one has no difficulty thinking that the Word's being symbol of the Father has significance for God's action *ad extra*. For Rahner this insight provides the crucial link to understand the relationship between the economic and immanent Trinity [cf., 4.03].

–Incarnation: The incarnate Word is the absolute symbol of God in the world—final and insurpassable. He reveals not merely something about God, but God's very self. Rahner is concerned that the dogmatic formula "the Logos took on human nature" can easily be misinterpreted to mean he assumed a guise and spoke through a reality that intrinsically and essentially had nothing to do with him. Rahner's analysis of the Thomistic doctrine that

the humanity of Christ exists by the existence of the Logos concludes that
"The humanity is the self-disclosure of the Logos itself, so that when God,
expressing himself, exteriorizes himself, that very thing appears which we call
the humanity of the Logos" (239). [All this is developed more fully in 4.05.]
   –Ecclesiology: The church, the persisting presence of the incarnate Word
in space and time, continues the symbolic function of the Logos. The fact it
appears in social, juridical form does not make it an arbitrary sign. In any case
the church is more than a social juridical entity. As the primary sacrament
(*Ur-sakrament*) of the grace of God it not only designates but possesses the
eschatological grace brought into the world by Christ.
   –Sacraments: This area of Catholic theology is where one is most likely to
find a discussion of symbol. To the recent controversy over the causality at
work in sacraments (physical or moral) Rahner argues that since sacramental
symbols have an intrinsic link to the grace signified (i.e., to God's self
communication through the church) these questions dissolve.
   –Sacred images: "Sacramentals" pose a difficult problem which, if he were
to explore it, Rahner would need to begin with Plato and Aristotle's theories
of image and representation. He does not chose to explore it here.
   –Eschatology: Rahner disagrees with those who say that in the beatific
vision all symbols disappear. He insists that though many signs will cease to
be (e.g., church, sacraments) the humanity of Christ will continue to have
eternal significance mediating the immediacy of the vision.
   Rahner summarizes Part II with two further principles: 3) The concept of
symbol is essential in all theology; 4) God, the reality of salvation, is actually
given and received by humanity in the symbol.
III. The body as symbol of man. These reflections bring us to the threshold
of understanding devotion to the Sacred Heart. The body serves as symbol
for human reality because, as Aquinas says, the soul is its substantial form.
The body is nothing else than the expression, the actuality of the soul itself
in the "other" of prime matter. Principle 5 (247). Principle 6 (247) states that
the individual parts of the body are not pieces which constitute one body but
parts comprising the whole in themselves, though to different degrees.
Hence, the heart can function symbolically for the whole person, and the
Sacred Heart can symbolize Christ and not just his love. Summary (252).

4.10 The Word and the Eucharist
   Wort und Eucharistie
{4.0}   M. Schmaus, ed., *Aktuelle Fragen zur Eucharistie*, (Munich 1960) 7-
        52.
Abstract: Because a theology of the efficacious word threatened the distinct
efficacy of sacraments, here Rahner sketches a theology of word, redefines
sacraments by rethinking *opus operantis*, applies all this to the Eucharist.

Topics: SACRAMENT, theology of; WORD, theology of; DOGMA, development of.

Subsidiary Discussions: Justification/sanctification (257ff); Grace (257ff, 261f, 270); Truths, hierarchy of (263f); Preaching (262ff); Sacraments, *opus operatum/operantis* (269ff, 274); Church as *Ur-sakrament* (272ff, 285f); Eucharist (282ff).

Precis: I. The Word and the sacrament in general. Word here means word of God on the lips of those charged by the church to preach it to the world. It is likewise the word heard and believed by the church which preaches it because it believes. How does this word stand in relation to sacraments? This question arises for two sets of reasons: **a)** Intrinsic. Affirmation made today about word and sacrament are so astonishingly similar; what distinguishes them? Since word and sacrament characterize fundamentally the nature of the church they cannot exist side by side unrelated. If word is formally constitutive of every sacrament how does this word relate to the word of God? **b)** Situational. The needs of present day preaching; advances in biblical theology; renewed attention in fundamental theology to revelation and grace; historical studies of the Greek Fathers and theology of Logos; closer communication with Protestant theologians for whom the word has always been a central concern.

Though a complete theology of the word is needed, all this essay offers in thesis form are "the characteristics of the word which are of immediate significance for the intrinsic relationship of word and sacrament" (257).

1) *"The word of God is uttered by the Church, where it is preserved inviolate in its entirety, and necessarily so, in its character as the word of 'God'."* Rahner insists this is a given.

2) *"This word of God in the Church is an inner moment of God's salvific action on man."* Rahner distinguishes the inner word of grace and the external, historical, social (ecclesial) word of revelation. God's salvific act inviting and empowering us to accept his self-communication is what Rahner defines as "word." But this inward self-communication is not normally adequate for the fully developed act of acceptance. It requires the proclamation of the church.

3) *"As an inner moment in this salvific action of God, the word shares in the special character of the salvific action of God in Christ (and the Church)."* The inner word of grace and the external word of revelation come together in every salvific act as mutually complementary moments of the one word of God to man. Every assertion about God's salvific acts is an assertion about this two-fold word of God.

4) *"This word of God … is the salutary word which brings with it what it affirms. It is itself, therefore, salvific event, which in its outward, historical and social aspect displays what happens in it and under it, and brings about what it displays. It renders the grace of God present."* To those made nervous that this definition of word sounds too much like sacrament Rahner urges calm. He sets out to prove the word of God is not simply a set of doctrinal propositions "about something," it is a revelatory, actualizing word in which and under which alone the thing designated is present. For proof he cites scripture's use of "word," and dogmatic theology. He ends this section with the concrete example of preaching (262).

5) *"This word ... takes place in the Church in essentially varying degrees of concentration and intensity."* Because "word of God in the Church" is used analogously it is no surprise it is capable of inner changes and broad variability. The same is true of the word of God as the revelatory presence of that which is announced in it. Although the goal of the word of God is always the same (i.e., God's self-bestowal on us and acceptance by us) like any historical reality it is reached only in stages. Rahner lists a number of causes for and types of inner changes in the being of the word of God (265).

6) *"The supreme realization of the efficacious word of God, as the coming of the salvific action of God in the radical commitment of the Church ..., in the situations decisive for the individual's salvation, is the sacrament and only the sacrament."* Rahner maintains "there can be no objection ... to the effort to determine the nature of the sacraments from their quality of 'words' ..." (268) because sacramental matter (rites and objects) insofar as they participate in the sacramental action are themselves "words." "For signs and words 'from the metaphysical and theological point of view' are of exactly the same nature" (267). Rahner reenforces this argument from the fact that two sacraments have no sign, and from the teachings of Vatican I. Attempting to answer those who have dealt with how a theology of the intrinsically efficacious word can be reconciled with the doctrine of efficacious sacraments, Rahner offers a long discussion of the concepts *opus operantis/ operatum* (269-272). He concludes by identifying two features which when taken together constitute the objective content of *opus operantum* in its unity: the word as the fullest actualization of the church in its absolute commitment, and the word spoken in the decisive situations of human salvation (272). These ultimately distinguish efficacious word from efficacious sacrament.

To understand these two factors Rahner sets them in the context of the church as primary sacrament (272-278). It is the source of all the sacraments which it decrees to be the eschatologically efficacious word of God, as its own absolute self-realization according to its essence as primary sacrament. After showing how this is true with six of seven sacraments (276f, he postpones discussing Eucharist) Rahner defines sacraments as: "basic acts of the self-realization of the Church with regard to individuals at decisive situations of their lives" (277). He argues this definition satisfactorily includes the notions *opus operatum* and institution by Christ.

One task remains: to show "that the efficacious word of God does exist in the Church outside the sacraments, and that this word does not first become efficacious and does not only appear as the presence of God's grace in the

Church, when it becomes sacramental in the strictest sense" (278). Rahner makes this case by noting that the sacramental word of God in the church and the other words of the church's preaching are related as sacramental and non-sacramental justification. These are not two disparate realities but two moments of the same process which are intrinsically connected and derive their value which climaxes in the sacramental word. Non-sacramental moments are not made meaningless or superfluous by sacramental moments as shown by the fact that grace can precede the sacrament as in the case of Cornelius in scripture. Summary (280).

II. **Word and Eucharist.** All that was said above comes to its unsurpassable climax in Eucharist which is itself word. It is the supreme case of all sacraments and the real origin of all others (281f). But how can such an exalted theology of Eucharist allow room for the word? Rahner insists Eucharist is the sacrament of the word absolutely. It comes into being through the words of consecration, not as an efficient but as a formal cause. The bread and wine is and remains Eucharist insofar as these words are uttered, understood, and believed by the church (not simply by the individual as some Protestants held). Thus, word is an abiding, constitutive element of sacrament. If the church did not exist Eucharist could not exist. Summary (286).

4.11 The Presence of Christ in the Sacrament of the Lord's Supper

Die Gegenwart Christi im Sakrament des Herrenmahles
{2.5} *Catholica* 12 (1958) 109-128.

Abstract: Separating the logical explanation for the real presence of Christ in the Eucharist (transubstantiation) from various ontic, theological explanations reveals Catholic and Lutheran positions are substantially the same.
Topics: EUCHARIST; ECUMENISM.
Subsidiary Discussions: Eucharist, transubstantiation (296ff); Explanations, logical and ontic (300f); Substance (307ff).
Precis: This a difficult subject because it is hard to say what the Catholic Church teaches on this matter. It is hard to distinguish what is explicitly binding in the dogma of real presence from the theological theorems surrounding it. Things are not supremely intelligible simply because they are made binding by the magisterium. New historical situations can make them clearer or more obscure to us by putting them in a context of new knowledge.
I. **Preliminary Remarks.** 1) This essay will not cover the history of the dogma of real presence nor the many questions connected to it (list, 289).

2) Preliminary remarks: a) A Catholic position on real presence cannot be dismissed out of hand on account of its realism. No one must suppose that only those things can be the true subject of dogma which lie completely beyond the realm of human experience. b) Even though certain truths of the

faith may have logical consequences, because they are meant for the salvation of all people at all times it is a priori improbable that a dogma must depend on one well defined philosophical system to be understood.

II. The doctrine of the Council of Trent on the real presence of Christ in the Eucharist. The following intends to present the doctrine of real presence and not necessarily the Catholic presentation of this doctrine and its history.

1) Trent professes the real presence of Christ in the Eucharist. **a)** Although its formulations vary, Trent makes clear Christ is present in a sacramental rather than a natural mode. This dogma is based on scripture especially on the Synoptics and St. Paul. Trent insists Jesus' words are not figurative or metaphorical. He gave his apostles his real body and blood. **b)** The whole Christ is present under each species: body and soul, humanity and divinity. **c)** Christ is present by reason of the consecrated bread and wine. Here form and matter constitute a unity. The words of institution are not an efficient cause but a permanent constitutive element of the sacramental sign. Part of the constitution of the sign is the relationship of the bread and wine to a meal and its character as nourishment. **d)** Real presence is not dependent on the faith of the individual priest or communicant, although when sinners receive the Eucharist they receive only sacramentally and not spiritually. **e)** Rahner concludes there is no essential difference between Catholics and Lutherans regarding real presence. Both believe an event takes place: the body of Christ which was not always present becomes present through the words of Christ.

2) Trent professes the real presence comes about by transubstantiation. **a)** This term dates back to Berengarius in 1079, and Pius XII's *Humani Generis* disapproves of theologians who maintain it rests on outmoded concepts of substance which need correction. **b)** Trent finds proof for this doctrine in the literal sense of the words of institution. There follows a succinct restatement of the Catholic doctrine (289f). **c)** What are the meaning and limits of affirmations which speak of transubstantiation? Here Rahner distinguishes logical from ontic explanations of a statement. The logical clarifies the statement by interpreting it on its own terms. It affirms nothing other than the matter at hand. Ontic explanations assert something in addition to the matter in question, something which makes the statement more intelligible (e.g., its cause, its history, etc.). Transubstantiation is a logical not an ontic explanation of the words of Christ. Hence, it does not explain *how* the real presence takes place (302) nor reduce the truth to something else that could be grasped in its own distinct content. No ontic explanation is identified with the doctrine of real presence. The proof that transubstantiation is only meant as a logical explanation is Trent's insistence this doctrine is derived from the words of Christ and the lack of unity among ontic theological explanations (summary, 304f). **d)** Why, then, do Lutherans reject transubstantiation? Rahner is at a loss. Perhaps they confuse scholastic ontic explanations which are not defined with the simple defined doctrine. Perhaps it stems from excesses of Catholic piety which adore Christ in the

sacrament outside the context of the meal. But those who reject it because it involves "a miraculous transformation" are not really Lutherans but followers of Calvin or Zwingli.

III. What remains obscure and open? 1) The Catholic ontic explanations of the doctrine need a thorough cleaning to reveal what is at stake in these ancient controversies. 2) A clearer line of demarcation must be drawn between the dogma and the theological propositions surrounding it. 3) A more precise definition is needed for *substantia panis*. No one today can seriously maintain bread is a "substance." It is at best an agglomeration of substances, a collection of elementary particles, accidents extrinsically denominated as bread. Applying transubstantiation to this complex substrata raises new difficulties (308f) among which is identifying the hermeneutic principle interpreting conciliar statements which reach the *agglomeratum substantiarum* from the *substantia panis*. 4) The treatise *De Eucharistia* generally begins with the concept of real presence. In the light of advances in biblical and ecumenical theology perhaps it would be better to begin with the event character of Eucharist, especially as sacrifice and food. 5) It is time to breathe life into the work on the history of Eucharist which has already been done, to turn it into a vital quest for truth. Too little of importance has filtered down to average believers. Popular piety concentrates too much on communion with the sufferings of Christ and too little on his death and resurrection or the eschatological future of the meal in the kingdom of God.

4.12 On the Duration of the Presence of Christ after Communion

> *Über die Dauer der Gegenwart Christi nach dem Kommunion-empfang*
> Originally, *Über die Dauer der Gegenwart Christi in der Kommunion.*
> {2.0}   *Geist und Leben* 32 (1959) 442-448.

Abstract: Rahner attempts to uncouple the notion of the duration of the real presence of Christ in Eucharist from a physico-chemical process of digestion. Christ is primarily present in the Spirit under the sign of bread and wine.
Topics: EUCHARIST.
Subsidiary Discussions: Substance (314ff).
Precis: This essay defends and expands Rahner's reticence to instruct people to offer thanksgiving after communion because Jesus is "still" present with the communicant in the moments after communion. "[A]ll these assertions are false or at least not sufficiently well founded in theology" (312). He asks how one can explain and justify thanksgiving after communion in theologically valid ways and not in pious sounding talk.

First, Rahner disagrees that "all theologians" oppose his view. Few theologians say anything about how long the presence of Christ endures in the Eucharst beyond the binding truth that he is present as long as the species exists. Secondly, these theologians maintain their view on the principle the real presence of Christ lasts as long as the Eucharistic species exists. Rahner takes exception to this principle. He argues that bread is not, strictly speaking, a substance but an agglomeration with the anthropological rather than the physico-chemical designation of bread. Hence, the real presence of Christ lasts only as long as the humanly intelligible unity of bread exists. Here Rahner enlists Aquinas. Summary (315f).

The question remains: can bread, once eaten, still be regarded as bread? Rahner asserts, "bread once eaten is not a human reality, whose meaning is that of food, of being eaten. And from this we deduce that the presence of Christ no longer persists" (317). This is not a matter of chemistry but of human usage. The human act of eating bread and not the involuntary physiological act of digesting it is the sacramental sign of grace. The opposite view leads to all kinds of awkward consequences (316f).

Only a rather confused piety resists these obvious truths. It does not distinguish clearly enough between the presence of Christ in the depth of our being and the bodily presence of Christ in the sacramental sign and hence in the eating. "This latter type is not the higher and sublimer [sic] … but the sign and the means of the permanent presence of Christ through the Spirit, which is indicated and increased by this sacramental sign" (319). Even popular piety, by showing so little concern with the hypothetical but on some accounts important moment when the bread ceases to be bread and the soul's audience with Christ is over, argues in Rahner's favor. Summary (320).

4.13 The Hermeneutics of Eschatological Assertions

Theologische Prinzipien der Hermeneutik eschatologischer Aussagen
{3.5} *Zeitschrift für katholische Theologie* 82 (1960) 137-158.
Abstract: If the presence of salvation in Christ sets the strict limit of what we say about the *eschata*, then we avoid both false apocalypticism and the false demythologizing of eschatological statements.
Topics: ESCHATOLOGY, statements; FUTURE; STATEMENTS, eschatological.
Subsidiary Discussions: Mystery (329f, 332); Christology (334f); Salvation/ damnation (338ff); Hylomorphism (340ff); History (343); Image (344f).
Precis: Rahner admits it is impossible to cover satisfactorily here the dogmatic principles governing the hermeneutics of eschatological assertions in the bible and in the church's preaching. He offers only hypotheses in this seldom visited area of Catholic theology. He hopes to grasp consciously and formulate expressly some theological principles for the hermeneutics of special eschatology. Advances in cosmology show the need to inquire into what kind of knowledge can adequately understand eschatological assertions. After outlining the "correct method" for such a study based on

scripture, Rahner outlines his admittedly more problematic method based on dogmatic considerations (325).

Thesis 1. Christian faith must contain an eschatology which bears on the real future in the ordinary, empirical, temporal sense. Any attempt to reduce eschatology to decisions made here and now by an individual is theologically unacceptable. In this sense eschatology is really prophetic.

Thesis 2. It cannot be ruled out a priori that God's omniscience does not include knowledge of future events or an ability to communicate them to us. Thus, any restrictions mentioned in what follows flow from the history of salvation and affects only us. They are not restrictions imposed on God.

Thesis 3. The sphere of eschatological assertions and hence of their hermeneutic is constituted by the dialectical unity of two limiting statements: a) Only because the end has the essential character of hiddenness is there room for faith and hope. The *eschata* are present as hidden. They are revealed precisely as mystery. This provides an essential criterion for distinguishing eschatological assertions from apocalyptic ones: the latter exclude absolute mystery and hence hiddenness from the event being described. b) Human beings are essentially historical. We cannot understand ourselves without relation to a genuinely temporal past (*anamnesis*) and future (*prognosis*). Since eschatology is concerned with salvation (i.e., fulfillment) of the whole person the real future must involve all aspects of our being. To omit any dimension would really be to mythologize the human person.

Thesis 4. A statement can only bring the future into the present and retain its quality of hiddenness if such knowledge of the future is knowledge of the futurity of the present. Thus, eschatological knowledge is knowledge of the eschatological present. It is an inner moment of our self-understanding. If it were merely an account of the future then human history would lose its connection to mystery. The content of any eschatological assertion about the future: a) must be something impenetrable and uncontrollable or it would leave no room for human freedom; b) must leave the future as something still to come, something beyond present existence: the fulfillment of the whole person by the incomprehensible God—a salvation already assigned and granted by God in faith to the individual and to humanity in Jesus Christ.

Thesis 5. The heart of the essay. Christians know the future insofar as they know themselves and their redemption in Christ through divine revelation. Their knowledge of the *eschata* is not a supplementary piece of information added to dogmatic anthropology and christology, but simply their transposition into the guise of fulfillment (335). Thus, Christian anthropology and eschatology are ultimately christology. If eschatological assertions were mere reports of the future there would be no way to maintain the mystery of the human future, and the images employed in scripture could be harmonized. Rahner's approach offers a path between false apocalypticism and a totally existential (gnostic) de-mythologizing interpretation. Summary (337).

Thesis 6. Consequences. **a)** Since the content and certainty of eschatological assertions is based on the *salvific* action of God in our regard, we cannot speak of salvation and damnation in a parallel manner. Though at present we have two equally possible futures, we are never entitled to claim knowledge of a universal apocatastasis or of the certain fate of any individual prior to his/her death. **b)** Because eschatological assertions concern the one, indivisible totality of humanity they are all marked with the same irreduceable two-fold dynamism unavoidable in anthropological assertions (e.g., we are individuals and members of society, personal spirit and corporeal being). **c)** There is no point in creating a fundamental, absolute opposition and antagonism between an immanent and a distant expectation of the *parousia.* All eschatological assertions both reveal what is and conceal what is to come. **d)** Summary of the basic thesis that anything which cannot be read as a christological statement is not an eschatological statement (234f). **e)** Certain formal principles of theology of history allow us to derive from our experience of Christ all that can and may be said objectively in the Catholic theology of eschatology. (List of the 5 formal principles and their conclusions, 343.)

Thesis 7. Although Rahner's basic principle provides a fundamental criterion to distinguish between the "form" and "content" of an eschatological assertion, he knows it can never perfectly distinguish between "thing" and "image." Images such as those found in scripture are not a primitive form of picture-thinking we eventually move beyond. They are a constitutive element of thought. In time new images may be offered as substitutes, but the adequacy of the new must always be measured against those found in scripture. Rahner concludes with a discussion of what would be needed actually to prove the hypotheses he outlines in this essay (345f).

4.14 The Life of the Dead

Das Leben der Toten

{1.5}   *Trier. theologische Zeitschrift* 68 (1959) 1-7.

Abstract: The dead live in eternity, neither the endless continuation of time nor the cessation of time, but the fruit of time wherein human freedom becomes definitive. Its reality is known through key human experiences and revelation.

Topics: DEATH; TIME/ETERNITY.

Subsidiary Discussions: Love (348f); Moral acts (349f); Salvation/Damnation (351); Resurrection of the body (352); Eschatology, intermediate state (353); Spiritualism (353f).

Precis: In speaking of the dead who live we must take care not to leave the impression of a rectilinear continuation of empirical reality after death. We do not merely change horses and ride on. "No, in this regard death puts an end to the *whole* man" (347). The problem is time. We cannot think of it as simply going on; we cannot think of it as merely ending. "In reality, it is *in* time, as its own mature fruit, that 'eternity' comes about" (248). Through death (not after it) one's freely matured existence is made definitive.

Even today we can know this really happens through revealed dogma and human experience. Rahner argues from such experiences as radical love which would be impossible if its inner reality were, of its nature and essence, something that perished or something that wished to be no more (349). He offers a similar argument from moral decision when we act in absolute obedience to a higher law. Even the act of doubting the reality and validity of such commands is only possible from inside the experience. Summary (351).

Even in the face of time's threat of total dissolution these human experiences allow us to claim that something in our personal existence is eternally valid. But only God's word of revelation announces clearly the actual concrete meaning of our being. The choice for eternity, either salvation or damnation, is open to the humblest person. "Scripture knows of no life which is not worthy to be definitive, it does not recognize any life as superfluous" (351). Scripture employs innumerable images to describe this blissful reality (list, 352).

The essay ends with brief thoughts on three themes: 1) "Resurrection of the flesh" which he treats as an allusion to the salvation of the *whole* person; 2) Purgatory, which Rahner sees as the opportunity for the full ripening of the whole person after death as the basic decision made during one's life penetrates the whole of one's reality; 3) Rahner denies the possibility of spiritualism or communing with the dead because they no longer share time with us in the same way as we can experience it. "We meet the dead," he says, "when we open our hearts to the silent calm of God himself, in which they live; not by calling them back to where we are, but by descending into the silent eternity of our own hearts, and through faith in the risen Lord, creating in time the eternity which they have brought forth forever" (354f).

4.15 Poetry and the Christian
Das Wort der Dichtung und der Christ
{2.0}   Previously unpublished.

Abstract: Because the capacity and practice of hearing the poetic word is a presupposition to hearing the word of God, Christians should defend all great poetry which, like itself, speaks to and about "the mystery that is man."
Topics: ARTS, poetry; FAITH, pre-evangelization; WORD.
Subsidiary Discussions: Grace (358, 363); Mystery (358f, 366); Heart (360); Love (360f); Logos (361f); Humanism (364); Anonymous Christian (366).
Precis: Rahner's starting-point is admittedly theological: how we should be if we wish to be a Christian. This raises two questions: 1) whether we searche for something which afterwards is seen to be poetry; 2) whether before

becoming a Christian we must develop a receptive capacity for the poetic word.
Before discussing four requisites for hearing the gospel without misunderstanding (358-363) Rahner makes clear that even this capacity is itself a gift from God who gives not only the invitation to share his life but also the capacity to hear and accept that invitation. The four requisites are: 1) the power to hear the word through which the silent mystery is present. This leads into a discussion of God as absolute mystery—the background silence in and against which alone it is possible to hear any word; 2) the power to hear words which reach the heart. This leads to a discussion of the heart as symbol for the whole person, not merely sentiment or intellect. Words spoken from the heart are sacramental, affecting what they signify; 3) the power to hear the word which unites. Ultimate, authentic words unite not only the manifold dimensions within the human person, they also unite that person with others in bonds of love; 4) "the capacity of recognizing the inexpressible mystery *in* the word which speaks of its bodily form, inseparable from the word but not confused with it: the power of becoming aware of the *incarnational* and incarnate incomprehensibility, of hearing the Word become flesh" (361). Here Rahner develops the notion of Logos, the second person of the Trinity, as incarnate in each authentic sacramental word. Summary (362f).

What do we call the word described above if not poetry? The capacity and practice of hearing the poetic word is a presupposition to hearing the word of God. "[T]he poetic word and the poetic ear are so much part of man that if this essential power were really lost to the heart, man could no longer hear the word of God in the word of man" (363). Conversely, whatever heart admits the word of God cannot remain completely unreceptive to poetry.

For us today this means three things: a) Poetry is necessary. Christians must love and defend the human word (culture and humanism) since God himself has assumed it into his eternal reality. This does not, however give us a priori the criteria to judge good poetry. We can only say good poetry is not confined to past forms. It always possesses the new and unexpected. b) Though they are not the same thing, really great poetry and really great Christianity have an inner kinship because their subject is man in all his multiplicity and true depth—man as mystery. Rahner classifies many great poets as anonymously Christian. c) Today with the ease and low cost of publishing the world is awash in books of every kind. Christians tolerate a great deal of this material just as they tolerate a good deal of daily life, but always looking for the true joy which marks the serious call to be children of God.

4.16 Theological Remarks on the Problem of Leisure

Theologische Bemerkungen zum Problem der Freizeit
{2.0} *Oberrhein. Pastoralblatt* 60 (1959) 210-218; 233-243.

Abstract: The subject of the 5-day work week inspires Rahner to reflect on work and leisure. They find their meaning and relationship in an anthropology which sees both as spiritual exigencies and not mere physical necessities.

Topics: CHRISTIAN LIFE, leisure and work; THEOLOGICAL ANTHROPOLOGY.
Subsidiary Discussions: Economics (370ff); Freedom (379, 383ff).

Precis: Modern discussion of the 5-day work week by philosophers and doctors leaves Rahner confused as a theologian. He attempts to define basic concepts of work and leisure more clearly in terms of theological anthropology.

I. Primitives spent most of their time at work—strenuous activities that provided for sustenance and survival. When they could not work because of darkness or exhaustion they rested. Modern people are often engaged in work not directly related to sustenance except insofar as they draw a salary. Modern recreation is often quite strenuous. How can this be explained?

1) Rahner considers and rejects the notion that work and leisure can be properly understood purely in terms of *political economy*. To say work is what we are paid to do poses two problems: **a)** It cannot properly distinguish work from leisure since many useful contributions to society are not remunerated, pensioners are paid not to work, and scholarships are given simply for study. **b)** This view cannot explain why work should ever be curtailed. No good case can be made that work today is more strenuous than it was for primitive people who worked longer and hence that we would need more "regenerative time." To say we should work less because we can produce all we need in less time ignores the needs of three quarters of the developing world. Summary (375f).

2) Rahner considers and rejects the notion that work and leisure can be properly understood purely in terms of *medicine*. This approach reduces all activity to the physical capacity for people to work. Rahner offers two pages of unanswered questions raised by a medical model of work and leisure.

3) Only *anthropology* can explain the proper nature and relation of work and leisure. Human life has a two-phased rhythm. In leisure the receptive exercise of freedom predominates. It is an unplanned, unpredictable, confident surrender to the uncontrollable forces of existence, the reception of grace. In work the activity of self-determined freedom predominates. It contains calculation, deed and performance, conquest and accomplishment, the effort to implement a project. Neither is found in a chemically pure form. These two dimensions spring from the fact that we are spirits who must perform our bodily activities spiritually. The degree to which work and leisure blend is greatly a function of historical circumstances. In our technological age more leisure time is needed not because our work is more

strenuous but because this more purely concentrated form of work incorporates very little leisure. It is a constant task to restore the proper balance between work and leisure. Only this anthropological view can explain why even strenuous hobbies might not be considered work, or why a second paying job could even be considered leisure.

II. The value of reducing the work week is only self-explanatory if work were viewed fundamentally as something to be avoided. Rahner's anthropology (383f) suggests something different. People are doers. We determine ourselves in what we do. We are also determined by elements of our environment. We are irreducibly paradoxical beings: body and spirit, social and individual, free and determined, who only find ourselves when we give ourselves away. Spirit becomes aware of itself in a history the major theme of which is the way we modify ourselves and our environment. We work to free ourselves from the burdens imposed by the brute necessity of our nature and our surroundings.

We only understand our hard won freedom when we know what it is *for*. If freedom is for the pursuit and accumulation of more economic goods (the only true reality as a materialist communism insists) then a shorter work week makes no sense. But in reality the spirit frees itself in order to come to itself, to act according to its real nature. "The spirit only attains the proper heights and depths of its express self-realization in non-biological terms where it is no longer a mere means of sustaining biological life but where man exercises an activity which no longer has *any* immediate material usefulness" (386). Hence, the real purpose of a shorter work week is not biological recuperation or pleasure, but the spiritual work and the spiritual leisure of man...love, fellowship, joy, dance, music, art, etc.

Rahner concludes with a final point. Spirit is essentially transcendental spirit—transcendence oriented to the mystery of absolute being. When translated into concrete form we have religion. Hence, the liberation of man for his express spiritual existence is also liberation for a more intensive religious existence. From this Rahner concludes that modern societies with the means to do so should subsidize those who are involved in such pursuits, e.g., contemplatives and artists, just as it now subsidizes those involved in more "useful" pursuits aimed at producing material goods. Summary (389f).

4.17 The Theology of Power
Theologie der Macht
{2.0}   Previously unpublished 1960 hektograph, 16 pp.

Abstract: Power (brute force) is ambiguous. Though it should not have existed, it is now an inescapable human existential through which our freedom is made definitive. Only the wise who exercise it in faith redeem and sanctify it.
Topics: POWER, coercive; FREEDOM and coercion.

Subsidiary Discussions: Concupiscence (393f); Existentials, natural (397ff); Salvation/damnation (402ff); Morality, natural (403); Anonymous Christian (403); Cross, theology of (408f).

Precis: All power is a share in God's almighty power. It is an ambiguous term. All beings possess power to some degree simply because they exist. The nature of this power changes essentially based on its specific nature, the region in which it is exercised, and the means it uses to bring about its end. This essay confines itself to the lowest form of power: brute force— physically intervening in the sphere of another to change it without its prior consent. Rahner offers three theological theses regarding this type of power:

1) [Power] *"ought never to have existed. In the actual order of salvation, as it is and as it was originally willed by God, it stems from sin"* (393). Rahner justifies this thesis on the Catholic view of human nature before the fall (i.e., original integrity and concupiscence). To violate another's freedom in a pre-lapsarian setting would have been irrational and hence impossible. It follows that although power is something we should work to abolish with spirit, love, and grace, it will never be eliminated in this world. Anyone who disagrees has fallen away from the truth of Christianity and is a heretic. Force exists in this world because of sin and must be struggled against. Yet in this world its use may be necessary and even justified. Hence, its ambiguity. It can only be used rightly by those aware of its danger and ambiguity. Summary (395).

2) *Power is "not itself sin but a gift of God* [and a charge], *an expression of his power, an element of the reflection of God in the world"* (396). Like all created things power is ambivalent, good in itself but subject to perversion and misuse. As an existential of our existence (like suffering and death) it cannot be eliminated. In fact limiting the freedom of others by the use of power is a conditions for the possibility of exercising our freedom. Although it is an inevitable consequence of every action, we can never renounce it not even by choosing to die since even this has an uninvited impact on others. Force can be considered natural even if it was not originally intended by God because it is not in itself sinful. However, to say power is good and natural does not mean it is obviously intelligible (398). Rahner proceeds to evaluate power as a reality of experience in the light of natural reason (review, 399f). He concludes the total renunciation of power is not only impractical it is also immoral since it would mean renouncing the exercise of human freedom. The only real questions concerns the proportionate use of power in each case. The proper balance between force and resistance, power and freedom, cannot be known before hand but must constantly be created anew. Summary (402).

3) *"In the actual order of things its* [power's] *exercise...is not irrelevant to salvation: it is a process of either salvation or perdition"* (402). After discussing whether acts of natural morality are salutary (including the notion of anonymous Christianity), Rahner proceeds on the assumption that "the whole of the free action of man...is either a salutary act inspired by faith, or

sin, even where it seems to be only a matter of natural morality" (403). And power is not just any act. Since it pervades the whole of life it is one of those acts in which salvation or damnation is decisively achieved. Insofar as it freely brings into existence a contingent concrete circumstance it is irreversible. By imposing this circumstance on another and thereby limiting his/her eternally valid freedom, the one who uses force spreads oneself beyond himself. About those whose freedom has been curtailed we cannot glibly say they remain free in their chains, because the realm of freedom available to them to work out their eternal destiny has actually been involuntarily restricted. Nor can the wielder of power take refuge in the claim he had no choice, because exactly insofar as his/her act was contingent it was free.

In all such situations the wielder of power should have canvased those at his mercy and employed power as a last resort and as something provisional. All power should be used to bring about its own abrogation. This is power as service. When it tries to maintain itself definitively, that is sin. But when power is wielded by the wise they are always struck and humbled by the dignity of the free person over whom they exercise power. People who use power to bring about life redeem and sanctify power. To use power without faith is to misuse it. This lesson is not discovered simply from the fact that an almighty God created the world. It is revealed only in the theology of the cross, and hence, it is a truly Christian reality. Summary (409).

V. LATER WRITINGS
V. *Neuere Schriften*

German edition: Einsiedeln, Benziger, 1962
U.S. edition: Baltimore, MD, Helicon Press, 1966
Karl-H. Kruger, translator

5.01 Thoughts on the Possibility of Belief Today
Über die Möglichkeit des Glaubens heute
{0.5}   Previously unpublished.

Abstract: Rahner identifies and addresses three major obstacles he sees to belief today: philosophical skepticism, the seeming mythology surrounding Jesus of Nazareth, and the sinfulness of the church.
Topics: FAITH; CHRISTIANITY, belief in.

Subsidiary Discussions: God as mystery (7f); Anonymous Christian (8f, 11, 20f); Skepticism (8ff); Christology (11ff); Hypostatic union (12ff); Church, of sinners (15ff); Church, controversy in (18ff).

Precis: The belief Rahner is speaking of is the courage to believe in the infinite, unspeakable mystery we call God; in the fact this infinite mystery has communicated itself to us absolutely and come infinitely near to us in Jesus Christ; in the fact the legally constituted community of those who confess the grace-giving nearness of God in Christ for the salvation of the whole world is to be found in the Catholic, Apostolic, and Roman Church. Rahner speaks of belief in uncharacteristically personal terms for he is not talking about conventional belief but belief engaged by a personal decision with the power to change the heart. He apologizes in advance if his remarks are not academic enough.

Born and raised in a Catholic home and culture, Rahner claims never to have encountered a good reason to cease believing. Because roots are crucial he insists we must never abandon our spiritual heritage except for something stronger which calls us to greater freedom and into a more inexorable light. He admits there are many intellectual difficulties in the realm of faith, but compared to the reality of existence they are too slight to warrant rejecting belief. There are other obstacles to belief which reside in the heart: loneliness, emptiness, the seeming absurdity of death, weariness with the finite, etc. But when faced honestly and humbly these very things which confront us with the ultimate questionableness of existence can be the labor pains of the true birth of Christian existence. The real arguments against Christianity are these dark experience of life. The simple message Christianity speaks to this darkness is difficult to accept because the mystery it proclaims is often darker than our own darkness. Is one not justified in accepting this "Infinity of Fullness," albeit as mystery, rather than the hellish torment of a meaningless existence?

Whoever accepts life has really already accepted God. Whoever really accepts himself accepts the mystery of the infinite emptiness that is man along with the One who has decided to fill this emptiness with infinite fullness. So why could one not be a Christian if it means basically accepting oneself in a spirit of infinite optimism? (8). One reason is the sin we experience within ourselves. This engenders skepticism and agnosticism which cannot face the reality of sin but avoid it by burrowing into the wretchedness of everyday life. But why should the abyss of skepticism be more true than the abyss of God which gives us the courage to believe in it?

What of the many who never have or never could embrace Christianity? This does not trouble Rahner who professes belief in a nameless or anonymous Christianity (9f). Even a pagan who embraces life is braver than the agnostic who remains aloof. Rahner challenges those who see Christianity as one among many philosophies of life which, however inspiring, do not solve the ultimate question of human existence in the face of death. Though it is admittedly difficult to synthesize every aspect of Christianity it does not insurmountably contradict legitimate human experiences. Rahner concludes one must be open to hearing the Christian message and not be dismayed by the wretched disputations of theology. For Christianity says only one thing: God has drawn near all people in Christ whether or not they are fully conscious of this truth.

This mystery that God draws near us in Jesus Christ, the God-man, cannot be deduced a priori. This presents a second obstacle to belief. But Rahner insists it is easy to believe in Jesus because of the doctrine of the hypostatic union, which is clearly not mythology (12). Why not dare to believe there is a man in whom God's absolute promise of self-donation to every spiritual creature, and the acceptance of this promise by the creature, are both true and rendered credible? If we believe ourselves to be partners with God in an absolute, mutual self-engagement through our transcendental orientation, why not acknowledge this partnership is so radical in Jesus that the answer given to us in him is the very Word of God? No one can be forced by arguments to believe in Jesus of Nazareth as the absolute presence of God. But it is easier to believe in him once he is seen to reveal what is ultimately meant by "man." Rahner concludes this discussion with an analysis of why Jesus is the final unsurpassable event.

A third and final hindrance to belief is the church itself. It is indisputably holy. But even a casual look at its history reveals it, and not only its individual members, is also sinful. Rahner lists its sinful failings in great detail (15ff). All these sins tempt one not to believe. They are a stifling burden. "But...are we ourselves not part of this burden which weighs on us and threatens our faith? Are we not ourselves sinners too?" (17). We know truth is only found in concrete, messy history, and also that we only find ourselves in community. Hence, we must bear the burden of the community of faith. So long as the church strengthens us with the body and blood of Christ we are empowered to remain within it and helped to bear its burdens.

Faith can mature. It need not be killed. This presents young people today with great challenges and duties (list, 18ff). First among these is to distinguish between real Christianity and the many competing ideas and programs in the church with are not matters of faith. Disagreements among believers are natural and good. But we must never lose sight of the kingdom of God. Young people will never build a true future by disavowing the genuine past. They must not become bitter but must grow in courage and humility.

All Christians today must put their beliefs into practice, and they must pray. "This means having the courage to speak into that silent immensity which yet lovingly embraces us—with a will to trust oneself to it and with the belief that one has been accepted by the holy mystery we call God" (20). Those who pray face up to the question of existence and do not run away. In this way they learn whether Christianity is the truth of life. Whoever follows light will find grace, whether or not they are counted among the official members of the church. For it is not easy to run past the Infinite Mystery which embraces us in silent love, despite what some narrow-minded Christians think. For they think of God too much in the image of their own puny hearts. Summary (21f).

5.02 Theology in the New Testament
Theologie im Neuen Testament
{2.5} *Einsicht und Glaube. Festschrift für G. Söhnen* (Freiburg, 1962) 28-44.

Abstract: Because the New Testament contains both original revelation and theological reflection Rahner can defend development of dogma, interpret ambiguous biblical statements, and disentangle kerygma from complex theology.

Topics: REVELATION and development of dogma; THEOLOGY; SCRIP-TURE, exegesis. SCRIPTURE, New Testament.

Subsidiary Discussions: Dogma, development of (25ff, 29f); Scripture, inspiration of (29); Sin, original (33); Christology (33ff); Kerygma (36ff); Faith (38); Mystery (39); Mysticism (40).

Precis: Rahner investigates whether there is already a theology in the New Testament itself and, if so, what significance it has for us today? He begins by offering a "sufficient" definition of theology and of the immediate, original event of revelation. From this he establishes that all theological reflection, although it is active "building on the data of revelation, of starting from and returning to them, of explaining and developing them, of relating them to the totality of the one system of human consciousness and knowledge, etc., [it never claims] to having been received from God himself in a direct event of revelation in such a way that it would be the direct result of this divine activity in its content or correctness" (24). Having made this distinction Rahner asks whether there is theology in the New Testament or whether all its statements are merely the objectification of an original event of revelation.

At first the answer seems an obvious no. But Rahner argues since dogmas exist today which are the product of deeper reflection on revelation (on its causes and logical consequences) without ever claiming for themselves the status of original events of revelation, why should this very process of reflection *not* be present in the New Testament? Hence, Rahner answers his question in the affirmative. This is made even more clear when we consider that no one ever hears or receives a word of revelation or any other word without engaging many phases of the mental process of understanding. Thus, it would not be surprising to find the authors of the New Testament pondering and reflecting on the data of their faith, solving problems to the best of their ability with theological reflection. It is unlikely they received answers "to all these questions simply by ever new, separate revelations from God (in the sense 'thus spoke Jahweh')" (28). Rahner identifies this process as inspiration as opposed to revelation.

What conclusions follow? First, since there is already theology in the New Testament which nevertheless is dogma, such theology can also be found in the church of later ages. This opposes a Protestant view which admits theology is possible in post–New Testament times but not new, binding dogma (summary, 30). Second, it must be possible to approximate a line of demarcation in the New Testament between the content of the original expression of revelation and the theology based on revelation. This is not to suggest one is more binding than the other or that there is some inner canon of scripture. The desired demarcation, however imprecise, would reveal what "the real basic content of Christianity [looks like] and can therefore be grasped as true when (and in so far as) it signifies a divine proclamation beyond which it is absolutely impossible to go" (31). Rahner illustrates how this demarcation would affect christology and soteriology (31f).

The ability to demarcate revelation from theology has an essential function. It can determine the meaning of a statement; what it is meant to convey and the limits of what it is meant to convey. When one learns where a New Testament author learned of a saying whose meaning is doubtful to us, it is easier to discern what he is trying to say. Rahner cites for example Paul's teaching on original sin (33). Catholic exegesis and biblical theology rely on this very method much more than dogmatic theology does, for example to understand the self-consciousness of Jesus. Superfluous as it may seem to use this method in dogmatic theology, where it is difficult to grasp the meaning of a particular statement of Christ it can be significant indeed (examples, 35).

A further benefit of applying this method to dogmatic theology would be to simplify the often bewilderingly complicated system of theological assertions. Although the truth which attempts to embrace the infinity of God cannot be completely simple, the message of the gospel is meant for average people. People today look for mystery, for God as always greater, and not for a system which claims to have completely captured God. Theology may need to be complicated to insure the kerygma is not diluted. But in relation to kerygma theology must always be seen as something derived and secondary. "For the kerygma, properly understood, is not an additional discourse about something, but is the reality itself" (36). "[K]erygma (if it is really itself and not a devitalized theology) is precisely in this way necessarily simple, for ultimately the simplest is also the most unfathomable and vice versa" (37).

Since faith does not necessarily grow though the study of either biblical or dogmatic theology (just the opposite may happen) it is also possible to explain the real growth of faith in another way. Rahner outlines a speculative process: reflection on the fact the mystery has drawn near us in grace which as such should be accepted in faith and love. The ambiguity of scripture and the Incomprehensible encountered existentially by modern people converge in this mystery. Rahner attempts to clarify and summarize the relationship between revelation and kerygma on the one hand and theological reflection on the other by drawing a parallel with mystical experience and its conceptual communication, interpretation, and reflex objectification (40f).

5.03 What is a Dogmatic Statement?
Was ist eine dogmatische Aussage?
{2.0}   *Catholica* 15 (1961) 161-184.

Abstract: After enunciating five theses about dogmatic statements Rahner distinguishes them from statements of original revelation (sacred scripture) by the fact the former are the permanent ground of the latter.

Topics: DOGMA, formulation of; REVELATION, statement of.

Subsidiary Discussions: Truth, propositional (44f, 54f); Sin, *simul justus et pecator* (45); Analogy (46f, 59f); Faith (48ff); Church (51ff); Sin, original (55f); Mystery (58f); Revelation, two source theory (63f).

Precis: Determining what is a dogmatic statement is difficult in no small measure because it is seldom explicitly asked in Catholic textbook theology. Rahner presumes part of the question is whether, how, and why there are intrinsically different forms of speech in the church, one of which is the dogmatic statement. In addition he must definitively distinguish dogmatic statements from kerygma (and hence from original revelation found in scripture) and from ordinary discourse. To this end Rahner offers five theses. 1) *Dogmatic statements must be true in the ordinary sense of everyday language and knowledge. They must fulfill all the inner structures and laws governing ordinary statements of truth* (examples, 44). This is because they are human, natural words (but not only this) subject to how Catholics understand nature and grace. Thus, "dogmatic propositions are inevitably also propositions of a natural, noetic nature...not an abstract one...but a concrete and thus infralapsarian nature which bears the stamp of the guilt of man" (45). This is why it is possible for such statements to be true and at the same time dangerous, rash, equivocal, seductive, and even sinful (summary, 46). Rahner further illustrates the human nature of dogmatic statements (46-48) by reference to their being intentional, analogous, not equally true or false, and marked by aptness. Dogmatic statements have these qualities because they refer to a truth grasped by personal act and not simply in the objective-conceptual statement. This gap found in all human statements between what is said and what is meant is especially pronounced in dogmatic statements. 2) *"Dogmatic statements are statements of faith."* They are not ordinary statements about some theological object; they are themselves exercises of faith. This is because they develop from faith and can never completely separate themselves from their source. This is not always obvious in Catholic theology. Here Rahner disputes the post-Tridentine notion that grace is too supernatural to enter human consciousness (49f). He concludes by insisting faith is a prerequisite to theology. Believers and non-believers, even when they cite the same dogmas, are not saying the same thing (summary, 51).

3) *"Dogmatic statements are in special measure ecclesiological statements."* Just as kerygma has an essentially ecclesial dimension, dogmatic statements are bound to the church because theology (definition, 52) essentially takes place in the church and theologians essentially address the church. In addition there must be an authoritative theology in the church for which the church itself is responsible: the magisterium. Above this there is scripture, the *norma normans non normata* which demands obedience and which the church merely interprets. At this point Rahner introduces a long sub-thesis about communally linguistic rulings on terminology which, though obligatory, must never be confused with the mystery of the thing being defined (54ff). Examples include original sin, Trinity, concelebration, church membership.

4) *"A dogmatic statement is a statement which leads into the 'mysterium'."* Both dogmatic and kerygmatic statements draw hearers beyond themselves into the very mystery of God. Both possess an element not identical with the represented conceptual content: reference to mystery. Rahner suggests a fuller appreciation of analogy would help to show whether theologians themselves are responding to the mystagogy of dogma or only to its conceptual dimensions.

5) *"A dogmatic statement is not identical with the original Word of revelation or the original statement of faith."* Rahner approaches the heart of this many-sided matter by reminding the reader of the distinction between the original proclamation of revelation and reflex dogmatic statements, a distinction he finds prototypically in scripture itself (cf., 5.02). It is not easy to distinguish these two because both arise from faith, both are qualified by the magisterium in the same way, and every revealed statement is cloaked in human words, the product of reflex thought. Hence, these two kinds of statements cannot be distinguished as pure word of God vs. human reflection. Were this the case development of dogma would be impossible to justify (61).

There is, however, an essential difference between dogmatic statements and the original testimony of faith. Rahner locates it in the history of revelation where events and statements are fixed in time and place, to which later ages are permanently bound, and to which all later proclamation and theology are referred. This permanent ground of all further statements is sacred scripture. Rahner criticizes the two-source theory of revelation (63ff) arguing that appeals to tradition must always refer back to scripture.

Hence, a theological word is only a theological word in as much as it is not the word of scripture. The same is true of statements of exegesis and biblical theology. Here Rahner draws an analogy between the individual theologian and the mystic. Both may have correct insights into the truth even though both may be at odds with the formulations given by the magisterium. Theologians work to illuminate the faith of their readers. It would be suspicious and perhaps wrong for them to claim to be supplying additional knowledge to the content of faith.

Rahner concludes by admitting he has not said everything on this topic. He suggests it would be fruitful to explore the difference between dogmatic statements which are directed to the reflex self-possession of knowledge about something, and dogmatic statements which regard the reality itself— a distinction rooted in the nature of human knowledge.

5.04 Exegesis and Dogmatic Theology
Exegese und Dogmatik
{0.5} *Stimmen der Zeit* 168 (1961) 241-262.

Abstract: In chatty, open letter format Rahner addresses shortcomings first of exegetes and then of dogmatic theologians. He ends by warning the magisterium of the potentially severe, unintended consequences of censorship.

Topics: SCRIPTURE, exegesis; THEOLOGY, dogmatic, MAGISTERIUM and theology.

Subsidiary Discussions: Error (74f); Preaching (75f, 86); Christology (76); Resurrection (82f); Sin, original (83); Certainty (85f); Intellectuals (87f); Censorship (90ff).

Precis: This essay offers observations on the growing estrangement between exegetes and dogmatic theologians over New Testament studies. Dogmatic theologians claim exegetes are insufficiently attentive to the church's binding teachings; exegetes claim dogmatic theologians would preemptively restrict their scholarship. More particularly this essay was occasioned by a scandalous controversy that arose in preparation for Vatican II (68 ftn1).

To the exegetes: a word from the dogmatic theologian. Exegetes do not always have sufficient regard for dogmatic theologians and theology. They seem to forget as Catholic theologians they are bound to observe all the principles proper to Catholic theology. Catholic exegesis is a science of faith not just of linguistics. The magisterium must represent for them not merely a negative norm but an inner positive principle of research. All too often when their research leads to difficulties they seem content to hand them to dogmatic theologians to solve. However, when dogmatic theologians try to solve these problems exegetes complain they are not trained to interpret scripture!

Rahner admits exegetes must be critical and not dishonestly cook their data. Still, part of their task is to harmonize their results and the church's teaching (e.g., Marian doctrines, 72). Rahner takes issue with exegetes who do not give a basic exposition of their exegetical principles (73). He also chides them for their inexact knowledge of scholastic theology (and dogmatic and fundamental theology (76), and offers examples where greater familiarity would help them in their *own* work (74). Rahner admits a Catholic theologian may have misgivings about non-defined doctrinal pronouncements of the magisterium. But one should state these openly and not merely shrug one's shoulders.

Finally, exegetes must take more seriously their responsibility to those whose faith is weak—who must see theologians working together to build up and defend the teaching of the church and not merely to show where our knowledge is imprecise. Exegetes must also take special care to train preachers. They must not weaken the tender faith of future homilists or send them out half-baked to propound an exegesis which weakens the faith of others. Rahner closes by reprimanding those who would discredit exegetes by labeling their findings "Protestant." Protestant exegesis too has much to offer that is correct.

To the dogmatic theologians: a word from a colleague. Dogmatic theologians know less exegesis than they should. Too often their knowledge is out of date. Though they have a right to do exegesis, it must convince modern exegetes. Dogmatic theologians should be patient with exegetes since their field is vast and complicated. They must not complain that exegetes give dogmatic criteria, norms, and sources too little attention if they are not willing to pay due attention to the tools of exegetes. Exegetes have as much right to engage in fundamental theology as dogmatic theologians have to engage in exegesis. When it comes to the historicity of scripture, dogmatic theologians must admit exegetes have to speak with more nuances. Overall, Rahner suggests dogmatic theologians have an easier job than fundamental theologians since they "can use every word of Scripture right away as an equally inerrant and inspired word in your dogmatic proofs" (80).

There are many problems dogmatic theologians could and should pose that would make things easier for exegetes, including questions of resurrection, the Trinity, christology, knowledge (list, 80ff). Too often dogmatic theologians fail to show how wide and accommodating their metaphysical principles actually are (e.g., Christ's resurrection, 82f; original sin, 83).

As much as dogmatic theologians should be cautioned not to pronounce something "historical," it would be wrong to suppose exegetes have destroyed all historical certainty. Still, being prepared to accept that different parts of scripture are more or less historical does not reveal which ones are more possibly Christ's actual words and deeds. Here the work of the exegete can actually make the dogmatic theologian's job easier (examples, 85). One must never expect or imagine the certitude the exegete can furnish is the same as the absolute certitude of metaphysics or faith. One cannot for this reason contradict the exegete's method, although this lack of certitude raises important questions about the role of modern exegesis in preaching (86).

Some additional considerations. Both exegetes and dogmatic theologians must understand they serve the magisterium which Christ entrusted to Peter and the apostles, not to professors. Nonetheless, it cannot be disputed that masters are also dependent on their servants. All theologians must be trusted with the freedom to fulfill their tasks. Today exegetes must align themselves with the church to speak to and enlighten modern intellectuals (87) who too often get the impression theologians are not answering their questions (examples, 88). In the past, as long as the church felt competing schools of theology were conserving its basic principles, it felt comfortable to let them contend with one another. Today it is harder to face questions squarely without at times giving the impression basic principles are being questioned. But what are the options? To tell the world to wait until theologians come to a consensus? To give an answer now which later may prove false? Even true answers may require incubation. Whatever the course of actions the magisterium does have the right and duty to keep such discussions in bounds and to halt heretical tendencies. Nevertheless, the process of discussion should never be curtailed by the magisterium at the outset. It is not after all empowered to explain every open question. This is the indispensable role of theologians.

Rahner ends with a discussion of the magisterium and censorship. He proposes the dilemma of a theologian who concludes a colleague has in good faith stepped over the line into false teaching, but fears that addressing it will bring severe, even unjust consequences to his colleague at the hands of legitimate authority. Does the theologian speak or remain silent? This dilemma underscores the need for the magisterium to be as forbearing as possible. For censoring one theologian runs the risk of paralyzing all honest discussion. This is more likely a greater risk to the church than leaving unremarked the error of a single person.

5.05 History of the World and Salvation-History
Weltgeschichte und Heilsgeschichte
{2.0} Previously unpublished.
Abstract: Beside profane history Rahner distinguishes two kinds of revelation- salvation-history: general and specific. The first explains how the world and its history are graced in the Logos; the second how they connect to Jesus.
Topics: HISTORY; SALVATION/DAMNATION; REVELATION, general and specific.
Subsidiary Discussions: Freedom (98f); Motives (101); God as horizon (103f); Word (106ff); Israel, history of (108f); Renunciation, *fuga saeculi* (113f).
Precis: **1. Salvation history takes place within the history of this world.** First Rahner defines salvation: our accepting God's free self-offer which perfects us. Salvation is not a moment in history but the cumulating cessation of history. This notion reveals as false any utopian idea of salvation-in-the-world. History remains forever the realm of the provisional, the unfinished, the ambiguous, the dialectical. Second, he insists salvation takes place within world history, for salvation is not a completely future reality. It is now. God's self-communication is not provisional. Even though God's grace supports our freedom to accept that self-communication it remains

real. It determines our salvation or damnation and is always exercised through an encounter with the world. It never takes place in an isolated religious sphere. Third, the content and reality proper to salvation-history lie hidden in an ambiguous and undefined profane history. Although in the resurrection of Jesus the history of the world becomes transparent in regard to salvation at least to the eyes of faith, the same truth remains obscure to profane history.

2. Salvation history is distinct from profane history.

a) This distinction rests first on the fact one cannot see unambiguous salvation/damnation taking place in profane history. This is because salvation depends on human freedom and human freedom can never be fully objectified since our motives are never transparent. Our conscious reflection is always provisional. This distinction rests in turn on the fact that we never create our own salvation, but if we are saved at all we receive salvation as a gift from God. Since this gift can only be experienced in beatitude we cannot grasp it within profane history. Summary (102).

b) Nothing said yet establishes the material difference between revelation- and salvation-history, and the profane history of the world. Rahner begins with God's salvific will which he maintains is a genuine subjective possibility for every person. This does not occur completely outside the realm of consciousness. Rather in every act of love or knowledge God is approached as the horizon which makes such acts possible. Thus, we are graced at our very roots. Our supernaturally elevated nature has the quality of revelation. Accepting and acting on this nature can already be called faith. "It follows then that there is a history of salvation, revelation and faith which co-exists with the general profane history. We have called [t]his the general salvation- and revelation-history" (104). Attempts to objectify this history produce the history of religion, something which on the basis of the account given above can be seen as quite legitimate.

c) Salvation-history and profane history are distinct because God has interpreted a particular part of the latter by his word, making it the actual, official, and explicit history of salvation. Rahner recalls here that something can be history even without clear, cultural objectification such as constitute a human community. Even without these forms it can make itself felt. At the same time salvation-history is always also the hidden foundation of profane history. The religious element is everywhere the meaning and root of history and is never merely the most sublime flower of merely human culture.

Whenever general salvation-history becomes tangible and objective it begins to pass over into specific salvation-history (examples, 108). Rahner goes on to say even the Old Testament history of Israel was only provisional until God sent the Logos into the world. In Christ and in the church saving history finds its clearest and absolutely permanent distinction from profane history as something destined for all people of every future age.

3. Salvation-history explains profane history.

a) General salvation-history represents the most profound character and basis of profane history; special salvation-history manifests this ultimate character of all history in the revelation in which salvation takes place while showing itself historically. In this way it demythologizes and undeifies the history of the world. Creation is not God, nor is history. Neither is self-explanitory. Though we have been thrown out into this undeified world, it is here we work out our salvation precisely by taking upon ourselves the soberness of the profane which is not yet itself salvation. Summary (111).

b) Salvation-history interprets the history of the world as something antagonistic and veiled. Precisely because salvation is not simply the immanent fruit of profane history, Christianity is skeptical towards profane history. It knows all our tasks are radically threatened by incompletion, failure and finally death. It knows life in the world is futile. The oppositions found in the world, rather than diminishing, often grow ever more acute.

c) The Christian existentially devalues the history of the world. This does not establish the right simply to flee from the world and its history, something which in any case is impossible. We have a duty toward history. We must suffer it because the eternal is only found in the temporal. But for this very reason the Christian relativizes the world. Thus, Christians do flee the world whenever it represents itself as absolute. Summary (114).

d) For Christianity the history of this world is a history interpreted in a Christo-centric sense. This summarizes all that has already been said. The world has been created by, and its history designed for the Logos because God who is love has willed to communicate himself to it. Thus, God willed the difference between nature and grace, salvation-history and profane history—differences already enveloped by Christ. Hence, the history of the world, precisely as profane, is part of the pre- and post-history of Christ. Natural history is the condition for the possibility of the human spirit to hear and accept God's offer of self-communication and so to find salvation.

5.06 Christianity and the Non-Christian Religions

Das Christentum und die nichtchristlichen Religionen

{2.0} *Pluralismus, Toleranz und Christenheit* (Nürnberg 1961) 55-74.

Abstract: Since it appears religious pluralism will always endure Rahner suggests four theses to aid in approaching non-Christian religions. These treat among other things revelation, salvation, and anonymous Christianity.
Topics: RELIGIONS, non-Christian; SALVATION and non-Christian religions; DIALOGUE, inter-religious; ECUMENISM.
Subsidiary Discussions: Religions, non-Christian (validity of) (118ff, 125f); God, salvific will of (122ff); Israel, history of (125ff, 130f); Revelation (125ff); Anonymous Christian (131ff); Faith, *fides implicita/explicita* (131f); Mission mandate (132ff).

Precis: "Open Catholicism" in a religiously pluralistic world involves two things: acknowledging the existence and significance of forces in the world contrary to the church; understanding and overcoming this pluralism to the degree it is an offense against God. The rise of militant, state-sponsored atheism is an unexpected weapon in advancing these initiatives. Catholicism, with its claim to be absolutely *the* one and only valid relation to the one living God has more problems than most to enter inter-religious dialogue. The very existence of pluralism, of non-Christian religions, despite two thousand years of evangelization is for it a scandal. It is all the more acute for individual western Christians who now live side by side with Muslims, Buddhists, and others in our modern cities. Hence, the urgency of this question. Rahner offers four theses he hopes describe the Catholic dogmatic (though unofficial) interpretation of the meaning of non-Christian religions.

Thesis 1: *"Christianity understands itself as the absolute religion, intended for all men, which cannot recognize any other religion beside itself as of equal right."* A religion is valid and lawful not because of the relationship we have developed with God but because of God's action toward us: God's free self-communication which rests on the incarnation, death, and resurrection of Jesus. On this basis Christianity enters "with existential power and demanding force into the realm of another religion and—judging it by itself—puts it in question" (118). But Christianity itself has a pre-history. It has not always and everywhere been the way of salvation for all people. Here Rahner discusses when the objective obligation of the Christian message begins, whether at the close of the apostolic age or at different times depending on the actual historical circumstances of those being evangelized (118-120). He concludes that although as regards "destination" Christianity is the absolute and only religion for all people, the point at which it becomes an obligation for them remains an open question. He finds implicit in this a sub-thesis: that since in concrete human existence religion is social we are commanded to seek and accept a social form of religion.

From all this it follows that when approaching paganism or non-Christian religions it is vital to concentrate not on the fact of their having refused to accept Christianity, but on Christianity's failure as of yet to proclaim its message with sufficient power to attract them. Seen in this light the call to dialogue becomes all the more urgent.

Thesis 2: *Even before the Gospel really enters into the historical situation of a non-Mosaic religion a) it contains supernatural elements arising out of the grace which is given as a gratuitous gift on account of Christ. Hence, b) it is a lawful religion without thereby denying the error contained in it.*

Regarding a), Rahner maintains aberrant elements of non-Christian religions are harmful. They have been and must be continually protested. But this does not mean there can be no God-pleasing pagans. Rahner summarizes his argument: if there is no salvation apart from Christ, and if

God has really, truly and seriously intended salvation for all people, then "every human being is really and truly exposed to the influence of divine, supernatural grace which offers an interior union with God and by means of which God communicates himself whether the individual takes up and attitude of acceptance or of refusal toward this grace" (123). It is legitimate to take this optimistic view because of the power and effectiveness of God's will and word. Summary (125).

Regarding b), Rahner defines as lawful any institutional religion whose "use" at a certain period can be regarded as a positive means for gaining right relationship with God and thus for attaining salvation. Such a religion is, therefore, positively included in God's plan of salvation. Rahner bases this conclusion on the fact that before Christ, Judaism was such a valid religion (125ff). Such a view frees us to face non-Christian religions without the dilemma that either they come from God and everything in them is willed, or that they are purely human constructions. Rahner reinforces this argument by insisting that since we are by nature social and religious, the maker of religions, then the pre-Christian religion at one's disposal and the morality of a people of a given age can be a legitimate and concrete form of divine law (129). This seriously undermines the notion of "natural religion." Rahner concludes this section developing the notion that elements in non-Christian religions can vary greatly in terms of their validity. Summary (131).

Thesis 3: *Christianity confronts members of non-Christian religions as those who have already been touched by God's grace and truth, and so in some respect or another are anonymously Christian.* After grounding this *fides implicita* in theological anthropology Rahner insists this in no way undermines the missionary thrust of the church. Explicit preaching of Christianity is never superfluous. Extending baptism and reconciliation cannot be dispensed with. "The reflex self-realization of a previously anonymous Christianity is demanded (1) by the incarnational and social structure of grace and of Christianity; and (2) because the individual who grasps Christianity in a clearer, purer and more reflective way has ... a still greater chance of salvation than someone who is merely an anonymous Christian" (132).

Thesis 4: *"The Church today must see itself not as that community which has a claim to salvation but rather as the historically tangible vanguard and the historically and socially constituted explicit expression of what Christians hope is present as a hidden reality even outside the visible Church."* Though Christians must hope, pray and work for the unity of all under Christ, we must nevertheless expect the pluralism we know today will not disappear in the foreseeable future. Herein lies the value of seeing non-Christians as fundamentally united with believers albeit in an anonymous way. Some find it presumptuous to impute the status of anonymous Christian to non-Christians. Rahner counters that Christianity cannot renounce this "presumption." It is the only true basis on which the believer and the church can be tolerant, humble, and yet firm towards all non-Christian religions.

5.07 Christianity and the "New Man." The Christian faith and utopian views about the future of this world

Das Christentum und der "neue Mensch"
{1.0} *Wort und Wahrheit* 16 (1961) 807-819.

Abstract: Although Christian eschatology often clashes with secular utopias over time and finitude, Christians have no right to opt out of planning for the word's future. Many modern, secular impulses have Christian origins.
Topics: ESCHATOLOGY; UTOPIAS; FUTURE.
Subsidiary Discussions: Theological anthropology, self-manipulation (137f); Finitude (140); Time (143ff); Hylomorphysm (147f); God as world's future (148f).

Precis: Christianity is a religion with an eschatology. It looks into the future; it guides present actions with binding statements about what is to come. With Jesus the last age has already begun. Salvation history has been decided. It is no longer open. Therefore, Christianity cannot be indifferent to planing or to the utopian futures suggested from other quarters which are often based on the "new man" endowed with the power to create and conquer oneself. How are these two conceptions of the future related? Rahner begins by offering some clarifying remarks on modern extra-Christian thought concerning the future. He sees in the man of today the beginnings of the man of the future...more global in outlook, more technological, more able to manipulate and control not only his environment but himself. Summary (138).

I. The eschatology of Christianity is no intra-mundane utopia. It sets no intra-mundane tasks or goals. It cannot relieve the anguish of planning or the inevitable darkness of the unknown. Each individual Christian must convert the general principles of religion into a specific plan of action. This is not to say planing for the future is unimportant. In fact the future is a problem Christians today show far too little concern over. Simply because Christianity offers no clear-cut program for the future does not mean every future program is compatible with it. Christianity must offer more than defensive criticism.

II. Christianity insists that whatever future we envision, we will always be drawn back to ourselves as finite creatures. Even though we have redefined many previously static barriers, others remain, especially our spacio-temporality, our biological constitution, and our mortality. The permanent finitude these represent cannot be overcome socially since society too is comprised of finite individuals however much a society may work to deny it.

III. The Christian notion of time as individual and existential differs greatly from the insufficient view of time held by most utopian dreamers. Whatever great utopia is proposed it can never solve the problem of personal existence by saying it will be solved by others in the future. The future of the human, spiritual person in no way lies in that future which will be brought about later. Rather it is the eternity which is brought about as the result of the spiritual act of the person (144). This is what Christianity means by personal, existential time: the coming to be of the unconditioned finality of the free decision of existence. This works in time by overcoming merely continuous time. It is eternal life which has already begun in every moment of the free decision of believing love.

IV. Christianity has also surpassed all ideologies and utopias (in which the new man looks strikingly like the old) by its teaching on the incarnation and the universal salvation it has ushered in. Rahner summarizes the Christian proclamation (146f) by saying, "In the actual world, creation no longer means merely the bringing into existence of something out of an infinite foundation and the perpetual keeping of this originated reality distant from its incommunicable source, but means rather the production of the finite as something on which the Infinite lavishes himself in the form of Love" (147). This fulfillment extends to the whole of created reality and to the human person, body and soul, in a glorified manner. Concretely Christianity can say very little about this state other than God is its consummation. It can only speak of it negatively. It is something unattainable by us—a gratuitous gift of pure grace. By the fact this coming of God is our true and only infinite future, Christianity has already surpassed and embraced all utopian intramundane futures. This fact in no way lessens our Christian obligation to take an active part in working for the progress of the world.

V. The Christian must live at present in this world which is always a world of the future already begun: a new world full of earthly goals, tasks, and dangers. But all too often Christians give the impression of being people of yesterday. Christians can only achieve their own proper nature if they live in the present and future, not just in the past. Rahner lists many long-postponed tasks facing the church (151f). Far from being bewildered by the impetus of the modern world toward globalization, greater freedom, and increasing self-manipulation, the church can take pride in the fact these impulses are the natural outgrowth of the Christian spirit itself.

5.08 Christology within an Evolutionary View of the World
Die Christologie innerhalb einer evolutiven Weltanschauung
{4.0}   Previously unpublished.
Abstract: An attempt to fit christology into a view of a cosmos which evolves towards that spirit who attains absolute self-transcendence and perfection through and in an absolute self-communication given by God in grace and glory.
Topics: CHRISTOLOGY and evolution; HYPOSTATIC UNION; EVO-LUTION.
Subsidiary Discussions: Theological anthropology, unity (161ff); Matter and spirit (161ff); Self-transcendence (164ff, 171f); Becoming (164ff);

Freedom (168); God as goal of transcendence (171ff); Jesus Christ as savior (174ff); Creation and incarnation (184ff); Incarnation and creation (184ff); Ideology (188); Utopias (190ff).

Precis: This essay presupposes rather than details both christology and an evolutionary view of the world. When Rahner speaks of including christology in an evolutionary view of the world he does not mean deducing the doctrine of the incarnation from an evolving world, nor that the incarnation raises no contradictions. He seeks to clarify the affinity of these two doctrines and to explain the possibility of their being mutually related. His theme is to assert God's presence in the world. This section concludes with a helpful preview (159ff): Part I, matter and spirit; Part II, human transcendentality as the point at which the cosmos achieves its goal; Part III, the hypostatic union; Part IV, redemption, the historical Jesus, eschatology, utopias.

I. 1) Faith in the spiritual and material world means not only that these two principles arise from the same cause, but that they form a unity in origin, self-realization and determination. In short they together form the one world.

2) This unity shows itself first and most clearly in the human person. We are a unity of matter and spirit logically and objectively prior to the diversity of distinguishable elements which are only understandable as elements of this one person. Since consummation comes for the whole, materiality is never simply a provisional element of human existence.

3) Natural science sees matter quite differently. Although it knows a great deal about matter and how it functions it cannot know matter itself. Matter can only be known in relation to the human person. The remainder of this section defines man as spirit, who "returning to himself" is referred to the absolute totality of all possible reality, and who as matter "returns to himself" in the encounter with the concrete individual. Matter is the condition for the possibility of otherness considered as the material of freedom.

4) This dense section argues "a really higher, more complex organization can appear also as a step towards consciousness, and finally towards self-consciousness, even though *self*-consciousness at least does include a real essential self-transcendence of the material as opposed to its previous condition" (168). Though matter and spirit have irreducibly different natures they are interrelated in the fact that matter develops out of its inner being in the direction of spirit. Were this not so it would be impossible to explain the phenomenon of becoming. Rahner argues true becoming must be understood as real, active self-transcendence (164f) based on a proper understanding of being. "[S]elf-transcendence includes also transcendence into what is substantially new, i.e., the leap to a higher *nature*" (165). This "essential self-transcendence" is only possible (not necessary) because of the finite being's relationship to God. This is not only metaphysically logical it is confirmed by observed facts (166f). Insofar as the self-transcending always remains present in the particular goal of its self-transcendence, and insofar as the higher order always embraces the lower as contained in it, even the highest can be understood as a change of something previously existing. Rahner ends by recasting these insights in Thomistic language (167f).

5) "If man is thus the self-transcendence of living matter, then the history of Nature and spirit ... develops towards man, continues in him as *his* history, is conserved and surpassed in him and hence reaches its goal with and in the history of the human spirit" (168). This explains why man and nature can only reach their one common goal by activity which is spiritual and spirituality which is activity. This is why the Christian knows the history of the cosmos as a whole will find its real consummation despite, in, and through human freedom.

II. What stage has the self-transcendence of the world reached in humanity?

1) Unfortunately many natural scientists even today think of human existence as an accidental fluke of blind nature. This contradicts both metaphysics and Christian thought which places humanity as the goal of a nature become conscious in it. Any other approach ends in a Platonic dualism with us as the enemy of nature. To reduce human existence to mere chance contradicts the scientist's own creed.

2) What is unique in our essential self-transcendence is "the fact of being present to oneself and of being referred to the absolute totality of reality and to its first ground as such" (169). If this is seen to be the goal of the history of the cosmos then the established world finds itself in us. This self-presence has a one-way history and ordination even if particular individuals are incapable of experiencing the final outcome of this process because of their present circumstances. Christianity calls this finality and consummation the immortality of the soul.

3) This self-transcendence of the cosmos in us reaches its consummation only when it receives the ultimate self-communication of its ultimate ground itself, when the direct self-communication of God is given to the spiritual creature in grace and glory. God creates in order to give himself to this other. The world receives God as its innermost life. God does this without ever ceasing to be infinite mystery.

III. The place of christology in this evolutionary world-picture.

1) After a quick review in the form of presuppositions, Rahner asks how exactly we can conceive of God's self-communication to spiritual creatures. Because it presupposes both freedom and the history of intercommunication among spiritual subjects, God's self-communication can be expected to take the form of a concrete historical event.

2) This event occurs in the person of a savior: "that historical person who, coming in space and time, signifies that beginning of God's absolute communication of himself which inaugurates this self-communication for all men as something happening irrevocably and which shows this to be happening" (174f). The coming of the savior is not necessarily the beginning of God's self-communication. It is however its climax. Two factors are

included in this notion: God's free communication and its free acceptance. Summary (176).

3) This dense section shows how the hypostatic union and the incarnation of the divine Logos is precisely what is meant by the evolutionary view of the world. The doctrine maintains Jesus is true man. This means simply that he is an historical moment in the history of God's communication to the world. He is part of the history of the cosmos itself. Like all of us Jesus received the self-communication of God. Unlike us, by his obedience, prayer, and freely accepting the destiny of his death he has also achieved the acceptance of his divinely given grace. This doctrine contradicts gnosticism and other heresies and links the creation and incarnation as "two moments and phases in the real world of the unique...process of God's self-renunciation and self-expression into what is other than himself" (177f).

Exploring what is necessary for God's self-communication to be definitive and irrevocable also implies the limit-notion of savior and of the hypostatic union. How does the hypostatic union of one individual fit the basic conception of grace and glory being the real possibility and final consummation for all? He argues that either the hypostatic union is the still higher stage of an essentially newer and higher kind of divine self-communication given to just one person, or regardless of the fact only one person enjoys its essential characteristics, it is precisely the way the divinization of the spiritual creature must be carried out if it is to happen at all. After clarifying the question (180) Rahner argues the latter must be the case because this divinizing event must be a concrete, tangible phenomenon in history; it must be irrevocable; it must become conscious of itself (summary, 181). If the necessarily finite vehicle for God's absolute self-communication were not in the strictest sense the divine reality itself, then it would in principle remain surpassable by some new finite reality. Hence, to say God's pledge is irrevocable implies what is meant by the hypostatic union. Summary (183f).

IV. A few concluding remarks to avoid misunderstandings on this subject.

1) Nothing has been said so far about guilt, sin, or redemption. To the potential charge Rahner has deviated unlawfully from traditional christology he maintains he follows Scotus to whom the magisterium has never officially objected. He views incarnation as an eternal part of God's plan for creation and not just something occasioned by the need for redemption. Second, Rahner defends his view against a misreading that, given the relationship of spirit and matter, sin is somehow unavoidable and hence innocuous. This cannot be the case since sin is dependent on freedom, and freedom is always a property of transcendent spirit, not matter. Finally, Rahner maintains that embracing an evolutionary view of the world does not make redemption a human achievement. The evolutionary view underscores the fact that the communication of divine grace always and only happens at God's initiative.

2) Rahner insists that although the evolutionary view allows for such a thing as the incarnation it does not necessitate it, nor does it prove that the

hypostatic union has in fact been realized precisely in Jesus of Nazareth and only in him. One is a Christian only after accepting the concrete person and not merely the idea of a savior. Hence, the evolutionary view maintains Christianity is an historical, revealed religion and not an ideology.

3) From an evolutionary point of view how is one to view the historical point in time of the incarnation? Rahner describes why it is legitimate to think of it as both the definitive end of one age due to the unsurpassable and irrevocable nature of Christ's revelation, and as the beginning of a new epoch as the cosmos now moves inexorably forward to its consummation in Christ.

4) Christology both frees and constricts all intra-mundane ideological and utopian views of the future. It liberates by insisting on human dignity without imposing a particular task; it constricts, sobers and subdues utopianism by insisting no intra-mundane plan in itself brings about salvation.

5.09 Dogmatic Reflections on the Knowledge and Self-Consciousness of Christ

Dogmatische Erwägungen über das Wissen und Selbstbewußtsein Christi

{2.0}   *Trier. theologische Zeitschrift* 71 (1962) 65-83.

Abstract: Rahner reconciles modern exegetes and dogmatic theologians over the divine knowledge and self-consciousness of Christ by offering a notion of human knowledge and self-consciousness as pre-thematic and non-objective.

Topics: JESUS CHRIST, self-awareness; THEOLOGICAL ANTHROPOLOGY, consciousness; KNOWLEDGE.

Subsidiary Discussions: Knowledge, nescience (201f); Freedom (202, 214f); Beatific vision (202ff, 206f); Hypostatic union (204ff); Knowledge, infused (213).

Precis: Many claims about Jesus' self-knowledge and possession of the direct vision of God seem almost mythological today, especially in light of modern exegesis. They seem to contradict Jesus' full humanity. The usual distinctions drawn by dogmatic theologians to overcome this tension seem artificial and improbable, achieving no more than a verbal harmony. Rahner hopes to offer exegetes a dogmatic conception of Christ's self-consciousness and knowledge more compatible with their findings (method, 198f).

Skipping the history of this problem, Rahner launches into an analysis of human knowing which he maintains has a multi-layered structure. This allows that something can simultaneously be known and unknown depending on the dimension of consciousness and knowledge engaged (examples, 200). Despite the many distinctions they have drawn, theologians generally assume objectified knowledge. Such knowledge is analogous to viewing an object in a mirror. Rahner points out two facts: 1) there is also an a priori, unobjectified knowledge about oneself, and this is the basic condition of the spiritual subject, the condition for the possibility of knowing or freely choosing any particular thing; 2) the nescience so abhorred by the Greeks is actually something positive: an opening out of space for freedom and action which can be more significant than the mere presence of a certain reality. It is also a condition for the possibility of human freedom.

Rahner comes to the heart of his reflection by asking the valid theological reasons to "ascribe to Jesus even during his life on earth the kind of direct vision of God" (202). Broadly speaking two groups of answers are given. The *extrinsic view* holds it is morally necessary for Jesus to have certain perfections (not ontologically bound up with the hypostatic union) for the furtherance of his mission. But prophets can be prescient without access to an immediate vision of God. Any appeal to the magisterium merely begs the question. The *intrinsic view* holds that any special knowledge is intrinsic to the hypostatic union, and whatever is not part of it is not part of Christ's knowledge and self-consciousness. Rahner maintains this view and uses a Thomistic metaphysics of being and self-awareness to defend it (205f).

How is one to conceive the direct union of Christ's human consciousness with God as implied by the hypostatic union? Rahner insists we rid ourselves of the imaginative schema of the divine essence being present as if it were an object being looked at by an observer standing opposite it. This view is both unnecessary and false. Consider instead the direct presence of God within Christ's soul as grounded in the substantial root of his created spiritual nature. Then awareness of divine sonship need not be thought of as object-like confrontation with God. Situated at the subjective pole of Christ's consciousness, it is comparable to any human being's knowledge and consciousness of one's direct presence to God as a spiritual self.

Rahner offers concluding remarks. The view he proposes is reconcilable with a genuinely human spiritual history and development of the man Jesus. Just as we come to ourselves only in the course of long experience through which we learn to express to ourselves what we are and have indeed always been, so Christ's consciousness also realized itself only gradually during his spiritual history. "We can, therefore, speak without qualms about a spiritual and indeed religious development in Jesus" (211). This can be seen not as pedagogical accommodation but as the personal history of his own self-interpretation. This theory has the added value of being able to lay aside the troublesome question of infused knowledge. To those who might object that Rahner's approach introduces nescience and therefore diminution into the soul of Jesus, Rahner argues first there is no binding magisterial teaching the preclude some form of nescience, and secondly, without it Jesus lacks an essential condition for the possibility of exercising human freedom. Rahner concludes with a succinct summary in thesis form (215).

5.10 Reflections on the Concept of *Jus Divinum* in Catholic Thought

Über den Begriff des "Jus divinum" im katholischen Verständnis
{2.5}   *Existenz und Ordnung. Festschrift für E. Wolf* (Frankfurt/M. 1962)
62-86.

Abstract: Rahner suggested modification of the concept of an unalterable *jus divinum* insures the notion of genuine divine law and at the same time explains historical development more easily and less artificially.

Topics: LAW, divine; MAGISTERIUM; REVELATION and historical development.

Subsidiary Discussions: Nature and form (221ff); Revelation, close of (231ff); Revelation as decision (233ff); Revelation, post-Apostolic (241f).

Precis: Divine law is the declaration that a certain norm of positive law which neither flows from natural law nor is simply a positive decree of the church is unalterable and cannot be repealed because it can be traced back to a positive ordinance of the founder of the church. Difficulties surrounding this notion for the most part center on proving the historical connection between a particular law and the will of Christ (objections, 220f).

Two subsidiary remarks. 1) One must distinguish between the concrete historical form of a divine law and its nature, just as in Thomistic metaphysics one must distinguish between an image and its concept. No divine law can ever be imagined apart from some historical form. And since one must admit that a thing of one nature can appear in a variety of forms, it is no telling criticism when historians complain today's form of a law cannot be found in New Testament times. The important question raised here is how to conceive a change of form which, while leaving its nature untouched, does justice to the way it obviously developed historically. 2) After a summary of point 1 (223), Rahner asks how theologians are to identify what is essential in the permanent nature of divine law throughout its changes in history. This question cannot easily be dismissed. Nor can one simply appeal to what tradition has handed on since the foundation of this statement begs the same question. It also leaves unanswered whether a particular law was meant to be binding when it first appeared (summary, 225f). Five considerations follow.

1) *"The historical development of a historical structure is not necessarily reversible simply because the development in question is a state which did not always exist. There are one-way historical processes which are no longer reversible. This is true even if these processes were not necessary, i.e., even when the preceding state was neither a fact nor a necessity which was bound to lead to the state in question."* Rahner argues this is true even for laws which though they came into being at a particular time can nevertheless be valid for all time. Whether, how, and why this logical possibility is actually true is argued below.

2) *"There are processes within a historically existing reality which at least can be recognized as legitimate by nature of this existing reality, even though they spring from a free decision and even though these processes and decisions cannot be proved to be the only possible ones, and hence cannot be proved to be the only obligatory means for the nature of the historically evolving reality."* Just as it is possible for an individual to make a free, contingent and yet binding decision (to marry or remain celibate, the choice of career, etc.) it is equally possible for an institution to do so (state, church, etc.).

3) *"It is possible to conceive of such a historical decision—a decision in conformity with nature even though not necessarily by nature—which is both of a juridical nature and itself creative of law...and irreversible."* Some attribute or dimension of a thing may be actualized at a later stage in its existence and nonetheless be a necessary part of its nature, as sight or the ability to laugh do not exist as actualities in an embryo but belong with absolute necessity to human nature. It remains difficult, however, to judge whether something which is historically established only later belongs necessarily to something's nature or is merely in conformity with its nature and is as such reversible.

4) *"An irreversible, law-establishing decision of the Church which is in conformity with her nature ..can be regarded as jus divinum when it took place at the time of the primitive Church."* Rahner prefers the term "primitive Church" to "apostolic age" because it can include as revelation such things as the writings of St. Paul and the Letter to the Hebrews, and because in this view the apostles were not merely the first generation to transmit revelation but were themselves vessels of revelation. Rahner imagines revelation itself not so much as passively hearing some message as the process of the apostles freely deciding something (e.g., not circumcising gentile converts). As a corollary Rahner discusses the fact such law-establishing, now irreversible decisions could easily have taken the form of a choice among several equally possible physical, moral, or juridical options. Summary (236).

If the process of revelation can be seen as the outcome of free decision it still remains to be discovered what exactly has been revealed in this process of decision. Presuming such a law-establishing process of decision did occur in the primitive church, Rahner bases the legitimacy of calling such decisions revelation because they conform with the nature of the church. The church was fully capable of being convinced that through this process it was fulfilling and developing its nature. The claim the church made decisions binding all future generations is intelligible from the fact it is exactly what one expects the church to do in light of its freedom. Summary (239f).

5) *It must be possible to ask whether there can be a jus divinum which is decided on by the **post-apostolic** Church by an irreversible decision in conformity with her nature.* Rahner merely asks the reader not to be too hasty in refusing to consider this question. A developed theory of post-apostolic revelation (revelation in the early church rather than in the primitive church) might do

more justice to the findings of historians and exorcise the weak notion of *fides ecclesiastica* (in distinction to divine faith) from the theological lexicon.

5.11 On the Theology of the Council
Zur Theologie des Konzils
{1.0}   *Stimmen der Zeit* 169 (1962) 321-339.

Abstract: On the eve of Vatican II, based on dogmatic reflection on the nature of an ecumenical council in general, Rahner asks what can be expected from a council and what would it be dogmatically unjustified and unjust to expect.
Topics: CHURCH, structure of; ECUMENICAL COUNCIL, theology of; EPISCOPATE.
Subsidiary Discussions: Petrine office (248ff); Church, charismatic element in (251ff); Laity (256ff).

Precis: Whereas earlier councils were called to meet particular dogmatic controversies the theme of Vatican II is veiled. To call it a council of renewal hardly distinguishes it from previous councils. Its ecumenical concern is to be met by self-renewal rather than dialogue with separated churches. All we know is it will address sufficiently universal issues appropriate to a general council. Examining the theological nature of a council yields more important insights into possible conciliar agendas than reflecting on various topics.
The structure of the church.
The nature and task of the council arises from the nature and task of the church. The church is constituted and ruled by the college of bishops with the pope at its head. This does not exhaust the nature of the church which also includes a truly charismatic and non-institutional element which is not clearly controllable.

The church as an official institution. The church is not a voluntary association. It is a structured society instituted authoritatively by Christ. Some of its historical changes were determined by his instituting will.

The collegial structure of the official institution. The college of bishops is not a subsequent, secondary union of individual bishops. The college precedes the individual bishop and his rights. The college with the pope at its head is an objectively and juridically superior entity compared with the territorial function of individual bishops. This makes infallibility intelligible as well as a bishop's rights and duties toward the universal church. The ordinary magisterium of the college with the pope at its head exists at all times and not only when assembled in council.

Primacy and episcopate. The college of bishops possesses the highest powers in the church only insofar as it itself is given its unity under and with the pope. We may say, therefore, that in the church there is one supreme holder of the fullness of powers communicated to the church by Christ.

The one ruling power in the church. Conceived of in this way there can no longer be any question whether there is one bearer or two inadequately distinguished bearers of supreme power in the church. This does not deny this one power can be exercised either in the pope acting as head of the college or in council.

The charismatic element in the church. Its institutionally hierarchical constitution does not exhaust the nature of the church. It is easy to get the impression the church and everything in its nature is bureaucratic and totalitarian. But there is also a free, charismatic element in the church. There are unexpected things in the church inspired by the Spirit among the faithful which cannot be planned or institutionalized.

The official and the charismatic element. Although the charism of office and free charism can be united in one person this is not necessarily the case nor is it fair to the office holder to expect or demand it. The church is seen correctly only as the unity between the official and charismatic functions adequately administered by God alone.

The council as an expression of the structure of the church.

The episcopate as a whole. The above permits an understanding of the nature of a council. Canon law merely restates divine law when it says the council possesses the highest authority in the church. This power does not come into being with the convocation of the council, it is merely another way in which the college of bishops can exercise its pre-existing powers.

Representation of all the faithful. Although a council is not representative in the democratic sense, the assembled bishops represent the people as their pastors. This bond between pastors and the faithful has been mandated by Christ in whose eyes, because they are constituted by their mutual faith, both are united as believers and as obedient subjects. This is not to say the current form of representation is optimal or that in the future it could not be constituted differently.

The council and the charismatic element in the church. A council by its nature is the concrete way the whole, always existing, official element of the church (episcopate) can exercise its function. This means it cannot be demanded or expected that a council should be the acting subject and representative of all the charismatic elements in the church. Thousands of demands are made on a council, many of which are contradictory, too parochial, or not yet ripe for consideration. This leaves open the question of whether the church at a given point in time may have within it some defect which keeps it from seeing clearly what the Spirit is urging. Though a council must consider and sometimes judge the charismatic element in the church it can never replace it.

Expectations from the council. A council cannot proclaim essentially new insights into dogmas. It could however attempt to proclaim these doctrines in new ways accommodated to the nature of modern culture. Without altering the truths the church can attempt to rid its teachings of unnecessary obstacles to belief. Rahner is pessimistic the magisterium is capable of many advances where even relatively unfettered theologians have made little progress. This he finds discouraging in today's situation where Christianity is on the defensive world-wide due in great part to the poor way in which it formulates and proclaims the faith. In any case he sees this kind of renewal as more the function of the charismatic element of the church than of the magisterium. In addition, councils have poor track records of reading and responding effectively to the signs of their times (examples, 263, 266). One can only hope the council will not feel compelled to justify itself by reaching for more precise dogmatic formulation of doctrines which in Rahner's opinion are highly inopportune for comment (e.g., role of psychoanalysis, limbo, evolution).

Regarding church discipline there is much the council could and probably will do. These concerns have incubated long enough and only the official function of the church can address them (e.g., relation of pope and episcopacy, decentralization, ecumenism, liturgical reform, renewal of religious orders). Though some of these issues may seem slight and inconsequential they may have an incalculable effect in the future. Still one must be sober, remembering that no law mandating renewal in the church can substitute for the work of the Spirit who alone can change and renew hearts. Hence, we must not expect miracles from the council not even in the area of church discipline.

5.12 The Theology of the Restoration of the Diaconate
Die Theologie der Erneuerung des Diakonates
{1.0}   K. Rahner, H. Vorgrimler, eds., *Diaconia in Christo* (Freiburg 1962) 285-324.

Abstract: Rahner contributes to this complex issue by reframing the question: it is not a matter of restoring a nearly extinct office but of extending the rite and grace of ordination to lay men who are already filling this office.

Topics: DIACONATE; ORDERS, sacrament of;
Subsidiary Discussions: Law, divine (273ff); Celibacy (279f, 292ff); Sacraments (286ff, 304); Orders and women (292); Marriage (294f); Eucharist (298f); Laity (299ff); Priesthood (301ff); Vocation (305ff).
Precis: Synthesizing what is known about diaconate from historical revelation presupposes knowledge of scripture, church history, and the magisterium.
1. Concerning the legitimacy of the question of restoring the diaconate.

   a) Why is it legitimate and potentially fruitful to suggest the restoration of the diaconate despite centuries of suspension by the church?

   b) Presuppositions for an answer to this first question. i) The diaconate is part of the sacramental office instituted by Christ for the church. ii) From New Testament times deacons shared in this office through sacramental ordination to assist church leaders in fulfilling their office. This one nature of diaconal service took many forms. iii) Although it can be a step to priesthood this is not an essential element of diaconal ordination.

c) How to understand the legitimacy of the question about restoring the diaconate. i) Viewing diaconate as a step to priestly ordination is not universal in the church. ii) The fact that for centuries it has been the practice to ordain as deacons only those intending to become priests does not prove this is the best approach or that it is unchangeable.

2. Remarks on the mutual relationship between individual church offices.

a) What is the exact relationship between diaconate and priesthood?

b) It is impossible to argue the division of bishop/priest/deacon goes back to the historical Jesus. Nonetheless, the variability in transmitting office in apostolic times argues the apostles never felt bound by any fixed stipulations of Christ. Since even a partial transmission of office preserves its essential sacramental character the ordination of a deacon remains a sacramental action.

c) This allows Rahner to say the diaconate is undoubtedly a sacrament willed by God insofar as the church is competent to delegate the power of office as it sees fit. From this one cannot insist the church must continue to divide the powers of office in its current manner. It depends on the will and intention of the church. Here arises the possibility of investigating whether the church has "anonymous deacons" those whom it has invested with the duties of office without conferring on them the rite and grace of ordination.

3. Questions concerning the opportuneness of the restoration of the diaconate.

a) A more exact definition of the question. Rahner admits the question of opportuneness can legitimately be posed in ways other than his. Here he is speaking about a diaconate which: i) is transmitted through the sacramental rite of ordination; ii) is not merely a step to priesthood (without judging the value or contemporary practice of transitional diaconate); iii) involves no obligation to celibacy (cf., Section 4); iv) without insisting a restored diaconate is equally pressing in all parts of the world.

b) The basic starting-point for a correct answer of the question. Office and sacramental transmission are not identical. The rite receives its ultimate justification from the office. The opportuneness of reviving the sacramental rite of transmission, therefore, is based on the opportuneness of the existing office. Rahner insists the office of deacon actually exists today in the church and has no need of being restored. The only active question is whether or not those who exercise this office should be strengthened for it with the graces conferred by the sacrament of orders. This would clarify the office, make it more permanent, and enhance its estimation among the faithful.

c) The reasons for the opportuneness of the thus understood restoration of the diaconate. i) Although these factors do not prove it is opportune to restore the diaconate, Rahner mentions shortage of priests; new ministerial needs; the dignity of certain offices now held by laymen which aid the hierarchy; relieving priests of non-essential duties. ii) Rahner lists as decisive

reasons: the office already exists; sacramental transmission of the office is possible; sacramental transmission is fitting (i.e., that where the grace to perform an office is available it should be conferred). Restoration would in no way jeopardize the transitional diaconate. iii) There are no serious objections to the opportuneness of restoring the diaconate, especially since a lay person currently exercising the office without ordination is for all practical purposes a cleric. iv) Rahner admits compelling arguments can be made along other lines by those who disagree with his approach. He neither challenges nor defends the practice of limiting diaconal ordination to men.
4. Diaconate and celibacy. This question must be viewed from the nature of the office or from its intrinsic significance for the church. Unlike priesthood, Rahner finds no inner affinity between celibacy and the office of deacon. Not imposing celibacy does no harm to the status a celibate priesthood.
5. Office and grace of office.

a) Not only has the office of deacon assumed many forms over the years, its essence remains comparatively fluctuating and contradictory. Although it's two major elements, liturgical and pastoral, can be performed together or independently, the two are essentially united in Eucharist as the central self-realization of the church in love and service.

b) It is as difficult to establish clear boundaries between the tasks of deacon and laity as between those of laity and hierarchy. Rahner suggests the lay person is called to practice the love of Christ in his proper situation in life. The hierarch is sent out to make every situation in life his proper area of ministerial concern.

c) The offices of deacon and priest are also difficult to differentiate. Their relationship is clouded because in the Latin church priests are generally also ordained deacons. This does not, however, preclude bishops from asking deacons to assist them directly even with work seldom entrusted to a priest.

d) Ordination is not magic. It is God's promise to aid the ordained over the course of his lifetime to the extent he opens his soul more and more to this grace by trying to do justice to his office with God's help.
6. Full-time and part-time diaconate. Vocation is not distinguished from job as full- or part-time activities. Vocation/apostolate, whether full- or part-time, is the existential formative principle of one's life. Only those disposed to such a commitment should be ordained. It is not an honor or reward.
7. Remarks about certain practical norms for the restoration of the diaconate. The following self-evident conclusions reveal that a restored diaconate is not as radical a proposition as some may think.

a) A permanent diaconate would not threaten the transitional diaconate.

b) Diaconal ordination is appropriate where the office already exists (catechists, administrators, etc.). One need not create artificial offices. Not every area of the world would restore the diaconate. Skeletal legislation should leave ample room for local interpretation and implementation.

c) Skeletal legislation which allows for local variations should include the requirement that bishops assess candidates' qualifications. It should set any rules for celibacy, and provide for easy laicization where necessary.

d) Deacons will have the right to assist at liturgy, perhaps in an expanded role. The more pastorally useful it is the more it will be respected.

e) Regarding dress and demeanor it is enough for the general instruction to say deacons should follow the direction of their bishop. Any specific rules should flow from what is required by the office, not by ordination to office.

f) The obedience the ordained owe their bishops includes: i) exercising one's office as perfectly as possible; ii) assisting at liturgy to the degree desired by the bishop; iii) leading a life in keeping with his ordination.

g) After ordination the church must continue to provide the deacon's livelihood at least at the previous level. Ordination increases the church's obligation to see to the welfare of the deacon and his family.

h) Diaconal training: α) He must receive a general level of education comparable to that of an educated Christian layman in that region; β) be professionally trained to fulfill any particular office entrusted to him; γ) the formation period will be relatively long to insure his quality; δ) religious/ spiritual instruction should accompany training for liturgical service.

i) The bishop will aid the deacon to live a wholesome Christian life, whether the deacon is married or single. Daily Eucharist will be central.

j) It seems inappropriate to insist deacons receive minor orders.

5.13 Some Remarks on the Question of Conversions

Einige Bemerkungen über die Frage der Konversionen
{1.5}   *Catholica* 16 (1962) 1-19.

Abstract: Rahner examines the many factors in today's world which cast doubt on the urgency of Catholics proselytizing other Christians: e.g., growth of neo-paganism, the ecumenical movement, the complexity of modern theology.

Topics: CONVERSION; ECUMENISM.

Subsidiary Discussions: Church, true (325ff); Neo-paganism (319f, 327); Motives (321f); Mission mandate (323, 326); Heresy/schism (330ff); Petrine office (333f).

Precis: Since the Catholic Church claims to be the true church of Jesus Christ to the exclusion of all others, it must oblige adults to join through a free act regardless of the political or social consequences converts might suffer. This applies to non-Catholic Christians and to non-Christians. But the ecumenical movement, insofar as it aims at Christian rapprochement, must not aim at individual conversions. Hence, bishops are justified in assigning a low priority to such proselytizing activities. This does not, however, abrogate the responsibility of the church to seek individual conversions, especially insofar as the church sees itself as not simply helpful but necessary for salvation. Because Catholics cannot embrace the view that all Christian sects share equal rights, they approach conversion differently from non-Catholic Christians.

Although non-Christians have a grave objective obligation to become Catholic there is a difference between this objective obligation and one's subjective realization of such an obligation. This sensitivity is markedly different from the attitudes prevailing in Reformation times. Because today we realize the immeasurable subjective conditioning of individual knowledge we can presume "good faith" on the part of the unconverted. Although this presumption raises problems (319), not presuming good faith either supposes the unconverted are stupid or that God's salvific will is ineffective.

Many psychological influences can obscure the church's claim in concrete cases, both for the individual and for an entire society. Rahner offers two observations: 1) the rise of anti-religious hostilities in the last century weakened the effectiveness of the church in areas not already predominantly Catholic; 2) the growth of neo-paganism has obscured the boundaries and lessened the existential urgency of denominational affiliation. These and other complex factors may influence people's religious decisions without their being fully conscious of them. This makes it difficult to assess the moral correctness and obligation for conversion in concrete cases. It is almost impossible to achieve absolute certitude regarding the motives for conversion either by converts or by their mentors.

In this climate (322) how can one encourage conversions? Conversion has a twofold meaning: objective belonging, and subjective increase in access to saving grace. Both of these "values" are at the root of the divine command to belong to the church. But these two values must often be balanced against one another. Concrete circumstances (education, fervor, physical access) can call into question whether conversion would lead to a subjective increase in saving grace. "In such a case one must surely ask oneself: does the subjective side of such an actually possible Catholic Christianity surpass a non-Catholic Christian life so decisively that this consideration demands going to great pains for the conversion of a Christian?" (325). Nor can Catholics feel malicious joy when non-Catholic Christians lose members to neo-paganism since this diminishes the kingdom of God. As "the whole of Christianity will either live or die together" (328) we must not wish catastrophes on one another.

Rahner next enumerates important areas where Catholics and other Christians could work effectively together: evangelization, exegesis, missionary efforts, pastoral theology, homiletics, etc. (328f). Much of what separates us is not theological, but differences in historically conditioned life-styles, forms of piety, and church polity. Too often theology has exaggerated or invented differences. Recasting our common faith in terms meaningful to modern people could do much to foster unity.

Rahner asks about the permissible time interval between realizing one's obligation to become a Catholic and actually fulfilling this obligation. Deferring for ecumenical considerations is tantamount to denying the obligation (330). Nor is one allowed simply to wait for a denomination to unite with the Catholic Church. This brings up the difference between schism and heresy, and the relationship of church members to their legitimate pastors (330f). Although the situations of the baptized and non-baptized cannot simply be equated (331f) the pastoral approach to one could shed light on the other.

Rahner concludes by questioning the subjective capability of a potential convert to grasp objectively sound reasons for conversion. Today theology is so complex it might be better to leave the question of conversion to the collective reflection of a whole church and not to individuals (333). Or, if one is unwilling to go this far, one must ask whether it is permissible to base the moral and theological lawfulness of conversion on considerations of an indirect or global kind (e.g., basing belief in the Petrine office indirectly on the need for an historical church to have a clear form of apostolic succession). In any case Rahner hopes the church will soon realize how much within itself presents an unnecessary stumbling block to those who earnestly seek salvation. It's clericalism, centralization, and incomprehensible liturgy do not present an inviting picture to the world and must be re-evaluated if the church is to fulfill its mission.

5.14 Dogmatic Notes on "Ecclesiological Piety"

Dogmatische Randbemerkungen zur Kirchenfrömmigkeit
{3.5} *Sentire Ecclesiam. Festschrift für H. Rahner* (Freiburg 1961) 9-44.
Abstract: The church is a reality grasped only by faith. Rahner unfolds three ways the church is significant for Christian piety: it mirrors our existence; it flows from belief in God; it embodies God's universally saving will.
Topics: CHURCH, faith in; ANONYMOUS CHRISTIAN.
Subsidiary Discussions: Faith, *fides explicita/implicita* (345f); Mystery (345f); Dogma, development of (347f); Love of God/neighbor (350); Death (359f); Conversion (361); Mission mandate (361ff).
Precis: *The Church accepts by faith everyone's existence in its ordinariness and burdensomeness, so that we experience our own fate as the fate of the Church and experience ourselves in* **this** *way as her members* (337-349). Although the church is an object of faith one does not believe in the church. Our tendency to personify the church, to think of it as a collective person, introduces this confusion. We are in fact members of the church, parts of its mystical body. This is hard to grasp insofar as one knows oneself to be a pilgrim, far from home, groping in the dark, a sinner filled with chaos. But can't we admit without scandal the same is true of the church? One must struggle to understand the teaching church must also believe; the illuminating church

must endure the darkness; the holy church is also sinful. How can the church not be a pilgrim when we ourselves so clearly are pilgrims?

Rahner expresses this insight in terms of dogmatic theology. The church can be seen in Vatican I's terms as an empirical motive of credibility or as an "object of a necessarily difficult faith which consumes the whole power of one's heart and which is possible only by the miracle of grace" (341). Though these two aspects are intermingled, people today are more apt to struggle to believe in the church because of what they see of it. What does this mean for ecclesiological piety (i.e., for belief becoming active in love) that one believes *in* God but not *in* the church, and that the church is merely an object of one's belief? [This discussion presumes familiarity with Augustine's distinction *credere Deum, Deo, in Deum*.] To believe in God does not mean grasping a proposition. It means encountering and possessing the one who is believed in by a graced act of personal relatedness supported and affected by the reality of the one who is the object of faith. Such faith can only refer to God.

The church can be said to be the "ground of faith." It supports the faith of the individual (344). How else except in union with the church could one have the courage to believe, to make the daring absolute claim that God, infinite Mystery, has communicated his own reality to his creatures in love? The church is also the ground of faith in that it passes on the message of Christ by its teaching and its faith, not only in what is taught authoritatively (*fides explicita*), but more importantly through that faith (*fides implicita*) which overcomes the self and enters into the unspeakable mystery of God. This mystery which abides forever is not achieved by a "formally empty leap away from the propositions into the Mystery, ...[but]... by surrendering one's faith into the faith of believers in general and taking this as the norm of one's faith" (346). This is the ecclesiological character of faith. Rahner now entertains a "limiting digression" into how such faith avoids relativism, how it both humbles and liberates believers, and undergirds development of doctrine.

The Church is an object of faith because we believe in God, and never identify its actual condition with what she believes (349-353). The faith discussed above is not, however a *credere in Ecclesiam* but only a *credere Ecclesiam*, for unlike entrusting oneself to God, one can never personally entrust oneself to the church which is provisional, non-personal, not self-conscious, unable to justify itself or to decide. The church can neither give itself in personal surrender nor can it accept such a surrender. One loves, respects, or is loyal to the church only in a derivative sense. More than likely one loves the people who form the church. But in this very act one loves God and hence the church as well (350).

This distinction between "faith of the church" and "faith in the church" is not petty. Very few people today find their empirical experience of the church a motive for faith compared with the supernatural experience of God's self-testimony. The church is an object of faith because one believes in God. The church becomes for believers an object sustained by faith—a faith always affected anew by God's grace (summary, 352). Rahner concludes this section by taking issue with Augustine's dictum that he would not believe the gospels if the authority of the church did not move him to do so. *The Church is the promise of salvation even for that world which has not yet recognized itself explicitly as a part of the Church* (353-365). Believers today see themselves more as the vanguards of salvation than as it heirs. They do not doubt the church is the ark of salvation, but with a keener appreciation for God's universal salvific will and a deeper awareness that mere church membership never insures salvation, they feel permitted to hope the victory of grace promised to them will be achieved by everyone. People of today think about this far differently than people of Augustine's time. We extend the presumption of good faith even to those outside the official membership of the church. Why? People live side-by-side today with neighbors or even family members with completely different worldviews in an irreducibly pluralistic society. Hence, the only question is how Catholics can simultaneously maintain that the church is the universal path of salvation for everybody *and* hold fast to the practical hope in the certainty of God's universal salvific will.

The answer to this question is to "see the Church as the 'vanguard,' the sacramental sign, the historical tangibility of a saving grace which goes beyond the sociologically tangible and the 'visible' Church, i.e., the grace of an anonymous Christianity which 'outside' the Church has not yet come to itself but which 'within' the Church is 'present to itself'" (356). This view changes everything. Non-believers are not simply outside the stream of salvation; their good will has yet to come to explicit faith. When Christians see themselves as the vanguard of salvation, surrounded not by enemies of the gospel but by people of good faith who are themselves on the way to God, they are no longer anxious. Filled with missionary zeal they aim not at converting others but at making them more conscious of what they already are.

Hence, Christians of today and tomorrow will experience the church not as one sect among many but as "the genuine representation of the nature of man as planned by God" (361). They will see it as the promise made to the non-Christian world to be saved by the church even where it does not become the church we can experience historically. Rahner bolsters this hope for future salvation of anonymous believers with reference to the way Christ was able to save even those who lived before him and knew nothing of him (362f). This does not take the sting out of sin, error, darkness, and the possibility of damnation. We must all continue to work out our salvation in fear and trembling.

5.15 Latin As a Church Language
Über das Latein als Kirchensprache
{0.5} *Zeitschrift für katholische Theologie* 84 (1962) 257-299.

Abstract: John XXIII's apostolic constitution *Verterum sapientia* focuses on Latin as a church language. Rahner offers neither commentary nor criticism. He merely intends to avoid misunderstanding the text or applying it too strictly.

Topics: LATIN; CHURCH, official language of; PRIESTS, formation of.
Subsidiary Discussions: Language (367ff); Liturgy, language of (386ff); Theology, study of (397ff); Philosophy, study of (408ff).
Precis: I. General Consideration.

   1. On the theology of a church language. Any valid comment on Latin as a church language must be based on a theology of language in general and of the church. (Rahner notes that assessing the cultural value and advantages of Latin are not within the ken of the magisterium.) Because language is a constitutive element of human nature each of us has a natural right to employ our mother tongue. The pluralism of languages is both an expression of the sinful gulf between God and us, and a manifestation of God's saving will. Hence, the church while attempting to restore unity to the human family cannot be out to destroy linguistic pluralism. Rahner points to Pentecost as the paradigm when one message was heard by all in many languages, not in one language. Every language is inherently adequate to convey the good news. Though Latin may have an historical advantage in conveying theological or legal concepts, it has no absolute prerogative. Though Latin may be the language of many clerics it is not thereby the language of the church.

   2. Latin as the common language of the one church—in general. Following a brief summary Rahner insists the unity of the church is not merely spiritual. It is also the unity of an historically tangible society which could not do without a common language. What is decisive is not how Latin came to prevail but the practical need for a common language. What reason could there be to renounce Latin as the common language? What can substitute? This is true even for those cultures which owe little to Latin as a formative influence.

   3. Latin as a "secondary" ("dead") language. Latin is unquestionably a dead language. This gives Latin an advantage over the living languages of rival nations. But this does not mean it is immutable, especially since the theological ideas are themselves generated in ever changing modern languages and then translated back into Latin. Summary (282).

   4. Latin as an essential part of a classical education. The church for years has insisted on Latin in junior seminaries. But insofar as their education must make seminarians men of their increasingly complex times, one should not be surprised to find less room for Latin in today's curriculum. In addition one can hardly expect Asians and Africans to have the same relationship to Latin as those raised in western cultures.

II. Latin in the liturgy. Many parts of the Catholic liturgy are no longer in Latin (e.g., penance, benedictions, sermons). Hence, the real question is establishing the proper proportion of Latin in the liturgy. There is no "sacred language" in an absolute sense. God does not speak only Latin. Again Rahner dismisses Latin's claim to immutability and hence to greater clarity. Modern languages are equally clear and have the advantage of being broadly understood. The only serious argument that can be offered for retaining Latin in the liturgy is the unity of a neutral language of worship for the many linguistically differentiated people. But does this value outweigh the spiritual benefit of adopting the vernacular? Rahner wonders whether Vatican II will allow greater use of the vernacular to achieve full, active, meaningful participation in liturgy.

III. Latin as an administrative language of the universal church. The utility and necessity of Latin is seen most directly and self-evidently in the administration of the universal church, especially in magisterial teaching. All priests should be proficient enough in Latin to read church documents. But this argument has its limits especially since local councils use vernacular languages. One must also question the reasonableness of insisting that those working in mission areas write to Rome in Latin.

IV. Latin as the language of the ecclesiastical sciences.

1. Latin as the language of present-day theological research. Latin has almost completely disappeared as the language of theological research. In all fields of theology publication of serious books or periodicals in Latin has ceased. Rahner maintains this change is legitimate because new intellectual insights into our existence arise in the heart and can only be reached in the mother tongue. In addition the sciences with which theologians must stay in closest contact (without ever becoming subordinated to them) also use modern languages. If theologians are to address more than clerics they must abandon Latin. Latin is declining not because theologians are lazy but because of the difficultly in translating the spirit of today into a dead language. Rahner again disputes the claim Latin is superior because it is unchangeable. Though the truths of faith are eternally valid, the concepts and vocabulary in which they are formulated are constantly changing. Theological language may change more slowly than that of other fields but it still changes (summary, 403f).

2. The use of Latin as a teaching language for theology. Latin undoubtedly affords many advantages in the study of the history of certain areas: exegesis, canon law, dogmatic and moral theology, etc. Priests should be able to read Latin documents issued by Rome. Hence, Latin should be taught in seminaries. One can also argue the value of doing some teaching in Latin. But these advantages must not be overestimated. Nor should one be so naive as to overlook the fact that every advantage has disadvantages. Wise choices are always a matter of balance and compromise. Among the disadvantages of Latin is the unfair burden it places on non-Western priests and theologians;

its inability to reach a student's heart; the difficulty of translating what is learned in Latin back into sound pastoral preaching. Rahner also discusses the special problem of studying biblical exegesis in Latin (414f) when most of the scholarly articles, theological and scientific, are in modern languages. The study of philosophy presents a similar problem (408ff).

Rahner offers some practical suggestions. Training to read Roman documents does not demand using Latin for instruction in every field of theology. Latitude must always be given in applying these standards to various countries. Since Rome would never oblige any course of action which brought grave disadvantages in its wake, Rahner proposes a compromise. Exegesis, dogmatic and moral theology, and canon law should be taught basically in Latin while allowing for the use of ancillary materials, lecture summaries, question and answer sessions, and seminars in modern languages.

5.16 Some Theses on Prayer "In the Name of the Church"

Thesen über das Gebet "in Namen der Kirche"

{3.5}   *Zeitschrift für katholische Theologie* 83 (1961) 307-324.

Abstract: Prayer is efficacious only to the degree it manifests supernatural faith, hope, and love. Simply offering prayer "in the name of the church" (whether Mass or obligatory Divine Office) adds nothing to God's glory.

Topics: PRAYER, ecclesial; CHURCH, prayer in name of; SACRA-MENTS, efficacy of.

Subsidiary Discussions: God, glory of (420ff); Grace, sanctifying (422f); Anonymous Christian (425f); Church, treasury of (429); Divine Office (435); Eucharist, value of (436f).

Precis: 1. The nature of prayer in general. Rahner's defines prayer as an act by which the whole person is actualized and surrendered to God.

2. The value of prayer in general. Prayer's nature/value depends on the nature/dignity of this self-surrender, its intensity and existential depth.

3. The increase of the (external) glory of God. Rahner distinguishes objective (material) from formal (subjective) giving glory to God. Every creature gives objective glory merely by existing. Formal glory is given when free creatures acknowledge God's infinite superiority through morally good acts. Objective giving of glory is only a means to giving formal glory. It is possible God may be glorified objectively without there being any formal glory, although such a material expression may subserve those beings who are actually giving formal glory to God through participation in those acts.

Hence, all human acts which are not absolutely good give only objective glory to God (e.g., when sinners pray, celebrate sacraments, or exercise authority in the church) even though these acts may be effective instrumentally by the power of Christ who willed them. Such prayers as these said "in the name of the Church" are effective by reason of ecclesiastical commission alone. Pious people could attain the fruits of a such prayers or sacraments by their objective sign when made in the name of the church. But such prayer does not produce any new supplicatory value before God. And where neither priest nor believer pray with devotion, even if they pray in the name of the church, such prayer is not only unproductive, it is an insult to God.

4. The nature of prayer, insofar as it takes place by supernatural sanctifying grace. A person whose nature has been divinized through sanctifying grace (God's self-communication through uncreated grace) is actualized by acts of faith, hope and love exercised in prayer. One's nature is surrendered to God and actually united with God in this way. Only such prayer aroused and animated by supernatural grace can be called a salvific act. It would be blasphemous to account some simply objective, material form of prayer to have greater dignity, even if it is mandated by the church.

5. Increase in the value of prayer. The dignity, merit, and intercessory power of prayer increase in the same measure as the divinization of the individual. This divinizing grace itself is increased by prayer. Prayer can become more zealous and intense when one is conscious of being commissioned and juridically obliged by the church to say certain prayers (e.g., Divine Office). But merely fulfilling the objective, material obligation has no value before God, even if it is done in the name of the church.

6. The prayer of the just, insofar as it takes place in and through the church. What has been said about the nature and value of supernatural prayer can also be deduced from Christ's union with the believer who prays. Insofar as union with Christ is also union with his mystical body, the church, the value of prayer can be seen as a consequence of this union. To the difficult question of the efficacy of the prayers of those just people who are not officially members of the church, Rahner suggests the notion of anonymous Christianity. He concludes the prayers of church members are not by dint of membership of higher supernatural value than the prayers of non-members.

7. Prayer in common. **a)** Communal prayer possesses a special efficacy because it is apt to be said with greater zeal, and because of Christ's promise to be with those gathered in his name. **b)** Communal prayer also receives special efficacy from the mystical body of Christ. God calls us to salvation as members of one community—the kingdom of God. Nowhere does this interdependence become more apparent than in communal prayer. It was for this very reason Christ promised special graces to this type of prayer.

8. Prayer as an act of the church. Two extremes must be avoided when speaking about the church: personalizing the community of the church as if it were an individual; underestimating the true unity of the church and its members. **a)** There are several ways of speaking of an act of the church: i) when a duly authorized person exercises the *potestas jurisdictionis* or *potentia ordinis* (although this does not proceed from sanctifying grace); ii) when any member of the church performs any saving act (always an act of grace, and hence an act of the church which builds up the mystical body of Christ); iii) when the ordained call forth, direct, or intensify those saving acts of the members (e.g., administer the sacraments). **b)** It follows: i) Every supernatural prayer (even if not commissioned by the hierarchy) which flows from the grace of Christ, and hence takes place within his mystical body, is an act of the church. ii) This is more the case with communal prayer, even if it is non-liturgical. The dignity of this prayer comes from the grace which inspires it not from its being commissioned. "The *objective* value of strictly liturgical prayer can never, purely as such, replace that value of prayer ... springing from a pure and humble heart" (432).

9. The notion of *opus operantis Ecclesiae* as applied to prayer. **a)** Any prayer can be called *opus operantis Ecclesiae* if and insofar as it takes place at the command of and in accordance with church norms, even though when said by an impenitent sinner it possesses no meritorious power, no formal glory being given to God. Any grace which flows from it arises from the unfailing intercessory power of the church. To say such rites were efficacious apart from this power would be to invoke magic. **b)** Prayer offered in the state of grace is an *opus operantis Ecclesiae* insofar as it springs from the formal, predefined and efficacious grace by which God wills the church to be holy. The mistake here is to think all prayer is efficacious simply because the term *opus operantis Ecclesiae* is applied to it. This confuses sign and thing signified.

10. The prayer of the breviary in particular. All that has been said above applies to the recitation of the Divine Office. Its value springs from the grace with which it is recited. Nothing is gained or lost if it is imposed as an obligation by the church.

11. The Mass celebrated in the name of the whole church. No Mass adds anything to the value of Christ's one sacrifice. Any added value comes from the formal glory given God by a worthy celebrant and zealous congregation. The whole church benefits from a particular Mass in that the prayers of those actually participating give God formal glory and thus build up the church.

5.17 The "Commandment" of Love in Relation to the Other Commandments

Das "Gebot" der Liebe unter den anderen Geboten

{4.0} *Wanderwege. Festschrift für I.F. Görres* (Paderborn 1961) 129-150.

Abstract: Rahner asks how love is related to other moral virtues. How can love sum them up without subsuming them? In what sense is love a command, and what precisely does it command? How are faith and love related to justification?

Topics: LOVE; VIRTUE, moral.

Subsidiary Discussions: Becoming (441f); God as horizon (446f); Aquinas on love (447ff); *Engagement fondamental* (448f); Sin, mortal/venial (449f); Morality (454f); Justification/ sanctification (448ff, 457f).

Precis: The New Testament commandment to love may seem like one among many commandments. But it is also *the* first commandment, which fulfills the whole law. Is this commandment simply the collective name for all the other commandments? Are they all merely partial formulations of this one command? Hence, the dilemma: "love is everything and not yet everything; where there is love, there is everything, and yet there are other values besides love which must not be excluded from the realm of what is moral" (439). This dilemma cannot be solved by saying love can be possessed only if all the other virtues are possessed, or one can have other virtues without having love. How are love and the other virtues related? How can love include every virtue and every virtue include love, and there still be a real plurality of virtues?

Virtues must not be regarded statically in their nature, but dynamically in the history of their realization. Morality is the free personal acceptance of one's own nature which is the mystery of love. This happens only gradually in an act of becoming. Applying the philosophical notion of becoming (441f) to this journey of existential self-realization Rahner concludes that any "already" acquired individual virtue becomes perfect only once it is really integrated into the totality of the acceptance of one's own nature, i.e., love. Hence, every virtue which is not love may be regarded—insofar as it tends towards love—as a moment in the movement towards it, and only in this way can we speak of it as a *moral* virtue; or it may be regarded as a moment in and of love, and only to this extent is it complete in its own nature" (442f). This explanation does not, however, simply reduce love to the sum of its preceding moments. Love can only be explained in terms of those moments when individuals learn who and what they are as a whole person when they love.

This does not mean love comes only at the temporal end of the history of the whole person. Love may be present at the beginning in the very core of the person yet need a lifetime to realize itself. Before they are fully self-realized we are dealing with individual virtues which are not the same as love. When one is completely self-realized then we have only love. Rahner attempts to clarify this further in the realm of sin and forgiveness (444ff). There mere "attrition" would seem to be impossible since even imperfect contrition (which presumes the love of God) would seem indistinguishable from perfect contrition. Rahner disposes of this difficulty by pointing out that faith, imperfect contrition, etc. are really a beginning of love—a dynamism which need not necessarily have reached its goal to the degree that this beginning stage can always already be named after its natural goal: love. This preserves the distinction between real virtue and love.

It is imperative to conceive the moral virtues from the very start as an internally connected history of realizing one's nature. This history is grounded in the fact that unlike other virtues, the formal object of love is not one object alongside others but *God*, the source and transcendental ground of all values. This absolute value is the goal in which every object and thus every single value is grasped. Love, which also tends to this goal is the free and explicit acceptance of this basic dynamism which is the root of everything else. Insofar as the free acceptance of any morally lawful individual object is already an implicit acceptance of this transcendental dynamism, such moral decisions are already love. Since one can decline any particular moral good, this tendency toward love is not inevitable. The historical nature of freedom and the development of love can be seen as this dialectic of "already love" and "not yet necessarily love."

Rahner comments on Aquinas placing love at the very beginning of human self-realization (447ff) due to his inability to conceive a free act except in virtue of an original orientation to its goal as such: the love of the absolute Good or Being. This explains Aquinas's indifference to psychological stages in the process of justification, and his presumption that accepting justification is a momentary event without temporal duration. Modern theology, on the other hand, assumes a temporal succession of acts prior to justification without carefully explaining how or why this can be the case.

When love is seen as simply the last in a series of moral tasks the problem of temporal series seems to disappear. But if love is seen as the total act of self-realization and commitment the question actually becomes more difficult. It seems to demand at least a formal act, an *engagement fondamental* at the outset in light of which "the individual virtues in their very individuality can no longer be understood as anything more than particular interpretations and expressions of the one basic virtue of love (the *mater et radix* of all virtues, as St. Thomas puts it), the other virtues being individual virtues insofar as they do not fulfill the whole of the ground on which they all necessarily stand from the very start" (449). Rahner enlists the distinction between mortal and venial sin to argue that such partial acts are possible: one can commit one's freedom without committing the whole of it.

Modern theology has thereby reached a much more serious consideration of the historical dimension than Aquinas had, although he is right to warn against conceiving of temporal succession too naively. As the source of our spiritual history, love governs the development of our spiritual lives into individual virtues. The fundamental decision to love roots these virtues in the core of the spiritual person and helps perfect them. Hence, individual virtues can exist because: 1) they are based on the many facets of human nature; 2) one can realize and accept them in temporal succession without having already realized oneself completely in one love.

There is another way to regard the mutual relationship between love and the other virtues. Other virtues and commandments demand certain tangible achievements. Love demands the entire person. But love is never fully performed or negotiated. It is always on the way to itself. It is measureless. It is only true love today "to the extent in which it reaches out to become more than it is today, only if it is really on the way and forgets what is now, reaching out for what lies ahead of it" (452). This raises the question of what is really demanded by the Christian moral law of love. With every other virtue one knows what is demanded. One can weigh its risks and benefits. Other virtues can be justified in relation to something else. But this is impossible with love. Love is its own justification when it is radical and complete.

Love, the strange, incomprehensible movement of an unconditional and trusting surrender to the unknown, is the real concern of Christian morality. This answers a number of questions (list, 454). [Rahner pays special attention to how this understanding combines the Synoptic's teaching on love with the Pauline notion of *Pneuma*.] Our basic capacity to love is our ultimate structure which alone expresses us perfectly. This capacity is boundless. Sin is the lesser love which, because it refuses the greater love is no love at all. This truth is objectified in the various commandments. One may speak of a "command to love" insofar as it commands one to fulfill oneself. It commands one to accept the love in which God gives not some thing but himself. This can be called a commandment only in an analogous sense to the other commandments which we are released from only when we fulfill them. Love, on the contrary, commands the freedom to love. This is only possible because God has already given what God commands. Love is not the power to fulfill a law; rather this law is given because love is already there as a possibility to be liberated.

Rahner finds this reconciles somewhat the Catholic/Protestant controversy over justifying acts (457f). "Faith *as* a 'different' 'virtue' from love is not indeed the whole of man's grace-supported attitude towards God and hence cannot by itself constitute the process of justification" (457). At the same time it must be admitted that faith is the source of justification. Every age and individual has certain "catch words" (faith, love, etc.) which encapsulate its grasp of existence. These only become false when the part is mistaken for the whole. Thus, even love must humble itself and divide and enter into the different moments of moral existence which are not love.

5.18 The Saving Force and Healing Power of Faith
Heilsmacht und Heilungskraft des Glaubens
{1.0}   *Geist und Leben* 34 (1961) 272-277.
Abstract: Faith has the power to transform otherwise meaningless suffering into a share in the redeeming death of Christ. By comparison, physical healings (miracles) though they occur, are secondary to what they signify.
Topics: FAITH; CHRISTIAN LIFE, illness; DEATH.
Subsidiary Discussions: Miracles (465ff).
Precis: This is a brief look at faith and illness which the New Testament insists are connected, though Christian opinion differs greatly over exactly

how. To begin with, faith is not indifferent to illness. It is seen neither as the product of personal guilt nor as a mere sign of psychic conflict. Two factors are always present together in concrete illness: an element of imposed fate and an element of freedom. Freedom allows one to accept an imposed illness in an absolutely definitive way and thus to transfigure it. Faith sees in illness the essential human condition, i.e., fated yet free and invited to make a free response. To the eyes of faith illness is a sign of the sin and brokenness of the world in general.

Illness also reveals to the eyes of faith that life is a continuous dying which ends and climaxes in death. Death is not merely the wages of sin. It is the manner of our redemption wherein we have the power to make the death of the Lord our own. How we undergo illness and suffering readies us for death. Illness has a profoundly dialectical nature which manifests sin and redemption, despair and belief. Because of the differences in their attitudes two people can have the same disease and yet two very different illnesses.

In this light we can see the real and ultimate nature of the saving power of faith. In the Christian understanding faith always saves because it changes illness from a degrading occurrence to an overcoming of sin by sharing in the death of Christ. Faith offers a way for us to accept death in union with Christ. Thus, faith transforms something senseless into a saving gift.

Although faith can restore health this is a secondary matter, but one which should not surprise us since restoration of health is a sign—a pledge of absolute health and eternal life. Indeed, the New Testament teaches the eschatological reign of God has already begun. It is difficult to determine empirically exactly how the saving power of faith affects illness (464f). For as much light as psychology may bring to the subject it neither rules out nor explains away the action of the always incomprehensible grace of God.

This brings Rahner to Jesus' miracles which do not so much authenticate his mission as reveal the content and nature of that mission. His miracles make free faith possible without making it necessary. Instead of performing spectacular physical events Jesus heals. By touching the inmost unity of the sick, Jesus invites their free response of faith. Rahner examines and then discards the notion that miracles call for a suspension of the laws of nature. Summary (467).

5.19 What is Heresy?
Was ist Häresie?
{2.5} A. Böhn, ed., *Häresien der Zeit* (Freiburg 1961) 9-44.
Abstract: The unavoidable pluralism and ambiguity of today's social and intellectual situation insures the existence of a new kind of "cryptogamic" heresy...diffuse, pervasive, ambiguous, and thus extremely hard to combat.
Topics: HERESY; TRUTH.

Subsidiary Discussions: Apostasy (470, 484ff); Revelation (469ff); Truths, hierarchy of (474f, 490f); Anonymous Christian (474f); Propositions (478ff, 506ff); Pluralism, gnosiological (493ff); Magisterium (505ff).

Precis: I. The Christian attitude towards heresy. Because of its definitive ethos of truth, Christianity is uniquely sensitive to heresy. Two factors contribute to this ethos: knowing a unique divine revelation of truth occurred at a particular moment in time and space, and knowing this truth is significant for salvation. Because revelation is essentially historical Christians continually refer back to definite authoritative events. Heresy only arises where the same events are interpreted differently to such a degree the genuine clear relationship among these events is broken. Heresy is only possible where a common religious sphere binds people together. Apostasy occurs when one no longer acknowledges the authority of those events.

As to the saving significance of revealed truths, Rahner notes the tremendous changes in the very notion of truth since 1900 (470ff). Today, apart from brute facts, truth claims are seen as relative opinions of little importance. Salvation seems to depend not on what a person believes but on why and how one has come to believe it. Rahner calls this "a strange subjectivist idea of 'interiority'" which separates the inner world from the outer (472). Because what we think about the outer world changes our relationship to it, Christianity rejects this indifference toward truth and insists some truths can be missed only in a culpable manner. By proving this point (473-475) Rahner hopes to dispel the scandal that surrounds this proposition today and also to clarify Christianity's anti-heretical attitude (475-481).

Without exonerating the excesses of the past, the Christian attitude towards truth explains why the falsehood of heresy was so vehemently opposed. Heresy is an absolute threat to human existence here below and in eternity. Unlike pagans who miss the essential point of Christianity, heretics threaten to lose the clarity which faith has already won. Heretics combat the real and final truth of Christianity in the name of Christianity itself. Rahner dismisses the notion that all differences in truth claims with heretics are simply terminological. Propositions embody meaning in a sacramental unity. To tolerate erroneous formulations reduces life to a game of endless chatter. Finally because Christians know they are not more intelligent than most people, and because they confess to being sinners, they see heresy as a temptation, a seduction and delusion from which they know they are not immune. They must defend against the heretic and themselves.

II. The traditional notion of heresy and of the heretic and the problematic nature of this notion. The church defines a heretic as someone who, after baptism and while retaining the name of Christian, pertinaciously denies or doubts any one of the truths of divine and Catholic faith. This definition itself is problematic. Although one can distinguish material heretics (guiltlessly caught up in error) from formal heretics (subjectively culpable), these categories do not fit the facts. What these two forms of heresy share is both retain the name Christian. Yet if faith is indivisible, in what sense can it be said heretics retain the name Christian (questions, 483)? The vagueness of this characteristic of heresy cannot be solved by reference to the totality or partiality of either the inner attitude of the heretic or of the deposit of Christian doctrine. Heretics retain the name Christian because they hold to enough of the faith which can constitute a salvific reality. Rahner admits this leaves the boundary between heresy and apostasy quite vague along with the question of how much belief in what things constitutes saving faith.

"Retaining the name Christian" gives rise to two further considerations: whether apostasy is possible in an existential environment influenced by the Christian tradition (485-488); the inner essential ambiguity of heresy and the heretic (488-492). On the first issue Rahner argues apostasy is impossible in a unified world society necessarily conditioned by Christianity. His arguments constitute the sociological underpinnings of anonymous Christianity. On the ambiguity of heresy Rahner begins by insisting on the real unity of Christian doctrines which is based on more than the formal authority of the church. Hence, it is possible that in embracing just one doctrine a person may at some level be embracing them all, and conversely that in explicitly denying only one doctrine a person may be rejecting them all. Two things must be remembered: there exits among the doctrines of faith a certain hierarchy such that one may be affirmed and another overlooked or denied (similar to how one can love God yet commit venial sin). Secondly, no heresy is simply error. It is formed and supported by an original experience of some reality and truth. This ambiguity can never be overcome by reflection. Hence, no one can claim to know where the heretic stands in regard to the truth of the faith.

III. The change in form of heresy. Rahner begins with a critique of today's intellectual situation. Compared to past times people today can never hope to master all there is to know. This has an new impact on our spiritual situation insofar as what we do not know includes important perceptions, theories, opinions and postulates. The known world has become pluralistic. Each person comes to a physical limit of what can be known. We cling to islands of meaning in an amorphous mass of information to which new materials are added faster than they can be organized or assimilated. This can be seen in the Babel of modern terminology. It flows from the profusion of experiences which can no longer be reconciled by one individual either outside or within the spiritual realm. As stated earlier this pluralism meets with ambiguity even in the camp of orthodox believers who can never have absolute certitude about what they themselves believe (summary Part II, 497f).

Rahner is now ready to explain his theses about today's new form of heresy. "There is far more 'cryptogamic' heresy today than ever before.... [It] exists also in the Church, alongside her explicit orthodoxy.... [It] has an essential tendency to remain unsystematized, and this fact constitutes its peculiar and extraordinarily dangerous nature.... [It] is very difficult to distinguish it from legitimate tendencies, from the justified spirit of the age, etc." (498). Although theology can analyze this phenomenon in an a priori manner (498f), Rahner prefers an a posteriori approach which combines what has already been said about insurmountable pluralism with the ambiguity surrounding one's faith (499ff). Our spiritual, existential environment is undoubtedly formed in part by heretical influences which can often remain hidden among healthy aspects (e.g., new-found reverence for the human body). This is the essence of a cryptogamic heresy (500).

Because we all conform in some part to the spirit of our times, everyone today is infected with such heresy, although not everyone has succumbed to the disease. This is no less true of the church, an institution made up of people, although it is never overcome by heresy or falls completely away from the truth. Since this heresy exists in and together with its orthodox beliefs no one can take comfort in the mere fact of being a member of the church. Only repeated examinations of conscience can help insure that practical heresy has not arisen even where no theoretical heresy exists.

Cryptogamic heresy finds an ally in the reluctance of people today to be tied down by conceptual formulations in religious questions which they see as "impious, smart, and typically clerical" (503). Such an attitude often leads to a reaction of unthinking traditionalism content with childish formulations of faith. In addition people labor against reflecting on religious concepts since it might disrupt the uneasy truce they have made to have a strong religion which can secure for them the benefits of social community.

The tactics cryptogamic heresy employs to remain latent include an attitude of mistrust and resentment against the magisterium (505f) seen in theologians who skirt difficult or sensitive issues to retain an untroubled position in the church—heresy wearing the garb of indifference. Though God's truth is one and always remains the same and is final, every age must express this truth in formulations appropriate to itself. Dead orthodoxy, freezing the form, is merely one more dangerous form of indifference to the truth of the gospel.

The magisterium is always tempted to combat such heresy with formal authority rather than proper teaching, i.e., positive formulation of the true teaching which alone can uproot error. It often suppresses precisely those theological movements which hold the key to new more adequate formulations. Today's heresy is combated by the conscience of the individual. Only there can one confront the sneaking heresy of false emphasis, balancing as best one can the laudatory initiatives of society's new directions with the doctrines of faith (examples, 509ff). "In this matter, the individual is set and called to a task and responsibility no one else can accomplish for him" (511).

VI. Concerning Vatican Council II
VI. *Neuere Schriften*

German edition: Einsiedeln, Benziger, 1965. Dedicated to his brother
Hugo Rahner on his 65th birthday, 3 May, 1965
U.S. edition: Baltimore, MD, Helicon Press, 1969
Karl-H. and Boniface Kruger, O.F.M., translators

Five essays in the German edition are not in the English edition: *Kirche im Wandel*, 455-478; *Konziliare Lehre der Kirche und künftige Wirklichkeit christlichen Lebens*, 479-498; *Grenzen der Amtskirche*, 499-520; *Der Anspruch Gottes und der Einzelne*, 521-536; *Zur "Situationsethik" aus ökumenischer Sicht*, 545-554.

6.01   The Man of Today and Religion

Der Mensch von heute und die Religion

{1.0}   October 1962 lecture. *Der Seelsorger* 35 (1965) 18-33, revised.

Abstract: People today have become uniquely the world's co-creators along with God. Despite making God seem more remote, God is in fact as accessible to this new age as to any previous age. The church can boldly engage the modern world.

Topics: THEOLOGICAL ANTHROPOLOGY, hominization.

Subsidiary Discussions: Nature (5ff); Creativity (5ff); Ecology (5ff); Freedom (10ff); Responsibility (14f); Death (16f); Church (18ff).

Precis: No single modern trait exhausts human complexity. The tendency to reduce humans to one dimension poses a great danger since openness to our complex nature and its mysterious depths opens us to religion and to God.

1. "[M]an today has clearly and definitively entered in his historical development into the phase of a peculiar creativeness and has become the rationally planning master of action and power both with regard to himself and with regard to his environment" (5). Consequently nature has lost its numinous quality. We no longer simply live in nature. We change it. We are surrounded by things we have made. Even our environment is our creation. We no longer find God in nature as our ancestors did for we are delivered into our own hands and have become our own subjects. We carried the Copernican revolution through from cosmocentrism to anthropocentrism.

2. "[T]he development described above is something inevitable and, in the last analysis...corresponds to the nature of Christianity itself" (9). Christianity maintains our destiny is to become full, free partners with God: co-creators.

3. What is the religious relevance of this situation? God seems more distant. Our inability to see God in nature makes scripture seem quaint—the echo of a long-lost world. But since hominization of the world is inevitable, and the product of Christianity, it possesses a positive meaning and constitutes an undeniable religious task in three ways:

   a) However much we control nature we must still face a future which is ultimately dark, unknowable, and uncontrollable. In this limiting experience the wise rediscover the disposed nature of their existence before God as our ancestors learned it from their contact with nature.

   b) The more we subjugate nature the more responsible we become. Facing the immense burden of our freedom is the peculiarly modern experience of God.

c) The world we construct for ourselves is hard, schematic, and impoverished, having been created by finite beings whose lives are so short. Such a world brings mortality home to us in a new way. Christians who accept this suffering, pain, and death participate in the death of Christ through which God has already irrevocably assumed and transformed death.

Insofar as this new situation is the necessary outgrowth of Christianity, however skeptical Christians may be of the modern scene it is not worse, it is no further from God, no less redeemable, than any past age.

4. Two final points:

a) To Catholics the world is sanctified though not yet sacralized. In this state grace is not co-terminus with the explicit message of faith offered by the visible church, the sacraments, etc. In such a world the effectiveness of the mission of the church remains hidden in silent mystery.

b) In relation to such a world the church itself is constantly changing. Though it remains tentative in its approach to the new order, it can minister in this world without fear for itself or its mission because God has already saved even this modern world. Summary (20).

6.02 A Small Question Regarding the Contemporary Pluralism in the Intellectual Situation of Catholics and the Church

Kleine Frage zum heutigen Pluralismus in der geistigen Situation der Katholiken und der Kirche

{1.0} *Stimmen der Zeit* 176 (1965) 191-199.

Abstract: Given today's irreversible, insurmountable intellectual pluralism how can one honestly embrace or responsibly act on a given worldview. Rahner explores grounding objective certitude in induction à la J.H. Newman.

Topics: PLURALISM; CERTAINTY; FAITH, assent of.

Subsidiary Discussions: Philosophy (25); History (25f, 29); Faith, simple (28f); Dialogue (30).

Precis: Rahner hopes to be excused for raising a seemingly unanswerable question due to the fruitfulness of the discussion it engenders.

A statement of the situation. A rational, apologetic foundation for the Catholic worldview requires many facts, proofs, and solutions to a wide range of questions. Unlike the past when the educated could rightly claim an approximate grasp of all relevant fields, today, due to the explosion of knowledge and increasing specialization, this is impossible. Nor is it sufficient to rely on second-hand reports or on the fruits of teamwork since "One has to travel the road oneself in order to reach the goal in any real sense" (23).

This insurmountable pluralism is true not only between one field and the other but also within each field, e.g., philosophy and theology (25), history and the natural sciences. This situation affects the basic task of creating a valid worldview, even leaving aside the problems introduced when findings in one field contradict those in another. Summary (26f).

The question: In this situation of insurmountable and irreversible pluralism how can we accept responsibility for the worldview we adopt and in good faith base our decisions on it? Must we extend probablism to embrace the whole of the intellectual and moral life? It is not enough to insist on the theoretical unity of truth which eludes our practical grasp, for faith cannot be built on the sacrifice of the intellect. Must our knowledge be direct or can it be proximately adequate, as in the manual's discussion of simple believers (*rudes*)? Or could one opt for a more inductive approach, the convergence of probabilities outlined by J.H. Newman, allowing that objective certitude could be founded on particular rather than universal deductive premises? (28).

It is necessary in today's intellectually plural world to specify how we have the right and duty to believe even before we have adequately worked out all the actual problems of fundamental theology presented by the Catholic worldview. Such an approach would liberate many believers who find it difficult to maintain that those who do not share their worldviews are either unintelligent or obdurate. A move away from deductive analysis would lead to a greater appreciation for how history influences the decision to believe. It would also help define a productive approach to dialogue with non-believers.

6.03 Reflections on Dialogue within a Pluralistic Society
Über den Dialog in der pluralistischen Gesellschaft
{0.5} June 1965 speech upon receiving the Reuchlin Prize in Pfortzheim. *Stimmen der Zeit* 176 (1965) 321-330.
Abstract: Dialogue between worldviews with competing universal claims is uniquely essential today. It can be grounded in the attempt to grasp shared terms and concepts, and the personal existential appropriation of the other.
Topics: DIALOGUE; PLURALISM.
Subsidiary Discussions: Power, coercive (32f); History (36ff); Atheism (37f).
Precis: Our world is pluralistic. This is a problem when those holding diverse attitudes, convictions, and orientations all claim universality and desire to convert everyone else. If diverse worldviews are meant to coexist and to dialogue, then how is this possible? Real dialogue must be free from coercion. But once we exchange force for talk is dialogue ever more than propaganda? Does it necessarily degenerate into polite tea party conversation? "Is there something like an unending dialogue which is meaningful even though it never comes to a conclusion in the realm of final and yet tangible 'results' but merely has an 'eschatological' hope and therefore meaning?" (34).

This need for dialogue is unique to our times. Formerly people lived isolated from other points of view. In today's society which is heterogeneous, united by technology, and aware of world history, and in which particular worldviews necessarily continue to live concrete cultural and institutional lives, dialogue is essential for co-existence. But is it possible?

One view says no: dialogue in permanently pluralistic societies becomes senseless either because it must remain without success or because it annuls the universal claim of a particular worldview. Rahner counters that dialogue is possible and potentially fruitful because: 1) Every worldview is subject to the laws of history. There is a difference between where it is and where it is going, between what it means and the historically-bound words and concepts it uses to express itself. 2) Dialogue is possible where one seeks the total inclusion of the existential experience of the other, without which we cannot understand or judge the other's universal claim. These are the grounds for ongoing dialogue which today demands more than toleration. It demands risking oneself. It demands commitment, humility, and in the final analysis, love.

6.04 Ideology and Christianity

Ideologie und Christentum
July 1964 talk to Catholic students of the University of Erlangen.
{1.0} *Concilium*, I (1965) 475-483, German Edition.

Abstract: Contrary to appearances Christianity is not an ideology. Humility and tolerance must always guard against its tendency to become one.

Topics: IDEOLOGY; CHRISTIANITY.

Subsidiary Discussions: Metaphysics (48ff); Pluralism (48ff); Experience, transcendental (50ff); Grace (51f); History (52ff); Anonymous Christian (56ff); Society and responsibility (55f); Tolerance (56f).

Precis: 1. What is ideology? It is a voluntary, fundamental closing oneself to the "wholeness" of reality by turning something partial into an absolute with a view toward determining the norm of life for the whole of society. There are three forms of ideology: immanent absolutizing a particular thing (e.g., nation); transmanent absolutizing a general ideal (e.g., brotherhood); transcendent absolutizing a process of overcoming every self-proclaimed absolute, a program of unrestrained "openness" (e.g., Communism).

2. How Christianity resembles ideology. **a.** To a skeptic or relativist who reduces valid experience to the empirical, Christianity is necessarily an ideology. **b.** Having often been co-opted by society to further political aims Christianity can be confused with politics and thus appear as ideology. **c.** Confusing the forms in which Christianity necessarily expresses itself for the substance of Christianity can make it seem an ideology. **d.** A radically pluralistic society will be uncomfortable with any institution making universal claims and will call it ideology.

3. Why Christianity is not an ideology. **a.** It is illegitimate to reduce experience to what is empirical. A pluralism of worldviews does not prove every worldview is false. Such claims are themselves metaphysical and go beyond the strict empiricism of their proponents. **b.** Since Christianity finds its fulfillment in the midst of human transcendence (which rises above all intra-mundane transcendence because of its orientation to the absolute mystery of God) it cannot be an immanent ideology. **c.** Insofar as Christianity is an historical religion which finds its ultimate moment in the unsurpassable act of the incarnation of Jesus, it cannot be a transmanent or transcendent ideology. **d.** Ideologies are by nature exclusive. They cannot admit the validity of any other approach to their goal. Christianity does not restrict that which constitutes its proper reality to itself (cf., anonymous Christianity).
4. Consequences. **a.** While Christianity can set forth norms of human conduct based on the ultimate truth of human life, it remains open regarding specific programs which are determined by historical circumstances. It follows: i) the church cannot be the standard bearer of particular reform programs; ii) individual Christians remain responsible for addressing their own social milieu. **b.** to avoid ideology Christianity must be characterized by tolerance among its members, between churches, and towards non-Christians. **c.** Christianity must always be on guard against becoming an ideology. It does this by trusting in God more than in its own doctrinal and institutional forms.

6.05 Marxist Utopia and The Christian Future of Man
Marxistiche Utopie und christliche Zufunft des Menschen
May 1965 talk in Salzburg to Paulists on "Christianity and Marxism."
{1.0}   *Orientierung* 29 (1965) 107-110.
Abstract: Christianity viewed as the religion of the absolute future will always play a role in planning the world's categorial future.
Topics: UTOPIAS; FUTURE; ESCHATOLOGY; CHRISTIANITY.
Subsidiary Discussions: Marxism (59f); God (62f); Atheism (63); Grace (63); Ideology (64); Anonymous Christian (65); Church (67f).
Precis: 1. Christianity is a religion of the future: "the proclamation of an absolute becoming which does not continue into emptiness but really attains the absolute future which is indeed already moving *within* it" (60). Human nature is the possibility of attaining the absolute future and not a contingent state which will itself be surpassed.
2. Christianity is the religion of the absolute future. The decisive question for metaphysical anthropology is whether the future towards which we project ourselves is merely a categorial future or the unsurpassable, infinite future. Christianity holds the latter. This future and its acceptance is our ultimate task, the condition for the possibility of engaging meaningfully in

the spacio-temporal world. It is both the absent world of possibility and hope, and the already communicated and attained future. It follows that the future cannot simply be another object in the world but is the unspeakable mystery which precedes and surpasses all individual cognition and each individual action *on* the world. This future is God; it is grace (62). Summary (63).

3. Christianity has no utopian ideas about a future in this world. Although Christianity insists all will be judged as to how we opened ourselves to this absolute future, it has nothing to say about the collective. By remaining silent regarding categorial plans it avoids becoming an ideology. It does insist that planning should move the world towards our greatest possible liberation from the dominion of nature, and the attainment of the greatest possible scope of freedom. The value of each individual is provided solely by the absolute future of each. Where the absolute future fuses the love of God and neighbor into one commandment there can be no purely intra-mundane future.

4. Christianity has inestimable significance for the movement towards genuine and meaningful earthly goals. Christians have no monopoly in creating the world's future since all who serve their neighbors selflessly are implicitly serving God. Christianity does have the explicit responsibility:
-to defend the present and future from being sacrificed for some purported good that is yet to come;
-to defend against equating anyone's worth with his/her ability to contribute tangibly to the future;
-to insist on love as the only acceptable path to the true future.

5. Christianity as the religion of the absolute future will always remain.

a. Insofar as the question of the ultimate meaning of intra-mundane activities will never disappear (but will in fact increase as we become more free from the fetters of nature) Christianity will never disappear.

b. Insofar as the true striving for the future must always manifest itself concretely there will always be a church, although we cannot predict its concrete form other than to say it will be controversial, and therefore a small group of free believers in the absolute future. It is therefore, in the church's best interest to live in a free and pluralistic society in which it will in all probability remain a minority.

6.06 Philosophy and Theology
Philosophie und Theologie
September 1961 lecture in Salzburg to a symposium on "The
    Significance of European Culture for Universal History."
{1.5} *Kairos* 4 (1962) 162-169.
Abstract: Since philosophy is an essential part of theology which exists both as an independent science and as the condition for the possibility of theology, perhaps Western philosophy should be enlisted to proclaim Jesus Christ.

Topics: PHILOSOPHY and theology; THEOLOGY and philosophy.
Subsidiary Discussions: Nature and grace (72f); Grace and nature (72f); Revelation (73ff); Revelation history (77f); Anonymous Christian (79).
Precis: What constitutes the unity and diversity of philosophy and theology? Rahner discards the common view that they are two discrete sciences which occasionally meet to talk. He frames the issue in terms of nature and grace. Just as nature is an inner moment of grace, so philosophy is an inner moment of theology. Just as revelation is always already theology (insofar as any revealed message must find a place among the hearer's pre-existing knowledge), theology is always already philosophy (insofar as all our knowledge comes already wrapped in language, concepts, and thought). Rahner defines philosophy as "the methodically exact...representation and articulation of [one's] original and never quite attained self-understanding" (74).

How does theology retain its independence from a knowledge different from itself, i.e., from philosophy? Philosophical knowledge differs from revealed knowledge in being the condition for the possibility of revealed knowledge. There follows a complex investigation (74-77) of how theology can distinguish the philosophical moment within its own being as something other than itself and at the same time introduce it into its own autonomous being (this being the only way to make philosophy a separate but real condition of its own being).

Recalling the interpenetration of revelation salvation-history with the personal history of humanity, the unity of theology and philosophy becomes even clearer. For if one believes in the universal, supernatural, salvific will of God which elevates all of created reality by making it the object of God's offer of self-bestowal, then all reflection on the meaning and direction of life necessarily brings one into contact with God. It follows that philosophy can only be thought of as "pure" when it does not derive any of its concepts or language from institutional religion. But actual philosophy already engages invariably and unthematically in theology, since it has no choice as to whether people want to be pursued by God or not (79).

Given the role of philosophy in theology and the mission of theology in the world to proclaim Christ to all, it follows that: 1) Western theology need not be "purged" of philosophy; 2) philosophy used by the church must be evaluated in terms of its capacity to express modern existential concerns; 3) Western theology and philosophy must listen to the world in which they proclaim the Word to learn and thereby to rid themselves of unnecessary accretions.

6.07 A Small Fragment "On the Collective Finding of Truth"

Kleines Fragment "Über die kollektive Findung der Wahrheit"
{1.0} Franz Wiedmann, ed., *Epimeleia: Die Sorge der Philosophie und den Menschen. Festschrift für Helmut Kuhn* (Munich 1964) 61-67.

Abstract: The truth of human existence is found only in dialogue. The formulations which express these truths are provisional and succeed only insofar as they point beyond themselves to the nameless mystery they serve.
Topics: DIALOGUE; TRUTH, formulations of.
Subsidiary Discussions: Language (82); Prayer (84); Science, exact (83, 86); Dogma, development of (85ff).
Precis: Without the common possession of truth community ceases to exist. One need not start at absolute zero in the search for truth. It already exists to some degree in all people and groups. Dialogue is the indispensable process for finding the truth since it is the condition for the possibility of finding oneself and the absolute mystery which resides in the depth of one's being.

The remainder of the article (84ff) considers the formulations in which truth is expressed. Such formulations are important and the search for common formulations is the goal of dialogue. But every formula is embraced by an existential questionableness that can never be completely overcome. Every formula is an abstraction the truth of which resides not in the formula itself but in subjective experience (the more subjective the more true). It follows that every formula is inadequate, precarious, and provisional (85); those who feel they possess the truest formula must be most on guard against having shut the door to the absolute mystery at the heart of truth; anyone rejecting an important formula must ask whether s/he expects too much from a verbal abstraction; all formulations are subject to revision. Understood wisely they all serve as "sacrament[s] of initiation into the nameless mystery which all formulae must serve" (86).

What is held in common is the formula. It always remains an open question whether the partners in dialogue share the existential experience it is meant to express. Continued reflection on that experience necessarily leads to further interpretation of the formula. The certainty of formulations resides in how successfully they continue to express what humans commonly experience about the complex mystery of their lives. Knowing this, Christians and all wise and experienced humanity will not allow agreement on these matters to be reduced to scientific truths about us, nor will they let themselves be banished to the ideal realm of subjective loneliness.

6.08 Scripture and Theology
Heilige Schrift und Theologie
{1.5} H. Fries, ed., *Handbuch theologischer Grundbegriffe*, II (Munich 1963) 517-525.
Abstract: Exploring theology's relationship to scripture (with special reference to whether tradition constitutes a separate source of revelation) concludes that scripture holds a unique place as *norma normans non normata*.

Topics: SCRIPTURE, close of; THEOLOGY; TRADITION; MAGISTERIUM and theology; REVELATION, two-source theory.
Subsidiary Discussions: Faith (90f); Tradition, oral (90f).
Precis: 1. The notion of scripture. Revelation is closed in the sense that in Jesus, God achieved the final, victorious salvation of the whole human race. Until the consummation of that victory everything must be referred back to this point. This occurs in a unique way in scripture which is "the pure objectification of this eschatological beginning of the end … an absolutely normative *norma non normata*" (89). Comments on inspiration and inerrancy.
2. Theology. ."[T]heology is not merely a scientifically methodic reflection on the Church's consciousness of faith, but also an intrinsic element of this consciousness of faith itself" (90). By reflecting on itself faith develops over time and becomes capable of making new valid propositions in spite of the fact that revelation itself is closed.
3. Theology and scripture. The development of faith remains bound to its beginnings, to the revelation of Jesus in the apostolic age and to scripture as its only material, absolutely original and underived source (91). Insofar as nothing in the writings of the apostolic period is not attested to in scripture, any appeal to apostolic, oral tradition as a separate source of revelation is moot. Still, tradition, "if and insofar as it is an attestation to the Church's consciousness of faith and of the teaching of the magisterium, always remains an authentic norm for the individual theologians's interpretation of scripture" (93). Thus, scripture is always read together with tradition. The magisterium conserves but adds nothing to the deposit of faith.

Though the church can demand full adherence to what it attests, it is never able in an absolute sense to distinguish the divine element in tradition from the human (all tradition is a unity of the two). Development of dogma and the history of theology attest to this. Scripture on the other hand is completely divine, although since like all human truth it is characterized by historicity, it too stands in need of interpretation. Thus, the truths it proposes necessarily undergo a continual history—the history of dogma. In this process scripture is expanded by applying the discipline of theology not to scripture itself (which remains *norma non normata*) but to the reader.
4. Biblical theology and dogmatic theology (and other types of "systematic theology"). Dogmatic theology can never divorce itself from biblical theology if it is to remain the reflex listening to God's revelation in Christ. But theology is more than a search for proof texts in service of the magisterium. Reflection on the whole of scripture is the object and task of the theologian (96). All theological reflection leads one back to scripture. Summary (197).

6.09 Scripture and Tradition

Heilige Schrift und Tradition
{1.5} February 1963 lecture in Munich to Catholic Academy in Bavaria.
Wort und Wharheit 18 (1963) 269-279.

Abstract: Exploring the problematic relationship between scripture and tradition for Catholics, Rahner argues scripture is a materially sufficient source for revelation and offers a Catholic understanding of *sola scriptura*.
Topics: REVELATION, two source theory; SCRIPTURE, *sola scriptura*; TRADITION.
Subsidiary Discussions: Revelation (99f); Tradition, oral (101f); Church (101f); Dogma, development of (104ff).

Precis: After Vatican II withdrew "The Sources of Revelation" schema Rahner explores what is at stake for Catholic theology in its attempt to clarify the sources of revelation. For Rahner tradition is transmission. For Christianity it is not so much the transmission of abstract concepts as it is events, and the singular event of Jesus Christ who hands himself over to us in word and sacrament, especially in the Lord's Supper. Jesus Christ "is also the absolute norm for every future tradition since he is the absolute reality" (101). Jesus handed himself over to his apostles orally. Those who were open to his words formed a community: the church. Thus, this church is the normative norm for all subsequent ages. The Church hands herself on not only in her teaching but in what the Church is in herself, what she believes and celebrates (102).

Scripture is how the church has objectified itself, has made itself concrete and expressed itself. Here the church becomes tangible and readable for us today. Scripture is the word of the living church. It continues to be supported by the living tradition of the church itself. Summary (103).

Is scripture materially sufficient to ground all Catholic doctrine, or is an appeal to oral tradition required? Rahner makes three clarifications: 1) the formal authority of the magisterium cannot be abolished in favor of scripture; 2) development of doctrine is legitimate; 3) tradition is a material source and norm of faith. The heart of the question is whether scripture is materially insufficient to ground doctrine. History gives no answer to the question posed in this specific form. The question was simply not posed in the past; development of doctrine was unknown as a concept. No answer was given prior to Trent, at Trent, or after, although even scholastic theology seemed to insist on the unique role of scripture (106f).

The remainder of the article is Rahner's attempt to frame a legitimate Catholic sense of *sola scriptura*. This should be done out of ecumenical sensitivity and also to discredit the current reasons Catholic theologians propose to dispute the principle. It remains the duty of theologian to trace every dogma back to the beginnings of the church. But there is so little in the non-scriptural, apostolic tradition that is not also found in scripture that an appeal beyond scripture seems unnecessary (109). Furthermore, how can one argue God did not ordain divinely inspired scripture to include all that is necessary for salvation? Finally, the inner unity of the truths of faith argue they must stem from a single source. Summary (111f).

6.10 Reflections on the Contemporary Intellectual Formation of Future Priests

Über die theoretische Ausbildung künftiger Priester heute
{1.0}   *Stimmen der Zeit* 175 (1964) 173-193. Amplified in current footnotes.

Abstract: A new generation of theology students calls for a new approach to teaching theology based on its inner unity and today's existential questions. Here Rahner outlines his idea for a basic course in fundamental theology.
Topics: THEOLOGY, fundamental; THEOLOGY, basic course; PRIESTS, formation of.
Subsidiary Discussions: Faith, simple (124f, 127f); Theology, dogmatic (129); Transcendentalism (129f); Philosophy (130f); Scripture, exegesis (133); Laity as theologians (137f).

Precis: Presuppositions.

The pluralism of sciences in general and of theological sciences in particular leads Rahner to conclude that theology today is too vast to master, especially if young theologians seek to understand a faith they can honestly justify to themselves and others, and even more especially if it is taught in the traditional manner.

The existential situation of the young theologians shows they come seeking answers to and foundations for their own existential faith. It is no longer the purely formal academic pursuit it was in previous generations.

The level of intelligence of the theological student is markedly lower today. Theology no longer interests the sharpest minds.

Orientation towards practical pastoral care has led to a loss of emphasis on the study of academic theology.

The basic theological discipline. Attempts to meet the needs of today's young theologians by juxtaposing kerygmatic with scholastic theology have largely failed. Further change is resisted for fear of watering down theology or creating two-track training. But the basic course Rahner envisions is not watered down nor is it impossible because many people today actually are able to justify the grounds of their faith. Bringing out and reflecting on this lived justification of faith in a strictly methodic and scientific manner is the new discipline Rahner espouses. It differs basically from the old foundational theology in that the old reflects on everything given in faith whereas the new theology limits itself to what "must be given in the pre-scientific existential basis for the faith of the educated man of today" (125).

Rahner argues such a method can be scientific, and is superior because it does not separate the existence of revelation from its content. It is an inner moment of dogmatic theology which argues the credibility of the content of revelation while it establishes the credibility of revelation itself.

The existence of a basic justifiable faith among simple believers (*rudes*) encourages its use as the content of scientific reflection. To reflect on the cannons of reason for the possibility and duty of the faith of people today "in their unity, coherence and possibility of achievement, is the task of the 'new fundamental theology'" (128). Such a theology is necessarily more charismatic and transcendental than the old theology.

The basic theological discipline in the framework of the whole theology. The position of philosophy in Rahner's schema would be integrated in the basic course. Pure philosophy could be studied later.

"Old" and "New" fundamental theology differ not materially but formally. The formal object of new theology is today's existentially effective reasons for faith in the real event of Christian revelation and its central contents.

"Mystery of Christ" should lead the course of theological studies, according to Vatican II. The new theology begins with this focus and is suffused with reflection on this mystery.

Unity of formation cannot be guaranteed merely by immersing students in biblical exegesis. Dogmatic theology could supply this unity but it is too fragmented presently. The discipline Rahner envisions could supply this unity.

Further practical considerations maintain the value of such a course for students of all levels and suggests the course run 3 or 4 semesters.

Basic discipline and other subjects. Only a steady focus on the inner unity and structure of theology can address the proliferation of new subjects in the theology curriculum and other departmental considerations Rahner's new theology would raise in German universities and seminaries.

Theology and the spiritual life meld better in the envisioned course.

Lay theologians would also find such a course of value. Summary (137f).

6.11 The Secret of Life

Vom Geheimnis des Lebens

{2.0} Previously unpublished May 1965 lecture to the Catholic Academy of the Archdiocese of Freiburg i. Br. at Mannheim. Revised.

Abstract: This theological reflection on the nature of life begins with a review of scriptural notions (II) and ends with a qualified acceptance of evolution and a reaffirmation of the essential unity of body and soul (III).

Topics: THEOLOGICAL ANTHROPOLOGY, hylomorphism; ETERNAL LIFE.

Subsidiary Discussions: Vitalism (141f); God as cause (142); Death (145); Resurrection of body (144ff); God as living (146f); Jesus Christ (147f);

Evolution (148ff); Self-transcendence (149ff); God as goal of transcendence (152).
Precis: I. Though Catholic ideas about life are compatible with hylomorphic biological vitalism, the former does not depend on the latter. Human life's divine source and irreducibility to physical or biological causes is safeguarded "by man's knowledge 'from within' about his absolute transcendentality, his spirituality and freedom, even before he has understood anything about the mere biosphere and its relation to the inorganic world" (142).
II. Theological notions of life derive from refection on ordinary experience. They have their own history in the history of revelation beginning with the concrete experience of life and death and ending with eternal life. Eternal life is no metaphoric extension of earthly life. It is the original meaning of life progressively unfolded in revelation. Reflecting on what is personal, free, responsible, and dialogic are other valid ways to arrive at the truth of the goal of life. Thus, "life" must remain united with these concepts as well as with revealed notions such as kingdom of God, face to face knowledge, community, etc., but especially with the biblical concept of *Ruach/pneuma*: God's power and the content of eternal life which fills and transforms us.

Early biblical reflection envisioned a concrete life (long, fruitful, abundant). But already its depth derives from and depends on God. Thus, bodily life is never neutral or profane. Death seems alien to God's original plan and seems due to our guilty separation from God at the beginning of history. The history of salvation is revealed as the struggle between life and death. Victory is always a victory of the whole person, body and soul (i.e., resurrection of the body) which, due to its radical nature (our disappearing into the mystery of God and returning to the original experience of life) is beyond imagining. God is *the* living being not merely as life's origin and destiny but as its provident sustainer. God is life, truth, love, light. Jesus Christ is the historically tangible point of God's whole self-communication rendered present in his irreversible victory.
III. Evolution offers an acceptable way of conceiving the unity of matter and spirit so long as it includes an essential self-transcendence under God's dynamic influence. Interiority relates inorganic matter, living beings, and spirit (150f). Inorganic matter lacks interiority but has complete passive openness. Living beings achieve interiority. Spiritual beings possess infinite transcendence towards being as such and are able to receive the transforming self-communication of God. But all life remains bound to its corporeality, even if it is transformed in an unimaginable way from our present perspective.

6.12 The Unity of Spirit and Matter in the Christian Understanding of Faith

Die Einheit von Geist und Materie im christlichen Glaubensverständnis
{3.0} April 1963 lecture. *Religionsunterricht an höheren Schulen*, special issue (Düsseldorf 1963) 29-47.

Abstract: A technical discussion of matter and spirit concludes that Christians may hold that spirit evolves from matter in a restricted sense.

Topics: MATTER and spirit; SPIRIT and matter; MATTER, materialism; EVOLUTION.

Subsidiary Discussions: Dualism (155ff); Angels (158f, 172); Incarnation (160f, 170); History (171f); Self-transcendence (174ff); Becoming (174ff).

Precis: Today's widespread materialism makes it necessary for Christians to revisit their position on the unity of matter and spirit both to combat this new philosophy on its own terms and to purify their own understanding. **I.** Christian faith experiences a unity of spirit and matter in their origin, history, and goal.

1) To say God is the origin of both matter and spirit is to claim that God is the common ground of our experience of both. This is not absolutely self-evident. But Christianity is adamantly anti-dualist, calling God spiritual but only in an analogous sense.

2) Spirit and matter have a unity in their history. Matter cannot be thought of as a neutral stage upon which spirit enters and exits, however much it may seem that the history of nature takes no account of people. (There follows a discussion of angels whose spiritual existence does not denigrate matter 158f) Both Old and New Testament anthropology view humans as an essential unity of matter and spirit. Consequently Christian morality is concerned with bodily, social humanity not merely with private ideas or intentions.

3) Matter and spirit are united by their common goal. The eschatological goal of history is not the final separation of matter and spirit, body and soul, but God's halting of history and perfecting it in a way beyond what we can imagine for either spirit or matter—a social not an individual consummation. Summary (162).
II. In what follows it is enough if a unified Christian explanation does not contradict itself or the doctrine of faith.

1) The difference between spirit and matter. Without fully defining either term the church teaches that spirit cannot be a secondary product of matter. Spirit, not matter is the a priori datum of human knowledge. Matter is recognized as something "not myself." Thus the human person in the act of knowing is a unity and distinction (knowing subject, encountering object). Radical materialism can give no positive meaning to the term "matter." Whereas on the basis of the experience of spirit in any original act of knowledge, it can be deduced that matter is "that which is closed in its

individuality to the experience of the transcendence of being as such" (166). Spirit cannot be deduced from any combination of the material.

2) The unity of matter and spirit. These cannot be seen as absolutely disparate realities since they are found in mutual correlation in one and the same apprehension. For this to be possible there must be a real communication between reality and the capacity to apprehend, and, therefore, an inner relationship between knower and known (167). The limitation of matter (inner negativity) is constitutive of its essence and can be overcome only by spirit. Thus, matter is an openness and the bringing-itself-to-appear of the personal and finite world (170). Spirit and matter must not be seen as existing side by side but as "correlative constitutive moments in one reality" (171). Summary. (171)

3) The unity of the history of the spirit and of matter. Historicity, the notion that events move in one direction and possess an absolute meaning, is a uniquely biblical notion. Insofar as the material world shares in human history it too can be said to participate in its history. The relatively brief history of spirit in the long history of matter raises the question of evolution: whether spirit in some sense can be regarded as the result of the history of nature, granting always that "spirit cannot be simply regarded as the immanent product of material development and evolution, it originates from a new creative initiative of God" (173). Rahner first evinces arguments to the contrary. Then he offers positive indications: 1) ascribing the emergence of spirit completely to divine causality reduces God to one among many intra-mundane causes; 2) it tends towards dualism; 3) it looks like a bad compromise with modern science; 4) it threatens the substantial unity of human persons.

"Active self-transcendence" is Rahner's key to understanding the emergence of spirit from matter. In a) he defines self-transcendence in terms of becoming; b) argues for the real possibility of self-surpassing; c) argues that true self-surpassing implies the possibility of going beyond one's nature. Thus, Rahner concludes, "a development of the material in the direction of the spirit and the self-transcendence of the material into the spirit is, both philosophically and in the Christian sense, a legitimate conception" (177). Summary (177).

6.13 Theology of Freedom
Theologie der Freiheit
{2.0} Previously unpublished November 1964 lecture at Georgetown University at the Patrick F. Healy Conference on Freedom and Man. Text expanded.

Abstract: Christian revelation maintains that in every categorial free act we determine both ourselves and thereby our stance for or against God who is not one among many possible objects of choice but the ground and goal of freedom.

Topics: FREEDOM, theology of; GOD as ground/subject of freedom; THEOLOGICAL ANTHROPOLOGY, freedom.

Subsidiary Discussions: Salvation/damnation (183f, 186f, 191f); Fundamental option (185f); Love of God (186ff); Love of neighbor (189f); Justification/ sanctification (191ff); Sin, original (194f); Jesus Christ as ground of freedom (195f).

Precis: (Bibliography ftn1). **I. Freedom in the theological sense is freedom received from and directed towards God.** Freedom exists in our unlimited spirit of transcendence toward being as such. Human choice is indifferent only regarding its choice of objects since the ground and goal of freedom (i.e., God) remains the same. This gives freedom its theological character. In every act of freedom God is unthematically willed or denied. God is never chosen directly, but always and only in our categorial choices. Christian freedom always possesses the possibility of choosing for or against God in each and every particular concrete choice. Though some theologians disagree, Rahner argues this point and ends with a summary (182). He cautions that one cannot deduce the supernatural, self-giving ground or subject of freedom. Without revelation it remains simply the silent, repelling horizon of experience.

II. Freedom as total and finalizing self-mastery of the subject. Christian freedom can never be viewed as a merely neutral capacity, choosing among concrete things *ad infinitum*. Rather it is the capacity, the unrenounceable task, to determine and dispose oneself wholly and finally, and in that act to choose or reject God. Freedom is first of all freedom of being. Human acts are significant for salvation insofar as they determine one's being. Such self-realization is the total project of one's existence, an *option fondamentale* (discussion and summary, 186).

III. Freedom regarded as a dialogic capacity of love. Freedom is always the self-realization of the choosing person before God. It is achieved in one's capacity to love. Only the love of God is capable of embracing all our human complexities. Our dependent relationship with this personal God is the basis of our historicity. Since God is only available to us transcendentally and since all human acts of freedom are all categorial, we can only approach the love of God through love of neighbor in our concrete surroundings.

IV. The mystery of freedom springs from its origin: the fact that it derives from and is directed toward God, the incomprehensible mystery which is never self-evidently accessible to us. Steeped in this mystery it is impossible for us to judge objectively the salvation/damnation status of our own free acts or those of others. Participation in this mystery relativizes all our knowledge and judgments about ourselves and others. Freedom remains a risk.

V. Created freedom in an unavoidable situation of guilt. We know that human freedom is created freedom from the fact that we experience the transcendentality of our freedom as borne and empowered by its goal (i.e., by God). In addition, disposing ourselves is always mediated by the given

environment which is itself always co-determined by guilt. Though we remain free to interpret this as a no or yes to God, its ambiguity keeps the import of our choice a mystery even from ourselves.
VI. Freedom as liberated freedom. Freedom is always an act of trustful surrender to God. For wounded souls this act of trust depends on God's prevenient grace. God has manifested this final, irrevocable decision to liberate freedom in Jesus Christ in whom "God has surrendered himself in his innermost divinity to the freedom which surrenders itself into the unforeseeable ways of God" (195) thus liberating freedom from sin, the law, and death (summary, 196).

6.14 Guilt, Responsibility, Punishment within the View of Catholic Theology

Schuld–Verantwortung–Strafe in der Sicht der katolischen Theologie
{2.5}   January 1963 lecture at University of Zurich. E.R. Frey, ed., *Schuld, Verantwortung, Strafe im Lichte der Theologie, Jurisprudenz, Soziologie, Medizin und Philosophie* (Zurich 1964) 151-172.
Abstract: Theological reflection on responsibility, guilt, and punishment deepens and challenges the secular understandings of these realities.
Topics: THEOLOGICAL ANTHROPOLOGY, guilt; FREEDOM and responsibility; GUILT; PUNISHMENT.
Subsidiary Discussions: Salvation/damnation (200ff); Fundamental option (202ff, 209); Ethics (205); Morality, intention (212); Sin (210ff).
Precis: I. The theological concepts of responsibility, guilt, and punishment presuppose and deepen the pre-theological, profane, provisional and juridical understanding of these concepts. Methodologically, Rahner presumes this pre-theological understanding, shows how theology deepens these concepts, and clarifies and challenges these secular notions.
II. [Responsibility/Freedom]. These mutually clarifying realities are the only basis for a theological discussion of guilt and punishment. They are commonly known even pre-theologically as permanent aspects of human nature. Thus, an authentic albeit provisional and unreflected experience of freedom and responsibility is possible. Presupposing the ordinary understanding of these concepts, Rahner first defines their theological locus: "man disposes over the totality of his being and existence before God and this either towards Him or away from Him.... [H]is temporal decisions determine the eternal finality of his existence either in absolute salvation or damnation; on account of this freedom, man is responsible for his eternal salvation or damnation" (200). Though human freedom is God's gift, these two aspects of freedom, its givenness and its giftedness, are related in direct and not inverse proportion.

From the secular point of view freedom appears neutral; theologically, as the capacity to disposes the whole of one's self, it can never be neutral. It is not foremost freedom *to act* but an inescapable freedom *of being* which determines the heart and makes personal responsibility possible. It is our capacity for wholeness, for achieving our *option fondamentale*. The goal of free self-disposal is only achieved through concrete acts, not even their sum total constitutes one's final disposition. Summary (204).

In addition, it is impossible ultimately to objectify how free any act is, either one's own or another's, and therefore to know with certainty how one stands before God. Nor is it possible to develop formal principles for the subjective exercise of freedom. The power and duty to make reflex objective judgments about one's actions and moral state fall to the individual, even though such judgments will always be risky and provisional. The inability to arrive at metaphysical certitude and the need to settle for moral certitude about one's state never frees one from the task of judging one's self.

Finally, theological freedom and responsibility is subject to its own inner variability and gradation. On the surface this seems contradictory since freedom is the ability wholly to dispose of one's self toward God (a state which seems not to admit of degrees). But it demands gradation because the objective material offered to freedom varies, and the inability to judge one's actions definitively leaves them open to gradation.

III. [Guilt]. Applying to guilt what was said about freedom, Rahner insists that right and wrong, good and bad acts of freedom, do not share the same nature because bad acts of freedom fail to attain to the full nature of freedom, and because the victory of Christ over evil makes them peculiarly powerless. Guilt is essentially the definitive decision of man against God—admittedly a kind of metaphysical suicide, but still possible. Our denial of guilt is encouraged by 1) our inability fully to dispose of ourselves by any individual act; 2) our inability to judge our acts with certitude; 3) the fact that after Christ guilt can only be experienced as disarmed. Just as ultimate freedom is achieved through concrete, free acts so the sin that separates us from God is achieved through concrete, particular sins. Similarly it is impossible to make any definitive judgments about our own guilt. It is even more difficult by extension to make judgments about the guilt of others.

IV. [Punishment]. Rahner cautions against confusing the theological and secular models of punishment. In the former, punishment in an intrinsic moment, a direct consequence of bad freedom and guilt. In the latter punishment is imposed externally. He also warns against sacralizing human forms of punishment by equating them too facilely with divine punishment.

6.15 Justified and Sinner at the Same Time
Gerecht und Sünder zugleich
{2.0}   *Geist und Leben* 36 (1963) 434-443.

Abstract: Outlines the proper Catholic understanding of the Reformation insight that Christians are both saved and sinful, *simul justus et pecator*.
Topics: JUSTIFICATION; THEOLOGICAL ANTHROPOLOGY, guilt.
Subsidiary Discussions: Hope (224, 229); Sin (225ff); Fundamental option (225ff).

Precis: Ecumenical dialogue in dogmatic theology will only flourish where spirituality is shared deeply. One foundational spiritual insight of the Reformation is the doctrine that Christians are simultaneously sinful and saved, *simul justus et pecator*. This insight has much to teach Catholics.
I. The Reformation formula. A central reformation insight is that we are sinners before God and are only Christians if we capitulate radically before God. Looking at myself I see a sinner; hearing the gospel I know I have been justified. This presents a paradox at which I must not balk. I am called to an immense venture of trust in God's message. "Only where the radical experience of permanent sinfulness is combined with the consciousness given by faith of being nevertheless someone justified by the saving deed of God, is one a Christian, in the faith of this alone, i.e., in an ever new leap away from oneself, in an ever new capitulating admission of being a sinner" (221).
II. The Catholic rejection of the Reformation formula *"simul justus et pecator."* **a)** Since justification is a divine event it actually produces a lasting change within the real history of salvation. Hence, Catholic theology holds that sinfulness and justification do not exist in their fullness on the same plane. **b)** Though a gap exists between the reality of the salvation God has already achieved and our experience of ourselves as sinful, God's power is the only effective and decisive factor in our justification, a reality with which we never completely catch up. Since God's justification transforms/divinizes us, Catholics insist we cease to be sinners in the true sense. Summary (223).
III. The properly understood Catholic 'yes' to the formula *simul justus et pecator*. Catholics are sympathetic to the Reformed formula because: **a)** Uncertainty of salvation: Trent teaches that we can never know the objective status of our salvation/damnation. Since looking to ourselves fills us with fear, we must courageously cling to God in unconditional hope. **b)** The sinfulness of man through "venial" sins. We all continue to sin, if only venially. But we must beware not to minimize venial sins insofar as they can mask a real, definitive turning away from God (summary, 227). Justification must not be considered static. So long as we live on earth it is threatened. **c)** Man the pilgrim is justified and sinner at the same time. As pilgrims our concrete salvific activity is always simultaneously characterized by our starting-point, i.e., our sinfulness, and also by the goal which we already possess in hope but which we also still reach. "Seen as a future citizen of eternal glory, man always moves between the beginning and the end. This

'at the same time' is not a simultaneity of beginning and end, but an 'at the same time' in the tension between both" (229). Summary (229f).

6.16 Reflections on the Unity of the Love of Neighbor and the Love of God

Über die Einheit von Nächsten–und Gottesliebe

{2.5}   May 1965 lecture at Cologne to *Katolische Fürsorgeverein für Mädchen, Frauen, und Kinder. Geist und Leben* 38 (1965) 168-185.

Abstract: Argues the essential *unity* of love of neighbor (*caritas*) and of God.

Topics: THEOLOGICAL ANTHROPOLOGY, love; LOVE.

Subsidiary Discussions: Anonymous Christian (239f); Knowledge and freedom (241f); God, experience of (244f); Jesus Christ as God made visible (247).

Precis: Rahner commends his audience for exploring love, knowing how the Christian mission can degenerate into mere social work, and love into an empty feeling. This inquiry argues that love of neighbor never simply dissolves into love of God, nor are the two completely independent. In their essential unity, "one does not exist and cannot be understood or exercised without the other, and that two names have really to be given to the same reality if we are to summon up its one mystery, which cannot be abrogated" (232).

–Active love as the illuminating situation of modern man's existence. The essential unity of the love of God and neighbor is an urgent practical and theoretical question today when metaphysics is being challenged by sociology and a demythologized God seems to retreat into an unapproachable silence. To speak to tomorrow's generation it is not enough that Christianity be true. It must find a convincing way to proclaim the central gospel truth: love of neighbor. Love could be the key concept for the future but only if love of God and neighbor can be seen as identical, as the God in Christ, as the path to attaining our own proper nature and perfection.

–Love of neighbor understood as love of God. The declaration of scripture. Scripture is not completely clear on the essential unity of the love of God and neighbor. It speaks of them being two; it suggests loving one's neighbor "as if" loving God; it suggests love of neighbor is a "proof" one loves God. Still, Rahner sees in scripture enough evidence to support his radical identification of the two loves.

–The teaching of theology. Scholastic theology unanimously identifies love of God and neighbor at least in the supernatural potency of the infused theological virtue of *caritas*. Nevertheless, scholasticism: 1) cautions that *caritas* can manifest itself in acts of personal love which are not formal acts of charity; 2) often fails to embrace the radical consequences of this insight; 3) would probably deny the identity of the two statements claiming that not every act of love of God is also an act of love of neighbor. Still, according to Rahner, scholastic philosophy points in the right direction.

–Love as reflected and explicit mode of action and as an unconceptualized transcendental horizon of action. Rahner first distinguishes the explicit and formal objects of love, the latter being the transcendental horizon both as the subjective possibility of experience and also as itself a given object, albeit never alone and often unreflectedly. He concedes that not every act of love of God is also a formal act of love of neighbor (e.g., prayer), although whenever the neighbor is loved with transcendental depth, God is loved.

–The anonymous "Christianity" of every positively moral activity. Whenever one loves one's neighbor in true love and freedom one can actually be loving God even without reference to explicitly theological categories. Rahner rephrases the question yet to be answered.

-Love of neighbor as the basic activity of man. Love of neighbor is not one among many appropriate human responses to our surroundings. It is the basis and sum total of morality as such. Rahner argues this from the nature of human knowing whereby one discovers oneself, and from the nature of human freedom wherein one disposes oneself. This is only done in categorial acts directed towards a personal Thou, first and foremost another human being. "The act of personal love for another human being is therefore the all-embracing basic act of man which gives meaning, direction and measure to everything else" (241).

–Love of neighbor as man's manifestation of his wholeness and essence. The love described above participates in the quality of mystery. Rahner admits a complete phenomenology of love would be necessary to flesh this out. He is not prepared to offer it here. He reiterates, caritas must always be a matter of real love, not just a matter of fulfilling a divine command. Love for God's sake never means "love of God alone in the 'material' of our neighbour merely seen as an opportunity for pure love of God, but really means the love of our neighbor himself, a love empowered by God to attain its ultimate radicality and a love which really terminates and rests in our neighbour" (244).

–The encounter of the world and of man as the medium of the original, unobjectified experience of God. To the objection that the religious act directed toward God is the basic act of human existence Rahner counters: 1) God is never simply given concretely, but only transcendentally; 2) whatever we know and choose, we do so through concrete experience. "The act of love of neighbour is, therefore, the only categorised and original act in which man attains the whole of reality given to us in categories, with regard to which he fulfills himself perfectly correctly and in which he always and already makes the transcendental and direct experience of God by grace" (246).

–Love of neighbor as the primary act of love of God. Rahner rephrases the question quite clearly for the last time and gives his succinct answer: Whoever loves the neighbor he sees loves the God he cannot see, and whoever does not love the neighbor he sees cannot love the God he cannot see. Since Jesus is the face of God we see, this principle has obvious christological and eschatological elements which Rahner can only touch on here.

–The topical significance of the love of neighbor for modern man's knowledge of God. Every age has it's own key concept for expressing the incomprehensible mystery of God as it is made known to the whole person (such as has been laboriously argued above). St. Paul suggested faith, St. John suggested love, and the Synoptics suggested metanoia. Rahner suggests that love of neighbor might be the key insight through which people in today's world may come to know both their true selves and an otherwise seemingly silent and unapproachable God.

6.17 The Church of Sinners
Kirche der Sünder
{1.5}   *Stimmen der Zeit* 139 (1947) 163-177.

Abstract: The church not only contains sinners it is undeniably sinful. Though its sin is redeemed in Christ, its sin remains harmful. Mature believers are led to pray for the church and to repent for their own sins more earnestly.

Topics: CHURCH of sinners; SIN; CHRISTIAN LIFE, holiness; CHURCH, holiness of.

Subsidiary Discussions: Creed, "I believe in the holy church" (passim); Spirit (258 passim); Sacraments, *Ur-sakrament* (259).

Precis: The creed proclaims "I believe in the holy Church." Yet church history, human experience, and church doctrine concur that the church is sinful in its members, its leaders, its actions and inaction. This reality fostered many heresies, and scandal in and outside the church. If the church simply confessed its humanness this problem would be minimized. But the church steadfastly maintains she holds "the place of the all-holy God in the world ... that her 'extraordinary holiness and inexhaustible fruitfulness in all that is good' is in itself a powerful and permanent motive of credibility and an irrefutable testimny to her divine mission" (255). What follows is an exploration of two questions: I.) how the church regards its own unholiness dogmatically; II.) how its members relate to its unholiness of the level of human experience.

I. The church of God and of his Christ is a church of sinners.

1. *Sinners in the church.* That sinners are church members is understandable, if we view church membership like the membership roles of civic organizations. But viewed as the very body of Christ, the presence within the church of people who lack grace and seem destined to perdition is hard to fathom. Yet scripture concurs. Sinners do not, however, belong to the church in the same full sense as the justified since, lacking the Holy Spirit, their nominal but valid membership is not fruitful. Rahner explains their

status in terms of the validity and fecundity of the sacraments and the church as *Ur-sakrament*.

2. The church is sinful. We mustn't idealize the church. The real church not only contains sinners it is sinful. The sins of its members are a blot and blemish on the holy mystical body of Christ himself. Furthermore, the church is sinful in the sinful action and inactions of its leaders. Still, the church is not simply a pure paradox since holiness belongs to the church in a different way that its sinfulness. The former is a manifestation of its true nature, whereas the latter is present like a disease in a otherwise healthy body. Sin, insofar as it exists in the church itself is a "manifestation of the cross of Christ in the world and a sharing of its burden: the manifest consequence of sin can in Christ become the conquest of sin" (264). However true such redemption may be, sin in the church is never simply innocuous.

II. Sinful man before the holy church of sinners. How do we reconcile with the sinfulness of the church? Not by idealization, by flight, or by attempts to refound the church as a sect. Mature believers admit the sinfulness of the church without flaunting it. The sinfulness of the church speaks to the heart of the sinful believers who will weep both for their sins and for the sins of the church. Rahner compares the church to the woman taken in adultery (Jn 8).

6.18   The Sinful Church in the Decrees of Vatican II

Sündige Kirche nach den Dekreten des Zweiten Vatikanischen Konzils
{2.0}   Previously unpublished.

Abstract: Vatican II sees the church here and now as subjectively both holy and sinful. This is dogmatically possible only if such holiness is an eschatologically victorious gift of God in Christ, not its own accomplishment.
Topics: CHURCH of sinners; SIN; CHRISTIAN LIFE, holiness; VATICAN II, *Lumen gentium*; CHURCH, holiness of.
Subsidiary Discussions: Church, indefectibility of (288ff).

Precis: I. Some members of the church live in the state of grave sin. How does this square with the church's claim to be holy? Rahner examines scripture and church history. Though the New Testament never treats this problem explicitly, Matthew shows a church whose eschatological holiness is always threatened by temptation from without and within. St. Paul also sees the presence of the sinner as a threat to the whole community (1Cor 5:1-13). Revelations sees the whole community as sinful, needing conversion, and threatened by judgment.

The Fathers often refer to gospel passages involving women as types for the sinfulness of the church. They see warnings for a sinful church in the Old Testament. Against Pelagius, Augustine (and later the medievals) maintained the sinfulness of a church whose holiness was primarily eschatological. Only after Trent does this theme wane noticeably. Vatican I argued the holiness of the church arose from the objective holiness of her institutions, sacraments, and teaching, and from the holiness of many of her members. Thus, the church became hypostatised, standing as teacher and guide over against the people of God. Such a church remains holy in spite of the sinfulness of its members (summary, 278). This problem retains significance for the church's self-understanding, for the individual member called to repentance, and for Catholic relations with the Protestant community who often sees a triumphalist Catholic ecclesiology skirting the *theologia crucis*. **II.** *Lumen gentium* is not meant to be a complete ecclesiology and therefore it does not treat this question with explicit clarity, intensity, or detail (perhaps because a complete discussion inevitably would have raised the question of the sinfulness of the church itself). But the "church of sinners" clearly emerges as an important concern as will be shown it what follows. **III.** Vatican II uses "pilgrim church" and "people of God" to express its key ecclesial self-understanding. These emphasize a struggling church not a church of eternal consummation. Sinners clearly belong to such a church as Augustine says, *in corpore* if not *in corde*. Their membership is much like a sacrament which though valid, remains unfruitful. Their presence co-determines the quality of the church itself, allowing us to call the church sinful. Precisely how to conceive this effect theologically is not made explicit. But such people "wound" the church; lead it to need continual purification; subject it to temptation. The church is also affected by the sinfulness of its leaders. Yet one must never forget the church also has the power of Christ's cross to continually combat and overcome its sin. Vatican II's document on ecumenism also attests to the sinfulness of the church and its need for conversion. **IV.** *Lumen gentium* repeatedly calls the church holy without ever clarifying dogmatically how it can be simultaneously holy and sinful. Because it speaks of the church here and now as subjectively holy, the Augustinian eschatological solution does not suffice. Nor can it be simultaneously holy and sinful in the same way as the individual is simultaneously sinner and justified, for this could not explain the indefectibility of the church. Rahner builds his solution on the insight that holiness and sinfulness are not two equal, neutral options. Holiness is the ultimately determining predicate of the church, the holiness "affected in her by God's eschatological action, the sanctification bestowed upon her by God in Christ which constantly triumphs over sin" (289). Such an approach addresses ecumenical concerns because the holiness of the church is not its own work but God's gift. Summary (291f).

6.19 The Church and the Parousia of Christ

Kirche und Parusie Christi

{2.0} April 1963 lecture to Protestant and Catholic ecumenical working groups. *Catholica* 17 (1963) 113-128.

Abstract: The eschatological dimension of the institutional church reenforces it provisional and ambiguous nature despite its victory and indefectibility.

Topics: CHURCH and eschatology; ESCHATOLOGY and the church; FAITH.

Subsidiary Discussions: Eschatology, *parousia* (295f); Justification/sanctification (299ff); Grace (299ff); Hope (301ff); Church, indefectibility of (302, 306ff); Utopias (310ff).

Precis: "*Parousia*" here includes both the Second Coming of Christ and the Four Last Things in their relation to the fulfillment of world history. Rahner also presupposes the basic Christian understanding that salvation history is to be accomplished in a genuine temporal order. Here he considers the relationship of the church to the *Parousia* and the completion of world history.

I. The church is essentially and constitutionally the community gathered by Christ which in hope and love believes the *Parousia* of Christ is yet to come. The church is a means of salvation precisely and insofar as it lives this faith in a salvific event now taking place and moving inexorably toward fulfillment. A pilgrim church seeing itself as always provisional and moving toward the Kingdom of God knows its present form is never her ultimate form. The church has a permanent dimension: its essence as the historically concrete word of salvation. In short, "the essential nature of the Church consists in pilgrimage towards the promised future" (298). Summary.

II. The church's eschatological nature gives it a special relationship to the *Parousia* since her future fulfillment already exists in her as a present event. This eschatological element belongs also to the faith which constitutes its being. The church is an essentially eschatological entity: 1) as a consequence of the Catholic doctrine of justification. The grace enjoyed by Christians is nothing less than God's self-communication: eternal life. As such it is the unsurpassable, definitive eschatological human constitution. It is the existing inner reality that leads to the future; 2) insofar as the victory that comes with God's self-communication is at once permanently achieved and yet to come; 3) in its hiddenness which derives from the fact that the grace of God and its final victory is never simply given as a transcendental possession but must always manifest itself historically. We live now by faith and hope, not by sight or knowledge. Yet only the real experience of the things believed and longed for can anchor faith and hope. The church's concrete history is at once the means of faith and hope and the greatest temptation.

III. What is the relationship between the church as institution and official ministry and the church as eschatological entity? They cannot be distinguished as the means vs. the fruit of salvation, nor as the concrete historical vs. the eschatological church. Rahner focuses his discussion on indefectibility which he insists resides in the institutional office of the church for three reasons, most importantly the fact that this alone can make sense of the limits of indefectibility and the fact that it is impossible to distinguish absolutely (308) defective and indefectible statements (summary, 311f).

IV. Utopias. The modern situation of our mastery over nature and our ability to plan and construct previously impossible futures has a basically Christian origin. Christians must participate fully in building the new order not as resentful, ineffectual, and fearful hosts, but as those who point the world to the inevitable *kairos* of Christ, not to the pilgrim institutional church.

6.20 The Episcopal Office
Über den Episkopat

{2.0} *Stimmen der Zeit* 173 (1963) 161-195. The foreword was written especially for this volume, and the essay is in other ways greatly expanded.

Abstract: Ten ramifications arise from two theoretical insights: 1) bishops are bishops and enjoy territorial jurisdiction due to co-option into the college of bishops and not vice versa; 2) responsibility for the church and not territorial jurisdiction is sufficient for inclusion in the college.

Topics: EPISCOPATE; PETRINE OFFICE; CHURCH, office in.

Subsidiary Discussions: Church, constitution (320ff); Church, college of cardinals (325ff, 356 ftn20); Epsicopate, titular, auxiliary (328ff); Orders, relative/absolute (330ff); Diocese (333ff); Presbyterum (340ff); *Potestas ordinis/jurisdictionis* (344ff): Episcopate, conferences (354ff) Episcopate, senate (357ff).

Precis: Foreword (313-317): This defense of his position on the episcopate was precipitated by an attack from D.T. Strotmann. [Insofar as this foreword clarifies a number of detailed points found in the body of this essay it does not warrant a separate outline here. It is probably better read as a conclusion.]

The episcopal office: Written in the course of Vatican II, this essay speculates on the council's final position on the role of bishops (summary, 317f). Rahner senses many other important questions will remain open (list, 318f).

I. The church is a divine institution, an eschatological salvation-entity whose essential structure (a college of bishops under the pope) insofar as it is given *juris divini* participates in its indefectibility. As it always lives in contingent historical persons and their acts, the real essence of the church is "clearly, purely and effectively in evidence in the historical image presented by the Church" (320). Hence, developments from the apostolic church to early Catholicism (such as the college of bishops) can possess the character of divine law if one grants: a) every historical entity makes one-way, irreversible decision; b) decisions may be legitimate even if they cannot be proven necessary; c) such facts can still belong to the Apostolic Age and be taken as part of the process of revelation.

Rahner asks, "how exactly the co-option of a bishop into the college is related to his appointment as bishop, to the conferring of the office" (321). Do membership in the college and the granting of the office mutually implicate one another in a relationship of interdependence, or is membership merely a secondary consequence of the bestowal of individual office? (By analogy, how does the pope's primacy over the college relate to his office as Bishop of Rome?) Rahner refutes the notion that inclusion in the college is purely a consequence of being granted office. He posits a reciprocal dependence between the two. One is a bishop when admitted to the college (and Bishop of Rome when elected supreme pastor of the church). Rahner argues: 1) it is a doctrine that the college of bishops succeeds the college of apostles; 2) the fullness of its power is not delegated; 3) the apostolic college was not constituted by territorial apostles nor was the Petrine office originally localized. Hence, the authority of the college cannot be derived from the locally limited authority of its members as local bishops. Summary (323ff).

II. Ten practical ramifications of the theoretical principles set out above.

1) The college of cardinals. Since the college of bishops headed by the pope possesses supreme and fullest authority in the church it would seem most competent to elect a new pope, especially today when technology makes their gathering possible, though admittedly difficult. But even such an assembly would probably resort to an electoral committee—the precise function of the college of cardinals. Continued internationalizing of the college of cardinals would insure its representative nature. John XXIII went some way in clarifying matters when he raised all cardinals to the office of bishop. It seems clear that those who hold great positions of power in the church should also be represented in the supreme collegial body of bishops (unless one holds too narrow a view of the relationship between the bishop and his territory).

2) Titular bishops. If non-territorial bishops can legitimately belong to the college of bishops, the office of titular bishop is legitimate provided these men hold an office equivalent in responsibility to a territorial bishop (e.g., curial administrators, military ordinaries, heads of major religious orders, university rectors). Auxiliary bishops should be admitted to the college based on the same principle. Though territoriality is one important principle for inclusion in the college it is not the only one.

3) "Relative" and "absolute" ordination. Episcopal ordination was considered relative if one was designated to serve a given location, absolute if ordained without jurisdiction. Rahner refutes absolute ordination in an unqualified sense. Every bishop participates in the power of the church in every respect by inclusion in the college (summary, 333). Major responsibil-

ity for the welfare of the church and not territory should mark every ordination.

4) The essential nature of the diocese. How large a diocese should be depends on one's theological concept of a diocese. It must manifest the totality of the church—characterized by the same theological concept as the universal church itself. It must be more than a local Eucharistic community because this does not bear all the functions that necessarily belong to the universal church. It must be large enough to host and support these activities in a vital way. Summary (339).

5) The bishop and his priests. Bishop do not relate to priests simply as the pope relates to bishops. But the fundamentally collegial structure of the church offers some insights on how bishops relate to priests. By ordination priests enter a presbyterum, a *jure divino* college for the bishop (priests are ordained not for themselves or their own ministries but to aid bishops). The presbyterum is as old and as original as the college of bishops. Just as the Roman curia is taken from among the college of bishops to aid the pope, so a diocesan curia is taken from among the presbyterum to aid the bishop. Both pope and bishop have the moral obligation to convene a representative curia. Only by seeing a priest in the context of a presbyterum can one clearly see why a parish pastor is not a bishop, why a parish is not a diocese, why the territorial principle is not the only constitutive concept in the church. Though the exact relation of priest to bishop is fluid, the concept of presbyterum goes a long way to explaining their proper relationship.

6) The unity of offices and powers in the church. One supreme office in the church is constituted by two powers: *potestas ordinis* (the power to sanctify derived from consecration) *potestas jurisdictionis* (pastoral power which may or may not be given at consecration). Rahner argues the inner unity and ultimate indissolubility of the two. They are divided only in relatively secondary effects and applications. They appear as completely one power only where both are possessed of necessity: in the college of bishops under and with the pope. It is not enough to say that the power of orders can be lost whereas the power of jurisdiction cannot, since in the original bearer (college of bishops) neither can be lost, and in the individual both can be lost.

7) Exemption. After repeating arguments for legitimate inclusion of non-territorial bishops in the college, Rahner turns to the category of exemption which in the past indicated the subjection of non-territorial bishops to the pope. But not only does the term beg what it intends to prove, it adds nothing substantial to the pope's immediate jurisdiction over all the faithful. Exemption does not create non-territorial entities. It is merely the legal designation of a prior, theologically legitimate entity. This area could prove ecumenically important in protecting the expression of reuniting churches.

8) The duties of the bishop. Membership in the college extends a bishop's duties beyond his diocese to the care of the universal church.

9) The idea of the patriarchate. Collegiality has always expressed itself in less than universal forms, e.g., patriarchate. Though a product of human law it is a concretization of divine law such that it is hard to distinguish it from *juris divini* structures. Rahner opts for treating such canonical or para-canonical "part-Churches" (in which he includes bishops' conferences) as products of divine law, and as such to be encouraged. Such groupings could function more democratically than the college itself, though its head need not be thought of as simply a *primus inter pares*.

10) A consultative board of bishops around the pope. Paul VI expressed a willingness to be advised on the governance of the church by a consultative board. Rahner notes: 1) Such a body must remain consultative and cannot delimit the power of the pope who convenes it. He could conceivably work with it as an ecumenical council in miniature; 2) Even without such a board the fundamental theological necessity of cooperation between pope and bishops is well established. (Cf., discussion of Vatican I's formula *ex sese*.) Such a board has the advantage of helping to insure unity, avoiding national biases, and compiling data more quickly. 3) Such a board could be composed of bishops and other leaders, but should be clearly differentiated from the Roman curia.

6.21 Pastoral-Theological Observations on the Episcopacy in the Teaching of Vatican II

Pastoraltheologische Bemerkungen über den Episkopat in der Lehre des II. Vaticanum

{1.0} *Concilium*, Vol. I (German ed.) 1965, 170-174.

Abstract: Six pastoral-theological ramifications of *Lumen gentium's* teaching on episcopacy, and the related tension between local and episcopal churches.

Topics: CHURCH, office in; EPISCOPATE; VATICAN II, *Lumen gentium*.

Subsidiary Discussions: Episcopate, conferences (364f); Episcopate, senate (365); Diocese (365f); Parish (366ff).

Precis: To Rahner, *Lumen gentium* is the most important achievement of Vatican II, and its work on the episcopacy is its crown. After summarizing its teachings (361f) Rahner discusses six pastoral-theological ramifications.

   1) Bishops can no longer be thought to exercise their office as simply agents of the pope. Each derives authority from Christ along with his proper duty and responsibility for his own diocese and for the universal church.

   2) Episcopal ordination confers all three offices (teacher, priest, shepherd) primarily in a pneumatic, sacramental rather than canonical transmission. Spirit and not law informs a bishop's collegial ministry of service.

   3) Orders is legitimately divided into bishop, priest, deacon. Each must be seen as rooted in pneumatic unity.

4) Smaller regional episcopal groupings (patriarchates, national bishops' conferences, etc.) are clearly indicated by *Lumen gentium*. Rahner hopes each will find its appropriate voice and scope.

5) The pope needs to be supported in governing the universal church by a representative body of bishops whose exact nature is undetermined but for which Rahner has a few practical suggestions.

6) *Lumen gentium* offers some indications, positive and negative, for determining the proper size of a diocese.

Rahner concludes with a discussion of one significant unsolved problem, partly dogmatic, partly pastoral-theological: the tension between the theoretical and real structures of the church. *Lumen gentium* makes it sound as if the bishop alone preaches, teaches, sanctifies, and otherwise ministers to the people entrusted to his care. In reality such work is carried out by parish priests. As far as the document goes to describe the priest as the helper to the bishop and leader of the local community, the church still lacks a theology of the parish—the local altar community as an actualization of the church. So long as parishes regard themselves as mere diocesan branch offices, they miss their true dignity. Addressing this problem calls for greater reflection on the relationship between the episcopal and local church. Rahner suggests the local church is the concrete essence of the church, so that believers experience there what is really meant by church: the sacramental and divinizing and forgiving grace of God in the unity of the human family in love. If this reality can be experienced and understood locally, the deeper episcopal structure of the church will itself be more fully and easily experienced.

6.22 On Bishops' Conferences
Über Bischofskonferenzen
{1.0}   *Stimmen der Zeit* 172 (1963) 267-283.
Abstract: Theological reflection and seven wide-ranging "purely personal" suggestions on the future structure and function of bishops' conferences.
Topics: EPISCOPATE, conferences; EPISCOPATE; CHURCH, office in.
Subsidiary Discussions: Diocese (378f).
Precis: These considerations arose from watching the de facto functioning of national caucuses early in Vatican II and from a desire expressed by bishops themselves to give large episcopal conferences a much more secure canonical status and to entrust to them duties and responsibilities which up to now have not been possessed by any individual bishop or previous episcopal assembly.
Past and present forms. Without reviewing the entire pre-history of bishops' conferences Rahner remarks: i) their importance is seen by the fact that they pre-date the rise of the primacy of Roman jurisdiction (pre-Nicean); ii) since the middle ages their power has waned in the West parallel to the rise of papal jurisdiction, though this move is not definitive or irreversible.

Rahner concludes an account of the recent history (1830 to present) of bishops' conferences with two observations: i) their decisions cannot bind their members; ii) they can convene, discuss, and make limited decisions without the participation of the Holy See. Still, bishops' conferences [as of 1962] have no canonical existence nor is their competence fully defined.
Dogmatic considerations. Having summarized a dogmatic ecclesiology of bishops, Rahner underlines each bishop's obligation to defend the welfare and promote the saving activity of the universal church. On this the legitimacy of such conference rests, not simply on practical necessity. Their otherwise abstract call to insure the welfare of the universal church is made concrete in regional conferences. Thus, the notion of bishops' conference springs from the very nature of the church. They cannot be established or abolished at whim or for mere administrative convenience. Rahner cautions against too easily identifying existing bishoprics as *juris divini* structures.
Bishops' conferences. Rahner's personal suggestions for the future of bishops' conferences: 1) based on subsidiarity, they should be collegial bearers of superior authority and legislative power for their part of the church; 2) their optimal size might equal a nation, with a similar internal breakdown by administrative region. This does not rule out inter-state assemblies in missions or supra-national conferences at times; 3) their duties and competence should extend to those areas incumbent on a local bishop but impossible for him to affect alone, e.g., representation to national governments, supervision of inter-diocesan organizations; 4) they also have duties to the central government of the universal church to propose, inform, complain and petition; 5) they might run area-wide or world-wide development campaigns; 6) the Holy See might transfer to them decision making power in liturgy; 7) regarding its inner structure, Rahner suggest it have a president (perhaps it's senior bishop); that it make its decision in fraternal discussion but perhaps with a binding plurality or a 2/3 majority vote depending on the nature of the issue.

6.23 Anonymous Christians

Die anonymen Christen

{1.0}   Previously unpublished summer 1964 *Westdeutscher Rundfunk* broadcast review of A. Röper's, *Die anonymen Christen* (Mainz 1963). Expanded.
Abstract: Responding to one's true nature is implicitly but really responding to the historical Christ. This alone makes one an anonymous Christian. This important teaching is compatible with the teachings of Vatican II.
Topics: ANONYMOUS CHRISTIAN; THEOLOGICAL ANTHROPOLOGY.
Subsidiary Discussions: Incarnation (393ff); Church (396ff); Mission mandate (396ff).
Precis: Catholics must hold two seemingly incompatible premises: 1) to achieve salvation one must believe not merely in God but in Christ; 2) God

wills the salvation of all, which hardly seems possible given the overwhelming mass of people who never heard of Jesus or who reject what they have heard. For both these statements to be true one must hold: either everyone is capable of being a member of the church in an historically concrete sense; or just as people are visible members of the church in ascending degrees from mere baptism to living a life of exemplar holiness, so they can be members in descending degrees from baptized to anonymous Christian. How can this relationship be conceived?

A brief summary of Rahner's theological anthropology (grace, spirit, God, mystery, freedom, knowledge) concludes that people are not only capable of hearing a possible word from the hidden God, we positively expect it, although it is not simply part of our nature and we have no right to demand it. How does this theistic tendency refer to the incarnate God, Jesus Christ?

Rahner next turns to the incarnation, "the uniquely supreme case of the actualisation of man's nature in general [in which] he can recognize this unapproachable height as that perfection of his own being which can be effected by God" (393). This possibility of accepting God's self-communication is not optional. This "supernatural existential" is the goal of all creation. To refuse this invitation puts us in contradiction with ourselves and this always remains a real possibility at the level of the heart. But to accept it is to accept Christ, however inchoately. Summary (394).

The reminder of the article considers problems arising from the term anonymous Christian and its application. The tendency of the heart to draw near God and to find real peace naturally looks for ever more explicit expression. The term anonymous Christian is not so much intended for the anonymous believer who might in fact be put off by such an attribution, but for believers who are apt to panic as they witness the decline of explicit faith around them. This topic is by no means unimportant. Whoever interprets it as a license not to preach the gospel have misunderstood it and need to think harder about the fundamental data of traditional theology and contemplate the real situation of people today. Rahner concludes by showing how the concept of anonymous Christianity is supported by the teachings of Vatican II's *Lumen gentium*.

VII.   FURTHER THEOLOGY OF THE SPIRITUAL LIFE I

VII. *Zur Theologie des geistlichen Lebens* (later, *Ein Grundriß des geistlichen Lebens*)

German edition: Einsiedeln, Benziger, 1966
U.S. edition: N.Y., Seabury, 1971
David Bourke, translator

This volume in the English edition comprises the first 26 essays of *Schriften zur Theologie* VII.

7.01 Christian Living Formerly and Today
Frömmigkeit früher und heute
{0.5} December 1966 lecture. *Geist und Leben* 39 (1966) 326-342.

Abstract: Though authentic Christian living in the future may take many new forms all will show an appreciation of God's incomprehensibility, responsible involvement with the world, and a new asceticism of self-imposed moderation.
Topics: CHRISTIAN LIFE; GOD.
Subsidiary Discussions: Vatican II (3ff); Tradition (5ff, 24); Atheism (11ff, 17); Prayer, intercessory (12f, 16); Mysticism (14ff); Anonymous Christian (16ff); Religion "of the world" (17ff); Asceticism (19ff).
Precis: The contemporary unrest aroused by Vatican II is a mixture of anxiety in the face of the new and a reckless embrace of the new for its own sake.

1. The problem of Christian living today: The goal of Vatican II was the renewal of Christian Life: to help believers love God and neighbor more, and to accept with greater courage their own freedom and responsibility. This essay imagines how such post-conciliar Christian living will look.

2. Christian living in the church today as heritage and as commitment: Any new approach to Christian living should be tested by the discernment of spirits to see how well it preserves the heritage of Christian wisdom. "It is genuine only when it regains its living relationship with its own past" (9). Rahner gives many examples of reckless tendencies to embrace what is merely novel.

3. Perspectives of Christian living in the future: Mere conservation is never a worthy goal. The true and unchanging must continually be adapted to new situations. Although adaptations cannot be foreknown by theoretical theology but only through experimentation, theology can offer some direction. Rahner suggests three essential dimensions of any authentic future Christian life.

1) *The experience of God as incomprehensible.* Christian living will be rooted in one's direct personal relationship with the incomprehensible God, a God often seemingly distant or absent. Christian living will be less publicly supported and more modest. Simply remaining open to the incomprehensible God will constitute the core of Christian life. This too is the core of mysticism.

2) *Life in the world and service of the world.* Christian life will entail living fully free and fully human, giving up all attempts to reconcile on our own the intrinsic plurality within us. Whoever courageously lives this openness to self is already "baptized." That person already participates in the "religion of the world" where sacred and secular merge. Rather than flee the world Christians will accept their responsibilities for improving it.

3) *The new asceticism: imposing one's own limits.* In past ages asceticism meant accepting imposed limits. In future Christians must freely practice

moderation. This may seem unheroic by former standards but it is rooted in one's openness to God as always greater than whatever we forego.

These factors can only be harmonized in living practice, in ongoing, self-critical discernment of spirits. In the end it is false to divide the old and new in Christian life since "the new is genuine only when it preserves the old, and because the old only remains living when it is lived anew" (24).

7.02 Being Open to God as Ever Greater. On the Significance of the Aphorism *Ad Majorem Dei Gloriam*

Vom Offensein für den je größeren Gott

{1.0} 1959 lecture. *Geist und Leben* 39 (1966) 183-201.

Abstract: The Jesuit motto evokes openness to God as ever greater and reveals a new subjectivity and existential ethic of choice where God is encountered more immediately, thus transcending rationalism and conventional authority.

Topics: CHRISTIAN LIFE; IGNATIUS LOYOLA; SPIRITUALITY, Ignatian.

Subsidiary Discussions: Fundamental option (26f); Dogma, development of (29f); Freedom (35ff, 40f); Subjectivity (38f); Choice (41f).

Precis: I. The Jesuit motto, *Ad Majorem Dei Gloriam* is more obscure than it seems: i) is it applicable to all Christians or is it distinctly Jesuit?; ii) how can sinful humans give God any glory?; iii) having created the world imperfect it seems God may not will the greatest glory; iv) the glory of God (*doxa*) is God's gift to us not ours to God; v) people today hardly presume to know what is to God's glory or how they can contribute to it.
II. Although this notion arose at a specific moment in history it is no less authentically Christian. Nor is it any less Jesuit because it has not always and everywhere been understood by each Jesuit in one particular way. What is highest is often most easily misinterpreted and most imperfectly understood.
III. This notion arose with St. Ignatius in the context of the *devotio moderna* at a technological and scientific turning point in European culture. It marks a new interest in the subjective self. Its concern with self-responsibility is in many ways unique to the Renaissance (what Rahner calls here the New Age).
IV. The definitive element in this notion is its commitment to absolute self-surrender to the sovereign will of God. This entails: i) obedience to God and indifference or detachment as explained in the Exercises; ii) that prior to disposing ourselves to God's greater glory we are already disposed by God; iii) there is a fluid interplay between our self-disposal and the limits God and the world place on us (summary, 36); iv) despite all this we remain capable of planning and determining ourselves to a great extent.
   What is definitive in this fourth element is the explicit, conscious and constant awareness of our openness to the possibility further conditions will be placed on us by God, by others, or by ourselves. The motto represents not

a fact but an orientation. This fourth element was always Christian though it remained unthematic until the Renaissance. It performs a critical function in the exercise of choice by allowing a "withdrawal of one's self to an absolute point in order from *there* to reflect and to test what is to be done" (41). Thus, the motto implies "an openness to the direct personal love of God, which is no longer arrived at through intermediate causes, and, in fact, the end of legalism and the freedom of children of God in the Pneuma of Christ" (43). V. Potential dangers attending this attitude include: i) fatally damaging one's spontaneity and freedom from over-calculation leading one to assume the power of God; ii) reducing everything to rationalism rather than leaving the last word to God; iii) drifting into "aristocratic skepticism" from always doubting whether this or that is truly to God's greater glory. Summary (45f).

7.03 Intellectual Honesty and Christian Faith

Intellektuelle Redlichkeit und christlicher Glaube
{1.0}   March 1966 address in Vienna to Society of Catholic High Schools. *Stimmen der Zeit* 177 (1966) 401-417.

Abstract: After defining intellectual honesty and the essentials of Christian faith Rahner argues that belief is not intellectually dishonest.

Topics: CHRISTIAN LIFE, intellectual honesty; FAITH.

Subsidiary Discussions: Skepticism (48ff); Faith (55ff); Creed, brief (59ff); God (60ff); Creation (62f); Trinity (63); Jesus Christ (63f); History (63f, 69); Language (65); Incarnation (67ff); Resurrection (70f).

Precis: Whether belief and intellectually honest are incompatible depends on how the latter is defined.

I. Intellectual honesty must not be confused with skeptical reserve.

Intellectual honesty and human decision. Even the decision to reserve judgement is a crucial defining act of human freedom. "Intellectual honesty commands us to have the courage to take basic human decisions, however weighed down we may feel by uncertainty, darkness and danger" (49).

Intellectual honesty, responsibility in faith and the exploration of ideas. Intellectual honesty does not insist every detail and presupposition be scientifically verified prior to assent. Intelligent people, while admitting how little they know, still assent to truth as they best understand it. Yet the fact that more exists than can be intellectually confirmed ("existential difference") can never countenance an appeal to blind, uncritical faith.

"Faith is primarily concerned with the all-embracing meaning of existence, and Christian faith...makes assertions about human existence in *all* its dimensions" (55). Such faith rests not on complete theoretic validation but on trust in one's living experience. This is true because: it is a gift from God; faith alone provides the context for establishing meaning; conscience and morality command us not to abandon mystery for any lesser good; those who accept faith experience liberation. This experience justifies faith as intellectually honest even prior to exhaustive theoretical examination.

II. Christian faith considered as a whole. Faith as a complex reality which resolves itself in the mystery of God can only be rejected or accepted as a totality. Rahner next summarizes the ultimate essence of Christianity (60) beginning with "God in his divinity as the mystery of human existence" (God and creation), and moving to "God's self-bestowal in history in Jesus Christ."

How the theological assertions are rightly understood. Is this Christian message credible measured by the standards of intellectual honesty? The fact the language which refers to mystery is obscure does not make faith intellectually dishonest.

The qualifications and criteria for deciding how faith and intellectual honesty can be reconciled. So long as one does not limit faith to what one has already grasped, and since every act of knowledge leads us beyond ourselves, there is no criterion that prohibits belief on the grounds of intellectual dishonesty. Rahner next illustrates this point with reference to two specific doctrines: "The credibility of the dogma of the incarnation"; "Belief in the resurrection as reasonable for the human intellect of accept." Summary (71).

7.04 Do Not Stifle the Spirit!

Löscht den Geist nicht aus

{0.5} June 1962 address in Salzburg to Presidium of Catholic Action, Austria. Originally subtitled, *Problem und Imperative des Österreichischen Katholikentages* 1962 (Insbruck, 1963) 16-25. Edited.

Abstract: This stirring appeal to the laity on the eve of Vatican II offers seven ways to guard against stifling the charismatic element in the church.

Topics: SPIRIT, gifts of; CHURCH, charismatic element in; LAITY.

Subsidiary Discussions: Boldness (81); Obedience (82); Spirit, discernment of (85f).

Precis: This address first (72-79) develops the notion that each person has the power to stifle the work of the Spirit, a fact not immediately obvious. Rahner outlines Paul's notion of an essentially charismatic church alongside an equally essential official church structure. Today this charismatic element is treated in a theoretical manner by the official church due in great part to the greater complexity of modern life and the concomitantly greater bureaucratization in the church which is often hostile to charismatic initiatives.

Two dangers are present in this situation: i) regional identity and initiative are threatened by centralization; ii) ecclesial unity in love is threatened by imposed uniformity in thought and practice. All this underlines the urgent imperative today not to stifle the Spirit. This is especially true in Central Europe which tends to weariness, resignation to routine, apathy, and lack of enthusiasm or direction. Seeing this attitude in the church at perhaps the most revolutionary point in the history of the world leads Rahner to ask, "where is that bold, powerful, creative, 'self-confident' movement of the Spirit among us in the Church?" (78).

This leads inevitably to the heart of the essay: "What must we do in order to avoid stifling the Spirit?" (79). Although the answers will only be discovered by bold experimentation and not by theoretical reflection, theology can offer some suggestions: i) We must care. Fearing to stifle the Spirit we should humbly and keenly anticipate signs of the spirit and act boldly when they manifest themselves. ii-v) We must have the courage to take risks, especially the risk of interpreting obedience to the church as obedience to the prompting of the Spirit as much as to church authorities; enduring the inevitable antagonisms we will encounter in the church; saying "No" to the church precisely as members of the church when its tendencies are misdirected. vi) We must recognize that the higher, charismatic wisdom of the church may reside precisely with the rank and file of believers and not in its official organs whose responsibility it is to allow charisms to surface. vii) We must all pray for the insight to balance charismatic courage with loyal obedience to lawful authority in the church.

Demographic trends suggest that Christianity in general will continue steadily to lose ground in the next century. In such circumstances how can we afford to stifle the Spirit? How can we not be bold?

7.05 The Christian in His World
   Der Christ in seiner Umwelt
{0.5}   June 1965 inaugural lecture for Nordic "Catholic Day" in Hamburg. *Stimmen der Zeit* 176 (1965) 481-489.

Abstract: Christians must participate wholeheartedly in the rapidly changing, diverse world with love, presenting in ever new ways the ancient message that God has revealed the meaning of life in the death and resurrection of Jesus.

Topics: CHRISTIAN LIFE: CHURCH of the future.
Subsidiary Discussions: Politics (90ff); Ecumenism (96f); Death (99).
Precis: After describing some of the major bewildering factors which shape the modern world Rahner asks, "What part does the Christian play in this world?" He lists four elements of the Christian's stance toward the modern world.

First, Christians must participate fully in the world. They must neither flee nor hate it. They must accept it as the God-given arena where salvation is to be found, realizing well they do not have all the answers to its most pressing problems.

Second, Christians accept their minority "diaspora" status in the world. They seek no hegemony over others nor tolerate its imposition over themselves or others. The multiplicity of ideologies in the world today makes their faith commitment all the more powerful. It also makes them more self-critical. They do not shrink from participating fully in civic affairs simply because their ideals are based on faith. "Christians are willing to accept unreservedly the situation of our diaspora in a pluralistic society, and in doing so to guard against the error of taking refuge in the ghetto of a reactionary defense of the traditional for its own sake, or in the comfortable cowardice of renouncing all claims to influence the course of political life" (92).

Third, in a complex, heterogeneous society the church community changes from one based on social or ethnic identity to a community of believers grounded on personal commitment. This implies two things. First, for such a community of love to exist "the bond of brotherhood between all the members of the community must transcend all differences of individual functions in the community" (93). The task of such a community extends beyond itself to the world, to witness there the fundamental meaningfulness of the world and of human existence. The second task of the church is not to ghettoize itself but to remain open to influences outside itself. The church must never be a fire which warms only itself (96).

Fourth, Christianity is and will remain even today "the grace bestowed upon Christians and at the same time the task with which they are presented" (98). However much the world changes it will continue to raise in the hearts of all people the question of the meaning and purpose of life—"the question inexorably of the ultimate mystery of itself, God" (98). However challenging it may be to remain open to the world and to address its needs in ever new forms, the true gift of Christians to the world remains the same: their belief that the world has already been saved by God in Christ—that at the heart of the mystery of the world lies love.

7.06 "I Believe in the Church"

"Ich glaube die Kirche"

{1.5} *Wort und Wahrheit* 9 (1954) 329-339. Originally subtitled "The New Marian Dogma and the Individual" this essay explored how to understand the recently proclaimed dogma of Mary's Assumption. In this revised version most references to the Assumption have been eliminated.

Abstract: New dogmas command belief because: 1) faith in Christ embraces faith in church teaching; 2) there is no higher norm against which to judge dogma; 3) partiality, a human characteristic, cannot discredit new dogma a priori.

Topics: DOGMA; CHURCH, faith in; FAITH.

Subsidiary Discussions: Creed, "I believe in the holy church" (106ff); Trinity (107); Magisterium (113ff); Dogma, development of (115f).

Precis: The essay first examines our human subjective reaction to any new truth (100-106). Modern people find new definitive claims scandalous. Though encountering truth is meant to change us, we prefer it to confirm our preconceptions. Still, faith in ultimate things must rest on an infallible authority outside ourselves. In the case of dogma this is the Word of God revealed in Christ and proclaimed by the church. "The humility of a sensitive spirit, readiness for change, the courage to take the pain of a new idea, prayer for light from above—these will achieve what is necessary" (105) to overcome our initial revulsion at hearing a new dogma. Summary (105). The essay next examines the objective sphere: the church precisely as an object of faith (106-113). To hear, heed, and believe in a new dogma one must stand in the faith of the church. But what does it mean, "I believe in the holy Catholic Church"? The church is the object of faith and, in a mysterious way, also the dimension in which that faith exists. These two dimensions are mutually complementary. Where faith is found in its fullness both aspects are present such that belief in Christ is belief in the church. The Spirit of God exists in the church in a hylo-morphic way so that without faith in the church, faith in the Spirit of God is not fully realized. The abiding word of Christ is the word on the lips of the church authorized by Christ. Even scripture is secondary to the ecclesial community which bears it (108).

Faith in the church also enjoys a logical priority since "the objectivity of faith is guaranteed by the Spirit of God...and is judged by no one. But this Spirit is present in the Church as her subjectivity, and is present nowhere else. No one can attempt to measure this, the ultimate standard of all measures. This ultimate standard ... is the Church, since the Spirit of truth has united himself inseparably to her, and to me, the individual, only to the extent that I am standing within her ... believing what she believes" (111).

Rahner finally considers (113-119) "how the faith of the Church makes itself clearly perceptible to us in the Church" (113). Rahner reviews the three-fold magisterium (all bishops, bishops and pope in council, pope speaking for the church). After discussing factors which bring new dogmas to the fore he cautions that however imperfect or even scandalous they may be, the Spirit can use the most imperfect means to reveal sublime truths. Human imperfection in doctrinal formulations do not provide grounds for withholding submission to the magisterium.

7.07 Christmas, the Festival of Eternal Youth
Weihnachten, Fest der ewigen Jugend
{1.0} Christmas 1964 Bavarian Radio address.
Geist und Leben 38 (1965) 401-404.

Abstract: We understand and embrace the Christmas announcement of everlasting life by fusing the voice of history with the voice of interiority.
Topics: ETERNAL LIFE; LITURGICAL YEAR, Christmas; MYSTERY.
Subsidiary Discussions: God (122); Death (124).
Precis: Christmas has a vital contribution to make to a weary world. It celebrates the start of the definitive victory of God's eternal youth in the world: the escape from the despairing cycle of birth and death. At Christmas the core of life is revealed as the fullness of God's everlasting life offered to us in love. God is revealed as the inner dynamic of human history.

But how can one appropriate deep in one's heart this seemingly cold voice of history? By accepting *this* life, "opening yourself simply, trustfully, obediently and without protest to its single ineffable meaning.... But you, when you open yourself to the inner meaning of life in this sense, do not give life its meaning *ab externo*, but rather let that meaning that is already present, even if mysteriously, in its innermost depths, rise up from the roots of your nature, endowed as it is with grace, in a quite simple and unremarkable manner" (123). The harmony of the voices from deep within says, "I believe in eternal life" and helps overcome the cynicism that the offer of such life seems too good to be true.

In the celebration of Christmas these two voices, that of history and that of the spirit become one when we recall the one God who has created them both and sustains them in a single act of self-bestowal on the world.

7.08 Holy Night
Heilige Nacht
{0.5}   Previously unpublished.
Abstract: A highly poetic reflection on how the dawn of the incarnation redeems the otherwise bleak darkness of natural night.
Topics: LITURGICAL YEAR, Christmas; SALVATION; NATURE, role in salvation.
Subsidiary Discussions: Symbol (127f).
Precis: Celebrating Christmas and Easter at night points to their deep inner connection. Both are sacred nights in which the divine mystery of salvation enters our lives. "Taken together these...are the festivals of the beginning of our redemption...they signify the victory of a new beginning" (127). Ambiguity adheres to these symbols because they participate in the ambiguous history of the world where salvation has dawned but not yet in its fullness.

There follows a reflection on the ambiguity of the symbols night and darkness (128f). Rahner concludes that only Christians can contemplate night and darkness without false romanticism because "[S]aving history as Christians understand it is not simply an interruption of the natural order...rather it is the process by which the natural order itself becomes radically and all-pervasively transformed into something which only the eye of faith can recognize for what it is, because only to the eye of faith is it apparent that nature too is involved in the order of redemption" (129f). By entering the world, the Word made flesh becomes the law at the root of the whole natural order, and makes night a fitting symbol of what is to come. "In that one night, every night, night as such, is redeemed and consecrated" (130).

7.09 Peace on Earth
Friede auf Erden
{1.0}   Previously unpublished.

Abstract: Christmas heralds peace because the incarnation marks God's reconciling the world, accepting, encompassing and overcoming its strife.

Topics: CHRISTIAN LIFE, peace; LITURGICAL YEAR, Christmas; CHRISTOLOGY, reconciliation in Christ.

Subsidiary Discussions: God, glory of (132f); Mystery (133); Conflict resolution (133f).

Precis: Why do Christians associate peace with Christmas? As the angels said (Lk 2:14) peace flows from the glory of God revealed in God's condescending to come to forgive and redeem us—God's gift to the world not its gift to God. Whoever accepts this offer of salvation finds peace.

Why associate this with Christmas? Because it was then that the incomprehensible mystery of hidden blessedness in which we believe, and which we call God, entered into the world. The message of this mystery is twofold: i) the conflict between creatures is taken up into the unity of the one God their creator; ii) even while this conflict still rages it has already been transcended and reconciled in Christ. Hence, the center of all reality is the peace won by the cross of Christ. Those who accept this find peace.

7.10 See, What a Man!
Seht, welch ein Mensch
{0.5}   *Geist und Leben* 28 (1955) 103.

Abstract: This Good Friday meditation invites us to see in the crucified Christ the deepest question and answer to the problem of human existence.

Topics: LITURGICAL YEAR, Good Friday; THEOLOGICAL ANTHROPOLOGY, human predicament; REDEMPTION.

Subsidiary Discussions: Death (139).

Precis: We avoid looking at the true nature of our existence. If a picture of the essential human predicament were drawn it would be precisely the portrait of the crucified Christ in all its detail (136f). Such a portrait confronts us with the question of what we are. It also gives God's answer to that question, since in Christ, "all that was received and accepted is redeemed" (138).

There is no proof for this claim, but our faith in it is strengthened merely by kneeling at the foot of the cross, listening, and praying, "Lord I believe, help my unbelief." In contemplating the crucified Christ we come to understand all that he endured when we hear him cry, "My God, my God, why have you forsaken me?" We understand all that he has overcome when we hear him say, "Into your hands I commend my spirit."

7.11 The Scandal of Death

Die Ärgernis des Todes

{0.5}   Good Friday 1966 Bavarian Radio address. Revised.

Abstract: Good Friday meditation on Christ's death recalls our need to prepare for our own inevitable death by identifying it with the death of Christ.

Topics: LITURGICAL YEAR, Good Friday; DEATH.

Subsidiary Discussions: Eternal life (143); Anonymous Christian (143).

Precis: Good Friday solemnly commemorates the death of Christ. Why do we celebrate this death? How is it different from millions of others? First, it reminds us of our own inevitable death and prompts us to prepare for it. For we take nothing with us when we die except who we have become in life. We practice for death by valuing things correctly in light of this truth.

Good Friday also celebrates the death of one man. We recall how he accepted death and made it into his own act. He is the prototype. In spite of his goodness and innocence his death included all that makes death terrifying. Nothing we say about his death is designed to spare us from death as he experienced it when he cried, "My God, my God, why have you forsaken me." Not until we reach this nadir in death can true life begin in us. For true life is not simply a continuation of this life. It transcends time and has the quality of the freedom and faithfulness that comes from the love of God.

Death confronts us with the question whether we will reach for the consolation that comes from the illusion of control or stay loyal to conscience even when it appears to do nothing for us. There is a third alternative: believing that God has redeemed our death "in Jesus Christ the crucified one, in him in whom God himself took our death upon himself and made it his own" (143); believing that if his death has become ours, so his victory over death will become ours as well.

7.12 "He Descended into Hell"

"Abgestiegen ins Totenreich"

{1.5}   *Geist und Leben* 30 (1957) 81-84 as, "*Karsamstag.*" Heavily revised.

Abstract: Holy Saturday points out: 1) Jesus really died and so redeems our death; 2) he endured being in the state of death to an unparalleled degree and thus redeems even our being dead, i.e., our existence as a separated soul.

Topics: LITURGICAL YEAR, Holy Saturday; DEATH.

Subsidiary Discussions: Eschatology, Sheol (146f); Soul, separated (147ff); Creed, He descended into hell.

Precis: Holy Saturday celebrates the creedal formula, "He descended into hell." What does this mean? How is that past event relevant to our present or our future? Two truths are brought together under this formula: 1) that Jesus really died and that only his death can redeem our death; 2) his death brought release and redemption to those who had died before him. Rahner only examines the first truth.

Hell renders the Hebrew "Sheol" and is better translated "realm of the dead." On one level this formula emphasises the fact that Jesus really died. It does not herald the discovery of a new geographical location. But it also refers to Jesus' being in the state of death. Here Rahner follows Aquinas' account of death as the life of the separated (disembodied) soul. It is open to reality as such, but lacking the discriminating power of the senses it is painfully unable to distinguish and completely take in the reality present to it. This is an unpleasant prosect for any unredeemed soul, but particularly painful to Jesus owing to his special closeness to God.

Holy Saturday declares that Jesus not only died, he also embraced the state of being dead. Therefore, just as Jesus' dying transforms our dying, his enduring the state of being dead redeems our separated, disembodied state. Jesus has plumbed and thus redeemed every evil that can befall us.

7.13 Hidden Victory
Verborgener Sieg
{1.5} Good Friday 1966 Bavarian Radio address. 3 consecutive talks. Revised.

Abstract: A meditation on the meaning of Holy Saturday as the redemption of the disembodied state, and on Easter as the answer to our deepest human longing and the hidden meaning at the heart of the world.

Topics: LITURGICAL YEAR, Holy Saturday; LITURGICAL YEAR, Easter; JESUS CHRIST, death/resurrection of.

Subsidiary Discussions: Soul, separated (152f); Hope (153ff); Resurrection (156f); Creed, He descended into hell.

Precis: I. What is the meaning of Holy Saturday, and of the creedal statement, "He descended into hell"? First it means that Jesus really died. "He has made himself one with us in death. He has shared our ultimate fate" (151). Second it means he experienced the state of being dead, the painful, remote, passive and lonely fate of the separated, disembodied soul.

II. The truth of our disembodied state is summarized by Paul who says, "Our life is hidden with Christ in God." God's life is in us but in a hidden mysterious manner marked by hope. The dying, the withdrawal from the world we endure every day of our lives is a foretaste of the final state of being dead. It is precisely in this daily experience of descent that we can unite ourselves with Jesus who overcame not only this but also the pain of the separated state.

III. Easter can be celebrated with noisy jubilation or with a more modest joy by those who have become tired to death under the burden of everyday toils and disappointments. To understand resurrection we must understand our deep human desire to achieve a definitive state which applies "to us in our complete natures as physical beings" (156) even though we cannot predict or picture such a state. Fixing our eyes on the risen Christ we are emboldened, not forced, to say "He is risen" soberly and calmly. This is because we are only asserting what we are at basis longing for ourselves if we take our humanity seriously and do not evade our responsibility by fleeing into nothingness. There is no depth to which death can drag us that has not already been experienced and redeemed by Christ's victory over death.

Christ and his hidden victory are already at the heart and center of all the poor things of this earth—in our blind hope, in the seemingly random movement of history, in all tears and in every death, even in our wretchedness, feebleness and sin. His victory is the secret seal of this world's eternal validity. This is what it means to say, "He is risen!"

7.14 Experiencing Easter
Ostererfahrung

{1.0} A. Röper, ed., *Der Vierzehn Stationen im Leben des N.N.* (Kevelaer, 1965) 120-132. Rahner's meditation on the 14th Station of the Cross.

Abstract: To apprehend the *sui generis* Easter experience demands rethinking time and eternity and also what passes for proof, not relying on the testimony of witnesses but on the resonance Easter truth finds in our own experience.

Topics: LITURGICAL YEAR, Easter; ETERNAL LIFE; TIME/ETERNITY.

Subsidiary Discussions: Freedom (162f); Resurrection of the body (167); Anonymous Christian (168).

Precis: Why assert that at death everything of oneself disappears from reality and turns into pure nothingness? Clearly, no one wants to go on indefinitely taking part in activities on this temporal plane. When time is eternally extended "everything would fall into the void of absolute indifference, where it would have no value" (161).

But is it not possible that something absolutely proper to human existence came into being in time which at death is born into and survives in the plane of eternity? Failure to think clearly about eternity often stems from the limits of our imaginations as we contemplate time. "A time which does not ...act as a starting-point for the spirit and for freedom does not in any sense give birth to eternity .... The final and definitive state of man, therefore is something that pertains to the dimension of spirituality and freedom in his mode of being .... As such it transcends time" (162).

Why must reality be confined to the level of an existence which even the most stupid and superficial would not contest? Morally, anyone who has ever acted with complete selflessness in a life-and-death situation has already experienced the timelessness of eternity.

But what proof do we have for the truth of the Easter experience? Although there are many cases when something which is objectively real and valid can only be accessible in the experience of someone else, Easter is *sui generis*. Here the testimony of witnesses such as the disciples is trustworthy and reliable not because we have seen the same thing (or ever can) but because it speaks something valid into our own existential experience. "Without the experience of the meaningfulness of existence which we receive from faith...we cannot achieve the necessary trustful self-commitment to the Easter witness of the disciples" (166). In this circle, faith in either one strengthens faith in the other. How could it be otherwise when what is at stake is not simply the validity of one objective fact among many others but the ultimate meaningfulness of life and human history as a whole?

Nothing forbids us to think along these lines. Is there a better solution to the question of the meaning of existence? "Is it really more honest, or simply in the last analysis, more cowardly when confronted with this basic question, to shrug one's shoulders in skepticism and yet to continue ... on as if everything did in fact have a meaning after all?" (167f)

7.15 Encounters with the Risen Christ
Begegnungen mit dem Auferstandenen
{0.5}   *Geist und Leben* 28 (1955) 81-86.
Abstract: Unsystematic meditations on the gospels of the first two Sundays after Easter: The Emmaus story (Lk 24); The Good Shepherd sayings (Jn 10).
Topics: LITURGICAL YEAR, Easter.
Subsidiary Discussions: Hope (169ff); Christology, "I am" (173ff).
Precis: Emmaus: Hope of the despairing (Lk 24: 13-35). The disciples on the road to Emmaus have had their hopes completely dashed. How strange, that they seek one another's company—seek consolation in talking together while they run away from Jerusalem. This chatter is the beginning of grace. They invite a stranger into their discussion, unable in their own hopelessness to recognize their fellow companion as Jesus. He points out to them how the Messiah had to suffer and die and invites them calmly to consider that it was Jesus' unique destiny to encounter the depths of such darkness. In a listening silence their hearts begin to be reborn. They invite the stranger to stay with them and share a meal. They recognize him in the breaking of the bread. How often do we on our pilgrim way glimpse the risen Lord breaking through the deepest of our disappointments?
The Good Shepherd. (Jn 10: 14-18). Most often this gospel is approached from the homey image of the shepherd whom Jesus claims to be. But the story must be approached backwards from a linguistic point of view: not from subject to predicate but from predicate to subject. This story stands in the long line of "I am" statements. Only when we understand what it means for the one who utters "I am" to call himself the good shepherd will we

understand the import of this gospel. Only the one who has freely and lovingly entered the meaningless void has the absolute authority to gather from chaos and bring into one flock all who are scattered. Summary (175).

7.16 He Will Come Again

Er wird wiederkommen

{1.5} *Geist und Leben* 32 (1959) 81-83 as "*Er wird so wiederkommen wie ihr ihn habt zum Hillem auffahren sehen.*"

Abstract: The mystery of Christ's ascension warns us not to expect the definitive on earth until he fulfills his promise and returns as he left. His promise of self-same return assures our own eternal and enduring validity.

Topics: LITURGICAL YEAR, Ascension; JESUS CHRIST, second coming of.

Subsidiary Discussions: Time/eternity (179); Creed, He will come again (passim).

Precis: The words spoken by the angels at the ascension of Christ (Acts 1:11) convey both a refusal/dismissal and a consolation/promise. The dismissal informs the apostles he is gone. He will not come again in his unambiguous, apprehensible human form. Future generations will have to rely on the testimony of others and not on sight. Our Christian life is essentially provisional and transitory. The definitive and enduring cannot be found here. The finite and infinite will be reconciled only later, when he comes again.

By way of consolation we are promised that he will come again "just as" he went. The Lord who returns will be identical with the one who ascended. He will be the one we know and experience. Nothing in him will have been lost or diminished. What he suffered and accomplished is finished but not lost. It has been made definitive in his death and rising.

This word of the angel also promises our own eternal validity. Jesus left so that in his physical absence "we could live *his* life; in order that when he returns he may find in us that which he brings with him to us of himself: a human life which belongs to God" (179). He lives on in us in our struggles through his presence in the world, the church and its sacraments. If in spite of this way of remaining on earth for the duration "he will so return as he has gone, then the word which we are here considering is a promise that he will give us the grace to live his life, for otherwise he could not come as he has gone" (179f).

7.17 The Festival of the Future of the World

Fest der Zukunft der Welt

{0.5} *Korrespondenzblatt des Collegium Canisianum* 96 (1961-62) 6-8. 1961. Meditation on the Ascension. Insbruck. Originally "*Christi Himmelfahrt.*"

Abstract: Meditations on five dimensions of the feast of Christ's Ascension.
Topics: LITURGICAL YEAR, Ascension; SPIRIT.
Subsidiary Discussions: Faith (181f); Resurrection of body (183f); Materialism (183f).
Precis: Although the Feast of the Ascension is part and parcel of the celebration of Easter it has unique dimensions. The ascension is:

–the festival of faith itself insofar as it points to that "little while" during which the church is denied access to Jesus' physical presence and lives by faith in things unseen. Faith in his future coming means living in the future. It is an eschatological faith.

–the festival of holy pain insofar as the church feels his absence, despite the consolation offered by the Spirit he sent. In fact his presence in Spirit is more important than his physical presence since even among those who touched him there were those who betrayed him.

–the festival of the future of the world insofar as his redeemed and glorified flesh is the very future destiny promised as a gift to all matter.

–the festival of nearness to God insofar as in his resurrected and glorified state he can be even nearer to us in Spirit than in the unredeemed physical state. Flesh both promotes and defeats our longings for intimacy.

–the festival of our preparation for Pentecost insofar as it is the transitional feast between the Easter of Christ and our own Easter when the Spirit comes at Pentecost. Thus, we celebrate Christ's ascension by watching and praying for his Spirit. In the end the meaning of any liturgical celebration is achieved only when it is lived out in the daily lives of believers.

7.18 The Church as the Subject of the Sending of the Spirit
Die Kirche als Ort der Geistsendung
{1.0} *Geist und Leben* 29 (1956) 94-98.
Abstract: The sending of the Spirit celebrated at Pentecost differs from "the Spirit who spoke through the prophets" insofar as the latter is the continuing presence of the Word incarnate now embodied in the visible church.
Topics: LITURGICAL YEAR, Pentecost; SPIRIT; CHURCH, Spirit in; TRINITY.
Subsidiary Discussions: Creed, He has spoken through the prophets.
Precis: Pentecost is the culmination of Easter. Together with Christ's exaltation on the cross these three moments constitute one feast. Death and resurrection are fulfilled in Pentecost. But what is Pentecost? It manifests the fact that the Spirit will never more be wholly withdrawn from the world until the end of time. What began with the incarnation continues to be visibly manifest in the church.

But how does this sending of the Spirit square with the creed which states that the Spirit had already spoken through the prophets? The sending of the Spirit at Pentecost differs in more than degree from the Spirit speaking through the prophets. The Spirit is now in the world in a new way. He now imparts himself to us as more than the remote creator of nature which in itself remains open to the endless cycle of birth and death. At Pentecost the Spirit lifts us out of our bondage to finitude and sin.

But how does the Spirit come upon us? Is there a visible, apprehensible point at which one can say, Yes, the Spirit has come upon me? This happens with the incarnation of the Logos when Jesus Christ entered human history. "The Church is nothing else than the further projection of the historicity and of the visibility of Jesus through space and time, and every word of its message, every one of its sacramental signs is...nothing else than a part of the world in its earthliness, with which the Spirit has united itself indissolubly since the day on which the Logos became flesh" (188f). At Pentecost this Spirit has become manifest...the Spirit of the Son who has become flesh. And where the Spirit is, there is the church. "Because the Church is there, therefore there is also a continual Pentecost" (190).

If this is true why do we so seldom see great signs as at the first Pentecost? In this age of faith we must condition ourselves to receive the Spirit. Ultimately, the Spirit blows where he wills and we are commanded to believe in him even when we do not feel him. Our task is to regard our feebleness as a sign of his complete power, to live in hope against all hope. More often than not, this is how the Spirit is present and works among us today.

7.19 The Spirit that is over All Life
Geist über alles Leben
{1.0} 1960 meditation on Pentecost. *Korrespondenzblatt des Collegium Canisianum* 94 (1960) 34-40. Originally, "*Gedanken an Pfingsten.*"

Abstract: Pentecost, the celebration of God's final and irrevocable acceptance of the world begun with the Incarnation of the Logos, inspires two attitudes in believers: responsibility and trust.

Topics: LITURGICAL YEAR, Pentecost; SPIRIT.
Subsidiary Discussions: Incarnation (195f); History (195f); Responsibility (198f); Trust (199f).
Precis: What do we celebrate at Pentecost? What does it mean to us personally?
I. Initial questions (193-5) reveal the problematic nature of Pentecost: if it is more than a simple anamnesis of an historical event how is it different from the presence of the Spirit in Old Testament times? What did it alter in human history? What does it add to Jesus' founding of the church? Was the Spirit available to people before Pentecost that much less? Were they less loved by God? Was everything before Pentecost inconsequential? Etc.

One must first understand that Christmas, Good Friday, Easter, and Pentecost constitute one salvific event: "the definitive and irrevocable acceptance of humanity in the incarnation of the Logos" (195). What is unique in this event is its definitive finality. Since the Word has taken flesh everything has become final. Human history has arrived at its goal. The Spirit which descended at Pentecost is the eschatological Spirit as the irrevocable gift: the invincible spirit of Christ.

II. There are two points at which this message comes home to us personally.

1). Responsibility: "The fact that God's power is effective in all that is, does not diminish the autonomous power of the creature (199). Both powers increase in direct not inverse proportion." The eschatological triumph of the Spirit of Pentecost is manifested in accepting one's responsibility for creaturely freedom at its most radical. "The hour of victory for the grace of Pentecost is also the hour of responsibility in its most intense form" (199).

2). Trust: The Spirit of Pentecost also provides the grounds for absolute trust. Without knowing the form or manner in which the Spirit will triumph believers know the victory will come. Therefore, we reject nothing, since the Spirit can use suffering, defeats, and even death to bring about the final victory. Everything can be, and in fact has already been, overcome by the Spirit. Trusting this, believers can endure everything in hope.

7.20 Sunday, the Day of the Lord
Sonntag, der Tag des Herrn

{0.5} June 1960 Holy Hour address. *Statio Orbis. Eucharitischer Weltkongress 1960 in Müchen*, II (Munich, 1961) 195-197.

Abstract: Sunday is designated by God for us to celebrate mastery over nature. We do this by exercising our true nature, freely worshipping the mysterious source of nature definitively revealed in Jesus' life and victory over death.

Topics: LITURGICAL YEAR, Sunday; HUMAN NATURE; CHRISTIAN LIFE, leisure.

Subsidiary Discussions: Eucharist (208).

Precis: What is Sunday? The Old Testament reveals it as a gift from God, a day of rest meant to remind us that we are masters and not slaves of nature. "Sunday, then, is the expression in tangible and liturgical terms, of the power actively to dispose of things instead of being disposed of, as the creative exercise of freedom on the part of spiritual beings instead of the passivity of merely natural ones" (206f).

Thus, there can be no purely "materialist" celebration of Sunday. Celebrating it on a merely physiological plane demeans us. "Sunday can only be rightly observed if man realizes himself *as man*" (207), a being capable of meeting and committing oneself to God in self-reflection. God's self-bestowal occurs in Jesus in whose death and resurrection the question of the meaning of life finds its definitive answer. This is the mystery Christians celebrate in each Eucharist.

Consequences follow from this realization. i) Sunday cannot be taken up completely with leisure activities sponsored by the entertainment industry. ii) Christians have a right to civil protection to keep this day holy according to the dictates of conscience. iii) Today when we can no longer expect that Sunday will be upheld by the force of social custom, each believer and spiritual person must take personal responsibility to understand and creatively celebrate this day in a manner befitting the holiness of human nature.

7.21 The Eucharist and Our Daily Lives
Eucharistie und alltägliches Leben
{0.5}   *Der große Entschluß* 17 (1962) 391-396, 440-443.
Abstract: Sacred and profane, two seemingly opposite spheres represented by Eucharist and everyday life, are in fact complementary. They are mutually conditioning and must be interpreted one in light of the other.
Topics: EUCHARIST; CHRISTIAN LIFE.
Subsidiary Discussions: Death (217ff); Virtues, theological (223).
Precis: The essay first (211-216) sets forth all that seems dichotomous about the redeemed realm embodied in Eucharist and the profane world of the everyday which seems remote from God and dangerous to the human spirit (summary, 214f). This being said, Rahner proposes: "This sacrament of the eternal encounter with God, this climax of our personal saving history...which is the Eucharist, is in fact the sacrament of the everyday" (216).

Why should this be so? Because Trent solemnly taught that Eucharist: i) is to be regarded as our daily bread; ii) has a remedial function which cleanses and preserves us from everyday sin; iii) is the supreme sacrament of sacred fellowship with God and the neighbors we meet each day and to whom we are bound by bonds of faith, hope, and love. Thus, "the most holy sacrament of the altar, is manifestly the sacrament of our everyday lives" (217).

Rahner next examines who is bestowed on us in this sacrament: the incarnate Logos, the crucified Lord and his salvific death. Death represents the ultimate in what we mean by the everyday, and Christ's death expresses the concentrated, the pure essence of what is apportioned to us again and again gradually and piecemeal in our everyday lives which is in essence a *prolixitas mortis*, the drawn out act of dying (219). But in receiving the crucified Lord we are also receiving as the innermost law of our lives the precise counterpoint to this slow death: the glorified Lord who achieved glorification by enduring a life that led through the sheer and absolute ruin of death.

Thus, the primary significance of Eucharist is not the strength it provides us to endure the everyday, but the task it lays upon us. For the everyday is not our proper share by chance. It is the very bond we share with Christ in baptism and at the table of the Eucharist. Both Christ and the everyday are bestowed on us in each celebration of the Eucharist.

How can we make this abstract truth part of our practical lives? First, we must withdraw into ourselves and in this state of recollection face up to ourselves as we really are, face up to the everydayness of our lives and the anxiety it produces in us. Only true believers will not run away. Only they will surrender their whole beings to God daily through faith, hope, and love. The final pages of this essay (224-226) offer a number of summaries all reinforcing the one point: accepting and enduring the everyday world is transformed in the act of accepting and enduring the everydayness suffered, overcome, and glorified in the death and resurrection of Christ made present at each celebration of the Eucharist.

7.22 On Truthfulness
Über die Wahrhaftigkeit
{1.5} 1960 address in Passau to Conference of Youth Workers
   Katechetische Blätter 85 (1960) 413-416; 468-474; 511-520.
Abstract: Explores five facets of truth/truthfulness: the relation of the two concepts; truthfulness with oneself; truthfulness in private relationships; truthfulness in public life; faith in, and love of hidden truth.
Topics: TRUTH; CHRISTIAN LIFE, truthfulness.
Subsidiary Discussions: Being (233f); Analogy (234); Mystery (233f); Intellectual honesty (235ff); God as truth (240f, 248); Virtue (241f); Revelation, divine (244f); Witness (244ff); Anonymous Christian (254ff); Reality (257f).
Precis: I. **Truthfulness innately connected with truth**. Truthfulness is the attitude which reverences truth as something of intrinsic value which is due one's fellows. In the present age truth is not so valued. The rise of the physical sciences has recast truth in terms of a relativized, skeptical pragmatism of only instrumental value. This section ends (223-4) with a concise statement of the metaphysical relationship of truth to being. Rahner argues truth is found in the horizon of any concept we grasp. It is omnipresent, unconditioned, presuppositionless, freely given, uniquely self-authenticating, incomprehensible mystery. Accepting (or rather being accepted by) this ultimate essence of truth is the foundation of human subjectivity and freedom. Truthfulness signifies the assent of the free individual to such truth.
II. **Truthfulness with one's self**. People today lack interior truthfulness. This is not so much a moral deficit as a result of our complex, skeptical, and cynical times when it seems more honest and courageous to deny what seems to answer the heart's deepest desire. In fact it takes more courage to live by the spirit than to reject it. This cannot be argued except by directing one to look steadfastly within to the depth of experience. An honest person will discover that today's radical self-questioning can only be achieved from an Archimedean point outside one's self (authority, community, tradition,

church). Refusing to take one's self as the absolute standard and leaving that role to God inaugurates that truth which sets us free. Yet this remains a gift. Summary (239).

III. Truthfulness in private relations. Honesty is not primarily a moral question. Liars act from insecurity or from attempts to prop up a false sense of self. Only those who have hidden their own true and ultimate selfhood in God and delivered it into God's protection find it no longer necessary to defend themselves. Rahner singles out two dimensions of this facet of truthfulness which are problematic today: the need to defend one's self against the power of mass media (242), and the need to balance truthfulness and tact (243f).

IV. Truthfulness in public life. Christianity of its nature attests to the truth. Every Christian must witness to the truth as an act of personal engagement. Although truth has not changed, the mode of witness has changed over the years. To Rahner this is not due to cowardice, though that is always a temptation. He ascribes it to a deeper appreciation for God's mystery, greater modesty, and the greater complexity of modern life and thought. Today one must wait to find a favorable climate to speak of faith. One's positions must be more carefully thought out and appropriated. Furthermore, to witness outside the church one must be able to exercise free expression within it. Official utterances too must always be genuine and truthful.

V. Love toward and faith in the unity of hidden truth. We live amidst greater diversity in every form of human life than ever before. Differences among us seem so great Christians begin to feel like a remnant, a threatened minority. But there is another attitude toward the world and one's neighbors that can be cultivated: the faith and hope that those around us, in living out the deepest promptings of their hearts are themselves anonymously Christian. This category is no abstract concept. It is the ability to make apparent to oneself the truth hidden in one's fellows. It is the truthfulness to be bold enough to let truth emerge for what it is in itself (256).

The article concludes with a summary look at the complex relation of truth to truthfulness vis-à-vis reality and being (257-259). Truth, the givenness of a thing to itself, is an intrinsic element of reality such that any given entity has being and exists to the extent that it realizes itself, thereby disclosing to itself the truth of its own nature. Thus, truth is not primarily a moral prescription but a metaphysical description. The source of truthfulness to others is the imparting of one's personal truth—free self-disclosure manifested in love. Yet the truth we disclose is always already given to us. Christianity is nothing more than the joyful news that absolute mystery freely bestows itself, its truth, to us too. Truthfulness is the indispensable mode in which we discover our own truth.

7.23 *Parresia* (Boldness). The Virtue Christians Need for the Apostolate.

Parrhesia

{0.5}   *Geist und Leben* 31 (1958) 1-6.

Abstract: The boldness needed by Christians sent to preach God's word in a hostile world is an extension of God's boldness in speaking the Word, the Logos, into the void of the world and enduring its consequences.

Topics: CHRISTIAN LIFE, boldness.

Subsidiary Discussions: Word of God (262f); Laity, apostolate of (265f); Silence (266); Mission mandate (266f).

Precis: Christian perfection is found in loving God and neighbor. Such love is the missionary task of every Christian. It is the Christian apostolate. But even scripture attests to our reluctance to speak out, to speak this word of love to others. Why? Because the Word is provocative, dangerous, unsettling. It is always inappropriate. Thus, the Christian apostle needs boldness, the New Testament virtue called *Parresia* (difficult to translate into German).

Christian apostles feel sent to an alien setting. They feel like intruders because their message is unwelcome and because it is awkward to put the unnameable into words. From this arises an elemental embarrassment. All true apostles are reluctant. Out of modesty and respect for the unutterable mystery they would rather remain silent than speak. *Parresia* provides the strength to bear and overcome this reluctance and to speak out in spite of it, just as God overcome any reluctance to overcome silence and speak to the world and to endure having the Word rejected (264).

Consequences: i) Caution is needed to judge a reluctant apostle. Glibness is not necessarily a sign of boldness, nor is reluctance necessarily a sign of cowardice, though people can reject the missionary task out of fear. ii) No Christian, clergy or lay, is absolved from speaking the word boldly in his/her respective sphere. iii) Our very reluctance to break the silence and to speak the word along with the quality of silence which accompanies our speech gives our words the ring of truth and holiness. Speaking of God must always proceed afresh from our sense of mission and a background of prayerful silence. Whatever its difficulties and risks the word must be spoken.

7.24 The Works of Mercy and their Reward

Preis der Barmherzigkeit

{1.0}   Previously unpublished.

Abstract: The reward for works of mercy, surrendering to and bestowing ourselves on our neighbor, is to receive the fullness of our compassionate God.

Topics: CHRISTIAN LIFE, compassion.

Subsidiary Discussions: God (270f); Incarnation (271f); Freedom (272f); Anonymous Christian (272f).

Precis: Compassion seems to entail condescension which inspires pride in the giver and robs the recipient of human dignity. Thus, compassion seems to belong only to God because human compassion humiliates the very ones it seeks to raise up. All this is made worse when the pride kindled by the compassion of the giver comes to loggerheads with the pride of self-reliance in the recipient who refuses help. Summary (270).

It seems the only ones who can be compassionate without incurring the pride of condescension are those who are conscious of being themselves the objects of compassionate love and to that extent know they are merely giving what they have already received. [Note: much of this discussion presumes certain classical distinctions of love: eros, charity, agape, terms Rahner does not define here.] But in this case do we not all simply bear the humiliation of God's original condescension, and all our acts of compassion merely spread this humiliation about like a contagion? No. Not if in the bestowal of the gift we, like God, give ourselves as well. But can we do this in our acts of charity?

To answer this question Rahner sketches a tentative hypothesis (271f). In the act of divine compassion we call the incarnation, God becomes one of us, and becomes responsible to us. Hence, as one of us his acts of compassion can never be condescending. The miracle of human compassion is this: freely abandoning ourselves to the unknown in service of our neighbor as Christ did, we encounter Christ and win a place in Christ's life and death. This happens even to those of us who eschew explicitly Christian categories. Accepting without reserve our own humanity and that of our neighbor, we have thereby accepted the Son of Man, because God has accepted us in him.

7.25 Proving Oneself in Time of Sickness
Bewährung in der Zeit der Krankheit
{0.5}   *Geist und Leben* 29 (1956) 64-67. Originally, *Reflexionen zur Zeit der Krankheit.*

Abstract: Sickness acquires redemptive value when it leads us to accept the mystery of human nature and to entrust ourselves to God. This free, spiritual act turns mundane existential patience into the true virtue of patience.
Topics: THEOLOGICAL ANTHROPOLOGY, freedom; CHRISTIAN LIFE, illness; CHRISTIAN LIFE, patience.
Subsidiary Discussions: Hylomorphism (275ff); Resurrection of body (276); Mystery (278f); Freedom (280ff).
Precis: We necessarily experience ourselves as a unity of body and soul. We control certain things and are controlled by others. We act and we suffer. Even our final destiny is not the separated state but the resurrection of the flesh. We experience the truth of this natural unity most acutely in sickness.

Sickness underlines our spirituality and our freedom. It also imposes the task of finding the meaning of our existence by exploring the limitations forced on our freedom by illness. When sick we realize how impossible it is to separate what we choose from what impinges on us from outside. In this ambiguity we glimpse the mystery at the core of our being. To accept this mystery is to say yes to God. It is the redemptive value of sickness. Summary (279).

Patience: Patience is a basic human attitude (unnecessary for either eternal or non-spiritual beings). Our capacity to distinguish past and future reveals the inevitability of change. Our capacity to recognize and accept change is called existential patience. Change also presents a spiritual task: deciding how to respond freely to the mysterious and uncontrollable elements of change. Are they random acts or purposive interventions leading to an ultimate destiny? Those who cling to the present out of anxiety or fear of the mystery never transform existential patience into the true virtue of patience.

When sick we become acutely aware of change and the limits of our control. This produces anxiety and forces to the surface the question of the ultimate meaning of our lives—whether we are on a meaningless trip to the void or are being directed to the ultimate goal of blessedness. In short sickness ask us whether we possess the true virtue of existential patience.

Faced with this decision we can take refuge in doubt disguised as false optimism, or in drugs which suppress our consciousness. Impatience in the face of sickness points to our failure to embrace the mystery directing our lives, bearing in mind that due to our very natures which both act and suffer we can never fully know how much of this impatience is willful act and how much is a symptom of external factors. Only God can judge. Summary (283f).

7.26 On Christian Dying
Über das christliche Sterben

{0.5} *Wort und Wahrheit* 14 (1959) 653-657. Originally, *Zum Tode verurteilt? Über das Sterben im christlichen Verständnis.*

Abstract: For Christians death possesses eternal validity because only in death does human freedom achieve its definitive state by how we respond to the complete powerlessness which then overtakes us.

Topics: THEOLOGICAL ANTHROPOLOGY, freedom; DEATH; LITURGICAL YEAR, Good Friday.

Subsidiary Discussions: Freedom (287ff); Protology, pre-lapsarian state (288f).

Precis: The death of Christ illuminates our death. Examining death in general illuminates the full meaning of Christ's death. What follows is a Christian study of death. Without denying the physical or biological it insists that human death is equally a spiritual reality since humans are endowed with freedom and responsibility.

Reflecting on the universality of death drives home the reality that "I must also die." Christians assert that the universal necessity of death has an absolute validity. It is in fact the inevitable goal of life since human freedom cannot find its definitive expression in the physical world with its radical openness to further development. Never-ending life on this plane is living hell to free beings (summary, 288). There follows a discussion of Adam's prelapsarian state and how even without death there must have been some way for him to transcend the physical and achieve definitive freedom (288f).

Freedom achieves its fullness in death. Death constitutes the absolute climax of the process of enfeeblement and deprivation of our power. We are intermediate beings, able to direct and control ourselves, but not absolutely. In the ultimate act of freedom we either willingly accept or definitively rebel against our utter impotence in which we are utterly subject to the control of mystery which cannot be expressed—that mystery we call God. Only when the last vestige of autonomous control is removed at the moment of death can we make a definitive free decision (290).

To Christians death does not occur at the point of physical death. All of life is the process of dying. Such a life can be either an act of faith that our lives and destinies are being controlled and rightly directed, or an act of despair motivated by anxiety. We have models of both: the death of the Son of Man who accepted death and thereby redeemed it, and the death of Adam. While we live, both modes of dying are concealed within us beneath the surface. Far from being tragic, the very fact we cannot know fully which has the upper hand in us makes it possible for us to choose freely between hope and despair.

It is important to reflect on death, especially on the death of the Lord. For Christians find the meaning of their deaths hidden in Christ's death on the cross. The death he endured with the hiddenness of free choice it demanded of him is just like ours. The two thieves crucified with him present a kind of allegory about our choice of whether and how to die with Christ.

VIII. FURTHER THEOLOGY OF THE SPIRITUAL LIFE 2
VII. *Zur Theologie des geistlichen Lebens,* (later, *Ein Grundriß des geistlichen Lebens*)

German edition: Einsiedeln, Benziger, 1966
U.S. edition: N.Y., Seabury, 1977
David Bourke, translator, 1971

This volume in the English edition comprises the last 4 parts of *Schriften zur Theologie*, VII.

8.01 Why and How Can We Venerate the Saints?
Warum und wie können wir die Heiligen verehren?
{2.0} *Geist und Leben* 37 (1964) 325-340, revised.

Abstract: Veneration and invocation of saints are legitimate and existentially meaningful religious acts today if seen as faith- and hope-filled extensions of the love of neighbor which Rahner argues is the same as love of God.
Topics: SAINTS, veneration of; LOVE of God/neighbor.
Subsidiary Discussions: Intercession (9f, 23); Theological Anthropology (11ff); Incarnation (11ff); History (14ff); Faith (14f); Anamnesis (15); Transcendence (19ff).

Precis: *Lumen gentium* covers dogmatic aspects of venerating saints. Here Rahner attempts to bring this teaching into dialogue with today's realities.
I. The Veneration of the saints as an existential and theological problem.
After a brief summary of *Lumen gentium*'s teaching on the veneration of saints, Rahner notes the document's failure to address the subjective side of this devotion. It is not obvious today why or how such veneration is possible.

The decline of the veneration of the saints in our own time. Without judging the trend, it is unassailable that veneration of saints has dwindled in today's world, as if the world had lost the capacity to do so even among those who would sincerely like to.

The experience of the silent God in our own time. Perhaps it is because our own dead seem so removed. We think of them as they once were and do not imagine them still living among us. More radically, perhaps it is because God seems so incomprehensible, remote, and silent. The dead seem to disappear into this silence, our own dead along with the holy men and women of past ages. This raises a host of questions (list, 8).

The problem of how the veneration of the saints is reconcilable with the adoration of God. Further serious questions surround the intercession of the saints as well as the honor due them. The old distinction between *dulia* and *latria* fails to show the unity of the two on the subjective level. Rahner concludes with a preview of his thesis that the unity of love of God and neighbor provides the key to answering these questions.

II. Some preliminary theological considerations. Rahner lists what cannot be covered in answering "what can be said positively to explain veneration of saints, especially its subjective elements."

Christ our mediator with the Father. Accepting Christ as our basic act of religion in which we attain to God's self-communication implies two things:
i) The significance of the humanity of Jesus for our relationship with God; Jesus remains truly human forever. His creaturely humanity, though hidden from our eyes, never becomes a matter of indifference. Too often our connection with the risen humanity of Jesus is wrapped in falsely concrete, mythological notions. Based on the principles of human nature "when I love Jesus I perform that act which effectively achieves direct relationship with God" (13). We never achieve transcendence by rising above or leaving behind the finite either in ourselves or in the world.

Excursus: The proximity of the silent God in Jesus Christ. Every age has its own challenge to experience God. Ours is to overcome God's silent distance. We do this by developing greater faith in Jesus primarily in loving our neighbor. "[I]t is possible for Christ to be our mediator in bringing us to the immediacy of God through the 'thou' of another as accepted in love" (15).

ii) The "presence" of the historical Lord. Accepting Christ as our basic act of religion also implies *anemnesis*, recalling and rendering present his history in the Eucharist and in the tradition of the church. In one act of religion we connect with the Jesus of history and the Christ of eternity.

The love of God and the love of neighbor is one and the same love. One may say these christological considerations do not answer the basic question of how and why to venerate saints. But they do show the value of those acts whereby creaturely entities mediate access to God and are therefore religious acts. Exploring the unity of love of God and neighbor in a single act will show how our relationship with Christ applies to the veneration of saints.

Personal love as a basic human act. After positing that love between a spiritual "I" and a similarly constituted "Thou" is the fundamental human act, Rahner addresses the objection that such primacy is reserved for our relationship with God. For God is not one object among others. God is the ultimate basis of experience and as such is only experienced indirectly. Love of a "Thou" is a pre-condition for hearing and responding to God.

Love of neighbor as love of God. Interpreted against the background of traditional theology, the theological virtue of charity reveals the amazing fact that "the exercise of love of neighbour is *ipso facto* and in itself the love of God" (18) each and every time the neighbor (as charity) is truly loved.

The experience of God as transcendental and as an object of enquiry in itself. Experience is a more basic act than reflection. The experience of transcendence is always more basic than forming concepts about objects which stand out against the transcendental horizon and which serve to mediate the immediate transcendental. Love of neighbor is the worldly act which mediates the original transcendental experience of God in grace. Loving Jesus Christ is the unique and highest act of love of neighbor. Summary (20f).

III. The veneration of the saints as adoration of God. Saints belong to Christ, to his body. They can be loved and this love can bring us in closer relationship to God in the same way love of neighbor does. In fact this connection between love of the saints and the love of God is more explicit and permanent. This is its one advantage over love of neighbor, although this latter is always the prerequisite experience for the former. Still, veneration of saints is never demanded. For those with the courage to hope that those who are loved are saved by God's grace, veneration of the saints is a natural extension of love of neighbor. Intercession is legitimate not as a court of second instance but as an act whereby we take refuge in faith in the all-enfolding community of the redeemed. Summary (23).

8.02 All Saints
Allerheiligen
{0.5}   *Geist und Leben* 29 (1956) 323-326.
Abstract: All Saints Day and All Souls Day provide the chance to ask why we venerate saints and why the church has the right to canonize its members.

Topics: SAINTS; LITURGICAL YEAR, All Saints; LITURGICAL YEAR, All Souls.
Subsidiary Discussions: Saints, canonization (26f); Church, holiness of (27f); Hope (28f).
Precis: Though each feast has its own mystery, All Saints (Nov. 1) and All Souls (Nov. 2) share a common meaning: they celebrate those who have gone before us in faith. On the surface the special mark of All Saints is the solidarity we feel with those who have made it; the hope that *our* beloved too will share eternal bliss; that all human life is so precious it can be brought to this final outcome; that God can make us all into saints.

At the deeper theological level this day celebrates the many anonymous saints along with those who were canonized. But how, by what right can the church canonize saints? Can it see into the recesses of the human heart? The answer rests on the nature of the church. It is not merely a juridical institution. It is itself holy. Its holiness consists in a special way in the holiness of its members. Its mission is not simply to enforce rules. "Rather she is the compassion of God as eschatologically victorious. She is the victory of that grace which has not merely *sought* to save man, but actually *has* saved them" (27). The impact of Christ's victory is irreversible in human history because it has been accepted in the dead and risen flesh of Christ. The church is witness and representative of this truth. It is because of this that the church can canonize "because the grace of God is present in the world as eschatologically victorious, because this grace is attainable in the Church, which is the salvation of God actually come into the world ..." (27).

The glory of the canonized saints falls as well on the unknown saints. In praising All Saints we celebrate the church itself which remains the church of sinners and yet offers us all the promise and possibility of salvation. Thus this feast is our festival too—the day on which we make a fresh start. It is a feast of hope that what those saints already possess may be imparted to us too. Such hope is not mere optimism. It is hope in the victory of Christ. It is not a grace we earn but a grace bestowed. We hope because there are saints. All Saints is also a festival of love. On this feast we praise God for his love and mercy which gives us courage and trust.

8.03 Ideas for a Theology of Childhood
Gedanken zu einer Theologie der Kindheit
{2.0} October 1962 lecture to 2nd International Convention of the SOS Children's Villages, Hinterbühl. *Geist und Leben* 36 (1963) 104-114.

Abstract: Good parents foster the infinite openness of childhood which remains alive within us to develop into mature childhood and the ability of the adult to trust radically the infinite mystery of life.
Topics: THEOLOGICAL ANTHROPOLOGY, childhood.

Subsidiary Discussions: Time (33ff); Sin, original (39f); Mystery (42f, 47ff); Concepts, transference of (45ff); Analogy (45ff); God as father (46f). **Precis**: What does the revealed word say about childhood? What meaning does it have? What task does it lay upon us for the perfecting and saving of humanity?

I. The unsurpassable value of childhood; Influenced by the secular notion of time we tend to think of childhood as a temporary, provisional stage of life that completely vanishes with the coming of adulthood and whose value derives from the fruit it bears in later life. Rahner insists childhood has its proper validity. The exercise of human freedom draws together our past, present, and future into an enduring valid reality. The eternity promised us is not a further stage of life nor the prolongation of adulthood. It is the eternal validity life enjoys as a whole from the transcendent acts of loving freedom we have engaged in our whole life long. Thus, childhood endures. Its meaning remains always open. We do not move away from it but towards its definitive meaning and unique fruits. Childhood is valuable in itself ... "to be discovered anew in the ineffable future which is coming to meet us" (37f). Summary.

II. The Christian awareness of childhood; What do Christian scripture and tradition say about childhood? The child is already the adult, equipped by God with an allotted task and with the grace to perform it from the very outset, with all the inexpressible value and burden of responsibility it entails. The child is already a fresh and unique blend of spirit and body, nature and grace, nature and person, self-possessed but influenced by the world it enters and needing to actualize itself in freedom. Childhood is a beginning in two senses. The child is a fresh creation but never a completely pure beginning. The child is compromised by original sin *and* encompassed by the salvific love and grace of God.

The child is a child. Scripture never defines this state but expects us to draw its meaning from our experiences which are admittedly ambiguous, dark, complex, conflicting. The Christian view of childhood is realistic and idealistic. Without glorifying children or failing to recognize the radical insufficiencies of their natures Jesus does see in them those whom he can receive lovingly into his heart.

The child is a mystery (summary, 42). When we respond to life as mystery original childhood is preserved within us forever—"a state in which we are open to expect the unexpected, to commit ourselves to the incalculable, a state which endows us with the power still to be able to play, to recognize that the powers presiding over existence are greater than our own designs, and to submit to their control as our deepest good" (42). The kingdom of heaven is for those who are children in this sense, i.e., mature children.

III. The fullness of childhood consists in being children of God; What does it mean to be a child of God? A secure childhood among loving parents seems essential to develop radical trust in God as Father. Here Rahner goes into a detailed discussion of "transference" of concepts (the Thomistic notion of prime analogates) and concludes that applying the term Father to God is legitimate not as a simple extension of the term from the physical to the metaphysical, but because "the human concept of childhood and parenthood is only fully realized when it is transferred to God (47). He argues this in three steps: i) childhood remains an active stage of our lives as subjects; ii) when it remains an effective force at the roots of our lives we are able to endure the depths of our own mystery; iii) thus, human childhood orients us to God and achieves its perfection in our real identity as children of God. The remaining pages expand the ramifications of this point in various ways.

8.04 The Sacramental Basis for the Role of the Layman in the Church

Sakramentale Grundlegung des Laienstandes in der Kirche
{2.0}   *Geist und Leben* 33 (1960) 119-132.

Abstract: By sacramental consecration every Christian in the visible church is authorized, empowered, and equipped for the task of actively cooperating in the church's supreme task: witnessing to the victory of Christ.

Topics: CHURCH, membership; LAITY; SACRAMENTS.

Subsidiary Discussions: Baptism (55ff); Anonymous Christian (55, 58f, 62ff); Eschatology (63ff); Confirmation (68); Penance (69); Eucharist (69); Orders, sacrament of (69f, 73); Matrimony (70); Anointing of sick (71).

Precis: Since World War I the church exhorted the laity to become more active. Given its long history of clericalism and institutionalism it's hardly a shock to discover the laity did not respond. Today we are in the initial stages of an awakening authored by the Spirit. An honest look at the church today reveals: 1) a highly clerical institution which views its members primarily as objects to be taught and sanctified; 2) a membership whose identity is primarily negative, i.e., non-professionals, amateurs, those not equipped to administer the church. This essay explores the essential task every Christian receives with baptism, and how the sacraments equip us to fulfill our task.

Through baptism one is justified by becoming a member of Christ's body, the visible church. The essence of this baptism is not the salvation of the individual, for this is possible even for the unbaptized, but the building up of the visible church. Without it the grace of God in Christ would no longer be "present in the world as an event, and an event which is manifest and enduring in history and incarnate in a physical body" (56). All the baptized share thereby in the task of the church: "*being* the historical concretisation of the grace of God in the world" (57). What are the implications? The grace of incarnation has a real history so as to reveal itself as a free act of God and not as a necessity. In this form it is able to confront human beings in their history. Thus, the church provides an outlet for grace to break into every aspect of the human world to transform them all in Christ.

Baptized Christians differ from unacknowledged (anonymous) Christians by their visibility and by their absolute obligation to be the body of Christ everywhere they find themselves. The baptized bear the Word to others. Hidden Christians are special objects of their solicitude. The church relates differently to its visible members. She is more harsh with them because as members of Christ's body their failings compromise the church and its task (summary, 60f).

Baptism does not impart a hierarchic position but a new task: "establishing the dominion of God in truth, in selflessness and in love, and thereby making what is truly essential to the Church's nature present in the setting in which he is placed" (62). This is an eschatological announcement directed in great part to "Christians outside the visible Church" (64f). Summary.

The church cannot be known beginning with its distinctions, clerical and lay, however valid. Beginning with the unified whole and saying the church is the body of Christ reveals that it is primarily a charismatic and not a juridic entity. Every authentic element of the church, including its leadership of service, flows from above. None is an end in itself but all serve the one authentic task of the church. Rahner next (68-71) enumerates how each of the post-baptismal sacraments equip one in special ways to fulfill this task.

Rahner concludes that in the church the word "layman" has exactly the opposite meaning it bears in the world. Whereas in the world lay status excludes one from participation, through baptism each member of the church is invested with the supreme dignity of participating fully in the internal and external mission of the church. Though there remains a very real difference between clerics and the laity ("an ascending order of rank and degree") these differences only regard specific functions—not holiness, or one's being loved by God, or the significance of one's function for salvation, or the basic inescapable task laid upon all the baptized. Summary (73f).

8.05 The Position of Women in the New Situation in which the Church Finds Herself

Die Frau in der neuen Situation der Kirche

{1.0} June 1964 address to the Union of German Catholic Women, Munich. O. Brachfeld, et al., eds., *Die Frau im Aufbruch der Kirche* (Munich 1964) 120-145.

Abstract: Women will be best at creating models for women to take the message of Christ into the new world situation—a task derived from their baptism, and which, despite its secularity, is Christianity's essential function.

Topics: CHURCH and women; WOMEN.

Subsidiary Discussions: Future (76); Metaphysics, universal/particular (77f, 87f, 91); Society, globalization (78ff); Orders and women (82, 84f); Religious life, women (85f, 89); Religion, feminine qualities of (92).

Precis: This discussion is difficult because: i) the church is an extremely complex unity in diversity; ii) to speak of *the* situation in the world overlooks the plethora of nations and cultures; iii) to speak of *the* woman in the world overlooks their rich differences. It is risky to talk about the future of women because although it is easy to list the elements of the past one hopes to eradicate, it is impossible to know which elements will actually endure. Both the past and the future have value but they are only discovered when the two are held in loving, creative tension. Rahner lists six enduring aspects of human life in the world, the Christian response to which must remain positive without being naive, and critical without being defensive. The past never presents an ideal pattern for the future. Too much is beyond human control and our conception of the future is all too often rigidly abstract.

The church assumes a realistic detachment from the past and future which may seem tiresome. But to say anything meaningful about women in the new situation we must remain sanguine about the enduring gulf between the clear, eternally valid but abstract principles derived from the gospel and natural law, and their application in concrete and often messy circumstances. This gulf makes differences of opinion valid and necessary, and at the same time makes every historical application provisional.

I. The unity of the world and the consequences of this for the church: The "new situation" is increasingly secular globalization, a reversal of the tower of Babel, accompanied by a startling possibility of cosmic atheism. Nonetheless, this development is a child of the West and a flowering of Christianity which proclaims the responsible use of freedom to create a more humane world. Such a world necessarily affects the church and its self-understanding. As the church becomes more global it loosens its association with any particular culture. It is freer to create itself though conscious planning. The world of the future will undoubtedly be less directly shaped by the church. It mission will remain the same but its membership and resources will surely shrink to become more like leaven in the lump, a sign, an *Ur-sakrament*.

II. Concrete requirements for the equal status of woman to be made effective in the church: What is the significance of this new situation for the church? 1) *"In her own personal life too the Church must recognize without reserve the fact that women have equal value and equal rights with men."* Vatican II's pronouncements on the laity sharing in the mission of the church based on baptism is equally true of men and women. [In a brief aside on women and ordination (82) Rahner calls that discussion inopportune at this time in the church's history whatever its theological merits. He urges patience.] As women increasingly find themselves in new settings they will have the task of proclaiming Christ there. The church must work as aggressively as society to rid itself of sexual stereotypes and prejudices, allowing that women can do much the same work as men, bringing to bear the particular gifts of her sex.

2) *"In her preaching and in her cure of souls the Church must take into account the unmarried, independent and professional woman no less than the mother and the housewife."*

3) The priest shortage has impelled the church to ask women to assume a greater role in fulfilling its apostolic mission. It has given them *"a share in the apostolate of hierarchy itself"* (84). This is not a condescension on the part of clergy but women's rightful assumption of their baptismal charism. Rahner has no difficulty calling such women deaconesses (84f).

4) Less patriarchal relationships must be built between clerics/women.

5) *"The church must be bold and far-sighted in demanding that the religious communities of women shall be shaped in accordance with the needs of the time."*

III. The indispensability of women for the new tasks that are theirs:

1) The fresh problems presented to women by this new situation are best addressed and solved by them. Though the church has a legitimate role enunciating universal binding norms, deciding how to apply these in concrete circumstances is best left to women themselves. They must provide the models and patterns of their own future. Women must decide how best to fulfill their baptismal mission in a new world. Most likely there will not be one model, but the Spirit will suggest many with which to experiment. Women's worldly work as lay ministers constitutes a truly Christian task.

2) To address the new situation women will need both loving acceptance of the past and critical faculties—"the complex attitude in which she both gives herself to, and withholds herself from the historical reality with which she is confronted" (90). This in turn will demand a deeper theological knowledge based on scripture, church teaching, and existential experience.

3) Women have much to offer the religion of the future, by imbuing it with what Rahner sees as feminine characteristics (list, 92). Summary (93).

8.06 On the Situation of the Christian Intellectual

Zur Situation des katolischen Intellectuellen

{1.5} Previously unpublished May 1966 lecture at Frankfurt a. M. Originally, *Aufgabe und Varantwortung des Hochschullehrers in der Sicht des Konzilskonstitution "Die Kirche in der Welt von heute,"* expanded.

Abstract: Examines the post-Vatican II situation and new tasks confronting believing intellectuals (scientists/professors) to the extent their faith and their work influence each other.

Topics: DIALOGUE; SCIENCE and religion; FREEDOM, intellectual.

Subsidiary Discussions: Vatican II (passim); Vatican II, *Lumen gentium* (97ff); Magisterium (100ff); Creed, brief (105f); Mystery (106ff); Theological Anthropology (106ff).

Precis: I) The new situation: Vatican II opened a wider sphere of intellectual freedom to church members. Ancient principle became reality. Vatican I taught: that revelation was only one valid source of significant human knowledge; other sources of knowledge possess autonomy but remain interconnected; productive dialogue between them is possible. In short, faith and science are of vital importance to one another. *Lumen gentium* makes this connection explicit (summary, 97). Vatican II put this principle into practice by reconsidering monogenism, marital ethics and population, biblical scholarship and exegesis, it's openness to non-Western cultures and its willingness to go beyond neo-scholasticism. All this showed the impossibility of solving pressing world problems on the basis of revelation alone. Dialogue with science is essential.

The church still identifies itself as an "absolute system." Invested by God with an absolute teaching authority to fulfill its mission, the church is not a debating society tolerating any opinion. Intellectuals unable to embrace this or actively opposing church teachings have no compelling reason to call themselves members. Thus, believing scientists must assent to the church's teaching authority *and* maintain professional integrity of conscience. These need not conflict because: 1) truths, however arrived at, can never be opposed; 2) church teaching is guaranteed indefectible by the abiding presence of the Spirit. This allows that provisional, non-definitive church decisions can be false or exaggerated, just as scientific statements are open to revision. Not all conflicts are easily resolved. In the meantime patience and mutual respect are required. The existence of such conflicts should not cause surprise. The church and the scientific community work at different tempos; scientists and theologians often fail to grasp one another's methods; even the church has difficulty distinguishing definitive dogma from revisable doctrine.

II) **The new tasks:** To the question, "How do my work and faith fit together?" it is enough for scientists to have present in their hearts a basic awareness that their lives are ultimately oriented toward God and that God is responsible for the way they conducts their lives as a whole. But the work of scientists may and must remain worldly. A second task is to know the faith. Here Rahner provides a precis of the Catholic faith (106f) intended to show there is nothing in it which is irreconcilable with the modern mentality. All Christianity demands is that one concedes that Mystery lies at the center of one's existence. In developing the virtues demanded of good scientists they simultaneously say yes to this Mystery and achieve their salvation.

In the present situation the task of initiating dialogue rests largely with scientists. It need not be institutional. It could take the form of influencing public opinion. In short, scientists who fulfill their professional and human duty thereby perform their Christian task. For to serve humanity in love is to serve God. Summary (111f).

8.07 On the Task of the Writer in Relation to Christian Living

Der Auftrag des Schriftstellers und das christliche Dasein
{1.0} *Werke und Jahre* (Salzburg 1962) 66-86. Originally, *Über den Buchautor.*

Abstract: Authorship, a free human act with moral dimensions, is an inherently Christian act though not always explicitly grasped by author or reader.

Topics: CHRISTIAN LIFE, authorship; ANONYMOUS CHRISTIAN.
Subsidiary Discussions: Grace (113f); Responsibility (115f); Censorship (119ff).
Precis: I. The thesis, every author precisely *as such* is a Christian, leads Rahner to discuss anonymous Christianity. Each life is made up of chance circumstances (nationality, etc.) and transcendent conditions or "existentials." Christianity is one of the latter. It perdures even when not consciously grasped or when denied outright. No one can undo being loved by God, redeemed by the Logos, open to the infinite, invited to self-transcendence. Even where this knowledge remains unconscious, this openness to the infinite mystery at the heart of each human being makes us restless. Summary (114f).

In what sense is the author *as such* a Christian? As a free act, without regard to content, writing has moral relevance. Moral responsibility appears at several levels: the author must write truthfully, write the truth, write intelligibly, respond to the urgent needs of the day and take the consequences for writing. Such activities draw one into the Christian sphere because: i) such writing can only be accomplished with God's help; ii) every free act confronts one with the question of one's own salvation.

In addition, whenever authors write about humanity, whether about some or all of humanity, they either appeal to or deny the Christian message. This is true whether or not they fully understand what they are saying. Readers and critics must be cautious here since what may seem to be denial may simply be the inevitable product of the ambiguity which enters every discussion of the mystery at the heart of human existence. Thus, when it comes to censorship, although care must be taken to protect the immature, mature Christians must be fully and unreservedly free to explore all writings that are truly great, bringing with them an attitude of sympathetic love. "And in all this we must not judge those who do not share our Christian belief" (121). Summary.

II. Five kinds of authors can justifiably be called Catholic: **1)** Those who restrict themselves to the immediate foreground of experiences, and may be voicing a genuine Christian modesty and reverence for the ineffable mystery which should never be spoken of lightly. **2)** Those overwhelmed by questions, who address the mystery of life by emphasizing the problem of humanity and aid complacent believers. 3) Those full but anonymous Christians who, despite being unconscious of the Christian content of their work, often write more compellingly than professed Christians. 4) Professedly non-Catholic authors who fail to realize their position is in fact a Catholic one. Old denominational lines can result in different modes of expression while what is being said remains substantially the same. 5) Professedly Catholic authors. This category is completely legitimate. Though they write "privately" they should continue to write boldly about their experience of sin and grace. Rahner offers a third thesis without elaboration: "the author is wholly and ... always susceptible of being judged and criticised by Christian standards" (129).

8.08 Prayer for Creative Thinkers
Gebet für geistig Schaffende
{0.5}   *Der große Entschluß* 10 (1954) 9-10.
Abstract: Rahner asks God to aid thinkers, poets, artists in their activities which mirror the image of God: creator, incarnate word, source of inspiration.
Topics: CHRISTIAN LIFE, creativity; TRINITY.
Subsidiary Discussions: Courage (130f); Incarnation (131f); Eschatology (132).
Precis: Rahner invokes God the creator and source of creativity in praying for all who have a creative contribution to make to the world. We need poets, thinkers, artists who in realizing themselves in their creative efforts discover and express that nature which is an image and likeness of God's glory.

He prays that the Spirit will fill them with courage: to respond to their inner call, to bear the pain it involves, to resists self-betrayal for fame or gain. He prays God will grant them the experience that life is not a meaningless hell, but also a heaven of infinitude and freedom. Whether they speak explicitly of God or remain silent, he prays that God may always be the source of their inspiration, will give them the courage to find joy, to distinguish and decide good from evil, to constantly begin anew, to work with undivided hearts, and not to give in to frustration.

As through the incarnation Jesus put his heart at the center of the world, Rahner prays that every personal creative effort will participate in the personal history of the Word made flesh. He hopes creative people will understand that whatever they create is either a part of the cross which condemned Christ and contributes to their condemnation, or is a part of building the kingdom which is a moment of grace for them. Through their efforts may they proclaim and promote the eschatological reality of the coming kingdom.

8.09 On the Evangelical Counsels

Über die evangelischen Räte
{3.5}   *Geist und Leben* 37 (1964) 17-37.

Abstract: The evangelical counsels are acts of renunciation that make faith explicit and recall the church to its eschatological nature.

Topics: CHRISTIAN LIFE, holiness; RELIGIOUS LIFE, evangelical counsels; CHRISTIAN LIFE, states of perfection.
Subsidiary Discussions: Death and passion (154f, 162f); Faith (145, 154ff).

Precis: I. Statement of the problem. To address both the charismatic and juridic structures of the church, Vatican II needed to discuss religious orders. It did this in two places: in the context of the call to holiness of all the baptized, and in a special section. It taught that all Christians have a radical vocation to develop to the full all that has been given in God's own act in baptism. All are called to that maturity of the Christian life (i.e, "perfection" or "holiness" *Lg* V #39-42). By so upgrading the vocation of marriage this teaching seemed to eclipse the older teaching on the superior status of religious life. Still the council maintained that a life governed by the evangelical counsels (religious orders) has a special value and function (*Lg* VI #43-47). Here Rahner synthesizes these two truths through dialectical confrontation. The process deepens our understanding of each truth and purifies both of unconscious errors they have long carried.

II. Some theses. In the post-Vatican II theological situation religious orders must resolve the tension between their lives as characterized by the evangelical counsels and the universal call to holiness. Rahner hopes to aid in this by developing in thesis from an account of what is essential to the evangelical counsels.

1. *"The fact that all are called to perfection."* God offers each person the possibility and duty to love God and neighbor with all one's heart. This is the call to attain perfection, and apart from this there is no perfection. Precisely how each one does this may differ but the duty remains the same. (On every Christian's need for the spirit of the evangelical counsels, 140 ftn6.)

2. *"Man's concrete stations in life considered as a calling to perfection."* The concrete circumstances of one's life and calling can be, precisely as such, factors in one's vocation to holiness. One is not merely called to holiness *in* a state of life, one is also called *to* a state of life. Marriage is such a positive vocation for the majority, "addressed to them by the God of creation *and* of redemption, and not merely an element in the old order tragically perverted by sin, which is tolerated even in the case of the redeemed [by] reason of their weakness and hardness of heart" (143f). In what sense then is the virginity of the evangelical counsels a "better means" to perfection if it cannot mean better for the majority?

3. *"The character of every Christian vocation to perfection as pertaining to saving history."* The call of each baptized person has a significance as part of

saving history. Insofar as each life shares in the cross and resurrection of Christ it is a life of eschatological faith as expressed in the Sermon on the Mount and the evangelical counsels. Most people live out this spirit in a less permanent, organized, or focused way than those in religious orders.

4. *"The duty to strive for that perfection which is made possible for us by God."* All gifts along with the circumstances in which and freedom with which they are exercised come from God. Refusing a "better way" God clearly offers and gives one the wherewithal to follow is "an explicit denial of the will to a greater increase in the love of God, and therefore culpable and a sin" (146).

5. *"The evangelical counsels as a means of personal perfection."* Scripture assures us there is a divine vocation to the evangelical counsels which entails renouncing marriage. Every Christian must ask seriously whether s/he may be called to this life. For those who are called, this is the "better means" of attaining Christian perfection. This is self-evidently true. For why else is renouncing human love (barring unfortunate cases) not only legitimate but also a better means for some to obtain a greater love of God?

6. *"Renunciation considered as the realization and confirmation of faith."* "The essence of the evangelical counsels consists in the fact that they constitute the *concrete* and comprehensible realisation of belief … in the grace of God that overcomes the world and is our salvation" (150). Poverty, chastity, and obedience share one theological nature: renunciation of supreme benefits of life. This can only be genuine if these benefits are esteemed and renounced for the sake of an objectively connected higher good. This is only possible when renunciation becomes the concrete realization of one's will to a higher good which: a) is unmerited, b) opposes the world's sinful corruption, c) is bestowed as a future, other-worldly good. Such faith only becomes concrete in a surrender of this-worldly values which, though not identical with that demanded by the universal experience of suffering and death, makes this act the ultimate. Renunciation takes faith out of the realm of theory.

It follows: a) every Christian is called to asceticism; b) faith and asceticism are not synonymous; c) each Christian must blend flight from and assent to the world according to one's particular calling. Evangelical counsels (definition, 156) are one valid way to live out this faith. But it is only made explicit in renunciation "the element which specifies this faith, considered as the acceptance of divine grace from above" (157). This is because every positive act has an intrinsic meaning in this world, and simple suffering can as easily seem to point to the meaninglessness of this world.

Interpreting and justifying evangelical counsels are difficult because they are not needed to attain Christian perfection. Other forms of life are positive moral vocations. But because every positive act in the world is conditioned by sin, only renunciation proceeds directly from the love of God. Thus, the evangelical counsels express and manifest "*that* faith which, in laying hold of the grace of God, at the same time withdraws from the effort to achieve a position in the world" (159).

7. *"The status of Christians under the evangelical counsels and in the world."* For these reasons (summary, 159f) evangelical counsels can be called objectively better or more blessed but in a restricted sense (i.e., ontologically). They are not better for everyone, or because they always produce the end at which they aim, but only because they are objectively better ordered to their end. The counsels are the superior form of enacted faith because they alone have no meaning apart from faith. They prepare us for the renunciation of death—an irrational activity in the world's view. Summary (163).

8. *"The ecclesiological (symbolic) significance of the evangelical counsels."* The evangelical counsels (like martyrdom) have an essential status and function in the visible, charismatic church. They remind it of its eschatological nature. They also have a soteriological character. Christians in the world remind religious they cannot compel grace; religious remind those in the world they too are pilgrims whose worldly activities do not win salvation.

8.10 The Theology of Poverty
Theologie der Armut
{1.5} *Geist und Leben* 33 (1960) 262-290 as, *Die Armut des Ordenslebens in einer Veränderten Welt.* Delivered to a conference of religious orders.

Abstract: After detailing the essentials of evangelical poverty and outlining the difficulties living it today, Rahner concludes that sub-communities of large orders have the best chance of developing new modes of witnessing to it.

Topics: RELIGIOUS LIFE, evangelical counsels (poverty).

Subsidiary Discussions: Neighbor (185f); Grace (188); Work (199ff).

Precis: The difficult task of developing a theology of evangelical poverty is made all the more complex when one attempts to avoid ideology and abstraction and speak instead from the prevailing religious and socio-economic situation. The results from such an effort will necessarily be partial. But just as in many other important areas of life practical reason outstrips theoretical knowledge without thereby denigrating the latter, the results of this investigation do not denigrate the value of evangelical poverty as it is lived today.

I. Some traditional problems: 1) How can one maintain that a member of a rich order is actually poor? If one's poverty resides in the fact that permission must be sought to use the possessions of the order then "poverty degenerates into a mere modality of community life and obedience" (173). 2) Poverty is neither dependence upon others in the disposal of material goods, nor the juridical concept of the absence of private property. 3) Religious poverty and poverty in one's mode of life should not be confused for one another if for no other reason than "the Church has recognized as legitimate the various modes of poverty practiced in the individual orders"

(175). 4) Poverty as practiced by the orders, shaped as it is by varying histories, apostolates, and motives, will exhibit an irreducibly complex theology.

II. The theological interpretation of evangelical poverty: Three provisos attend this inquiry: these remarks will be very abstract; they may not lay bare all the roots of this complex reality; they must try to do justice to the various theological reason which inspire the practice of poverty. **1.** Preliminary observations concerning the limits within which we can and must find the theological essence of poverty. **a)** "[A]ll forms of the religious life are conscious of being authorised in their practice of poverty simply by the very fact that Jesus has recommended it ... *one* element in this poverty is precisely the inalienable connection with the Lord and his personal lot" (177). **b)** Poverty as practiced by the orders is ecclesial in that it concretizes the spirit of the church. **c)** The meaning of poverty in any particular order is determined by the broader more comprehensive significance which the community itself is intended to have. **d)** The mode of poverty practiced by any particular order will be affected by its apostolate. **2.** How to synthesize these points (summary, 180)? Foremost one must hold that the two elements of New Testament poverty (identification with Christ, and the command to sell all things to follow him) and the ecclesial dimension of evangelical poverty need not and cannot come into conflict. The three are intrinsically related in service of the kingdom. All of an order's apostolic aims can be achieved within the purview of religious poverty. **3.** Here Rahner reviews the New Testament warrant for evangelical poverty (excluding the 'communism' of Acts, Paul and James) and summarizes (186) that it is the outcome of of the situation of eschatological salvation requiring us to be in the state of radical preparedness for the kingdom of God, a means of setting the individual free and enabling one to devote oneself to missionary activities. It is more than poverty of spirit. **4.** From this Rahner draws three theological conclusions: **a)** "Poverty is a combination of interior attitude and exterior 'work'" (187). In poverty the heart is to be made visible. Simple compliance with external rules does not guarantee this. Material detachment is not yet faith and love. **b)** Poverty is a graced act of faith in the meaning of the world or the possibility of transcending it. In this sense one cannot view the poverty of the orders as a completely different way of life from that of other Christians. Nor is there a directly proportional relation between detachment from the world and drawing nearer to God. This can never be the religious ideal. **c)** Religious poverty is always ecclesial. Hence, "we must do our utmost to give the practice of this poverty a form such that it can maintain this function of bearing witness to the faith of the Church and in the Church, both internally and externally" (190).

III. On the contemporary situation with regard to the forms assumed by religious poverty: Since poverty and riches are not completely relative concepts, can the poverty of religious communities be made meaningful in today's socio-economic order? The following remarks are fragmentary. 1) Religious communities are poorer now but the higher general standard of living makes insecurity for most religious highly unlikely. 2) Life for most people is more secure, and a simple lifestyle makes life more secure. Today when wealth is represented not so much by goods as by the ability to make wealth, educated religious are not seen as truly poor. For them to beg is inadmissible. Common ownership of property is primarily a practical arrangement. The fact that today's religious poverty has little to do with any kind of insecurity threatens its witness character. 3) Juridical dependence on the permission of the superior (often little more than a legal fiction) can never substitute for religious poverty which must remain subjected to the yoke of genuine dependence. 4) Many of the goods owned and used by religious today (libraries, computers, etc.) are intended to make them more effective. Must efficiency be sacrificed for poverty? 5) Does present-day poverty still possess that formative power for religious? (Summary, 203f) Though it may not amount to anything more than consumer ascesis, might this be a sufficient ground to retrieve the meaning and practice of religious poverty? 6) How much of the compromise religious have made to today's socio-economic situation was necessary? How much of what has been retained of religious poverty is simply anachronistic? 7) Voluntary religious poverty had a clearer meaning in a much poorer society by pointing to something much greater than material wealth. But can voluntary material poverty speak to the existential poverty of this wealthier age? Here Rahner returns to the idea of consumer ascesis. 8) "In working out a mode of poverty that will be convincing to outsiders as well, the individual and the small units are the more important and have more chances of succeeding than major religious communities as such" (211f). Should such small groups not be given the chance? 9) More problems touch on religious poverty than have been examined here, e.g., the division of labor in religious communities. Answers to this complex problem will not be found by simply applying stricter rules but by coming to grips with today's reality and all the difficulties it entails.

8.11 The Theological Meaning of the Veneration of the Sacred Heart

Der theologische Sinn der Verehrung des Herzens Jesu
{1.5} *Festschrift des theologischen Konviktes Innsbruck 1858-1958* (Innsbruck 1958) 102-109. Originally, *Vom Ziel unseres Sterbens unter dem Symbol des Herzens Jesu.*

Abstract: The "Sacred Heart" is a key religious term which has the power to unite the diverse facets of Jesus Christ and the many dimensions of people today who can only find the existential unity they crave by possessing him.
Topics: JESUS CHRIST, Sacred Heart of; GOD-TALK.

Subsidiary Discussions: Metaphysics, one/many (217f); Incarnation (218f); Dogma, development of (219f); Heart (222ff); Mystery (224ff); Word, primordial (224ff); Transcendence (227f); Knowledge (227f).

Precis: Rahner offers "a few extremely subjective and peripheral observations" on the church's teaching on the Sacred Heart. Because man is not God we lack an existential unity which we are forced to seek. This law of our being makes life at once a rich varied adventure and a nagging pain. In the mystery of the incarnation Jesus Christ became that unity we seek. He redeemed our multiplicity so we need not flee it, and revealed the positive meaning of the unity we seek. Our only chance at unity is to possess him who is at once the all (of the many) and the one (the divine). Veneration of the Sacred Heart is the ultimate act of adoration of the unity in Christ which underlies the multiplicity of our lives (219).

This theological insight has a history. In another age the key term to epitomize the unity we seek might have been Logos, Son of Man, *sophia*, *gnosis*, or Spirit. The proper nouns God or Jesus Christ fail. The first needs to be filled with content and the second needs to have its multiplicity unified. In our age what key word in our actual situation can take the place of "heart" which is so evocative and rouses such a deep response in us? "This word has the function of adjuring the heart, that which is innermost and unifying, the mystery which defies all analysis ..." (222). It lays upon us a burden and a grace, a task and a mission. In sum, "the eternal Word of God, issuing from the heart of the Father, has discovered our hearts, has endured them and keeps them for all eternity" (223).

The proper response to this reality is twofold: a) to be reverent and therefore sparing in our use of this word since it is not a rudimentary fact of faith and overuse makes the hearer jaded; b) to learn the real significance of such a key word which is not a mere concept but an existential reality. It refers to a mystery which we do not grasp but which grasps us indirectly in contemplation. Summary (226f).

To anyone who finds this explanation too difficult Rahner suggests another approach: the Thomistic metaphysics of knowledge. Just as in every act of knowing there is the object known and the background against which it is known (the first grasped directly and the second only indirectly and upon reflection) so in every religious concept the reference to God is twofold. There is a conceptualization and objectification of the reality referred to, and the something more which makes the conceptualization possible. Through contemplation this "something more" can impress itself upon us ever more strongly and be received at an ever deeper more existential level into our hearts. It is in this awareness that we utter "Sacred Heart." Summary (228).

8.12 Unity–Love–Mystery
Einheit–Liebe–Geheimnis

{1.5} 1962 meditations for Sacred Heart Triduum, Canisius College, Innsbruck. *Korrespondenzenblatt des Collegium Canisianum* 97 (1962) 4-15.

Abstract: Three considerations flowing from meditating on the Sacred Heart (unity, love, mystery) have important implications which at first seem highly theoretical but are in fact quite relevant to the practice of one's faith.

Topics: JESUS CHRIST, Sacred Heart of; UNITY; LOVE; MYSTERY; THEOLOGICAL ANTHROPOLOGY, heart.

Subsidiary Discussions: Renunciation (234, 246f); Transcendentals (237ff).

Precis: Unity. 1) Veneration of the Sacred Heart does not encompass the whole of Christianity, neither is it simply one devotion among many. It is rightly called the *summa religionis* and "constitutes the ultimate and inner-most centre, the ultimate reality from which everything else draws its light … [is] united and held together" (229f). The heart is that interior center from which one goes out to encounter multiplicity, and to which one returns to establish unity. 2) The heart seeks unity. We are the act of seeking the concrete unity we have already grasped in anticipation. Failing to find it brings pain. This is no less true in the religious sphere where Christianity seems to present a bewildering multiplicity of doctrines and practices. 3) This unity is not to be found by selecting the elements of Christianity we prefer but by following back to its source our experience of the original unity bestowed on us by God: the super-essential unity, never left for us to achieve for ourselves but imposed on us from without and brought close to us in that reality we call the Sacred Heart. Its message to us ist twofold: **a)** "Go out into the multiplicity and complexity which is yours by nature. Do not fear it" (233); **b)** "Return! Do not let yourself be poured away" (234). **c)** We arrive at unity only by trusting enough to go forth into the manifold and complex and to gather it into a unity within our hearts. There is no formula for regulating these two movements. We do not grasp their meaning conceptually. It is hidden in God and we accept it as the mystery of our existence. It is the unity which love alone can achieve for us and which we see when we turn to the Sacred Heart.

Love. Veneration of the Sacred Heart is precisely a devotion to that love of God present in Christ, crucified and risen. It is far from self-evident that love is the mystery of reality itself. 1) Love is the basis of our existence—the love of God made visible in the heart of Christ which emptied itself for us. It defies the seeming blindness of nature and the seeming meaninglessness of human history. The Sacred Heart is not simply one heart, nor one among many which loved and suffered. It is the *fons et origo* of love and unity. For it reveals that divine love and unity do not exist simply above the chaos of this world, but that in the heart of Christ this chaos has been embraced, accepted and finally redeemed. 2) Love is an inexhaustible, transcendental concept, one which we do not grasp but which grasps and transforms us. It ceases to be a mere concept when we attempt to comprehend the whole complexity of life in a loving embrace. We see and respond to this in the all-embracing, transforming, self-emptying event of the Sacred Heart. 3) Such love brings joy, the sign to the world that our witness is credible and that we do indeed proclaim the good news intended to abolish pain, incomprehensibility, and death.

Mystery. True religion begins with the courage to face up to the mystery which comprehends and envelops all things—gathering all things up in love within its own unity. 1) What has the heart to do with mystery? They are both eternally youthful, original, and inexhaustible with no norm beyond themselves by which they can be defined or regulated. 2) The Sacred Heart, symbol of mystery par excellence, dominates and encompasses our entire lives, remaining mystery even in the beatific vision. Its message is that the ultimate basis, the real and true essence of our existence, is mystery. This is not an insight we achieve, but one to which we surrender by contemplating the heart of Christ. 3) We also encounter the mystery of our lives in the experience of freedom and in the fact that we experience our salvation as threatened because neither the depth of our freedom nor the status of our justification can be completely comprehended by us. This condition of ours calls again for self-surrender to the God of love manifested in the crucified and risen heart of Christ. Only his heart gives us the courage for such surrender.

8.13 The Future of the Religious Book
Die Zukunft des religiösen Buches
{0.5} Previously unbublished.

Abstract: Future religious books will undertake the most basic theological task: putting people in touch with the inescapable mystery of human existence.
Topics: THEOLOGY, future of.
Subsidiary Discussions: Ideology (252f); Scripture (253); Mystery (254); Science (255).
Precis: The religious book definitely has a future, although its exact future guise is unclear. It will treat diverse matters and have a diverse readership. It will be characterized by a lack of ideology, treating religion not as a remote, ideal way of life imposed *ab externo*, but as a revelation which illuminates our present existential situation. It will concentrate on the foreground of existence in order to burrow underneath superficialities to reveal their deeper religious significance. It will remain biblical but without pious exaggeration. Heavy scientific exegesis will inform it but will remain in the background.

Taking nothing for granted in the background of its readers, the future religious book will return to the basic theme of Christianity: God as the inconceivable, inexhaustible mystery at the heart of human existence. This focus will give new significance to other basic concepts such as prayer, death,

Christ, love, etc. Unlike the secular sciences which become less accessible as they become more scientific, books which return to these basic themes will be the most scientifically theological and the most accessible.

The religious book of the future will be more gentle and humble. Though it will unmask pseudo-religious attitudes it will never speak as though God were completely understood or could be expressed perfectly in its religious language. It will recognize and admit the interior complexity of people. It will not attempt to bring everything under the purview of religion but will have a more positive appreciation for the worldliness of the world.

The future religious book will be courageous. It will demand that people accept themselves as more than mere homo sapiens, but as creatures capable of transcendent dimensions of infinite depth.

IX. WRITINGS OF 1965-1967, I
VIII. *Theologische Vortrage und Abhandlungen*

German edition: Einsiedeln, Benziger, 1967
U.S. edition: N.Y., Herder and Herder, 1972
Graham Harrison, translstor
Dedicated to Johann Maria Hoeck

This volume in the English edition comprises the first 15 essays of *Schriften zur Theologie*, VIII.

9.01 The Vatican Council's Challenge to Theology

Die Herausforderung der Theologie durch das II. Vatikanische Konzil
{0.5}   Previously unpublished March 1966 lecture to International Theological Congress at Notre Dame University, USA.
Abstract: Rahner contends Vatican II inescapably reoriented the present and future tasks of theology. He applies this insight to seven concrete areas.
Topics: THEOLOGY, future of; VATICAN II.

Subsidiary Discussions: Theology, historical (8ff); Theology, biblical (11ff); Church, theology of (14ff, 25f); Theology, foundational (17ff); Eschatology (19ff); Creed (21f); Theology, ecumenical (22ff); Theology, pastoral (24ff). **Precis: I.** There can be no doubt Vatican II challenged Catholic theology by providing it with a more acute awareness of problems, pointing out new tasks, giving it a more dynamic impetus and a wider scope for free movement. The council proved that theology was not a nearly complete scholastic monolith lacking only a few peripheral details from professional theologians. **II. Eschatology:** The council's call for dialogue with the world presents new tasks to theology. The need it creates for "profane knowledge" and secular experts is a strange turn for ecclesiology, fraught with danger and promise. **III. Historical theology:** This area must be expanded/developed to include some day the history of theology itself. It must be done not completely retrospectively, but must ask about the future and about its implications for evangelization. It must let the past speak without prejudice in an attitude of receptive listening. It has the great capacity to separate true dogma from the mere theologoumena which necessarily accompanies it. **IV. Biblical theology:** The great contribution of the council was to sanction the use of critical methods and thus to give scholars more tools to probe longstanding problems. The new task for biblical theology is to show the relationship between the Jesus of history and the Christ of faith in a way that is adequate to Catholic dogma. It must also assume a greater role in the formation of clergy. This will entail the development of a new methodology. **V. Systematic theology (dogmatic and moral):** Another critical new task is to incorporate newly enunciated conciliar themes into ecclesiology (list, 14ff). A more biblical moral theology must be developed which is more oriented toward love and the common good and less concerned about private salvation. **VI. Foundational theology:** Theologians today must not turn inward. The council's aim was courageously to confront the world over basic questions: God, Christ, the human person. This calls for rethinking eschatology: the nature of Christian hope and the ultimate things concerning our deepest needs and our exalted vocations all wrapped in the incomprehensibility of God. There is also a need to consider a new short creed or basic statement of faith. **VII. Ecumenical theology:** Separated Christians have much to learn from each other in a context of dialogue. But we could learn even more as together we address the religious needs of tomorrow's world and today's non-believers. **VIII. Practical/pastoral theology:** This area needs the most development to mirror the council and become truly pastoral—everything from reforming canon law to including scientific data in the church's decision making.

IX. The council's challenge to update theology is perhaps greater than the council fathers ever realized. Efforts must be encouraged at every level, although in the end theology itself remains the Spirit's gift to the church.

9.02 Theology and Anthropology
Theologie und Anthropologie
{2.5}   March 1966 lecture at St. Xavier's College, Chicago, IL.
    P. Burke, ed., *Künftige Aufgaben der Theologie* (Munich, 1967) 31-60.

Abstract: Rahner argues why dogmatic theology today must be "transcendental anthropology" and illustrates the potential consequences of such a turn.

Topics: THEOLOGY, dogmatic; THEOLOGICAL ANTHROPOLOGY, transcendental.

Subsidiary Discussions: Christology (28f, 29f, 36); Angels (30f); Trinity (31f, 36); Philosophy (34, 38ff); Salvation (35); Demythology (40ff); Revelation (42f, 34); Church, theology of (43f); Sacraments (44); Theology, moral (44f); Eschatology (38, 45).

Precis: The study of human persons is the whole of dogmatic theology. Once we grasp that as subjects we are not one thing among others, anthropocentricity and theocentricity become the same thing seen from two sides. One cannot be comprehended without the other since true statements about God are statements about us and vice versa. The same holds for anthropology and christology.

I. "A *transcendental investigation* examines an issue according to the necessary conditions given by the possibility of knowledge and action on the part of the subject" (29). To purse dogmatics this way means that when confronted with an object of dogma one inquires as to the conditions necessary for it to be known by the theological subject, ascertaining that the a priori conditions for knowledge have been satisfied, and showing that they imply and express something about the object, the mode, method, and limits of knowing it. Rahner next considers the relationship between the a posteriori material content of the object being considered and the a priori transcendental dimension of the investigator. Rahner gives two illustrations: angels and the Trinity.

II. Why is this anthropological change in theology necessary?
    1. From the nature of theology and its object. Every claim to philosophical knowledge regarding the totality of reality and truth raises questions about the nature of the thing known *and* the subject who claims to know. Philosophical questions are theological when an object is seen with its origin and orientation towards God—not one thing among many but the fundamental ground and absolute future of all reality. Furthermore, all revelation is revelation of salvation. Thus everything of significance for salvation is illuminated by referring it back to our transcendental being—to our saving receptivity for the revealed object. Finally, if salvation is founded on God's

gracious self-communication in Christ, such grace must be understood in its anthropological context. Thus, "the most objective reality of salvation is at the same time necessarily the most subjective" (36). Otherwise everything ends up as meaningless mythology.

2. From the contemporary situation. One could object that if this were true, why has it not always been seen as the case? Rahner first distinguishes between proclamation and theology which generally achieves a higher degree of conceptualization and reflection, and this only insofar as there is more transcendental thought. In any case, theology cannot return to a former stage of philosophy (classical, scholastic, or idealist). Even modern philosophy which gave rise to transcendental thought is being eclipsed. The change to transcendental anthropology challenges both today's and tomorrow's theology.

3. From reasons of basic theology and apologetics. Theological statements today are not formulated such that we can see how what is meant by them is connected with our self-understanding as witnessed to in our own experience. This raises many problems and misunderstandings (list, 40f).

III. What consequences follow? Rahner describes five areas where applying transcendental anthropology would greatly aid the task of dogmatic theology: revelation and salvation history; salvation-historicity especially as it relates to ecclesiology and the question of infallibility; sacraments and the theology of symbol; moral theology and natural law; eschatology.

9.03 Philosophy and Philosophizing in Theology
Philosophie und Philosophieren in der Theologie

{2.0} Previously unpublished January 1967 lecture in Munich to a study group of German-speaking dogmatic theologians.

Abstract: Philosophizing is essential to theology. Since philosophy today is radically pluralistic so is theology. This poses new problems for theology and indicates its future dialogue partner will be "non-philosophical" sciences.

Topics: PHILOSOPHY and theology; THEOLOGY and philosophy.

Subsidiary Discussions: Philosophy, neo-scholastic (48); Revelation (49f); Scripture, biblicism (49f); Concupiscence, gnoseological (52ff); Magisterium (58ff); Science (60ff).

Precis: I. Regardless of its technical name, "There must be 'philosophizing' within theology if by 'philosophising' here one understands the activity of thinking about the revelation of God … with the support of all the means and methods of the intellect and by relating the act and content of faith to everything which man experiences, questions and knows" (47). This is all the more true since Neo-scholasticism has dissolved into a wealth of philosophies.

Two dangers are positivism: dogmatic and biblical. The former is false because its a-historicism imposes unjustifiable limits on theology. The latter falsely asserts its competence far beyond what Catholic theology grants scripture. Theologians must think about and not merely catalogue past dogmas. They must talk not only to believers but to doubters and non-believers in a language which presents its dogma as intrinsically worthy of belief.

II. The fact that philosophy today is radically and inescapably pluralistic and that this pluralism is recognized presents a new question for theology. Honest theologians must admit there is simply too much to know. This complexity originates in the pluralism of the human sources of experience (summary, 53f). Two consequences follow (III, IV below).

III. There is today an inevitable multiplicity of theologies. Not just schools of theology which share a worldview—but radically different theologies each employing its own philosophy based on its own source of experience. Theologians who respond to this by trying to know something of everything end up passing on a denatured, second-hand version of things that must nevertheless be lived and known. Therefore, theologians must study faith at the level prior to profane science, even if it will never lead to a complete synthesis. Today "[e]ach theology and philosophy knows too much to be merely itself, and too little to become the only Theology or Philosophy" (57).

IV. Theological pluralism does not invalidate dialogue or appeals to doctrine. But pluralism will affect the teaching office. In the future those entrusted with the magisterium will find it increasingly difficult to speak authoritatively on the validity of greatly divergent theologies. Perhaps the church will need as many teaching authorities as there are theologies (60).

V. Theology's future dialogue partner will not be philosophy so much as "the 'unphilosophical' pluralistic sciences and the kind of understanding of existence which they promote" as history and science have already shown (60).

9.04 The Historicity of Theology
Zur Geschichtlichkeit der Theologie
{2.0} November 1966 lecture in Barcelona. Expanded. D. Stolte, R. Wisser, eds., *Integritas, geistliche Wandlung und menschliche Wirklichkeit* (Tübingen 1967) 75-95.

Abstract: Accepting the historicity of theology demands trust that revelation can survive honest dialogue with the modern world, and the courage to admit that partiality, sinfulness, and error can attach to theological claims.
Topics: THEOLOGY and history; HISTORY and theology.
Subsidiary Discussions: Dialogue (64f, 81f); Revelation (66ff); Sin (74ff); Error (79ff).

Precis: Real dialogue implies mutual willingness to learn, and readiness to admit a capacity for and history of error. This is true even in doctrine because it is people who dialogue and everyone's command of doctrine changes. **I.** How does the experience of the history of revealed truth relate to God, the unchanging source of truth? Without answering directly Rahner illustrates the inadmissibility of an a-historical revelation. Revelation always takes place within history employing the concepts civilization makes available. **II.** Since revelation has a history, theology has a history. Theologians must always beware of latent rationalistic interpretations of the history of dogma, recalling that if theology were deductive, theologians could predict its developments. We possess the eternal truth of God in the forward-moving course of history. "We possess this eternal quality of truth in history, and hence we can only appropriate it by entrusting ourselves to its further course" (71). **III. Implications:** 1. Theology is about human experience not abstractions. Thus it must always take account of the whole historical situation. Theology is not a complete, self-enclosed system. This demands dialogue with science and courageous hope that the truth of God cannot be overcome by this contact.

2. Today's historical situation has three characteristics: a) it is dominated by the rationalistic (methodologically atheistic) worldview of the natural sciences which needs further study; b) its historical consciousness embraces all times and cultures and demands that theology address them as well; c) it is dynamic, capable of planning and creating its own future by questioning its historically conditioned conceptual models.

3. "The situation in which theology carries on its dialogue with the world is conditioned in part by sin" (74). This implies that: a) theology must confront the world's prevailing ideologies; b) theology must be self-critical.

4. Theology which has not been condemned by church authority may contain error or its effects. It is difficult to distinguish error and ignorance (77). Thus, theologians must be modest, self-critical and brave enough to discard error in a model or a formulation whenever a theological claim is untenable.

IV. Dialogue never demands that both parties be equal. Though the church always speaks as the historical and social representative of a truth from which it cannot fall away as a result of God's eschatological promise of grace, still it engages in real dialogue. This is because the church in its historicity is always a learning church.

9.05 Theology and the Church's Teaching Authority after the Council

Kirchliches Lehramt und Theologie nach dem Konzil
{1.0}   October 1967, U.S. lecture. *Stimmen der Zeit* 178 (1966) 404-420.

Abstract: Rahner's observations on Cardinal Ottaviani's 1966 warning to bishops of ten dangers and errors in the implementation of Vatican II.
Topics: MAGISTERIUM and censorship; EPISCOPATE: THEOLOGY, task of; AUTHORITY; VATICAN II.
Subsidiary Discussions: Dogma, development of (88f); Censorship (94ff, 97f).

Precis: I. The spiritual/intellectual climate [in 1966] of uncertainty and perplexity makes it difficult to know which tendencies are transitory and which are threats. The council insisted on speaking the truth to people today in ways they understand. Such dialogue rules out a retreat to old style monolithism or a laissez faire attitude. Theology must find a *via media*. Rahner emphasizes the modern tendencies alluded to by Ottaviani [then head of the Holy Office] are not formulated systematically, and other equally important concerns are not addressed, e.g., God, atheism.

Today the church gains nothing by simply saying No and repeating ancient forms. It is legitimate to ask the boundaries of dogmatic teaching. "[M]odern theology inevitably deals with a mass of problems and methods of conceptual expression and is so weighed down by the awareness of the ambiguity of all statements that it is not so easy as previously to replace a real or suspected error with another, positive and unequivocal statement in which men of good will recognize that not only something correct is said but also something which is equal to their 'concern'" (89). To insist on one language (Latin) in a theologically plural setting would make the church a sect. A further problem is the existence of two attitudes: a tendency to reinterpret dogmas without regard to church teaching, along with a desire to be accepted in the church whatever one believes. In today's new setting, what are the limits of personal interpretation?

II. Simple appeals to authority no longer work. Rahner sees this as an opportunity for local bishops to assume more authority—a responsibility they cannot hand off. They must try to foresee and forestall dangerous local doctrinal and practical tendencies, the solutions to which do not exist but must be discovered. In this context a fresh approach to episcopal censorship must be taken realizing there will always be continuing differences of opinion even over important matters. Ultimately the magisterium and not theologians must decide such issues, for although both bishops and theologians are aided by the Spirit, only the dogmatic teaching of bishops is preserved from error by the Spirit. Although bishops need the advice of theologians they must have the courage to teach authoritatively even vulnerable, reformable decisions.

III. What practical measures might follow? Rahner suggests insuring greater collaboration between theologians and bishops by establishing and funding special institutes; opening the censorship process perhaps by relying on national conference of bishops; relying more heavily on priest councils; encouraging academics; using mass media better; introducing better training programs for young theologians; assuming a more pro-active stance focused on a few key issues. Compromise may be called for as we patiently seek the center.

9.06 Practical Theology within the Totality of Theological Disciplines

Die praktische Theologie im Ganzen der theologischen Disziplinen
{1.0} Previously unpublished April 1967 lecture at Arnoldshain.
Abstract: Practical theology relies on other fields of theology. It also takes precedence in criticizing their effectiveness and determining their scope.
Topics: THEOLOGY, pastoral; CHURCH.
Subsidiary Discussions: Theology, biblical (107, 109f); Scripture, exegesis (107, 109f); Theology, systematic (107, 110f); Church, history (107, 111f); Law, canon (107, 112f); Liturgy (113).
Precis: I. Practical theology (a term Rahner prefers to pastoral theology) is the scientific organization of reflections on the church's self-actualization which, since it is a historical reality, must always take place in ever new worldly situations. This is a unique, fundamental, independent science, not a mere application of the results of other areas of theology. A critical science involved with the testing of spirits, it should be creative and prophetic.
II. Although to fulfill its critical function practical theology must rely on sociology, political science, history, etc., it critically distills their analysis within its unique theological and ecclesial perspective. Rahner wonders whether institutes of practical theology should be established akin to research institutes found in secular areas.
III. What practical theology expects from other theological areas: 1) recognition of its originality and significance as a discipline in its own right, deserving personnel and resources in academic institutions; 2) recognition and appreciation of its own proper elements (examples, 107). Practical theology will continually warn other theological disciplines that their tasks are not fulfilled in the unhistorical and sterile realm of eternally valid truths, but in the contemporary setting. Practical theology does not determine the content of the church's self-realization but it is competent to reflect on the performance of all the other areas of theology. The other areas must submit to this scrutiny and to the precedence practical theology has in setting their future tasks based on the needs of the times.
IV. Illustrations. **1.** Exegetics and biblical theology must be conducted in the service of the church's kerygma and contribute to the effective proclamation

of the gospel. Practical theology is right to insist other disciplines provide material appropriate for theologians and preachers. 2. Systematic theology too often addresses peripheral issues in an atmosphere of detached historicism. Practical theology has the right to demand that it address pressing questions of the day. 3. Church history is often perused for its own sake. Practical theology can legitimately ask how these studies illuminate the church's present and future. 4. Canon law could relate to practical theology as profane jurisprudence relates to politics and sociology (jurisprudence submitting to the observations of the two younger sciences). 5. Liturgical theology is helped by practical theology when it challenges liturgists to insure that sacramental celebrations are both liturgically correct and also effective.

9.07 The Need for a "Short Formula" of Christian Faith

Die Forderung nach einer "Kurzformel" des christlichen Glaubens
{0.5} *Geist und Leben* 38 (1965) 374-379, as, *Kurzer Inbegriff des christlichen Glaubens für Ungläubiger.*
Abstract: Argues the need for a short profession of faith more meaningful to modern people. Concludes with a sample creed.
Topics: CREED, brief.
Subsidiary Discussions: Mystery (122f); God (119f, 122f); Love (122f); Theological Anthropology (122f); Jesus Christ (120, 123f); Trinity (124f); Church (125); Sacraments (125f).
Precis: "In order to be effective *vis-à-vis* modern unbelief the mission of the Church calls for a kind of witness to the Christian faith which can be really intelligible to modern man" (117). This basic task is often neglected or fails to distinguish what is essential in the Christian faith from what is secondary. What is needed is not an ideology but an explanation of human experience. In today's pluralistic society such a creed would also help Christians discern what distinguishes them within their secular environment.
I. When one realizes how important such a short formula is today it is surprising how few attempts have been made. In arriving at such a creed Rahner cautions: 1) "short" is a relative term; 2) such a creed might have a brief useful life; 3) people must be able to assimilate it existentially; 4) it should begin from presuppositions and use a vocabulary intelligible today. He shows how the term God and the idea of christology are very problematic today. Rahner briefly reviews short formulations from the past (120).
II. Rahner's sample creed (122ff) is aimed at educated westerners. He makes no apology for this and hopes its partiality will inspire others to try their hand a formulating a short formula appropriate to the groups they know best.

Today many such creeds are needed. The sample creed Rahner presents here works from Mystery-as-God to the love manifested in Jesus of Nazareth, the God-man. Next he moves from the Trinity to the church and sacraments. He concludes with reflections on death and eternal life.

9.08 Observations on the Doctrine of God in Catholic Dogmatics

Bemerkungen zur Gotteslehre in der katholischen Dogmatik
{2.5} July 1965 lecture at University of Marburg. *Catholica* 20 (1966) 1-18.

Abstract: Knowledge of God and the nature of theological language argue that the doctrine of God always precedes the doctrine of Trinity and soteriology.
Topics: GOD, doctrine of; THEOLOGY, dogmatic.
Subsidiary Discussions: Salvation, theology of (129f, 133f); Trinity (131f); God, knowledge of (131f, 134ff, 137f); God, attributes of (132f, 136); Metaphysics (139, 143f); God, proofs for (139f); Atheism (132, 140f); God-talk (141f); Incarnation (143); Philosophy and theology (143f); Theology and philosophy (143f).

Precis: I. In these "unsystematic observations" Rahner disclaims any desire to revolutionize theology except to the degree that one must radically oppose all idolatry, i.e., replacing God with any theory about God, setting God as one object among others, or claiming control over God. Dogma about God must do justice to our unique relationship to God: 1) God commits himself to us precisely when we give up claims to any knowledge that conquers God; 2) God only appears when accepted humbly in worship and obedience, when not torn to pieces in all the talk of reflection; 3) all aspects of our relationship to God must be thought out in very strict terms. Reflex dialectic is a necessary preliminary which must remain calm and measured and never replace the true God with idols. In Part I, Rahner arranges his observations within the scholastic framework of Catholic dogmatics.

Dogmatics must begin with the doctrine of God despite developments in "foundational theology." Against those who hold that the doctrine should begin with soteriology Rahner insists that since saving grace is nothing less than God's self-communication one always in fact begins with God (130). Rahner next considers the priority of the doctrine of God over the doctrine of Trinity. After a brief history of the question (130f) Rahner takes a long run at the topic by discussing our knowledge of God with special emphasis on Vatican I's teaching on the "natural" knowledge of God (131ff). This leads to a discussion of how the attributes of God are known, whether though the events of salvation history or through metaphysics (133ff). Part I concludes with a discussion of the relationship between the treatise on God and our knowledge of God (134f).

Rahner's initial remarks on our knowledge of God suggest this theme should be deepened to make clear: 1) that Vatican I's teaching is the bottom line of the discussion and not its center which must remain the total, complex experience of God; 2) that knowledge of God is never knowledge of one thing among many, but is the fundamental source and ultimate horizon of all knowledge. This knowledge may lead to the formulation of a concept, but God and even our knowledge of God always remain more than the concept.

Rahner returns to the question of whether the treatise on God should begin with soteriology (133). He disagrees because: 1) we are only truly ourselves once we receive and respond to God; 2) God is greater than God *ad nos*, the God of our salvation. Because this treatise is theology (i.e., reflection) and not the original source of the history of faith, it must always include what we have learned about God through Christ in the events of salvation history. "Thus it will … strive against the danger of tacitly making an abstract metaphysical schema the *norma non normata* of what, how and who God 'can be'" (133f). As to the sequence of the treatise On God and On the Trinity, the traditional Catholic order seems more didactic than foundational. But one must guard against acting as though they appeared in this order in revelation history which is from the beginning a trinitarian self-revelation.

Returning to the topic of the knowledge of God, Rahner applauds its recent inclusion in the treatise On God for reasons related to theological anthropology. He would like to see the connection made radical, "not only one *piece* of the whole doctrine of God but the doctrine itself.… Expressed in Catholic terms this doctrine of the transcendental necessity of the priority of the experience of God and its necessary expression in explicit speaking about God…refers to knowledge which is both transcendental *and* unavoidable and is always sustained by the offer of God's self-communication in *grace*" (135). Rahner contends this knowledge, when it is accepted, is already faith.

Rahner concludes by urging Catholic dogmatic theologians to do a better job of distinguishing and relating metaphysically deduced attributes of God with those revealed by events of salvation history and known by reflection on our existential condition.

II. Further unsystematic remarks with application beyond Catholic dogmatics.

1. Presuppositions which characterize the Catholic doctrine of God. a) We calmly accept the fact that whereas God may constitute the objective unity of knowledge, all our subjective knowledge, our systems, are necessarily a partial and plural composite of concepts, ideas, and opinions. b) There is nothing revolutionary in theology. Every new insight is foreshadowed in previous teachings. The datum of theology itself is already given. c) Theology demands the courage to engage in metaphysics, however inadequate it may be.

2. The question of God must be asked rightly so that God is not seen as one individual existent among many others in space and time, but as the ground sustaining the question that we ourselves are.
3. Regarding "proofs for the existence of God" dogmatic theology should not assume they are guaranteed by metaphysics but should include them in its own treatise. This will lead to the conclusion that there is in the end only one proof: the ultimate mystery that grounds our experience of existence.
4. The Catholic doctrine of God must take atheism more seriously, especially the constant inner temptation of the theist to atheism, which is itself the condition of faith.
5. Rahner asks whether God-talk reveals or conceals God. He concludes that although it is impossible to speak directly and knowingly about God, when we speak honestly of our human condition and the mystery at its core we do say something authentic about God whom we possess not in concepts or language but in our love of neighbor. This is the hope given to us in Jesus.
6. The revelation of Jesus surpasses the distinction of God *in se* or *extra se*. For in him the infinite becomes flesh without becoming finite or violating our creatureliness.
7. Can there be an alliance between philosophy and theology today? Yes, and necessarily so because both seek to know the whole. (Perhaps the greater question is how they ever separated.) This leaves unanswered their precise relationship. We are presented today with a pluralism of philosophies which must be respected and embraced by theology. The *philosophia perennis* will be discovered in these and not beside them. Theology can be expressed in all these languages for it too is a human language and like every language points to the unutterable mystery with which alone theology is ultimately concerned.

9.09 Atheism and Implicit Christianity

Atheismus und implizites Christentum

{3.0}   October 1967 U.S. lecture. Concilium 3 (1967) 171-180, as, "The Teaching of the Second Vatican Council on Atheism." Expanded.

Abstract: Atheists come to share supernatural salvation not simply by obeying natural morality but by accepting their own supernaturally elevated nature.

Topics: ATHEISM; ANONYMOUS CHRISTIAN; VATICAN II.
Subsidiary Discussions: Supernatural existential (146, 162); Faith, *fides qua*e/*qua* (152ff); Knowledge (153ff); Freedom (157f); Mystagogy (159).
Precis: I: Implicit Christians live in a state of grace and justification even prior to contact with the explicit preaching of the gospel. After defending the terms "implicit" and "Christian" and challenging whoever takes exception to them to come up with better terms, Rahner maintains there are anonymous Christians, some of whom are atheists, and lays the anthropological

grounds for this claim with a synopsis of the supernatural existentiale. He argues human nature is always elevated by the offer of God's self-communication.

The thesis that an atheist can be an implicit Christians is not self-evident. It seems to have against it the witness of scripture and a long tradition of church teaching. However, these must be squared with the teaching of scripture that God wills all to be saved, and the unprecedented phenomenon of world-wide militant atheism. After pointing out the salient passages of Vatican II documents, Rahner demonstrates his thesis in two stages (see II).

II. 1) *"According to Vatican II not every instance of positive atheism in a concrete human individual is to be regarded as the result and the expression of personal sin."* Rahner finds the silence of the council on the older textbook approach to atheism remarkable. He interprets it to mean not every concrete case of atheism can be construed as a willful exclusion of God.

2) *"Such an atheist can be justified and receive salvation if he acts in accordance with his conscience."* This does not mean simply that an atheist can with God's help become a theist and thus be justified. Rather, Rahner includes atheists under the council's treatment of "all men of good will in whose hearts grace works in an unseen way. For since Christ died for all men and since the ultimate vocation of man is in fact one, and divine, we ought to believe that the Holy Spirit in a manner known only to God offers to every man the possibility of being associated with this Pascal mystery" (*Gs* 22).

III. By explicitly including atheists with the unbaptized and non-Christians in "salvation optimism" the council said something really new. This, however, requires real supernatural faith (albeit implicit) on the part of the atheist not just a life of natural morality. For Rahner's basic thesis this implies: 1) God wills to save all in Christ; God's grace is available to all; all people share one supernatural goal. 2) Not every atheist is a gravely culpable sinner. The latter position rests on the impossibility of judging another's salvation/damnation status, and the diminished culpability of one raised in an atheistic environment.

IV. Rahner refines the question: Do seeking truth and fulfilling the demands of conscience provide an adequate object of saving faith? Rahner says yes. He argues that to accept the existence of an absolute moral demand on one's freedom is implicitly to acknowledge and accept God. The degree that one is reflexively conscious of all this is inconsequential. Here Rahner reviews the dipolar nature of the act of knowing as it relates to God, concluding it is possible to respond to God on a transcendental level even while lacking or denying the proper categorial references to God.

V. From all this Rahner constructs a rough table of possibilities:

    a. Correct transcendental and categorial theism freely accepted: (true theism).

    b. Correct transcendental and categorial theism freely denied: (culpable atheism).

    c. Correct transcendental theism accepted, incorrect categorial denied: (innocent atheism).

    d. Correct transcendental dependence on God and insufficient categorial theism freely denied (culpable transcendental atheism).

VI. How and why is blameless atheism possible? How can culpable atheism consist not in transgressing a particular moral duty but in an ultimate "No" to God? (Rahner here adds another possibility to the chart: culpable theism, affirming theological terms but denying any real dependence on God.) The answer lies in the fact that the culpable atheist denies God in the act of misused freedom and not in an act of knowledge.

VII. Certain pastoral insights emerge from these distinctions: we never approach anyone who has absolutely no experience of God, only people who have not yet interpreted their experience correctly. Combating this categorial and conceptual atheism demands mystagogy: deepening one's transcendental awareness of God by reflecting on such experiences as one's acts of unconditional faithfulness, absolute honesty, selfless surrender, etc. Appeals to a posteriori proofs or scientific phenomenalism are not only ineffective, they run the risk of idolatry, reducing God to one object or cause among many others.

VIII. From blameless categorial atheism how does Rahner arrive at the implicit Christianity in which one, by grace, accepts the self-imparting God in faith, hope, and love? Recall first that God's will that all be saved along with our essential transcendentality already elevate us by God's supernatural grace. Thus, even so-called "natural" morality is already elevated by its orientation to God. Next Rahner couples the undeniable fact that salvation is possible for the unbaptized through an act of desire with Aquinas' contention that all our supernaturally elevated acts have a supernatural formal object which can never be reached by any intellectual or moral act of our own. "The supernatural elevation in grace automatically involves [transcendental] revelation and the possibility of faith" (162). This, however, never renders categorial revelation meaningless. Summary (162f).

    Rahner ends with an appeal to implement Vatican II by means of more serious dialogue with atheist and more theological reflection on the modern phenomenon of atheism.

9.10 "I Believe in Jesus Christ." Interpreting an Article of Faith

"Ich glaube an Jesus Christus"

{3.0}   Spring 1967, South German Radio broadcast. G. Rein, ed., *Das Glaubensbekenntnis* (Stuttgart 1967) 20-23.

Abstract: A brief summary of what the church means by belief in Jesus Christ as the Incarnate Word, fully God and fully human.

Topics: CHRISTOLOGY, incarnation; JESUS CHRIST, faith in;

Subsidiary Discussions: Faith (165); Hypostatic union (167f); Creed, I believe in Jesus Christ.
Precis: Faith is a human act with a specific content. It is not private subjectivity. It is an ecclesial act. Hence, the need for a creed. Faith results from placing absolute trust in another person. In so doing one embraces the rights and privileges of such total self-abandonment with an unreserved hope. Precisely how to address the one we trust matters little (e.g., Lord, Savior, Son of God). Much depends on the personal nature of one's experience. However one may understand this trusting relationship, "where someone is *justified* in trusting himself to another person *absolutely*, and where this other person *on his own account* is able to accept this absolute trust and give it a basis, authorized by God and by no one else, then this other person is in such a unique and radical union with God that the relationship" (166) coincides with what the orthodox christological formula affirms.

Most people misinterpret incarnation. It simply points to the unique union with God of the person "who is able to receive an act of unconditional trust in God authoritatively and on his own account" (166). The essence of a spiritual creature is its origin and destiny: that it issues from and proceeds to God. This is God's gift. To receive this gift purely and to actualize it so fully that one becomes God's self-expression and once-and-for-all pledge of himself to the world is what is meant by the incarnation (167).

The message of faith concerning Jesus Christ is his radical achievement of the ultimate possibility of human existence—complete surrender to and acceptance by God in faith, made plain by the resurrection. Jesus alone was able to do this because he alone had always been accepted by God.

From the view of the believer, whoever in faith experiences absolute trust in Jesus (that in him God makes an unbreakable pledge) that person experiences what the church calls God. Faith in who Jesus is, is based on the experience of faith. This circle cannot be broken. The ground of our absolute trust is revealed in our radical act of trust.

Every valid formula of faith must affirm that Jesus Christ is the absolute mediator of salvation now and always. Whoever professes this faith believes what the church believes.

9.11 One Mediator and Many Mediations
Der eine Mittler und die Vielfalt der Vermittlungen
{3.5} June 1966 lecture at Mainz to Institute of European History. Revised.
Abstract: Approaches mediation/s not by showing how the saints participate in the one mediation of Christ, but how Christ's one mediation is the eschatologically perfect, hence, unique case of human intercommunication before God.
Topics: CHRISTOLOGY, mediation.

Subsidiary Discussions: BVM, Mediatrix (169ff); Saints, mediation of (169ff); Theological anthropology, intercommunication (176ff); Love of God/neighbor (176f); Incarnation (179f); BVM, devotion to (182f).
Precis: I. All Christians insist that Christ is the one and only mediator of salvation. Church teaching on Mary and the saints leads Rahner to conclude that they function on the plane of solidarity in salvation because "salvation in Christ by grace always implies a significance *for everyone*; salvation is not solipsistic" (173). He ends by outlining his approach to mediation: "to understand the mediatorship of Christ as the eschatologically perfect and consequently the highest, the unique 'case' of human intercommunication before God and of the solidarity in salvation of all men .... [The latter is] the necessary precondition for Christ's mediatorship and also its effect" (173f).
II. Rahner rephrases his thesis (174) and proceeds to substantiate it (leaving aside how anthropology contains both natural and graced dimensions). Since the very concept of mediation is complex and needs demythologizing, "What and where is the unavoidable existential experience [the horizon of understanding] within the perspective of which we can really encounter the unique historical fact of the redeeming death of Jesus and find it credible?" (175).
III. "The horizon of understanding is man's experienced, intercommunicative existence, which is always committed to us for us to accept or reject freely" (176). No one is ever alone. One is always responsible and significant to everyone else. This "is made concrete in the absolute quality and unfathomable depths of the love of one's neighbour" (177). Whether conscious of the fact or not, in drawing near to one's neighbor in love, one is also drawing nearer to God. Whenever this happens, "Man is loved in God, and God in man" (178).
IV. When in concrete history this intercommunication encounters its apogee it achieves its goal and one-way history. Christians believe this occurs in the incarnation of the Logos in Jesus of Nazareth. Jesus' mediation is understood this way: "the Word made flesh is the Mediator of God's self-communication and, within this, of the ultimate, radical depth of human intercommunication as well" (179). Only on this reading can one hold that: 1) justification was possible before Christ; 2) yet all are saved through the merits of Christ; 3) and the Christ-event is the effect and not the cause of God's salvific will.
V. It follows: 1) salvation achieved for any individual to some degree mediates salvation for all; 2) Jesus is the God-given apogee of salvation history and precisely as such is its sole and absolute mediator.
VI. Two final considerations: 1) if Christ is not to remain an abstract idea, he must be capable of being encountered and loved, much as Mary is revered by so many. 2) Christ can be proclaimed as the unique and absolute savior only by proclaiming him as the apogee and goal of all human intercommu-

nication. This alone provides the context of respect necessary in approaching other religious and social points of view. Summary (183f).

9.12 Christian Humanism
Christlicher Humanismus

{2.5} April 1966 lecture to Conference on "Christian Humanity and Marxist Humanism" at Herrenchiemsee. *Orientierung* 30 (1966) 116-121.

Abstract: Christian humanism, claiming no concrete ideology except to insure the dignity of the individual and to fulfil the divine precept to love one's neighbor, can dialogue profitably with secular humanism to plan the future.

Topics: CHRISTIANITY and humanism; HUMANISM and Christianity; THEOLOGY, political.

Subsidiary Discussions: Love of God/neighbor (188f, 200f); Ideology (190f, 194ff); Theological anthropology (191ff); Death (190, 194, 197ff); Future, planning (200ff).

Precis: The difficulty to define either Christianity or humanism makes it difficult to discuss their relationship. This is compounded by the fact that Christianity contains many competing anthropologies and humanism contains many self-definitions.

I. Rahner outlines Christianity's credentials for being considered humanism: it values every individual; it preaches inescapable responsibility for oneself as witnessed only in radical and absolute love of neighbor, a love that is essentially political. The mystery of the incarnation makes its theology, anthropology and all salvation societal. It sees the whole world as a religious sphere. Finally it urges the struggle against sin which always threatens to make life and death seem meaningless.

II. This radical humanism (summary, 190) which is not some arbitrary or superfluous feature of Christianity, emboldens theologians to challenge liberal and Marxist humanism's appraisals of Christianity.

III. But does the theologian really know what and who man is? It is not enough to repeat church teaching or to list the secular discoveries of the last century. All theological anthropology can say, its ultimate touchstone, is that man is "the being who loses himself in God" (192) the ineffable, intractable mystery. What practical use is this *anthropologia negativa* to humanism?

IV. Such theism eliminates every particular, concrete humanism insofar as the latter claims to be eternal or absolute. "Theism relativizes every concrete humanism" (194). This does not rule out but encourages dialogue with humanism although it can never surrender the notion of man's radical openness to and dependence on God, thus ruling out a material historical determinism. Summary (197).

V. How does Christianity's embrace of the cross and death co-determine genuine humanism? As a political act the acceptance of death is a radical act of love to the remote neighbor which simultaneously affirms both God as the absolute future and the right of others to their own future. Summary (200). **VI.** Christians cannot be indifferent to the humanists' concern for the world's future because it is precisely in loving service to one's neighbor that Christians offer God true worship. The concrete unknowability of the future does not excuse Christians from responsible participation in planning. **VI.** Rahner concludes with a series of questions to non-Christian humanists: whether given this understanding of Christianity the two camps must continue as enemies; whether they could not work together to plan the future in an atmosphere of freedom and toleration.

9.13 The Experiment with Man. Theological observations on man's self-manipulation

Experiment Mensch: Theologisches über die Selbstmanipulation des Menschen

{3.0}   September 1965 lecture at The Hague. *Adelbert* 13 (1965) #11 197-208.

Abstract: Today the arena for self-manipulation, an essential part of human nature, has greatly expanded to include one's psyche, body, and society. Here Rahner addresses some of the new questions this raises for theology. **Topics**: HUMAN NATURE; THEOLOGICAL ANTHROPOLOGY, self-manipulation. **Subsidiary Discussions**: Science (206, 208f); Freedom (212f, 217); History (213f); Sin, original (218ff); God as absolute future (219f); Love of God/ neighbor (220f); Death (220, 221ff). **Precis**: Before theology can discuss whether people ought to manipulate themselves it must know what such manipulations are and how they are accomplished. The difficulty of knowing this is compounded by today's scientific pluralism. Still theology must speak to these issues because self-manipulation has consequences for salvation. The following abstract remarks are plainly theological.

I. 1) The new reality and the future of man's self-manipulation which has already begun. Self-manipulation is our capacity to change ourselves— everything from building houses, to shaving, to learning. Self-manipulation has entered a radical new stage: it is multi-dimensional; intended to cover the entire future of humanity; involves our basic fabric as a totality; intends to design and produce a new human being. This is happening in the hominization of the environment; in biology, biochemistry and genetics; medicine, pharmacology, and psycho-pharmacology; psychology, sociology, and politics.

    2) Theological comment. Rahner omits here: a) questions of a specialist and technical nature; b) moral questions (i.e., what is permissible or morally obligatory with respect to self-manipulation).

II. 1) *"Christian cool-headedness in the face of man's future."* The fact that we are essentially operable, and that in order to survive the future we must manipulate ourselves and must want to do so, is no cause for alarm. Jubilation or lamentation would both run counter to Christian cool-headedness.

2) *"Self-determination as the nature and task of man's freedom as understood by Christianity."* According to Christian anthropology, we are essentially the beings who manipulate themselves. Through our free actions we dispose of ourselves radically towards God and achieve salvation or damnation. Our free actions must not be viewed as external epiphenomenon but as touching and determining our inmost essence.

3) *"Self-manipulation as a new manifestation in our time of man's essential freedom."* All that has changed in the modern setting is that self-manipulation has assumed a clear and historical, categorial form. What we have always been now comes to light. The scope of active self-determination now extends to our psychic, physical, and social existence. Such a change, for all its dangers, is actually the product, the full flowering of Christianity.

4) *"The question of the normative essence, the 'nature' of man."* This raises the question of the true nature of man which forms the horizon and limitations of self-manipulation. (The question arises from an apparent dilemma framed abstractly here, 215). This nature has often been incorrectly identified with existing conditions.

To moralists who warn we must not do all we can do, Rahner says, 1) that since evil is never a positive act but the absurd desire for an impossibility, moralists must show the categorial absurdity of wrong choices in the area of self-manipulation. To skeptics who say we ultimately will do all we can do with dreadful consequences, Rahner recalls 2) what seem like "laws" bring systems back into balance "naturally." None of this, however, legitimizes a laissez faire attitude towards self-manipulation. It does, however, console the anxious. All the moralist can judge of self-manipulation are it's objective, categorial appearances, always leaving open the status of subjective sinfulness.

5) *"The seriousness of irreversible historical decisions."* The dogma of original sin which visited irreversible guilt on humanity warns us that any self-manipulation may have unforeseen and irreversible consequences.

6) *"Planning the future and the absolute future of man."* Christianity is the religion of the absolute future which we work out in concrete historical circumstances. The fact that God is not only "above us" but "in front of us" as our unalterable goal both relativizes and legitimates self-manipulation.

7) *"Shaping the future as a Christian task."* Self-manipulation insofar as it is the concrete expression of love of neighbor by which we determine our absolute relationship to God is not an interim activity, but one heavy with eternal consequences. Today the arena for expressing the love of God has

expanded dramatically. Society has entered a post-individualist phase when serving humanity has become a real task and challenge.

8) *"Death as the permanent door to the absolute future."* All attempts at self-manipulation or utopia building confront us with the inescapability and unalterability of our own death. This inevitably leads to the question whether life is surrounded by a void of absolute absurdity or the infinitude of the mystery of love—an absolute future which is reached through death. **III.** Rahner concludes with a list of questions theologians have yet to consider and hints that the answers may be found "in the simple experience that man really does *make* history (and thus himself) and that in this very activity he is not his own, but belongs to the mystery of love" (224).

9.14 The Problem of Genetic Manipulation
Zum Problem der genetischen Manipulation
{2.5}   Previously unpublished.

Abstract: Theology today seems unable to solve the pressing issue of genetic manipulation (A.I.D.). Rahner applies "the moral instinct of faith" to this issue along with his theological anthropology. This yields 7 observations.
Topics: THEOLOGY, moral; THEOLOGICAL ANTHROPOLOGY, self-manipulation (genetics).
Subsidiary Discussions: Human nature (227 ftn7, 230ff; 143ff); Artificial birth control, A.I.D. (236f); Faith, moral instinct of (238ff).

Precis: Genetic manipulation presents theology a tremendous problem: morally, how to evaluate new technical procedures whose details it cannot hope to master. Analysis begins with a review of traditional Catholic morality.

I. Catholic thought finds no solution to this issue in scripture, nor can it simply leave the matter up to individual conscience. Self-manipulation cannot be condemned outright since we must by nature exercise our freedom to manipulate ourselves and thereby determine our absolute relation to God. Genetic manipulation is one instance in the tremendously expanded arena of human self-manipulation recently open to us. Abstractly, there is nothing morally wrong or repugnant in freely manipulating genetic material. We do it routinely in choosing marriage partners, and historically in following folk practices which claim to determine the sex of a child. A concrete case of genetic manipulation could be justified based on the concrete subject (e.g., married, unmarried); the premeditated result; the concrete method. These reduce to one principle: a concrete reality must be adjudged according to its appropriateness to human nature. But is there an unchanging human nature? Can we correctly distinguish it from its present historical form? To judge the morality of a particular case of genetic manipulation these questions would seem to need answers.

II. Rahner insists our knowledge and understanding of our own nature can exercise a normative function in our moral evaluations. But how far can it take us in this particular inquiry? After sketching our transcendental nature he concludes that violating this nature is immoral. The converse is not necessarily true: what does not violate this nature is not necessarily morally acceptable. Can a rule be deduced to distinguish moral from immoral genetic manipulation? After a summary (234) Rahner concludes, no. Though the abstract concept of genetic manipulation is not immoral, one cannot make concrete moral decisions about genetic manipulation based on our abstract metaphysical nature except in the most extreme forms which never give rise to disagreement.

III. Is there another way of approaching the whole question? Rahner first clarifies genetic manipulation. He is not talking about criminal law, state sponsored eugenic measures, or experimentation with human genetic material. He confines this discussion to "heterologous artificial insemination" which is itself a complex personal, legal, and social issue. Before proceeding further Rahner suggests an epistemology which could support a moral judgement on the complex issue of genetic manipulation—the lynch pin of his essay.

IV. Rahner applies the "moral instinct of faith" to this otherwise intractable moral problem. It is an indispensable "instinctive" judgement which cannot and need not be adequately subject to analytic reflection. Though it offers reasoned arguments using conceptual terms, it is not the product of such reason (e.g., the justification for an appeal to natural law). Because this approach does have dangers it is legitimate to be critical towards it. This mode of knowing exists in real life and does not curtail or replace reason. It comes to the fore when conceptual reasoning gets bogged down and a decision is needed. It allows one calmly to take risks. "[A] particular contingent judgment of this kind can still be the only correct one *in its situation*. The making of it requires a universal knowledge of the current situation; this knowledge is correctly grasped in the 'instinctive' judgment which recognizes what is currently and properly called for, and this results in an 'appropriate' judgement" (239).

Such a judgement is not identical with a "prudential" judgment or an individual existential moral judgement. It is the foundationally synthetic knowledge formed by the two. Without describing how it actually happens, his examples include the decision for a marriage partner or career. Ignoring this universal instinct of faith and reason, or not having the courage to rely on it, results in moral paralysis. To those who say this method ignores the complexity of moral situations Rahner counters: 1) often one cannot wait for universal agreement; 2) silence issuing from theological uncertainty often leads to immoral practical consequences; 3) theological indecisiveness on important moral issues argues the possibility for another valid approach; 4) moral theologians are too apt to temporize in the face of the possibility that attitudes are likely to change soon.

V. Rahner applies his basic anthropological and ethical insights:
1) Human nature is predetermined, the gift of an incomprehensible love. Failure to accept this necessarily alien determination (*amor fati*) confidently in patience and humility subjects us to neurosis and fear.

2) The wrongness of genetic manipulation can be seen in the motive of those who propose it: the desire to rid procreation of the unknown, that part of human nature Rahner calls *fatum*. This in turn stems from neurotic anxiety in the face of our determinism, a fear and hatred of destiny.

3) Heterologous artificial insemination invades the area of intimacy where freedom itself resides. It separates marital union from procreation and removes procreation from the area of human intimacy. It deprives the child of its birthright: knowledge of one's own father. Simply achieving conception does not justify the ends used to bring it about.

4) The impossibility of implementing universal genetic manipulation does not make selective genetic manipulation acceptable. In fact limited genetic manipulation would set the stage for a new class of genetically enhanced or reduced individuals which in turn threatens dire social consequences.

5) Genetic manipulation could potentially give the state a powerful means of limiting the individual's sphere of freedom.

6) The slow pace of the past often reinforced the wisdom that not everything that can be done should be attempted. The rapid, far-reaching, and unknown consequences of genetic manipulation reduce the time available for feedback and evaluation and open a door to unseen irreversible consequences.

7) Some argue that novelty can never ultimately be resisted. What can be done will eventually be tried. This view never excuses us from resisting even the inevitable where it offends the moral instinct. Summary (251f).

9.15 Self-Realization and Taking up One's Cross
Selbstverwirklichung und Annahme des Kreuzes
{0.5}　G. Zacharias, ed., *Dialog über den Menschen. Festschrift für Dr. W. Bitter zum 75. Geburtstag* (Stuttgart 1968) 194-198.

Abstract: Modern day "frustration anxiety" which arises from our inability to accept human finitude is best addressed by Christian renunciation: a free, hopeful surrender to infinite mystery as embodied in the cross of Christ.
Topics: CHRISTIAN LIFE, renunciation; CROSS.
Subsidiary Discussions: Frustration anxiety (253f); Death (254ff).
Precis: Modern life with its inability to deal with finitude, its desire to miss out on nothing, to have it all, is characterized by "frustration anxiety" a force which ultimately steers life into the void. Saying yes to everything leads to never fully appreciating anything. The opposite strategy of renouncing the

thirst for existence is often only a thinly veiled rouse which secretly hopes by saying no to everything it will ultimately regain it all.

The ancient wisdom counsels proportion, calmly letting things go. Rahner sees Christianity going further. It counsels renunciation which scripture refers to as denying oneself and taking up one's cross. The fullness we seek is not cobbled together from particular finite possibilities. It lies ahead of us in the absolute future which is God who bestows himself on us as we freely let go of everything else. Every free act of renunciation is a preliminary exercise in accepting our concrete and inevitable death.

We do not know this through reflection. We grasp it in faith and hope. We come to know it through another: Jesus Christ who carried the cross laid on him by God who was his own fullness and thus became the source of salvation. Those who similarly relinquish themselves to the mystery of existence actually believe in the death and resurrection of Jesus even if they do not grasp it explicitly in these terms.

Taking up one's cross has many forms. Rahner cites two: accepting the disappointment with the world which comes from knowing death is inescapable; accepting the disappointment that comes when love demands we become truly selfless.

In the end there are only two ways to live: being driven by frustration anxiety or accepting the cross. Strangely these opposite ways often mimic each other to such an degree that we cannot judge which it is we follow. Those who choose the cross need not fear they will be rendered passive in the face of life's tasks. In fact only those who do not fear death can enjoy the good things of life, can risk themselves entirely, and are free to love unsparingly. They do not need to overtax this life's happiness and thus spoil it.

X. Writings of 1965-1967, 2
VIII. *Theologische Vorträge und Abhandlungen*

German edition: Einsiedeln, Benziger, 1967
U.S. edition: N.Y., Seabury Press, 1977)
David Bourke, translator
Dedicated to Johann Maria Hoeck

This volume in the English edition comprises the last four parts of *Schriften zur Theolgie*, VIII.

10.01   The New Image of the Church
Das neue Bild der Kirche
{1.0}   January 1966 lecture to Academy of Theology, Koblenz
Geist und Leben 39 (1966) 4-24.

Abstract: Vatican II supplements the image of church as institution with images of the church as the local community gathered for worship, sacarament of salvation for the world, vanguard, pilgrim community of love, etc.

Topics: CHURCH, new images of; VATICAN II.

Subsidiary Discussions: Church as *Ur-sakrament* (12ff); Salvation (13ff); Anonymous Christian (16ff); Israel (18); Mission (19); Supernatural existential (20f); Death (21); Love of God/neighbor (24ff); Church, collegiality in (24f); Authority (25f).

Precis: I. All Vatican II's constitutions and decrees are reflections on the church's self-understanding. Rahner finds this startling. Since the church does not exist for itself why does it speak only indirectly to the needs of the world? Recalling that issues are often forced upon the church and at times this proves providential, perhaps ecclesiology was the proper subject for this council. In discussing new conciliar images of the church Rahner does not mean novel images but images that are more vital and especially effective today.

II. The first trait in the new image of the church is its true, concrete presence in the local communities and regional churches (*Lumen gentium* #26). This does not deny the model of the universal church but supplements it as an alternative viewpoint. After a brief history of how this image came to be part of this conciliar document (9f) Rahner expands on what it means for the whole to be truly present and to achieve its fullness in the part. Rahner insists an immeasurable amount needs yet to be done to flesh out this insight.

III. Vatican II also taught the church is the *sacramentum* of salvation for the world. This notion binds in a dialectical unity two insights: the church is necessary for salvation; salvation is possible even outside the church. The church which is and will be a diaspora community (12ff) is related to the salvation of the world as sacramental word is related to grace—intrinsically connected but not identical (14). Though the message of the church takes root in individual hearts it is not essentially private revelation but Christ in the world–an *Ur-sakrament*. Thus, Christians see themselves not as one among many sects but as the vanguard of salvation. They see non-Christians as anonymously Christian. Their stance towards the world is fearless and untroubled. Filled with missionary zeal they approach the task with calmness and patience. They know in calling others to the church they are calling them back to themselves (summary, 23). The church is leaven in the dough of humanity.

IV. The two traits mentioned above are the ultimate basis for the collegiate and synodal principle in the church enunciated by the council. The love of those united in Christ makes them equal. People in today's increasingly alienated society will connect with others in an intimate bond gathered with Christ at the local altar community. This church may see its power to coerce decrease but its true authority, based on the mission of Christ and springing from love, will grow. In this community the unity of love of God and neighbor will be experienced in a new way, less individualistically and more communally.

V. Rahner admits that what he has said so far only scratches the surface of the church's new self-understanding ushered in by the council. The church is far more than an institution, it is the fruit of salvation which must act as such. Thanks to the council the church is no longer seen as that which acts upon us but as "she whom we all *are* in virtue of the fact that the grace of God has moved and inspired us and bound us together into a unity" (28). Rahner closes with another full page of new conciliar images of the church which cry out to be developed and take root in the hearts of the faithful.

10.02   Church, Churches and Religions
Kirche, Kirchen und Religionen

{2.0}   January 1966 lecture to a conference on "The Theological Academy," Cologne. K. Rahner, O. Semmelroth, eds., *Theologische Akademie* III (Frankfurt 1966) 70-87.

Abstract: Aided by teachings of Vatican II and his concept of the supernatural existential, Rahner clarifies the relationship of the Catholic Church, the unique bearer of salvation, to non-Catholic Christians and non-Christians.

Topics: CHURCH and the churches; SUPERNATURAL EXISTENTIAL; SALVATION, outside the church; ECUMENISM.

Subsidiary Discussions: God, salvific will of (33f); Beatitude, natural (33); History, salvation-, revelation (36ff); Jesus Christ as God-man (37ff).

Precis: Changes in modern society have forced the Catholic Church to reexamine its relationship to non-Catholic Christians and to non-Christians. Catholics cannot hold a religious relativism that all religions are equal except for unimportant details. But how can one make sense of the seemingly incongruous claims that the church is necessary for salvation; that God's salvific will extends to all people; that non-Catholics and non-Christians are neither unintelligent nor insincere? Rahner's answer is a faith response he hopes is reconcilable with Catholic dogma. The fresh and courageous teachings of Vatican II make his task much easier.

I. The fundamental principle on which Rahner bases his answer is the supernatural existential. Section I offers a synopsis of this thesis in the following steps: 1) God wills that all be saved and gives all people the genuine possibility of salvation whatever their circumstances. God's will can only be frustrated by the real, grave personal guilt of the individual. God's saving will consists in freely offering to bestow himself on creatures endowed with spiritual faculties. God is both the ultimate cause and real content of salvation which has the effect of uniting all the levels of the being who freely accepts God's offer. 2) God's self-bestowal on creatures endowed with spiritual faculties implies: a) a radical reorientation of one's nature towards the immediate presence of God whether or not one is reflexively conscious of this fact; b) every spiritual mode of transcendentality (e.g., knowledge, freedom, love) is activated when people engage in the concrete realities of life. Thus, transcendentality is not one compartment of life. It has a concrete history for individuals and society. Hence, a purposive, unfolding salvation-revelation-history coexists with world history (36f). This history can and did become explicit in the Old and New Testaments. It finds its climax and goal in Jesus Christ, the God-man, in whom God's self-bestowal and acceptance are accomplished in an absolute and definitive way. This history always remains dependent on the supernatural existential. Summary (38).

II. In this light what does it mean to say Christianity is the universal, absolute, and God-given religion, and how can this claim be justified? Obviously it does *not* mean salvation is confined to explicit membership in the visible church. It means human transcendentality finds its unsurpassable goal in Jesus Christ who is effectively present in the church he founded.

III. What does this mean for non-Catholic Christians and their churches? While maintaining it is uniquely the "one and total presence in history of the one God-man in his truth and grace" (41) the church cannot think of itself as simply one Christian church among many. But the unity Christ willed for his church is not simply a future promise. As the fervent will of all believers, it is a divine gift stronger than whatever may currently divide us. Despite the fact others cannot yet see the unique saving character of the Catholic Church, salvation remains accessible to them in their own churches through our common beliefs (list, 43). Until they can see the Catholic Church as the unique bearer of salvation they have an absolute duty to hold to the faith they have inherited. Such churches serve a positive function. They inspire the Catholic Church to explain itself more effectively and may also manifest certain truths of the faith with greater clarity and purity than the Catholic Church.

IV. What does this mean for non-Christians? Realizing his general comments apply differently to different non-Christian religions, Rahner first addresses the status of these religions before the coming of Christ. He sees them as positively willed by God—legitimate ways to salvation addressed to individuals as members of a community. They are not the mere product of human speculation but arise as a response to God's offer of self-bestowal which grounds the supernatural existential. This in no way denies such religions are often a mixture of disparate elements manifesting both sin and grace.

V. The coming of Christ signals the abrogation of the legitimacy of these non-Christian religions insofar as the definitive brings the provisional to an end. This does not, however, decide the question of the precise moment in time when these religions cease to be legitimate for particular societies. As for individuals, they have the duty to continue to practice these religions until the message of Christ so penetrates their conscience that the call to conversion can only be denied in bad faith. There is no particular point at which this can be known with absolute certainty either by the individual or by any third party. Summary (48f).

10.03   On the Relationship between the Pope and the College of Bishops
Zum Verhältnis zwischen Pabst und Bischofskollegium
{2.0}   *Euntes Docete* (Rome 1967) 41-57.

Abstract: In harmony with Vatican II, Rahner attempts here to define the relationship between the pope as supreme pastor of the church and the united episcopate which, as a college, is invested with the same supreme powers.
Topics: PETRINE OFFICE; EPISCOPATE; CHURCH, power in.
Subsidiary Discussions: Ecumenical council, power of (50ff); Spirit, unity in (54, 64); *Potestas ordinis/jurisdictionis* (67f); Sacraments (68).
Precis: **I.** On the question of supreme authority in the church the only advance Vatican II made over Vatican I was to frame this relationship in terms of the pope and college of bishops rather than pope and ecumenical council. In all other essential matters church teaching remains unchanged: the pope possesses full and supreme power in the church as does the college of bishops as a body. Were either to depend on the other for its power it would not be supreme. After analyzing the problems that arise from scholastic theology's attempt to untangle the notion of pope and episcopate as "two incompletely distinct subjects vested with supreme powers" Rahner urges a cautious approach.
II. *"The bearer of the highest and supreme power in the Church is the united episcopate with and under the pope as its head … there are two modes in which this supreme college may act: a 'collegiate act' properly so-called, and the act of the pope as head of the college."* Rahner insists this formulation in no sense derogates the dignity or primacy of the pope. Since the Bishop of Rome enjoys his plenary powers precisely as head of the church, he enjoys them in virtue of being head of the united episcopate. Each fact implies the other in the same sense and with equal validity. Rahner rebuts three arguments against his thesis having to do with the sense in which the pope can act "alone." He concludes, "In the strictest and most precise sense the pope has supreme power not as a figure over against the college or above it, for this college is in fact itself indisputably vested with this supreme power … the pope exercises this same power as an individual also" … (58f).

III. Rahner proves his thesis by eliminating opposing theories. Every attempt to derive episcopal power from primatial power meets with insurmountable difficulties theoretically and historically. No power enjoyed *juris divini* can be a derived power. Hence, the powers of the episcopal college are not a participation in the pope's powers. There are, therefore, two different subjects vested by God with the same power. After refuting the objection that his view is historically improbable he proceeds to consider the alternative view that supreme authority in the church is vested in two incompletely distinct subjects (61ff). Although this formulation avoids the problem of derived powers it is too obscure and imprecise. He concludes there can be only one subject invested with supreme power. On this view the terms "pope" and "college of bishops" must imply one another. After a few remarks on corporate persons, Rahner takes up the final question: whether the appointment of the pope *jure divino* can allow him to act in the name of the college in an act that is not collegial. Although at the formal level this possibility involves no intrinsic contradiction, it raises practical and historical difficulties.

IV. Rahner advances his thesis by moving from formal considerations to matters of content. The acts of any subject vested with supreme authority must reflect the distinctive quality of the church itself: unity in multiplicity and multiplicity in unity based on mutual love and respect of individual freedom. For this reason the power of the pope is never full or unrestricted in an absolute sense (66f). Rahner concludes this section by discussing the implications of Vatican II's teaching that bishops enjoy membership in the episcopal college because of ordination (*potestas ordinis*) not only by virtue of appointment (*potestas jurisdictionis*). By extension, collegiate acts can be so in the true sense or individually. But in the latter case the individual shares in the sacramental power of the church and hence is acting in the name of the church.

V. What practical difference does this thesis make? Though modest, it could help to increase the role of bishops in general synods and in the day-to-day administration of the church. They would not constantly be thinking in terms of balancing two separate powers but exercising one common power. Insisting on one supreme power in the church can help the pope to feel collaboration does not diminish his proper powers, and can help bishops accept initiatives of the pope without thinking their powers were being usurped.

10.04   The Presence of the Lord in the Christian Community at Worship

Die Gegenwart des Herrn in der christlichen Kultgemeinde

{3.0} September 1966 lecture at Rome to *Congressus Internationalis de Theologia Concilii Vaticani II.* A. Exeler, ed., *Die neue Gemeinde. Festschrift für Th. Filthaus zum 60. Geburstag* (Mainz 1967) 11-22.

Abstract: Christ and the church are present to each other in the cult of the local church through the medium of the Holy Spirit of Christ. Eucharist is the sublime case of this presence which is always single, active, and sacramental.

Topics: JESUS CHRIST, presence of in cult; SACRAMENTS, Christ's presence in.

Subsidiary Discussions: Theological anthropology, presence (71ff); Symbol, real (72); Becoming (73f); Spirit of Jesus Christ (74f); Church, local (75f); Eucharist (77, 80); Vatican II, *Lumen gentium* (78ff); Eschatology (81).

Precis: **1. Presence in general.** Presence signifies much more than the physical proximity of two objects (bibliography, 71 ftn1; cf. 10.05). Because it is capable of being extended to all levels of human life it cannot be defined any more precisely than the human person. It points to a primary experience incapable of being reduced to words. This shifting experience varies in intensity depending on the level at which it engages us. Presence always implies a third thing: a medium, a common ground which makes possible the presence of two objects to one another. Hence, a) presence is fundamentally an anthropological not a physical reality; b) such presence causes and affects presence; c) physical presence is merely what is presupposed by the *Realsymbol* of human presence; d) presence through love, knowledge, in the Spirit, etc., far from being a metaphorical extension of the concept of presence is its original and basic meaning; e) despite its originality something else can substitute for the anthropological concept of presence: "that by which this presence is constituted (in terms of its actual content), and in relation to this the 'presence' itself is, as it were, only subsequent and secondary" (73).

2. On the Presence of Christ in the cult. a) Christ and the church are present to each other in the cult of the church through the medium of the Holy Spirit of Christ. aa) Though the notion of medium is often overlooked it is the necessary condition for the possibility of two objects *becoming* present to one another and differs from that presence itself. bb) Here the medium is the Spirit of Christ in the church. It is the necessary prior condition for the further presence between Christ and the church in cult for two reasons: the cultic presence of Christ has a greater degree of actuality than his habitual presence in Spirit; the habitual presence of the Spirit of Christ in the church is the ontological presupposition for the actual presence of Christ in cult. For

Christ is only present when the church prays, teaches, believes, hopes, loves, and confers the sacraments in the Spirit of Christ. Only through the presence of uncreated grace can particular acts attain to God's very self.

b) Christ and the faithful are present to each other in the highest degree in the cult, the eucharistic sacrifice of the local church (summary, 76). This fact separates Catholic cult from the cult of the Old Testament and makes the church much more than merely a "perfect society."

c) The presence of Christ in cult must be seen as single and active. By "single" Rahner means that although the presence of Christ in the cult of the local community and in eucharist (77) contains very different elements these must be understood as different degrees in the actualization and intensity of this one unique saving presence which unites God and humanity. By "active" Rahner means "actively taking effect," i.e., God actually bestowing himself and his life on us precisely through signs.

d) This single presence of Christ in the cult considered as an active sanctifying force is constituted by these elements: aa) *By the word of the gospel,* which as kerygma makes present what it proclaims; bb) *Through the sacrament,* the exhibitive and effective word of Christ in the mouth of the church; cc) *Through the Eucharist,* the supreme act in which Christ's pascal sacrifice is made present to the Father by the visible cult of the church offered in the Spirit, while at the same time his body and blood are brought to believers; dd) *Through hope and love* which, as an eschatological event, the cult both manifests and instills in the faithful united at the altar.

e) [missing at 81] Rahner reiterates point (c): these diverse but mutually connected elements constitute the single, active presence of Christ (summary, 81f). Such a presence is always sacramental, constituted by the sign as that which is objectively symbolic, and by the reality signified itself and capable of unlimited intensification.

f) The effective presence of Christ is not limited to the cultic. Christ may also be explicitly present in one's other Christian activities, and "anonymously present" in seemingly secular activities. Christ is present and apprehensible whenever the church functions as a sign of salvation to the world—whenever one person shows heartfelt compassion to another.

10.05 On the Presence of Christ in the Diaspora Community according to the Teaching of the Second Vatican Council

Über die Gegenwart Christi in der Diasporagemeinde nach der Lehre des Zweiten Vatikanischen Konzils

{1.5} *Lebendiges Zeugnis,* Vol. 2-4 (1966) 32-45.

Abstract: Since Christ is fully present in the small, poor, local church united in love, preaching the gospel, and celebrating Eucharist, it is here that Christians of tomorrow will be inspired to believe and to act in faith.

Topics: CHURCH, Christ's presence in; JESUS CHRIST, presence in church; CHURCH, diaspora.

Subsidiary Discussions: Vatican II, *Lumen gentium* (85f); Spirit of Jesus Christ (91f); Sacraments, *Ur-sakrament* (94f); Church of poor (95ff); Church, future of (97f); Truths, hierarchy of (100).

Precis: These remarks apply to any local church gathered at the altar. Without idealizing or glorifying the harsh fate of diaspora churches Rahner sees them as the model of the church of tomorrow.

I. Rahner extends what Vatican II said about local churches to the small, often poor diaspora communities. After discussing the history of *Lumen gentium* 26, Rahner contrasts the scholastic tendency to understand "church" as the hierarchically structured universal church, with the New Testament and Vatican II's view of the church as the local altar community. "The Church, the one Church of Christ, is present in its entirety in every local community. In this local community *the* Church is made actually present" (88).

II. How is Christ present in this local community? In addition to union with its local bishop and with the universal church three other factors essentially constitute the local church: the preaching of the gospel of Christ for which the community assembles; celebrating the mystery of the Eucharistic meal which unites the members; the love and unity of the community which flows from these. All this happens in the Holy Spirit of Christ. The church which possesses Christ makes him present in its two dimensions: hierarchic order and spiritual charism. Both together constitute the single presence of Christ, much as any sacrament is composed of sign and reality signified. Hence, Christ is not only present in the church, the church is also the presence of Christ.

III. For whom is Christ present in this way? Obviously Christ's saving presence is meant for the members of the church which both receives and mediates his presence in Word, Eucharist, and love. Moreover Christ is present in the church for the salvation of the whole world. As the basic sacrament of salvation the church is a sign of God's offer of self-bestowal on us and a sign of that offer having been accepted and victoriously achieved in Christ.

IV. Rahner now turns to the diaspora community. Precisely because of its smallness and poverty, and not in spite of it, the diaspora community makes Christ so perfectly present, "and him crucified." Such communities help us avoid thinking of the church in terms of abstract theology and to think instead of the preaching of the gospel, the celebration of Eucharist, and the sharing of love in the concrete. Far from being marginal, the church of the diaspora most clearly embodies the essential nature and future of the whole church. For the church is not the actual glory of God but the sign and promise of the kingdom of God—not salvation but the sign of salvation.

V. It will take average believers a long time to assimilate the fact their local worship communities are the supreme actualizations of the church as such through the preaching, celebration, love, and unity which transpire there. These communities provide the impulse for belief and love. Their poverty and smallness will be the mark of the universal church of the future. All the other truths of the universal church will be realized and rooted in the faith and practice of the local altar community (summary, 100f). This theology of the church provides the real basis for ecumenical dialogue.

10.06   Dialogue in the Church
Vom Dialog in der Kirche

{1.0}   December, 1966 lecture to Fourth Plenary Conference of the Advisory Council on Culture of the Central Committee of German Catholics. *Stimmen der Zeit* 179 (1967) 81-95.

Abstract: Existing intellectual pluralism in the church necessitates open dialogue on matters of dogmatic theology. Wise bishops and theologians will balance the need for dialogue with the church's need to teach with authority.

Topics: CHURCH, dialogue in; DIALOGUE within the church; THEOLOGY, dogmatic.

Subsidiary Discussions: Pluralism (106ff, 117); Magisterium (111ff, 118ff).

Precis: An inquiry into the nature of dialogue between social groups and institutions over religious and ideological matters.

I. Because the Catholic Church possesses divinely revealed truth it cannot enter open dialogue with the idea of changing or discarding such truths. However, in open dialogue the church can learn more about its dialogue partners and itself (105). This essay concentrates on the nature of and the need for open dialogue *within* the church itself over issues of dogmatic theology.

II. Open dialogue within the church is possible and necessary. The need for dialogue arises from the insurmountable pluralism of modern society (106f) which is equally present within the church (history, 107f; examples, 108f). Because no one person or school today can grasp all facets of any doctrine there is no substitute for dialogue. This does not mean dialogue can substitute for decision, but magisterial authority can never substitute for dialogue. Dialogue both within and outside the church teaches Christians to be intellectually modest and prudent. It informs and enriches our minds and gives precision to our ideas even if we never reach full agreement on all issues. Every person and group in the church can benefit from engaging in dialogue.

III. Today a certain organization of dialogue has become inevitable. The institutions which have been set up to facilitate dialogue need continually to be tested for effectiveness and improved where needed. Leaders must open themselves to hearing diverse opinions especially from acknowledged lay experts in given fields. Institutions alone can never substitute for the

presence and action of the Spirit. Rahner suggests the German bishops establish a panel of theological specialists to advise them (115ff).
IV. The pluralistic situation of theology in the church necessitates dialogue. But it has limits. Rahner warns that theology is never an end in itself. It is always meant to serve the preaching and teaching mission of the church. He lists the specific prior conditions necessary for true dialogue in the church (list, 118). At times legitimate authority may need to put an end to dialogue. Theologians and the faithful must accept this unequivocally and obediently. Even if bishops do not understand the issues as well as theologians, they are the appointed judges of these matters. Conversely, authority is no substitute for dialogue. Issues must not be pre-judged. Contrary opinions must not be dismissed prematurely. The promise that the Spirit will keep the church from falling into error is no pretext for evading dialogue. Bishops need wisdom to know when to be bold and allow dialogue and when to be silent. Summary (121).

10.07 Penance as an Additional Act of Reconciliation with the Church

Das Sakrament der Buße als Wiederversöhnung mit der Kirche
{2.5} Previously unpublished.
Abstract: Vatican II was right to reestablish the link between sacramental penance, forgiveness of sin in God's eyes, and restoration of peace with the church. He gives an historical survey of the theological dogma [cf., 15. 1-8].
Topics: PENANCE, sacrament of; CHURCH, restoring peace with.
Subsidiary Discussions: Vatican II (125ff); Sin, mortal/venial (130f); Penance, binding/loosing (passim); Church, excommunication (131, 135f, 138f, 143); Sacraments, *res et sacramentum* (133, 141ff).
Precis: Vatican II taught the church not only bears the word that effects reconciliation with God but by the same act it restores to the repentant sinner the bond of peace damaged or broken by sin (*Lg* #11, *Po* #5).
I. Rahner finds this conciliar teaching astonishing since one of its few 20th century proponents, B.F. Xiberta, had been ignored for 40 years despite the preponderance of corroboration by the Fathers and the scholastics. In fact the history of penance remains a complete mystery without reference to the restoration of the *pax cum ecclesia* (bibliography, 128f ftns14-37a).
II. Rahner reviews the context in which this ancient truth was reasserted: Vatican II's emphasis on the ecclesial dimension of all the sacraments. Without debate the council dismissed prevailing theological opinion and insisted that since all sins have an eccleisal aspect, in every celebration of penance reconciliation with the church takes place as well. But the council left open the question of precisely how forgiveness of sin in the sight of God and reconciliation with the church are related (list, 130). The remainder of this section explains why this insight applies to venial as well as mortal sin

and its attendant excommunication. It refutes the notion the only reconciliation achieved in the sacrament is reconciliation with the church.
III. Rahner leaves aside whether reconciliation with the church is the *res et
sacramentum* of reconciliation with God, this in turn being considered as the
res sacramenti. He also clarifies that what he means by excommunication is
broader than the canonical notion. It refers to the loss of that state of grace
which leaves one a member of the church *in corpore* but not *in corde.*
IV. Rahner gives a history of the dogma of reconciliation with the church.
He begins with the New Testament notion of "binding and loosing" (Matt
16: 19; 18:18; Jn 20:23) which he says clearly gives the church the power of
the ban and the power to remove the ban (i.e., the power to consign or release
one from the power of Satan) and precisely in this sense the power to forgive
sins. "Sacramental penance as practiced in the early Church was penance
from excommunication" (136). Failure to understand this makes the discipline of the early church incomprehensible. In the Middle Ages the practice
of repeatedly conferring reconciliation led to the modification of the rite as
it is known today [1968] and the gradual loss of consciousness of its ecclesial
dimension.
V. Rahner details the history of these developments including *Pastor
Hermae*, Tertullian, Cyprian, Origen, Augustine. When the Middle ages
introduced the search for the matter and form of a sacrament, the penitent's
interior state came to be seen as the true matter of the sacrament. Although
the notion of penance as reconciliation with the church was pushed to the
background it was never completely forgotten, not even in the High Middle
Ages (Bonaventure, 144; Aquinas, 145f).
VI. From the Middle Ages on, the role of reconciliation within penance
became increasingly blurred due to the rise of private confession, the
increasing view of the church as an external juridical institution, and the
growing individualization of modern times. Despite all this it still was and
is possible to experience penance as reconciliation with the church. That this
doctrine was obscured for a long time is no argument against its correctness.

10.08   A Brief Theological Study on Indulgences
Kleiner theologischer Traktat über den Ablaß
{1.5}   *Stimmen der Zeit* 156 (1955) 343-355. Cf. p. 391 for revisions.
Abstract: Rahner attempts to explain the notion of indulgences and related
subjects using non-technical terms. In the process he unpacks three concepts: temporal punishment due to sin, treasury of the church, purgatory.
Topics: INDULGENCES.
Subsidiary Discussions: Theological anthropology (151ff); Sin, temporal
punishment due to (153f); Baptism (154f); Penance (154f); Love of God/
neighbor (157); Church, prayer for sinners (159ff); Church, treasury of
(160f); Eschatology, intermediate state (163f).

Precis: Rahner hopes this exercise can reveal aspects of the doctrine too often smoothed over or taken for granted and lead to a deeper understanding. **I.** We are complex multi-leveled beings. Actions and decisions made at the kernel of our being are objectified in attitudes, habits, and other elements of character. Even when our inmost being is transformed by God, such conversion does not immediately undo all the attitudes and habits embedded in other levels of our being. The "old I" can remain unconverted. Complete personal transformation can be a long, painful process. Christians call these ingrained elements of character "temporal punishment due to sin." Temporal because they endure and are only overcome in time; punishments because they are the consequences of sin and a judgment upon it. Sin occurs when we engage our personal freedom in ways that violate or distort our God-given nature. Such contradiction produces pain. Thus, we can say sin gives birth to its own punishment.

This stance of contradiction can become permanent alienation from God. When transformed into eternal punishment it must not be seen as God's decree imposed from without but the effect of our free actions unfolding from within. Because all our free decisions have objective, material objectifications we can see why even if our sins are fully forgiven temporal punishment due to sin may remain. (Baptism and penance differ in how they remove sin and punishment due to sin, 154f)

For all of our hard work and good will, the process of dissolving and transforming the after-effects of sin depends in the last analysis on God's disposition to the sinner. The process can be quicker or slower, involve more or less pain and suffering. Everyone has certainly experienced this (examples, 155f). We are not masters of our own course. How the effects of sin in us are healed is up to God. Nonetheless, we need not think of this process as completely external, juridical, or vindictive as if God were granting amnesty.

The decision we make to love in faith and hope, has the power to justify. The radical decision to love God and neighbor with all our heart and strength, containing as it does the will to achieve personal integration, accomplishes this very thing. Such blotting out of the effects of sin is not a reward for love, it is the co-natural consequence of love (157). Hence, an indulgence is an aid towards that perfect love which blots out temporal punishment due to sin and not a means which excuses us from following this one essential way of compensating for our past. This explanation does not mean our final decision for or against God can be changed after death. It merely allows for further integration of this decision into all the levels of our being after death, a position which does not contradict any doctrine of the church.

II. We can rightly entreat God to transform our lives and overcome the effects of our sin as quickly and beneficently as possible. We can also reasonably ask this for others. The church can and does support this prayer for it is not simply an external, controlling organization, it is the very body of Christ all of whose members live for one another, suffer with one another, and come to perfection for each other. When God hears the church pray, God beholds the victory of the Son and answers these prayers. This is precisely what is meant by the "treasury of the church": God's own will to save; God himself; Christ in union with his body the church. Hence, this doctrine does not teach about a commodity which can be exhausted or a debt God can be compelled to pay. This truth is embedded in the current rite of penance and Rahner hopes the renewed rite will make the reality even more clear. No one is excluded from this prayer of the church. We should be humbled to know the very bride of Christ stands at the throne of God interceding for us.

III. The dissolution of the effects of sin which the prayer of the church brings about is in no way a simple, external amnesty. Trent teaches the church has no power to grant such a thing. But the church's prayer of intercession can draw down a true remission of sin. The effectiveness of the prayer of the church always depends on the prior subjective disposition of the penitent. The prayer of the church can never replace the penance of the individual. It can only be aimed at securing the help of God more quickly and easily.

Rahner assumes the process of individual maturity is not necessarily or simply completed at death. Although at death one's disposition toward God is made definitive, it is possible to suppose it may take longer for the contradictions created by our improper use of freedom to be completely overcome, and for all the levels of our being to be integrated into this basic decision for God. The church calls this interval purgatory. Summary (165).

10.09   On the Official Teaching of the Church Today on the Subject of Indulgences

Zur heutigen kirchenamtlichen Ablaßlehre
{3.0}   *Catholica* 21 (1967) 261-268.

Abstract: Rahner attempts to prove Poschmann's "new theory" of indulgences is reconcilable with the 1967 Apostolic Constitution "*Indulgentiarum Doctrina*" and is better able to clear up some of its apparent contradictions.
Topics: INDULGENCES.
Subsidiary Discussions: Sacraments, *opus operatum* (175f, 194); Church, prayer in (178f); Sin, temporal punishment due to (186ff); Love (188ff); Church, treasury of (194ff); Dialogue, ecumenical (197f).
Precis: I. 1). Rahner presupposes the reader's familiarity with Poschmann's theory of indulgences (bibliography, 166 ftn1, 2) which he calls the "new theory" even though its teaching is quite ancient. 2) This essay is not a commentary on the Apostolic Constitution viewed as a whole (bibliography, 167 ftn3; 169 ftn9). It merely inquires whether the new theory is compatible with the Constitution. Many questions go undiscussed (list, 170). 3) By "reconcilable" Rahner does not mean to prove the two approaches are

identical, only that they are not in conflict. The Apostolic Constitution provides the common ground upon which theologians are free to speculate. Mere differences in terminology are never a proof of heterodoxy.

II. Criticism of the new theory is often based on a distorted interpretation to the effect that temporal punishment is remitted not by an official exercise of the church's juridical authority but by prayer alone. These critics hold that in remitting punishment, indulgences differ from mere prayer precisely in being juridical acts of the church. The difference is in the interpretation of the phrase *auctoritativa applicatio et dispensatio "thesauri Ecclesiae."* Is this a real or only a verbal contradiction?

III. Rahner argues this authoritative act (*potestas*) is not an act of ecclesial jurisdiction. Such an interpretation leads into "a whole thicket of thorny questions" (174). By leaving this question open we are in a position to deduce two facts from the Apostolic Constitution: 1) the importance of the disposition of the recipient of the indulgence and the subsequent real, valid, and effective "ability" of the church to blot out punishment due to sin which it achieved through recourse to the "treasury of the church"; 2) This ability does not consist merely in prayer.

IV. Does the Apostolic Constitution's rejection of the idea that the essence of indulgences consists in "prayer alone" on the church's part imply a rejection of the new theory?

1) Rahner begins with a word about method and approach. Many controversies in theology are merely verbal. They stem from the mistaken assumption that both parties are using a term in the same sense.

2. In this controversy "prayer" has a variety of meanings (list, 178f). Among them, Rahner argues, one is not only compatible with *potestas auctoritativa* but constitutes it. The only kind of prayer the Apostolic Constitution excludes as inadequate to define the nature of indulgence is one which is not conceived of as an act of the church's authoritative power.

3) Because the new theory always had this form of prayer in mind, it is not materially opposed to the Apostolic Constitution. This form of prayer is the intercessory prayer of the church on behalf of her members. Rahner gives four reasons why such prayer is infallibly heard (list, 180). This proves the new theory is not irreconcilable with the Apostolic Constitution.

4) This becomes even more clear when one recalls the two reasons the new theory seeks to interpret indulgence as prayer of the church: **a)** it diminishes the danger of misinterpreting the nature of indulgence as automatic or mechanical, reducing the role of the disposition of the penitent (precisely what the Apostolic Constitution aims to rule out). The ultimate object of the prayer of the church is for the penitent to receive the grace to perform penance in a spirit of love in order thereby to attain the blotting out of temporal punishment due to sin. **b)** This understanding precisely rules out a defective, essentially juridical notion of indulgence. Rahner previews the outstanding questions to be treated in the remainder of this essay (182f).

V. 1) The Apostolic Constitution treats the relationship between the inner disposition of the penitent and the effectiveness of an indulgence far more fully than any previous official statement. Realizing that no one can change completely overnight and that most people retain some "*affectus*" towards sin Rahner concludes: a) proper interior disposition is needed. b) Temporal punishment cannot be completely blotted out so long as one retains an *affectus* towards sin. c) The precise relationship between disposition and the effectiveness of indulgence is left an open question. 2) A discussion of temporal punishment due to sin follows.

VI. 1) Regarding temporal punishment due to sin the Apostolic Constitution makes no attempt at a precise definition. It appears to regard it as a co-natural consequence of sin rather than as an external act of God's vindictive justice. Because sin becomes materially objectified its effects perdure even when the sin itself is forgiven. For this reason the blotting out of temporal punishment cannot be thought of along the lines of an amnesty. The Apostolic Constitution sees indulgence as an "*auctoritativa dispensatio*" of the "*thesaurus Ecclesiae*" "*ad poenae temporales remissionem*" (188). Missing from this definition is the middle term which explains how this blotting out takes place. If the ultimate purpose of temporal punishment is the purification of the soul then this is the intention of the intercessory prayer of the church. Every means for blotting out sin must in some way lead to a closer union with God and Christ in the unity of love. Love alone sanctifies and purifies and in this way overcomes the temporal punishment due to sin. The fact this middle term is omitted does not deny its reality or effectiveness.

2) Summary (191). Seeing the increase of love as the sole means by which temporal punishment due to sin is blotted out clears up two apparent contradictions in the Apostolic Constitution. "*Facilius*" in the document cannot refer to some means "easier" than maturing in love. Thus, indulgence is never a substitute for *metanoia* or for acts of love and penance. It is rather the assistance one needs to accomplish these—assistance gained through the intercessory prayer of the church. Secondly, the new theory clarifies the fact that the "state of the soul in which, as the ultimate *effect* of indulgence, a specific 'measure' of the temporal punishments due to sin is blotted out...has this same effect of blotting out even when no indulgence is gained" (194). Without this understanding it would be impossible to distinguish indulgences from simple magic.

VII. A further concept the new theory clarifies is the "treasury of the church" which the Apostolic Constitution insists must never be reduced to a material or quantitative notion. By identifying the "treasury of the church" with the total Christ, head and members, upon whom and in whom God is gracious to the individual sinner, the new theory insures "the treasury of the church" is not susceptible to being divided into portions and so distributed. The only finite limitation on the effectiveness of Christ through the power of the church to blot out sin is the finite limitation of the recipient because of one's interior disposition. For all these reason the new theory is superior to earlier theories. Finally, the Apostolic Constitution interpreted in light of the new theory supplies fresh impetus for ecumenical dialogue.

10.10 Marriage as a Sacrament
Die Ehe als Sakrament

{3.5}   March, 1967 lecture in Vienna. *Geist und Leben* 40 (1967) 177-193.

Abstract: This dogmatic look at marriage clarifies its nature as a sacrament, the relationship between sacramental and non-sacramental marriages, and how the love of spouses parallels the love of Christ for the church.

Topics: CHRISTIAN LIFE, marriage; CHURCH as *Ur-sakrament*; SACRAMENTS.

Subsidiary Discussions: Sacraments, *opus operatum/operantis* (202, 214f); Symbol, real (202f, 209f); Love of God/neighbor (203f); Mystery (204): Supernatural existential (205f); *Caritas* (206).

Precis: A dogmatic examination of how Christians understand the heart and center of marriage contributes greatly to solving many of today's practical questions regarding marriage. What does it means that marriage is a sacrament?

I. Rahner first inquires into the nature of a sacrament in general—a dangerous field because for too long the unique history of particular sacraments has been made to fit a Procrustean bed of philosophical abstraction. But certain points are inescapable: sacraments take place in the church. They are events in which the church realizes its own nature and thereby "actualizes" itself. The event is both palpably historical and eschatological. Hence, in every sacrament one can distinguish a sign and the thing signified, elements which are connatural but not identical. Insofar as the sign proceeds from God's salvific will expressed through the church (the *Ur-sakrament*) "this sign always has an 'exhibitive' force as the effective and unconditional offering of salvation by Christ and the Church. In this sense, then, the sacramental sign is *opus operatum*" (202). But since grace only brings about salvation when it is freely accepted, the sacramental manifestation of grace remains radically indeterminate precisely from the human aspect. Prior to any theological consideration, marriage is a sacrament because marital love has a physical and social dimension of reality. It is a "real symbol," holding in a unity sign and the thing signified: its physical and social manifestation on the one hand, and personal love on the other.

II. Rahner develops three aspects of personal love, that most intimate and personal unity between two individuals signified in marriage physically, spacio-temporally, and socially.

  1) How this love relates to God. The long answer lies in the mutually conditioning relationship between love of God and love of neighbor. Love of neighbor is not merely a moral task, it is the means without which we cannot love God. The relationships we form with the world actualize our

transcendentality towards the Mystery which is our origin and goal and that of all creation. The self-surrender of one human being to another in love is based in its ultimate and connatural depths precisely on this orientation to God. The depth of love consists in its power to reach the other in the very deepest and most ultimate levels of his/her personhood and uniqueness. Only because this love is rooted in God can they hope their love and fidelity will succeed.

2) How this personal love acquires fresh roots through grace. Even outside the Christian context the personal love which creates the state of marriage is sustained and opened to the immediacy of God by the grace of God. Rahner bases this on his controversial notion of "supernatural existential" which argues that any moral act is also a salvific act. Applied to marriage this means "genuine love is de facto always that theological virtue of *caritas* which is sustained by God himself through his grace" (206). This *caritas* is salvific: attaining to God himself in his offer of self-bestowal.

3) How personal love unites us with the whole human community. Although marriage has the aspects of exclusivity and withdrawal, this partnership is essentially open to all. Marriage is essentially communal in its origin and orientation. Love is only love to the degree it includes and remains open to the "other," entrusting oneself to the other, putting oneself into his/her debt. The grace of God which sustains marriage is the grace of a covenant encompassing everything from the innermost dynamism of the world and of human history to the unique spiritual depth of each individual. This one grace unites each person with the whole human family. Hence, marriage unites one with God and neighbor. Summary (209).

III. What was said above about marriage as "real symbol" of personal love can also be said of the church. Allowing for the differences in the relationship between certain communities and individuals, Rahner maintains the same sign function which is found in marriage is also present in the church. As *Ursakrament* it is the historical manifestation in Christ (i.e., sign) of the love of God for the human family in his act of self-bestowal. Both in marriage and in the church the sign and the love signified can be so stretched as to pull apart. But whereas the sign function in marriage can sinfully become degraded into a lie, the church as a whole can never lose the intrinsic connection between itself and what it signifies because of the eschatological victory of Christ. Summary (211).

The unity of the church, which it presents as the model and basis for the unity of marriage, is constituted through the love of people in the church and the manifestation of this love at the level of social and communal life. Thus, "the love which unites married spouses contributes to the unity of the Church herself because it is one of the ways in which the unifying love of the Church is made actual. It is as much formative of the Church as sustained by the Church" (212). Hence, the parallelism between the church and

marriage does not rest in mere external similarity but in their common root: love.
IV. When marriage takes place within the church it becomes a sacrament precisely because married love is never merely a worldly affair. It is always an event of grace and love which unites God and humanity (summary, 213). For this reason theologians need not concern themselves to find Christ's historical "words of institution." It is enough that Jesus acknowledges the religious relevance of marriage and that it has been instituted by the church as an eschatological sign of salvation for the kingdom of God until the end of time.

Theologians have long been embarrassed because the theology of Ephesians 5 seems to offer no way of distinguishing a sacramental from a non-sacramental marriage. In Rahner's view we need not insist on this distinction. The two are related as *opus operatum* and *opus operantis*, the latter also being wholly an event of grace. Marriage (like baptism and penance) does not become an event of grace when it becomes a sacrament. The event of grace becomes a sacramental event of grace as *opus operatum* when it is celebrated in the church where it acquires the character of an unconditional pledge of grace from God. The grace of marriage gives rise to the grace of the sacrament by building up the church with its gift of love which the church itself sustains. This approach frees theology from forcing marriage to fit certain suspect postulates or hypothetical doctrines said to have existed from the beginning.
V. In what sense is marriage is a sacrament because it is an image of the unity between Christ and the church? Rahner finds Ephesians 5's emphasis on leadership and submission wanting. For him the key parallelism lies in the concept of covenant, for in Christ all creation understands its dynamism and finds its goal. This common orientation unites the love of two people in marriage and unites Christ with the church. Hence, the parallelism is no external similarity but a participation of one love in the other. Based on the multivalent unity of Christ and the church the unity of spouses cannot be limited to the culture-bound relationship of leadership and submission. It can equally well be recognized in other symbols, e.g., the cross. Summary (221).

10.11 The Teaching of the Second Vatican Council on the Diaconate

Die Lehre des II. Vatikanischen Konzils über den Diakonat
{0.5} October 1966 lecture in Rome to International Conference of Studies, "The Deacon in the Church and in the World Today." *Die Seelsorger* 36 (1966) 193-199.
Abstract: Midway through the council this essay summarizes the directions and motives for restoring the diaconate: to counter the priest shortage and

to strengthen with sacramental grace those already performing diaconal service.

Topics: VATICAN II; DIACONATE; ORDERS, sacrament of.

Precis: Three council documents treat the diaconate (*Lumen gentium* 3 #29; *Ad gentes* #16; *Orientalium ecclesiarum* #17). After a brief summary of how diaconal initiatives fared in council votes Rahner turns to the texts themselves.

I. Essentially, the diaconate can constitute a permanent official state and a sacrament in the church not merely a transitional step to priestly ordination. It is not a lay state but belongs to the three official states of hierarchy itself which Christ founded in his church. The tasks of the deacon participate in those of priest and bishop: to teach through preaching the word; to sanctify through leading the community in prayer; to lead by administering the charitable works entrusted to them by the bishops. *Ad gentes* supplies more detail regarding specific tasks than *Lumen gentium* (summary, 225).

II. *Ad genetes* sees the restored diaconate as useful and recommended; *Orientalium eccesiarum* urgently advocates it; *Lumen gentium* characterizes the tasks entrusted to deacons as supremely necessary for the life of the church. A restored diaconate could address present difficulties especially the priest shortage. *Ad gentes*, however, adduces a different reason: the need to fortify with sacramental grace those laymen already performing the tasks of deacon in the church. In other words, the official function already exists; the diaconate has sacramental status; so why deprive those already involved in these tasks of the sacramental grace that comes with ordination? (227).

The decision to restore the diaconate is left in the hands of the bishops' conferences with the full agreement and assent of the pope. These conferences have the duty to examine and decide whether or not this would be opportune in the regions entrusted to their care. Rahner does not believe an individual bishop could oppose in his own diocese the policy agreed to by the regional bishops' conference. Vatican II agreed to extend the possibility of ordination to the diaconate to more mature men, even if they are married, and to younger men with the proviso they remain celibate.

III. Rahner concludes with a look at some open questions. What age is mature? What constitutes a legitimate bishops' conference? What kind of diaconal formation is necessary? (Rahner assumes not much since the men already doing the work of deacons must already have sufficient formation.) Theologically, what do "higher" and "lower" indicate in the relationship among the three orders? Rahner ends by restating the argument for conferring the grace of orders on those laymen already entrusted with diaconal service in the church.

10.12 A Fragmentary Aspect of a Theological Evaluation of the Concept of the Future

Fragment aus einer theologischen Besinnung auf den Begriff der Zukunft

{1.5}   Part 1 of a September 1966 lecture at Darmstadt. E. Schlechta, ed., *Darmstädter Gespräch: Der Mensch und seiner Zukunft* (Darmstadt 1967) 149-160. Other parts of this essay are found substantially in 6:05.

Abstract: The true absolute future is Mystery—uncontrollable, incalculable, alien. While furnishing us with the material for planning it also relativizes all our plans, theories, and ideologies. It challenges us to self-surrender.

Topics: FUTURE, planning.

Subsidiary Discussions: Trust (238f); Hope (238f); Death (239); Ideology (240).

Precis: Theologians pay insufficient attention to the future. It is incorrect to believe the future is precisely that which we foresee and plan for. Any future encompassed by plans, by an evolutionary worldview, or by ideology are only dreams of tomorrow which are already here today. Without denigrating the human penchant for planning Rahner insists the real future can never be understood as simply our plans for the future.

The real future is mystery. We do not reach out to it, it comes to us of itself. It is uncontrollable, incalculable, and alien. Hence, we can never dispense with the need to deal with the future. Though the specter of the future can be suppressed or denied it is always there as incalculable mystery. On the one hand it empowers our freedom; on the other hand it condemns us as guilty whenever we insist that it remain at bay.

We must constantly come to terms with the true future. One attitude we may cultivate toward the future is trust—trust not merely that the future is beyond our comprehension and control, but that it is arriving *for* us. This becomes an attitude of hope in the future, and self-commitment to the mysterious future. What happens when we trustingly surrender ourselves to the true future? On one level apparently nothing. The world turns, swallowing up our plans in its infinitude. On the other hand everything would be different. (Here Rahner digresses over whether "would be" or "is" is the proper term, since it is quite possible to have this attitude of trust and not be explicitly aware of it. It may only become clear in death.)

"What does it mean, therefore, for a man to have this trust in the absolute future considered as that which is radically breaking in upon his own life?" (239). First, our planning continues. For one dimension of the absolute future presents us with the material out of which the future becomes temporal. This is a precious and indispensable gift which we must never confuse with the real future. At the same time our relationship with the absolute future relativizes all our plans and ideologies in the face of ineffable mystery.

No one can claim to be completely unacquainted with these two dimensions of the future. No one can be so naive as to equate completely one's own plans for the future with the real absolute future. As a result each of us must keep watch to see whether in human history there has ever been anyone in relationship with whom we can attain that attitude of pure self-surrender to the absolute future breaking in upon our own lives precisely as a promise for us. This is where Christian theologians could address the world beginning with the phenomenon of the future.

10.13   On the Theology of Hope
Zur Theologie der Hoffnung
{3.0}   March 1967 lecture at Graz. *Internationale Zeitschrift für das Gespräch zwichen verschiedenen Humanismen* 1 (1968) 67-78.

Abstract: Rahner draws from scholasticism the essential characteristics of hope and its relationship to faith and love: it is not provisional; it is unique and not merely a consequence of faith; it is cosmic and social.

Topics: HOPE, theology of; VIRTUES, theological; VIRTUES, perichoresis of.

Subsidiary Discussions: Theological anthropology, modes of transcendentality (245ff); Trinity (245f); God, possession of (248f); Despair and presumption (251, 255, 258); Faith (252f); Jesus Christ as ground of hope (255); Future (257f); Ideology (257ff).

Precis: Rahner offers this fragmentary contribution to the debate on hope (bibliography, 242 ftn2,3; 243 ftn4) based on scholastic philosophy. He hopes it will open a common approach to the topic, reveal hidden riches of scholastic insights, and correct some hypotheses of contemporary theology.
I. Rahner summarizes clearly the major insights of scholastic theology into the theological virtues in general and hope in particular.
II. Hope is one of the theological virtues, unique in its own right, irreducible to either faith or love. This is not always clear. Viewed in terms of the two basic modes of human (transcendental) self-realization, and given its subordinate role in the New Testament, hope could seem quite provisional. It would seem to belong to a relatively superficial triad of theological virtues postulated on an interrelationship of initially disparate concepts. Rahner disputes this and insists what is at stake is more than a squabble over terms.
III. Rahner dismisses a number of false solutions to this problem. He rejects a facile conceptual model of "possession" drawn from daily experience. On such a reading faith and hope appear to be completely provisional, as if once God were "possessed" there would no longer be a need for faith or hope. But the act of attaining to God in truth confirms rather than overcomes or solves God's unfathomable mystery. The act of attaining to God in love is a response to and an acceptance of a love which is radically and incalculably grace. Hence, "possession of God" "is that radical transcendence of self and

surrender of self which is entailed in the act of reaching out for truth into the
unfathomable mystery, and it is also the radical self-surrender and self-
transcendence of that love which ... lives totally by the love of that which is
beloved as based on nothing else than itself" (249). The interior unity and
common source of this surrender to God in truth and love is hope. "Hope
implies the one basic character which is the common factor in the mutual
interplay of truth and love: the enduring attitude of 'outwards from self' into
the incontrollability of God" (250). Where hope is achieved as the radical
self-submission to the absolute uncontrollable, there alone do we truly
understand who God is. Hence, hope is not provisional.

IV. Hope is not merely an inevitable consequence of faith, as if one could
only decline to hope in the truths revealed by the light of faith by an
incomprehensible and nonsensical refusal of the will. Leaving aside the
debate between Thomism and Scotism, Rahner maintains that what is
promised to faith and to hope are significantly different. Faith grasps general
theoretical truth, the universal promise. But it can never by itself reduce the
general promise to a particular, concrete promise to me as an individual. I
must hope. Hence, hope is a basic modality of human existence. It is not
simply a consequence of faith which can never provide the basis for hope.
Though hope grounds itself, it cannot do away with Christ, the one whose
death manifests the grace of God in the world in an historically definitive way
(255). Rahner summarizes with a definition of hope and its relation to faith
and love (256).

V. Lest the reader be left with the opinion that hope is for the most part a
private matter, Rahner turns to its social and cosmic dimensions. He cites
Lumen gentium (IV #35) which calls for a continually revolutionary attitude
on the part of Christians in the world toward the world. Hope directed
towards God as the absolute future cannot simply represent an attitude of
conservatism, traditionalism, or petrification. People find their fulfillment
through engagement with the world where theory becomes practice. Christians plan for the future, but not in such a way as to reduce the uncontrollable, incalculable, absolute future to the scale of their plans. In fact hope
rejects all absolutizing of this world and calls into question all intra-mundane
structures, plans, and ideologies. Hope is the courage to commit to as well
as to renounce the things of this world—to persevere or to set out on
pilgrimage. When to stay and when to leave is not revealed by theoretical
faith but only by hope. Rahner concludes with a gloss on I Cor 13.

10.14 The Theological Problems Entailed in the Idea of the "New Earth"

Über die theologische Problematik der "Neuen Erde"
{3.0} October 1967, U.S. lecture. *Neues Forum 14* (1967) 683-687, as, *"Mitarbeit an der Neuen Erde."*

Abstract: Collaborating with non-believers to make a better world is possible because Christians have no blueprint for the future beyond the conviction that human history will finally endure *and* it will be radically transformed by God.

Topics: FUTURE; ESCHATOLOGY, consummation of the world; HISTORY, consummation of.

Subsidiary Discussions: Vatican II (260f); Magisterium, future of (262ff); Material world (266ff); Marxism (267f); Death (269).

Precis: I. Vatican II urges Christians to collaborate with non-believers of good will for the betterment of the whole world. Christians are to impress upon the framework of secular life the stamp of their eschatological hope. But how can a precisely Christian vision of the world be an appropriate project for non-Christians to collaborate in? What is the precise material content of the Christian future? Is there a specific Christian blueprint? Do these questions reveal a veiled inconsistency in the teaching of the council?
II. The real difficulty lies neither in collaborating with non-Christians nor in engaging in a pluralistic society. It lies in determining whether there is a particularly Christian vision of the future applicable to the secular world. It would seem there is nothing peculiarly Christian in working for a world that is more peaceable, just, etc.
III. But there is another side. Vatican II speaks of the salvific manner in which even those outside the church contribute to the consummation of the world. Insisting that the "new earth" is presented as a gift from God and not as the result of a gradual earthly process does not mean replacing the already existing world but transforming it. In short, in the consummation of the world God transforms what we humans (not simply the church) have shaped. The council leaves open the question of how the secular formation of the future and the divine gift of the future are related.
IV. Rahner is now able to state the real question clearly: is the world we fashion simply the indifferent material realm in which we prove ourselves morally, and which God does away with at the consummation of the world? Or does the world we have formed somehow pass transformed into the *eschaton* properly so-called? The question would have made no sense in past times since people then contributed so little to shaping their world. The question arises today because our actions greatly shape the world, and also because of the differences between Christian and Marxist visions of the future (267f).

V. Can this question be answered, and how? [In this key section Rahner applies analogously insights drawn from theological anthropology to the problem of the consummation of the world.] The consummation is coming of itself. It is not the outcome of a human plan or a natural process, nor is it simply an ideal—a mirage which animates history. It will be the deed of God as the self-transcendence of history. Just as the consummation of our personal history brought about by death is not merely one more stage in that history but a real, unimaginable transformation, so it will be with the consummation of the history of the world. Just as one cannot discount the role of the body in the personal consummation of an individual, one cannot discount the role of the material, secular world in the consummation of the world.

Hence, there is a basic dialectical tension regarding the consummation of the world: human history will finally endure, *and* it will be radically transformed. "This tension maintains us in an openness to the future while still according a radical importance to the present" (270). Rahner bases this on what he knows of the relationship of body and soul definitively manifested in what is posited of the glorified body of Christ. Further proof is found in the fact the moral element in us consists precisely in that which takes place in concrete history, not simply in that which survives history. Hence, history must have definitive significance if the moral is to have such significance.

VI. For the above to be true the world in all its secularity must exhibit a secret Christianity. All human actions which aim to fulfill creation are implicitly oriented toward the consummation of the world. Even though this does not clarify what is distinctively Christian in this process, it does free us from having to choose between finding some specifically and exclusively Christian element or dismissing what mankind strives for as "merely human." The meaning and the Christian roots of many seemingly secular world-building initiatives are often only seen in reflection, e.g., the growing unity of humanity; the openness to the absolute future. Summary (272).

10.15 Immanent and Transcendent Consummation of the World

Immanente und transzendente Vollendung der Welt

{3.5} September 1966 lecture at Feldafing, Starnberger See to the Institute of the Görres Society for Achieving an Encounter between Natural Science and Theology. *Naturwissenschaft und Theologie* (Freiburg 1968) 174-184.

Abstract: Rahner defends matter as an essential, non-provisional factor in the unity of spiritual beings even after the world's consummation. He does this by imputing to matter a graced, immanent, self-transcending impetus toward God.

Topics: ESCHATOLOGY, consummation of the world; MATTER and spirit.

Subsidiary Discussions: Transcendent/immanent (277ff); God as goal of consummation (278); Creation (280f); God as goal of creation (282f); Nature and grace (282f); Merit (283); Self-transcendence (287); Becoming (287); Incarnation (288).

Precis: Since all the key terms of this discussion are philosophically controversial Rahner feels permitted to begin without clarifying each term.

I. Rahner lists five senses of the term "consummation." Its meaning in any particular circumstance depends on what is being consummated. He insists consummation cannot validly be applied to the physical world as such or to events taking place in it as such and in isolation. Consummation can only be applied to a temporal event which: 1) has an end (i.e., goal) different from itself; 2) results in something other than itself which is definitive; 3) the result is the goal of the event. Strictly material events "run out." They never become definitive. They exhibit no will to finality and produce nothing qualitatively different from themselves. There is nothing of higher value in the final stage than in the lower. Only material events with an intrinsic reference to spirit can be thought of in terms of the consummation of the material world. Biological life is a case in point, although if it brings about nothing more than its own ceaseless regeneration it cannot properly be considered consummation. Consummation can only refer to events worked out in personal freedom and attached to material reality as its intrinsic element and unifying principle (summary thesis, 276). Consummation cannot properly apply to the definitive state of perdition arrived at through the misuse of freedom. It is more accurately called the final, definitive state of non-consummation.

II. The immanent or transcendent consummation of the world can only be understood when these terms are grasped in their original sense, i.e., in terms of the consummation of the spiritual person in freedom. There immanent and transcendent do not differ as internal and externally given goals. On the contrary, for the spiritual being immanence is precisely transcendence. After summing up this insight in three formulations, Rahner concludes by insisting that it is only because we employ a false mechanical or biological model to spiritual beings that we can think of humans as having a purely immanent goal.

III. Here Rahner hopes to make more plain and precise the relationship between immanent and transcendent consummation by referring to the theological anthropology of Christianity, primarily the relationship between nature and grace. He intentionally avoids the controversial doctrine of justification (280). When the goal of creation is seen as willed from the outset to surrender itself to God's free act of self-communication, attaining God becomes at one and the same time the immanent and transcendent goal of creation. God becomes not merely the efficient but also the quasi-formal cause of the world. This insight breaks down the old conceptual model of nature and grace which clings to the notion of an inner and outer goal of creation.

IV. Rahner next applies all this to the term consummation. God is not only the goal of the movement of the spiritual creature towards its consummation, God is also the ultimate and innermost principle of that motion. Uncreated grace (considered as the quasi-formal cause) and created grace (as the necessary prior condition and consequence of uncreated grace) form a unity. Hence, the present is sustained by its future and the immanent and transcendent consummation of the spiritual creature are the same. It points to one consummation in which one aspect demands the other. Because creation has no mere natural end, no mere immanent consummation, beatitude can in no way be thought of as merited. Although one can imagine and construct the idea of achieving a "natural end" which entails the denial of God, this is a false construct and not a real competing natural end. Rahner concludes with a summary of why what is true of the individual spiritual being is also true of humanity as such (284).

V. What are the implications of all this when applied to the consummation of the material world? Purely as such, matter can have no consummation. It is only to be found in the unity it shares with spirit. Without materiality, which is the expression and medium of finite spiritual self-fulfillment, spiritual creaturehood at the finite level is totally inconceivable. Quite apart from metaphysical considerations, Christian dogma makes the unity of matter and spirit more probable (list, 285). Nor can one argue that temporal priority of matter to spirit invalidates these claims since in any case matter is ordered toward spirit to provide its true fulfillment. Rahner weaves together the notions of intrinsic development, self-transcendence, and becoming to prove the ultimate common bond between matter and spirit wrought by God who is simple and absolute spirit. It is God who freely implants in matter the creative impetus toward self-transcendence.

VI. The material world has a transcendent consummation (summary, 288). The gift of the impetus towards divine self-bestowal upon the material and spiritual world implies the manifestation in material history of the incarnation of the divine Logos as its goal. This struggle for self-transcendence takes place in an open future where sin and our refusal of God always remain possible. Rahner concludes by insisting that matter must never be thought of as superfluous or provisional—a transitional stage through which spirit passes, even though we cannot conceive of the mode of existence of matter once it is fully consummated and self-transcended. Summary (289).

10.16 On the Theological Problems Entailed in a "Pastoral Constitution"

Zur theologischen Problematik einer "Pastoralkonstitution"
{4.0} Composed for the commentary *Schema dertien. Tekst en commentar.*
In collaboration with J.-Y. Calvez, et al., *Vaticanum 2, No. 2: De Kerk in de wereld van deze tijd* (Paul Brand, Antwerp 1967) 315-336.

Abstract: Vatican II's "pastoral constitutions" are essentially instructions which draw their authority and binding force from the charismatic dimension of the church and from the immutability of the values they proclaim.

Topics: MAGISTERIUM and Pastoral Constitutions; VATICAN II.

Subsidiary Discussions: Decision, universal/particular (296ff); Church, pastoral function of (294f, 301ff); Spirit (304ff, 310f); Church, charismatic element in (304ff, 310ff); Inspiration (307f).

Precis: *Gaudium et spes*, Vatican II's Pastoral Constitution on the Church in the Modern World, embodies a new and unique intention to address a wide range of secular concerns. But on a theoretical level what precisely is a pastoral constitution? The document describes itself only negatively: that its teachings do not have supratemporal validity or universal binding force.
I. But what can be said of a positive nature? The designation "constitution" indicates the document's importance but in what does it consist? Insofar as all conciliar documents are an exercise of the church's pastoral office the designation "pastoral" reveals little. It does not help to distinguish it by opposing pastoral to doctrinal, or to insist it is an exercise of *potentia jurisdictionis* and not *potentia ordinis*. It is possible to call this document pastoral in the sense that it attempts to shed light on the contemporary world situation with instructions and warnings to Christians and all those who would hear, with hope they will shape their lives aright in this situation. These instructions are not eternally valid and binding doctrines but they do express a legitimate task of the church. But this raises more theoretical questions.
II. [Sections II-V attempt to clarify the term "instructions."] Instructions are based in doctrine, the message of the gospel. Hence, it is no surprise to learn the pastoral constitutions have a doctrinal character even though their instructions are not thereby offered as universally binding. But if these instructions are not binding why must they be taken as more than simply expressions of opinion? Rahner begins with this thesis: no concrete, free human decision can be fully deduced from universal principles (297). He is quick to add that this does not mean some universal norms cannot also be very concrete.
III. After defining an instruction (298) Rahner points out every instruction is itself a decision of the instructor, for no particular instruction can be fully deduced from the universal. Instruction is aimed at getting the hearer freely to choose a particular decision. But from where does instruction derive the

force of its demand? In the case of a "theological instruction" the binding force can be interpreted as coming from a summons uttered by God in the concrete to the individual directing him/her to take a particular decision. The church can legitimately issue such a summons even without knowing precisely to whom it is addressed.

IV. In addition to its other tasks, the church is authorized and empowered to guide the Christian actions of its individual members. It can do this by issuing commands or prescriptions to individuals, or by encouraging certain movements within itself, e.g., Catholic Action. It is to this realm that instruction belongs.

V. After summarizing the sense in which the church decides to issue instructions (303) Rahner asks how the church knows which individual instructions it should promulgate. Remembering these instructions are not simply derived from general principles and can also contain the element of divine summons, the church, like the individual, must issue such directives according to the highest dictates of its conscience.

VI. What separates the individual's decision from that of the church? The church is constantly being guided by the Holy Spirit. This gift is bestowed by God on the church to insure that it does not depart from the truth of Christ in any definitive doctrine, and that hope and love will always remain alive and manifested adequately in history. (This does not mean the church is devoid of sinners or free from sin.) This freedom from error can only be guaranteed by the charismatic element within the church and not merely by its institutional dimension (though the two are not mutually exclusive). This charismatic dimension can be manifested in very unspectacular ways even by the laity. All this leads Rahner to conclude that the instructions of the church are charismatic instructions formulated with the assistance of the Spirit in the church. It is this element which insures that an instruction is more than a mere opinion even though it is less than a law or commandment.

VII. Charismatic instructions, however divinely inspired, always take place in the context of a concrete encounter with a specific human situation. This situation is always recognized in a human process with all the prior restrictions that apply to human recognition. But to fulfill its own nature the church must act in and upon human history. The power so to act is part of the intrinsic nature of the church. Hence, while it is true the church draws its life from the unchanging revelation of Christ which we say is closed, it also draws its life from the knowledge of the situation in which it lives. Though the Spirit may aid in assessing this situation it never dispels the need for a non-revelatory kind of human knowledge in order for the church to act.

VIII. This fact was little reflected upon in earlier ages because knowledge of the world situation was previously very simple and uncomplicated. Today not only is the situation very complex, the church must rely on other specialists to grasp this world situation. Thus, the question arose on the council floor how the church can know precisely what to say if it cannot draw on the special sources of knowledge bestowed on it by God (310). The practical answer given was that since the church must instruct it must have the capacity to do so. Rahner seeks to know whether any more precise theoretical insight is available. Here he appeals to the charismatic element in the church which insures the church can do what it must to achieve its nature without thereby excluding the process of human reflection or insisting the church can never make mistakes of any kind. Rahner ends this section with a succinct thesis on what constitutes the essence of a pastoral constitution (312).

IX. But is there any such thing as a pastoral constitution as Rahner defines it? And does *Gaudium et spes* fit the terms of his definition? Rahner answers the first question by alluding to the history of the church which has often recognized and passed on as its own instructions the charismatic utterances of particular people (e.g., Catherine of Siena). The second question is more difficult especially because the document itself does not tackle directly the notion of a pastoral constitution. This lack of theoretical precision does not, however, entitle one to deny *Gaudium et spes* has the essential character of pastoral constitution outlined here. Rahner points to the similarities between this conciliar document and the great pastoral encyclicals of John XXIII. If the latter can be called pastoral instructions, then perhaps in the same sense and spirit this document can be called a pastoral constitution.

X. After reviewing the characteristics of a pastoral instruction Rahner explains how the unchanging value upon which it urges one to act gives the instruction its abiding validity. These values and not the theoretical nature of the instruction itself are what the council fathers had in mind when they issued the document. The fact the ultimately concrete element which constitutes the essence of a pastoral instruction is wholly incapable of being the object of theoretical speculation does not count against its truth or value. Speculation is always of secondary importance. Though the line between doctrine and instruction can never be made absolutely clear or unambiguous the attempt to achieve clarity is never meaningless. Rahner warns theologians not to dismiss a pastoral constitution hastily because in comparison with purely dogmatic statements it is finite, limited, and incapable of being made completely clear. For these pastoral documents are no less products of the working of the Spirit in the church than dogmatic statements.

10.17   Theological Reflections on the Problem of Secularization

Theologische Reflexionen zur Säkularisation

{3.5}   Previously unpublished August 1967 lecture in Toronto to Congress on the Theology of the Renewal of the Church.

Abstract: Secularization, the growing separation/autonomy of the world from church, is not an evil. It challenges the church to participate fully in the democratic process of society and find new ways to endure and serve the world.

Topics: CHURCH and secularization; SOCIETY, secularization.

Subsidiary Discussions: Atheism (319f); Integralism (321ff); Pluralism (325ff); Magisterium, instruction (331ff); Theology, political (336); Theology, pastoral (337ff); Concupiscence (342ff); *Agon* (344ff); Sin (346f).

Precis: I. This theological analysis of how the church relates with an increasingly secularized world begins with definitions. Rahner is concerned with secularization as the growing influence of the "world" as the outcome of human ingenuity, and the process by which it becomes increasingly separated and autonomous from the church as a social entity. Secularization never negates the fact the world is permeated by grace and plays a positive role in the history of revelation and salvation. The remainder of this section deals with the limits of the essay (preview, 320) and certain presuppositions with which Rahner expects the reader to be familiar.

II. *"A phenomenon frequently apparent in the history of the Church is a false integralism. By comparison with this the process of secularization is, judged by genuinely Christian standards, right and just."*

Integralism is the belief human life can be unambiguously mapped out and manipulated in conformity with certain universal principles proclaimed and managed by the church. Integralism fails to account for the autonomy of the practical intellect. It dismisses as hopelessly secular and of no account whatever falls outside its own universal principles. Two insights overthrow integralism: that the church does not have the power to determine in the concrete what the world should do in every case; that we cannot deduce what we should do from what we should not do (examples, 324f). The effect of taking historical conditions seriously reveals the limits of the church's ability to encompass the realm of free decision and the essential pluralism of the world in which the church is only one element among many contributing to the overall moral climate of the world. Since integralism is false in principle the church must leave the world free and responsible in its own right even though its acts do not cease to be moral or significant for salvation. Though the church cannot control the secular world it supplies to the process of secularization the grace of God, the principles of the process, and its ultimate boundaries.

III. *"The secularization of the world in the good sense implies that the Church has a quite new task, namely to create a new ecclesiastical integration between the faithful themselves within herself taken as a whole and in the individual communities."*

Churches are meant to be communities. In earlier times when society was more homogeneous this presented few problems. Today's more secularized world is also more pluralistic. Hence, the church today must create what it formerly presupposed as the social or "natural" substrate for the formation of its own community. The church must do this without becoming a "sect." It must remain an open society with room for all while at the same time integrating social and intellectual pluralism within itself. But how can the church do this without reverting to integralism? At an abstract level Rahner suggests the church does this by collaborating with the world in social welfare projects and by fully participating in the democratic process both in society and in itself.

IV. *"In its situation of pluralism and secularism the Church leaves society to develop along its own lines. Now precisely because she is incapable of shaping the course of society in its concrete decisions in an integralist, doctrinal or juridical sense, the Church herself has a quite new task in relation to this society, a task which might perhaps be characterised as 'prophetic'."*

Section III made clear what the church cannot do to control the secular world. What can it do? Even Vatican II fails to give a clear answer. It can do more than simply preach its own principles and collaborate on meeting human needs. In democratic societies the church can contribute its own opinions and attempt in all legal ways to convince public opinion how to act on certain matters. Such a concrete plan of action Rahner calls a rational instruction. Relying as it does on the practical intellect and creativity these instructions cannot claim to be fully comprehensive or convincing in the same way as speculative arguments. In offering such suggestions the visible church acts as leaven in the world and realizes its true and full nature.

How is the church able to do this? Rahner points to the "pastoral" approach embodied in the encyclicals of John XXIII, Paul VI, and Vatican II's *Gaudium et spes* [cf., 10:16]. Their analysis of the contemporary world is not given in revelation nor can it be established as brute fact. These can only be described as prophetic instructions (334f). Can the church address the world in this way with any hope of success? This is difficult, for on the one hand the official church can do far less than the church as a social group; on the other hand the church cannot compel its members to accept or pursue its pastoral instructions. What is needed to insure success is to develop a "political theology" (336) which Rahner hopes will overcome the excessive individualism of contemporary believers and spur them to engage in transforming the world by accepting the prophetic challenge of the church.

V. *"The relationship of the Church to the secular world as it exists today demands, within a framework of 'practical theology' that a special theological discipline* *shall be worked out and shall have a constitution of its own...a 'practical ecclesiological cosmology'."*

This new contemporary situation highlights a new need for the church to realize its essential nature—a need that can best be fulfilled by a new discipline which as yet has no name. Here Rahner describes and names this new discipline and shows where it fits in relation to existing disciplines. Such a discipline could remind the church it is more than an organization for satisfying the religious needs of individuals. It is also a free partner with the secular world in an open dialogue. It is not simply *the* representative of God.

VI. (Summary and section preview, 341). *The situation entailed in the secular world is one of permanent pluralism and "concupiscence" signifying that our existential context is one of contest and struggle threatened by sin. This situation must be accepted and endured by the Christian without falling into any ideologisation of this world in an integralist sense.*

Concupiscence, the interior pluralism at every level of our being, is not itself sinful but leads to sin when we absolutize one dimension of our existence in an attempt to escape the "contest and struggle" concupiscence brings in its wake. Because concupiscence is a part of us, when acted upon it becomes a part of our human world. Hence, Rahner imputes to the world three factors the Council of Trent imputed to concupiscent human nature: that concupiscence is not in itself sinful; that it imposes a permanent state of suffering upon us; that it implies an impulse to sin. Integralism is a great temptation for the church and its members to escape the pain of concupiscence by our own power rather than have it overcome in God, our only true and satisfying goal. Hence, this analysis reveals the secular world with all its pain and threatening complexity as the very world God loved so much that he laid down his life for it. This insight allows Christians both to endure and to minister to the world.

10.18   Practical Theology and Social Work in the Church
Praktische Theologie und kirchliche Sozialarbeit
{3.0}   June 1967 lecture to General Assembly of Swiss *Caritas* Foundation at Lucerne. *Caritas* 45 (1967).

Abstract: By exercising its right to engage in the same social work as society the church fulfills its duty to manifest the love of God and neighbor without controlling the world or losing the prophetic distance needed to critique it.
Topics: CHRISTIAN LIFE, *caritas*, science of; SOCIETY, social work; CHURCH, development work of; THEOLOGY, pastoral.
Subsidiary Discussions: Grace and nature (354f); Church, subsidiarity in (363); Pluralism (364f); God (365f); Community building (367f).
Precis: After confessing his personal and professional inadequacy to deal with this topic Rahner presents four key statements and lines of argument (I-IV). He concludes with a summary (Section V).

I. *"The teaching with regard to the Church's works of charity and social work is an intrinsic element in pastoral theology which should better be called 'practical theology'."*

Charity and social work because they are integral elements of the fulfillment of the church constitute a subject for practical theology. These works are not the sole responsibility of clerics and are often difficult to distinguish from an individual's private acts of Christian charity. In addition to the fact practical theology has its own rightful place within theology, it is an original and autonomous science not merely a collection of concrete conclusions deduced from an essential ecclesiology. It contains a prophetic dimension of its own. Hence, the concrete activities arising from the science of *caritas* have not always been the same, nor must they always stay the same. Despite its recognized importance this theological science still has no precise name. After ruling out certain possibilities (352f) Rahner suggests calling it "theological and ecclesiological cosmology." The quickly changing forms and modes of social work and the expanding role of practical theology make Rahner wonder whether the whole department of this science of charity should not be completely expanded and reorganized.

II. *"The difference between the Church and grace on the one hand, and 'the world as it has become worldly' on the other,...determines a further relationship between grace as 'caritas' and the Church as the historical and social manifestation of this ecclesiastical 'caritas' on the one hand, and that 'caritas' the forms of which have been secularized on the other."*

How is one to distinguish church and world? To Rahner they are a whole. "World" is not merely a creation but a task, the subject of human projects for the future. Hence, world is distinguished from grace and church not only as nature and grace but also in a temporal sense. As the world matures grace and the church relate to it differently. Far from being an unmitigated disaster, the growing worldliness of the world is the new mode in which grace itself enters more and more fully into creation. It is not the task of the church to control the development of the world but to accord it due responsibility, to teach people how to accept and endure its concupiscent pluralism.

The church contributes to the liberation of the world by communicating with it in its wordliness. *Caritas* is that form of communication constituted by grace as such. Divinely bestowed, it is manifested in the church in a special and unique form. It has the basically sacramental significance of being a sign and effective within history. This is principally what distinguishes the church from the world. The church sends it members to dialogue with the world without any desire to control it. This keeps the church from becoming an accomplice with the world and helps it achieve the detachment it needs to critique the world and imprint its hope upon it. It follows that no particular social work is or should be the sole concern of the church. In addition the church cannot of itself arrive at any theoretical or adequate judgement of the necessity, urgency, or concrete form of social work. The world the church addresses with prophetic instruction always remains free. **III.** *"The Church must affect the world with works of charity and social welfare. This work cannot a priori and in all cases materially be distinguished from the same work and institutions catering to those that belong to the world. All lines of demarcation are products of particular circumstances."*

After explaining his preference that the term social work stand for all the works of *caritas* (357f) Rahner insists the church has the right and duty to engage in social work because it is not merely the recipient and witness to the world of the faith and of the future in hope, it is also the basic sacrament of unity in the ministry of love. Hence, the subject of social work is the church in the broadest sense, especially but not exclusively as it refers to the initiatives of its official institutional organs, to the charitable work of local faith communities, and to the free initiatives of the faithful, whether or not they enjoy official approbation. There is continual interplay between these church efforts and worldly institutions.

No firm line of demarcation can be drawn between the respective areas for social work of the church and of the world since all such lines are the product of practical reason geared to particular circumstances. They are not deduced from formal principles. Such clear lines are impossible, impractical, and unnecessary (360f) since the nature and quality of the love that inspires social work is known only to God. Though material lines of demarcation have been drawn in the past they are not permanent. The church is free to drop traditional activities and to assume new ones, fitting them into society by a process of free competition. [Rahner adds a word on subsidiarity, 363.] Rahner concludes the church need not fear insoluble conflicts will arise in this area between itself and the world. The need to dialogue over their differences will be good for both the church and the world.

IV. *"There can be a form of social assistance which can be fully and legitimately exercised only by the Church and by the Christian as a member of her."*

Just as the individual person is a unity in plurality so is society. Just as a disturbance in one area of a person's life can be felt as a disturbance in another area, so it is in society. One can treat the symptom in one area without actually removing the cause which resides in another. It is conceivable there are social disturbances which can only be removed or diminished in the religious dimension of faith, hope, and love in the strictly theological sense. Likewise, social conflicts can arise precisely because we lack a right relationship with God and/or neighbor based on true *caritas*. Breakdowns can take place at the interpersonal level or in the conceptual/cultic arena. In fact no one whose relationship with God is broken can accept or endure the pluralism of the world and the responsibilities it involves. Rahner adds that a right relationship with God can be had outside the church, and that God is never a means for controlling life but, as the goal of life, God makes life meaningful and therefore bearable.

This is how the church precisely through its specifically religious activities, and as mediating salvation, is also socially effective. Rahner sums it up, "When there is a specific *work* of love to be performed or expected, a work which, in the long run, can never be performed at all without a love that is reinforced with faith and hope, and when there is a failure to perform such a work, then the situation arises in which the religious question can be explicitly and consciously borne in upon man in the concrete, and this is the place for a kind of social work which is specifically appropriate to the Church" (366). Hence, no clear line of demarcation can be drawn between the spiritual and social mission of the church. Such work is not limited to the ordained, although Rahner mentions a potential role for deacons. Though such work has a personal nature it never rules out the possible contribution of the institutional church through the sacraments. Rahner describes in some detail a new task of the church to form community among the members of local churches (368f). He also mentions some ecumenical considerations (369).

V. After again apologizing for the abstract and formal nature of his talk Rahner concludes with a very helpful summary.

10.19   The Peace of God and the Peace of the World
Der Friede Gottes und der Friede der Welt

{1.5}   September 1966 lecture at Württemberg to Conference for the Directors of Colleges of Advanced Engineering. *Streit um dem Frieden* (Munich-Mainz 1967) 64-85.

Abstract: After outlining the complexity of peace and its Old/New Testament roots, Rahner argues the inevitability of conflict and the need for Christians realistically to balance love and justice to avoid all ideological extremes.

Topics: SOCIETY, peace; POWER, coercive; IDEOLOGY.
Subsidiary Discussions: Theology (379); Justice (383ff); Love (383ff); Love of God/neighbor (386); Eschatology (387).
Precis: I. Peace is a multi-level topic of almost incalculable breath. 1) A theology of peace involves peace with God, self, neighbor, the sexes, classes, and nations, as well as the unity among all these forms of peace. 2) The forms of peace are subject to wide variations from the absence war to the absence of all conflict. 3) Understanding peace means understanding power, an essential condition of human life sinfully misused (cf., III). 4) Peace must not be romanticized as absolute rest or permanent equilibrium since conflict in one's self and in the world is a product of universal concupiscence. 5) How does one reconcile peace with the dynamism of history and the need at times for revolution? 6) Looked at internationally, understanding peace entails the question of secularization and the growing unity of world history. 7) How is peace related to justice and love? What does it imply for understanding the unity of the love of God and neighbor? 8) Can Christians and secular

humanists agree on the meaning of peace or find common ground to work for peace? **II.** Peace is a central biblical concept. Old Testament *shalom* is far broader and deeper than our modern notion of peace. It is a gift of God, the central content of salvation, the key word for messianic expectation. In the New Testament God is the author of peace mediated by Christ in the Spirit. Christ is our peace, having restored our peace with God. Peace touches every branch of theology (list, 379). **III.** *"So long as this world in which we live endures, so long as the kingdom of God is not made present by the act of God himself, the 'conflict' which is 'war' is an abiding reality, an insuperable 'existential' of human living. In spite of this the Christian has an abiding task to create peace."*

Christianity is realistic and anti-ideological, recognizing as it does the inescapability, necessity, and legitimacy of power (definition, 380) in the life of the individual and of society, despite its potential for sinful misuse. This power should not be completely controlled by any one earthly authority, nor should the attempt be made. Thus, Christian realism stands at a halfway point between the total rejection of power and those who absolutize and monopolize power as an ideology. No authority, not even the church, can set itself up as God's absolute representative on earth. Christians have the duty to strive to restrain and avoid this inevitable conflict. Summary (382). **IV.** Catholics attempt to humanize power and conflict with justice and love. Peace cannot be imposed, it is the outgrowth of justice. But where justice leads at best to organized egoism, saying, "give me my own," love says, "what's mine is yours." There is an irreducible pluralism between love and justice. Christians cannot abandon one for the other but must come to terms with the demands of both for the sake of peace. There is no ready-made, unambiguous formula for doing this. This fact also argues against the legitimacy of any ideology. **V.** The only way to renounce a legitimate claim in this world where such renunciation does not benefit the renouncer, is if I feel radically loved by someone such that what is truly mine is constituted by the infinite fullness of life. Only this assured love of God for me and for my neighbor brings peace with God and opens the way to peace with others despite the fact we will still have conflicts over our legitimate rights. No formula process resolves this. We risk because we hope in an eschatological process still unfolding, the goal of which is brought about not by our deeds but by God. Hence, the Christian must face and address the various conflicts in the world to preserve and establish something which holds out the prospect of a tolerable peace.

XI. CONFRONTATIONS I
IX. *Konfrontationen*

German edition: Einsiedeln, Benziger, 1970
U.S. edition: N.Y., Seabury, 1974
David Bourke, translator

This volume in the English edition comprises the first 14 essays in *Schriften zur Theologie*, IX.

11.01   Pluralism in Theology and the Unity of the Creed in the Church

Der Pluralismus in der Theologie und die Einheit des Bekenntnisses in der Kirche

{1.5}   April 1969 lecture. Concilium 5 (1969) 462-471.

Abstract: In this new age of insuperable theological pluralism credal unity is assured more by unity of practice (table fellowship, sacramental celebrations, care for the poor, etc.) than by agreement on theological propositions.
Topics: PLURALISM; MAGISTERIUM and theology; THEOLOGY.
Subsidiary Discussions: Theology, history of (4f); Philosophy (5); Ecumenism (6, 9f, 22f); Eucharist, transubstantiation (10f); Propositions (14ff); Dogma, development of (20); Orthopraxis (21f).

Precis: How can the unity of belief be assured in the new situation of radical theological pluralism? One cannot wait for an answer slowly to mature but must speak personally, courageously, out loud, and in public, even if one's contribution is flawed and incomplete. **I.** The problem of pluralism is new. Although in the past there were different schools of theology they developed from a common intellectual worldview (terminology, philosophical presuppositions, unanalyzed attitudes and feelings). Since one could completely comprehend an opponent's position, differences of opinion could be attributed either to stupidity or bad faith. Today's situation is essentially different. Quantitative changes in the amount of historical knowledge available, proliferation of disciplines and methodologies, the new pluralism in philosophy have given rise to a qualitative transformation. Not even teamwork can overcome the problems created by this explosion of knowledge for in theology one cannot rely on the conclusions of others but must arrive at them and test them on one's own. There have always been contradicting ideas within theology. But in today's theological pluralism there is not enough common ground to reduce these points of view to logical alternatives within the same system. On a personal note Rahner outlines the reactions of traditional scholastic theologians to this pluralism (8f) and follows with three examples (9ff). Theologians encountering alien theologies must ask whether the school they represent may not be equally alien to others.
II. What is to be done in this situation of insurmountable theological pluralism? Realizing no answer will be completely satisfactory Rahner makes two points. 1) Radical theological pluralism of today can neither be simply eliminated or accepted. It must be constantly struggled against. 2) The inevitability of pluralism does not annul the magisterium's right to draw new, unequivocal boundaries around its teachings even to the point of declaring certain positions heretical. Rahner advises, however, that in this new situation such discipline must be administered in new ways.
III. We fail to grasp the nature of today's pluralism when we fail to grasp the fact that the formulations used by the magisterium to convey the creed include an implicit element of linguistics conditioned by social and historical factors. Our assent to such formulations is never the same as our assent to the truths they are meant to convey. This too is a dawning reality. Hence, Rahner suggests that in the future really important statements of theology will no longer be magisterial statements. Attempts to canonize any set of theological propositions over and above credal statements are doomed to fail (examples, 17). The pluralism among theologies is made possible and justified by the linguistic conditioning present in all credal statements.
IV. How can we insure the unity of the creed while allowing for this pluralism in the forms of language used by the theologies? In this matter the magisterium must to a great degree leave the task of policing to the various theologies themselves. Even so, it may be forced to rule that a certain position

or school is irreconcilable with the creed. When it does so it is not simply ruling on the truth of a particular statement but on the epistemology and sociology embedded in it. In this environment: 1) the old creedal formulations and doctrinal decisions attain a new status; 2) the possibility of new doctrinal statements is greatly reduced; 3) pluralism comes to be seen as a necessary enrichment fostering new pastoral impulses in the church. It does, however, signal the demise of the idea cherished by some of the development of doctrine into a complete system of individual pronouncements (20).

V. Faith and creed cannot be present apart from words. Common sympathy, cult, actions, etc. can never substitute for a common creed. Insofar as the word is always more than the word, pointing as it does to the inexhaustible mystery of God and us, the unity of the word is possible. This is what gives rise to the assurance of the unity in diversity which underlies irreducible theologies. Such assurance is not produced by concepts held in common but by a common physical life, common statements, common concrete actions, etc. Concrete actions are common not merely as the consequences of a prior conviction, they are just as much elements through which this common conviction is realized and achieved. There can be no breaking out of the circle. Creedal unity is not maintained only at the conceptual level, but at the level of common action. We must express the creed together and thus achieve unity despite the pluralism of theologies.

VI. What is the ecumenical significance of what has been said? Rahner wonders whether the theologians of separated churches have not already entered into that pluralism of theologies which certainly has its place in the one church. This may be a result of recognizing the distinction between theology and creed. Perhaps the ecumenical future will be based more on common life and action than on having to hammer out common theologies.

11.02   On the Theology of Ecumenical Discussion

Zur Theologie des ökumenischen Gesprächs

{2.5}   O. Semmelroth, et al., eds., *Festschrift zum 65. Geburstag von Bischof Hermann Volk: Martyria, Leiturgia, Diakonia* (Mainz 1968) 163-199.

Abstract: This inquiry into the nature of ecumenical theology concludes that what makes it possible also makes it necessary: a common, justifying faith already shared by the churches despite differences in their dogmatic formulae.

Topics: ECUMENISM; THEOLOGY, ecumenical.

Subsidiary Discussions: Theology, controversial (25ff); Theology, pluralism in (27ff, 53f); Dialogue (28ff); Truth (30ff, 53ff); Faith (35ff, 66f); Theological anthropology (37f); Propositions, theological (40ff, 58f); Heresy (42ff, 56f); Sociology, religious (45ff); Truths, hierarchy of (54, 58). Relativism, confessional (54f); Theology of the future (59ff); Knowledge (62f); History (62f); Conversion (65f).

Precis: I. Starting with the history of ecumenism Rahner leaves open the question how old the discipline actually is. He tries to distinguish it from controversial theology but ends up showing they have the same tasks: first and foremost to present the teachings of one's church in all its breath and depth; to present the doctrinal view of other churches in respect to one's own origin, development, and current positions; with courage and obedience to the revealed will of God to identify error when they see it in their teaching or in that of other churches. Despite their reliance on scripture and the Fathers the ecumenical theologies of different churches appear very different from one another. Discussion among them will be immensely difficult. Therefore, we must ask how discussion is even possible because prior to all conscious insight on our part this possibility already exists.

II. Dialogue describes how the churches are to conduct their discussions. But can Catholic Christians participate in open dialogue with others on a footing of equality? If by dialogue one meant merely imparting information there would be no problem (leaving aside whether even this exchange is possible). But theology is meant to impart truth or else it is merely an exchange of opinions. Pluralism also raises problems. When each church makes contradictory claims of universal validity is open dialogue possible?

III. What constitutes the ultimate basis of ecumenical theology is the unifying belief of all parties that the others already possess justifying grace. Though liberal humanism is the occasion and context for modern ecumenism it is not its true ground. Ecumenical dialogue depends on mutually recognizing one another as Christians, i.e., that one's dialogue partners live in the grace of God, are truly justified by the Holy *Pneuma* of God, and share in the divine nature. This conviction was not always accepted. Even though it was taught by Vatican II it is not immediately self-evident and is only slowly coming to be accepted by the faithful (summary, 35). This conviction implies that the God-given faith that unifies us is different from the way we have objectified that faith in words and concepts. Rahner argues the inevitability of this conclusion (36f) and he grounds the possibility in theological anthropology (37f). Once this unity is recognized ecumenical dialogue is seen as the attempt "to render intelligible to the other parties the fact that what is being expressed to them in conceptual terms is simply a more correct, fuller and a more precise expression of something which they have already apprehended as their own faith through the Spirit in the ultimate depths of their lives as already justified, and which they have laid hold of as their own truth" (39). This alone explains how open dialogue is possible.

IV. Rahner returns to the difference between ultimate faith and the explicit objectification of that faith in propositions. He concludes that even in Catholic formulations (list, 41) there is a concealed element of linguistic relativism which keep them from ever completely expressing the reality to which it alludes. Often ecumenical dialogue is not disagreement over what is believed but over how it is expressed.

V. Everyone involved in ecumenical dialogue must have the courage to reject whatever is found in their own church or in another's church which is contrary to the gospel. Even amid legitimate pluralism there are positions incompatible with Christianity. Partners in dialogue can help one another recognize and reject such positions and in this way aid the leaders of their various churches. Without this Christianity becomes little more than an umbrella organization under which any opinion however arbitrary would find a home. If it embraced everything Christianity would end up standing for nothing.

VI. Rahner analyzes ecumenical theology, which seeks to establish the truth or error of the propositions it uses to express its faith in the context of contemporary religious sociology. In earlier times this search was carried on mostly by clerics who felt the legitimate right to speak for their churches. Today, though ecumenical theology is still largely carried on by theologians, they no longer speak for their churches. In fact few believers pay heed to theologians. Most remain separated from or unite with other churches without any convincing theological supports for their actions (47). Theology is almost irrelevant when it comes to the de facto unity or separation of the churches. Sociological considerations are much more important. What does this mean a) for the future of ecumenical theology; b) for the question of truth itself?

a) The gulf between the institutional status of individual churches (Protestant and Catholic) and the de facto faith of their members will continue to widen leading to the heresy of indifferentism. Many will separate themselves officially from their churches while perhaps remaining sympathetic to their old homes ("Christian oriented groups"). Churches themselves may delineate their positions more clearly and boldly. Rather than hamper unification, greater interior unity and homogenization could make it easier for churches to discuss the doctrines they hold and finally to commit themselves to the kind of binding assent needed for unification (summary, 51). This process of internal concentration will not focus on issues which have historically divided churches but on the issues central to the faith (i.e., hierarchy of truths) addressed to modern society in a way meant to evoke a response. Formerly these basic truths were merely presupposed. "[I]n the future it is precisely *these* which will be the sole body of truth constituting in all the Churches the power to form a Church" (53). A particular doctrine may remain absolutely true but on a practical level be completely unimportant. The growing pluralism within Catholic theology which makes it easier to distinguish the epochal from the objective significance of its doctrine helps the church clarify its hierarchy of truths and so aids its ecumenical dialogue.

b) Regarding truth as such, a de facto situation of religious relativism already prevails among church members. Although theologians clearly cannot subscribe to this error (55), rejecting relativism raises problems

Rahner only mentions here: the relationship between truth and institution
(55f); whether every disparity between the individual and the institutional
expression of faith is always illegitimate. But even where there is clear
disagreement over doctrine, separation need not be inevitable since it is
possible that one may hold a cardinal truth in such a way that one implicitly
encompasses a second, less important truth. One can maintain the distinction between objective truth and its subjective salvific significance which
may vary over time, without falling into the error of subjectivism (summary,
58f).

VII. *"Ecumenical theology is for the most part the theology of the future which
has to be worked out by all the Churches, each from its own starting-point as
previously determined by its past history."*

"Theology of the future" means "that theology which is necessary as a prior
condition for any proclamation of the gospel in order that the gospel may
appear credible in a future conditioned by science, technology, cybernetics,
the social unification of mankind on a global scale, a future which has already
begun" (59f). Admittedly, ecumenical theology has made little headway,
perhaps because Catholic theology remains too bound to scholastic theology; perhaps because Protestant theology is too inclusive. In any case Rahner
sees the only chance for ecumenical theology lies in embracing a theology of
the future—working together to make the Christian message credible to a
new age.

Rahner concludes by reflecting on the limits to determining the meaning
and the possibilities of ecumenical theology (62f). Change in human affairs
is never brought about solely by rational speculation, nor can history be
comprehended adequately by any such process. This includes theology.
(Rahner uses theological anthropology to establish these two points, 62f)
Hence, ecumenical theology as a science is addressed ultimately to the
element of the incalculable in history—the sphere of the Spirit where God
moves freely. Experience bears this out. Historically almost nothing has
taken place in ecumenism. It seems ecumenical theology faces two choices:
either accept all churches as equally valid, or achieve unity through individual conversions. But neither of these is happening. Rahner finds this
consoling. For him it points to the existence of the common, God-given faith
at the heart of each church. Were the churches not anchored by the Spirit
they would be as unstable as systems of modern philosophy. Rahner
concludes, "We must arrive at the unity of faith in the dimension of
conscious thought and social living too, because we already possess this unity
at the level of the justifying grace of God. The unity of faith already present
at this level, points both to the possibility and also to the necessity of
ecumenical theology" (66f).

11.03   Reflections on Methodology in Theology
Überlegungen zur Methode der Theologie
{4.0}   Previously unpublished, August 1969 lectures to International Symposium of Theologians in Montreal.

Abstract: In 3 lectures Rahner presents the pluralism of today's theology; defines transcendental theology; challenges theologians to relate theological mysteries/propositions to the one mystery: God's offer of self-communication.

Topics: THEOLOGY, method; THEOLOGY, transcendental; MYSTERY.

Subsidiary Discussions: Pluralism, theological (70ff); Theological method (indirect) (74ff); Church, theology of (79ff); Knowledge, subjectivity of (81ff); Magisterium (83, 112f); Hermeneutics (83f); Philosophy, transcendental (85ff); History (88f); Faith (91f); Supernatural existential (92ff, 100, 109); Trinity, transcendental theology of (93ff, 108); Christology, transcendental (95ff, 108); Eschatology, transcendental (98f); God, incomprehensibility of (104); Theological anthropology (104f); God as creator (107); Eucharist, transubstantiation (108f); Propositions, theological (111f).

Precis: I. Asked to speak on his own theological method Rahner demurs saying he has no personal method and has given little time or interest to the subject. In these three lectures he makes partial and "arbitrary" remarks on the method that seems best suited to the current situation of theology. **The situation which provides current theology with its starting-point** (70-84).

1. *"In contrast with earlier ages the theological situation today has a special and peculiar element which renders it less capable of analysis and calculation."* Rahner first describes the closed, shared, predictable situation of Catholic theology prior to Vatican II he calls "Denzinger Theology" (70f). Today's situation is marked by radical philosophical and theological pluralism which cannot be mastered. Rahner traces this pluralism in biblical theology and history of dogma. As a consequence theologians today are alienated and isolated. Acutely aware of being historically conditioned the only way they can uphold the absolute binding force of their propositions is by developing indirect methods (75). Only these will satisfy the demands of the individual conscience on the question of intellectual truth. After further defining this indirect method Rahner applies it to the example of justifying belief in the Catholic Church as opposed to a Reformation Church (76ff).

2. *"This situation ... is precisely determined by the ecclesiastical context in which the theology of today must, more than ever before, be practiced."* Rahner presupposes that ecclesiology has always been an essential element of Christian theology. Here he examines how the role of ecclesiology is altered by the new pluralism. The inescapable historical conditioning of theology today presents greater threats and fresh opportunities. The dangers are self-evident. The fresh opportunities reside in the fact that as individuals become more aware of the historical conditioning of their own knowledge they may

value the kind of institutionalized, social knowledge present in the church. Theologians, too, become less individualistic and more reliant on the church. Theology today is only of interest when it constitutes a process of reflection on the faith of a church (81). Hence, any sound theological method will take as its starting-point the average and representative awareness of the faith as it is found in the concrete church (summary, 81). This in no way denies the subjective nature of knowledge born of faith. There is an unbreakable circle in the process of our thought which moves between the subjective and the objective forms of ecclesial truth and carries with it an unconscious interplay of the most varied elements. This situation makes criticism within the church possible, although theologians may go astray or the church itself may squelch criticism prematurely. This calls for courage on the part of theologians. Rahner is skeptical of any attempt to reduce theology to the methodology it employs, especially the modern fascination with hermeneutics.

II. Transcendental theology (84-101). Transcendental theology is hard to define. Though it is inseparable from transcendental philosophy it is not simply a method transported into theology from without. Since every authentic metaphysics (including Origen, Augustine, Aquinas) must proceed along the lines of transcendental philosophy it is not completely new. Though it begins to emerge reflexively in the work of Descartes it remains obscure. This lack of general philosophical consensus does not, however, invalidate its use.

For Rahner, "A transcendental line of enquiry...is present when and to the extent that it raises the question of the conditions in which knowledge of a specific subject is possible in the knowing subject himself" (87). This is legitimate since the act of cognition involves the mutual conditioning of the object known and the knowing subject. Knowledge is always knowledge of the metaphysical structure of the known object in itself. Rahner further distinguishes transcendental method from Hegelain idealism (88) with its tendencies to absolutize human spirit and human freedom or to reject history, although these remain dangers for transcendental method. It is enough to recognize two things about transcendental philosophy: the question of the knowing subject is not simply one department of knowledge but is prior to every other kind of knowledge; we only arrive at real philosophy or metaphysics and can only recognize the objectivity of the reality investigated when we include the investigator as an object of conscious reflection. Since theology is essentially philosophical theology, and since philosophy is essentially transcendental, it follows that theology must necessarily be transcendental theology, even if in the past this was not always known in an explicit way.

Rahner lists five principles he uses as a starting-point (94) and illustrates transcendental theology with four concrete applications: Faith (91ff) with

reference to the supernatural existential; Trinity, both economic and immanent (94f); christology (95ff) in terms of Christ as absolute savior and the
logic of the incarnation of the Logos; eschatology (98f) in terms of human
consummation which distinguishes eschatological and apocalyptic statements. In each example Rahner seeks to render intelligible and assimilable
that particular object in each topic which is actually being called into
question. He does this by pointing out an already existing reference to this
object within the knowing subject due to which each example can be
understood in a transcendental-theological sense despite the variations
among them (93).

Rahner concludes this lecture noting the limitations of transcendental
philosophy. Any transcendental philosophy which claimed the exclusive and
total ability to express what was necessary for human existence, and hence
salvation, would leave no room for historical revealed religion. The task of
fundamental theology is to prove the positive possibility of saving history
and revelation. When it does this it constitutes transcendental theology: "the
act of consciously reflecting upon the fact that the creaturely subject as such
is of its very nature rooted in that history which is precisely that of the
[transcendental] subjectivity most proper to its own nature as such" (99f).
Grace takes place in history. Transcendental theology shows the two factors
condition one another. It renders intelligible the fact that the concrete
element in history can really affect us at the ultimate level of our existence
and subjectivity. For the saving nature of historical events can never be
known simply a posteriori. We must discover our very natures are oriented
toward them. This is the object transcendental theology considers.

III. *Reductio in unum mysterium* (101-114). This phrase serves as a
methodological guard against the illusion that mystery is only provisional—
that as scientific knowledge increases the role of mystery and theology
decreases. Theology refutes this false characterization (101f) insisting it is the
science of mystery as such. It does not grow by systematic deduction but by
incessantly relating us back to that ineffable and obscure mystery called God.
Rahner begins by saying something about mystery as such (103). Too often
even the church presents mystery in a false, negative aspect as provisionally
restricted to our pilgrim mode of existence on earth. In fact the dogma of the
incomprehensibility of God reveals that mystery is permanent, and that
comprehensive knowledge is a comparatively deficient mode of knowledge.
Rahner makes the same point based on an analysis of our transcendental
subjectivity (104f).

Rahner next explores the relationship between the one mystery and what
seem like the many mysteries of Christianity (105ff). He asserts, "there is,
and these can be, only one single absolute mystery in the strictest sense of the
term, God himself and in relation to him all those aspects under which man
with his finite knowledge has to conceive of God" (105). After showing how
this flows from the relationship between being and knowing, Rahner

concludes that *God as remote* constitutes the mystery at the heart of the world and worldly knowledge; *God as near* constitutes the whole content of the Christian mysteries. Theology has the task of reducing all seeming mysteries to the one mystery—to demystify theology. Rahner proceeds to apply this to the doctrine of creation (107f) and Trinity and incarnation (108) the two central mysteries of Christianity which constitute a unity. He adds a word about transubstantiation which he considers mystery in a derived sense (108f).

The true significance of this *reductio in unum mysterium* is to be found in how grace relates to the incarnation in history. The incarnation is addressed to a human nature already elevated by grace (i.e., supernatural existential, 109). Scripture itself is addressed to this pre-existing transcendentality. Hence, "the task of theology must precisely be to appeal ... to this basic experience of grace ... the truth, namely, that the absolute mystery ... that permeates all things, upholds all things, and endures eternally, has bestowed itself as itself in an act of forgiving love upon man" (110). Theology must constantly move beyond the conceptual to the transcendental. It should constitute a "mystagogia" leading all to the experience of grace.

This theological task of *reductio* has a number of consequences. The propositions of theology must constantly be referred back to one mystery and to our grace-given experience of that truth. Theological statements cannot demand silent adoration of themselves. Realizing the radical incommensurability of mystery and theological statements the church must be much more indulgent of pluralism and its theologians much more modest in their claims.

11.04   The New Claims which Pastoral Theology Makes upon Theology as a Whole
Neue Ansprüche der Pastoraltheologie an die Theologie als ganz
{2.0}   *Gregorianum* 50 (Rome 1969) 617-638.

Abstract: Pastoral theology, which considers how the church at every level is to achieve its nature in the world, should serve as the organizing principle of theological studies for priestly in formation.

Topics: THEOLOGY, pastoral; PRIESTS, formation of;

Subsidiary Discussions: Theology, political (120f); Theology, research (122ff); Scripture, exegesis (129); Preaching (134); Theology, pluralism in (135f).

Precis: Vatican II gave pastoral (practical) theology a higher status and more central role especially in the formation of priests. This is true even though theologians cannot agree on its nature or essence (history, 116ff). However, two features stand out: 1) Pastoral theology is not confined to the work of the clergy. It extends to everything the church must do at every level to achieve its nature. 2) It presupposes a thorough scientific and theological investigation of the situation of the church and the circumstances in which it finds itself. Rahner adds a note on the relationship between pastoral and political theology (120f).

Two consequences flow from accepting this definition of pastoral theology. 1) It must be included prominently in the formation of priests so they can assume active responsibility for the church fulfilling its nature; 2) all theological disciplines must be given a certain pastoral orientation. They can no longer be taught for their own sake or for the sake of research.

Rahner offers some preliminary considerations for the reform of theological studies along more pastoral lines. He begins with the nature of a university and the mutually conditioning relationship between teaching and research. Given the complexity of theology and today's world Rahner suggests uncoupling teaching and research and establishing an intermediary school between high school and university for "advanced specialist studies." This would not only safeguard the quality of university research it would begin to address the rivalry among the many legitimate theological disciplines for a seminarian's time (summary, 126). The future preparation of priests can no longer be organized to do justice to the academic disciplines themselves. Though theology forms an academic unity at the theoretical level for the purpose of teaching theology, as distinct from researching into theology, the subject matter must be organized along different principles (limits, 128f).

Leaving open the exact content of such a program (the role of philosophy, exegesis, etc.) how should theological teaching be structured? [Rahner distinguishes two possible approaches, the *existentielle* and the vocational (130) which he later admits amount to much the same thing (132).] He describes what a curriculum would look like if it were organized anthropocentrically, awakening in students questions about human nature itself and how Christian revelation condescends to the human condition. Rahner provides an example of such an interdisciplinary course of studies implemented at Heerlen (130ff). Admittedly, critics might ask whether this approach includes enough dogmatic and moral theology, and whether philosophy and church history are too reduced.

All in all, pastoral theology can no loner be seen as one special department of study among many. It must provide the organizing principle for theology especially in seminaries. The advantages of this approach include: clarifying how various subjects fit in an overall curriculum; paring back non-essential studies; making better use of limited time; allowing the emergence of fresh themes. Pastoral theology also imposes new demands on theology as a whole. Rahner cites significant changes necessitated in the teaching of homiletics (134f) and extends this thought to include canon law, liturgy, exegesis, church history, and biblical theology. Pastoral theology cannot contain in itself everything the church needs to achieve its nature but it can and must form the other disciplines to aid in this objective.

Today practical reason enjoys a higher status than theoretical reason. What does this imply for practical theology? It will continue to grow in ways we cannot now begin to perceive and will take its place in the constellation of insuperably pluralistic church theologies. Although it will never be *the* theology of the church in an exclusive sense, pastoral theology will be the special signature of the church of the future.

11.05 The Future of Theology
Die Zukunft der Theologie

{1.0}   December 1968 Bavaria Radio talk in the series *Abschied von Trient*. J. Bielneier, ed., *Abschied von Trient. Theologie am Ende des kirchlichen Mittelalters* (Regensburg 1969) 121-130.

Abstract: Rahner lists for a general audience some of the elements he imagines will characterize Catholic theology in the future.

Topics: THEOLOGY, future of.

Subsidiary Discussions: Creed (137f); Magisterium (138f); Theology, pluralism in (138f, 143); Boldness (139f, 144f); Philosophy in theology (139f); Propositions, theological (141f); Ecumenism (142f); Truth, communal (145).

Precis: No one knows the future. But here Rahner extrapolates into the future some trends he sees in the church and in Catholic theology today. Without guessing how large or influential the church of the future will be Rahner insists it will endure as a community centered on the ancient creed. Although that creed may be understood and expressed by future theologians in new ways they will continue to live in historical continuity with the ancient creed. Since the church will also continue to be a community hierarchically ordered and taught by those officially endowed with magisterial authority, theology in the future will continue to follow the lead of these legitimate teachers.

Theology of the future will include a high degree of pluralism impossible for any individual to overcome. The church will no longer claim one official theology. There will be an irreconcilable diversity of methods, philosophies, outlooks, and terminologies demanding constant dialogue among theologians. In this setting the magisterium will need to allow for greater latitude among theologians. Theologians will have to be at once more humble in their claims and more bold in making their opinions known.

Future theology will concentrate decisively on the heart and center, the ultimate, basic questions of the Christian message. Such theology will be done at a comparatively high level of abstraction. It will continue to use analogous terms, cognizant of the unavoidable gap between idea and its expression, image and the reality it is meant to signify. Though it will retain colorful figurative language, future theology will work hard to demythologize it. Future theology will also be more ecumenical because theologians of different denominations are increasingly more united by the common methods of their disciplines than they are divided by their individual confessions.

Rahner raises a number of other questions, possibilities about future theology which he leaves open: its exact content; whether it will be more anthropocentric; whether it will be more practical, political, and pastoral than theoretical; how it will relate to the other sciences; whether it will be more transcendental. Whatever the case, theology of the future will need the courage to help the church make decisions and engage in concrete actions to shape the future. Hence, theology will have to be more prophetic. Finally, theology of the future will be more ecclesial since as people come to accept the limits and radical subjectivity of individual knowledge they will look to the truth embodied in institutions. Theology in the future must work to help both the church and individual Christians to realize their true natures. To do this it may need to be more critical, but it must also be more prayerful.

11.06   The Experience of God Today
Gotteserfahrung heute
{2.0}   October 1969 lecture at Cologne. O. Semmelroth, K. Rahner, eds., *Theologische Akdemie VII* (Frankfurt 1970).
Abstract: The experience of God displays four unique characteristics today: it is more transcendental and mundane, less personal, and less overtly Christian.
Topics: GOD, experience of.
Subsidiary Discussions: Nature and grace (154); Mystery (155f); Atheism (159ff); Jesus Christ (164f).
Precis: People continue to experience God today. Their experience is unique because of the times—not absolutely unique but significantly so. Experience of God always has a paradoxical character: it is more basic and inescapable than physical causality, but it is never imposed in a irresistible way. Experience is integrated through reflection, though one never substitutes for the other. The final interpretation of experience is left to the individual.

After listing characteristics of this experience (153) Rahner concludes that God is not one among many other objects of experience, but the asymptotic goal of the human spirit's exercise of freedom and knowledge, present not simply as an anonymous power but as the initiator and sustainer of the goals towards which spirit is drawn. "The experience of God constitutes...the ultimate depths and the radical essence of *every* spiritual and personal experience (of love, faithfulness, hope and so on), and thereby precisely constitutes also the ultimate unity and totality of experience, in which the person as spiritual possesses himself and is made over to himself" (154).

How does one undergo this experience? Pointing to it indirectly leads to the assumption that it is a vague poetic feeling. Describing it in precise philosophic terms makes it seem a mere concept. One is often met with blank incomprehension because what is being pointed to is a mystery, "the underlying substrate which is presupposed to and sustains the reality we know" (155). The path to boundless mystery is apprehension of human finitude. Retrospective abstraction can never bring one to the experience of God. It is achieved in everyday life whenever one is forced to make sense of the radical depth of one's loves and loyalties, knowledge, responsibilities, and yearnings.

Experience of God is no private mood or interior feeling. It is full of social and public significance (159) since each and every person must respond to and make sense of the mysterious depths found within. This would remain true even if all organized religion were to vanish from the face of the earth.

Rahner concludes with four special characteristics of this experience of God today: 1) God is seen as more transcendental, not simply another object in the world but as the very depth of the world. 2) God is mediated to people more through experience of oneself and one's subjectivity than through the experience of the outside world. 3) Where it becomes difficult to establish a personal relationship with a transcendent God, and 4) where the experience of God is less explicitly Christian, the role of Christ becomes more crucial.

11.07 Theological Considerations on Secularization and Atheism
Theologische Überlegungen zu Säkularisation und Atheismus

{1.5} September 1968 lecture in Vienna to Conference of the Secretariat for Non-Believers. *Bollettino di Informazione*, III/4 (Rome 1968) 18-20.

Abstract: Understanding the unique atheism engendered by modern secularization can help the church frame an effective pastoral response based not on "self-evident" scholastic concepts but on experiencing one's transcendental nature.

Topics: ATHEISM; GOD, belief in.
Subsidiary Discussions: Secularization (168f); Anonymous Christian (174, 176f); God, proofs for (182f).

Precis: At the close of Vatican II, Paul VI inaugurated the Secretariat for Non-Believers to further dialogue with atheists. Except for recognizing the varied new forms of atheism, Rahner characterizes the efforts of this Secretariat as stagnant. It has aimed at nothing new on the theological level. But there should be a new effort on the level of social psychology to address the newly emerging form of atheism arising from the secularization of society and culture—the growing "worldliness of the word," the loss of any connection to the numinous, and skepticism over anything metaphysical (169).

I. Though atheism follows in the wake of secularization it is not the sole cause or form of contemporary atheism. The various forms of atheism (list, 170f) although they influence one another, cannot be reduced to one system and

hence, cannot be addressed by one approach. The church must develop new means and methods for addressing the newly emerging forms of atheism.
II. Theism cannot be defended adequately simply by insisting "we cannot manage without God." The wretchedness of human history would seem to count against the truth and utility of such a claim, especially when it seems the greatest advances in relieving human misery have come from human initiatives. Nor would it seem that human society requires belief in God to be orderly and free. Theistic societies have no better track record than secular or atheistic ones. Individual atheists seem to live as morally and as productively as believers do; natural law would seem to argue that even non-believers are oriented to God, albeit anonymously; those most acutely aware of their own neediness find the idea of God "too beautiful to be true."
III. God's salvific will extends to all. Hence, there is in principle no form of human life where God cannot be encountered even if the encounter remains non-thematic. Therefore, Christians today can maintain without fear that even if their message becomes less effective God may be no less present to people in a salvific albeit non-explicit way. In fact a decline in an overly abstract, conceptual form of theism may bode well for the historical theism embodied in a concrete church. In short, secularization will advance atheism world wide not on conceptual grounds but with a certain psychological compulsion. The Church may actually benefit from this new situation if it reacts honestly and adopts new more effective pastoral approaches to non-believers.
IV. Rahner argues Christianity should think of its task as "wooing an elite." Embracing the truth of Christianity today demands many intellectual and personal abilities (as does logic, aesthetics, ethics, etc.). Rahner admits the idea of God widely accepted in former societies was at best a pale shadow of the actually existing, inconceivable God. God can no longer be presented as self-evident as would have been the case in primitive societies. Theism can only make sense today to those who have at least some capacity to adore mystery which withdraws itself from us into its own ineffability.

The particular kind of atheists formed by secularization are not stupid or malicious. Rahner sees them as "narrow minded" insofar as they have "not yet advanced to the stage of being able to achieve an overall view of the functional interconnection between the individual elements in their existence and in the world and explicitly to objectify this at the conceptual level …. [T]hey cannot yet face up to the absolute mystery which ultimately, but silently encompasses this totality of the world" (181). Knowing this attitude and seeing itself as having advanced to a higher stage than atheists helps the church form an appropriate response to this new kind of atheism. It also helps reduce the shock theists often feel towards the advance of atheism.
V. This new kind of atheism calls for more than the old scholastic proofs for the existence of God (critique, 182f). More is needed than such indoctrination at the conceptual level. "What is needed is an initiation, an 'inaugura-

tion' into an experience of God that is ultimate and basic" (183). Rahner sees
this happening by putting secular atheists in touch with their transcendental
reference to the mystery called God. Unfortunately most people eager to
proclaim the message of Christian theism begin with a sense that their
position is self-evident and socially sanctioned. For them the idea of God is
indoctrinated from outside. They cannot clearly experience or express the
nature of God as mystery and so continue to address others on the theoretical
level. No wonder they have so little success.

11.08 The Position of Christology in the Church between Exegesis and Dogmatics

Kirchliche Christologie zwischen Exegese und Dogmatik
{3.0} Previously unpublished May 1968 lecture, Theological Academy of
Berlin.
Abstract: Even the reduced scope of Jesus' self-understanding posited by
modern exegesis is sufficient warrant for dogmatic theologians to attribute
to him the full Chalcedonian claims of post-resurrection christology.
Topics: CHRISTOLOGY; RESURRECTION.
Subsidiary Discussions: Salvation, history of (185ff, 200f); Certainty (189ff);
Dogma, development of (209f).
Precis: Preliminary remarks (185-189): Claims of contemporary exegetes
about the self-knowledge of the pre-Easter Jesus challenge the validity of
dogmatic statements for the post-resurrection Christ. If the exegetical view
is taken too far the connection between the historical Jesus and the work of
salvation is lost. Jesus becomes just another prophet or religious genius and
the resurrection merely seals an abstract religious idea with no eschatological
meaning for others. But ignoring current exegesis leads to Monophysitism:
Christ becomes indistinguishable from God. Rahner argues that modern
exegesis leaves enough scriptural warrant regarding Jesus' self-understanding to ground the church's claims about the universal meaning of his
resurrection.
The historical Jesus as dogmatic problem (189-206): Rahner begins with
two epistemological claims about certainty (189-193): 1) there are two types
of certitude, one based on faith (lived experience) and the other based on
proof (history and science). These two are incommensurate. One can never
exclude or replace the other; 2) it is impossible to rid the search for objective
knowledge of all subjectivity. Faith is a part of certitude. This is true even in
discerning which of the words we hear constitute the revealed Word. Since
what is true of all human attempts to discern the Word of God is equally true
of Jesus, his own grasp of revelation had its individual history and development. What exegetes discover about Jesus' self-understanding a posteriori
(summary 194), dogmatic theologians presume a priori. Thus, there is a deep
harmony between the positions of exegetes and dogmatic theologians.

"This brings us at last to the real theme, the central question of our considerations" (196). Dogmatic theologians need not fear exegetes have removed or weakened their basis for a dogmatic christology. Proof begins with the correct understanding of the church's teaching on christology. But it is difficult to maintain the hypostatic union of Chalcedonean christology without succumbing to either Monophysitism or monothelitism (mono-subjectivism) (199). Dogmatic theologians must hold to the true, full humanity of Jesus. And while insisting on his unique and unsurpassable place in salvation history, they must also fit Jesus into the long history of salvation. Jesus' unique role in salvation history is the locus in history where God's freedom and our freedom, God's self-offer and our acceptance, become irreversible (201).

"We can now apply ourselves directly to the consideration of our basic thesis" (201). Even within the limits established by modern exegetes it can be said that the pre-Easter Jesus understood himself as the absolute eschatological event and bearer of salvation. Jesus saw himself as more than one person pointing to a message about a pre-existing relationship between God and humanity. "He understood himself...as the one in whose message (precisely as *his*), and in whose person that which he preached was actually made present in a new and irrevocable form as a new and unsurpassable summons of God" (202). Jesus' true nature is understood only when it is seen as absolutely one with his function in saving history. Thus, in preaching the kingdom Jesus is revealing his nature. This is what the church's later christological statements make clear (summary stressing the unsurpassability of Jesus, 205f).

Resurrection (206-214): Lingering dualism makes it difficult for ontology and philosophical anthropology to appreciate the definitive human state, i.e., the state of being redeemed and having attained salvation which is the same as resurrection. Rahner sees Jesus' resurrection (107) not as a miracle unexpectedly inserted into the spiritual situation but as an a posteriori realization of an a priori perspective of hope already transcendentally present within us. Theologically the claim of resurrection means the individual, his fate and history, have attained to God. Jesus' simple bodily resuscitation and a return to this plane of existence would have had no universal significance.

Rahner draws from this distinction the physical qualities which can be posited of a resurrected person. He applies them to Christ and by extension to the interpretation of post-resurrection narratives (208f). Much remains obscure as to how the resurrected Jesus appeared to his disciples. Paradoxically, the more physical the experience the more like resuscitation it would have been. All that is maintained by the appearances is that the disciples experience of the risen Christ was not simply a vision or subjective state of mind.

The question returns, are the disciples' post-resurrection experiences susceptible to abstract investigation and explanation in rational terms, or do such investigations lead to their invalidation? Far from insisting on scientific proof the Christian "believes with the disciples" (211). Here the exegete and dogmatic theologian share common ground. Rahner concludes with a parting shot at those who claim the resurrection was the product of the apostles' loneliness (213). He challenges skeptics to consider embracing the resurrection as an appropriate human goal instead of suspecting and rejecting it simply for that reason and ending up with a meaningless world.

11.09   Christology in the Setting of Modern Man's Understanding of himself and of his World

Christologie im Rahmen des modernen Sebslt- und Welt-verständnisses

{2.5} Previously unpublished. 1970.

Abstract: Rahner incorporates into christology modern views of the world as dynamic and evolving, and of God as more immanent to that process.

Topics: CHRISTOLOGY, transcendental; EVOLUTION.

Subsidiary Discussions: Revelation history (215ff, 226f); Matter and spirit, unity of (217ff); Angels (219); God: immanence/ transcendence of (222ff); Freedom (226); History (228f); Eschatology, second coming of Christ (228).

Precis: Even though revelation takes place in and is shaped by history it is not ultimately subject to historical conditions. Though public revelation ends with the close of the New Testament period it has never been frozen in some definitive form. The task of theology is to interpret dogma within ever new historical contexts. How is christology to be interpreted in today's world?

"Our age is certainly characterized by a profound conviction of the unity between spirit and matter" (217f). Rahner sees in biologically organized materiality an impulse to ever-increasing levels of complexity and interiority toward spirit—a self-transcending, divinely inspired process through which matter becomes spirit. This bears on christology insofar as it sheds light on 1) the significance of the incarnation for angels and why the Logos became man and not (also) an angel; 2) why incarnation has radical significance for the material world and how incarnation is essentially related to creation (220).

A second characteristic of modern thought sees people and their world as evolving, and God as more immanent. Evolution has always been the Christian view of things even when Greek philosophy introduced a static view of the world with God quite outside and beyond it (222). In this evolutionary view "God is the dynamic impulse toward self-transcendence present in all being in virtue of the immanence of God" (224). Rahner bolsters the claim for divine immanence by a further theological argument which sees the act of creation as the act of grace: God's offer of self-communication to what is not God (225).

What does this modern view (summary 225f) mean for christology? The incarnation is no less than the historical point at which in an irreversible act of freedom "man attains to God in an ultimate act of self-transcendence" (227). God's own self-bestowal upon us in its most radical form has taken place precisely in Jesus of Nazareth. This truth cannot be deduced, it is a faith experience. That this transcendental christology is developed a posteriori does not invalidate it. Is the "Jesus-event" too modest to bear such transcendental meaning? In response Rahner points to the second part of that event: its completion in the Second Coming. The Christ event does not bring history to an end. By definitively establishing the proper goal of history and human freedom it provides a reason for hope even for "this worldly" history.

11.10   Reflections on the Problems Involved in Devising a Short Formula of the Faith

Reflexionen zur Problematik einer Kurzformel des Glaubens
{1.5} *Der Seelsorger* (1970) 4-30.

Abstract: Though a new short creed is desirable, today's intellectual/cultural situation will at best yield many creeds. Although these will differ from one another in many details they will all be fundamentally Trinitarian.

Topics: CREED, brief; FAITH, short formula of.
Subsidiary Discussions: Truths, hierarchy of (230, 236); Theology, pluralism in, (234f); Trinity (239f, 243f); Love of God/neighbor (241f); God as absolute future (242f).
Precis: This is Rahner's contribution to a discussion on the necessity of a modern short formula of faith to accomplish today what the Apostles' Creed and others did in their times. Traditional creeds find little resonance in the contemporary intellectual climate when the very idea of God can no longer be taken as self-evident. The task of creating such a brief formula, however, raises many important questions.

Because the contemporary intellectual climate is oriented to practical action rather than to theoretical reasoning any new creed would probably counterbalance previous excessive conceptualizing, over-defining and dissecting of what is properly signified in the Christian faith.

Could a single basic formula of the faith be acceptable to all Christians and replace all former creeds? No. The world is too pluralistic to expect all the hearers of one creed would find it directly intelligible. Rahner notes the opposition to a universal catechism (233). A less imperial and colonial church will no longer simply export a single creed and expect it to be universally accepted. The irreducible pluralism among theologies today also militates against the very possibility that a single creed could be formulated even by an ecumenical council. Hence, in the future one can expect to see many brief formulations differing among themselves due to the historical and cultural situations out of which they arise.

What should such a creed include, what should it set aside? Because no creed can contain every truth of the faith it must appeal to Vatican II's notion of the hierarchy of truths. Each creed will attach greater importance to those truths which speak most directly to its social, religious, historical setting. As to how much should be included in such a creed, although they will most likely differ in length, Rahner hopes they will all strive to be brief.

Any future creed must face the question of how to be christological without negating the possibility of anonymous Christianity: that even those who do not ascribe to Christianity explicitly are not thereby beyond God's saving will and power.

Rahner offers three examples of a short formula with brief commentaries on each: a theological formula (238ff) which emphasizes the experience of God as mystery and the workings of the Trinity; a sociological formula (240ff) which emphasizes the self-transcending love of neighbor and how it is rooted in love of God; a futurologist formula (242f) which emphasizes the eschatological theme of God as the fulfillment of human transcendence. Rahner concludes by insisting that any future short formula will necessarily be Trinitarian because the God of Christianity is triune.

11.11   The Sin of Adam
Die Sünde Adams
{3.5} Previously unpublished March 1968 lecture at Paderborn. 28th Conference of the Ecumenical Study Group of Protestant and Catholic Theologians.

Abstract: Rahner offers a theology of original sin in unique theological terms which he hopes will be accepted by the church as a truly Catholic position.
Topics: SIN, original; THEOLOGICAL ANTHROPOLOGY, mono-/polygenism.
Subsidiary Discussions: Protology (249ff, 253f); Freedom (254, 261).
Precis: In today's state of theological pluralism it is difficult to identify a Catholic or Protestant theology of "the sin of Adam," even though Catholic theologians have clear parameters within which to work. In this setting individuals must risk stating in their own terms the contemporary meaning of this doctrine in the hopes the church will find it compatible with the faith and will accept it as "Catholic." By beginning with the question of original sin Rahner hopes to clarify the sin of Adam, since by contrast the latter shares with our sinfulness the quality of being "derived."
I. Methodological presuppositions:
1) Our knowledge of the "fall of the first man" along with the doctrine of original sin is deduced from a more primary revelation: the awareness of ourselves as sinners who obtain forgiveness and salvation only in Christ. The value of this etiological approach (understanding causes by examining the present) is that it focuses us on the New Testament where this doctrine first

appeared and it points to the transcendental horizon. Rahner finishes these reflections by insisting the interpretation of Romans 5 remains an open question for Catholic theologians.

2) One must distinguish between the reality of "original sin" and the ecclesiastical, disciplinary terminology that accrues to it. Rahner notes the Orthodox Church avoids the term sin in this connection, and even seminary theology sees sin and sinfulness (i.e., our condition as descendants of Adam and our condition apropos to our personal choices to go against God) as only analogous. Sin and sinfulness arise from two different causes external to the conditions themselves. We are not sinners merely due to our descent from Adam.

3) Original sin can be rethought in this way without regard to the question of monogensim and polygenism. Even though when Rahner uses the term "Adam" he means "humanity," this does not explain away original sin in existentialist terms as though it applies to "man as such."

4) To explain adequately the doctrine of original sin one would need a formal "theology of beginning" since only this can justify a retrospective etiology (sketch, 253f). This approach argues that the beginning of a sequence has a unique character which determines all later events. It is never merely the first in a series of common events. Whoever fails to appreciate this will always see original sin as pure mythology. Summary (254).

II. **The nature of original sin:** Every doctrine is couched in its unique theology. Here Rahner attempts to present a Catholic interpretation of original sin, albeit in idiosyncratic terms he knows are not universally accepted.

1) Rahner frames the entire discussion in terms of God's self-bestowal on us, the singular fact which sanctifies us prior to any decision of our own. God gives this gift to all humanity in virtue of the fact of our common historical reality which derives its existence from Christ and is oriented to him. Christ and not human derivation or descent is the basis and the medium of our justification and sanctification.

2) God, however, willed that this gift of justifying holiness be communicated through the medium of human descent, prior to one's personal existence (whether or not one takes a Scotist view of creation). Original sin (*peccatum originale originatum*) is precisely the lack of this existential, grace-bestowing modality communicated through human descent as God willed.

3) The failure of human descent to provide the medium through which holiness is imparted to all people is only conceivable as the outcome of the guilt of those who existed at the beginning of the human race and provided the origin of the rest. This explains why sin and original sin are analogous concepts. Explanatory observations: a) The circumstances surrounding personal guilt at the very beginning is radically withdrawn from us. We cannot imagine states so different from what we experience. b) Personal guilt at the beginning does not produce personal guilt in us. It simply removes

from us the mode of sanctification by God's self-bestowal in Christ precisely as descendants. c) What is missing in this "state which ought not to be" is not some personal moral failing against God but the inhibition of the will of the creator to endow all humanity with grace in a particular way, i.e., through human generation. d) This rules out interpreting original sin as collective guilt. e) Original sin does not precede God's effective will to save all through Christ. The two exist in dialectic counterpoint. f) There are two ways we know God intended human generation to be the medium of grace: i) the solidarity which still remains within the human community; ii) the fact salvation is extended to us in Christ because we are sinners and not because we are not due the grace of God. The universality of sin points to its prior origin and sui generis character. g) The doctrine of original sin is implied in the fact that sinners must be redeemed by Christ who does not simply liberate us from guilt but imparts his own holiness to us in his Holy *Pneuma*.

4) Rahner distinguishes "the sin of Adam" (*peccatum originale originans*) from original sin which applies to us. a) Before the fall the human race existed in a state of original freedom. b) It makes no difference whether we think of this humanity as an original group or an individual. c) It is possible the decision of even one individual in the original human unit could have destroyed the grace-mediating function of original humanity. d) Scripture does not settle the question of monogenism or polygenism. e) The reality of sinful history argues that the doctrine of original sin is no mere mythologem.

5) There is much more to this topic than Rahner can treat here.

11.12 On the Encyclical *Humanae Vitae*
Zur Enzyklika "Humanae vitae"
{2.0} *Stimmen der Zeit* 182 (1968) 193-210.

Abstract: Without commenting on the content of this 1968 encyclical Rahner addresses the theological problems raised by the widespread opposition to it, concentrating on the binding force of such reformable papal teachings.
Topics: MAGISTERIUM; DOGMA, reformable.
Subsidiary Discussions: Marriage act (265); Theological Anthropology, self-manipulation (265f); Morality, sexual (266f); Morality, ideal norm (273f); Artificial birth control (278f, 282); Episcopate (280f); Priests (282f); Theologians (283f); Dogma, development of (286).
Precis: I. **Preliminary observation.** Catholics must take this encyclical seriously because: it is a papal pronouncement; it is the outcome of mature thought; it is backed by doctrinal tradition. Pride and emotionalism are inappropriate responses. This essay is not concerned with the core teaching of the encyclical nor with the many important subsidiary questions it raises (list, 265f). Rahner in no way dismisses the important Catholic convictions maintained by the encyclical: that sexual life and marriage are subject to

moral prescriptions based on natural law; that the state can never claim exclusive rights in regulating birth.

II. The encyclical as a reformable statement of doctrine. This encyclical is not a papal definition. Rahner offers a long quote from the German bishops to convey the encyclical's real significance and implications (268ff). The encyclical is authentic but non-definitive. At least in principle it is susceptible to revision. As to its binding character, Catholics in general and Catholic theologians in particular have the right and duty to take such a teaching seriously. To say it is reformable does not mean it is false or stands in need of revision. But it does allow for legitimate disagreement. Rahner points to the recent history of similar papal pronouncements which have in fact been revised (list, 272). Making the case for reforming such teachings is not un-Catholic nor does it become legitimate only after revisions have been made.

Turning to the content of the encyclical Rahner insists a distinction must be made between the content of a statement and its correctness. Is it not possible the content of this teaching is true insofar as it constitutes a moral ideal Catholics should strive to appropriate and implement rather than as an effective universal moral obligation? Is it not possible people today may evidence invincible error in regard to this teaching? How else can one explain the theological significance of the rejection of this teaching by such a large part of the Catholic faithful? Summary (274).

III. Deviant decisions of conscience. Rahner presents possible grounds over which an individual Christian could justifiably deviate from this papal teaching in good conscience by a psychological process we can understand. a) One must not too quickly see this conflict as a choice between what is easy and what is hard. Rahner sees it as a conflict between valid duties on both sides. b) This conflict in conscience cannot simply be solved by recourse to logical argument based on the formal authority of the church. Since real people do not make decisions based solely on logic, such an appeal can easily be over-strained from a psychological point of view. c) No one can assume the absolute certainty of the objective correctness of this papal norm. d) This lends a far greater effectiveness to the arguments against the papal norm. e) The more a teaching is intrinsically based in natural law the more compelling it is psychologically. f) The less a moral norm can be seen to connect with one's concrete circumstances the more abstract and theoretical it will seem to be. Summary (277).

Rahner now turns to notable arguments against the papal norm, not to supply an unambiguous proof against the teaching but to explain how a believer might hold a contrary opinion in good faith. a) The encyclical is too brief to be convincing at the psychological level, especially insofar as it fails to connect the teaching intrinsically with the natural law. b) Because this teaching runs contrary to the recommendations of a notable majority of the Papal Commission empaneled to study the question it is psychologically

harder to accept. c) Analysis of the "safe period" in human fertilization and how it is affected by this teaching has the psychological effect of making the teaching seem like so much hair-splitting over biological techniques.
IV. The de facto situation among Catholics since the encyclical. The living practice of most Catholics remains largely unchanged by this encyclical. Most in good faith will apply to it the principles stated in the letter of the German bishops. Far from being unique, this situation closely resembles the reaction to the papal teaching on biblical scholarship issued at the turn of the century. Nothing positive is to be gained by ignoring or censoring the dissenting voices. Rahner suggests ways bishops, priests, theologians, and the Christian faithful should respond in this current situation.
V. The significance of the current situation as constituting a representative example. Today's situation is nothing absolutely novel as the history of the development of dogma clearly shows. What is new is the rapidity of change and the wide dissemination of information to an increasingly educated laity. But the church is and has always been an open system. For as essential as the magisterium may be in enunciating the faith it has no exclusive grasp of the truth. The church must rely on many of its members to contribute to the proper development of doctrine. Christians retain the individual responsibility to arrive at sincere decisions in their own personal lives before God. The two factors, free responsibility to arrive at the truth and paying due heed to the magisterium, are united and combined in the process of decision making.

11.13   Theological Observations on the Concept of Time
Theologische Bermerkungen zum Zeitbegriff
{3.5} Previously unpublished September 1967 lecture at Feldafing to a Conference of the *Görres-Gesellschaft*.
Abstract: The dogma that the world was created in time leads Rahner to speculate on the nature of time. Any true theory of time must allow for the definitive exercise of responsible freedom in relation to God's self-communication.
Topics: TIME/ETERNITY, theology of; FREEDOM.
Subsidiary Discussions: Dogma, development of (296f); Matter and spirit (300f, 304f); Nature and grace (305f); God, immutability of (307f).
Precis: After justifying the narrow scope of this essay Rahner points to the sad fact that although so much of Christian theology concerns time (list, 289ff) a complete theology of time is still lacking. Rahner attributes this to the widespread, naive assumption that everyone already understands what time is. In this essay Rahner hopes to show that in order to accomplish its aims theology must concern itself with the concept of time even when this takes theologians outside the borders of their own discipline.

I. Rahner examines the Catholic dogma that the world is not "eternal" but has been created in time. Leaving aside whether this is a statement of revelation or of natural science, he warns against falling into the "transcendental fantasy": confusing the existence of time in the world for the existence of the world in time (294). Since understanding finite time as material ends in an intractable dilemma [modeled on Kant's antimonies], Rahner feels justified in insisting that theologians must consider time not within the parameters of natural sciences but within the context of "saving truth," i.e., insofar as it allows for the possibility of our achieving definitive freedom. Summary (297).

II. Rahner starts from the assumption that dogmatic pronouncements regarding time are meant to safeguard the material and spiritual unity of the human person whose nature finds its true consummation in the definitive exercise of freedom. Rahner develops this in two parts: a) the qualified temporality inherent in us; b) what can discreetly be extrapolated from it. After listing the limits and advantages of this approach Rahner insists that only finite, one-way, irreversible, material time is consistent with the human experience of responsible freedom which can and must reach definitive consummation. Although this reading based on "saving truth" leaves open a great deal about the intrinsic nature of time, material time can never be imagined in such a way that precludes the possibility of how Christians understand human freedom. Nor can it claim to solve all the philosophical and scientific problems of time.

III. By means of summary and to point out further avenues of study Rahner adds: a) For theologians the primary heuristic norm for understanding time is its relationship to saving history: to the possibility of a definitive, free, human response to God's self-communication. b) Any extrapolations from this must be very cautious and will meet with only limited success. It will, however, shed important light on the relationship of matter to spirit. c) The relationship of secular, scientific time (time-in-itself) and the saving time of theology are best understood as analogous to other distinctions Rahner makes between pure and graced nature. d) Although eternity can be understood in many ways it is not primarily the endless succession of time. It refers to that consummation made possible in and through time because of God's free self-communication. e) As to how time belongs to God, Rahner insists we think of God as immutable and timeless *in se*. f) God's self-communication makes true *kairos* possible in time. It lifts time from neutral homogeneity to the realm of privileged time where irreversible decisions of tremendous importance are made. Summary (308).

11.14 Theological Considerations on the Moment of Death

Theologische Erwägungen über den Eintritt des Todes

{2.0} November 1968 lecture in Vienna to 22nd Congress of Austrian Doctors of the Van Sweiten Society. *Artz und Christ* 15 (1969) 24-32.

Abstract: Considering the limits of a doctor's duty to prolong life leads Rahner to distinguish mere biological life from human life which finds its proper consummation in the presence of God either as blessing or judgment.

Topics: DEATH; ETHICS, medical.

Subsidiary Discussions: Organ transplants (311); Life, human (312f); Life, consummation of (314ff, 319f); Life, prolongation of (315f); God as consummation of life (318f); Hylomorphism (317); Jesus Christ, death of (320f).

Precis: Theology brings to the interdisciplinary question of the limits of a doctor's duty to preserve life a certain a priori perspective which resolves into two interpenetrating concepts of life. The first, biological, leads to the seeming truism that a doctor can only relinquish care for the patient when the individual is dead and not before. But it is not so easy to distinguish the point of death even on the biological level (e.g., organ transplants). Just as in particular cases the theologian depends on input from the natural sciences to determine the borderline between death and dying, medical professionals also depend on theologians and philosophers who consider the human being as such to fully understand death and dying. Especially at its beginning and at its end it is possible for human life to be present in the biological sense although not at what philosophers or theologians would call a human level. For all these reasons Rahner is comfortable in identifying brain death as the point at which the process of human dying comes to an end and that point at which medical intervention can justifiably cease (313).

Rahner is comfortable with the fact the scientist's notion of death does not always completely coincide with the theologian's even though the two remain intrinsically interconnected. The ultimate value of the life the doctor struggles to prolong arises precisely from the person's spiritual mode of existence which has its own intrinsic limits. Biological life is not meant to be prolonged indefinitely into an indeterminate future. Spiritual life, one's personal history, has and seeks its own proper consummation. Hence, the patient's death is not the doctor's ultimate failure. It marks the effective completion of the patient's life task. Not surprisingly a doctor will feel differently about losing a patient who seemingly had many years of full personal living ahead as opposed to one whose underlying condition made such a life impossible.

Doctors face death both as professionals who continually fight to stave it off and as people who must learn humbly to endure the reality of death (both their patients' and their own) and its inescapable questions (317). These questions can never be answered on the biological level alone for it reveals nothing about the disposition of our responsible freedom. Biology alone cannot explain the consummation of our personal history.

To those who patiently endure these questions the best the Christian and theologian can do is ask whether the answers faith supplies do not correspond to the seeker's deepest longings. Faith does not rationalize death away. It offers God as the mysterious fulfillment of our own personal histories. Death is not a phenomenon of this world. It is the moment when our lives are brought into full relationship with the mystery of God either as a consummate blessing or as judgment. Whatever formula one uses to express this truth (resurrection of the flesh, separation of body and soul, etc.) each is meant to indicate that death brings us into the presence of God where we must give an account of ourselves. It is no wonder that neither death nor its effects are completely discoverable within the restricted realm of the empirical.

Medical personnel endure in a special way the tension of struggling against death at the biological level while seeking death as their own personal, final consummation. Christian faith in eternal life in no way cheapens biological life nor does it denigrate the heroic efforts physicians make to prolong life. Believing in the cross of Christ we seek to follow Jesus who died as we shall die in terrible darkness.

XII. Confrontations 2
IX. *Konfrontationen*

German edition: Einsiedeln, Benziger, 1970
U.S. edition: N.Y., Seabury, 1974
David Bourke, translator

This volume in the English edition comprises the last two sections of *Schriften zur Theologie*, IX.

12.01   The Teaching Office of the Church in the Present-Day Crisis of Authority
Das kirchliche Lehramt in der heutigen Autoritätskrise

{2.0} March 1969 lecture to Ecumenical Study Circle of Protestant and Catholic Theologians at Priory of Hardehausen on the theme: authority in crisis.

Abstract: The formal conceptual model of the church's teaching office is inadequately related to the believing church as a whole. It can be more democratic. To be convincing today it cannot simply appeal to authority. It must show the relationship between its teachings and fundamental Christian truths.

Topics: MAGISTERIUM; CHURCH, democracy in; CHURCH, authority in.

Subsidiary Discussions: Infallibility (8f, 15f); Revelation history (9); Theology (11f); Law, divine/human; (16f); Society, minority rights (18ff); Propositions, theological (21ff) Truths, hierarchy of (23ff); Power, coercive (26ff); Theology, pluralism in (28ff).

Precis: This parochial and somewhat fragmentary discussion of authority and the teaching office of the Catholic Church has ecumenical implication. After setting out the official formal model of teaching authority in the church (4) Rahner proceeds to examine inherent problems in this conceptual model. First it lacks adequate reference to the church as such, as if the teaching church were a one-sided affair to which the listening church had nothing to offer. But all official teachers are themselves first believers and hearers who always preach as members of the community. However much it may seem a self-evident truism, Rahner insists the authority of the official teachers derives from the church itself as a whole, although not in the same sense as secular leaders are invested with authority in a democracy. All teaching authority in the church, even papal infallibility, derives from Christ through the church, just as the church itself derives from Christ (7). Unfortunately, this truth is often overlooked. Too often it is made to appear that the office and its teachings derive directly from God. But not only does the content and the mandate of the magisterium derive from the church, so does the actual power to teach including the authenticity and effectiveness of the teaching (9f).

Self-evident as these principles may seem they are easily obscured by the formal conceptual and juridical model of teaching authority put forward by the church. This is especially dangerous in today's cultural atmosphere which is skeptical of authority as such. Rahner contends there is no necessary division between the formal authority invested in an official body and the authority inherent in the realities it upholds, however difficult it may be to show the link between them. This means church authority must never be afraid to reveal its true nature. It must never obscure the fact that it relies on many human sources to come to conclusions. What it teaches is often primarily an "infallible" confirmation of the absolute assent to an article of faith it has discovered within itself (allowing that the means by which such discoveries are made vary greatly over time). In any case the teaching office must never make it seem that what it proposes is authoritative precisely where and to the degree it is derived independently of human efforts. This only plays into the modern skepticism of authority, even if tender believers may be less edified with this approach.

Rahner turns to how the church comes to understand what it believes—the question of the teaching authority and democracy (13-23). He lists a number of caveats, insists the discussion not be controlled by reactionary prejudice, and distinguishes between two kinds of realities in the church:

divinely revealed truths and institutional factors and practices in the church. Voting, he maintains, has a long history stretching from the apostles to Vatical II. After showing how voting is not incompatible with papal infallibility (14f) Rahner considers the binding power of such votes on the consciences of individual believers (16), and the extent of the mandate to participate in voting (16f). After a brief summary (18) Rahner returns to the weight or significance of a majority vote on the dissenting minority (18f). Since the truth of a position is never guaranteed simply because it is embraced by the majority, even if it does not contradict the faith of the church in earlier ages and is agreed to by the pope, such decisions are never absolutely binding on individual conscience. Summary (20).

After a few words on the dangers inherent in allowing all the baptized without regard to their degree of personal identification with the church to vote on matters of faith, Rahner considers the distinction between the faith of the church and the formulations in which that faith is professed. Although he cannot prove it Rahner assumes (a priori) that church members first and foremost agree on one faith and disagree only over secondary questions: the terms in which that faith is expressed. Certainly in this situation the minority would be free to express these common truths in its own analogous way. Thus, in an age of theological pluralism when increasingly it is less likely that the church will be stating new doctrines than it will be teaching new ways to express commonly held truths, the dangers that democracy in the church would tyrannize a minority are greatly reduced.

Rahner next considers the essential relationship of the teaching authority of the church to the actual truths to which it attests, as well as to the forms this relationship assumes today (25-30). The formal authority of the teaching office is not (St. Augustine not withstanding, 23f) the first or most fundamental datum in the content of faith. Although it has its legitimate place in the hierarchy of truths, the magisterium has a duty to show the intrinsic relationship between its pronouncements and the original basis of the Christian faith in general. No longer can mere appeals to power or authority sway the conscience of believers. Today appeals made to formal authority will be largely ineffective. By relating its teachings more closely to the common truths of faith the teaching authority will make itself, in a sense, "more and more superfluous" (28). Rahner believes the future task of the magisterium will be to preserve the basic substance of the common faith in a far more radical and concentrated way than ever before. This also holds the greatest opportunity for advances in ecumenism.

12.02 The Point of Departure in Theology for Determining the Nature of the Priestly Office

Der theologische Ansatzpunkt für die Bestimmung des Wesens des Amtspriestertums

{1.5} Concilium (1969) 194-197.

Abstract: Starting from an analysis of ministry of the Word, Rahner radically reappraises the mutable and immutable elements of priesthood. He concludes: 1) one is justified in embracing this vocation today boldly and confidently; 2) the church possesses almost unlimited freedom to determine the concrete form of the official institution of the priesthood.

Topics: PRIESTHOOD; WORD, ministry of.

Subsidiary Discussions: Mediation (33); Church as *Ur-sakrament* (33ff).

Precis: Attempting to addresses the growing crisis in priestly identity Rahner looks for a theological starting-point from which to distinguish the changeable from the abiding elements of the complex reality of Catholic priesthood.

Preliminary remarks: Rahner examines and discards two possible theological starting-points: 1) sacramental powers, because these are not based in scripture; 2) the concept of mediator, because this power is not unique to priesthood. Rahner next enlarges the discussion by recalling: 3) that although the church possesses the power of office this power has been and can be divided up sacramentally in many different ways; 4) the church fulfills its own nature as the sacrament of God's self-utterance to the world by effectively proclaiming the word entrusted to it in *anamnesis* and *prognosis*.

The point of departure itself: Rahner summarizes his definition of the priest with the remark, he is "sent by the Church to proclaim the gospel in her name" (36). He does this in the supreme mode by celebrating Eucharist. On the basis of this definition the priestly office is not clearly separated from that of the bishop; it is not reduced to a cultic role; it retains its missionary and communal character. From this starting-point it becomes clear that the office of the priest can vary greatly in form as circumstances warrant (list, 37). One must not identify the essence of priesthood with any one of its concrete manifestations, however venerable a tradition it may have.

This radical reappraisal of mutable and immutable elements of priesthood leads Rahner to conclude: 1) one is justified in embracing this vocation today boldly and confidently; 2) the church possesses almost unlimited freedom in determining the concrete form of the official institution of the priesthood.

12.03 Theological Reflections on the Priestly Image of Today and Tomorrow

Theologische Reflexionen zum Priesterbild von heute und morgen

{2.5} June 1968 lecture to Conference of the Catholic Academy in Bavaria.

Abstract: Despite its changing forms the essence of priesthood lies in its ministry of the Word through which the church realizes its sacramental

nature in the world as the sign of salvation. Because it involves the whole person it remains a vocation even if secular society fails to see it as a profession.
Topics: PRIESTHOOD.
Subsidiary Discussions: Mediation (43ff); Diaconate (47f, 58); Sacraments (48); Church, nature of (50ff); Church, future of (54ff); Celibacy (58f).
Precis: I. After admitting his approach to this complex problem is subjective, Rahner remarks on the age of rapid transition in which we live. Today when the old image of priesthood has come into question and a new image has not yet appeared there is a right and a wrong way to hold to what is of value. Rahner calls for calm, patient endurance in a spirit of openness. Attempting to glimpse the future image of priesthood calls for more than imaginative speculation. It involves a realistic confrontation with a future state of affairs from which we deduce consequences which in turn must be reconciled with the unchanging faith of the church. Rahner concludes this section asking whether priestly ministry will or must continue to be a professional calling in the secular sense as it has been since the Constantinian era.
II. Today's culture is essentially skeptical in matters of religion. This has the effect of calling many elements of traditional priesthood into question (list, 42f). Without addressing this whole array of questions Rahner intends to argue that Catholic priesthood today (though vital and capable of change) is still identical with the priesthood of traditional theology. He does not start from the notion of mediator between sacred and secular spheres, but from the priesthood insofar as it participates in fulfilling the essential nature of the church. The world is not divided sacred and secular. The church is the historical and symbolic manifestation of God's offer of salvation. Priesthood derives from the universal priesthood of the faithful to direct their activities at the historical and social levels. The activities of the priest (whose commission is from above and not simply from below) are determined by the mission of the church. This explains why the celebrant of the sacraments always arises from and works for the community of the faithful. Summary (46).

This being so, Rahner warns against determining the essence of the priesthood by specifying those unique activities which in the past have constituted a full-time profession. The proper way to view the case is to ask whether certain members of the church are not already carrying out a unified complex of activities which further the nature of the church and to whom a sacramental seal could be legitimately extended (e.g., the Diaconate). The sacrament does not create a set of activities *de novo*, but strengthens those already engaged in these activities with the grace of the sacrament (48). However much the content of this complex of activities may change over time it will always include presiding at Eucharist and preaching the gospel, even though the latter is never the exclusive task of the priest.

Since priesthood cannot be understood by beginning with the historically late three-fold division of orders (bishop, priest, deacon), Rahner examines how it is rooted in the nature of the church as "medium of salvation" (50). The church is the abiding actualization of the now eschatologically victorious Word of promise God uttered to the world through Christ in history. This Word finds its supreme proclamation in the Eucharist. This Word must not only be formulated it must also be persuasively uttered and lived afresh. Whoever does precisely this is a priest, whether or not he has yet been officially commissioned. For the sake of establishing order in the community such persons should be ordained. An office of this kind cannot be reduced to the cultic. And whether or not secular society recognizes it as a "profession" it remains a full-time vocation and calling in the ecclesial sense insofar as it lays claim to the whole person. It should come as no surprise that an increasingly secular society might not see priesthood as a true profession since the Word of God will always be a sign of contradiction in the world.

III. Rahner next considers some more practical elements of priesthood of the future. Some of these have a more European flavor. Whether priests will continue to enjoy the status of professionals in secular eyes depends on, 1) the form the local worshiping community will assume; 2) the function priests themselves will be asked to fulfill. Rahner senses today's large, nominally Catholic "national churches" will be replaced with smaller communities of believers who gather as an act of free commitment. While these groups will have to struggle against the tendency to ghettoize, their missionary impulse will be limited by their more limited resources. They may not be able to afford to educate their priests to the same level as we are accustomed today. In addition, people who come freely to worship will be less tolerant of poor preaching and poor liturgy. They will expect to be inspired and led by the living faith of their priests and will remunerate them accordingly.

Rahner asks whether "part-time" priesthood (in a civic sense) might not be possible; whether elders in the community might be ordained having undergone a very different formation than is now the standard; whether the parochial structure is necessary; whether celibacy can be reconsidered. In any case the outward form of the priesthood has changed and will continue to change. We need not fear or resist the future. We need not simply suffer it. We can be among those who create it with hope that Christ will continue to lead us.

12.04 On the Diaconate
Über den Diakonat
{2.0} Previously unpublished December 1968 lecture at Freiburg.

Abstract: The theology of the diaconate leaves its future shape an open question. Responding to current needs (especially the need to build community) will provide the key, not abstract reasoning or strict historical restoration.

Topics: DIACONATE; ORDERS, sacrament of.

Subsidiary Discussions: Priesthood (60ff); Mediation (72); Community building (73ff); Laity as theologians (76); Grace, sacramental (77ff); Sacraments, grace of (77ff); Laity, diaconate of (79f).

Precis: Since Vatican II reestablished the permanent diaconate fresh problems have arisen surrounding the priestly office of the church which call for a reexamination of the content, significance, usefulness, and necessity of the permanent diaconate. There are two salient elements of this new theology of priesthood: 1) that the essence of priesthood resides in its special mission to preach the Word and to lead and guide the community; 2) the fluid nature of the divisions of the one *ordo* into three offices. In addition, the concrete situation of the priest in society has changed. The fact he is not so clearly seen to have a well-defined role (profession) in the secular world along with the shortage of priests has brought up the question of part-time priests.

Given the fluidity of the lines of demarcation among the three orders (bishop, priest, deacon) and the fact that Vatican II did not insist on any one set of tasks for deacons, Rahner feels justified to reconsider the role of deacons not simply from a theoretical angle but also with the hope of affecting real change.

Rahner can identify only three invariable factors in the permanent diaconate: the deacon receives his office; office is sacramentally conferred by a bishop; its powers do not include presiding at Eucharist. Hence, the question today is not how to restore the historical diaconate but how to create its dynamic future. How is this new conception to be arrived at? Rahner makes two points: 1) it will take creative experimentation; 2) one must be prepared to see a wide variety of forms appear depending on local conditions. Rahner approaches this question in three steps:

-Preliminary methodological remarks (69-71): Rahner admits his former line of argument to justify the restoration of the diaconate (cf., 5.12) is no longer adequate insofar as it was overly influenced by historical forms of diaconate. Since the concrete form of the diaconate is a response to the needs of its times Rahner no longer sees it as essential that today's forms should have existed in the past. There is no need to evolve any absolutely uniform type of deacon, just as there is no such form of priesthood, even though both have an essential nature. Lines of demarcation will necessarily remain somewhat obscure, and changing situations will call for ever new solutions.

-Negative boundary lines (71-73): All Christians share the universal duty to serve their neighbors in ways appropriate to their life situations. Without prejudice to this universal *diakonia* there is a *diakonia* proper to those officially ordained because: 1) ordination authorizes such service; 2) as a concrete social structure the church needs such specified offices. This being said, Rahner insists on certain restrictions: the function of ordained deacons cannot consist in the function of leadership itself; the existence of this office does not negate the duty of the laity to serve others; the deacon is not a mediator between laity and clergy; the true nature of diaconate cannot be defined in terms of cultic powers; priests and bishops cannot permanently transfer to deacons the specifically diaconal elements of their orders. Such functions are marked by graded participation and not strict exclusion.

-The future shape of the diaconate (73-80): The future form of the diaconate will depend on the needs of society. Pointing to the widespread fragmentation of human communities and the consequent alienation people feel today, Rahner maintains deacons of the future will be called on to use their special talents to foster community, both societal and ecclesial. This is true whether or not deacons performed this role in earlier ages (summary, 75). From this starting-point Rahner goes on to mention certain questions which the theology of the diaconate leaves open: the need for professional specialization among deacons (with a special note on teachers and lay theologians); the full-time or part-time nature of the call; the optimum age of deacons; whether they work solo or as part of a team.

The essay concludes with remarks on the grace conferred by the sacrament. [What at first seems like a digression reveals itself to be a word of encouragement to those who are currently doing those things Rahner has defined as the work of deacons even though at this time they are not seen by the church as proper candidates for diaconal ordination ("lay deacons").] After identifying the sacramental character of orders as empowerment to serve others, Rahner goes on to show how this very grace (as well as every other sacramental grace) is already present prior to the juridical conferral of the sacrament (79). Given this notion of pre-sacramental and extra-sacramental grace Rahner concludes that there are many lay practitioners of the complex amalgam of functions usually identified with the sacramental diaconate. These lay people should enjoy the same grace and its effects as those who have been juridically ordained.

12.05 Observations on the Factor of the Charismatic in the Church

Bemerkungen über das Charismatische in der Kirke
{2.5}   *Geist und Leben* 42 (1969) 251-262.

Abstract: The charismatic element in the church does not exist on the same plane with the institutional factor as its opposite. Rather it is the first, most ultimate formal characteristic inherent in the nature of the church.

Topics: CHURCH, charismatic element in.

Subsidiary Discussions: Church, holiness of (81ff, 86f); Grace (83f); Orders, grace of (86); Petrine Office (89ff); Theology and discovery of truth (92f); Future (93f); Church, obedience in (95ff).

Precis: I. From the Reformation onwards Catholic ecclesiology stressed the institutional factors in the church at the expense of its charismatic dimension. Even holiness was seen to reside in the church as a byproduct of its institutions (hierarchy, sacraments, etc.). Since Vatican II a more explicit theology of the charismatic factor in the church has developed (bibliography, 82 ftns.2,3). The church today is seen not only as the means of salvation but also as the fruit of salvation. Spirit, grace, *charismata* are now seen as constitutive of the church as much as its institutional factors. The two elements are not opposed or hostile. The church is holy not only as a dispenser of the goods of salvation, but also on account of the victorious grace that resides in it by virtue of the love of its members for God and neighbor. As such the church both demands faith and provides the basis for it.

After saying it is not important here to distinguish between actual, effective grace and the charismatic gifts of grace in the narrower sense, Rahner does just this (83f) in order to make the point that "the charismatic element belongs no less abidingly and necessarily to the nature of the Church than her official institutions and the sacraments" (84). This was taught by Pius XII and Vatican II. Summary (85).

This being said, Rahner warns against thinking the charismatic element should exercise such a primacy that the institutional factor becomes a minor function which simply regulates the charismatic element. It is wrong to see these two factors as simply opposed, especially since the institutional factor is itself a charism given to the church by the Spirit. As proof Rahner points to the fact that those called to orders often live lives of heroic virtue. But clearly all the faithful, the entire "holy people of God" and not only those called to office in the church, enjoy graces and charisms. It is in this way that the whole church fulfills its task to be "the sacrament of the world." However true it may be that the institutional element in the church must examine and cultivate charisms, these gifts will not always manifest themselves through official channels. The institutional church must not suspect such movements simply because they come from below for it is always possible for the institutional church erroneously and culpably to suppress legitimate movements of the Spirit.

II. "*The charismatic element in the Church designates that point in the Church at which God as Lord of the Church presides over the Church as an open system.*" Rahner distinguishes open from closed systems. An open system can only be defined by reference to a point outside itself. Hence, it cannot be monolithic, absolute, definitive, or totalitarian. After arguing against a "papalist" view which sees the church as a closed system (89ff) Rahner concludes that a proper understanding of the papacy, the means the church uses to discover truth, and its openness to the absolute future, all reveal the church to be an open system. "It is from the nature of the Church in this sense, as constituting an open system in a radical and abiding sense, that the charismatic element in the Church derives its ultimate and truest essence" (94). Hence, for Rahner the term charismatic stands for the ultimate incalculability which belongs to the mutual interplay among the many factors in the church. The charismatic is transcendental in character, not one element in the system but a special characteristic of the system as a whole. It is creative freedom.

III. "*The interplay between the official institution and free charisma as it exists in the concrete.*" In concrete Christian life, conflict between the institutional and charismatic elements in the church is inevitable. This raises the question of obedience. After showing how obedience differs in open vs. closed systems, Rahner maintains that in an open system such as the church there are no formal principles on the basis of which all conflicts can be settled. The necessary balance between personal initiative and obedient fulfillment of directives from above cannot be arrived at by appeal to general principles. It must always be rediscovered afresh in concrete circumstances. Although one could say that as a practical rule of thumb "the last word" should be given to the official institution, in a truly open system there can be no "last word." Summary (97).

12.06   Schism in the Catholic Church?
Schisma in der katolischen Kirche?
{2.0}   *Stimmen der Zeit* 184 (1969) 20-34.

Abstract: Not only is it difficult today to distinguish heresy and schism, great caution must be exercised not to label certain trends in the church as schismatic (e.g., subsidiarity, theological pluralism, democratization).

Topics: HERESY; CHURCH, schism.
Subsidiary Discussions: Authority (103); Church, local (autonomy) (105ff); Power, coercive (106f); Hope, eschatological (107f); Theology, pluralism in (108ff); Church, democracy in (110ff); Faith, incomplete identification with (112ff).

Precis: The possibility of schism has immediate relevance in the church today.

Heresy and schism: It would seem the distinction between schism and heresy is clear. As opposed to schismatics, heretics separate from the church because they formally reject its dogmas. But in light of Vatican I's teaching on papal infallibility, for a schismatic to withdraw obedience from the pope seems now to entail heresy as well. Though heresy is not innocuous, Rahner feels there is little danger of fresh heresies primarily because people today are not interested in theoretical questions of faith. Due to the ascendancy of practical reason one is more likely today to separate from the church over practical issues of life. But according to Rahner this new type of dissent is actually a modified brand of heresy because in these cases the speculative reason is carried along by practical reason.

Schism as a contemporary phenomenon: Though its modern form is not well understood, schism remains no less possible today than in earlier times. Today it is most likely to erupt as a reaction against specific modes of living in the church which seem outmoded. This form and not flagrant heresy (which is still possible) interests Rahner. Rejecting modes of life which seem outmoded raises the question of the legitimacy and binding force of such regulations. Insofar as only very few of the church's teachings are binding *de fide*, theoretically there are many opportunities for disagreement over specific regulations. As such these cannot be settled either by excommunication or by appeal to theory or formal law. They can only be settled at the level of practical reason with "patience and a Christian attitude of readiness to renounce and to serve" (104). Although schism and heresy are possible today, one must be cautious not to condemn every new development in the church as schismatic or heretical. Rahner proceeds to describe three legitimate tendencies in the church which must not be confused at the outset with schism or the danger of schism.

The degree of autonomy of the subsidiary churches: At the theoretical level (having in mind primarily the Eastern churches) Vatican II reaffirmed the right of local churches to a high degree of autonomy. This legitimate tendency must not be thought of as schismatic even when it appears in the Western churches. How to strike a proper balance between unity and autonomy of the local churches remains obscure today. Rahner is interested in how this balance is to be discovered afresh in the concrete. The decision to change will always, he insists, contain an element of power or compulsion. It is naive and dangerous to deny this. However, one must never use schism or the threat of schism to compel change. This would be a denial of our eschatological hope. The church can only be reformed from within.

Pluralism in theology: For many reasons we live today in a time of irreducible theological pluralism. No theological system or outlook can claim hegemony. Though dialogue is essential, assimilation or systematization are asymptotic goals. In this atmosphere one must trust that all these various theologies are in fact striving to be faithful to the same creed even if they express their faith in irreducibly alien terms. Each particular theology must refrain from over-hastily concluding that it can discern heretical or schismatic tendencies in another. This situation demands from the magisterium ever greater patience, prudence, and caution, along with a deeper commitment to dialogue.

The formation of groups within the church: The legitimate process of greater democratization in the church derives in great part from the formation of formal and informal groups from below. These groups do not need authorization from the hierarchy. They can legitimately spearhead change which makes sense locally without regard to the effect these changes would have if universalized in the church. Such groups have always existed (e.g., religious orders, secular institutes). They are indispensable and should not be suspected of heresy simply because they stand apart in some ways from the *corpus ecclesiae*. Their justification springs from their origin in and through the charismatic element of the church. The church today must accustom itself to the presence of such grassroots groups, bearing in mind that although they are not a priori schismatic, they can separate themselves from the church by the programs they champion or the tactics they employ. **Incomplete identification:** Rahner returns to another face of schism stemming from the fact that many Catholics today identify themselves only partially with their church (examples, 113). He admits that harboring such reservations about church dogma can constitute an interior state of schism even if this never becomes public knowledge. But he warns that these reservations which seem to be heretical very often do not entail any subjective guilt. There have always been such situations in the church. Assuming good will and a low public profile on the part of those incompletely identified with the church, there is no reason to think they are not good Christians or to trouble their consciences over the issue. All the more so if this incomplete identification is the result of a failure to have achieved a positive harmony among the many various propositions of the faith. Finally, not every dissenting opinion or individual act of disobedience to the official church is ipso facto schism or heresy. In fact such acts can perform the positive function of helping the Spirit usher the church into a new future.

The schismatic or heretical status of these many situations can never be decided by appeal to formal rules alone. In the concrete such circumstances must be solved by practical reason which includes patience and modesty on all sides, efforts to overcome intolerance, humility and charity, faith and hope. Rahner is not surprised to find such conflict in the church since its nature derives from the Spirit which uses many human means without ever identifying completely with any one of them. In such situations one does better by examining oneself to see how much self-will might be involved in one's own position rather than by trying to play God and judge the positions of others.

12.07   Heresies in the Church Today?

Häresien in der Kirche heute?

{2.0}   December 1967 lecture at Essen on the theme: theological academy.
Abstract: Heresy is possible today and must be condemned publicly. Understanding the legitimate ways to distinguish one's own beliefs from official church teaching can assuage the felt need for heretical separation.
Topics: HERESY; MAGISTERIUM.
Subsidiary Discussions: Pluralism (120f); Authority (122f); Truths, hierarchy of (123); Theology, disputed questions (124f); Theology, dissent (124ff); Theology, pluralism in (128ff); Creed (131f); Preaching (138ff); Faith (140f).

Precis: I: In the post-conciliar situation people are asking whether doctrines are emerging unchallenged today, or are even being put forward within the church itself, which measured against traditional teaching would have to be rejected as heresies. Rahner hopes to probe the phenomenon of people holding dissenting positions yet staying in the church. What factors today contribute to this new situation?

Vatican II is not the cause but the catalyst through which already existing heresies surfaced into the church's public life. The real cause is the complex new intellectual and social situation which Vatican II boldly sought to address. This new, radically pluralistic situation forces the church to interpret and express itself afresh. People today are in a strange state of transition: wanting simultaneously to exercise their own authority independent from the group while still wanting to belong to the group, and all the while being skeptical about the value of their own philosophy of life and hoping to be able to harmonize their own sense of truth with the convictions held by the believing community. This situation is further complicated by the existence in the church of a hierarchy of truths, legitimate disputes over matters of theology, and the public recognition that the church can and has erred in its non-definitive teachings.

II. Rules for a right understanding and a right attitude toward the existence of what seems like heresy in the church.

1) *"There is both an illegitimate and a legitimate way of distinguishing between the individual and collective conviction of faith."* The illegitimate form is heresy strictly speaking which occurs in the heart even if one does not publicly distance oneself from the church (although one cannot judge whether it carries with it a subjective state of guilt). The legitimate form consists first and foremost in the fact that one need not personally be in possession of all the truths of the faith in perfect clarity and harmony. One can and must concentrate on the truly central elements of the faith. With regard to the less central truths it is enough if one leaves them more or less to the side without denying them (127). Such an attitude avoids many difficulties. Attempting to attain personal appropriation of every church teaching can lead to frustration and ultimately to formal heresy. One sees this dynamic in many areas of modern life.

2) *"The justifiable pluralism arising from the theological freedom within the Catholic Church must freely be accepted as a given fact."* This situation makes it impossible clearly to distinguish between the body of doctrine held in common and various theologies that interpret it and hence make it difficult to be genuinely obedient to the magisterium. What is true of technical theology is also true at the level of the individual believer. Summary (131).

3) *"This inevitable pluralism in theologies...must not and need not surrender the unity of the Church's creed even at the verbal level."* Since such unity based on verbal agreement can be established in sufficient measure it is inevitable

and legitimate to insist on a linguistic norm from which there can be unjustified deviations which must publicly be labeled as heresy.

4) *"There is a possibility—indeed under certain circumstances a necessity and a duty—for the Church to reject a doctrine arising within her as heretical."* This does not, however, settle the question of subjective, culpable error. When it is a matter of rejecting a defined dogma, dissenters must either change their positions or separate from the church. When it is a matter of rejecting a non-defined dogma, the "censured" individual must discern how to resolve the call of conscience and obedience to the magisterium. Many options are available short of separation from the church. After a long quote from the German bishops on this matter (134f) Rahner returns to the fact that the church must at times invoke anathema against both those who separate themselves from the church as well as those who would stay within it. Rahner recognizes that such condemnations will seldom be fully effective (137) because they may simply induce those who hold false opinions to keep a low profile within the church, and because often the only way to combat such errors is to reformulate the official teaching in a way that can be fully assimilated more easily. Paradoxically the best way to safeguard an irreformable dogma is continually to reformulate it in more convincing terms.

5) *"Throughout this discussion a distinction must be drawn between the pulpit and the classroom; the essential differences between preaching the faith and theological speculation."* There is plenty to preach about without risking embroiling the faithful in potentially disturbing or even scandalous theological controversies in the public forum.

III. In these days of immense spiritual upheaval the existence of heresy should not surprise anyone. But it is wrong to conclude the church's teaching has become ambiguous, obscure, or untrustworthy. After listing a number of unchangeable Christian beliefs Rahner goes on to say faith is never simply a fixed sum of statements formalized once and for all. Faith centers on the realities to which these statements point and not simply on the formulations which are always open to the future, and hence to reformulation.

12.08   Concerning our Assent to the Church as she Exists in the Concrete

Über das Ja zur konkreten Kirche

{2.5}   October 1968 lecture at Frankfurt on the theme: theological academy.

Abstract: Assent to the church in the concrete is a burden. It is, however, more intellectually honest to assent to the institution and its authority than to maintain a skeptical distance. With assent comes the right to be critical.
Topics: CHURCH, visible; CHRISTIAN LIFE, intellectual honesty; FAITH, assent of.
Subsidiary Discussions: Church, authority in (143f, 154ff); Truth (155ff).

Precis: This essay focuses on Catholics' assent to the church not in the abstract but as it exists in its historical and seemingly contingent concreteness, even though this can be expressed only at an abstract level. Throughout the essay Rahner is applying J. H. Newman's notion of assent.

I. Honest Catholics must admit that belief in the concrete church does not come easily for many reasons: it imposes and exacts duties and a concrete way of life upon us through concrete individuals who are not always exemplary. We cannot pick and choose among its teachings even though they are legion and hardly present the aspect of a harmonious synthesis. Many can appear exotic, impractical and old-fashioned. Its teachers seem out of touch insisting certain issues which seem irrelevant are crucial, and ignoring issues which seem critical. Summary (145).

II. How can Catholics give wholehearted assent to such a concrete institution? Rahner first mentions that many of these same factors are burdens in other areas of human life. He also points to the fact that throughout modern culture there is a tension between ever greater social organization and ever increasing individualization. This makes patience, prudence, and the courage to endure all these burdens ever more necessary. Rahner offers three distinct aspects of reality which he feels serve as starting-points for the possibility of a hopeful and committed assent to the church in the concrete:

a) *"Human living in the concrete is not artificially developed by a process of speculation as though in a test tube."* Here Rahner argues against Descartes' method of skeptical reduction. We can never begin from zero. To withhold action until we achieve complete clarity would result in absolute immobility. "And for this reason anyone engaged in genuine living freely accepts, by an ultimate act of trust in life itself, the impossibility of totally comprehending life in his own speculative processes" (147f). Life is never mastered. It is bestowed as an incomprehensible reality called grace. Insofar as assent to the concrete church permeates our entire lives, the grounds for this assent can be held with intellectual honesty even if they cannot be completely sorted out by critical reason beforehand. Catholics commit themselves to the concrete church in a spirit of trust. When it comes to assent we must not allow ourselves to be swallowed up in the morass of universal doubt. Summary (150).

b) *"Global decisions of life, which affect the totality of our human lives and which are therefore incapable of ever being totally subsumed under our critical speculations, should endure throughout those unresolved tensions which arise between the decisions themselves and our critical reflections upon them."* We cannot be expected to solve all the complexities of life. Once we have honestly done all we can to resolve them we must endure them in a spirit of confidence and patience.

c) *"It is only in the act of striving for that which is greater, more enlightened, a greater force for life, that man has the right to relinquish something that belongs to his life, to surrender it. And it is only for the sake of greater meaningfulness that he has the right to abandon that which has hitherto been meaningful to him as meaningless.* "This makes assent to the church intellectually honest despite all its temptations and difficulties. Separation from the church leads one into either the lethal darkness of skepticism or into a life of impoverished isolation.

III. Since the church is the most complex, manifold, variegated human entity extending into all levels of personal existence and society, it is no wonder it is so difficult to comes to terms with it.

a) The church once again becomes a simple and self-evident fact for us when we see it as one of those ultimate realities of life towards which we can adopt a critical attitude only if we commit ourselves to it immediately and without reservation. Rahner compares it to a love relationship or a relationship with parents whom we know well enough to love and trust without knowing all there is about them. Thus our relationship includes reservations. To abandon the church in its concreteness leaves us with an abstract God, the mere projection of our own subjectivity.

b) Many Catholics today find their assent to the legitimate, concrete teaching office of the church entails a heavy burden. From among the many questions this topic raises Rahner concentrates on the proposition that the truth which sustains and illuminates human existence as a whole is inherently connected with concrete institutions. Rahner is amazed at the level of naive self-opinionatedness and emotional aggressiveness directed toward the church today. He suggest those critics might be more critical towards their own opinions especially when it comes to church teaching. Only by submitting to legitimate authority can one transcend the capriciousness of subjectivity. The truth of salvation in particular demands such an Archimedean point outside ourselves which only authority can provide.

c) Even allowing what has been said, assent to the church always remains a fearful burden (list, 158f), one to which individual Catholics often contribute by the incomplete ways we live our faith. But all that we find burdensome due to its concreteness has the one single significance of passing on the one faith (summary, 159). We endure the church in faith, hope, and love as we journey together to God, our true future. We are critical of the church in its concreteness precisely because we assent to it with constantly renewing hope.

12.09   Anonymous Christianity and the Missionary Task of the Church

Anonymes Christentum und Missionsauftrag der Kirche

{1.5}   Previously unpublished.

Abstract: The presence of justifying grace in those outside explicit Christianity does not render the universal missionary task of the church superfluous. Grace always seeks to express itself in its richest concrete incarnation.

Topics: ANONYMOUS CHRISTIAN; MISSION, theology of; SACRAMENTS, grace of.

Subsidiary Discussions: Theological terms (164f); Grace, justifying (168ff); Supernatural existential (169ff); Baptism (171ff); Penance (173f); Word and grace (174).

Precis: This essay attempts to reconcile anonymous Christianity with the universal missionary task of the church. Rahner first examines two questions concerning anonymous Christianity: 1) the adequateness and appropriateness of the term; 2) the objective reality described by the term. On the first point he insists one must either accept the two terms together or reject them both. "Anonymous" modifies Christianity in the sense of showing that the inherent tendency of human nature to find God is fully realized only in Christianity, whether or not one is explicitly aware of this fact. Whenever adjectives are introduced an element of ambiguity arises. But the reality not the terminology is paramount. On the second point Rahner admits the definition of anonymous Christianity (165) leaves open the question of exactly who it applies to and whether they are culpable for remaining anonymously Christian. He closes with a brief history of the development of the concept (166f). About the missionary task of the church Rahner is content to say it is universal (i.e., fundamentally directed to all people), leaving aside the question of precisely who has this missionary obligation and to what degree.

Rahner now turns to his true theme: "whether these two realities can exist in unison or whether the one removes the other" (168). He answers this question by pointing to the fact that all missionary work presupposes a kind of anonymous Christianity in those to whom it is directed: the grace of faith (at least at the level of an offer) that can hear and respond to the word preached to it. The word becomes actual, effective, and demanding "precisely in virtue of the fact that it has been present all along and belongs to the enduring existential modalities of man" (170). Hence, the missionary task of the church can exist together with anonymous Christianity.

Rahner next attempts to show that even though anonymous Christianity precedes explicit Christianity logically and temporally it does not thereby render Christianity superfluous. He bases his argument on the reality seen when pre-sacramental grace presses forward towards a sacramental incarnation of itself. He shows how this is the dynamism in adult baptism (173ff) and is most clearly seen in penance (173). He concludes his argument with an analysis of the relationship between grace and the word. Summary (174). All this points to the need for a fresh interpretation of the theology of mission. Former missionary efforts were aimed at individuals out of fear that without embracing explicit Christianity they would be lost. Pre-moderns could not appreciate the vast numbers of non-Christians or the tremendous length of non-Christian history which if taken serious call into question the effectiveness of God's salvific will as extended to all people. Today's deeper view of mission allows that salvation is possible even for those who do not embrace explicit Christianity. It concerns itself not simply with proselytizing individuals, but with transforming cultures and civilizations. For Christ did not come to rescue a chosen few from the world, but to transform the earthly dimension of the world in his image. Far from demeaning outreach to individuals this new theology of mission which clarifies a person's metaphysical status actually improves the situation for an individual to attain salvation. Love always strives for what is greater. Because we believe anonymous Christians will find the fulfillment of their true nature in explicit Christianity, our love of neighbor will always fuel the church's missionary task.

12.10   The Question of the Future
Die Frage nach der Zukunft
{2.5}   June 1969 lecture to KHG Cologne. H. Peukert, ed., *Diskussion zur "Politischen Theologie"* (Mainz, 1969) 247-266.

Abstract: Rahner distinguishes two mutually conditioning futures: the absolute future and a this worldly future. While working critically to improve this world, hope in the absolute future keeps us from absolutizing finite utopias.
Topics: FUTURE.
Subsidiary Discussions: Eschatology (182ff); God as absolute future (184ff, 188f); Logos, incarnation of (189f); Freedom (194ff); Freedom and determinism (196f); Utopias (198f); Future, *docta ignorantia* (181, 198ff).
Precis: About this world's concrete future theologians are not futurologists. What theologians essentially bring to a discussion of the future is their insistence on the radical unknowability of the absolute future.
I. By its very nature Christian theology is concerned with the future as a question, and not so much with the question of the content of the future. Far from being a peripheral study, eschatology constitutes for Rahner the whole of Christian theology or at least the formal structural principle for all theological statements (list, 182f). But because we have a greater capacity than ever before to choose and shape our future we are in a position today to distinguish two distinct futures: a "this worldly future" which we plan, and an absolute future which comes to meet us and fulfills our eschatological hopes. This essay considers the relationship between these two futures.

II. Rahner more clearly defines the two futures.

"The absolute future" is God himself. This future both allows and demands that we continually engage in a radical critique of the present and of our plans for the future. The absolute future is not one specific event within the world but as a transcendental it comprehends and determines the consummation of the whole. Although it is freely bestowed, the absolute future leaves room for human freedom and in an important way is brought about by our acceptance of it.

"The this-worldly future" comes about as an event within this world which is always open to further modification by other future events. As such it does not signify consummation. Some elements of this future are determined by past events and are only understood by tracing these events back to their sources. But there is also in this future an element which is genuinely and radically new. God is not so much the cause of this free element as the condition for its possibility. These two futures do not sit side by side but interpenetrate. They demand and dialectically condition one another. This allows us both to extend our past and present into the future and to transcend them.

III. *"First Thesis: The content of the Christian preaching consists in the question...into the absolute future and properly speaking in nothing else besides."* Rahner takes exception to the common perception that Christianity is a highly complex affair. He argues it is utterly simple: it is the question, maintained in openness, of God who is the absolute future. The meaning of the world and its history is found in God's free desire to communicate himself to us as absolute incomprehensible mystery. God bestows himself only in the mode of the radical question which shatters every idol offered as a finite answer. Christians await the coming of this future as eternal life or beatific vision. In short, Christianity is radical openness to the question of the mystery of the absolute future which is God. Rahner concludes by outlining how this truth comes to fullest expression in the incarnation of the Logos.

IV. *"Second Thesis: The 'this worldly' future of man always constitutes an open and, abidingly open, question."* Rahner begins with a fuller description of the "this worldly future." He insists Christian engagement with the absolute future in no way diminishes or eliminates their responsibility for a this worldly future. In fact the one gives radical depth and meaning to the other. It is because both futures are always unknown, unpredictable, and surprising that the this worldly future can be a medium for the absolute future. Granting that our plans and programs actually can influence the future, Rahner offers three reasons why a this worldly future is indeterminable: 1) on the physical level this world is too complex even at the level of cause and effect (192-194); 2) human freedom adds another layer of complexity insofar as when one free choice is realized other free choices cease to be possible (194-196); 3) even though after the fact it is possible to trace the root

of free decision in such a way that it can appear to have been a determined act, to deny human freedom is tantamount to denying personal history and hence, any real future. In short, human freedom makes a this worldly future unknowable (196-198).
V. *"Third Thesis: In the very nature of his function the theologian is the guardian of this docta ignorantia futuri."* When one has the right attitude to both a this worldly future and to the absolute future a third thing arises: a utopian future which constitutes a prior condition for every change and provides a standard by which to criticize the present and to impel it forward to a new historical future (summary, 200). Theologians, who guard the *docta ignorantia futuri* as not merely provisional but as necessary and irremovable, keep alive the true hope for the future and preserve the meaningfulness of human freedom. Though Christians may disagree on which specific plans to enact they are united on the need to shape the this worldly future and to remain open to God as the absolute future. They have no stake either in upholding the status quo for its own sake or in uncritically introducing novelty.

12.11   Perspectives for the Future of the Church
Perspectiven für die Zukunft der Kirche
{1.0}   October 1967 lecture at Bochum to the Protestant *Michaelsbruderschaft.*
Abstract: Rahner imagines the implications of four tendencies he associates with the church of the future: its smaller size, its renewed sociological structures, its reformulated theology, its relations with separated churches.
Topics: CHURCH of the future.
Subsidiary Discussions: Church and society (204f); Heresy (205, 215f); Church, authority in (207); Priesthood of the future (209f); Demythology (210f); Creed (211f); Theology of the future (212f); Ecumenism (213ff); Theology, pluralism in (215f).
Precis: Rahner prefaces his few brief ideas about possible future changes with a proviso setting out certain basic unchanging elements of the church.

1) The church of the future is destined to be a "little flock" both religiously and on the empirical level of social living. As such it will struggle to retain its missionary thrust and not become a sect or ghetto. The days of a broad, homogeneous "Christian society" are over and could only be restored though a totalitarianism the church must reject. In the future the church will live as one element among others in a pluralistic world. In the concrete this means the church must freely give up every vestige of power in society. It must not be afraid to denounce heresies within itself even through excommunication. The sphere of freedom of conscience and the sphere of the church are not identical. This smaller church will have to overcome feelings of inferiority and the temptation to overcompensate by considering itself an elect remnant. It will do this by recalling it is the recipient of a graced vocation, even though the grace of justification extends to those outside the fold.

2) The Christian community of the future will have a quite different sociological structure. Since little in its social structure is mandated by its essence, this presents no problem for Rahner who outlines three implications: a) The future church will be a church of brethren, freely united in their faith and love of Christ. Authority in them will not be earthly honor but a ministry flowing from the recognition of one's free faith, willingness to obey, and brotherly love. b) In an age when society no longer serves as a source of integration the churches will have to develop other means of social unity in addition to reliance on one creed and one liturgy. But it must not attempt to develop such bonds at the expense of isolating itself from its neighbors and the culture around it. c) These communities may develop a new kind of internal leadership, identifying and ordaining to priestly service trusted elders in the community regardless of their formal theological training. This may call for the reevaluation of priestly celibacy.

3) To insure the true gospel continues to be proclaimed it will have to be preached in new and more accessible forms. a) Rahner sees as one such option a "demythologized theology properly understood." b) He also suggests the development of new brief statements of the faith for our modern age serving much the same role the Apostles Creed played in its culture. c) In an age when people are no longer even sure what they mean by the word "God" Rahner suggests a radical redesign of theology with different starting-points and new points of arrival. d) Theology which speaks to modern people about the most basic Christian truths will also be the most ecumenical theology.

4) Rahner concludes with a few ideas about the future attitudes of separated churches towards one another. a) All the churches of the future will live a diaspora situation. Some will be lucky to escape all-out persecution. In this situation what they share in common will become more apparent. In spite of doctrinal differences they will work closely together on social issues of common concern. But they will have to be careful not to paper over their real remaining differences nor build union on insufficient footings. b) All the churches will experience an increasing degree of theological pluralism within themselves. This may lead to new cross-confessional understandings. Insofar as some of these new theologies tolerated in one's own church might prove to be heretical, believers might reassess the real doctrinal differences between themselves and those churches from which they were formerly estranged.

In an age when all religions of the world mutually condition one another Rahner sees Christianity playing a leading role in inter-religious dialogue because, "it is the most comprehensive religion, the one that allows for the most variations and is least of all attached to a specific cultural milieu" (217). Whatever the future of religion, it is not a set product of blind fate. It is wrought from the solitary decisions of the heart. This future is not one we merely suffer. It is one we create with faith and hope in the promise of God who is the absolute future.

12.12   Of the Structure of the People in the Church Today
Zur Struktur des Kirchenvolkes heute
{0.5}   Previously unpublished, 1970.

Abstract: Embracing the human element of the church highlights the need to: celebrate its charismatic side; accommodate individuality; re-evaluate the place of non-practicing Catholics; discover new means of sustaining *communio*.
Topics: LAITY; CHURCH, visible.
Subsidiary Discussions: Church, nature of (218ff); Church, charismatic element in (220ff); Saints (221); Orders, sacrament of (221f); Individualism (222f); Church of sinners (223ff); Community building (227f).
Precis: The church is not an idea. It is essentially a concrete, social entity, a visible church, the people of God, an institution in the world with a particular history and all that entails. It is and always will be an irreducibly human institution. Yet the church is always tempted to imagine itself in abstract, theoretical categories, in terms of what it should be. In spite of this truth little attention has yet been paid to the sociological structure of the laity whom Rahner calls the "people of the church."

1) The church does more than mediate salvation. As the visible community of those who genuinely believe, hope, and love, it is the historical manifestation of the event of salvation as effectively achieved and victoriously imposing itself. Hence the church must continually find ways to manifest and celebrate the charisms of its members, living and dead. To a large extent this is the role of religious orders and other charismatic movements led "from below." Since the church is increasingly composed of those who freely embrace it rather than those who belong to it for historical or social reasons, it is increasingly individualistic. This is not to be regretted because it signals the true flowering of faith. The church must maintain sufficient scope within itself to accommodate these individuals and the protesting sects which inevitably flourish in this more individualistic time.

2) Rahner is dissatisfied with over-simple divisions within the church between nominal members (*in corpore*) and zealous members (*in corde*). The theological and sociological reality is much more complex. He treats in particular non-practicing or borderline Catholics who he insists are real members of the church. No one's faith can be judged by such external things as Mass attendance or by how well they seem to fulfill the laws of the church. To this he adds the complex problem of degrees of individual commitment to the faith of the church. He concludes with a call for the official church to be more tolerant of "non-conformist" groups within itself, humbly recalling that we are and will always be a church of sinners.

3) If one takes seriously the contemporary social situation marked as it is by increasing alienation and cultural disintegration, the sociological composition of the church would be very different. With the help of professional sociologists the church must constantly be on the lookout to identify and support new social means to form and sustain human and religious community.

12.13   The Function of the Church as a Critic of Society

Die gesellschaftskritische Funktion der Kirche.

{1.0}   October 1968 lecture to Society for Socialist Studies, Westphalia.

Abstract: The church functions properly as a critic of society when in preaching the gospel it reveals the relative, transitory nature of this world's plans and projects without making them seem indifferent or inconsequential.

Topics: CHURCH as social critic.

Subsidiary Discussions: Church, visible (230f); Dogma (232); Creed, brief (232); Church and politics (233f); Power, coercive (234, 247ff); Scripture, Gospel (235f); Secularization (236f); Salvation (237f); Community (238); Future (237f); Love of God and neighbor (240f); Cross, theology of (241); Instruction, prophetic (243ff); Laity (245f); Society, revolution (246f).

Precis: I. A critique of the church is implicitly involved in the church's understanding of her own nature. Self-criticism is a necessary prior condition which enables the church to criticize society. As an essentially social entity the church is subject to all the dangers of any human institution (list, 231). Hence, the church must always be an *ecclesia semper reformanda*. To this Rahner adds that only a church with a clear, unambiguous creed and dogma can be subjected to sociological or political criticism since only from such a starting-point can the institution be shown its internal inconsistencies. But merely because the church is legitimately criticized in the name of the church does not mean all genuine struggle or conflict is eliminated.

II. The self-critical church as an authoritative critic of society. Why can the church assume the role of social critic based on its understanding of its proper nature?

1) The distinction between criticism of society on the church's part and political action: Social criticism must be distinguished from active political engagement. Although the church and its members have a right to participate in politics like any other legitimate group, it can never use power to manipulate society. Rahner defines the church's function as social critic as, "opening up ever anew a perspective which transcends the concrete social reality such that within this perspective the social reality concerned appears in its relative value, and so as capable of alteration" (235). This is true even though the church neither can nor should supply any absolute political alternatives.

2) The origins of the perspective provided by the church as critic of society as found in the gospel itself: Why and how does the gospel provide the critical perspective the church needs to criticize society? Secularization, which is legitimately rooted in Christianity, is the primary condition which allows the church to criticize society (236f). The salvation mediated by the church is not purely individualistic. It is addressed to humanity and to the individual precisely as a member of society. There is no sacral sphere. Salvation is achieved precisely in the sphere of human existence in general to

which believers commit themselves (237f). In addition, the fact that the infinite God is the absolute future of the world relativizes all human plans and goals without thereby making them insignificant or indifferent. For only through them can faith and hope in God's absolute future be asserted (239f). Gospel teaching which identifies love of God and love of neighbor implies an attitude of protest and criticism of society (240f). Finally, the gospel is always a gospel of the cross. Neither the fate of Jesus nor the fate of any individual is without its social dimensions insofar as how our fate is accepted has a transforming effect on the world (241).

3) The upholders of the function of criticizing society in the church: Who upholds this function in the church? Rahner admits that although no complete theology of social criticism has yet been thought out no one should simply assume it is the function of the hierarchy, especially since social criticism cannot wholly be subsumed into any of its three offices: teaching, priestly, or pastoral. Notwithstanding, Rahner points to an emerging *topos* for this kind of social criticism employed in Vatican II's *Gaudium et spes* which he calls "prophetic instruction" (243f). So far these kinds of pronouncements of the official church have been echoes of criticism voiced by charismatic movements from below. Rahner employs a long quote from *Gaudium et spes* to argue the legitimate role of the laity to develop such criticisms and initiatives whether or not they are commissioned or even encouraged by the official church. The laity can legitimately appeal directly to the authority of the gospel rather than to any authority granted by the official church.

III. The problems entailed in a theology of revolution. The abstract and ambiguous nature of the terms "revolution" and "power" make it impossible to distinguish revolution from evolution, or a just from a bloody application of power. These distinctions belong to the realm of practical rather than theoretical reason. Thus, although Rahner maintains it is impossible for Christians completely to eschew the use of force to affect social change based on the Beatitudes, it is equally impossible to draw clear dividing lines between just and unjust institutions and our proper response to them.

Rahner concludes by asking whether the church today is adequately fulfilling its role as social critic. Not surprisingly he finds as a whole the church is not doing so, since usually it only reacts when its own interests are threatened. But Rahner warns that in posing this question and answering it in the negative one is accusing oneself, for it is inescapably true that we are the church.

XIII. THEOLOGY, ANTHROPOLOGY, CHRISTOLOGY
X. *Im Gesprach mit der Zukunft*

German edition: Einsiedeln, Benziger, 1972
U.S. edition: N.Y., Seabury, 1975
David Bourke, translator

This volume in the English edition comprises the first 15 essays in *Schriften zur Theologie*, X.

13.01 On Recognizing the Importance of Thomas Aquinas
Berkenntnis zu Thomas von Aquin

{0.5} Previously unpublished December 1970 lecture on Bavarian Radio.

Abstract: Contemporary Catholic theologians should not forget Thomas Aquinas because as one of the initiators of the anthropocentric approach he stands at the threshold of modern thought.
Topics: AQUINAS, importance of; THEOLOGY, history of.

Subsidiary Discussions: Mysticism (8f); Thomism (9f); Philosophy (10f).
Precis: Rahner begins his argument for the perennial value of Aquinas with the proviso that although he retains the function of a Father of the Church, in this new age of theological pluralism he can no longer be thought of as providing *the* textbook for theology. His importance lies in that fact that he is one of the initiators of the anthropocentric approach. In philosophy and theology fashions come and go. But for these speculative disciplines to stay alive, more than for the natural sciences, they must retain contact with the ideas and thinkers of the past. "Again and again we must think with a thinker if we are to achieve a genuine and a radical insight into his ideas" (6).

What makes Aquinas great, unique, and deserving of special study is the tremendous breadth of his work and the gentle magnitude of his spirit (7f) along with his mysticism (8f). Rahner cautions against identifying Aquinas with the various streams of "Thomism" which developed after him. He insists that intellectually this age is not far removed from Thomas for in turning to the subject his philosophy parts company with Greek philosophy oriented as it is towards objects and an objective world. Although he must be seen as first and foremost a theologian, Aquinas championed philosophy as an autonomous discipline. This places him at "the origins of that reflexive process in theology in which Christian faith explicitly recognizes the status of the world as autonomous and responsible for its own destiny" (11). He underscores the truth that however much it may be misrepresented, what is special to our age (e.g., secularization, individualism, pluralism) derives from the spirit of Christianity. Rahner closes with a call for theologians to study Aquinas even at the risk of being "unmodern" for such study helps the church remain free and immune from the cult of the new.

13.02   Thomas Aquinas on Truth

Die Wahrheit bei Thomas von Aquin
{4.0}   Previously unpublished January 1938 lecture. Revised.
Abstract: A brief but thorough overview of Aquinas' philosophy of truth according to the school of transcendental Thomism à la Maréchal, et al.
Topics: AQUINAS on truth; TRUTH.
Subsidiary Discussions: Judgement, philosophical (16ff); Knowledge, sense (18ff); Ontologism (22f); God as the unity of pure being and knowing (29).
Precis: This study presents two immediate problems: 1) because Aquinas is primarily a theologian his treatment of truth is seldom his main concern; 2) since Aquinas' original line of reasoning must be reconstructed from other more theological treatises it calls for an interpretation. Rahner is satisfied if his interpretation is internally consistent. He is not concerned whether in all particulars it agrees with later schools of Thomism. Rahner develops his ideas in three stages.

1) **The judgement.** Truth at the human level is located in the judgement (the content not the act) and not in the formation or synthesis of concepts. "The reason that our judgement is valid is that the concretizing synthesis is merely the reproduction in the conceptual dimension of that synthesis achieved in the objective one between a subject ... and quiddity ... by which that subject is specified" (17f). But how does the judging subject know a reproduction and application of the objective synthesis is actually valid and does in fact correspond? Rahner investigates the relationship between the sensible and intellectual elements contained in any judgement. He concludes sense knowledge can never be true or false in a proper sense. As a genuine reality it supplies the basis for the truth of the material content of particular judgements.

2) **The light of the active understanding.** Because a judgement constitutes something more than the mere passive reception of the impression of a particular sensible object as such, what is the truth of a judgement based upon? Rahner locates Aquinas in a camp with Aristotle, Kant, and Hegel in insisting that truth consists in a light of the understanding rather than in some *fundamentum* of truth viewed as an object. Three lines of transcendental argument lead to the conclusion that any act of judgement always involves a simultaneous awareness of the self as "over against" the known object (21).

The assurance of truth is derived by a reduction from certain self-evident ontological rather than purely logical first principles. Rahner next explores the basis of the self-evidence of these first principles. It cannot be found in some pre-existing Platonic idea (ontologism) or in their objective conceptual content (Anselm's ontological proof). They cannot be gained by some process of induction since processes based on sense perception never lead to universal conceptions in a metaphysical sense. "It follows that it can only be a formal a priori principle of the spontaneous intellect itself. Aquinas calls this the *lumen intellectus agentis*" (24). This light is a hunger for being itself which, when it encounters an object presented by sense experience judges it to be finite. This transcendental openness to being itself is the condition for the possibility of abstraction and so the condition of expressing a judgement.

Aquinas disagrees with Kant over the extent and range of this transcendence. He insists the powers of the intellect extend beyond the senses and open onto the knowledge of being itself. Without actually supplying transcendental proof Rahner suggests what such an argument looks like (25f). Rahner next revisits the self-evidentness of his first principles which he argues is metaphysical, i.e., their validity is based on the a priori structures of being itself and confirmed by the principle of non-contradiction. The summary and conclusion to this section are meant to refute a charge that Aquinas' notion of truth is based on naive assumptions (27f).

3) **Pure being and pure thought.** Rahner addresses the heart and center of the metaphysical concept of truth: the ultimate unity of being and knowledge. On this unity hangs the validity of the formal a priori of the

intellect as wholly reasonable and intelligible. In Aquinas' view knowledge is not essentially confrontation with the knowledge of the other but a coming together of knower and known, a return to the self in the act of knowledge. In the act of knowing we possess ourselves as that which does not know everything and is not everything. The more the act of knowing reveals being itself the more it confronts us with our finite self. Rahner concludes with a recapitulation (30f).

13.03   Possible Courses for the Theology of the Future
Über künftige Wege der Theologie
{1.0}   H. Vorgrimler, R. van der Gucht, eds., *"Ausblick,"* *Bilanz der Theologie in 20. Jahrhundert, III* (Freiburg 1970) 530-551.

Abstract: Conjectures on what elements will shape theology in the year 2000.

Topics: THEOLOGY, future of.

Subsidiary Discussions: Pluralism (36ff); Mystagogy (41f); Preaching (42ff); Dogma, development of (48f); Scripture. exegesis (49ff); Ecumenism (51ff); Theology, pluralism in (52f); Theology, political (56ff).

Precis: A. General traits in a theology of the future. Although Christianity insists the future is unknowable because it is always open to the influence of God, some planning is possible and desirable not to dominate or control theological speculation, but to make eternal truths credible to new generations. The four general and formal characteristics of future theology are:

1. Pluralism in theology. As it comes to terms with the church's role as world church, theology will be forced to recognize and value the tremendous unsynthesizable diversity in the world. Each culture will develop its own irreducible theology from its particular starting place with its own vocabulary.

2. Missionary and mystagogic theology: Future theology will be missionary insofar as it will address not co-religionists but the uncatechized world in terms it can understand. It will be more mystagogical in displaying how every theological truth has a reference to the self-communication of God in every person.

3. "Demythologizing" theology: Theology will have to be expressed in newer terms than those developed in the first five centuries of Christendom without losing the truths contained in scripture and the ancient formulas. The mystery inherent in faith can never be invoked to cover up flabby thinking.

4. Transcendental theology: Future theology will be more transcendental not by limiting itself to anthropology, but by beginning and ending every inquiry asking how it pertains to the human subject's transcendental nature.

B. Points of emphasis in a theology of the future. Historical and biblical theology are in crisis. Both will endure but in very different forms.

1. The history of dogma: History of theology must broaden to embrace the history of dogma, but not like a prospector looking for hidden nuggets. The historian proceeds deductively, trying to ascertain the meaning and limitation of original dogmatic formulations free from the context of later development.
2. Exegesis: Exegetes have the right to use every modern critical method to point out boldly the extent to which any dogma has biblical underpinnings.
3. Ecumenical theology: Future theology as it becomes more missionary, mystagogical, transcendental, and biblical, and as it addresses itself to a more pluralistic world will become in turn less divisively confessional. Will theologians then manufacture new distinctions or boldly move towards unity?
4. Political theology: Future theology, insofar as its sees the human person as social, will necessarily be more political. It will spread eschatological hope, critique social institutions, and combat totalitarianism.
Summary (59f). Theology will have a future so long as theologians study it out of love for others and in service to God who first set them on that path in hope.

13.04 On the Current Relationship between Philosophy and Theology

Zum heutigen Verhältnis von Philosophie und Theologie
{2.0} November 1971 lecture at Munich for the opening of the *Hochschule für Philosophie/Menschen. Theologie und Philosophie* 47 (1972) 1-15.
Abstract: The complexity of both philosophy and theology makes their enduring relationship difficult to define. However, their state of monogamy is over. Their future includes an open dialogue with the social and natural sciences.
Topics: THEOLOGY and philosophy; PHILOSOPHY and theology.
Subsidiary Discussions: Supernatural existential (62ff, 67f); Revelation, universal (64f, 67f); Sin, hidden (65f); Vatican I (67f); Pluralism, gnoseological (68ff); Pluralism in philosophy (70ff); Science, social and natural (72ff); Metaphysics (75); Secularization (77); Dialogue (78).
Precis: I. The universality of theology. After briefly describing theology Rahner points out that not all revelation is identical with Old and New Testament revelation. In keeping with God's will that all be saved there is a universal revelation bestowed on all as a transcendental determination of human life prior to any preaching of the gospel [i.e., supernatural existential]. Hence, whether it is known reflectively or not, there is no such thing as pure philosophy. Rahner concludes "the primary and most radical history of philosophy is the history of Old and New Testament revelation" (63). Insofar as it becomes reflexively aware of this it can no longer be called

philosophy but theology. It is legitimate for philosophical thinking to abstract from this ultimate orientation to God, but it can never completely succeed without reference to this reality. "From this point of view philosophy is properly speaking a theology that has not yet arrived at the fullness of its own nature" (65). It is possible at times for philosophy to overtake theological reflection in delving into the truths associated with universal revelation. Since philosophy and theology are fundamentally incommensurable, theologians must exercise great caution in judging philosophy and confine themselves to laying bare any hidden sinfulness or grace in the work of philosophers.

II. The problems entailed by philosophy. Philosophy is as complex and obscure as theology. After a comment on the need for philosophy seriously to consider its own hidden sinfulness, Rahner moves to the "utterly astonishing" teaching of Vatican I that something "takes place in man which is significant for his salvation ... and yet which is, independently of Christianity or the Church, present inescapably and always" (67). If we call this knowledge philosophy, then Vatican I is saying that basically philosophy has a similar or even equally important significance as revelation. For all this, the unity of this universal revelation and particular revelation in the church finds its unity in God alone. There will always be a somewhat tense "gnosiological pluralism" between philosophy and theology due to the fact that neither can wholly reconcile or subsume the other.

a) Pluralism in philosophy. There are many philosophies. Insofar as theology is involved with them it divides into many theologies. After outlining the history of the development of pluralism in philosophy and its impact on the church Rahner chides the magisterium for failing to find ways to embrace this pluralism without the fear that it will destroy church unity.

b) Philosophy as it affects the specialist in modern scientific disciplines: Today philosophy no longer constitutes the sole meaningful discipline for integrating knowledge as such. To the speculative sciences must be added the natural and social sciences which are no longer subordinated to philosophy and actually have an important influence on theology today. If theology intends to deal with the person as a whole it will have to develop meaningful links with these other sciences.

III. Aspects of the future partnership between philosophy and theology. After affirming the inseparable but changing nature of the bond between theology and metaphysics Rahner insists that in the relationship between theology and philosophy "the state of monogamy is over" (74). What their new relationship could or should be is properly the question of philosophy. But insofar as thinking will always remain a part of theological reflection philosophy will always be a part of theology. Far from being a fall from grace, the new found autonomy of philosophy and the other sciences (secularization) is actually the legitimate fruit of Christianity itself. Only autonomy allows for real partnership among the sciences.

After recapitulating earlier points (77f) Rahner concludes with the vision of how in the future the dialogue among all the sciences will be so mutually co-conditioning that it will be increasingly impossible to draw precise distinctions among them. For everything human belongs to God—the ineffable and insuperable Mystery.

13.05   Theology as Engaged in an Interdisciplinary Dialogue with the Sciences

Die Theologie im interdisziplinären Gespräch der Wissenschaften
{2.0} September 1970 lecture at the Center for Interdisciplinary Research at the University of Bielefeld. J.B. Metz, Tr. Rendtorff, eds., *Die Theologie in der interdisziplinären Forschung* (Düsseldorf 1971) 27-34.

Abstract: Theology's unique contribution to interdisciplinary dialogue is not its special material content but its ability to insure the pluralism of the sciences by combating the totalitarian tendencies of the other disciplines.
Topics: THEOLOGY and interdisciplinary dialogue; DIALOGUE, interdisciplinary.
Subsidiary Discussions: Science, pluralism in (81f, 89f); Mystery (88f); Concupiscence, gnoseological (90f); Science, natural (91f); Science, social (93).

Precis: Whether theology has any part to play in dialogue with the sciences and what that role is depends on the meaning of interdisciplinary dialogue.
The problems entailed in an interdisciplinary dialogue. A careful look would seem to show interdisciplinary dialogue is actually impossible since either the various disciplines talk with one another to the degree they overlap, or one of the disciplines is not truly autonomous. It appears that professionals dialogue simply as people and not from within their disciplines. No science today would be willing to capitulate its autonomy to a third discipline (e.g., logic or metaphysics) for the sake of dialogue.
Interdisciplinary dialogue as a fact. But dialogue exists as a fact. Professionals do engage in it before knowing exactly what it is or what results it may yield. It always contains a degree of aggression, however well cloaked by conventional politeness. This tendency of each discipline to monopolize stems from the paradox that although every science is autonomous, each discipline secretly believes that if pursued far enough it and it alone holds the key to the unity of human knowledge. Hence, all the disciplines are bound in a love/hate relationship by this often unacknowledged and hidden adversarial stance.
The human factor and science. Precisely this "human factor" (formerly called metaphysical or transcendental) grounds all interdisciplinary dialogue.
The standpoint of Christian theology. Rahner makes clear he is working as a Christian theologian. (He leaves aside any division into Catholic or

Protestant, and the question of theology as a science and the legitimacy of other disciplines to exclude it from dialogue a priori). In any case, without regard to how it is viewed by the other disciplines, an autonomous theology is actually in a position to lead any interdisciplinary discussion, although not because of its distinct material contribution.

Theology and the human factor. From all this it might seem the role of theology in interdisciplinary dialogue is precisely to uphold the human factor, to defend mystery, to insist the other disciplines submit themselves to the most radical questioning. But not only could this be done by philosophy (as in the past), all professionals by dint of their humanity bear this responsibility.

The task for theology. The real task of theology in interdisciplinary dialogue is to conduct itself in such a modest and self-critical way that it upholds self-criticism on the part of the sciences. "It must persuade them to be modest in outlook, to be aware of their provisional nature and their limited perspective.... In this way theology will be the defender of any given science against any other" (89). Theology helps other sciences restrain their totalitarian tendencies to subsume and subordinate all other sciences to themselves. It is the defender of pluralism among the sciences.

A situation of "gnoseological concupiscence." Rahner calls this unique role for theology "the guardian and defender of gnoseological concupiscence." Older disciplines like theology learned the hard lessons of hubris and are less susceptible to the lure of hegemony. Younger disciplines present the big problem.

Possible factors deriving from dialogue with the intellectual disciplines, natural sciences, and social sciences, which may be of further assistance. Rahner concludes with brief observations on the special contribution theology can make to the history of ideas, natural sciences, social sciences.

13.06   On the Relationship between Theology and the Contemporary Sciences

Zum Verhältnis zwischen Theologie und heutigen Wissenschaften

{2.0}   Previously unpublished March 1971 lecture at Rome to *Pax Romana*.

Abstract: The basic and original distinction between theology and the sciences resides in their ability to address and express transcendentality: the absolute "once and for all" character of natural and social phenomenon.

Topics: THEOLOGY and science; SCIENCE and theology; STATEMENTS, theological; EXPERIENCE, transcendental.

Subsidiary Discussions: Concupiscence, gnoseological (95); God as mystery (97ff); Jesus Christ, death of (98f); Death of Jesus (99).

Precis: The unity of knowledge and the fact theology and science concern the human subject make the quest for common ground reasonable. Rahner leaves aside the relationship of theology and philosophy and "gnoseological concupiscence."

The contrast between theology and the sciences. Every science is a particular branch or category of knowledge which chooses particular phenomena to study and its method to study them. They are not concerned with such questions as scientist as subject, knower and knowledge, the original unity of reality. Theological statements, however, are concerned with the experience of human transcendence as such even prior to conscious reflection. "This transcendental experience is oriented toward that absolute Mystery ... which we call 'God'" (96).

The heart and center of theology. Christianity makes very few statements about God but they are dogmatically very important. Its statements differ from those of science in their quality and source. Their rational structure belies the fact they all point to the original, pre-thematic, transcendental experience. Only on this condition are they comprehensible. They point to the actual self-bestowal of absolute Mystery which makes it the innermost consummation of the movements of our being and a goal to be immediately possessed. In the historical person Jesus of Nazareth, and precisely in his death, this bestowal is made victorious and irreversible (98f). Every transcendental experience is also an historical one. This is the point at which social sciences and theology meet, although history, for example, is precisely incapable of addressing what is absolute in any experience and can only concern itself with the common dimension of "this-worldly realities."

Theology and the sciences in their relationship with one another. Rahner concludes with a few arbitrarily selected points on the relationship of theology and modern sciences. After distinguishing faith (transcendental experience) and theology (secondary reflection), Rahner locates the difference between science and theology in their concern with "this-worldly" vs. transcendental experience. This distinction does not, however, create an absolute disparity because transcendentality is impossible apart from concrete experience. Science and theology also find common ground insofar as the limits of science often serve as a first intimation of transcendence. This is also glimpsed when science's quest to extend the limits of rational explanation come into contact with the mystery of human freedom and the reality of an uncontrollable future. Science and theology, each in its own way, help orient us to Mystery, even though their absolute reconciliation is achieved in God alone.

13.07 Institution and Freedom
Institution und Freiheit

{1.0} November 1971 lecture to Institute of Education of the BASF/ Mannheim. *Die BASF* 20 (1970) E-1–E-8.

Abstract: Institutions which are products of human freedom inevitably trigger in us the desire to be free from them. Christians work to reform institutions while realizing that true freedom will only arrive with the kingdom of God.

Topics: FREEDOM and institutions; UTOPIAS; THEOLOGY, political.
Subsidiary Discussions: God and freedom (106f); Society, change in (113f).
Precis: Because today in the name of freedom a certain kind of atheism
rejects the idea of God as the author of institutions, the question of whether
freedom and institution are reconcilable is a properly theological question.
"Institution and freedom" as a question for the theologian. Freedom is a
central New Testament concept. Spiritual freedom can only be known in our
attempts to realize social freedom. Insofar as God is the author of those
structures in the universe that make the realization of human freedom
possible, God is at once the original source of both institutions and freedom.
Freedom as a slogan: a key factor in modern life. Freedom is a key issue in
modern life even though it is only quite imperfectly grasped. Although this
generation is perhaps more free than any other it continues to desire even
greater freedom with ever greater urgency. This is because we are increasingly
unwilling to accept our environment as fixed or unalterable. On this
showing freedom is "a condition in which it is possible to get rid of a situation
which is regarded as undesirable and capable of being abolished" (110), often
without sufficient regard to the value of what would replace it.
Reality and institution. The institutions Rahner is considering here are
those human institutions (laws, attitudes, taboos) which constrain human
freedom and are capable of being changed by it.
Compulsions and changes. It is easy to see how freedom can oppose
institution. Youth with no recollection of how things were before the current
institutions were created tend to be impatient with institutions. After a
"digression" on inter-generational conflict over fashion and novelty (113f)
Rahner insists it can be as materially and morally capricious and reprehen-
sible to obstruct institutional change as it can be to press for change for
change sake.
The ambivalence of creative freedom. The paradox of social institutions is
that these objectifications of human freedom over time become obstructions
and engender a call for freedom from the restrictions they are now seen to
embody. Rahner makes two points here: social institutions will always be
imperfect and ambivalent, allowing freedom to a greater or lesser degree;
social institutions can always be made better. To this theology adds that one
is only free from the diabolical "temptation to freedom from freedom itself
when he recognizes, and accepts in a spirit of hope, a dimension of freedom
which transcends this ambivalence inherent in the forms in which freedom
is objectified. We mean that dimension of freedom which is the kingdom of
God" (118).
The institution of freedom. Just as over time judicial systems arose to insure
freedom, in the future more such institutions should be formed with an eye
to insuring human freedom. After touching on the legitimacy of revolution
to force change and insure freedom Rahner concludes with a brief recapitulation.

13.08 Experience of Self and Experience of God
Sebsterfahrung und Gotteserfahrung
{3.0}   J. Tenzler, ed., *Urbild und Abglanz*. (Regensburg 1971) 201-208.

Abstract: The experience of self, God, and neighbor form a radical unity.

Topics: EXPERIENCE, transcendental; TRANSCENDENCE, experience of.

Subsidiary Discussions: Knowledge (123f); Love of God/neighbor (126ff); History, personal (129ff).

Precis: After a brief discussion of the ties between metaphysical anthropology and philosophical theology Rahner examines the following four questions:

I: What do the phrases "experience of self," "experience of God" mean? (123f). At issue here is not categorial knowledge of God or self, but the original unthematic experience which logically precedes and grounds any other specific knowledge. When the self experiences depth (i.e., its invitation to participate in incomprehensible mystery at the root of its being) it is experiencing God. This is true even if one wholly eschews all such categorial language.

II: What is the relationship between these two experiences? (124ff). Although experience of self and experience of God always remain distinguishable, they constitute a unity in their shared transcendentality. In every experience of God the subject is made present to itself. Without the experience of God the self cannot know itself and vice versa. Here Rahner summarizes philosophy's transcendental deduction of this insight (126).

III: How does this relationship make possible the unity of love of God and love of neighbor taught by Christianity? (126ff). "The only way in which man achieves self-realization is through encounters with his fellow man...who is not a thing or a matter, but a man" (127). Failing to encounter the Thou in others, one fails to encounter the I in oneself. Love of God, self, and neighbor "ultimately constitute a single reality with three aspects mutually conditioning one another" (128).

IV: What is the relationship between one's concrete, historical experience of the self and the ultimate transcendental experience of God? For many reasons an appeal to the faculty of memory is not enough to account for the experience of personal unity. But if personal identity is upheld by the history of the experience of God, then another problem arises. The real history of experience of God and the self cannot constitute a simple unity, for then the history of the self would be so overwhelmed by the history of God that subjective freedom would be impossible. Rahner insists that the history of freedom, which from one perspective seems to interrupt at least potentially the history of the experience of God, is itself part and parcel of the history of God since it is God present to the self which alone makes personal freedom possible.

13.09   Does Traditional Theology Represent Guilt as Innocuous as a Factor in Human Life?

Verharmlosung der Schuld in der traditionellen Theologie?
{3.0}   Previously unpublished.

Abstract: Even classical Christian descriptions of guilt/forgiveness if pushed to their radical limits portray guilt as an innocuous factor in human life. Rahner approaches guilt in a paradoxical but more existentially resonant way.
Topics: GUILT.
Subsidiary Discussions: Freedom, finite (137f); Hope (139f); Evil (140ff); Forgiveness (144ff); Death (147).
Precis: Today guilt is often portrayed as relatively innocuous. To those who are not Christian theists one must simply insist that without understanding what is meant by God they shall never be in a position freely to accept the notion of guilt (135). But even within Christianity guilt is often portrayed as innocuous, not simply by those influenced by the secular impulse to demythologize, but also by those who maintain the classical definition of guilt (definition, 136) and forgiveness. The bulk of this essay (136-149) describes five ways classical Christian definitions of guilt, when pushed to their logical, radical conclusions, make guilt seem innocuous.

Guilt presupposes finite human freedom—finite in its object (never being presented with completely good or completely evil choices) and in its ability ever to be definitive. Thus, all human choices would seem to be murky compromises and thus the guilt attached to them would seem innocuous.

Christians hope God's mercy will overcome guilt. The effect of this universal hope either diminishes the lively sense of hell, or reveals God as complicit in perdition by actively tolerating evil which God could stop.

Following Augustine's theory of evil as material privation one must either see guilt as innocuous or affirm that God is not responsible for human failings without ever being able to explain why this must be so.

The doctrine of God's power to forgive and remove evil (both provisional, particular faults and even seemingly radical exercises of freedom which cut one off from God and which seem to be unforgivable) make guilt innocuous.

The theory of evil as intellectual privation also fails. People choose lesser goods out of ignorance. But lived experience and the approach of death clarify the value of one's choices. Where choices are so refined guilt becomes innocuous, and where they cannot be refined due to unrelenting ignorance, guilt also seems innocuous.

Rahner's summary (148f) insists one must either embrace the arguments that guilt is innocuous, or admit something is wrong with traditional premises. None of them seems able to do justice to the Christian conception of the radical nature of evil and still preserves God's absolute goodness and omnipotence. Obviously, theology must move in a new direction. Based on existential experience it must insist on two facts: we fear for our salvation; we hope for our salvation. Though these constitute an unsynthesizable pluralism, all one-sidedness must be avoided. "In guilt a reality is present which can be understood only on the basis of living practice, in which man hopes for something more than that which his theoretic reason can tell him about" (150).

13.10 Theological Observations on the Concept of "Witness"

Theologische Bermerkungen zum Begriff "Zeugnis"
{3.5} Previously unpublished 1972.

Abstract: By revealing the essential dogmatic elements of "witness" Rahner highlights the ontological importance of Jesus' death and of the individual believer's surrender to death as the proper response to the witness of Jesus.

Topics: CHRISTIAN LIFE, witness; CHRISTIAN LIFE, martyrdom; JESUS CHRIST, death/resurrection of; SAINTS, martyrs.

Subsidiary Discussions: Theology and philosophy (154f); Mystery (155f); Transcendence (156ff); Jesus Christ (156f); Anonymous Christian (158f); Statements, theological (153, 161); Miracles (161f); Church (164); Eschatology (167f); Resurrection (165f); Spirit (166f); Donatism (168).

Precis: Rahner begins his dogmatic (non-exegetical) investigation of religious witness (bibliography, 152 ftn1) with a provisional description: imparting oneself to another by the intense use of one's freedom in such a way that a corresponding decision is evoked in the other. This assumes a number of things about freedom and the human subject (list, 153f). Rahner hopes an examination of the theological implications of this provisional description will reveal what belongs to it necessarily and absolutely. Rahner refutes criticism that his approach is too philosophical by pointing to the fact that grace is already active in the heart of philosophy.

The key point of this six-page paragraph (155-160) is to prove that what in the provisional description of witness appears to be purely a human self-impartation is actually always an attestation of the grace of God revealed in Jesus Christ, whether or not one is reflectively aware of it. "The witness is always a theological one" (157). The argument rests on the fact that human transcendentality is always directed to and upheld by Mystery (i.e., God) not as an ever-receding goal or mere possibility but as a hope fulfilled in the historical person of Jesus Christ (156). One can give transcendental witness in an "anonymous" sense, i.e., without being fully aware of all its underpinnings and implications at the level of conscious reflection (158). All this assumes that self-communication to another at this level is possible (158f). Rahner argues it is, but only because the love of God is the ground which affirms the uniqueness of the two unique individuals, unites them in providing their common basis, and sustains and guarantees the absolute character of their mutual self-communication and commitment (159).

Rahner's second point concerns the fact that witness necessarily has a content classifiable "in terms of this-worldly categories" (160). Since transcendental decisions are always and only communicated in categorial forms Rahner rules out the possibilities that this content is either a mere verbal statement or a miracle. Witness can only be "a blessed death," i.e., one which as it takes place leads to the absolute life of God (162, cf. 160 ftn7). Though its categorial nature makes this event apprehensible to us, it cannot insure its absoluteness. Not even the absolute quality of Jesus' death can be transcendentally deduced.

Witness is directed to one's fellows not in their private individuality (which would be love) but insofar as they exist socially and politically. Hence, witness has a political character. It is public proclamation (163). Insofar as it is rejected we call this political milieu "the world." Insofar as it is accepted it is called "the church" (164).

This blessed death of Jesus can "only be realized aright when he who bears the witness has in principle decided to accept his own death" 165). This is the real and effective link between witness and martyrdom. The truth which is attested to in the verbal witness of Christianity is precisely the truth of death as constituting salvation. At this point (165f) Rahner weaves the threads of New Testament exegesis into his dogmatic account: Luke's notion of eye-witnesses to the resurrection of Jesus (165f); John's notion of witness as an attestation to the Spirit (166f). He concludes with two points which link the historical event of Jesus to the eschatological hope of his "return." With a nod to Donatism, Rahner acknowledges that individual preachers who attest to the content of the witness may themselves lack the very self-surrender they proclaim. Their message, however, is guarantied by the "Holy Church." There are, he allows, derived and deficient forms of witness (168).

13.11   Ideas for a Theology of Death
Zu einer Theologie des Todes

{2.0} Previously unpublished November 1970 lecture at Regensburg to *Katholische Akademie*, Bayern.

Abstract: Connects death with hope for eternal life and with human freedom.

Topics: DEATH; ETERNAL LIFE; HOPE and death; FREEDOM and death.

Subsidiary Discussions: Language (173ff); Resurrection of body (175f).

Precis: Not even theologians speak of death and afterlife with the authority of experience. Often what theologians say is suspect because it is less empirical, more mythological, and intended to comfort. Here Rahner considers death and eternal life, religious topics surrounded by many unanswered questions. He takes personal responsibility for his statements realizing his starting-points and sources are chosen arbitrarily. He warns skeptics not to dismiss this discussion as the product of wish fulfillment. He warns believers not to approach this study uncritically, remembering how the Old Testament is mute on this important point. **Linguistic forms and reality.** Language always struggles with the distinction between signifier (word) and signified (reality). Although Christian language about death and "life beyond" employs mythological concepts this does not ipso facto invalidate the reality behind them. The language can be honed with time. **The end of the temporal dimension.** Two misinterpretations about "continuance of life after death" must be dismissed: 1) It does not mean more of the same in the spacio-temporal sense. Death is a radical end. 2) It is not a realm where further self-defining choices can be made. Does this make afterlife inconceivable? No, for the radical mystery, love, and freedom experienced in life provide sufficient content to imagine an eternal life which is not "the other side" as far as our personal history is concerned, but is rather the radical interiority of our personal freedom (174). This conceptual approach avoids all discussion of the body/soul dichotomy, and does not force one to posit a temporal interval between death and "resurrection of the flesh."

The hope of eternal life. Christian hope for eternal life is "the most radical exercise of the human spirit when subject to the bitterest pain" (176). Theological hope is not for some difficult outcome or obscure thing. It is hope against hope, hope for the impossible, for what the subject can never bring about. It may seem irrational, but such hope contains its own light in the exercise of human freedom which commits itself to the unity it can no longer synthesize. It is a unique mode of knowledge and a pure gift available both to Christians and to anyone endowed with intellect and freedom. **Dying and death.** Death and the dying process (which affects the whole person, not just the body) constitute hope which depends precisely on the ability to embrace death as comfortless and absurd—the arch-contradiction of existence. "Death as a conclusion is the absolute powerlessness of man" (179). But the free man "confronts death with the demand that it must constitute the sum total of his life as an act of freedom in which the whole of life is gathered up" (180). Freedom cannot consent to a mere empty draining away of life. **The exercise of freedom in death.** (Summary.) "Death constitutes precisely the true and necessary situation of Christian hope" (181). But if death represents absolute powerlessness, how can one engage in active hope when faced with death? One does this in the midst of life by the attitude one assumes toward death. "And what [man] hopes for is a unity, a reconciliation of the contradictory elements, a meaning for existence, an eternal validity for love as freely entered into, an assent to absolute truth, so that all this that is hoped for is truly *hoped* for" (182), i.e., is neither manipulated nor controlled by one's own powers.

Nothingness and finality. Why not opt for death as nothingness? Because it would not explain the sway radical decision making exercises over us—the feeling of absurdity that attends this option; and because our radical acts of love or loyalty in themselves attain a kind of eternality. Hope is offered a choice which must be made. Hope opts "for the eternally valid, and rejects death as the final definitive factor, and gives the name of God to that power which is not its own, yet which removes, by reconciliation, the absurd arch-contradiction present in existence through death" (183). Even those who die despairing, raging against the perceived absurdity of death, may in fact achieve the same radical acceptance of death alluded to in Christian hope, but in a veiled way (184).

Freedom as the event of definitive finality. The biggest problem which haunts this discussion is our propensity to think in spacio-temporal terms. For then the problem of eternal life becomes one of duration. But the ruling metaphor for human freedom is not spacio-temporal but the achievement of definitive finality which contains the real meaning of eternity for human beings.

13.12   Human Aspects of the Birth of Christ
Menschliche Aspekte der Geburt Christi

{1.5}   Previously unpublished. *Tribuna Medica* 7 (Madrid 1970) #368, 14-15.

Abstract: In retrospectively deducing Mary's status as *virginitas in partu*, Rahner allows that she was subject to pain. But due to her sinlessness and integrity she experienced pain in a mode subjectively different than we do.

Topics: BVM, *virginitas in partu*; JESUS CHRIST, birth of; THEOLOGY, method (retrospective deduction).

Precis: In this address to physicians Rahner concentrates on the physical aspects of Jesus' birth, in particular that it involved no pain, and that Mary remained *virginitas in partu* during and after the birth. Rahner numbers this doctrine among those valid doctrines which are not found in the New Testament but which are legitimately deduced "retrospectively." Retrospective deduction is legitimate if it upholds the substance of a doctrine even without upholding every concept and mental image used over time to illustrate its significance.

Rahner argues: Jesus birth was a real human birth. Jesus and his mother were genuinely human and thus capable of suffering. There is no reason to think it was unfitting for them to experience pain. But all doctors know people experience pain differently. In childbirth much depends on the disposition and attitude of the mother. Insofar as Mary was free from sin and concupiscence she was able to integrate the physical side of her nature and those factors deriving from her environment within her personal decision as a subject. Her birth experience was different from ours because she was different from us in her sinlessness and integrity. Rahner even wonders whether the term "pain" can be applied to her and to us in the same sense. If this is the true starting-point for understanding the doctrine of *virginitas in partu*, then one can easily see why it is of no importance to insist that the concept of *hymen virginale* should necessarily be attached to the doctrine of Jesus' birth.

13.13   The Quest for Approaches Leading to an Understanding of the Mystery of the God-Man Jesus
Auf der Suche nach Zugängen zum Verständnis des gott-menschlichen Geheimnisses Jesu

{1.0} *Geist und Leben* 44 (1971) 404-408.

Abstract: We are at root a three-fold question about the meaningfulness of love, death, and the future, to which Jesus of Nazareth in his life, death, and resurrection is the definitive answer uttered to us by God.

Topics: JESUS CHRIST, death/resurrection of; LOVE of neighbor; DEATH; FUTURE.

Subsidiary Discussions: Dead, our relationship to (196f).

Precis: In the simple act of living, by taking love of neighbor, death, and the future in their full and radical seriousness, we understand what the faith of the church says about Jesus of Nazareth. What is this relationship to Christ? Since he has died and is removed from our presence can our relationship with him really be anything more than ideology, mere allegiance to an idea? An analysis of the living relationship we have with our own dead and the enduring claim their lives have on us lead Rahner to conclude that we can and do have a living relationship with the living Christ when we accept the demands his life, death, and resurrection place on us.

Love of neighbor asks from us an absolute commitment of our personal existence to our neighbors. But we can only do this in the hope that despite what we see, such a commitment is reasonable and will not necessarily meet with disappointment. This hope finds its confirmation in the fate of the God-man.

The absolute character of love of neighbor seems to be threatened by the death of the beloved. But insofar as we are all united in death, and Jesus Christ rose from the dead, we can hope that our individual deaths will share in his resurrection.

We all hope for a final and definitive victory as the outcome of the history of humanity, even if we are incapable of stating in concrete terms what that future would be or how to achieve it. Such a hope must search history to see how far this consummation may have come towards us. This is because hope must render an account of itself in the concrete. With the eyes of faith one sees in the resurrection of Jesus the dawn in time of the insuperable victory, the absolute future, God alone can and will bring about.

13.14   Remarks on the Importance of the History of Jesus for Catholic Dogmatics

Bermerkungen zur Bedeutung der Geschichte Jesu für die katholische Dogmatik

{3.0} G. Bornkamm, K. Rahner, eds., *Die Zeit Jesu. Festschrift für H. Schlier* (Freiburg 1970) 273-283.

Abstract: This sketch of a strategy to liberate modern Catholic exegesis from the hegemony of dogmatic and fundamental theology centers on separating the question of Jesus' messianic self-awareness from faith in his resurrection.

Topics: THEOLOGY, dogmatic; THEOLOGY, fundamental; THEOLOGY, biblical; CHRISTOLOGY; JESUS CHRIST, death/resurrection of.

Subsidiary Discussions: Jesus Christ, historical existence of (201f); Dogma, development of (206); Jesus Christ, self-awareness of (207ff).

Precis: How and to what degree can Christian beliefs and Christian dogmatics be emancipated from history?

First Thesis (201-204): *Catholic faith and dogma have been and will be indissolubly bound up with not only the historical existence of Jesus of Nazareth, but also with the historical events of a specific kind which took place during his life.* Today this may not be so self-evident. Some Catholic dogmatic and exegetical theologians would even say it is affirmative in the dogmatic sense but negative as it pertains to fundamental theology. But Rahner maintains any absolute denial of this thesis is thoroughly false and heretical. This position leaves open the precise nature of the relationship between fundamental and dogmatic theology, between the light of faith and the basis of faith as capable of being reflected upon by human reason (history, 203f).

Second Thesis (204-208): *Catholic fundamental and dogmatic theology must develop new approaches due to problems raised by present-day exegesis with regard to the historicity of the events of the life of Jesus.* These theologians must realize that even within the New Testament there are different levels and a wide variety of theologies which cannot be easily harmonized. This thesis may seem commonplace until we ask certain pointed questions (list, 207) about precisely what in the life of Jesus the fundamental theologian must insist are historical. Rahner concentrates on two: a) Jesus' messianic self-awareness prior to his death; b) whether the resurrection of Jesus is a figure in the realm of the disciples' conscious faith or an event prior to their conscious faith.

Third Thesis (208-212): *Catholic dogmatic theologians have yet to pose or answer the question whether they can dispense with the historical witness of a "messianic" awareness of the pre-Easter Jesus and construct an orthodox Christology solely on the basis of Jesus' resurrection.* To say this question remains open in no way prejudices the outcome of the inquiry. Rahner leans toward an affirmative answer to this question for reasons he does not fully pursue. The benefit of an affirmative answer is that it would afford Catholic exegetes wider scope and greater freedom for their historical research into the self-understanding of the messianic pre-Easter Jesus. Rahner concludes the essay by refuting the objection that it is of no real importance which way this question is decided (211f).

13.15 The Two Basic Types of Christology
Die Zwei Grundtypen der Christologie
{2.0} Previously unpublished December 1971 lecture to *Katholische Akademie*, Munich.

Abstract: Though the two basic types of christology, ascending and descending, are legitimate, they cannot find a higher synthesis except at the cost of becoming more remote from the concrete conditions of life.

Topics: CHRISTOLOGY, ascending; CHRISTOLOGY, descending.

Subsidiary Discussions: Theology, pluralism in (222f).

Precis: Rahner distinguish *the* two basic forms of christology: saving history (ascending) and metaphysical (descending). These two forms already exist in the New Testament; they often appear mixed; both can be formulated in orthodox or heterodox ways. Rahner leaves open whether metaphysical christology is already logically contained in ascending christology, and how to classify Calcedonian christology.

The christology of saving history. Ascending christology finds its starting-point and touchstone in the man Jesus Christ, his full human reality and his definitive, unsurpassable, and victorious fate: resurrection and glorification. The role of the cosmos does not enter into this view.

Metaphysical christology. This christology is "metaphysical" insofar as it goes beyond the original experience of the believer. Although it finds its point of departure and criteria for verification in the first type of christology it has two unique characteristics. First, it concentrates on the pre-existent Logos who descends to earth—God made man. It justifies this approach in the words Jesus used about himself. Second, it encompasses the cosmic and transcendental significance of the incarnation touching on such areas as creation, humanity, the world, and saving history.

On the relationship between the two basic types. Rahner limits christology to *two* basic types because they arise from the two poles of our basic understanding of humanity: historicity and transcendentality. Just as human events find their fullest meaning in transcendental reflection and all transcendental reflection is rooted in concrete events, the second form of christology is rooted in the first and must repeatedly appeal to it for intelligibility and justification. Hence, metaphysical christology remains legitimate, inevitable, and sanctioned by the church from the earliest times to the present.

On the significance and credibility of the two basic types. Even though people today find the first form of christology more credible, significant, and compelling, theologians continue to present christology in its second form. This can lead to seemingly exaggerated christological claims which cannot be substantiated solely by recourse to ascending christology but must appeal to magisterial authority. Rahner insists this needs to be examined. These two forms of Christology, beginning as they do from different points of departure for a decision of faith in Christ, can never be fully harmonized in a higher synthesis except at the cost of becoming more remote from the concrete conditions of human life on which all human understanding ultimately rests.

XIV. Ecclesiology, Questions in the Church, The Church in the World
X. *Im Gesprach mit der Zukunft*

German edition: Einsiedeln, Benziger, 1972
U.S. edition: N.Y., Seabury, 1976
David Bourke, translator

This volume in the English edition is composed of the last three sections of *Schriften zur Theologie*, X.

14.01   Basic Observations on the Subject of Changeable and Unchangeable Factors in the Church

Grundsätzliche Bemerkungen zum Thema: Wandelbares und Unwandelbares in der Kirche.

{1.0} November 1970 lecture in Krefeld. F. Groner, ed., *Kirche in Wandel. Festschrift für J. Kard. Höffner* (Cologne 1972) 23-36.

Abstract: Clearly the church contains changeable and unchangeable elements. Each generation must work to separate them as best it can with theological acumen, patience, and the courage to experiment.

Topics: DOGMA, development of; INFALLIBILITY.

Subsidiary Discussions: Vatican II (3f); Petrine office (17f); Human nature (14ff); Episcopate (18f); Patience (20); Theology (21); Courage (21f); Spirit, discernment of (21); Experimentation (21ff).

Precis: After Vatican II the church seems divided into two camps over the issue of change. What in the church is changeable and what is unchangeable? Clearly unchangeable elements exist in dogma, morals, and the constitution of the church. The difficulty lies in deciding where to draw this line (7).

For Rahner, "The changeable and the unchangeable are not two entities simply existing side by side as immediately empirically apprehensible each in its own right" (7). They exist at different points on the same scale. The more concretely we experience something, the more apprehensible it is, the more it is subject to change. The unchangeable is always the more hidden factor which necessarily calls forth Christian faith and hope. Three discussions regarding the changeable and unchangeable elements in church follow.

Unchangeable dogma?: (8-14). How can one distinguish the kernel of gospel teaching enshrined in dogma from the manifold ways in which it has been developed in human history and formulated in human language and concepts? No dogma ever appears or can appear in a "chemically pure state." The process of separating dogma from its historico-linguistic amalgams is never complete, e.g., transubstantiation and monogenesis (13).

An unchangeable ethic? (14-16). Ethics is subject to all the same difficulties with the added problem that apart from wholly universal norms of an abstract kind "there are hardly any particular or individual norms of Christian morality which could be proclaimed...to have the force of dogma" (14). Nor is it easy to distinguish what is unchanging in the concrete nature of human beings.

How far is the basic constitution of the church changeable? (17-20). The basic constitution of the church has clearly developed since the primitive church. How then does one distinguish divine from human law in church polity? Granting papal primacy, are the modes in which it is exercised matters of human or divine law? Though scripture establishes the office of bishop, is it divine law that the office be administered by one person or could it be exercised by a synod (19f)?

The nature of this complex relationship between the changeable and unchangeable calls for Christians to be patient towards the church (20). It also calls for the proper "discernment of spirits," the basic task of theology (21). Finally the church needs the courage to experiment (21ff). It is impossible to draw full or adequate distinctions between the changeable and unchangeable solely by means of theoretical reason. Spirits are distinguished by practical reason. Such experiments may take quite a long time to be recognized, tolerated, or rejected definitively. The essay ends with a summary.

14.02   The Faith of the Christian and the Doctrine of the Church

Der Glaube des Christen und die Lehre der Kirche

{1.5}   July 1971 lecture in Munster to Union of Catholic Students.
Stimmen der Zeit 190 (1972) 3-19.

Abstract: By living fully and with great patience the truth they actually do believe, today's students can in good faith remain Catholics despite any real gap between what they may actually believe and official church teachings.

Topics: DOGMA: FAITH, assent of.

Subsidiary Discussions: Church, excommunication (24ff); Pluralism (29ff); Vatican I (32f); Concupiscence, gnoseological (34f); Mystery, *reductio in mysterium* (35); Truths, hierarchy of (37ff); Faith, act of (39f); Creed, brief (44); Orthopraxis (37, 46).

Precis: **I. The possibility of a heresy that separates men from the church.** The church has always held, "that if an individual Catholic Christian explicitly and publicly contradicts any dogma of the Catholc Church as upheld by her official teaching authority, then this Christian is cut off from the Roman Catholic Church" (24). This leaves open a person's salvation/ damnation (26), and never gives the church the right publicly to vilify any individual (27). What does this mean in the current historic and sociological context?

II. The modern pluralism of ideas and its significance for the conviction of the believer. Until recently societies had a ruling elite with power to enforce a particular worldview. In today's pluralism of living human thought (30) believers are more likely to find their faith challenged than confirmed. In addition, even one's own thoughts can no longer be completely harmonized except by willfully ignoring much information. Faith is no longer a system of ideas. It is only one element in a complex world of ideas. Still, one can hope to experience the unity of truth in its eschatological fulfillment, and people need not tolerate opinions they hold as seriously wrong (32).

III. The attitude of the Christian towards the official teaching of faith.

1) *Accepting the difference between one's own "personal" truth and the official teaching of the church.* Christians experience this irreducible pluralism as a

gap between what the church holds and teaches and what they have so far been able to appropriate (realizing that both are developing). Believers are in a state of irresolvable "gnoseological concupiscence" (34f) knowing they cannot know the unity of truth, yet having to strive step by step in that direction often in the dark.

The intrinsic harmony of church teaching is not simply available to the individual living in a pluralistic world, not even to those who assent to this teaching in faith (36). This difference does not necessarily mean they stand in radical or total contradiction. At this juncture Christians must rely on their own truth and on the personal history of their own achievement of self-identity. Believers are justified not by assenting to true propositions about the good, but by practicing the good they have come to believe (37).

2) *Paying due heed to the hierarchy of truths.* Although there is an essential unity among the truths of the church, believers possess only a subjective hierarchy of truth. One may even be impelled to forego probing into certain matters of faith (38). But this is alright because the act of faith and not the object of faith (*fides qua* not *fides quae*) is salvific (39). Finally the complex faith of the church lives in the act of faith of individual believers.

3) *Awareness of the historicity of the truth officially proclaimed by the church.* Christians must also be sensitive to the historically conditioned nature of the language and concepts used for official teachings. These too await definitive consummation through a human process of development which separates temporal accretions from the eternally true.

4) *Any absolute contradiction of dogmas is false and unnecessary.* Rahner concludes that persons are Catholic if and to the extent they do not declare any absolute contradiction between those truths they recognize in their own concrete personal existence and those taught by the church. Indeed whoever disregards one's conscience in order to maintian Catholic teaching risks damnation (42). This insight itself is unclear because people often misapprehend church teaching, believing it teaches or denies what in fact it does not.

Why are people today so insistent on contradicting the church? Would it not be more prudent when it appears one's personal understanding differs from church teaching to take a wait and see attitude. In time both the individual and the church may see things in a different light. One should surrender church teachings only in favor of some better and more liberating position and never in favor of a weary skepticism (43).

5) *The ultimate basis of faith.* This is easily summarized in a few general principles (44). Though some intelligent people of good will cannot accept this faith, we need not assert that anyone who does not understand these basic tenets in some particular way stands in absolute contradiction to this faith. One copes with the complex and often incomprehensible official teaching of the church by living by the truth which is prior to and transcends all verbal expression—the truth of the inconceivable God. One lives this by participating in the fate of Jesus. "Even today we can be Catholics" (46).

14.03   Does the Church Offer any Ultimate Certainties?

Bietet die Kirche letzte Gewißheiten?

{2.0} Previously unpublished December 1971 lecture in Garmisch-Partenkirche.

Abstract: The church offers ultimate certainties, but in a restricted sense. Ecclesial certainties rest on a more basic and radical trust in the meaningfulness of existence. In addition, all magisterial propositions are subject to the same reformability as any human proposition.

Topics: DOGMA; CERTAINTY; CHRISTIAN LIFE, trust; FAITH, assent of.

Subsidiary Discussions: History (53ff); Faith, *fides quae/qua* (53ff); Church (56ff); Magisterium (60ff); Dogma, formula (62ff).

Precis: This essays questions Hans Küng's statement ("Infallible? An Inquiry" N.Y. 1971) that the Spirit preserves the church in truth even though none of its propositions are infallible (47f). After a long discussion showing how the church can offer certainty in a derivative sense, and arguing the need to revise even binding dogmatic propositions, Rahner asks whether theologians like Küng by discarding dogmas they judge erroneous are not simply avoiding the hard theological work demanded in the process of revising doctrine (64f).

Each word in the question, does the church offer ultimate certainties to believers, needs clarification. Rahner insists that any "certainty" rests on the logical and psychological priority of a basic attitude, wholly subject to human freedom and decision, of radical trust in the meaningfulness of human existence and the possibility of all-embracing, and definitive salvation (48).

This basic attitude cannot be wholly derived from the church. In fact ecclesial faith rests on this radical trust. Ultimately the conviction one places in this basic trust rests on the movement of one's own heart. No church teaching can replace the need for a free personal decision regarding this attitude. This attitude is never fully conscious. The propositions in which this attitude is formulated are often not metaphysical or religious. In addition, all these propositions contain elements of concrete human history (53), and are thus somewhat contingent. Summary (53).

Historical contingent reality and basic human trust are co-conditioning. Basic trust helps individuals believe in Jesus Christ as savior of the world, and this belief strengthens one's basic trust. Still, one can have this basic trust without reference to Christ, and faith in Christ remains itself a gift (54). Rahner summarizes his conclusions, "we cannot truly expect any other certainty or sureness than that which is inherent in the ultimate basic attitude of trust [which remains] liable to the assaults of temptation, always to be achieved afresh in freedom and responsibility" (55).

Can the church itself offer believers any ultimate certainties? Yes. To believers, faith in Jesus as absolute savior implies faith in the indestructibility of faith in Christ, the world, and humanity in general, not as an autonomous human achievement but as a gift of God. This faith in Christ implies faith in the survival of the church. This in turn implies faith in the propositions which articulate the faith of the church, both of which are indestructible, infallible and inerrant (57).

This surety applies only to believers, and never replaces the need for that interior assent predicated on basic trust. Christians who fail to arrive at this intrinsic connection should be permitted to leave the derived proposition alone, hoping to grasp it fully some day. Finally, just as human decision making is an amalgam of ultimate convictions and provisional opinions, so too the faith of the church. Thus, theology distinguished dogmas from other non-binding and possibly erroneous opinions to which respect is due nonetheless.

The church is an organized society which claims a teaching authority or magisterium as an essential part of itself. Its legitimacy is not self-derived but rests on its correlation to the basic trustworthiness of the experience of Jesus Christ (61). Whoever holds to the propositions put forward by the magisterium can enjoy the certainty of not departing from the truth of Christ. This sureness is, however, subject to provisions:

1) it is offered to believers;
2) there are different ways of assimilating dogmatic propositions;
3) understanding dogma may be hindered by non-dogmatic accretions;
4) the terms used for dogmatic propositions are analogous, imbedded in human awareness, subject to time-conditioned parlance, style, and language. For all these reasons it is difficult even for theologians to recognize clearly and unambiguously what parts of a true and infallible proposition are subject to error. To declare a proposition infallible is not to say it is irreformable. Dogma even in its most binding form is open to the future (64).

14.04   On the Concept of Infallibility in Catholic Theology
Zum Begriff der Unfehlbarkeit in der katolischen Theologie
{2.5} January 1971 lecture in Rome for a symposium, *L'Infaillibilité, Son aspect philosophique et théologique*. E. Castelli, ed., *L'Infaillibilité* (Paris 1970) 57-72.

Abstract: Examining the doctrine of infallibility not in terms of its locus and exercise but as a dogma about the truth of individually defined propositions, reveals its modest scope of application both now and for the future.

Topics: INFALLIBILITY; DOGMA, development of; DOGMA, formulation of.

Subsidiary Discussions: Magisterium (68); Spirit (68); *Memoria* (74f); Theology, pluralism in (72ff); Truths, hierarchy of (76ff); Theology, moral (83).

Precis: One must refrain from seeing the doctrine of infallibility as a totalitarian imposition on a believer's conscience because: 1) the church is a free association of believers; 2) absolute assent to a proposition and critical regard are not mutually exclusive. Only the belief that any doctrine is authored by the Spirit frees one from fear of totalitarianism.

I. The historicity of the dogma of infallibility. What implications flow from the fact that this dogma is subject to the same limitations as every other historical proposition which asserts to be true? As applied to the pope, this dogma is a recent datum (69). The meaning of a dogma of this kind is expressed in elements that need continual re-definition. Thus, the dogma has a history and future never to be definitively concluded (71).

The dogma of infallibility as an historical proposition. Rahner doubts there will be "new" dogmas in the sense envisioned by Vatican I because no genuinely new proposition can be formulated so as to be felt to be the conscious expression of the whole church, and so capable of definition (73). This flows from the new irreduceable pluralism in the church both sociologically and theologically. Then does the dogma of infallibility become insignificant? No. It will always be a datum the church must reckon with in understanding truth. It will still be exercised to defend the ancient faith from error, albeit more modestly (75). The fact that over the last 100 years the doctrine has not become a blank check for writing new doctrines indicates that it will not become such in the future.

II. The development of the dogma of infallibility since 1870. The dogma of infallibility within the totality of the truths of faith. As one proposition in a system this dogma does not ground the system but is grounded by it. Thus, its scope is limited to a secondary check within the system applicable to secondary conflicts. As a purely formal principle it can never be the basis of faith. It can only be accepted if the system which upholds it is accepted without prior recourse to infallibility. The surety that pope and council will never produce false declarations cannot be greater than the doctrine of infallibility as it has come to be recognized (77). This secondary function of infallibility makes it more historically conditioned than basic doctrines of Christianity. As such it is of less vital subjective importance now than when it was promulgated, especially in today's world where the radical question is whether one can believe at all (78).

Teaching authority as having an authorized language. Every proposition is formulated in time-conditioned language and concepts. Because religious discourse uses analogies to communicate the mystery of God, two verbally contradictory propositions could be affirmed or denied simultaneously, depending on which dimension of the analogy was at the forefront.

On the character of new dogmatic formulae. Practically speaking no new definition could be proven false today because the legitimately wide range of interpretations brought to bear would make it impossible for any proposition to exclude all error. The very notion of development of dogma limits the possibility of new doctrines because any new dogma would have to be a further explication of an old one, which remains logically prior and more compelling to faith than any new one. Rahner defends this point in some detail (1-3a-c).

Rahner concludes by arguing that whatever was said here about metaphysical propositions is equally true of moral statements because they too are propositions of faith implying a relationship to God and only achieve their true nature when accepted in their relationship to absolute mystery. They too are historically unfolding and linguistically determined.

14.05   The Dispute Concerning the Church's Teaching Office

Disput um das kirchliche Lehramt
{1.0}   *Stimmen der Zeit* 185 (1970) 73-81.

Abstract: A stinging refutation of the claim that non-infallible formulations of the magisterium must not be thought of as "provisional."
Topics: INFALLIBILITY; MAGISTERIUM.
Subsidiary Discussions: Error, in teachings (92); Dogma, development of (93f); Conscience (94f).
Precis: **On the problem of non-infallible doctrinal decisions on the part of the church. The document of the German bishops.** A 1967 document of the German bishops touching on the relationship between believers and the magisterium was criticized in a paper circulated among "higher ecclesiastical circles" (88).
Critique of the document. The criticism focused on the bishops' distinction between a provisional statement of doctrine and an infallible doctrinal decision. In the case of non-infallible teachings (which they characterized as provisional) the situation of the individual is, "analogous to that of a man who knows that he is bound to accept the decision of a specialist even while recognizing that it is not infallible" (88f). The Roman critique rejects this analogy and insists no church teaching is to be thought of as provisional.
Interior contradictions within the critique. Rahner finds this criticism "theologically and practically speaking radically mistaken" (89). It is logically inconsistent since it cannot simultaneously maintain a position the bishops authoritatively reject, and claim to do so on the grounds of the church's magisterium. The critic disputes the very point he is trying to make: the need to accept magisterial teachings as virtually infallible.

The medical analogy, Rahner argues, is quite appropriate, the point of comparison being that one individual is presenting another with a decision both recognize as potentially erroneous. Though authoritative the opinion is open to error, and therefore can be rejected in good faith with sufficient reason. Often people reject authority without sufficient reason. They will have to answer to God for this. But there are times one has the right and duty to depart from official, non-infallible church teachings. **Examples of erroneous decisions.** Rahner enumerates many erroneous official teachings of the last 100 years which have been silently dropped though never officially rescinded. This shows the provisional nature of such teachings (list, 92f). Where would progress in addressing the errors contained in such teachings come from if each norm had to be received as absolutely binding? In the past the church counseled dissenters to maintain a *silentium obsequiosum*. How is this possible in today's fast-paced, media-saturated world? **Provisional decisions and the advance of doctrines.** The principle set out by the critic, "leads to heresy hunting, stagnation in Catholic theology, and the falling away of many from the faith" (95). It is true that accepting authoritative teachings as provisional puts a burden on the conscience of the believer. But even infallible doctrines firmly accepted do not relieve the burden of conscience in the most pressing matters of personal life.

14.06   The Congregation of the Faith and the Commission of Theologians
Glaubenskongregation und Theologenkommission
{1.5}   October 1969 lecture in Rome to International Commission of Theologians. *Stimmen der Zeit* 185 (1970) 217-230.

Abstract: Rahner suggests a post-Vatican II agenda for the Congregation for the Doctrine of the Faith and by extension to the International Papal Commissions of Theologians.
Topics: CHURCH, Congregation for the Doctrine of the Faith; PLURALISM.
Subsidiary Discussions: Faith and theology (104); Dogma, development of (106f); Theological method (109f); Ecumenism (110f); Church, Constitution of (112f).
Precis: At the close of Vatican II, Paul VI established a Commission of Theologians to aid the Congregation of the Faith. This address to its first assembly offers an agenda derived from the logically prior task of the Congregation of the Faith: "to guard and defend the Christian and Catholic faith against all errors and dangers to which it is exposed whether from within or from without" (99). How can this be done in today's situation?
I. The nature and function of the Roman Congregation of the Faith.
The situation. The undeniable pluralism in today's world (which even the erudition and good will of the Congregation can't overcome) make it impossible to defend the faith as in the past. The Congregation can no longer assume that theologians or the secular world to which it speaks share one set of theological or philosophical terms, assumptions, or even a common worldview.

The Congregation's recent history is one of lost opportunities, avoidable errors, "and many decisions which were objectively false" (101) including its teachings on modernism, biblical statements, scientific progress, etc. Previously censured Catholics had two alternatives; to submit or to leave the church. Today many such individuals stay in the church insisting that the condemned ideas were not properly theirs but the church's false interpretations. What can the church do when people refuse to accept appeals to formal authority and the church lacks the means to back them up (103)? In addition, the link between faith and theology today is tenuous at best (104). **Consequences.** In this situation the Congregation must first admit it does not know precisely what to do (106) in either teaching the faith or even recognizing it. The Congregation must have the courage explicitly to withdraw past errors or risk losing its credibility. Methodologically, scripture can no longer simply be used as a storehouse of *dicta probantia*, and any appeal to tradition cannot rest on one historically favored era for proof. Legalism must be overcome to arrive at a more original revelation (107).
II. Tasks for the Commission of Theologians.
General themes: the possibility, limitations, and methods which can be used by the church today to defend and proclaim the faith (108f); church membership in a pluralistic and ecumenical setting (110f); the distinction between morality and justice in the church especially in the realm of marriage and canon law (111f); the constitution of the church, how much of its organization is a matter of divine law (112f).
Particular themes: mixed marriages; *communicatio in sacris*; infant baptism; indissolubility of marriage; priestly celibacy.

14.07   On the Theology of a "Pastoral Synod"
Zur Theologie einer "Pastoralsynode"
{1.0}   October 1969 lecture to Catholic faculty of the University of Munster. J. Schreiner, ed., *Die Kirche im Wandel der Gesellschaft* (Würtzburg 1970) 1-14.
Abstract: Three considerations for any particular pastoral synod are: the legitimacy of a local synod; its pastoral nature; its binding legal power.
Topics: CHURCH, synod.
Subsidiary Discussions: Theologians, role of (116f); Law, divine/human (124ff); Church, subsidiarity in (120ff); Petrine office, election to (126f); Church, democracy in (129f).
Precis: In the wake of Vatican II the German bishops convened a local pastoral synod (winter 1969-70). Rahner argues that theologians can help prepare for such synods by offering their critical reflection through which the essential nature of the church is separated from its trappings and accretions.

Since the Middle Ages there has been a growing homonization in the western Church. Local initiatives and customs have been brought into line with Rome. Though Vatican II asserted in principle the possibility of legitimate pluralism within the church, it never showed in concrete terms how this would be reconciled with the authority of the pope in the unity of the church.

Clearly the desire for local autonomy is not a call for a separate church. But how autonomous the German church should be is admittedly unclear (121). Its unique character calls for more than tolerance on the part of Rome. It must also be seen to posses a positive theological dimensions along with the right and duty to frame its own solutions to problems within the local church in its own way while remaining within the one church. Summary (121f).

Secondly, a "pastoral" synod must consider "the concrete modes in which the Church *as a whole* has to achieve its own fullness in *all* of its members and in all its dimensions ... in the light of the situation of the Church in the world as reflected upon theologically" (122). Starting here the synod can discern which particular matters to discuss. These discussions should not end with authoritatively promulgated declarations but practical plans of action.

Finally what is the scope of a synod's legal powers? This leads Rahner into a long discussion of the distinction between divine and human law. What are a synod's legal powers vis-à-vis local bishops and the pope? Can bishops bind themselves to the decisions of a synod comprised largely of lay members? How does one insure adequate representation at a synod?

All these discussions point to greater democratization in the church, a move stongly resisted by both the pope and local bishops in their eagerness to preserve the purity of the faith (129). But recalling that the faith subsists in the entire church and not simply in its leaders opens potentially fruitful avenues of discussion for those preparing for the synod.

14.08   What is a Sacrament?
Was ist ein Sakrament?
{1.5}   January 1971 lecture to the faculty of Catholic Theology at Mainz. *Stimmen der Zeit* 188 (1971) 19-25.

Abstract: Developing a fuller theology of the Word, or viewing the church as sacrament could overcome the ecumenical stalemate arising from the controversy over the number of sacraments and how they are all "instituted by Christ."
Topics: SACRAMENTS; WORD, theology of; CHURCH as *Ur-sakrament*; ECUMENISM.
Subsidiary Discussions: Sacrament, *res et sacramentum* (137f).

Precis: Catholic sacramental theology today is not monolithic or universally accepted. New approaches might overcome the impasse Catholics and Protestants face over the number of sacraments and how they are "instituted by Christ" (136 ftn3). One promising starting-point is an enhanced appreciation of the distinctive theological character of the Word uttered in the church as the eschatological presence of God.

Word of God and sacrament. Despite Vatican II, a Catholic theology of the Word remains meager. In the past the Word was seen primarily as the bearer of true propositions. A hylomorphic approach to sacraments which opposed word to matter failed to account for the sacramental status of matrimony and penance. Today religious words are seen to share in the variability of all human speech. But the Word uttered in the church is an event of grace, possessing an exhibitive character as the eschatological presence of God's salvation in the world (138).

Three factors suggest developing sacramental theology from a theology of the Word: 1) it provides a good account of institution; 2) it builds on Vatican II that: a) the proclamation of the Word is bringing about salvation; b) the church is the basic sacrament of salvation (139). Rahner examines a and b. **The saving character of the Word.** All Christians hold that the Word pronounced in the church at the behest of God and Christ is in principle exhibitive (it affects what it signifies). As human words differ in degree of significance, so do words in the church (140 ftn10). That the church's Word is effective is the action of grace. These are divine words, not simply human words about divine things. Sacraments are the consummate, most effective of these words.

The function of the church as sign. The church is a sacrament—the sign which manifests in history (and thereby also affects) that will of God towards the world which creates salvation and unity (134). The church both proclaims this Word and receives it. This Word is eschatological: irrevocable, unsurpassable, victorious, ultimate, definitive. In bearing this Word to the world, God affects what the church believes and proclaims. Summary (144).

Concerning the nature of the sacraments. Sacraments constitute the highest stages in the Word of grace in the church as exhibitive and as event. Its efficacy rests in its eschatological nature, not in its acceptance by people. Thus, it is *opus operatum*. Sacraments are "instituted by Christ" because and to the extent they were instituted by the church and as such derive from him (145f ftn14). Although the existence of seven sacraments is an historical decision of the church, historicity does not make a decision arbitrary (147f).

14.09   Introductory Observations on Thomas Aquinas' Theology of the Sacraments in General

Einleitende Bemerkungen zur allgemeinen Sakramentenlehre bei Thomas von Aquin

{3.0} Previously unpublished in German. 1970. Commentary.

Abstract: Rahner's brief, catalogue-like observations on Aquinas' treatment of the sacraments also indicate fruitful approaches for completing his treatment.

Topics: SACRAMENTS; AQUINAS on sacraments.

Subsidiary Discussions: Sign and causality (150f; 155f); Church, as *Ur-sakrament*(151f); Word, theology of (152f); Causality, sacramental (157ff).
Precis: Rahner summarizes Aquinas' treatment of sacraments in *Summa Theologia* (III, Qq. 60-65) and concludes that this profitable work leaves much "unsaid which nowadays calls for explicit and extensive consideration" (151). He singles out Aquinas' vague treatment of the relationship between the sign function and instrumental causality of the sacraments. Insofar as the *Summa* contains no developed ecclesiology, Aquinas lacks the connector between christology and sacraments. Without a developed theology of the Word, the relationship between word and sacrament also remains obscure.

Rahner intends next "to draw attention to certain points...in Thomas Aquinas' teaching on the sacraments in general which would not be recognized clearly enough on a simple reading ... to present a few random examples of starting-points, and so to afford fresh insights and to habituate our readers to an approach which is indispensable if we are to take due account of the work both of Thomas Aquinas and of tradition in general in a way which is necessary and fruitful even today" (153). His comments follow the order of questions in the *Summa*.

[Note: Without a copy of the *Summa* at hand Rahner's text is difficult to follow and his comments seems positively cryptic. Almost the entire content of this essay is expressed more clearly in 14.08 "What is a Sacrament" and 14.10 "Considerations on the Active Role of the Person in the Sacramental Event."] The value of this essay derives from showing at precisely which points Rahner finds the work of Aquinas must be interpreted or augmented. He also cautions at quite specific points not to forget this or that dimension of sacraments, not to overly physicalize an analogy, etc.

14.10 Considerations on the Active Role of the Person in the Sacramental Event

Überlegungen zum personalen Vollzug des sakramentalen Geschehens
{1.5} *Geist und Leben* 43 (1970) 282-301.
Abstract: Viewing sacraments as the fullest expression of the ongoing work of God in the world and not as islands of light in a dark world of evil profoundly changes the way individuals participate in the sacraments.
Topics: SACRAMENTS; EUCHARIST.
Subsidiary Discussions: Grace (166ff); "Liturgy of the World" (169f); Symbol, real (177f); Church as *Ur-sakrament* (179ff); Anonymous Christian (179).
Precis: Applying his "Copernican" theology of grace to the sacraments (in particular to Eucharist) demonstrates their true significance and renders them intelligible to a contemporary world. Sacramental grace consists, "in an intellectual and spiritual movement of the sacramental event outwards to

take effect in the 'world' and backwards in a spiritual movement leading from the world to the sacrament" (162).

The old model: sacrament as isolated encounter with God. The old model viewed sacraments as isolated encounters with God. Catholics retreated from the secular world into a sacral sphere to encounter and be strengthened by God, and were sent back into the world to pursue their monotonous lives. This model is under attack as unrealistic, ritualistic, and ideological (165). This is not the best or only way to consider the sacraments as apogee of Christian life.

A new model: using the whole of life to bring the sacrament to its fulness. Rahner sees grace and divine life present everywhere, brought about and made manifest in the concrete conditions of history and of human life (166). Though sacraments are specific events of God's grace as forgiving, sanctifying, and imparting the divine nature, they do not impinge on the world from outside. "The world is constantly and ceaselessly possessed by grace from its innermost roots, from the innermost personal centre of the spiritual subject (166).

God's grace as creating salvation at the roots of human existence. Grace is simply the ultimate depths and radical dimension of everything the spiritual creature experiences, all of which finds its only true fulfillment in the silent infinitude of God (168). Grace's clearest manifestation and irrevocable victory is Jesus Christ. All those who believe this promise has also been made to them affirm what is essential in classical Christology. Grace unites all believers in love and in a common destiny.

Sacraments a symbolic manifestations of the Liturgy of the World. "The sacrament constitutes a small sign, necessary, reasonable, and indispensible, within the infinitude of the world as permeated by God .... [It] reminds *us* of this limitless presence of divine grace" (169). Thus, in terms of Eucharist, "the world and its history are the terrible and sublime liturgy...which God celebrates and causes to be celebrated in and through human history in its freedom" (196). This history has the cross of Christ as its sustaining center. One only genuinely reenacts Christ's liturgy by drawing strength from the liturgy of the world.

The Eucharistic meal. At Mass the individual is united to the longings and movement of the world through union with Christ. Nothing new is initiated at Mass, but God's plan for the salvation of the world is consciously manifested. It is believed and proclaimed, and thus affected. By participating in this great drama in everyday events believers are oriented to the absoluteness of God. To avoid the temptation to denigrate Eucharist as mere ritual believers need only to recall the divine depths inherent in real life. Whoever fails to grasp this should refrain from celebrating the sacraments altogether.

The Eucharist and the Liturgy of the World. Seeing the Mass as the "Mass of the World" restores its importance. It is the supreme moment insofar as in it is an exercise in hope-filled self-surrender—a dry run for death.

Believing that sacraments celebrate the definitive and irrevocable outcome of freedom makes them more and not less important, nor does it obscure their significance or efficacy (176). After all, since grace is required even to approach the sacraments, they cannot be seen to affect all grace upon their reception.

The effectiveness of the sacrament in the sign. Rahner discusses sacramental efficacy by referring to his notion of the "real symbol" in which spiritual beings simultaneously cause in themselves what they actually do. Sacraments, arising as they do from God's continuous offer of grace to the world, further the course of that grace by manifesting it. The proper understanding of the relationship between the church and the world clarifies this.

The church as the basic sacrament of the salvation of the world. The church is the sacrament of salvation for the world when its confessing members make salvation manifest sacramentally to the world (180). They do this precisely to receive and maintain their own salvation.

The application of the sacrament in the concrete circumstances of human life (the frequency of the sacraments). Rahner concludes that individual sacraments "are nothing else than acts in a process of concrete self-fulfillment on the part of the church as the basic sacrament of salvation for the world as applicable to the individual and to the specific situation of his own personal life" (181). Their effectiveness derives from Christ's union with the church as the church projects and actualizes itself in the world. Since the same grace which sustains the Church infuses and directs the world, sacraments are never extrinsic.

Religious and secular. Does this new model of the sacraments put too heavy a burden on the believer? Any model rightly understood demands a great deal. This model has the simple advantage of helping believers "realize in concrete personal terms what is meant by the grace of God and to realize it *in such a way* that the idea of receiving such a grace is also really credible" (182). Modern people can feel this grace to be verifiable because it proceeds from everyday experience and avoids narrowing the concept to individualistic terms. Frequent reception of the sacraments can easily blunt the experience of *kairos* they present (183). Properly understood, Rahner's model overcomes the distinction between sacred and secular. It both urges and allows believers to work out their salvation in the midst of the world.

14.11   Aspects of the Episcopal Office
Aspekte des Bischofsamtes

{1.5} Previously unpublished January 1972 lecture in Innsbruck to the General Assembly and Study Conference of German-speaking Pastoral Theologians.

Abstract: Rahner suggests new ways the episcopal office could be exercised without jeopardizing its proper authority.

Topics: EPISCOPATE; CHURCH, office in.

Subsidiary Discussions: Church, as founded by Christ (187f); Law, divine (187ff); Church, paternalism in (194f); *Potestas ordinis/jurisdictionis* (195f); Parish (198ff); Base communities (198ff).

Precis: Rahner accepts *de fide* the necessity and legitimacy of the episcopal office in its monarchial form. Here he explores reshaping the exercise of that office in ways not closed by prior dogmatic limitation. Here the task of dogmatic theologians is a negative one: revealing to pastoral theologians and canonists how much in a given area is still open to receive new content (186).

Rahner first examines the sense in which Christ "founded" the church and by extension its hierarchical structure. Only in a very limited and indirect way can Jesus be said to have instituted the office of bishop. It is justified "on the grounds that in the concrete it constitutes the legitimate and, in the long run historically speaking, indispensable way of ensuring the necessary continuity of the community of Jesus with its origins" (188).

In what sense then is there a *jus divinum*? "[T]he episcopal office derives from the will of Jesus to found the Church … in a process which, while in the eyes of modern theologians it may seem to be conditioned by historical factors is nevertheless in terms of its meaning perfectly reasonable and irreversible" (189). Though the monarchial episcopacy developed over time, Rahner argues that even historically contingent events can bear the unalterable will of God.

Given the legitimacy of a monarchial episcopacy and the fact it is exercised in a collegial way, the open question for theologians is what rules for the exercise of collegiality will insure the proper discharge of that office. Rahner first asks whether the office, which has traditionally been vested in one person, could not be vested in a *collegium* (191f), especially insofar as the full power of the church itself is vested in a *collegium*.

Second, can a bishop invest any kind of binding juridical power in other bodies which share in the direction of the local church [e.g., synods] (192f)? Rahner argues such a move is both doctrinally possible and opportune. It would be a hedge against unwarranted ecclesial paternalism (194f).

Since even popes are "elected from below" without prejudice to that office, could the same principle apply to selecting bishops (195)? Also the relation between bishops and priests in the realm of *potestas ordinis* and *potestas jurisdictionis* remains unclear. By what right can any authorized leader of a faith community be denied the powers now reserved to bishops (195f)? Realizing that orders have been parceled out in many ways in the history of the church, who today possess the power to reshape not only the office of bishop but other ministries, and according to what criteria (196f)?

However the episcopal office of the future is reshaped, it will never be done through the mere application of risk-free theory to practice. It will be born afresh though free decisions which by their nature will be autonomous and unique. They will be achieved through experimentation at the local level in widely varying cultures (197f).

The Church today "survives in a diaspora situation in the midst of a pluralist environment or one which is in principle and in its institutions hostile to the Church itself" (198). This marginal situation in which the church finds itself today invites it to reach out in a special way to all the marginalized in society. Such an outreach would lead to a revolutionary restructuring of parish communities, perhaps along the lines of South American-inspired base communities, and possibly with a concomitant revolution in the exercise of the episcopal office (198ff).

14.12 How the Priest should View his Official Ministry
Zum Selbstverständnis des Amtspriesters
{1.5} Previously unpublished November 1969 lecture in Venice to its priests.

Abstract: History and dogma show the church has great latitude in organizing sacramental ministry. Rahner suggests many ways priesthood might be reshaped.

Topics: PRIESTHOOD.

Subsidiary Discussions: Law, divine (204ff).

Precis: With a laity come of age, and biblical and historical studies showing a wide variations in priestly ministry, this essay suggests possibilities for reshaping priesthood which in no way question its abiding nature. The first part of the essay examines Catholic dogma on priesthood (203-209). The second part suggests consequences which are doctrinally possible, though not necessarily opportune ecclesially, spiritually, or pastorally (209-219).

Even without establishing a moment when Christ instituted priesthood, it is legitimate to accept it *jus divinum* insofar as it arose from the church's need for leadership to fulfill its mission from Christ (204). In time the single office of leadership was articulated in distinct, secondary functions (207). In the early church leadership, not the power to celebrate Eucharist, was reserved and passed on by the laying on of hands. Leadership and the ministry of preaching the Word were the two New Testament notes of priesthood. Trent and IV Lateran highlighted the role of priest in Eucharist.

Rahner concludes, "the Church has at her disposal an extremely wide scope for developing variations within her necessary and ultimately *single* official ministry, in accordance with the needs of a particular age, the variations of cultural milieu etc., and of subdividing that official ministry into various individual offices, regulating the relationships between these offices, establishing and defining the functions of the particular officials, and, without prejudice to the sacramentality of the process by which offices are conferred, defining the concrete conditions under which they are to be handed on" (209f).

Thus if opportune, orders might be conferred differently; candidates might be selected differently; functions might be distributed differently among the three orders; office could be vested in a *collegium*. Change will come not from above but from experimentation from below, by priests of today working to shape the priesthood of the future (212). Rahner's own concrete suggestions include: greater specialization among priests, requiring different training (212f); the possibility of part-time priests (214f); candidates for ordination arising from the communities in which they live (215f); priestly service limited to a set term (216). Relations between priests and local bishops could also be reshaped along more collegial lines (217f); many episcopal powers could be exercised by a bishops' conference (218f).

However the priesthood changes, priests today know what they are and what they must do: believe, preach, and embody the truth of the Lord crucified and risen whose grace "pervades our life [and] imparts himself to us as our goal and as the strength of our life which we call God" (219).

14.13   The Relationship between Personal and Communal Spirituality and Work in the Orders
Das Verhältnis von personaler und gemeinschaftlicher Spiritualität und Arbeit in den Orden

{1.0} June 1971 lecture in Würzburg to Union of German Religious Superiors. Expanded version in *Ordenskorrespondenz* 12 (1971) 393-408.

Abstract: Rahner's analysis of the generational tension felt within religious orders in the wake of Vatican II and its impact on apostolic activities.
Topics: RELIGIOUS LIFE; SPIRITUALITY.
Subsidiary Discussions: Solitude (235f); Liturgy, experimentation in (239f).
Precis: This essay is not strictly dogmatic. It is Rahner's analysis of the source and meaning of the tension felt within religious orders in a time of transition, the late 1960s and early 70s. It is both a generational problem (old vs. young) and a problem arising from conflicting worldviews.
Nineteenth-century individualism and socialism. The older generation works from a model of religious life he calls "nineteenth-century individualism" (personal); the younger generation from "socialism" (communal). These terms are general and difficult to define. Each has its own historical genesis, strengths and weaknesses, applications and abuses.
Reality in the orders. The values of the individualist model are self-sufficiency and personal competence manifested in a life spent following the rules and thus contributing to the common good, albeit often in large communities of remote "institutionalized hermits." The work of the group was decided by someone beforehand and open discussion centers on how best to do the work (225).
Transition. The communal model seeks fraternal community constantly being formed afresh from below through a collegial process. It seeks to

introduce greater maturity and personal responsibility and tends to favor small communities as the best way to achieve a fully human way of life. It demands intelligibility as a criterion for obedience in religious life. The glue of community life is the personal commitment of the individuals to one another. Apostolic service is marked by teamwork in deciding both the ends and the means (227ff).

The interplay between the personal and the communal aspects. These two views are not mutually exclusive. They always exist in society and can be co-conditioning in a healthy way. Nonetheless, communities must become more communal (however threatening this may be to older members) because: 1) The homogeneous Catholic worldview which sustained the individualist model is irretrievably gone. Its remaining principles lack clarity and force, and so one appeals to the truth found in personal experience and relationships with others. 2) The interior world of newer members is significantly more complex and calls for a greater reliance on community to find and hold one's bearings.

What remains and what follows. Whatever changes a move towards a more communally-oriented religious life of the future might take, solitude will always remain its hallmark due to the very nature of the individual's relationship with God. This is the great gift older religious have to offer the young (235f). Discovering the future will come gradually as the result of risky, messy experimentation. This demands especially from religious superiors the courage to embrace ongoing experiments, especially in the liturgy (239f).

14.14 Some Problems in Contemporary Ecumenism
Einige Probleme des Ökumenismus heute
{1.0} Previously unpublished. 1972.
Abstract: Progress toward Christian unity rests on two bold actions: admitting the already existing unity we share in possessing the one saving grace; laying aside old controversies to proclaim the basic good news to a neo-pagan world.
Topics: ECUMENISM.
Subsidiary Discussions: Theology, ecumenical (248f); Creed (249ff); Theology of the future (252f).
Precis: "Particular questions in ecumenism often become difficult and even insoluble precisely because we have not achieved a sufficiently deep realization of what ecumenical theology really is, its starting-point and its aims" (245). After reviewing the current ecumenical situation Rahner suggests two theses concerning the ultimate assumption on which ecumenical theology is based and the future path of ecumenical progress.
The crisis of ecumenical theology. Currently more is being done among Protestant groups than between Catholics and Protestants because: 1)

Catholics have not yet made their dogmatic positions sufficiently intelligible and open to dialogue; 2) Protestants have difficulty acting in concert even about their own beliefs. Thus, despite all the talk of unity and its importance, "nothing or almost nothing ever happens …. Despite all ecumenical resolves the real frontiers still remain stiff and immovable" (248).

The ultimate basis for ecumenical theology. Rahner proposes as the ultimate basis for making progress in ecumenical theology "the unity, apprehended in hope, of a belief in justifying grace which already exists and is identical on both sides, yet which, so far as theology is concerned together with the creedal formula which gives it conceptual expression, is still in process of being achieved" (248). This premise implies, "we are convinced of the fact that the partners to the dialogue on both sides live in the grace of God, are truly justified by the Holy Pneuma of God, and are sharers in the divine nature" (249).

What then of creedal differences? Such problems exist at a level of secondary reflection. Either these truths implicit in the faith have not been reflected upon consciously enough, or they have been formulated poorly. Since any creed is by its nature a product of secondary reflection, the task of ecumenical theologians is to move beneath creedal formulations and to meet in the area of shared reflections and lived experience of our one faith (251).

The future of ecumenical theology. Ecumenism will not advance by returning to correct controversies and definitions of the past. Progress will be made when Catholic and Protestant theologians enunciate a theology of the future (252f). They will meet and find union in their mutual cooperative attempts to formulate and proclaim the good news in a credible way to an as yet unknown future which has already begun.

14.15 Ecumenical Theology in the Future
Ökumenische Theologie der Zukunft

{1.0} February 1971 lecture at the University Extension at Bocholt. J. Brosseder, ed., *Begegnung. Festschrift für H. Fries* (Graz 1972).

Abstract: Suggestions for making theological progress towards Christian unity.
Topics: ECUMENISM.
Subsidiary Discussions: Secularization (255ff).

Precis: Dialogue with a secular world. Ecumenical theologians will progress toward the unity of separated churches indirectly. It will arise "from the common task of the separated Churches and their theologies and will be concerned with the theological study of the common substance of the Christian faith and with preaching it in such a way that it can be assimilated afresh and in more effective ways by men in the so-called Christian countries even when either explicitly or tacitly they have become remote from the gospel message despite the fact of still outwardly and publicly retaining their membership of these Churches" (255). Churches will cease competing and collaborate to re-Christianize a secular world of "post-Christian pagans" (256). Their new "post-Christian theology" will be the true ecumenical theology of the future —a theology addressed to the needs of the modern world, not to doctrinal controversies of the past. **"Non-theological" aspects of an ecumenical theology.** In the future, "non-theological" aspects of old doctrines will be carefully examined (i.e., those aspects of a doctrinal problem often overlook by traditional theology). Studying the historical, intellectual (260 ff), and sociological context out of which controversies arose, and the linguistic context in which they were formulated (263f) will lead to deeper understanding and eventual reunion. **Church Christians without any confessional awareness.** Today the theological differences which separate the churches are known and appreciated by only a handful of scholars. The faith of most believers is devoid of confessional awareness at the doctrinal level. Separation is a more socio-historical matter than a matter of conscience. What would it mean for mixed-marriage, joint catechesis, inter-communion, etc. if ecumenical theologians took this fact seriously (264ff)? **Is it possible to achieve a church that is institutionally one?** Might it not be possible for the churches to unite institutionally on the basis of the one faith they already share and at the same time tolerate among themselves a plurality of creeds on less essential matters (268f)?

14.16   The Unreadiness of the Church's Members to Accept Poverty

Die Unfähigkeit zur Armut in der Kirche
{0.5}   *Neues Hochland* 1 (1972) 52-59.

Abstract: The church's unreadiness to embrace poverty in order to eliminate poverty reflects the sinfulness and reticence of its members.
Topics: SOCIETY, poverty.
Subsidiary Discussions: Church of sinners (274f).
Precis: This loosely argued essay (a response to Vatican II's concern for the "church of the poor") is more hortatory than dogmatic. The New Testament harbors a dualism regarding the poor. It urges remedying the poverty of one's neighbors while embracing a life of voluntary poverty oneself. For Rahner eliminating poverty is the only relevant reason freely to embrace poverty.

Today the poor are everywhere. Though the church responds by preaching for justice, the real question is the will of the church to eliminate poverty (272). How can the preaching of the church be credible when its efforts are so inadequate? Why is its preaching so ineffectual? Some claim it is because the church and its clergy do not practice what they preach. They are themselves rich and prefer wealth to poverty. But these reasons are only superficial. They merely point to the fact that the clergy shares the same cultural deafness that affects all believers in their concern for the poor.

Can priests alone motivate the laity to eradicate poverty in the world? Probably not (274). History has shown that the church was and remains a church of sinners, always capable of failing even in matters of greatest urgency.

The church is often better at preparing excuses than proposing or implementing solutions. Its response mirrors secular society. Only when unavoidable, undeniable historical circumstances coincide with the gospel mandate is change likely. Even then it is slow. Actual attempts to overcome poverty by embracing poverty will always be the work of heroic individuals (276). Yet no one can justify lack of action before the judgment throne of God simply by claiming to have been caught up in the spirit of one's times.

14.17   Observations on the Problem of the "Anonymous Christian"

Bemerkungen zum Problem des "anonymen Christen"
{1.5}   Previously unpublished January 1971 lecture in Mainz to Department of History of Religions of the Institute for European History.
Abstract: Restates and defends the concept "anonymous Christian" as the most adequate explanation of Vatican II's teaching that salvation is possible even without membership in the church or explicit knowledge of Christ.
Topics: ANONYMOUS CHRISTIAN.
Subsidiary Discussions: Knowledge (287ff); Mission mandate (292ff).
Precis: The essay begins with a bibliography of Rahner's work on this topic and selected theological responses (280). He notes opposition to the term but is still waiting for someone to suggest a more adequate word.
The reality of the "anonymous Christian." The incontestable existence of those living outside the church who enjoy a salvific relationship to God, leads Rahner to define such an anonymous Christian as, "the pagan after the beginning of the Christian mission, who lives in the state of Christ's grace through faith, hope and love, yet who has no explicit knowledge of the fact that his life is oriented in grace-given salvation to Jesus Christ" (283).
The theological meaning of the reality signified by the term "anonymous Christian." Despite its being taught by Vatican II, no clear theological demonstration of this thesis can be given through scripture or tradition, though there are some signs of its development (283). This definitive teaching contains two points: the need for faithfulness and obedience to one's own conscience; the need for supernatural faith, not simply philosophical faith (285). Rahner's chief concern in this article is to make an intelligible case for this optimistic teaching of a primitive and ultimate revelation which is consonant with modern paleontology, anthropology, and exegesis and ongoing missionary work (286f).

How could it be possible for there to be an "anonymous Christian"? Rahner builds his case on an insight from Thomistic anthropology: "the difference and the unity between objective knowledge and that which is known on the one hand, and a non-objective, non-thematic awareness and the reality thus known on the other" (287). Rahner makes two assumptions in applying this to pagans: 1) God's universal salvific will is constantly being freely offered as the goal and dynamism of human existence; 2) this dynamism is at work even without one's explicit consciousness of it (288). In developing this concept Rahner briefly touches on grace, freedom, history, and revelation.

Further implications of a thesis. Rahner summarizes the problem and answers the question of how anonymous Christianity leads to supernatural faith (290). This section (291f) summarizes his entire thesis.

Perspectives. This final section (292ff) suggests areas in which the concept of anonymous Christianity needs further refinement: New Testament exegesis; the ongoing need for missionary activity; theology and history of revelation.

14.18   The Church's Commission to Bring Salvation and the Humanization of the World

Heilsauftrag der Kirche und Humanisierung der Welt
{1.5}   October 1970 lecture to Theology Academy at Frankfurt
Geist und Leben 44 (1971) 32-48.

Abstract: In an age of "horizontalism" which sees its only legitimate task as humanizing the world, the church must preach the proper relationship between the love of God and love of neighbor which grounds and completes humanization.

Topics: LOVE of God and neighbor; HUMANISM and horizontalism.
Subsidiary Discussions: Demythology (298ff); Atheism (300f); Ideology (312f).
Precis: "Horizontalism" in Christianity and in the contemporary church. The church today is faced with a new heresy of radical horizontalism which claims the church's only function is to humanize the world. In the process, "'God' is reduced to a mere cipher.... Jesus is simply the most fruitful and perhaps... indispensable example of this commitment on behalf of one's neighbor and of a better society" (296). Prayer, Eucharist, and creed are similarly devalued.

What are the reasons for the sudden appearance of "horizontalism"?

1) The tendency to demythologize. This modern tendency leaves un-named whatever is not fully understood (298ff);

2) The experience of God in a world colored by the natural sciences. Modern scientific method disregards whatever is non-empirical (300f);

3) The new responsibility for the world as the meaning of human life. When being responsible for the world becomes the meaning of life, appeals to God, prayer, grace, etc. seem mere distractions (301ff).

The response of faith to the challenge of "horizontalism." It is not enough to say love of neighbor is a moral duty imposed by God. There must be a greater unity between love God and neighbor than saying the latter is a condition for winning God's favor. 304-308 summarizes the relationship of love of God and neighbor. (God can only be loved through neighbor; self-transcendence achieved in loving one's neighbor is itself orientation to God and thus salvific; these two loves are co-conditioning. They are not two separate duties, but one.)

The new relationship between "horizontalism" and "verticalism" which has emerged in our particular epoch. Given the spirit of this age "horizontalism" manifested in love of neighbor enjoys a certain legitimate priority of emphasis in the proclamation of the gospel over verticalism, love of God.

What has the church to contribute to the humanization of the world? In a society committed to humanizing the world, the task of the church is not to control how the world thinks about and expresses itself, or to reestablish a sacral sphere. It must preach "that the whole of human existence, and so the entire world in all its dimensions, ultimately reaches out to the life of God; that there is no horizontal dimension which is *entirely whole and complete* in itself without a vertical one; that it is only through God's grace that we are set free [so as] to use and enjoy the world, and open ourselves unreservedly to our neighbor without becoming enslaved by this social and material environment of ours, without having to idolize it in order to endure it" (312).

14.19   On the Theology of Revolution
Zur Theologie der Revolution

{1.5}   Previously unpublished October 1970 lecture in Rome to International Commission of Theologians.

Abstract: The church must preach the legitimacy of revolution especially today in a global revolutionary situation between northern and southern hemispheres.

Topics: SOCIETY, revolution; THEOLOGY of revolution.
Subsidiary Discussions: Horizontalism (316, 327); Love of God/Neighbor (316f; 327); Power, coercive (318; 325); Church, change and future of (321f; 324ff); Church and Spirit (329); Poverty (329).
Precis: A true theology of revolution can not be built on fashion (revolutionary chic), nor can it be promoted as the sole key concept of a theology which portrays Jesus as the prototypic revolutionary.

Concepts: As a critic of society the church opposes "horizontalism" which equates the task of the church with the humanization of the world and leaves no room for God [cf., 14.18]. Yet love of neighbor, the indispensable medium for a relationship with God, today appears irreversibly social. This allows one to speak legitimately of a theology of revolution.

The concept of revolution is much broader than a study of force or violence. Revolution differs from evolution in that "the decisive forces which a revolution brings to bear are...not immanent within the system" (318), although they are not so foreign as to constitute an invasion. The goal of a revolution subjectively and objectively is a greater scope for freedom and an increase in justice and harmony among all. Revolution has a negative aspect (eliminating unjust conditions) and a positive aspect (introducing new, more liberating conditions). A revolutionary situation is one in which the majority is marginalized in terms of influencing society or benefitting from it.

In this schema the concept of "permanent social revolution" is only true or possible in a special, restricted sense (320f). In this special sense the church itself might be seen as an institution in a state of permanent revolution. As a pilgrim its task is not simply to conserve, but in dialogue with society, continually to discover its original meaning (321f).

A revolutionary situation exists when a sufficiently large group within society is marginalized. When this situation affects all nations it is said to be global. Rahner saw the situation existing between the Northern and Southern hemispheres as a global revolutionary situation, even though many developing nations did not view it as such (322ff).

Church and revolution. The church is not the proper propagandist for global revolution. But it must recognize and boldly preach the legitimacy of revolution and even of force where that proves necessary (324f). As the church interacts with the global revolutionary situation it clarifies its own divine mission. Nonetheless, it will never be able to work out a complete, concrete, normative world order which Christians simply impose on society. Believers must apply their practical wisdom to the social situation as well as they can, with or without the approbation of the church (328). Finally, the church must not be silent about its own historical guilt in this area; it must sever ties with repressive regimes, and never employ or tolerate torture, murder, etc.

XV. Penance in the Early Church
XI. Frühe Bußgeschichte in Einzelunterschungen

German edition: Einsiedeln, Benziger, 1973
U.S. edition: N.Y., Crossroad, 1982
Lionel Swain, translator

15.01   The History of Penance
Bußgeschichte.
{2.0}   1973, previously unpublished.

Abstract: This survey of the history of penance explains the meaning and significance of the essays in Volume XV. This analysis of the sacrament and its theology corresponds with theoretical and practical attitudes towards sin.
Topics: PENANCE, history of: SIN, remission of.
Subsidiary Discussions: Baptism (4f); Penance, binding/loosing (6ff); Church, excommunication (8, 10); Sin, serious (9); Montanism (9f); Novatianism (9f); Aquinas, on penance (16f); Poschmann, B., on penance (18ff).
Precis: I. **Explanation of the notion and outline of the problem.** (Bibliography of Rahner's work, cf., Preface, vii-viii; 329 ftn1). A brief description of the elements involved in Christian penance makes clear that any precise notion of penance will correspond to prevailing notions of sin and justification. After insisting that all acts of penance are God's graced response to a graced invitation, Rahner's argues the notion of the forgiveness of post-baptismal sin through a separate sacrament of penance is rooted in the New Testament.

II. The history of Christian penance.
1) The teaching of scripture. Rahner finds New Testament legitimization for the forgiveness of post-baptismal sin in the authorization of the leaders of the community to bind and loose (Matt. 16, 18). Antecedents are seen in Qumran and the synagogue's imposition of a ban. Summary (8).
2) The teaching of the Fathers of the Church. Hermas, the first theological reflection on penance, allows for a one-time forgiveness of post-baptismal sin for the truly contrite and for their reintegration in the church. The third century was marked by the twin rigorist heresies Montanism and Novatianism with their innovations: a class of unforgivable sin, and martyrdom as the only mode for the one-time forgiveness of less serious sin. At this time the form of penance was excommunication from Eucharist. The contrite entered a special penitential order, often for life, until sin was remitted by the local bishop's laying on of hands. The *pax cum ecclesia* was considered the means of reconciliation with God. The next major development came from the Irish Anglo-Saxon monks in the sixth century. In spreading the popularity of a simple form of repeated, private, auricular confession to a priest for the forgiveness less serious sin, penance became confession.
3) The theology of the sacrament of penance in theologians since the twelfth century. Scholasticism codified the sacraments using Aristotelian concepts, notably matter and form. Whereas up to this time there had been a lively appreciation that the sign (matter) of the sacrament consisted in the acts of the penitent and its form consisted in the words of absolution (cf., Aquinas), this approach lost out to Scotus' more instrumental-effective view that absolution affects the infusion of justifying grace. Summary (17).
III. Research in the history of penance. Modern research into the history and dogma of penance has its roots in the apologetic controversies of the turn of the century (e.g., Harnack). The first major Catholic studies were B. Poschmann's *Paenitentia secunda* (1940), another work on indulgences (1948), and a final work on sin and last anointing (1951). Rahner offers a summary and criticism of the main points of these three works (18-22).

15.02 Sin as Loss of Grace in the Early Church
Sünde als Gnadenverlust in der frühkirchlichen Literatur
{2.0}   *Zeitschrift für katholische Theologie* 60 (1936) 471-510. Revised.
Abstract: Rahner grounds the nature and effect of penance in the rise to prominence from New Testament times to the third century of the notion that serious sin is the culpable loss of sanctifying grace bestowed at baptism.
Topics: SIN as loss of grace; GRACE, baptismal; PENANCE, history of.
Subsidiary Discussions: Death as a consequence of sin (25, 31ff); Shepherd of Hermas (38ff); Gnosticism (40f); Irenaeus of Lyon (41f); Tertullian (42ff); Sin, serious (44ff).

Precis: This attempt to understand the historical beginnings of the teaching that sin is a loss of sanctifying grace contributes to the history of dogma and to the development of a new, more mature method for presenting historical treatises based on scripture and the Fathers of the Church.

I. The question. Though in the New Testament baptism signals a turning away from the kingdom of darkness, believers are always threatened by sin. Analysis of scripture reveals three main categories for the effects of sin: i) the juridical-ethical or moral view which sees sin as a transgression of the law which changes our relationship with God and neighbor and provokes anger and retribution; ii) the eschatological or end-of-time view which sees sin in terms of one's final destiny, i.e., being excluded forever from the kingdom of God; iii) the graced view concentrates on one's interior life and sees sin as loss of baptismal grace whereby the Spirit is expelled from one's innermost being and the seal of baptism is broken. These three views are so closely related they are often used interchangeably. Although this three-fold distinction may not have a large impact on dogmatic theology, it has value for historical study since one particular view may have more important pastoral or personal resonance at a particular point in time. Summary/preview (26).

II. The New Testament. The New Testament stresses the juridical-ethical and eschatological consequences of sin clearly and strongly. The meaning of sin for the interior state of grace achieved by faith and baptism receives no emphasis and is mentioned in the New Testament only in passing.

1) *The juridical-ethical and the eschatological approaches.* Details how the Synoptics and John stress judgement and hell as the punishment for sin.

2) *The approach from the point of view of grace.* Passages in the New Testament which seem to point to sin as loss of grace are so terse and vague their meaning remains questionable. Rahner details in turn a) Paul; b) the Letter to the Hebrews; c) death as the consequence of sin; d) images and parables. He concludes with a summary (34).

III. The Apostolic Fathers.

1) *The early apostolic Fathers.* This group considers the consequences of sin in much the same way as the New Testament and for the same reasons. In his analysis of these witnesses Rahner enunciates a methodological principle for interpreting these texts: "general and vague phrases can justifiably be understood in a precise sense only if the idea in question occurs clearly in at least one other place in the same author" (36).

2) *The later apostolic Fathers.* Especially in the so-called Second Letter of Clement and Shepherd of Hermas the approach to the consequences of sin from the point of view of grace appears very clearly. This shift of interest is quite noticeable even though it is by no means used exclusively (summary, 40). Rahner assumes these developments were a reaction to gnosticism which taught that one's external actions had no impact on the life grace. Hermas is the first text explicitly to consider the possibility of a second metanoia after a post-baptismal fall. Summary (41).

IV. The rigors of Montanism. After the notion of sin as the loss of grace and exclusion from the kingdom is clearly expressed (cf., Irenaeus of Lyon), Tertullian turns to the question of the different consequences incurred by particular sins. Rahner examines the presuppositions of Tertullian's insistence that the only guaranty of the forgiveness of serious post-baptismal sin is martyrdom, the baptism of blood (summary, 43). This solution arose from his attempt to reconcile two contrary truths: that post-baptismal sin resulted in the loss of grace and the death of the soul forever; the church can forgive post-baptismal sin and restore the life of the soul. Whereas the church maintained these two contradictory truths until they were solved at a later date, Tertullian solves this dilemma by falsely denying the second truth and adopting a rigorist position. To make this rigorism practical he had to restrict the number of unforgivable sins as much as possible (44). This section ends with detailed textual analysis in two parts:

1) The loss of grace in general.
2) The consequences of the teaching of the loss of grace. Summary (51).

V. The basis of further development. During the first half of the third century rigorist errors died out; the doctrine survived that serious sin leads to loss of baptismal grace; the distinction remained between serious and light sin based on their nature and their effects on grace. Rahner summarizes three positions which remained universally accepted throughout these centuries: one must take care to preserve what was received at baptism; God's free mercy lifts one to mysterious participation in God's nature and life which transcends human comprehension; one must safeguard this gift by a way of life that corresponds to the dignity of one's call to share God's life.

15.03   The Penitential Teaching of the Shepherd of Hermas

Die Bußlehre nach dem "Hirten des Hermas"

{3.5}   *Zeitschrift für katolische Theologie* 77 (1955) 385-431. Revised.

Abstract: This exposition, which is also a critique of Grotz, concludes Hermas is primarily concerned with sinners' relations to the church, and that penance as a church-sacramental event and penance of excommunication are identical.

Topics: PENANCE, history of; SHEPHERD OF HERMAS on penance; CHURCH, excommunication; GROTZ, J., on penance.

Subsidiary Discussions: Sin, forgiveness of (67ff); Penance for sin (72ff); *Metanoia/aphesis* (74ff); Church, *pax cum ecclesia* (106ff).

Precis: Conventional wisdom holds that B. Poschmann (1940) proved conclusively that Shepherd of Hermas did not announce through a new revelation a previously unheard of jubilee of a second penance for forgiveness of post-baptismal sin.

I. The state of research. J. Grotz (1955) made a frontal assault on Poschmann arguing the basic form of penance has always been private, and excommunication from the church is a secondary, later disciplinary addition. Rahner refutes Grotz on the basis that his proofs are confined to very subtle, indirect arguments (60); his ecclesiology tends to Nestorianism (61); he lacks a precise consideration of what excommunication is (61f); methodologically he fails to take into account the New Testament witness (63f). He argues Grotz's thesis finds no confirmation in Shepherd of Hermas because it fails to reveal a group of sinners who needs a special sacrament for the forgiveness of sins and reconciliation with God without needing to be reconciled with the church.

II. The Shepherd of Hermas—the author and his work. After discussing date, authorship, and key passages, Rahner summarizes the problem Hermas presents to history of dogma with his announcement that post-baptismal sin can only be forgiven once. This admits of three interpretations: such forgiveness is an innovation; it attests to the practice of forgiveness in the church but adds a degree of urgency due to Hermas' view of the immanent end of the world; this one-time limit represents a *via media* between church practice and rigorists who disallow any possibility for the forgiveness of post-baptismal sin.

III. The limitation of the accepted possibility of penance. Hermas teaches all sin is forgivable by genuine sorrow and repentance, and this is not a new possibility. All he does to modify the traditional belief is to limit it in view of his conviction the end of the world is immanent. Renewing this eschatological proof is for him an urgent exhortation, a consolation, and an assurance of salvation all rolled into one.

1) *Forgiveness is possible.* a) All sins are forgivable. Hermas is aware of apostasy and holds it is irremissible not because of its gravity but because the apostate is generally unwilling to return and do penance. He rejects anything like Tertullian's category of unforgivable sin. b) The limit. The limit Hermas sets for post-baptismal forgiveness of sin is based on his conviction that not enough time remains from now till the final day for baptized Christians who sin from this point on to completely fulfill their penance.

2) *The situation before Hermas.* a) The possibility of a penance for all sins. Does the revelation to Hermas of the forgiveness of sin though penance mean that previously there was no such possibility, or does the new limit for penance stem from his eschatological conviction? Only the second interpretation is possible because the possibility of forgiveness is pre-supposed (72). As to what "Hermas has heard from certain teachers" that there is no other penance than baptism, Rahner takes to be an ideal prescription for all the baptized rather than a principle which does not admit of exceptions in practice. Rahner lists the difficulties involved with any other interpretation (list, 75). He concludes by pointing out the "nucleus of truth" in Hermas' eschatological teaching on sin and repentance (76).

b) Baptism and further penance. Hermas distinguishes between the quick, sure, and effortless forgiveness of sin (*aphesis*) in baptism and the arduous, long-lasting, and unsure possibility of forgiveness (*metanoia*) after baptism through penance. This distinction would be superfluous if there were not a tradition of a different kind of forgiveness available for post-baptismal sin.

IV. The unrepeatable character of the granting of penance. Hermas teaches that although the possibility of forgiveness for post-baptismal sin is not a new revelation, from now on there is only one chance left to attain it.

1) *The fact of the unrepeatable character.* To understand the meaning of the once-and-for-all character of metanoia one must understand the basis of the irrepeatability of penance.

2) *The basis and meaning of the unrepeatable character of the granting of penance.* Though reasons vary, for Hermas the decisive (though not unique) reason sin is unforgivable is that the nearness of the end of the world makes further penance impossible. There is the added possibility that penance which needs to be redone is neither true nor effective, and there is the parallel to be drawn between the irrepeatability of post-baptismal penance and the irrepeatability of baptism. Yet there is always a question for Hermas about the effectiveness of penance before God vs. its effectiveness before the church. Finally, Rahner sees an essential connection between the irrepeatable character of penance and its ecclesial character. Summary (82).

3) *The fate of recidivists.* Because this happened so seldom, recidivism is only a peripheral concern to Hermas and thus it is "solved" only vaguely. Because recidivism reveals the clear lack of earlier sorrow and repentance the position of the recidivist is pretty hopeless, especially when it comes to reintegration into the community of the church.

V. Church penance.

1) *The church and salvation.* The visible, earthly church which always fails fully to embody its ideal image plays an important role in the theology of Hermas.

2) *Church and penance.* a) Penance of excommunication. The church excommunicates sinners to express empirically as well as it can the holiness of the church and the actual spiritual state of sinners as separated from grace. After distinguishing excommunication in the early church from its modern form, Rahner spends the remainder of this section refuting Grotz's reading of Hermas. Rahner's central insistence is that however far stones "expelled from the tower" may lie, they all share the fate of excommunication. He does not reject the notion of a graded penance in Hermas, but he does reject the notion that only those "under the punishing angel" are actually excommunicated (97-98).

b) *The church form of penance.* Hermas is not attempting a systematic treatment of penance. He is attempting to stir the conscience of sinners. Because in Rahner's reading of Hermas actual spiritual excommunication is not always accompanied by church excommunication, Grotz is wrong to conclude that "Hermas recognized an excommunication which, independently of a sinner's definitive obstinacy, excludes him from full communion with the Church, even though he has not yet received the one *metanoia*, and which banishes him as a matter of principle and for ever [sic] to a 'lesser place'" (105f).

c) *Church reconciliation.* Rahner argues sacramental reconciliation is precisely reconciliation/readmission to the church. "In the final analysis the whole of Hermas' theology of penance revolves around the question of the right relationship of sinful man to the *Church*" (108). For how could the seal of baptism be restored by subjective penance alone?

VI. Conclusions on Hermas' penitential teaching. "Penance as a church-sacramental event and penance of excommunication are identical in Shepherd of Hermas" (109). Hermas recognizes different grades and lengths of penance for sins involving different degrees of separation. Grotz's work, flawed as it is on New Testament witness and Hermas, is probably equally flawed in some of its other treatments. It is more likely modern forms of excommunication developed in a process of separating themselves from early penitential processes than to think excommunication became attached to penance at a subsequent stage.

15.04   The Post-baptismal Forgiveness of Sins in the *Regula Fidei* of Irenaeus

Sündenvergebung nach der Taufe in der "Regula Fidei" des Irenäus
{1.5}   *Zeitschrift für katolische Theologie* 70 (1948) 450-455. Revised.

Abstract: Since according to Irenaeus the deposit of faith holds that even after baptism a person can return to Christ's love through penance, the church in his time must have restored such people to full church fellowship.
Topics: PENANCE, history of; IRENEAUS OF LYON on penance.
Subsidiary Discussions: Angels (115ff); Gnosticism (118).
Precis: Does Irenaeus provide any evidence for the possibility of penance after baptism?

I. Explanations of the possibility of penance according to Irenaeus. Scholars disagree in interpreting Irenaeus. Was he the last advocate of the old ideal of holiness, the representative of a rigorist theory of baptism, or did he hold the possibility of post-baptismal penance? B. Poschmann disputes the latter interpretation. He interprets the text on attaining salvation through repentance to refer to angels not to men based on a certain textual symmetry.

II. The reference to men. Rahner disputes Poschmann and argues that the text refers to the salvation of those *men* who persevered in love only after a (second) penance. He cites four proofs (117) and concludes Irenaeus follows Hermas in identifying two groups of Christians: those who never knew sin and those who have kept the "seal" only after a second post-baptismal penance. He ends with remarks on the anti-gnostic context of the *Regula*, and warns it is perilous to offer any definitive interpretations of Irenaeus' silence on other controversies (unforgivable sins, repeatability of penance, etc.).

III. The text. Rahner includes the Latin and English versions of the salient sections of the *Regula Fidei*.

15.05   Tertullian's Theology of Penance
Zur Theologie der Buße bei Tertullian
{3.5}   M. Reding, ed., *Abhandlungen über Theologie und Kirche. Festschrift für K. Adam* (Düsseldorf 1952) 139-167. Revised and extended.

Abstract: This overview of Tertullian's complete theology of penance concentrates on the relationship between the formal act of the church to reintegrate its members and the assurance of God's forgiveness of guilt.

Topics: PENANCE, history of; TERTULLIAN on penance.

Subsidiary Discussions: Sin, serious (127ff); Sin, confession of (130ff); Episcopate, power of (138ff); Prayer of the church (139f); Church, *pax cum ecclesia* (142, 146ff).

Precis: This look at Tertullian on penance offers something new by taking the broad view and examining how all the elements of his theology fit together.

I. The object of public penance. Judging from *De Paenitientia* Tertullian would seem to hold all sin which destroys baptismal grace should be submitted to church penance. Never in his Catholic or Montanist phases did Tertullian draw up a systematic list of which sins fell into this category. Rahner maintains the only way they can be discovered is to examine his work as a whole. This shows Tertullian distinguishes broadly between daily faults, lesser sins, and serious sins, any of which could be public or secret. Although in theory the potential realm of application for obligatory, public church penance was quite broad, in practice (like excommunication today) it was probably quite narrow. This may be what led theologians to limit to three the actual number of mortal sins which needed to be submitted to the church for penance.

II. The performance of public penance.

1) The obligation to do penance. Tertullian insists that since without penance sinners will find no salvation they should set aside all false shame and submit to public church penance.

2) The confession. Penance consists first of all in public confession. This took place before the community in a liturgical action. It is unclear whether the request for penance called for a full enumeration of sins (including secret sins) either to the assembly or privately to the bishop.

3) Penitential practices. Penance is also comprised of certain penitential practices of a private nature (fasting, prayer, etc.) before and during one's time of public penance. Previous penance may shorten the duration of public

penance. The penitent's aim is to regain peace and fellowship with the church. The form of church penance has two stages (133) a public act outside the doors of the church in which the sinner begs forgiveness and reentry; a penance of longer duration, Sunday after Sunday, inside the church.

4) Reconciliation. Penance came to an end at a particular point with an official act of church reconciliation in some kind of rite of forgiveness and readmission at the hands of the bishop by means of an act of absolution. Such an act was supported by the prayers of the whole church. Rahner discusses in turn the repeatability of such a penance, the necessity of concluding penance with a formal act of readmission, and the interdependent roles of the bishop and the community in effecting this formal act of readmission.

III. The effects of *paenitentia*. When Tertullian speaks of the effects of penance he refers to penance as a whole—its subjective and public elements (list, 141). These two dimensions cannot be separated. Tertullian takes it for granted that subjective penance only has a meaning and effectiveness as church penance. Rahner next examines the effects of penance.

1) The *pax* with the church. Reintegration is the aim of all penitents.

2) Reconciliation with God. Penitents also seek remission of sin before God. Rahner explores the Montanist controversy over the church's power to forgive sins before God by analyzing how Tertullian connects the subjective and public components of the one penance with the reconciliation with God and the forgiveness of guilt before God. The relationship between subjective penance and divine forgiveness is clear. But how is the church's public act of forgiveness related to pardon before God? Tertullian offers what at first seem like two irreconcilable theories: i) the infallible efficacy of the prayer of the church (142f); ii) the theory of episcopal absolution (144f). Rahner harmonizes these theories somewhat by arguing for a third term (not explicit in Tertullian) to connect them: that the act of the church forgives sin (145f).

3) The inter-relationship between both effects of the church's act. The harmonization suggested by Rahner above leaves unsettled how the *pax cum ecclesia* and the *venia* before God, both of which are affected by the action of the church, are in fact related. Clearly the decision of the church is never infallible. Tertullian saw clearly that a mere external act of the church could never force God to forgive nor make up for a lack of subjective penance. Having ruled out other alternatives Rahner concludes, "Insofar as the Church's judgment is considered as *praejudicium* of God's judgment, the *humana pax* ... must therefore, be the actual effective cause of reconciliation with God" (147).

But more precisely, how is reinstatement with the church the middle point between the act of the church and the forgiveness of guilt before God? And how is the granting of peace with the church community related with the forgiveness of guilt by the church? As to the first question Rahner follows Tertullian and rejects Poschmann's solution as being too materialist, i.e., it fails to take seriously the spiritual reality of the church as the true body of

Christ. For it always remains possible for a sacrament to be valid yet not fruitful. The second more difficult question Rahner settles by reference to the fact that insofar as the church is the actual bearer of the Spirit, the church is the effective and indispensable mediator of grace (150f). Finally, how is the penitent's subjective penance related to this whole procedure? In this connection Rahner finds Tertullian too semi-Pelagian. In fact the whole movement toward healing and reconciliation with the church is already the very work of Christ's body, accomplished by the Spirit.

15.06 The Penitential Teaching of Cyprian of Carthage

Der Bußlehre von Cyprians von Karthago
{3.0} *Zeitschrift für katolische Theologie* 74 (1952) 257-276. Revised.

Abstract: This analysis of Cyprian of Carthage's approach to penance covers such topics as the penitential liturgy, imposition of hands, serious sin, excommunication, satisfaction for sin, private and public penance.

Topics: PENANCE, history of; CYPRIAN OF CARTHAGE on penance; PENANCE, liturgy.

Subsidiary Discussions: Imposition of hands (156ff); Confirmation (157ff, 168f); Heretics/schismatics, reconciliation with (160ff); Baptism of heretics (163f); Sin, serious (173ff); Sin, remission vs. satisfaction (178ff, 193ff); Church, *pax cum ecclesia* (200ff); Penance, private (208ff).

Precis: This essay on penitential discipline in Cyprian's time in North Africa and Rome focuses on the penitential liturgy and his corresponding theology.

I. The external form (152-171). Rahner distinguishes three stages in the penitential process in this order:

1) The performance of penance. Even if it may be performed privately such penance always remains public insofar as it is always an ecclesial act.

2) The exhomologesis. Cyprian sees this confession as part of a liturgical act which takes place before the community just prior to readmission to the church. This does not deny the possibility of an earlier private confession of sin to the bishop before one undertook public penance.

3) Reconciliation and imposition of hands. Though the action is considerably older, Cyprian is the first to testify that reconciliation was affected through imposition of hands by bishop and clergy. Sometimes the rite was accompanied by anointing, and always by the prayer of the church begging for the forgiveness of guilt and the restoration of the life of the Spirit.

a) The origin of the rite. Is imposition of hands intended as confirmation? If not, what does the action mean? Is it identical to imposition of hands in the reconciliation of heretics?

b) The imposition of hands and confirmation? Rahner insists in Cyprian's time penance and confirmation are clearly distinguished. He cites the unity and irrepeatability of the sacraments of initiation and the witness of the *Didascalia Apostolorum*. Cyprian's own approach to the imposition of hands in penance is less clear, tangled in the similarities with the impositions of hands at the reconciliation of heretics. But the fact that Pope Steven insists on imposing hands for penance, and appeals to an ancient tradition shows the principle was not determined by theological considerations but by custom.

c) The imposition of hands and the reconciliation of heretics. The origin of imposing hands for the reconciliation of all heretics lies in the practice of receiving back into the peace of the church through an imposition of hands *in penitentiam* those heretics who had been baptized in the Catholic faith. In time the practice extended to all returning heretics even those who had received heretical baptism (valid but lacking the conferral of the Spirit reserved to confirmation). The fact Pope Steven's private theology on this topic was filled with contradictions and obscurities argues theology did not dictate the practice of reconciliation of heretics. A theory was developed later to account for an existing practice. This inquiry shows the autonomous sacramental nature of penance along with the sacraments of initiation.

d) The meaning of the imposition of hands. This gesture is particularly apt to convey reconciliation (restoration of interior grace received at baptism) because it always expresses the communication of something the person imposing hands possesses, and because the original bestowal was symbolized in this way. Though Rahner sees it as parallel to confirmation because it bestows the Spirit, he is open to the possibility it is the last of many impositions of hands by those blessing the penitent. In any case, "A perfectly clear and unified explanation of the imposition of hands in the reconciliation of penitents and heretics in Cyprian's day on the basis of the available material is not possible today, and it probably did not exist in the third century" (170). Rahner sees in this very obscurity an argument for the possibility the gesture had apostolic origins.

II. The theology of penance (171-222).

1) The sins of daily life and their private remission. Cyprian knows even the baptized fail daily in struggling against sins. Unlike the sins that are fully remitted in baptism these daily faults are forgiven through one's penance. The semi-Pelagian character of this practice gives rise to Cyprian's anxiety over the adequacy of *satisfactio* in individual cases.

2) The nature of serious sin. Although his technical terminology is still imprecise, Cyprian maintains sins differ in seriousness and effect. *Mortale crimen* not only bring about hell they also cause the death of the inner life of the Holy Spirit. Cyprian is very sensitive to the ecclesial dimension of serious sin: it separates one from table fellowship in the church prior to any disciplinary sanction imposed by a bishop (summary, 175). As to which particular faults carry the effects of serious sin Cyprian makes no final list and is content to rely on passages from scripture, common sense, and everyday moral judgments. Whereas in theory the range of such sins is great, in practice it appears quite limited.

3) The necessity of personal and church penance for serious sins. For Cyprian the only avenue to forgiveness of post-baptismal sin is long-lasting, personal penance which moves God to forgiveness. This personal penance is at the same time ecclesial. It is imposed, controlled, and supported by the church, and ends with the reestablishment of peace with the church. Although the individual can by his individual actions separate himself from the church, only by acting in union with the church can one obtain reconciliation.

4) The effect of the personal act of penance. Cyprian's approach to the forgiveness of post-baptismal sin is primarily moral and eschatological, emphasizing the fact sin offends against God and merits damnation. Whereas sins committed before baptism and their concomitant punishment are simply remitted by baptism, post-baptismal sin constitutes a debt which can only be canceled through sufficient penitential satisfaction made in this life or the next. Whatever doubts surround this theory they involve not God's willingness to forgive but whether the sinner has fulfilled the pre-scribed conditions.

To appreciate the deficiencies and advantages of this theory Rahner considers two points: the notion of sin and its remission entails guilt and punitive expiation (181-184); the opposition of baptismal and post-baptismal forgiveness of sin (184-189). On the first matter Cyprian seems to hold that when the sins committed before baptism are forgiven, the punishment due them is simply waived. Post-baptismal sin (daily and serious) is liable to punishment and the remission of these sins through penance eliminates this liability. For him penance is sorrow made visible. Feelings of sorrow or regret not put into action through penance mean nothing. This psychologically naive position has theological strengths.

On the second matter, justifying the difference between the remission of sin in and after baptism, Cyprian points to scripture and to the tradition of the irrepeatability of baptism. An examination of the relationship of guilt and punishment and their remission ends in a dilemma. Either the practice of penance is semi-Pelagian, or it is merely a practice in the church with no dogmatic significance (186). Rahner argues there is a practical reason for the practice of penance: the objectively more justifiable suspicion toward the sincerity of a change in attitude in the sinner after baptism than in the catechumen before baptism. Only penance as sorrow made manifest could reassure both the church and the sinner of his/her commitment to the struggle to recover that attitude which would make him/her worthy of the spirit of God and peace with the church. After suggesting taking more seriously the analogy of penance working to heal the soul injured by sin, Rahner observes that the healing analogy raises the real theological problem not of how punishments due to post-baptismal sin could remain despite sorrow manifested in penance, but why they are totally waived in baptism.

5) The effect of reconciliation by the church. a) The effectiveness of the church's act in penance (apart from in the actual reconciliation). The effect of the church's acts in penance is not restricted to restoring fellowship. Insofar as it involves the intercession and consent of the whole church, Christ's body, church penance also involves eschatological *satisfactio*. b) The effect of the reconciliation by the church. The decisive act of the church is readmitting the penitent to Eucharist. One can be assured the judgment of the bishop and the mind of Christ are never at odds by reference to Matt. 18. (For Cyprian's reservations in citing Jn. 20, cf., 193f) Cyprian knows reconciliation with the church has effects in the next life insofar as "membership is an absolutely indispensable precondition for a real possibility of salvation" (195). Hence, readmission is as essential to salvation as *satisfactio*. The imposition of hands renews the Holy Spirit in penitents and makes them worthy to rejoin the Eucharistic fellowship. This idea is not new with Cyprian. It is not the *satisfactio* that bestows the Spirit (for its full effects are eschatological) but the *pax*. Cyprian's insights rest on his theology of the church (198f), membership in which is never an external precondition but the actual life-giving union with the Spirit of Christ.

6) The unity of *Satisfactio* and *Pax* in their remitting of sins. It would seem Cyprian is caught in a vicious circle: *satisfactio* is necessary to restore peace with the church, and this peace is needed for complete *satisfactio*. Furthermore if *satisfactio* depends on the effort of the penitent then Cyprian would seem to be semi-Pelagian. Whatever categories might be used to solve the question today (201f), Rahner concludes the problem is solved if we grasp "the subjective act of man and the act of the Church in their unity in such a way that the one causality can be predicated of both acts with regard to the one effect which is both the reception of the Spirit and the remission of sins together" (205).

7) The sacramental nature of church penance. For Cyprian is penance a "sacrament"? If one keeps in mind the historical and terminological problems associated with identifying sacraments, and allowing that for Cyprian full *satisfactio* is an eschatological reality, nevertheless Rahner concludes the forgiveness of post-baptismal sin Cyprian describes is in fact a sacrament.

8) Lasting consequences after complete reconciliation? In Cyprian's time penance prior to readmission to the church was very lengthy and overseen personally by the bishop. Hence, Rahner does not see at this time a lengthy post-reconciliation period of penance. Nor does Cyprian seem concerned over the irrepeatability of penance, perhaps because it was seldom needed.

9) A "private" sacramental penance in Cyprian? a) The question and its treatment. The precise meaning of these terms is difficult to establish both historically (209f) and liturgically (210ff). This difficulty cannot be clarified by reference to the extremely variated practice of "private" penance in the seventh-century church (214f), nor by comparison to the twentiet-century practice of "private" penance (215ff). For these comparisons beg the

question of what constitutes the essence of penance. The only essential element different in today's practice of penance concerns its repeatability, not its being public or private. Hence, according to Rahner, the church before the seventh century did not know a sacramental "private" penance besides its "public" penance (conclusion, 218).

b) A look back at Tertullian. Rahner grants that Tertullian recognized different "species" of penance. These, however, arose from his increasingly rigorist theology and the subsequent need to distinguish serious from less serious sin. It was not based on nor did it lead to there being two forms of penance, public and private.

c) Variations of the penitential process in Cyprian. Rahner does not believe the different forms of penance known to Cyprian justify the conclusion that a public and a private penance existed side by side. They are for Cyprian variations within one form of penance. Rahner leaves open the nature of the encounter between priests and wounded souls who need to unburden themselves.

15.07 Penitential Teaching and Practice according to the *Didascalia Apostolorum*
Bußlehre und Bußpraxis nach der "Didascalia Apostolorum"
{1.5} *Zeitschrift für katolische Theologie* 72 (1950) 257-281. Revised.

Abstract: Rahner's analysis of the *Didascalia Apostolorum* pays special attention to whether or not penance is repeatable. He concludes it is.
Topics: PENANCE, history of; *DIDASCALIA APOSTOLORUM* on penance.
Subsidiary Discussions: Church, excommunication (227ff); Church, excommunication (liturgical) (231ff); Church, *pax cum ecclesia* (233f); Imposition of hands (234ff); Church, excommunication (ban) (243f).
Precis: This is an important early source canonically, liturgically, and dogmatically. It is unique in holding that penance is repeatable.
I. The question of penance. Rahner's analysis of the text concludes it should be taken as a unified treatment of penance in Syria about the middle, or even the first half, of the third century.
II. The theology of sin. This theology is not very precise.
III. Excommunication. Serious sinners must be excommunicated. This circle is very wide. Rahner surmises this community was quick to excommunicate in part because it did not know of the irrepeatability of penance. After listing the many reasons for excommunication Rahner turns to its two-fold implementation.

1) The real excommunication. The first step is the sinner's voluntary withdrawal from the community, either because s/he has given up the faith, or because shame or sorrow cause them to avoid the liturgical assembly. A less tactful person might be involuntarily and publicly expelled by the

bishop. To all these people, should they repent, reconciliation remains open after an official period of penance and a public, liturgical act of readmission.

2) The liturgical excommunication. Rahner describes a rite to formalize the status of the repentant sinner not yet fully readmitted to Eucharist. It involves a scrutiny by the bishop, a relatively short period of penitential ostracism, and the assembly's ratification of the bishop's actions accompanied by prayers for the penitent.

3) The effects of excommunication. It is more than disciplinary. It has other-worldly effects in that it separates one from the possibility of salvation. The text waffles on the effects of an illegitimate excommunication.

IV. Reconciliation. All repentant sinners can be reconciled to the church. The act of God and the act of the church are one in the same. The only unforgivable sin is obdurate heresy—the refusal to repent.

1) The rite. Lists the elements of the rite.

2) The meaning of the rite. After listing the parallels between the rites of baptism and penance, Rahner calls special attention to the fact that both rites in their entirety (including imposition of hands) take place apart from the celebration of Eucharist. This parallel points to the fact imposition of hands in both cases represents the communication of the Spirit, each in its own way. Because it is repeatable, penitential imposition of hands is not a repetition of confirmation even though according to Rahner it is modeled more on confirmation than on rites of exorcism or healing.

3) The theological meaning of reconciliation. The ecclesial and sacramental nature of penance is underscored by its parallels with baptism, the teaching on the bishop's power to bind and loose in God's name, and a communication of the Spirit through the imposition of hands. The bishop's obligation to support the penitent with prayer and guidance apart from the rite does not, in Rahner's opinion, point to the existence of a separate, private penance.

4) The repeatable character of reconciliation. The argument for the repeatability of penance is an argument from silence, with all the difficulties that involves. For Rahner the key argument in favor of this thesis is the broad distribution of sins for which excommunication is prescribed. Practically speaking, such freedom to excommunicate must have been accompanied by relatively unrestricted access to penance and reconciliation (242).

5) Parallels to the ban practice of the synagogue. In view of the affinity between the synagogal practice of the ban and the Syriac practice of excommunication Rahner finds it difficult to believe penance in this community was irrepeatable. Rahner concludes with a brief but complete summary (244f).

15.08   The Penitential Teaching of Origen
Die Bußlehre des Origens
{3.0}   *Rescherches de Science Religieuse* 37 (1950) 47-97, 252-86, 422-56, as,
La doctrine d'Origène sur la Pénitence. Thoroughly revised.

Abstract: Rahner unhesitatingly describes the excommunication/reconciliation in Origen as "sacramental" even though it was firmly embedded in the general reconciling activity. He finds no case for a "sacramental" private penance.

Topics: PENANCE, history of; ORIGEN on penance; PENANCE, binding and loosing; CHURCH, visible (and internal); CHURCH, excommunication; SIN.

Subsidiary Discussions: Church, mystery of (247ff, 296f, 321ff); Sin, postbaptismal (250f); Sin, mortal/venial (252ff, 254ff, 286ff); Sin, forgivableness of (261ff); Penance, subjective (266ff); Punishment (276); Penance, ecclesial (279ff); Church, *simul justus et pecator* (279ff); Donatism (285f, 320f); Church, *pax cum ecclesia* (293ff, 311ff); Penance (293f, 311f, 324ff); Church, office and holiness in (293ff); Saints, power to loose (297ff); Imposition of hands (303f); Baptism and penance (312ff); Sacraments, *res et sacramentum* (317ff); Symbol in Origen (321ff).

OUTLINE

I. Teaching on penance, theology and the church.
II. The personal penance of the sinner.
   1. Sin committed after baptism.
      a) The differences between sins.
      b) Light sins.
      c) Mortal sins.
      d) Concrete mortal sins according to Origen.
   2. The forgivable character of sin.
   3. Penance.
      a) The fire of penance.
      b) The penance of the sinner.
III. Church penance.
   1) The ecclesial meaning of penance.
   2) The church's saving action with regard to the sinner.
   3) Excommunication.
      a) The object of excommunication.
      b) Excommunication in practice.
      c) The theological meaning of excommunication.
   4) Reconciliation by the whole church.
      a) The different functions within the church community.
      b) Reconciliation achieved by the church of the saints.
   5) The official power of the church.
      a) The lifting of excommunication: the fact and the terminology.
      b) The extent of the church's power of reconciliation.

6) The meaning of excommunication.
   a) The lasting consequences of excommunication.
   b) The theological meaning of official church reconciliation.
   c) A systematic survey.
7) Penance as sacrament.
   a) Church penance as a sacrament.
   b) "Private" sacramental penance in Origen?

Precis: Origen is the first theologian of penance, the first who attempts to organize the data of transmitted revelation into a powerful system. To guard against misunderstanding, Rahner first looks at fundamental methodological preconceptions of Origen's whole theology.

I. Teaching on penance, theology and the church. What is prescribed by the gospel and taught by the church are the self-evident and inviolable norm of Origen's thought. He is radically anti-gnostic. His speculations are in no way superior to the common formulations the church teaches the masses. For Origen the principle object of theology is mystery—the unique movement of spirits from God and back. All created reality is interrelated in this hierarchically structured movement. Every level finds its meaning and truth in the highest level which never threatens or denies the lower. Thus, everything when seen properly is the image and likeness of the Logos. Every reality has two levels: its inner truth and its external presentation (e.g., the church, 249). The forgiveness of sin is necessarily connected to all these levels of mystery within the church. Rahner follows Origen's lead and presents the forgiveness of sins in two parts below: II the subjective aspects (the penance of the sinner under the influence of grace): III objective aspects (ecclesial).

II. The personal penance of the sinner (250-279).
1) Sin committed after baptism. With Origen the dream of the church as God's sinless bride comes to an end. He squarely confronts the reality of sin within the Christian community. His enthusiasm for baptism is remarkably less intense than his predecessors'. He sees it as a mere beginning of a long struggle against sin during which post-baptismal relapse is expected. Because Origen is concerned with the real sins of real people his treatment of sin itself is sometimes obscure. His terms and categories are often imprecise or fluid.

   a) Differences between sins. According to scripture sins differ in their seriousness—not merely in degree but in kind. His divisions, however, do not correspond completely with the modern concepts of mortal and venial sin.

   b) Light sins. Certain sins do not lead to death and co-exist with holiness. Even saints can simultaneously be sinners. Such people preserve baptismal grace and enjoying fellowship in the church.

   c) Mortal sins. Other serious sins incur death. Such sin causes death the moment it is committed because Jesus no longer dwells within. The Spirit which came with baptism is not preserved. In Origen "incurable" sin connotes sin which is terminal not necessarily unforgivable. Fallen Christians are in a worse state than pagans. For Origen the "sin against the Holy Spirit" attested to in scripture is not obduracy but any sin unto death. There follows a long discussion of the concept of *aphesis* in connection with Origen's idea that it is no longer possible for the baptized who have fallen into serious sin (255-259). Rahner concludes this is true for Origen because these sins cannot be remitted through a second baptism, nor by the regular intercession and sacrifice of the church because the sinner is no longer part of its fellowship. "Rather they must be expiated through the undergoing of the punishment which they deserve" (259).

d) Concrete mortal sins according to Origen. Origen never attempts to establish any theoretical, objective norm for distinguishing which sins lead to death and which do not. Nor does Rahner think it is likely he held there were essential distinctions among serious sins.

2) The forgivable character of sin. Given Origen's optimism regarding universal salvation in the future life, the real question here is whether serious sin is remissable before God in *this* life. Rahner maintains Origen holds this possibility since it is in keeping with his theology and his rejection of rigorism. Being a man of the church it is also likely Origen sees his teaching as one with the church. Rahner offers examples from Origen's works (263ff) all showing that mortal sins are remissable in this life even if after baptism this requires not *aphesis* but the interior fire of penance.

3) Penance. a) The fire of penance. The subjective penance of a person guilty of mortal sin is first and foremost a grace. After refuting the imputation that Origen's theology of grace is semi-Pelagian (266f) Rahner insists the raising of a person dead in sin is always the work of God, similar to but not identical with the modern notion of *gratia efficax*. The grace which makes penance possible resides in the experience of divine judgment on sin. Blessedness dawns for those lucky enough to feel their faults and the punishments they deserve. This "inner fire of judgment" is kindled when one's sins come into contact with the inalienable existence of the Logos of the Lord within a creature. "This impulse is the awakening experience within the human being of the burning contradiction...between one's personal decisions and the inalienable real, ontological, supernatural orientation towards God which is an indelible mark of human existence. It is at this point, at the very ground of being, that God's fire burns, that God's voice constantly calls the sinner from the grave of his sin" (270).

b) The penance of the sinner. This burning which begins in the heart must extend to the whole person, particularly to one's corporeity—the manifestation of original sin and the means of overcoming it. Hence, the torment of the heart overflows naturally in external works of penance: tears, sleepless vigils, groans, and fasting. In time, willing acceptance of this penance imposed by God can lead to the death of carnal cupidity. Such a punishment is always medicinal, never vindictive. It is not external but an intrinsic, connatural consequence of sin. This does not lead to the gnostic notion of an automatic effective self-destruction of evil in the sinner because guilt is never taken away except by human freedom. One must freely accept these consequences of sin to overcome them effectively.

Because Origen's views on punishment rule out a juridical notion of penance two points must be clarified: his distinction between mortal and non-mortal sins cannot be as clear-cut as today's; Origen offers no clear distinction between guilt and punishment, and their remission (276). All this raises the question of the relationship of personal penance to grace. Rahner brings the question to a point by asking what the "ideal" grace of the Logos within the sinner (which leads to the interior fire of judgment, which in turn leads to penance) has to do with the grace of Christ and his redemptive cross. If the mystery of the incarnation and death of the Logos consists in overthrowing the dominion of devil and flesh, then the sinner's penitential struggle participates in that of Christ. Insofar as Christ's death makes possible the experience of opposition between flesh and spirit and elevates the order of the flesh to heaven, penance is a grace. This insight has the effect of making it more difficult for Origen to incorporate the *aphesis* for pre-baptismal sin. To Rahner this proves he must have accepted this view as part of traditional church teaching without integrating it into his system.

III. Church penance (279-328).

1) The ecclesial meaning of penance. Sin is never a purely private affair. It changes sinners' relationship to the church, putting them beyond its healing influence. Sin also changes the church itself, making it simultaneously sinful and holy (an irresolvable dialectic for Origen). As this sense of the effect of sin on the church is lost excommunication grows increasingly insignificant.

2) The church's saving action with regard to the sinner. The status of the sinner in the church is ambiguous. Excommunication (for which Origen has no technical term) imposed by the bishop as an official and not necessarily as a spiritual person, because it is meant to bring the sinner back to it, is the church's first saving act with regard to the sinner. But the τέλειοι (perfect believers) also possess the power of the keys. Rahner examines this teaching in terms of Donatism and concludes Origen need not be interpreted in a Donatist sense because in this context he is focusing on the problem of unjust excommunications and on the power of the τέλειοι to loose them.

3) Excommunication.

a) The object of excommunication. All mortal sins, whether publicly known or secret, are subject to excommunication at the discretion of the bishop. Rahner enumerates serious sins.

b) Excommunication in practice. The bishop's task of supervising Christian life was a burden. Rahner outlines the situations in which excommunication was imposed, noting Origen does not describe the liturgy itself.

c) The theological meaning of excommunication. Excommunication is no added, arbitrary discipline imposed by a bishop. It is the public acknowledgment of the actual state of the sinner who has separated him/herself from table fellowship and has temporarily lost salvation by losing a place in the church which for Origen is always a spiritual and a visible reality. So to ask how church excommunication stands in God's eyes misreads Origen completely.

4) Reconciliation by the whole church.

a) The different functions within the church community. Rahner returns to the question of Origen's anti-Donatism insofar as it seems to be undermined by the "perfect believers'" role in loosing. He begins with the methodological remark (293ff) that treating the remission of sins in the categories of modern sacramental theology leads to very misleading and unsatisfactory results. Origen sees the whole church playing a role in reconciliation insofar as all the members participate in the reconciling work of Christ the head. Both the interior and exterior hierarchy play their roles, even if these cannot always be clearly distinguished. Rahner concludes that perfect believers, far from usurping the power of the external hierarchy in reconciling the sinner, are performing their proper function in which bishops participate insofar as they are spiritual. Summary (297).

b) Reconciliation achieved by the church of the saints. Only sinners are excluded from the reconciling work of the church which takes place in numerous activities (list, 298f). Hence, for Origen the loosing power of the church is essentially far more widely distributed than its power to bind. All it presupposes both in the bishop and in other members "is holiness and the living, grace-giving union with the holy Church, the body of Christ" (299). The bishop's spiritual power to remit sin is expressed in two official acts of the church: reconciliation and the Eucharistic sacrifice. Summary (301).

5) The official power of the church.

a) The lifting of excommunication: the fact and the terminology. Excommunication can be lifted and after suitable penance the sinner may be reconciled with the church as a real member. Origen uses the term *solvere* to refer to the bishop's power to lift excommunication. The rite of reconciliation consists of prayer, the imposition of hands, and perhaps an anointing. Rahner connects the meaning of the imposition of hands with a parallel gesture associated with confirmation.

b) The extent of the church's power of reconciliation. Since for Origen all sins are forgivable all sinners are able to be reconciled with the church. Rahner's analysis of Origen's *De or.* 28 (305ff) does not dispute this.

c) The conclusion of reconciliation. The duration of penance prior to reconciliation varies case by case according to the objective seriousness of the sin and the evidence of sincerity given by the penitent. Three years would not have been abnormal. Origen makes no mention of life-long penance.

6) The meaning of excommunication.

a) The lasting consequences of excommunication. The rights of reconciled persons are diminished. They cannot hold ecclesial office, and a second church penance is closed to them. Origen accepts this as self-evident.

b) The theological meaning of official church reconciliation. According to Rahner it is unfair to style Origen's excommunication and reconciliation as "sacramental" in today's sense of the term. Once again Rahner calls attention to the fact that for Origen salvation entails church membership. Only the sinner who inwardly repents can be reconciled with the church in an official act. Here Rahner sees a parallel between baptism and penance (312ff) where reception of the Holy Spirit in an ecclesial act is preceded by interior purgation from sin and its effects. Rahner answers the objection that Origen's approach reduces the scope of the ecclesial act by insisting that for Origen excommunication and reconciliation are two phases of one simple event, the whole of which takes place in and through the church (315f).

c) A systematic survey. The fact that repentance is a very interior process in no way precludes the mediation of created sanctifying powers (list, 316f). The process of penance in all its phases is visible as a reality of the church. Rahner presents a schema of this process (318) which sheds light on three later theological concepts: *sacramentum, res et sacramentum, res sacramenti* (317ff). Origen's unique contribution is that the sacramental event (*sacramentum*) and its immediate (*res et sacramentum*) and mediated (*res sacramenti*) effect themselves have three stages each. This schema clarifies Origen's notion that reconciliation bestows the Spirit. Rahner shows how Origen keeps this notion free from Donatist tendencies (320f). The schema also illustrates the relationship between what happens in the official church sphere and its effect in the depth of the human soul. Here Rahner discusses Origen's notion of symbol (σύμβολον), similar in many ways to his own (321ff).

7) Penance as sacrament.

a) Church penance as a sacrament. Rahner does not hesitate to describe the excommunication/reconciliation in Origen as "sacramental" even though questions remain as to the relationship between the sacramental sign and the grace signified. "Origen knew of a *sacrament* of penance" (324), even though at his time it was still firmly embedded in the general reconciling activity of the church through which it constantly renewed its own holiness.

b) "Private" sacramental penance in Origen? Rahner finds no evidence in Origen for a real "sacramental" private penance.

XVI. Experience of the Spirit: Source of Theology

XII. *Theologie aus Erfahrung des Geistes*

German edition: Einsiedeln, Benziger, 1975
U.S. edition: N.Y., Seabury, 1979
David Morland, O.S.B., translator

Dedicated to his mother on her 100th birthday. This volume in the English edition comprises essays 1-16 in *Schriften zur Theologie* XII.

Foreword (vii-xii). These introductory remarks situate the experience of the Spirit at the heart of this moment in the history of the church and Rahner's own theology, especially insofar as it was influenced by Ignatian discernment of spirits. The reality of the Spirit in Christian faith confronts theology with limit questions: the foundations of faith, the experience of grace, living from faith, etc. Since the Spirit is at work in concrete signs of the times this study significantly broadens the scope of theological reflection.

Separately these essays may seem to lack detail and originality. But reading them with the title of this volume in mind will bring to light fresh connections and insights. Whoever lives in radical hope digs from the rubble of daily existence what Rahner calls the experience of the Spirit and what Christians call the definitive victory of Jesus Christ. At this deep level can be found the spirit of joy and courage needed to carry on in an atmosphere which threatens fragmentation. Rahner hopes these essays contribute to the transmission of this Spirit.

16.01   The Foundation of Belief Today
Glaubensbegründung heute

{1.0}   Previously unpublished December 1973 paper to preachers and catechists at *Bildungshaus Stift*, Zwettle. Revised and expanded.

Abstract: Rahner grounds belief in our human experience of hope which Christians find sealed in the cross and resurrection of Jesus Christ.

Topics: FAITH, foundations of; HOPE.

Subsidiary Discussions: Concupiscence, gnoseological (5ff, 11f); Truths, hierarchy of (8f); Trinity (9ff); Infallibility (11f); God (14ff); Jesus Christ as ground of hope (15ff); Cross (17f); Church, necessity of (18ff); Love of neighbor (20f); Religions, non-Christian (21); Atheism (21); Death (18, 22).

Precis: Rahner offers only fragmentary remarks on this difficult and necessary investigation into the grounds of belief. Catholic apologetics has always respected and appealed to the intellect both through metaphysics and narrative theology. "Giving an account of our hope" is always external and internal, rational and spiritual. Catholic theology since the 19th century has been too external and rationalistic, and has relied too exclusively on appeals to formal, magisterial authority.

The situation of belief today. The church today is a cognitive minority. The intellectual climate in and to which theology speaks today is characterized by what Rahner calls gnoselogical or mental (as opposed to moral) concupiscence. The knowledge which is important for our worldview no longer admits of positive and complete ordering into a coherent whole.

The consequences of the modern situation. The reality of mental concupiscence prompted Vatican II to speak of a hierarchy of truths. This permits one to profess belief in the central tenets of faith without having synthesized them all into a single whole. The only way to provide grounds for belief is to concentrate on the innermost kernel of one's faith. Rahner has no fear this anthropological approach will end in reducing faith since the question of human existence finds its only satisfactory answer in God. Rahner answers the objection that an anthropological approach may never lead to the fulness of faith (e.g., to the doctrine of the Trinity) by insisting that not only does the doctrine subsist at the deepest level of anthropological inquiry, but also that approaching faith from the outside with appeals to formal authority is doomed to fail. Rahner also notes people today have a tremendous capacity to endure mental concupiscence. They do not seem to want or to seek a complete theology of everything, nor do they need one in order to be saved.

From the experience of faith to the establishment of belief. No one can escape the desire to be free, faithful, loving, and responsible. One can only accept oneself in the hope that "the incomprehensible element in all that is beautiful will in the end be made plain and that this meaning is final and blessed" (13). The ultimate ground of this hope is what Rahner calls God. Thus, the act of accepting personal existence in trust and hope means surrender to the incomprehensible mystery in silence and adoration. Christians call this mystery which sustains our hope "grace" or "Holy Spirit." Our fear of unbelief and the threat posed by our own capacity to deny ourselves are overcome by hope.

Jesus Christ: the synthesis. Those who are humble in the face of incomprehensible mystery find this basic human hope and the experience of Jesus sustain and justify each other. The basic unity which underlies all Christians' experience of Jesus gives them the strength to affirm from the center of their own experience, and from the hope that lies in it, that he is risen. His total surrender in faith was completely vindicated by God and opens new, decisive, and unsurpassable opportunities for all, whether or not one uses explicitly Christian terms to express or understand this truth. Cross and resurrection belong together in any authentic witness to Jesus and in genuine and responsible faith in him. Christianity is at once the simplest and hardest thing.

The task of the church. Many believe in the eternal validity of Jesus' resurrection. These believers necessarily form a visible community, the church, because of their common relationship to him, their active witness, their social nature and history, and their human solidarity. (Rahner also mentions the sociology of knowledge.) At the same time the church is a scandal. Its members inevitably deny with their actions what they profess with their lips. But where else can believers turn? Finally, faith must be embodied in a church because God can only be loved in one's neighbor. Rooted as it is in the death of the Lord, the Christian responsibility for the social sphere can never be ideology, false optimism, or pure humanitarianism. After a brief word on non-Christian religions and atheism, Rahner ends with a summary (21ff).

16.02   Experience of the Spirit and Existential Commitment
Erfahrung des Geistes und existentielle Entscheidung
{3.5}   1974 contribution to a festschrift for E. Schillebeeckx's 60th birthday. Revised, cross references added.

Abstract: Faced with a number of worthwhile possibilities one can only come to an existential decision before God by assuming a synthesis of the transcendent experience of Spirit and the encounter with the categorial object of choice.

Topics: SPIRIT, experience of; SPIRIT, discernment of; FREEDOM and choice; TRANSCENDENT/CATEGORIAL.

Subsidiary Discussions: Commitment, existential (24ff); God (25); Anonymous Christian (26f); Nature, pure (26); Freedom (26f).

Precis: The topic of this essay is a sub-set of the topic "transcendence and history" about which Rahner can make only a few brief remarks. He insists the gift of grace through the Spirit of God is a genuine self-communication of God to the transcendent human self and not some internal or external categorial reality of human consciousness (an idea, thought, datum, or insight).

Characteristics of existential commitment. The essence of existential commitment cannot be completely defined. It signifies the free act of human beings in which they have ultimate control over themselves before God. (Insofar as God is implicitly co-known in any choice of the good, Rahner is not concerned whether a person explicitly accepts/rejects God.) The basic tenet of Christian anthropology is that free behavior isn't limited to the categorial and finite object of choice or to a concept of God in one's objective consciousness. It extends to God's own self. This is why categorial choices can constitute salvation/damnation, the acceptance/rejection of God's self-communication. This assumes that our transcendent nature is graced. (Rahner argues pure nature is never an acceptable starting-point for any anthropological discussion, 26.) Whoever surrenders without reserve to one's transcendent nature is raised by grace to communion with the direct reality of God whether or not reference is made to explicit Christian revelation. This always takes place through an existential decision involving historically limited, categorial material. How freedom which involves categorial objects is related to the freedom of the subject toward self and God is very complex. This is seen in the fact that there is no absolutely fixed relationship between the categorial content and the transcendental significance of free decisions. Conclusion (27).

Spiritual experience. The essential nature of genuine experience of the Spirit does not consist in particular objects of experience found in human awareness. It occurs when one experiences the radical re-ordering of one's transcendent nature in knowledge and freedom towards the immediate reality of God through God's self-communication in grace. It is not a particular divine operation from without, but God's self-communication to the human spirit by which God becomes a constitutive element of human transcendence. This innermost depth of the person can be understood as "nature." Leaving aside cases of mysticism, this transcendent experience of a personal other is mediated through categorial objects. Although transcendental experience can be given objective form it must never be mistaken for it. To assume that only certain categorial objects (i.e., religious objects) can bear transcendental experience is a basically mythological view of the world.

Commitment and the Spirit. How are experience of the Spirit and existential commitment (choice of vocation, marriage partner, etc.) related? How are these categorial decisions related to the basic acceptance or rejection of God? Rahner spends the remainder of this section outlining the ambiguities of choice: a wrong categorial choice can lead to a positive relationship with God whereas an objectively good choice need not necessarily do so. It is also possible that among many good choices perhaps only one is God's will.

The problem of choice. How can one come to an existential decision in the face of a number of worthwhile possibilities if one is to proceed, not arbitrarily, but before God and in conformity with a choice willed by God? Setting aside the mythological talk of ordinary Christians, and steadfastly maintaining there can be no "new revelations," the only possibility for making a specific choice is to posit a synthesis of the transcendent experience of Spirit and the encounter with the categorial object of choice freely offered here and now. The transcendent experience of God is the experience of a person; the experience of freedom is experienced as a gift of God—the continuation of God's creative act in our lives. This makes the synthesis of the categorial and transcendent conceivable. "The categorial which is freely willed can be experienced as the fixed purpose creatively determined by God's freedom" (31).

As regards the choices we are given by God, though the synthesis Rahner describes may not mask or disguise the transcendent experience, it may still be difficult for an individual to make the choice. This is because it is possible God had not intended one particular outcome, and has even willed the obscurity or ambiguity one feels. At the same time this synthesis can be experienced in a more positive way. A categorial option may not only lessen or distort the experience of the Spirit, it may provide a concrete and practical means of expression for it.

Though he realizes his remarks are very general and abstract Rahner challenges anyone who does not see practical applications to his discussion by asking whether they fully appreciate the distinction between transcendent experiences which have been thought out and given objective, verbal expression and those which have not. For those who say they never experienced the synthesis, Rahner suggests that although perhaps these experiences are rare they nonetheless retain the ability to determine the rest of one's life.

16.03 Religious Enthusiasm and the Experience of Grace
Die enthusiastische und die gnadenhafte Erfahrung
{3.0}   November 1973 paper to Swiss Theological Society at Berne. C. Heitmann, H. Mühlen, eds., *Erfahrung und Theologie des Heiligen Geistes* (Munich 1974) 64-80. Originally, *Das enthusiastich-charismatische Erlebnis in Konfrontation mit der gnadenhaften Transzendenzerfahrung*. Expanded.

Abstract: The best way to analyze charismatic experience is under the rubric of mysticism. Strictly speaking, the categorial content of these experiences counts neither for nor against their spiritual authenticity.

Topics: SPIRIT, charismatic renewal; MYSTICISM; GRACE, experience of; TRANSCENDENT/CATEGORIAL.

Subsidiary Discussions: Grace and human consciousness (36ff).

Precis: Though there is much about religious enthusiasm which dogmatic theology cannot comment on, Rahner hopes here to establish the *locus theologicus* in which to situate charismatic enthusiasm and to offer some basic guidelines about the discernment of spirits. He realizes this leaves many issues open. Chief among these is whether the Spirit enters human consciousness as the Spirit or is only accepted as present because of the external teaching of scripture and the magisterium. After describing this older, established theory of grace in detail (37f) Rahner insists that if dogmatic theology wants to speak of Christian enthusiasm it must break definitively from this school and return to an even older school according to which *Pneuma* means a "genuine *self*-communication of God in himself" (39). This is not to say the first school has nothing to recommend it (list, 39). Its strengths even lead some to suggest that it alone can rescue the specific essence of Christianity from the onslaught of charismatic enthusiasm which would reduce Christianity to the level of other religions. From this safe position dogmatic theology could declare itself to have no interest in the phenomenon of religious enthusiasm.

Outline of a contemporary theory of grace. The theory of grace Rahner proposes is justified by its usefulness in interpreting the phenomenon of religious enthusiasm. For him the essence of grace is "the self-communication of God to the transcendent spirit of man ... [which] divinises man and bestows upon him a share in the holiness of God" (40). Not only does this view allow for the communication of grace in explicitly non-Christian settings, it also avoids all the problems accompanying the older theory. Rahner's theory assigns no categorial object of consciousness to this grace, although at a later point the transcendent experience of grace can be the object of reflection and categorial expression. Hence, grace is never tied to a particular inner-worldly phenomenon.

Rahner next asks whether the various expressions of religious enthusiasm can be brought under a single heading (42f). Although identifying their common element does not enable one to say anything at all about religious enthusiasm as such, Rahner suggests all genuine expressions of religious enthusiasm "bring more clearly to a person's consciousness the experience of transcendence" (43). These rare occurrences are found "in homeopathic states and in unreflective mysticism (by mysticism is meant here a transcendent experience through grace which is not categorial) .... Religious enthusiasm is, as it were, mysticism in ordinary dress" (43). Rahner links this mysticism with the *kenosis* of Christ's death.

The meaning of religious enthusiasm. Rahner summarizes: expressions of religious enthusiasm are not specifically religious or experiences of grace. "However, through these phenomena a man comes face to face in a particular way with his own transcendence and through it with his freedom and so with one's inner reference to God" (43f). For ordinary Christians in their daily piety the true meaning of religion is hidden and made remote by the dominance of its traditional, everyday expressions. Through religious enthusiasm the objectification of religion is dislodged from its system. This experience of being taken out of oneself makes the institutional church seem provisional, questionable, and incommensurate with the meaning it is supposed to signify. We are then thrown back on our subjectivity which we can no longer control but must find the courage to trust. All this is sustained by God's self-communication.

Consequences. Religious enthusiasm is a sort of "mysticism of the masses." Within certain limits (list, 47) the phenomenon of religious enthusiasm can rightly be subjected to human critical analysis. One is not faced with the alternatives that either these experiences are the unadulterated operation of the Spirit or they must be discounted from the start as rubbish. Because no one can deny the human origin of the categorial content and conceptual framework of these experiences, they cannot be interpreted as guaranteed divine inspiration. Strictly speaking, their categorial content counts neither for nor against their spiritual authenticity, although it cannot be said that their categorial content is simply irrelevant. For Catholics the criteria for assessing these experiences is found primarily in mystical theology, though similar criteria are used to assess the truth of theological statements (49f). Rahner ends by listing (51) other departments of dogmatic theology which in their own way deal with the same problem raised by this study: the relationship of the categorial and the transcendent.

16.04 Anonymous and Explicit Faith
Anonymer und expliziter Galube
{2.5} *Stimmen der Zeit* 192 (1974) 147-152. Footnotes added.

Abstract: Rahner grounds the possibility of salvation for non-believers on two theological principles: human transcendence and God's universally efficacious will. Historical revelation in Christ embodies transcendent revelation.

Topics: FAITH, anonymous; ATHEISM; ANONYMOUS CHRISTIAN.
Subsidiary Discussions: Revelation, transcendent (55f); God, salvific will of (56f); Revelation, historical (58).
Precis: Anonymous faith is necessary and effective for salvation even though it occurs without an explicit or conscious relationship to Christian revelation or to God. This topic has ramifications for atheism. Rahner assumes genuine faith is necessary for salvation and justification. Since non-believers who do

not offend against conscience can be saved by their faith, what precisely is the "faith universally necessary for salvation"? (53)

Faith necessary for salvation. Rahner lists (53) and dismisses previous explanations of how non-believers achieve the faith necessary for salvation. He posits "anonymous faith" which, though sufficient, possesses the dynamism towards full and explicit faith. The possibility of such faith rests on two valid theological principles drawn from theological anthropology: the unlimited transcendent nature of the human spirit in knowledge and freedom; the dogma of God's universally effective will. Rahner rephrases his thesis (55).

The transcendent character of the human spirit. The inner dynamism of human spirit is directed towards God. This goal is mediated through categorial objects. Neither these objects nor their goal needs to be expressed in explicitly religious categories. "There then exists a conscious reference to God which can be freely accepted, although this is not explicitly reflected upon or treated under the heading of 'God'" (55). People, even atheists, accept God whenever they accept themselves in their own unlimited transcendence.

The saving will of God. The supernatural grace offered to all by God as self-communication: 1) is not episodic. It is an abiding possibility of human freedom. 2) It transforms human consciousness in the Thomistic sense of bringing about a new, a priori, formal object beyond the reach of any natural act of human reason. This fact makes it impossible to distinguish grace as such from one's natural spiritual essence merely by reflecting on particular objects of consciousness. Because God's saving will is universally operative this transforming grace is universal in time and place. This whole process also goes under the title "transcendent revelation." Summary (57).

"Anonymous" faith. Why, then, is Christian revelation not simply superfluous? After a one paragraph synopsis of his thesis Rahner clarifies the relationship between transcendent revelation and historical Christian revelation. Because God wills transcendent revelation to become present in history the two have a mutual reference. Historical revelation only realizes its proper character through its transcendent counterpart. Those who refuse to give objective structure and shape to their transcendental being jeopardize their salvation.

16.05   Faith between Rationality and Emotion
Glauben zwischen Rationalität und Emotionalität
{3.0}   K. Rahner, ed., *Ist Gott noch gefragt?* (Dusseldorf 1973) 125-144. Revised and expanded.

Abstract: Because faith is the single fundamental whole composed of rationality and freedom (emotion) it is possible to think rationally about faith both in itself and in reference to the other sciences.

Topics: FAITH; FREEDOM; THEOLOGICAL ANTHROPOLOGY, emotion; THEOLOGICAL ANTHROPOLOGY, rationality.
Subsidiary Discussions: God as ground of rationality (66ff); Grace (68ff); Revelation (68f); Mystery (70f); Concupiscence, gnoseological (73f); Faith, *fides quae/qua* (73); Theology and science (75ff); Science and theology (75ff); Dialogue between theology and science (75ff).
Precis: Rahner proceeds slowly, beginning with a few preliminary remarks.
The approach to faith. Simply because the terms emotion and reason are obscure does not make it illegitimate to try to situate faith between them. For Rahner rationality is not directed to the content of a proposition. It refers to the tendency to build systems connecting propositions into a logical whole. It includes such concerns as verification and its presuppositions. If faith is a reasonable act of worship then faith and rationality must be related. Emotion is more difficult to define. Negatively it is what escapes the control of rationality. Rahner insists the reality of human freedom and its historical expression fall within the category of emotion for a number of reasons (list, 63f). Freedom can never be subjected to adequate rational investigation insofar as rationality is primarily concerned with the effectiveness of means and not with the creative establishment or justification of ends. Summary (64).
Faith and freedom. Faith "between rationality and emotion" equates to faith "between rationality and freedom" (64). Rahner insists the essential nature of freedom is not in itself a neutral possibility of choice among various categorial objects. It is the capacity of spiritual subjects to exercise definitive control over themselves. Freedom means the capacity to act once and for all for oneself. Thus, for Christians faith is identical with freedom (65).
The reference to God. Rahner's thesis that faith equates with freedom rests on certain indisputable theological assumptions. Faith is a free act conceivable only in and through the transcendent reference to human freedom whom we call God. In fact freedom is freedom for or against God. Whenever we accept ourselves as the mystery we are, we are accepting God. Rahner finds the justification for this thesis in the efficacy of God's universally salvific will (leaving aside here precisely how this is the case).

Rahner returns to the topic of rationality, insisting, "the ultimate condition of possibility of rationality is the transcendent reference of man to the unfathomable mystery we call God" (67). All the functional connections among particular phenomena are grounded as a single whole in the dynamic structure of the human spirit. This in turn is focused upon the ultimate goal of the whole movement which Rahner calls absolute mystery or God. To call this goal irrational would be to deny all rationality.
Radical transformation through grace. For Rahner grace refers to the unfathomable mystery of God which is above reason, at least in the form of an offer. Grace refers not simply to a datum of revelation but to the whole dynamism. Hence, for Rahner "the history of revelation is the history of

human rationality under the influence of grace in which reason grasps ever more plainly this mystery as its foundation and master and freely accepts it" (69). Christian faith, therefore, is not a particular event among others, but the primordial act of human rationality as such grasped in its ultimacy in the freely offered and accepted death of Jesus Christ. It is the ultimate event of rationality and emotion in a single whole...the simplest and the hardest thing (70f). The remaining content of the Christian faith (including the church) are particular formulations deduced from this truth. The acceptance of the single totality of rationality and emotion can never be equated with any formulation of it in conceptual terms. Although such formulations are always secondary to faith they are not thereby unimportant or unnecessary.

Tension. Though faith, rationality, and emotion form a unity there is always an essential tension among them. Rahner returns to the distinction between faith itself (*fides qua*) and the secondary reflection and conceptualization of faith (*fides quae*). The tension in today's intellectual situation in which we cannot hope to synthesize all we know, Rahner refers to as gnoseological concupiscence. Christianity can neither deny this basic inner conflict nor use it as an excuse to avoid coming to terms with the tension.

Characteristics of the relationship. Rahner analyzes faith and science, looking in turn at natural science, history, psychology, and social science. He maintains that even though there will always be opposition to faith it is not necessarily deadly for two reasons: sciences no longer presume to hold sway over all knowledge; faith is no longer seen as a particular set of propositions but as the single totality of rationality and freedom. Summary (78).

16.06   The "Spiritual Senses" according to Origen
Die "geistlichen Sinne" nach Origenes

{2.0}   *Revue d'Ascetique et de Mystique* 13 (1932) 113-145, as, *Le début d'une doctrine des cinq sens spirituals chez Origène.*

Rahner's first major theological work. Substantially abridged.

Abstract: This overview of the five spiritual senses in Origen situates the doctrine within his overall theology and traces its use by later thinkers.

Topics: ORIGEN on spiritual senses; SPIRITUALITY, Origenist.

Subsidiary Discussions: Life, active/contemplative (90ff); Evagrius (97ff).

Precis: Mysticism must express itself in images drawn from sense knowledge. This essay sketches the history of Origen's idea of spiritual senses.

The points of departure in Origen. "[M]an possesses, over and above his bodily faculties, 'a sense for the divine, which is completely different from the senses as normally described' or simply 'divine faculties of sense'" (84). Only the "perfect" are endowed with these faculties which they have brought to a higher level of operation through constant practice. Origen is the first to formulate this doctrine (83) which owes its inspiration solely to scripture.

The development of the idea. His polemic against Celsus forced Origen to interpret all genuine religious experience psychologically. Unbelief is shown precisely in the lack of spiritual senses in certain people who are then incapable of perceiving spiritual realities. It is possible to develop only some of the five spiritual senses, and each to a different degree.

The exercise of the five senses. Sin obstructs the spiritual senses. To vitalize them takes grace and practice. For their correct use the Logos itself is the indispensable foundation. The angels also help. Practice consists in such things as faith, attentive study, prayer. Rahner concludes with a look at Origen's obscure distinction between soul and spirit (88f).

The place of spiritual faculties within the system. To see how this doctrine fits into Origen's system Rahner first outlines two basic principles: his distinction between the active (practical) and contemplative (theoretical) life (90ff); the three stages of the spiritual life (*moralis, naturalis, inspectiva*) (92ff). The "perfect" are those contemplatives who have arrived at the third stage of the spiritual life and who are in full possession of all five spiritual senses.

The use of the spiritual senses. Grace is required to use the spiritual faculties. They can grasp nothing unless God bestows his merciful grace. For all this, it would be a mistake to equate Origen's spirituality with the mysticism of contemporary theology. Origen applies his theory to his understanding of final beatitude (the five senses remain active) and to prophetic inspiration.

The later influence of the doctrine. Rahner briefly comments on the later use of Origen's doctrine of the five spiritual senses in Evagrius of Pontus (97ff); Diadocus Photicus (100f); Pseudo-Macarius (101f); Simeon Logothetes (102) and the Greek and Latin Fathers as well as the Scholastics (102f).

16.07   The Doctrine of the "Spiritual Senses" in the Middle Ages

{3.5} "Die Lehre von den 'geistlichen Sinne' im Mittelalter: der Beitrag Bonaventuras." *Revue d'Ascetique et de Mystique* 14 (1933) 263-299, as, "La doctrine des 'sens spirituels' au Moyen-Age en particulier chez St. Bonaventure." Expanded in *Zeitschrift für Aszese und Mystik* 9 (1934) 1-19, as, "Der Bergriff der Ecstasis bei Bonaventura."

Abstract: As Part II of 16.06 this essay analyzes Bonaventure's contribution to the notion of spiritual senses, especially the relation of touch to ecstacy, and sketches the history of the idea from Bonaventure to the present.

Topics: BONAVENTURE on spiritual senses; SPIRITUALITY, Bonaventuran; THEOLOGICAL ANTHROPOLOGY, ecstacy.

Subsidiary Discussions: God, object of spiritual senses (113ff); Eschatology, *raptus* (117f, 120); Beatific vision (122); Dark night of the soul (123ff); Ignatius Loyola (130); John of the Cross (131); Mysticism (133f).

Precis: The contribution of St. Bonaventure. All that was achieved from the time of Origen and Augustine to Bonaventure (by Bernard of Clairvaux, William of Thierry, Alcher of Clairvaux) was to keep the idea of the spiritual senses from falling into complete oblivion. Rahner notes developments in the term *sensus* and the tendency of the scholastics to domesticate classic concepts such as the spiritual senses within their own systems in a way which rendered the older concepts almost superfluous.

The idea of the high middle ages. Rahner examines briefly the doctrine of the spiritual senses in William of Auxerre, William of Auvergne, Alexander of Hales, and Albert the Great respectively.

St. Bonaventure. After refuting Bonnefoy's argument that Bonaventure is so inconsistent in his use of the term "spiritual senses" that it is an error to expect to find any coherent thought, Rahner proceeds to outline what he sees as Bonaventure's doctrine presented not in connection with psychology but with grace. The soul in the state of grace has three modes of operation: through the virtues, the gifts of the Holy Spirit, and the blessings of beatitude. Each corresponds with one of the stages of the spiritual life: purification, enlightenment, perfection. Those who are perfect stand on the threshold of contemplation which is exercised precisely in the acts of the spiritual senses. For this reason the spiritual senses are not new powers but new application of existing acts. Rahner concludes this rather obscure preview with a look at how these acts are related to beatitude, the gifts of the Holy Spirit, and virtues, with special attention to intellect and will (112f).

The object of knowledge of the "spiritual senses." Bonaventure's *Breviloquium* and *Itinerarium* provide a forced, rhetorical treatment of spiritual senses (114f). Other texts offer a more complete view. Rahner begins with spiritual sight which is indebted to the act of faith, the gift of understanding, and the blessing of purity of heart. These three modes of operation correspond with Bonaventure's three stages of the supernatural knowledge of God. Rahner concentrates on the third which is characterized by "simple vision," "an infallible fore-knowledge of the eternal foundations which comes through particular images bestowed upon our spirit" (116). Next Rahner turns from acts of understanding to acts of will which Bonaventure associates with the spiritual sense of taste. Above both of these, however, is the ecstatic union with God of a more direct love characterized by spiritual touch, the highest spiritual sense.

Ecstacy. Rahner distinguishes ecstacy from the extraordinary occurrence of *raptus*, a foretaste of beatific vision. Ecstacy is also distinguished from knowledge of God mediated by the created effects of grace. "According to Bonaventure, therefore, we should assume [in ecstacy] a *cognoscere* or better a *sentire* of God which is a direct process ... without any intermediary means of perception ..." (119). Rahner proceeds further to distinguish ecstacy from *raptus* and to argue why and how it differs from beatific vision.

How can this direct experience of God be made comprehensible? Ecstacy takes place in an affectivity higher and more interior that the intellect. Since God dwells exclusively in this innermost part of the human being one can see the whole of Bonaventure's spirituality as "the gradual return of a man to the interior domain, as ascent to the highest point of the soul" (123). Because it is achieved as affectivity, in ecstacy one leaves all intellectual activity behind and enters an intellectual darkness, a divine obscurity. How are we to conceive the direct experience of a union of love? The problem Bonaventure encounters here is how we can will something we do not know. This can be solved if one sees the will lying at a deeper level of the soul than the intellect, and God (the dark fire of love) the ground of the soul, as deeper still. Summary (125).

Ecstacy and spiritual touch. Rahner argues spiritual touch is nothing else than the act by which the soul grasps the substance of God in ecstacy. "Contact" conveys better than "touch" the sense of directness and darkness in this highest, direct grasp of God. Rahner rounds out this discussion with a sketch of how the doctrine of spiritual senses was developed by those who followed Bonaventure: Roger Bacon, Meister Eckhart, Rudolf of Biberach, 15th and 16th century authors (with a special note on Ignatius Loyola), Theresa of Avila and John of the Cross (with special concern for the dark night, 131), modern and contemporary thinkers.

Rahner concludes with a few observations (133f). Mystical experience is always described in images drawn from sense perception. For all its value this approach also shares the limits of analogy. A key problem is why to retain the notion of five senses, especially if one analyses mysticism in terms of intellect and will. Bonaventure proves that the analogy to senses is valuable and necessary, although the analogy of precisely five sense seems superfluous.

16.08   Modern Piety and the Experience of Retreats
Moderne Frömmigkeit und Exerzitienerfahrung
{1.5}   *Geist und Leben* 47 (1974) 430-499, as, *Über den geistesgeschichtlichen Ort der ignatianischen Exerzitien heute.* Expanded.

Abstract: The close of the modern era calls for a new form of the Ignatian exercises with the local church as an active subject. It would aim to discern the movement of the Spirit in groups such as parishes and religious orders.
Topics: IGNATIUS LOYOLA, Exercises of; SPIRITUALITY, Ignatian; CHRISTIAN LIFE, retreats.
Subsidiary Discussions: Church history (136f); Society, modern era (138ff, 146); Vatican II (146f); Church, local (142ff; 146ff); Spirit, discernment of (142ff, 146ff).

Precis: Ignatius' Spiritual Exercises were a product of the modern era. What does the close of that era signify for their future? Though the topic may seem overly general Rahner insists it has important practical consequences for retreat ministry today.

Presuppositions. Rahner begins with a discussion of change and continuity. To say the church is genuinely historical means new and unpredictable things actually arise continually in the church while at the same time it preserves its essential character. Only the passage of time reveals the deep historical roots of these innovations. This process of development touches dogma and every other area of church life. Because these developments are always the product of human freedom change is never a simple growth in perfection. It also necessarily involves obstruction, guilt, and infidelity.

The Spiritual Exercises as a characteristic document of the modern period. Thesis: *"The Exercises of Ignatius had a decisive influence on the history of the post-Reformation church of the modern era. The Exercises brought something new into the church which in the present situation of the 'end of the modern era' is both passing away and being maintained."*

a) The modern foundation. Leaving aside the question of when the modern era began, the central fact of the modern period is that of the individual subject, not as a member of a group but as personally directed to God (139). Modern individuals see themselves as radically free. They engage in plans to extend their control over themselves and their environment.

b) Self-discovery before God. The Exercises are modern insofar as they place the creator and creature in solitary contact with each other. They do not aim to instill a general principle into the subject but call for a subjective act of free decision.

c) The individual and the church in the Exercises. The church does not figure as "active subject" in the Exercises. The church is merely a reality to which the individual is related before God. It is never the controlling agent in the Exercises but is at most a supporting agent. Rahner questions whether this must continue to be the role of the church in the Exercises.

Ignatius and the "end of the modern era." Ignatius did not consider himself the sole founder of his order. He saw that as the work of his first companions united as they were by the spirit of the Exercises which they used to discern the makeup and direction of the group. In addition the new epoch which is gradually emerging, and in which the Exercises must continue to function, is characterized by people searching for higher forms of social structures "to reconcile the dignity and value of the individual with the social character of man and also face the social and material demands which are necessary for survival both now and in the future" (146).

The church after the end of the modern era. After listing the ways in which Vatican II positioned the church to engage this new age and to participate in building its new, higher forms of socialization (list, 147) Rahner suggests the initiative now rests with local communities.

New questions—new praxis. All this allows a fresh look at the Exercises. Rahner asks whether the church could assume the role of an active subject in the Exercises finding expression in a specific community of believers. If this is possible what might this mean for the Exercises and for retreat ministry? Rahner insists on an affirmative answer for empirical and theological reasons (the existence of such groups, and a newly emerging ecclesiology). **The Exercises: Possible self-expression of the church.** Insofar as Eucharist, choral office, common prayer, etc. are all moments of genuine self-realization of the church, it is clear this capacity exists even outside the acts of the official institutional church and in the acts of the local community. Rahner suggests that discernment of spirits is simply another legitimate local expressions of church. "Collective acts of decision made by an ecclesial group, a community, can therefore be ecclesial and be, in the strictest sense, self-expression of the Church" (151). Though Ignatius never states it expressly, in Rahner's view such collective discernment of spirits by parishes or religious orders constitutes the proper form of spiritual exercises proper to the post-modern era. Obviously this would call for modifying the Exercises to yield an entirely new form of a perennial reality. **Practical Consequences.** After a one-paragraph summary (153) Rahner suggests the logic of existential decision inherent in this new form of the Exercises could be of benefit to today's Pentecostal movement. It would not replace but supplement the classic individual Ignatian retreat. Between these two types of retreats (two extreme points of what may be termed Ignatian) many variations are conceivable.

16.09   Reflections on the New Task for Fundamental Theology
Einige Bemerkungen zu einer neuen Aufgabe der Fundamental-theologie
{1.0}   *Estudios Eclesiasticos* 47 (1972) 397-408.

Abstract: The Exercises of St. Ignatius contain all the elements needed for the new task of fundamental theology: connecting the relative conclusions offered by rational reflection with one's need for absolute commitment.

Topics: THEOLOGY, fundamental; THEOLOGY, method (indirect); IGNATIUS LOYOLA, Exercises of.
Subsidiary Discussions: Concupiscence, gnoseological (156ff); Newman, John Henry (165).
Precis: The state of fundamental theology today. How can fundamental theology, scientific and systematic reflection upon the grounds of credibility of Christian revelation and the obligation of faith, accomplish its task in today's cultural and human situation of gnoseological concupiscence? Today's intellectual world differs from that of the past insofar as no one person today can hope to encompass totally any field of knowledge. Not even teamwork can overcome this difficulty, especially not in fundamental theology which is a reflection on one's personal decision of faith.

Indirect method in fundamental theology? An indirect method must be found to enable fundamental theology to speak into this new irreducibly plural situation. Rahner asks how a person can make an absolute, irrevocable commitment when reflection can only provide relative grounds. The various theories offered to address this problem "either do not pay sufficient attention to the radical difference between the grounds of faith provided by fundamental theology and faith itself, or they simply appeal to the decision of 'the will'" (160).

Methods of "choice." Rahner suggests a clearer theological explanation of the Exercises of St. Ignatius possesses the elements necessary to bridge the gap between relative reasons and absolute commitment. They are found in the "rules of choice," especially to first and second choice (Bibliography, 161 ftn6; 163 ftn7). Rational reflection on the object of choice results at best in relative certainty regarding whether a particular choice is God's will. The conviction it is God's will and demands absolute commitment comes only from an experience of grace. This implies a lived synthesis of the categorial object of choice and the absolute freedom of the spirit directed to God's immediate reality. Here are all the elements needed to overcome the impasse outlined earlier.

The significance of the "choice" for fundamental theology. Rahner concludes the task for any genuine fundamental theology is to develop a theology of Ignatian choice as a precondition for an absolute decision of faith (summary, 164). After showing how contemporary theologies of grace fail to connect rationality and commitment Rahner briefly discusses J.H. Newman's contribution to this problem: the "illative sense" (165). He concludes with comments on the "depressing" state of Jesuit reflection on the theology of the Exercises.

16.10   The Acceptance in Faith of the Truth of God
Glaubende Annahme der Warheit Gottes

{2.0} W. Kern, G. Stachel, eds., *Warum Glauben? Begründung und Verteidigung des Glaubens in einundvierzig Thesen* (Wurzburg 1967), as, *Nicht das Weltbild der modernen Wissenschaft vermag dem Dasein letztlich Sinn zu geben, sondern esrt die glaubende Annahme der geschichtlich uns zugesprochenen Wahrheit Gottes.* Slightly revised.

Abstract: Religion and knowledge of God are prior to the scientific world-view. Though God-talk never breaks free of its historical limits, its very opacity in some ways preserves the transcendent mystery of God.

Topics: GOD-TALK; THEOLOGY and science; SCIENCE and theology.
Subsidiary Discussions: Atheism (170); God, transcendence of (171f); Demythology (173ff); Statements, eschatological (174f).

Precis: If the contemporary situation were looked at in the proper way, far from making people more deaf to God it could perhaps be seen to bring them to a more acute sensitivity to the mutual dependence of faith and knowledge. **The present situation: a God-less world.** In prior times God was universally seen as a piece of the world. Today the world seems self-contained and God increasingly seems nowhere to be found. This gave rise in the 18th century to a superficial theoretical atheism. Today it engenders an existential kind of "atheism of anxiety." This atheism is a false interpretation of a genuine intuition of the depths of existence which actually indicates "the growth of God in the spirit of man" (170). **Prior conditions.** We inherit our worldview with its two faces: metaphysical and historical. The first principles of metaphysics are never fully verified from without. They are only revealed as legitimate to those who freely entrust themselves to them. We think and act out of a tradition we renounce but never fully jettison. The only question for Rahner is how to insure our renunciation does not involve a *fatal* loss. **The basic first principle.** The truth of religion (i.e., the knowledge of God and faith in God's historical revelation) is prior to the scientific worldview. These do not constitute two truths but one. Religion is the higher reality since it arises from a more fundamental level of existence. All understanding occurs within and is directed towards God, the incomprehensible infinity lying behind the world's multiplicity—the personal spirit who is the foundation of all personal beings existing in the world. God, the precondition of the world and of knowledge of the world, can only be known indirectly. Only today is this knowledge explicitly entering the real heart of human existence. **Christianity and religions.** For this reason the Christian religion (comprised of history, institution, authority, commandment) is not a rival to science. The competition is between Christianity and a pre-scientific worldview which colors Christianity's analogical language about God. To some the pictorial character of this inexact talk about God must be demythologized. But all God-talk is inadequate stammering which leaves the mystery of God intact. **The language of the Bible.** It is unnecessary to demythologize because mythological language retains its same meaning even after the worldview in which it originated disappears (e.g., eschatological propositions, 174f). Greater opacity also harbors a gain: it lessens the danger of naive reduction of religious realities and makes even clearer the inexpressible greatness of God. **Listening to the word of God.** The change Rahner describes means we grasp the word of God precisely insofar as we grasp our historical situation in the world. God is never grasped in prior intellectual reflection (scientific, philosophical, or theological). Religion, knowledge of God, reception of the word of God, supply the answer to our lived situation. "[P]rior to and behind science there lie metaphysics and faith, higher and more comprehensive forces ...essentially ordered to freedom and commitment" (175f). The roots of unreflective understanding and harmony of being must never be cut off. They must penetrate as deeply into the subsoil of existence as science. Rahner finds it remarkable that modern science and philosophy are beginning to accept this idea. Referring to history and tradition in this way helps us hear the word of God as the object of hope, the saving answer to the question of the meaning of existence. Though spoken in image and parable it contains the promise of absolute truth which justifies and makes possible all creative thought and action.

16.11   The Old Testament and Christian Dogmatic Theology
Altes Testament und christliche Dogmatik
{2.5}   1972 paper in Regensburg. Revised and expanded.

Abstract: Rahner defends Old Testament inerrancy with a hermeneutic principle which assesses the material truth of a religious proposition by its conformity with its proper object: God's self-disclosure in free, open-ended history.

Topics: SCRIPTURE, inerrancy; TRUTH, formulations of; REVELATION, biblical; GOD-TALK; SCRIPTURE, hermeneutics.
Subsidiary Discussions: God, heno-theism (180, 186); Eschatology, afterlife (180f, 186f); Israel (181, 187); Prophesy (181f, 187); Scripture, canonicity (183f); Jesus Christ, self-awareness (189).
Precis: Given their allegiance to the last hundred years of papal teaching on the inspiration and inerrancy of scripture how can dogmatic theologians deal with the Old Testament?
The range of the topic. Rahner cannot align himself with those theologians who solve the problem of inerrancy by allowing that errors of all kinds (material, historic, and theological) occur in the inspired text.
Specific difficulties in the Old Testament. Realizing exegetes and dogmatic theologians will identify different problems in the Old Testament, Rahner lists four: heno-theism (180); silence on individual survival after death (180f); egotistic nationalism (181); materially inaccurate prophecies (181f).
The higher unity of theological truths. Since Old Testament statements must be judged true or false only in relation to God, the intended object of theology, Rahner's solution concentrates on theological statements. Taken in isolation the material content of a proposition merely points to an innerworldly state of affairs and thus is not the right sort of object to be revealed in a personal, divine self-disclosure. An inner-world reality can only be an instance of revelation insofar as it is set within the spiritual movement by which a person accepts God's self-disclosure in faith. Inerrancy does not demand that propositions are essentially and in every instance true in a

factual sense. In Old Testament revelation the ultimate horizon of understanding is grasped and made actual in particular objects of knowledge. In New Testament revelation one goes beyond this to the direct presence of God.

The openness of the Old Testament. First Rahner bolsters his argument on the fact that only Christianity establishes a single binding canon. This it does by reference to the New Testament. Second, insofar as the movement of Old Testament revelation leads to Christ, only in the context of the entire Old Testament can particular statements of particular books be correctly interpreted and understood as free from error. Third, since the Old Testament is essentially open to the uncontrollable activity of the God of history, the goal of which is Christ, its inerrancy is found in understanding it as open.

Rahner comes now to the critical point of his theory. Statements about inner-worldly realities can be theologically true while being false on an inner-worldly assessment. No one can seriously doubt that inner-worldly confusion and the error attached to it can still be the medium of saving action. Rahner warns against calling these statements simultaneously true and false. Summary (186).

The application of the solution. Rahner applies his solution to the four problems outlined earlier (180f) showing how erroneous or incomplete positions in the Old Testament actually i) constituted positive steps toward the truth to be finally revealed in Christ, and ii) expressed the religious truth of radical openness to the sovereign freedom of the grace of God.

The concept of truth. Rahner's concept of truth has a specific religious character which distinguishes it from truth in the usual sense. The conformity of a religious proposition to the reality it signifies refers here to the reality of the direct self-communication of God. When the material and categorial content of religious propositions cannot be reconciled to this divine self-disclosure they should be called false. Clearly it is possible for them to be true in relationship to God's self-disclosure but materially false. Rahner gives as an example the eschatological expectation of Jesus (188f).

The solution and the New Testament. Rahner ends with a caution against hastily applying this hermeneutical principle to the New Testament. There is a basic difference between statements in the Old and New Testaments. Each has a specific concept of truth proper to itself. "The propositions of the Old Testament are true on condition, and for the reason, that they signify the realisation of a commitment to the God of an unknown and open-ended promise; the propositions of the New Testament are true in that they proclaim the death and resurrection of Jesus, in which the absolute future has already arrived and is no longer a mere possibility presented to the freedom of man" (190).

16.12   On the "History of Revelation" according to the Second Vatican Council

Zur "Offenbarungsgeschichtes" nach dem II Vatikanum

{1.5}   *Neues Testament und Kirche. Festchrift für R. Schnackenburg* (Freiburg i. Br. 1974) 543-549, as, *Kritische Anmerkungen zu Nr. 3 des dogmatischen Dekrets 'Dei verbum' des II Vaticanums.* Revised and expanded.

Abstract: *Dei verbum* is seriously flawed. It presents the history of revelation in a naive temporal framework unintelligible to most people today rather than treating it retrospectively from the starting-point of Jesus Christ.

Topics: REVELATION- SALVATION-HISTORY; VATICAN II, *Dei verbum.*

Subsidiary Discussions: Adam/Eve (194f); Abraham (195ff).

Precis: Rahner's critical remarks on section 3 of the first chapter of *Dei verbum* are intended to show how the conciliar text leaves open important questions which demand an answer if the history of revelation is to be grasped by the modern person.

The text and its presuppositions. After presenting the text in question Rahner describes its place in Chapter 1. If one ignores its "objectivist structure" its sequence seems quite reasonable. It does, however, presume a traditional mental model of nature and grace which is no longer self-evident or even valid, ignoring as it does God's universal salvific will and the essential unity of the human experience of God.

Stages in the history of revelation. The document divides revelation history into three stages climaxing in Jesus Christ: the original revelation of God to the first parents (194f); the period between them and Abraham and Moses (195f); Old Testament history up to Jesus Christ (196f). Rahner discusses each stage and details the important question the council left open.

The essay concludes with a summary (198). Rahner does not fault the council fathers for not answering all these open questions. But if they had recognized their urgency and necessity they would have written a very different document. They would have replaced the naive chronological framework with a retrospective view of the Old Testament from the starting-point of Jesus Christ. Such a view would offer a survey of the whole of human history as the history of salvation and revelation. The Old Testament would then have been presented as a theological deduction rather than a piece of historical description.

16.13   The One Christ and the Universality of Salvation

Der eine Jesus Christus und die Universalität des Heils

{3.0}   Previously unpublished.

Abstract: The concepts "sacramental causality" and "anonymous Christianity" explain how all people are saved through Christ's cross and resurrection.

Topics: SALVATION, universal; CROSS, theology of.

Subsidiary Discussions: Theology (199f); God, salvific will of (202f); Logos (205f); Pelagianism (206f); Reparation, theory of (207f); Jesus Christ, merit of (208ff); Humanity, unity of (210f); Causality, sacramental (212ff); Symbol, real (214f); Anonymous Christian (218ff); Christology, questing (230ff); Love of God/neighbor (222f); Death (223f); Hope for the future (224).

Precis: Theological clarity results when defined truth is grasped and express-ed by means of theological opinion. The truth examined here is how the salvation of any and every person depends on Jesus Christ. Rahner devotes the first 11 pages to clarifying the problem (199-209).

The theological meaning of the question. This essay concentrates on the "possibility" of salvation for all people after original sin, not on its realiza-tion. Rahner understands salvation as the strictly supernatural and direct presence of God afforded by grace. By "all" Rahner means all those who have achieved the full exercise of freedom. This leaves aside infants and so-called adults who are actually incapable of freedom.

God's salvific will in the contemporary understanding of faith. Rahner maintains that after Vatican II the universal possibility of salvation has absolute binding dogmatic force, even though it was not always taught explicitly by the church. There are no empirical criteria which *prima facie* preclude the possibility of a person's being saved. We can judge no one.

The direct and saving presence of God. Since the Spirit of God directs the whole world toward its proper goal, in an ultimate sense God is equally near everywhere. It is not required that people change their existential circum-stances in order to be saved, although failure to respond to what one believes is a true call from God to change can be a culpable choice. The question is how one can claim salvation comes entirely from Christ.

The problematic. The material connection of all physical events alone cannot explain the universal significance of the cross insofar as it fails to explain how an event can cause something prior to itself. In addition arguments based on "objective redemption" or predestination do not give sufficient room to human freedom. Finally, appeals to the "cosmic Christ" leave unanswered how a particular historical event (e.g., the cross) can have fundamental importance.

Self-redemption and redemption by another. Rahner allows that the salvation of which he speaks could be construed as "self-redemption" but only in a very restricted, non-Pelagian sense.

Cross: consequence or cause? The crucifixion cannot be seen as the cause of God's uncaused salvific will. Contrary to Anselm's theory of satisfaction, Jesus' death did not originate in an angry God who demanded reparation, but in a God of love and mercy. It is metaphysically impossible to think the cross somehow transformed God's intentions towards humanity.

The merit of Christ. Much is made of the grace of salvation being made available before the fact (e.g., Immaculate Conception) *"in meritorum*

Christi." But this line of thought merely connects human salvation with the cross without explaining *how* the connection is to be conceived. Events inside history can hardly be explained by reference to forces operating outside history (summary, 209). Rahner is ready at this point to begin his investigation proper. He starts with Jesus himself and then turns towards us. "[T]he double perspective will open up questions which otherwise might have been overlooked" (209).

Jesus and all men. Of the many questions raised by the relationship of Jesus to all people (list, 211f) Rahner concentrates on one: how to imagine the connection between Jesus' death and universal salvation. Obviously, Jesus is related to all humanity in the same way we all are: by participation in one genuine history. Rahner emphasizes here that the genuine unity of humanity is founded not merely on biology but on the reality of human freedom. If redemption were achieved though the incarnation this physical connection would be sufficient. But if Jesus' death is the cause of universal salvation one must look farther for an explanation. It is insufficient to say that Jesus' death and resurrection alone contain the power to convince all people of God's love and forgiveness since many never knew this event. Nor can we give up the notion of causality, however it is expressed. Rahner suggests the cross has a primary *sacramental causality* for the salvation of all insofar as it mediates salvation to all by means of a prior salvific grace which is universally operative in the world. The cross is the sign of this grace and of its victorious and irreversible activity in the world. "The effectiveness of the cross is based on the fact that it is the primary sacramental sign of grace" (212).

Sacramental sign and grace. Rahner proposes to show how a single historical event can uniquely possess universal meaning for all human history. The universal effect of the cross must be obtained from a theological investigation of the cross itself: "sign causality" must be proper to the sign itself and not something added to the sign. In sacramental causality "the sign is the cause .... [I]nsofar as a sacrament can and should be conceived of as a 'real symbol,' as a historical and social embodiment of grace, where grace achieves it own fulness of being and forms an irreversible gift (*opus operatum*), to this extent the sign is a cause of grace, although the sign is caused by this grace" (213). Grace and sign of grace are not two separate realities but two moments in one process of historical and ontological fulfillment.

To make a case for the cross as sacramental sign of universal salvation Rahner begins by outlining the constituent elements of the logical possibility of salvation (God's free offer of self-disclosure accepted definitively and irrevocably at one moment in time and space in total freedom, thus freeing history of its ambivalence and making its outcome fixed and irreversible). If salvation history is irreversibly directed in this sense to salvation through a concrete event, then this historically tangible occurrence must be a sign of the salvation of the whole world in the sense of a "real symbol" and so possess a type of sacramental causality where salvation is concerned.

Christian faith sees in Jesus' cross and resurrection just such an event. "*Because* Jesus died and rose again, therefore salvation is offered and given to the whole of mankind" (214). As the church which derives its nature from Christ is the basic sacrament of salvation, Jesus is the primary sacrament (*Ursakrament*). Rahner answers the objection that although a sign may cause awareness it cannot cause salvation. He does this by pointing to the essential unity of sign and signified in sacramental sign. He concludes by alluding to dimensions of the topic this discussion has left open.

Man and the cross of Christ. For all this to be true it is necessary not only for Christ to be related to all people but also for all people to be related to Christ. How is this true for those who through no culpable guilt have never heard of Christ or cannot in good conscience find a way to accept him? Rahner assumes what Vatican II taught: i) all people only achieve salvation through Christ; ii) all people who do reach salvation must have a relationship to Christ in the faith necessary for salvation. For Rahner the only way these conditions can be fulfilled is with a kind of implicit and unthematic faith he associates with anonymous Christianity. This he defends in some detail and distinguishes from explicit Christian faith (218ff). But precisely how does one have implicit faith in the historical Jesus and not simply in the idea of the God of the philosophers?

A christology of quest. Rahner dismisses as too thin the idea that a relationship to Christ is established by aligning ourselves to the realities objectively connected to Jesus and his history. Rahner suggests an unconditional "christology of quest" which involves searching in eschatological hope for something specific yet unknown, and being related to the unknown by means of the search.

The claims upon human existence. [Rahner is unclear whether the next remarks refer to the christological quest of the anonymous Christian or of the explicit Christian, or to both. In any case] "it" demands three things: absolute love of neighbor realized only in the radical unity it has with love of God in Christ (222f); readiness for death not as absurd negation but as expectant hope in the free and willing acceptance of one's powerlessness (223f); hope that in the future which has already definitively begun, self-alienation, the gap between what we are and hope to be, is finally overcome (224).

16.14   The Hiddenness of God
Über die Verborgenheit Gottes
{3.5}   *Le service théologique dans L'Eglise.* Festschrift for Y. Congar (Paris 1974) 249-268.

Abstract: Treating God's abiding hiddenness (incomprehensibility, mystery) as a central theological concern leads Rahner to reappraise radically the traditional notions of revelation, revelation history, and human knowledge.

Topics: GOD, incomprehensibility of; KNOWLEDGE; MYSTERY; REVELATION.

Subsidiary Discussions: Creation (299f); Beatific vision (230f); Virtues, perichoresis (233f); Mysteries (234); Transcendence (236f); Trinity (240); Christology (241f); Justification and grace (241f); History, theology of (242f); *Theologia gloriae* (243).

Precis: This radical reflection on God's hiddenness has three parts: review of the traditional data; problems raised by the traditional approach; attempt at a positive synthesis between modern systematic theology and the tradition. **"The hiddenness of God" according to classical theology.** Catholic theologians prefer the term incomprehensibility to hiddenness. It flows "from the essential infinity of God which makes it impossible for a finite created intellect to exhaust the possibilities of knowledge and truth contained in this absolute fullness of being" (229). God is simultaneously known and incomprehensible. In this sense God and the mystery of the Trinity are not "transparent" in this life not even after revelation. Though God is somewhat disclosed in the act of creation (and salvation history), God remains incomprehensible insofar as creation does not restrict God's freedom. Traditional theology also holds that God remains incomprehensible even in final beatitude. **The problem of God's incomprehensibility.** Rahner is struck by the way desire for theoretical understanding dominates the traditional discussion, based as it is on a certain model of knowledge in which an object is penetrated and mastered. In this context the incomprehensibility of God is grounded in a negative view of the creature's finitude. But doesn't such a view engender indifference towards an object which can never be understood? Doesn't God's incomprehensibility end up a trap for the finite intellect?

Secondly, the hidden character of God's personal freedom in relation to creation is not so easily intelligible as traditional theology imagines. God's free choices, once they are made categorial, are intrinsically commensurate to the finite but still transcend human intellect. In this case it would be a matter of indifference what God kept hidden.

Thirdly, traditional theology does not make clear that the problem arising from the direct vision of an incomprehensible God (i.e., that knowledge comes to grief and despair confronted with God's continuing hiddenness) can only be solved in the context of love. Here is the first hint of Rahner's synthesis: a more fundamental notion of knowledge than the accepted notion of seeing through an object (233).

Finally, the traditional approach spawns (without ever fully justifying) numerous distinctions among the "grades of mysteries." It fails to ask "how any finite reality, created by God and distinct from him, can be a *mysterium stricte dictum* for an intellect possessing unlimited transcendence" (234f). **Outline of a synthesis.** The starting-point, as philosophical as it is theological, is the assertion that "God himself and nothing else is our eternal life" (236). *The* Truth occurs in the basic experience of the mystery itself. Here is the heart of Rahner's argument: knowledge of mystery is no secondary, defective form of knowledge. Knowledge according to the common usage is secondary and defective. "[T]he essence of knowledge lies in the mystery which is the object of primary experience and is alone self-evident" (236). After briefly distinguishing his notion from Hegel's and Heidegger's, Rahner argues that both freedom and knowledge find their origin and goal in mystery, the a priori pre-condition of all categorial knowledge and history. Rahner immediately expresses the same point for readers who insist on the primacy of knowledge in the commonly accepted sense of clear understanding. For them he stresses that mystery is the unthematically co-known condition for the possibility of any act of knowledge. What is co-known can, however, be misinterpreted or missed entirely or denied. In any case, the hidden God is the source of truth which is freely bestowed and determines our identity. "Knowledge is primarily the experience of the overwhelming mystery of this *deus absconditus*" (238).

Rahner's synthesis demands new definitions. Revelation, far from being the unveiling of something previously hidden which leads to greater worldly awareness is now seen as the radical manifestation of abiding mystery. Thus, revelation is never overcome by *gnosis* bestowed by God. It is the history of the deepening perception of God *as* mystery to which the blessed abandon themselves, and in which the theoretical intellect is set free to love the mystery which lays hold of us by its direct presence. Summary (238f).

Rahner's treatment of the hiddenness of God has implications for other elements of Christian dogma. Rahner remarks on five: Trinity; christology; grace and justification; eschatology and theology of the future; *theologia gloriae*. On this last issue Rahner suggests his approach would allay the criticism leveled against Catholics by showing how, rightly interpreted, any *theologia gloriae* is always a theology of *deus absconditus*. "The 'gloria' is nothing other than the loving surrender of man to the incomprehensibility of God which is now a directly present reality" (243).

16.15   An Investigation of the Incomprehensibility of God in St. Thomas Aquinas

Fragen zur Unbegreiflichkeit Gottes nach Thomas von Aquin
{4.0}   *Thomas von Aquin 1294-1974* (Munich 1974) 33-45. Slightly revised.

Abstract: Argues the centrality of divine incomprehensibility in Aquinas, not as a negative characteristic of God but as an anthropological statement which when radically understood establishes the positive quality of human finitude.
Topics: GOD, incomprehensibility of; AQUINAS on incomprehensibility of God.

Subsidiary Discussions: Aquinas, metaphysics of light (247f); Creation (249f); God, *lumen gloriae* (251f); Finitude (252f); Virtue, perichoresis (254).

Precis: Rahner assumes here the basic substance of Aquinas' teaching. Regarding God this refers to the permanent incomprehensibility which results when a finite intellect attempts to grasp an infinite God. From a hermeneutical point of view Rahner cautions against oversimplifying Aquinas on this crucial point—the key to all the heights and depths of Thomistic theology and philosophy.

The proposition of faith. The incomprehensibility of God is a theological proposition affirmed by revelation and not simply a philosophical proposition. It must always be grasped against the revealed truth that beatitude consists in a direct vision of God. This fact alone gives depth to the doctrine while at the same time it poses difficult problems. For in beatitude God is present precisely in incomprehensibility which is not an obscure remainder or a part of God. It is a mysterious dialectic.

The interpretation of Aquinas. Although Aquinas deals with this topic in terms of his metaphysics of light, Rahner leaves that aside. He concentrates instead on Thomas' central ontological concerns. This immediately raises two problems: the relationship of divine, infinite being and finite being; the relationship between grace and glory as the condition for the possibility of the vision of God, and grace and glory as the direct vision of God. How can one explain a real, direct vision of God while preserving God's incomprehensibility? Rahner takes each problem in turn.

On the relation between God and finite being (249ff) Rahner argues the causality that links the two is more complex than is generally appreciated. He argues the need for a more radical appreciation of the unique nature of causality in creation. God is not another potential object of knowledge and encounter. God remains the condition for the possibility of being and knowledge. This section closes with the clearest statement of the problem (251).

On the *lumen gloriae* as condition for the possibility of vision and the content of vision (created vs. uncreated grace), Rahner argues their relationship is more complex than generally assumed. Any explanation of beatific vision must show why it not only permits but demands divine incomprehensibility.

The finite nature of man. Aquinas' doctrine of divine incomprehensibility is primarily a statement about us. Making divine incomprehensibility a negative character of God fails to give the doctrine its proper weight or value. By endowing us with divine incomprehensibility God invites us to participate in that incomprehensibility. Failure to grasp this makes incomprehensibility seem like a completely negative, finite limitation which we can only endure.

"Excess" in God. The incomprehensibility of God is present in an *excessus*, i.e., the primary movement of spirit and its activity directed toward unlimited being and the incomprehensibility of God. This is the ground of all knowing. It is not simply a transcendent characteristic of consciousness, it is a free human act by which we surrender ourselves unconditionally to incomprehensibility as the true source of our fulfillment. Only then do we discover the reality of faith, hope, and love. Rahner ends with a brief discussion of the central role of perichoresis (254).

16.16 The Mystery of the Trinity
Um das Geheimnis der Dreifaltigkeit
{3.0} Originally appeared as a footnote in M. de França Miranda's study which attempted to systematize Rahner's work on the Trinity (cf. 255 ftn1).

Abstract: Rahner offers a few unsystematic reflections in response to certain objections to his theology of the Trinity.
Topics: TRINITY.
Subsidiary Discussions: Person (258f).
Precis: The lack of a coherent framework of faith makes theological speculation on Trinity inevitable. Though the Trinity remains a question of central importance in Christian doctrine and preaching, today it is in danger of being relegated to a backwater either because it is taught without practical application to Christian life and spirituality or because it is overshadowed by a one-sided emphasis on liberation or christology from below. Rahner insists a valid speculative Trinitarian theology will necessarily be practical.

After a brief word of thanks to M. de França Miranda for compiling his own scattered work on the Trinity, Rahner defends his own work against what he considers unjust objections:

The present work cannot possibly present the many lines of thought or ideas connected to the Trinity (e.g., exegetical questions concerning Jesus' awareness of his divine Sonship). Rahner contends it is enough if he explicitly recognizes the need to fill out his work with such material contributions. The same can be said to those who object to the excessively formal character of his thesis that the justified possess real relationships to the Trinitarian God and not simply those of appropriation.

He dismisses out of hand those who say he does not sufficiently distinguish between self-communication and the self-communication of God.

He defends his use of the term "distinct modes of subsistence" by clarifying this term's relation to the classical notion of distinct "persons" in the Trinity.

He ends by arguing that in the future Trinitarian theology should solidify the relationship between immanent and economic Trinity, and forever banish the idea that any purely speculative doctrine of the immanent Trinity is possible or desirable.

XVII. Jesus, Man, and the Church
XII. *Theologie aus Erfahrung des Geistes*

German edition: Einsiedeln, Benziger, 1975
U.S. edition: N.Y., Crossroad, 1981
Margaret Kohl, translator

This volume in the English edition comprises the last four sections of *Schriften zur Theologie*, XII.

17.01   Christmas in the Light of the Ignatian Exercises
Weihnacht im Licht der Exerzitien

{3.5}   1974 Christmas sermon preached to Jesuits. Slightly revised.

Abstract: Ignatian indifference reveals how the particular and the transcendent form a unity perfectly expressed in the hypostatic union of Jesus we celebrate at Christmas. It reveals the true nature of the human person.

Topics: LITURGICAL YEAR, Christmas; IGNATIUS LOYOLA, Exercises of; TRANSCENDENT/CATEGORIAL.

Subsidiary Discussions: Ignatius Loyola, *Indifferençia* (3f); Choice, Ignatian (5f); Hypostatic union (6f).

Precis: These few highly theoretical and fragmentary suggestions attempt to relate the mystery of Christmas to the indifference and freedom characteristic of Ignatius' Exercises.

Indifference. Rahner equates Ignatian indifference with Pauline freedom over all the powers and forces in our human existence (inner and outer) conferred by the Spirit of God. Ignatian indifference sees things from the viewpoint of the free individual; Pauline freedom views these same things from the vantage point of God's liberating grace. Indifference and freedom signify the infinite open space in which we encounter God in mute adoration of the ineffable mystery, albeit a place of emptiness and darkness.

Assignment to action. This encounter event, however, can only be the object of hope. Far from ending in mystical retreat, Ignatian indifferent freedom for this tremendous mystery of God offers no permanent resting place. It impels us to return to the concrete reality of everyday life to decide and to act. For Ignatius the event is only truly conferred when we let ourselves be sent back and freely choose the assignments sent to us out of the freedom of God. "In this way Ignatian choice is, in unadulterated and undivided unity, the place at which divine freedom, the consolation of indifference and our earthly decision in freedom for something specific are simultaneously consummated" (5). For Rahner this marks the point at which [categorial] history and transcendence are united. "In Ignatius indifference and choice of the particular possess an ultimate unity in diversity; freedom becomes concrete and what is concrete becomes free" (6).

Christmas? Viewing Christmas as the supreme instance of the free acceptance of this unity of transcendence and particularity allows Christians to see in their own experience what happens uniquely in the birth and death of Christ. Relating this insight to the potentiality of the hypostatic union of God and an undiminished and untruncated humanity reveals what it is to be human. Jesus' hypostatic union (as distinct from ours) is an efficacious promise revealing what grace means as the act of divine freedom towards us.

Practically speaking, Ignatian indifference allows the unadulterated and undivided unity of the categorial and the transcendent to grow in us. "We then find God in that unity, even in the down-to-earth triviality of our everyday life; and we cease to be the selves of that triviality" (7). When we let this unity happen, lay hold of it, die and live, then Christ is born and the mystery of that birth lays hold of us as our own salvation.

17.02   On the Spirituality of the Easter Faith
Über die Spiritualität des Osterglaubens
{3.0}   *Geist und Leben* 47 (1974) 88-94.

Abstract: After criticizing two most common devotional approaches to Jesus' resurrection, Rahner offers a view which by uniting history and transcendence grounds our hope that Jesus' resurrection will be effective in our lives.

Topics: RESURRECTION; TRANSCENDENCE and history.
Subsidiary Discussions: Revelation (8).
Precis: All revelation is meant to further human salvation. Therefore, one is absolutely justified to question every tenet of faith with regard to its anthropological significance. Here Rahner asks what the Easter faith means for Christian spirituality which he defines as the conscious and methodical development of faith, hope, and love.

Textbooks which approach the question of the Easter faith from the vantage point of dogmatic or fundamental theology generally have no spiritual relevance. They fail to illuminate the connection between the destiny of Jesus and the existence of the individual believer. Traditional devotional approaches separate the historical and transcendental aspects of the resurrection so severely as to obscure the real meaning of the resurrection for the life of the believer. One devotional approach fixes its gaze on the historical past. It sees the resurrection as the final vindicating episode in the life of Jesus but cannot show how the believer participates existentially in this past event (10). The other devotional approach gazes upward to Christ in glory. In this transcendent approach the life and person of the historical Jesus tend to be lost or made irrelevant in light of Christ's assumption into glory.

The deep spiritual background of Easter faith lies in the indissoluble unity between transcendence and history. Devotion must insist that "the consummated encounter with God as he is in himself actually means encounter with the consummated history that is ours" (12f). It is a question of identity. "[T]he risen Lord *is* the One who was crucified.... [Jesus'] earlier life itself is completed and has found eternal reality in and before God" (13). History is never completely left behind. "[I]t has itself been accepted by God and acknowledged as real; from the human subjectivity of Jesus, it has been gathered out of the mere flux of earthly time into the Now of eternity, and taken into irrevocable possession" (13). So it is for believers as well.

Rahner harmonizes and corrects the backward- and upward-looking devotional approaches. Resurrection is not simply a new phase of life. Neither does it make personal history irrelevant. Resurrection means "the ultimate, God-given form of the earthly life belonging to history. And this history has an ultimate meaning because in the incarnation and cross of the eternal Logos, it is the history of God himself" (14).

17.03 Jesus' Resurrection
Jesu Auferstehung
{2.5}   Previously unpublished 1975 lecture at Louvain.
Abstract: The meaning of Jesus' resurrection does not arise from examining biblical/historical facts but from applying experiential knowledge of theological anthropology to the proclamation, "He is alive."

Topics: JESUS CHRIST, resurrection of.
Subsidiary Discussions: Resurrection of body (16ff); Hope (18); Death (20f).
Precis: Some observations drawn from systematic theolgy. This dense treatment of the meaning of Jesus' resurrection begins with systematic theology (16ff). Hope that one's own history of freedom will be conclusive is already hope for "resurrection." This notion in turn assumes the resurrection of the body insofar as one cannot imagine existence without corporeality. "[R]esurrection in its theologically valid sense refers primarily to the acquiring of a final and ultimate form by the whole, individual person in his own history of freedom; it applies to his 'body' only in a secondary and derivative sense" (17). Thus, philosophical knowledge of resurrection is in some ways prior to revelation, although hope for resurrection has a long history in the Old and New Testaments, and accepting this hope is always only possible with God's grace (18).
The Lord's resurrection. This philosophical anthropology forms the transcendental context which alone makes possible the belief in Jesus' resurrection—not only the fact but also its meaning in itself and for us. These two factors (the concrete history of our hope and the transcendence of Christ's resurrection) are circular (i.e., because Jesus is risen, I believe in and hope for my own resurrection; because I have hope for my own resurrection I can grasp the nature of Jesus' resurrection). For these reasons the statement "He lives" is more primal and basic than accounts of the post-resurrection appearances (19). In the risen Christ hope for our own resurrection is vindicated.

There is also a theological justification for the close link between our own personal hope of resurrection and the unique character of Jesus' resurrection. The grace to believe in his resurrection is based on the hope of resurrection which springs from human nature, itself a supernatural gift from God. "[T]he Lord's resurrection means the ultimate deliverance of actual human existence by God and before him. This means that human history acquires its real validity for the first time; it neither simply goes on continuing into vacuity, nor is it simply destroyed" (20).

It is not simply Jesus' "cause" that lives on in an ideological sense. The person of Christ is vindicated, and victory is given to his claim to be the absolute mediator of salvation once and for all. The resurrection of Christ is the eschatological victory of God's grace in the world—a victory in which each human person longs to share.

17.04 Christology Today?
Christologie heute?
{2.5}   December 1973 lecture at Saarbrücken. Revised.
Abstract: Classical christology which stresses the descent of the pre-existent Logos and tends toward monophysitism finds a corrective in modern,

horizontal christology which takes as its starting-point the full humanity of Jesus.

Topics: CHRISTOLOGY.

Subsidiary Discussions: Christology, Calcedonian (26f); Death (33f); Resurrection of Jesus (34f); Statements, ontological and functional (36); Christology, communication of idioms (37).

Precis: Christology is always topical.

Traditional christology. Survey. Each generation must make Christ its own. But this can never be done by leaping over or discarding 2,000 years of christological speculation for three reasons Rahner outlines (26ff).

The limitations of classical christology. A vertical, incarnational theology of descent tends to idealize the humanity of Christ so much he appears at times a demi-god. "[I]n actual fact classical Christology not infrequently strayed unintentionally into a monophysitism" mingling the two natures of Christ in "a curious deification of the man, in place of a radical acceptance of the bitterly finite character of the person in whom God appeared among us" (28). In addition Calcedonian christology fails to connect the incarnate Logos and his function as mediator of salvation (29f). Finally, it is insufficiently "fundamental," i.e., it gives too little weight to the experience of Jesus as the saving word of God to us. It is difficult to get from a Christ-in-himself to a Christ-for-us (30f).

New approaches. By today's new approaches to christology Rahner means "something very simple: quite plain statements about the meaning of Jesus and what he did for us, statements which give us the impression that, in spite of their *relatively* easy accessibility, they still contain in full the classic, essential Christology. This requires that that, on the one hand they are taken really seriously, in a thoroughly radical way; and on the other, people do not again interpret them in a monophysitic sense" (32).

Here at the heart of the article Rahner sketches his own horizontal approach to christology beginning with the experience of Christ (32ff). He concludes, "the simplest experience of faith with Jesus, the crucified and risen One, therefore leads inescapably to statements which in actual fact include an ontological Christology of descent and incarnation, but which also from the very beginning simultaneously include, seriously and effectively, the horizontal Christology of salvation history and fundamental theology" (34).

Rahner ends the article discussing ontological and functional statements (36f). He insists that one is never left to choose one set over the other because in christology every functional statement leads inexorably to an ontological statement and vice-versa. This in turn leads to a brief discussion of the communication of idioms (37). He concludes with a brief summary (37f).

17.05 Jesus Christ in the Non-Christian Religions

Jesus Christus in den nichtchristlichen Religionen
{2.5} G. Oberhammer, ed., *Offenbarung, Geistige Realität des Menschen* (Vienna 1974) 189-198.

Abstract: Jesus is present and active in non-Christian religions in his Spirit which orders all history to its zenith (i.e., his incarnation and cross). Non-Christian savior figures anticipate this hope for salvation sought by *memoria*.

Topics: CHRISTOLOGY and non-Christian religions; RELIGIONS, non-Christian; HISTORY.

Subsidiary Discussions: God, salvific will of (40f); Revelation, original (42f); Jesus Christ, merit *(Intuitu meritorum Christi)* (44f); Spirit (46); *Memoria* (46ff).

Precis: What dogmatic principles and reflections must be postulated prior to historical investigation when we ask whether Christ can be present in non-Christian religions? Although historians of religions can and should approach this question in an a posteriori manner, dogmatic theologians can only approach it in an a priori investigation. Rahner presupposes two things: Vatican II's teaching on the existence of a general supernatural divine will to salvation which is already efficacious in the world before the death of Christ (40f); non-Christian religions can play a positive role in their adherents' winning salvation through faith, hope, and love (41f).

How is Jesus Christ present and efficacious in the faith of individual non-Christian believers, and hence in the non-Christian religions? Rahner answers, "through his Spirit" (43). After showing how the Spirit equates to the eternal Logos, Rahner looks more closely at how the Spirit of Christ is active in the non-baptized. Without dismissing the notion of *"intuitu meritorum Christi"* Rahner details the problems with this theory (list, 45f).

The only way out of these difficulties is to see Jesus' incarnation and cross as "the 'final cause' of God's universal self-communication to the world, given with God's saving will, which knows no reason outside itself and which we call the Holy Spirit; and if we view the incarnation and cross in this sense as the cause of the imparting of the Holy Spirit at all times and in all places in the world" (46). This Spirit is always the determining principle (entelechy) of the history of revelation and salvation. Directed toward the zenith of history, human transcendentality is necessarily always directed towards the incarnation and cross of Jesus Christ.

"Jesus Christ is always and everywhere present in justifying faith, because this is always and everywhere the seeking *memoria* of the absolute bringer of salvation" (46). Rahner clarifies this statement with a brief treatment of the concept of *"memoria"* (Plato's *anamnesis*). It is the *"a priori* principle of expectation, seeking and hope in man's finding and retaining subjectivity" (47). It offers the possibility of perceiving something in history, of distinguishing it, and of assigning it a certain place. It is the a priori possibility of historical experience *as such*, always on the lookout for the absolute bringer of salvation—the hope that one's radical dependence on incomprehensible mystery will not be eternally frustrated but will be fulfilled by the direct self-communication of God. Although in non-Christian religions this hope could be objectified in many ways, Rahner simply suggests historians of religion be alert for "savior figures" in non-Christian religions which might anticipate the hope Christians find realized in Jesus.

17.06 The Theological Dimension of the Question about Man

Die theologische Dimension der Frage nach dem Menschen
{3.0} September 1972 lecture at Dortmund. *Donauwörth* (1972) 9-28. Revised.

Abstract: By posing the most radical questions about man, Christian anthropology can be seen as the only true anthropology which offers a new starting-point for evangelizing today's secular world: man's experience of himself.

Topics: THEOLOGICAL ANTHROPOLOGY.

Subsidiary Discussions: Pluralism, gnoseological (56f); God (58f); History (63f); Faith (64f); Grace (66); Creed, brief (69f).

Precis: Points of departure. Rahner assumes: 1) even some social scientists deny the validity of anthropology; 2) this study must rely on a method to discover where philosophical anthropology and theology meet; 3) this is not a sectarian Catholic analysis; 4) evangelization begins today with an appeal to the inner truth of human existence which itself grounds belief in scripture.

Questioning man. Anthropocentric theology never nullifies theocentric theology since, given the nature of salvation in Christ, one always implies the other. Whether or not one accepts its claim to have the most decisive thing to say about us, theological anthropology is not just one more irreconcilable point of view in the insurmountable pluralism surrounding anthropology. Were this so, we would be left with a concept of God and revelation deeply opposed to the contemporary mentality (59). Theological anthropology "actually bursts these secular anthropologies radically apart, thereby making access possible, for the first time and finally, to the one mystery which we call God" (57).

Man's experience of God. The discussion is premised on three Christian convictions: 1) God exists; 2) God exists in a particular relationship with the world; 3) thus, statements can and must be made about us which include the word "God." The real question is whether a place can be found in human self-understanding for an experience of God which allows this relationship with God to become more than just another individual fact. Rahner is not seeking a reality parallel to those in which secular sciences are interested, but the radical form of these human realities themselves—not an additional anthropology but the radical depth of any and all anthropology.

It is a matter of radicality. Theological anthropology warns against stopping with any statement about man which falls short of an apophatic anthropology which drops the question into the incomprehensibility of God—our hidden depths. This is the only position from which God and our relationship with God is preserved from being just one more fact among facts. "Theological anthropology is only truly anthropological when it really sees itself as *theology* and loses itself in that. But theology is theology only when it becomes the acknowledgment of God's incomprehensibility" (61). **The loss of revelation.** Calling Christian anthropology the radical form of secular anthropology does not lead to the dissolution of theological anthropology based on revelation. Radical anthropology does not nullify revelation. Rather in a non-systematic way it reveals within the person the very same divine self-communication in grace which finds its zenith in Jesus Christ and which scripture proclaims.

Insights and proclamations. In an age when appeals to authority, whether of the church or of scripture, fail to convince, this new approach "allow[s] orthodox Christian teaching to start unabashedly with man, with his experience of himself, with his existence" (67). Then the Christian message is not seen as something alien or external, but something which already exists in the ultimate depths of human existence. True, this approach has been tried in the past and failed [Modernism]. But it failed not because the approach is wrong, but because it was never pushed radically and courageously enough.

17.07   The Body in the Order of Salvation
Der Leib in der Heilsordnung
{2.5}   K. Rahner, A. Görres, eds., *Der Lieb und das Heil; Probleme der Praktischen Theologie* (Mainz 1967) 29-44. Style improved, notes added.
Abstract: The Catholic teaching on the body which Rahner summarizes here has significant, unexplored implications in morality, ecology, eschatology, etc.
Topics: THEOLOGICAL ANTHROPOLOGY, hylomorphism.
Subsidiary Discussions: Creation (71ff); Sin, original (73f); Creed, Word became flesh (74f); *Sarx* (74f); Redemption (75ff, 82f); Resurrection of body (77f); Trinity (80); Dualism (85ff); Eschatology (88).
Precis: Revelation by way of the body. From the seven Catholic teachings on the body Rahner hopes to form one theological concept of the human body. These teachings are (71-78):
  1) because God created the body it is good and intended to be as it is;
  2) the body is made of dust of the earth, lowly yet a partner with God;
  3) original sin is transmitted through procreation, not to demean sex but to insist that no child of Adam and Eve is immune from the effects of sin;

4) "the Word became flesh" refers to the truth that when the Logos utters itself in time and space a human person is what comes forth;

5) all human beings are redeemed through Christ's death. We participate in the event of his suffering and death by our common bodily heritage;

6) "resurrection of flesh" refers to our hope the whole person is saved;

7) unity of body and soul is real, true, radical, substantial, original.

The consequences of a theology of the body. As a consequence of these truths one can understand "why the Church as a concrete, bodily, sociologically constituted community sees itself [and the sacraments consisting of physical elements] as the Church that is necessary for salvation" (78). In fact the church is exclusively interested in bodily existence, and leaves to God any purely spiritual elements in us. Thus, the church judges what people do, not what they think (79). Even the Trinity is an object of concern for the church only insofar as the Word became flesh.

Sections a, The fundamental concept of the body; b, Indivisible unity; c, Man as spirit (80-85) restate Thomistic teaching on the body and soul as an original unity. In section d, Christian Dualism?, Rahner admits to a Christian dualism very different from Greek Neoplatonic dualism. In the latter there is a direct encounter between so-called bodies and souls. But in Christian dualism, although there is a clear metaphysical distinction between prime matter and spirit, every actual encounter is always already an existential synthesis of the two.

This means two things: 1) that our spiritual self-expression returning to us through our material experience is always ambiguous, i.e., we can never clearly say what comes from within and what comes from without (86); 2) all self-expression, however personal or intimate, puts us into contact with the wider physical, social world (86f). Thus, the world and its fate can never be a matter of indifference. "Through bodiliness the whole world belongs to me from the start, in everything that happens" (87). Thinking of ourselves as "open systems" we connect with others in intercommunication, and in original sin and redemption. What might this mean for the common sphere of being when we contemplate the transfiguration of the world in the end time?

17.08 Mystical Experience and Mystical Theology

Mystische Erfahrung und mystische Theologie

{2.5} Revised preface to C. Albrecht, *Das mystiche Wort. Erleben und Sprechen in Versunkenheit* (Mainz 1974) vii-xiv.

Abstract: In the light of his theology of grace Rahner concludes that mystical experiences are not of a higher nature than other Christian experiences of God in terms of content, but represent a unique natural mode for such experience.

Topics: MYSTICISM; GRACE.
Subsidiary Discussions: Faith (93); Revelation (94f).
Precis: Rahner suggests a framework for a systematic theology of mysticism. Although there is no generally accepted Catholic theology of mysticism, three factors call for one: to safeguard Christian life from ending up a "flat, humanitarian affair" (99); to aid charismatic movements towards deeper self-understanding; to open Western Christianity to more sympathetic dialogue with the East.
The mystic and his experience. Past attempts at a systematic theology of mysticism have not dealt adequately with the ultimate fundamental questions. Too often they were dominated by "an 'extrinsic' conceptual scheme, according to which direct divine 'intervention' is thought of in the case of mystical phenomena" (91). For Rahner the fundamental question in mystical theology is identity and difference. Mystics must be asked to explain as best they can what, if anything, remains of the distinction between subject and object in the mystical experience (92).
Grace and faith. This raises a second crucial question: the relationship between mystical experience and grace and faith. How does the grace of mystical experience differ from God's universal offer of self-communication? Viewing mystical experience as a participation in beatitude seems to negate the need for faith. But by definition this cannot be. Where the mystic is competent to describe the mystical state, "The dogmatic theologian can only determine that on earth there cannot be any higher experience in the *theological* sense than the experience of faith in the spirit of God. But this means that every genuine mystical experience...can also be understood as merely one mode of the experience of grace in faith" (94). Rahner argues for the validity of non-Christian mysticism in the sphere of revelation theology.
Nature and grace. A third question arises. Since it is the mode and not the graced content of experience which is different in mysticism, are the special phenomenon connected with it (suspension of senses, etc.) best understood as purely natural or are they also somehow preternatural? This depends on one's theology of grace. Rahner opts for the second explanation. "[M]ystic experiences sustained by the Spirit, which make God's spirit accessible, do not differ from normal Christian existence because they are of a higher nature simply by virtue of being mystical experiences of the Spirit. They are different because their natural substratum ... is as such different from the psychological circumstances of everyday life" (97f).
The normal way of salvation and mystical experience. Is mystical experience a necessary step in Christian maturity? Rahner argues no. People have proven capable of complete surrender to God without it, though he admits future psychological research may prove him wrong.

17.09   The Liberty of the Sick, Theologically Considered
Die Freiheit des Kranken in theologischer Sicht
{2.0}   *Stimmen der Zeit* 193 (1975) 31-40. Noted and cross referenced.

Abstract: A theological reflection on human freedom grounds Rahner's approach to pastoral care of the terminally ill. It highlights such issues as patient autonomy, advanced directives, euthanasia.
Topics: FREEDOM and death; CHRISTIAN LIFE, illness.
Subsidiary Discussions: Fundamental option (103f); Death (104f); Anointing of the sick (106ff).
Precis: On the essence of liberty. In this essay freedom is not meant sociologically (freedom from constraint) or psychologically (freedom to choose) but theologically. Whenever there is a radically responsible, true freedom of choice there is also a definite relationship to God. This is true whether or not one is conscious of it, and without regard to whether one accepts or rejects the claim. Thus, freedom is not the capacity to act capriciously. It is the ability to dispose totally and finally of oneself and one's life.

This raises two problems: i) the relationship between theological freedom and the finite objects through which freedom is realized; ii) the relationship between freedom and time. All freedom is mediated through individual objects. It is quite possible to achieve great freedom even within the most restricted circumstances (e.g., terminal illness). Regarding freedom and time, there is no necessary relationship between one's final moments of life and the moment of one's irreversible free decision for or against God (107).

The liberty of the sick person. Proximity to death is "a radical challenge to liberty to decide finally for God on the very basis of the 'material' offered by the process of dying, with its helplessness and loneliness. It should decide for God by accepting serenely and hopefully this 'hopeless' situation of radical helplessness and of being engulfed by the incomprehensibility of what we call God" (105). From these points certain consequences follow:
  —one ought as far as possible to die consciously, though free from pain;
  —one ought to be informed of one's terminal status;
  —one should be given every opportunity to mold one's situation;
  —one should be kept as free as possible from debilitating pain.
Styles of dying. "Styles of dying" have changed greatly, from a personal, historical, free event in which the dying participate, to a mere biological event they simply endure. Rahner allows that medical death and death as an act of liberty do not always coincide. The latter can take place much earlier.
Human and religious help in dying. Caregivers should never exploit the weakness of the ill to clothe their death in hastily donned garments of religion (108). Wishes should be respected even if that means denying a pastor access. Compared with arriving at a religiously existential attitude toward death, "Last Sacraments" are secondary. Making peace with family

can be of greater benefit to achieve this final disposition than reception of sacraments (109).

The free choice of doctor. The dying should have maximum choice in selecting a physician (109f) with whom to work out in advance how to exercise their right to die within the parameters of Catholic teaching (110f).

The right to die. Church teaching requires further refinement in principle and application (e.g., How valid are advance directives? Can they be communicated through a third person? Must a physician accept them?). Rahner ends with a poetic summary (113) encouraging physicians to see themselves as companions and ministers to the dying.

17.10 "The Intermediate State"
{2.0}   *Über den "Zwischenzustand"*

Abstract: The "intermediate state" between death and the final consummation of history is not a dogma. As an element of an intellectual framework it is not a necessary part of Christian eschatology and is open to theological discussion.

Topics: RESURRECTION of the body; THEOLOGICAL ANTHROPOLOGY, hylomorphism; ESCHATOLOGY, intermediate state.

Subsidiary Discussions: Time (118f); Immortality (121); BVM, assumption of (122).

Precis: Rahner argues that no heresy is involved in holding that "the single and total perfecting of man in 'body' and 'soul' takes place immediately after death; that the resurrection of the flesh and the general judgment take place 'parallel' to the temporal history of the world; and that both coincide with the sum of the particular judgments of individual men and women" (115). The dogmatically binding statements of Benedict XII (1334-42) were not concerned directly or thematically with this question. It is rather an unconsidered assumption which lies behind his central teaching on the perfecting of the soul and the glorification of the body. If one can uphold these dogmas without recourse to an intermediate state one is free to do so.

What do the scriptures say? Scripture contains two quite different series of statements on this issue: i) resurrection of the flesh (which always means the destiny of the one and total person who as such is "flesh"); ii) reference to Christian death as "being with Christ." Although traditionally the intermediate state reconciled these two notions, it is a later theological notion not taught explicitly in scripture.

Implications for the history of theology. Though the intermediate state only represents a stage in the history of theology, theologians must still grapple to integrate the individual in the final consummation as one element of a progressive transformation of world history and the cosmos. The intermediate state also entails considerable intellectual difficulties: the notion of "time after death" (118f) and the status of the separated soul (119f).

Philosophical background. Though modern philosophy upholds the distinction of body and soul, its overriding concern is the substantial unity of the human person who as a transcendent being acquires finality before God through the responsible use of freedom. Hence, modern philosophical anthropology not only cannot prove an intermediate state, it must refute any state which entails the absolute liberation of soul from body. Theology can follow the lead of philosophy so long as it safeguards the responsible use of freedom before God, and the enduring validity of our historical (i.e., bodily) character.

Theological objections. Theologians might object by recalling the Assumption of Mary. Rahner counters that nowhere does the doctrine state this privilege was reserved to her alone. To the other texts from scripture and tradition that could be used to adduce the existence of an intermediate state Rahner argues they are not meant to establish the dogma of an intermediate state but are simply part of a naive worldview which advances in theology and philosophy allow us to dispense with today. He lists other such dispensable ideas which accompanied the presentation of other valid dogmas (list, 123).

17.11 Opposition in the Church
Opposition in der Kirche

{1.0}   *Stimmen der Zeit* 192 (1974) 812-820. Notes, cross references added.
Abstract: The church not only permits criticism it requires it of its faithful members. Although it can take many forms it is legitimately limited by common faith, the bonds of love, and its refusal to seize its goals by force.
Topics: CHURCH, opposition within.
Subsidiary Discussions: Church membership (128f); Utopias (133f); Power, coercive (137f).
Precis: The possibilities and the limits. Positive criticism must always be taken seriously. Here Rahner has in mind criticism within the church. He realizes the nature and value of criticism will vary greatly based on the nature of a particular critic's faith and association with the church.

The possibility and necessity of criticism within the church. There can and must be opposition and criticism within the church. It is not only permissible or unavoidable. It is required of its members. The scope of legitimate criticism is fundamentally identical with the scope of human existence. Absolute commitment and critical inquiry can co-exist. The church desires this kind of criticism since it always wants faith to be a matter of free assent. Criticism is underpinned by an absolute assent of faith continually renewed by hope. Much within the church is alterable and hence, open to criticism. Summary (131).

The possible directions which criticism of the church from within may take. Criticism need not be formal, explicit, or raised by particular groups. It can also be diffuse. Rahner cites as examples criticism of theology for failing to bridge the gap between the contemporary situation and the way the faith is proclaimed. The church can also be criticized for its lack of commitment in its tasks towards "the world." Criticism is not a right reserved for office-holders in the church. It can extend to the rank and file. **Forms of criticism with the church.** One must reject any form of criticism which seeks to transform the church into something contrary to its nature: into a proponent of some form of this-worldly utopia. The most effective criticism is often informal: movements and ways of thinking. He cites the triumph of Greek metaphysics and the modern attitude towards the possibility of universal salvation. Formal criticism is, however, more common. **Groups and parties.** Groups can exert a considerable critical function. Rahner mentions religious orders, the charismatic movement, worker priests, etc. Within ecclesial institutions there are such things as parish councils and synods. Rahner warns, however, against the formation of parties along political lines. These are contrary to the freedom of the members of the church. Should they arise they must avoid party discipline, never reject compromise, and be willing to leave controversial questions open. The true goals of the church can never be achieved by coercion.

17.12 "*Mysterium Ecclesiae.*" On the Declaration Made by the Congregation for the Doctrine of the Faith on the Doctrine of the Church

"*Mysterium Ecclesiae*"
{1.5} *Stimmen der Zeit* 191 (1973) 579-594. Slightly edited.
Abstract: A brief account and critical appraisal of the six sections of this Vatican document lead Rahner to conclude it is best to leave the controversial aspects of these ecclesiological issues open to further discussion.
Topics: MAGISTERIUM and infallibility.
Subsidiary Discussions: Church of sinners (142); Ecumenism (142); Truths, hierarchy of (148); Dogma, development of (148ff); Propositions (150ff); Orders, sacrament of (154f).
Precis: Insofar as this 1973 document was promulgated by the Congregation for the Doctrine of the Faith it cannot claim to be infallible. Although it contains some binding truths it is open to theological criticism.
The one church of Christ. This section stays within the teachings of Vatican II. It could have developed more fully the idea that the essential notes of the church are realized to varying degrees (sometimes only potentially) in its various parts. It lacks any discussion of ecclesial sin and seems not to appreciate how much the situation of the separated churches has changed.

Much remains unsaid about the Catholic role in the separation of the churches.

The infallibility of the church. The first part of this section which deals with infallibility in the universal church. Rahner praises for subordinating magisterial infallibility to the fact that the whole church abides in the truth of Christ. It could have developed this more precisely and carefully. Missing is any discussion of how one distinguishes firm conviction and opinions (which are often wrong) from an infallible "assent of faith." The second part presents certain axioms concerning the magisterial functions of pope and bishops compared with the total faith of the church. Rahner argues these axioms are stated in overly exclusive language and fail to show how the various elements of the church co-condition one another. Overall the document fails to link the function of the magisterium with the infallible faith of the whole church. It relies too heavily on a simple appeal to authority.

The infallibility of the magisterium. The document repeats Vatican I on infallibility without any attempt to give reasons for it. Clearly an appeal to formal authority cannot ground its own legitimacy. The Congregation seems unaware of the new intellectual situation among the faithful they address. To make its authority effective it must share with them the process it uses to arrive at decisions.

Warnings. This section fails to offer any clarity which would help implement its warning against slippage in the doctrine of infallibility. It offers no help in understanding Vatican II's teaching on the hierarchy of truths.

The historical character of dogmatic formulations. Rahner finds this section best insofar as it courageously teaches the development of dogma. However, in its concern to ward off "dogmatic relativism" it fails to explain adequately the relationship between the form and content of propositions. Summary (153).

The priesthood of the church. Rahner assumes this section is a response to a statement by German ecumenical university institutes on the possibility of the mutual recognition of orders (154 ftn12). Rahner finds its argument based on the sacramental character of orders to be disingenuous. He concludes that the confusion surrounding the current state of ecclesiological discussion would argue for allowing these questions to remain open for further discussion.

17.13   The Area Bishop: Some Theological Reflections
Theologisches zur Aufgabe Regionalbischofs
{3.0}   H. Fleckenstein, et al., eds., *Weltkirche. Festgabe für Julius Kardinal Döpfner* (Würzburg 1973) 478-487.

Abstract: Irrevocably endowing a person with power to administer a particular area of a large diocese which cannot be split cannot be understood as anything other than sacramentally conferring episcopal consecration.

Topics: EPISCOPATE; ORDERS, Sacrament of; SACRAMENTS, theology of.
Subsidiary Discussions: Diocese (160).
Precis: This essay on the tasks of "area" bishops, their status and relationships to other bishops was occasioned by the 1968 appointment of three episcopal vicars to three geographic regions of the Diocese of Munich and Freising.
Presuppositions. Because even within the church things can differ in form while remaining essentially the same, it is possible for a sacrament to be conferred even if the person administering it does not think he is conferring one. Conversely, a sacrament need not necessarily be present even when the administrator believes he is conferring one. To prove a sacrament is instituted by Christ it is enough to maintain that Christ willed the church to extend his saving work, making its decisions in fact *jure divino*.
The area bishop. In many ways the status and legitimacy of area bishops is easier to defend than that of curial appointees with no geographic responsibilities and whose office is purely titular. The legitimacy of area bishops rests in their having a tangible flock, and in the fact that it is often impractical to split a large diocese. The real theological problems arise in trying to understand what it means when the church says such episcopal vicars need not be bishops. Based on a theology of orders what justifies not consecrating such vicars?
Ordination (episcopal). If the position of episcopal vicar is valid then one must concede to the office holder "the powers and rights which naturally emanate from his membership of [sic] the entire episcopal body" (162). Rahner makes a second case based on the hypothetical situation where a bishop selects such a vicar and confirms his choice through prayer and the public laying on of hands. In this case a sacrament is conferred even if the administrator is not consciously aware of it. Were this not so it would be impossible to make the case for what a sacrament is. But in this case an important, new, and highly central ministry now exists. [The remaining discussion meant to answer a number of objections is very confusing, seeming simultaneously to allow and disallow the thesis that the conferral of this office is a de facto episcopal consecration.] Rahner concludes by affirming the logically necessary combination of episcopal powers and orders in the matter of area bishops.
Summing up. After a brief summary Rahner examines a few outstanding problems: how to rectify the equal yet subordinate status of an area bishop to a local ordinary; whether the office of area bishop is a new order falling somewhere between that of bishop and priest. In any case he insists such area bishops be treated with full respect and as equals by their brother bishops.

17.14   Transformations in the Church and Secular Society
Kirchliche Wandlungen und Profangesellschaft
{1.0}   1974 lecture in Madrid. Revised with notes.

Abstract: Despite their differences church and society face similar problems (e.g., freedom and authority). Rahner believes the solutions the church finds on a small scale could supply society with models for transforming itself.
Topics: CHURCH, change in; SOCIETY.

Subsidiary Discussions: Law, divine (167f); Pluralism (169f); Theology, pluralism in (170); Society, grassroots (171, 178ff); Power, coercive (173f); Truths, hierarchy of (176); Freedom and authority (176ff).

Precis: What effect could changes taking place in the church (i.e., not change in the nature of the church but in its institutional form) have in society?

What transformation? Rahner illustrates three characteristics of the transformations which have been provoked in the church by its new minority status and its subsequent efforts to submit to the laws of a pluralistic society. First, the mind of the church is no longer identical with the mind of society. In this new complex relationship the church is everywhere the weaker partner even though much in society is inspired by Christianity. Second, theology itself is insurmountably pluralistic because of its attempts to speak to an increasingly pluralistic society. Finally, "grass roots" believers have assumed greater importance. Today the effectiveness of authority in the church depends on the good will of the faithful. This will lead to greater democratization of the structure of the church.

The practical consequences for secular society. After narrowing the question Rahner suggests three effects structural alterations might have in the church. Rahner is optimistic the church can/must be a pace-setter for society.

a) Shared basic convictions. The state has the right and duty to provide (regenerate and change) a basic stock of common convictions for all its members. Though these choices affect everyone they are generally made by the stronger members. The real question is not whether these choices will be made but *how* they will be made without infringing unduly on the freedom of individuals. The historical nature of truth makes this a never-ending task.

b) The formulation of fundamental convictions. Rahner believes institutional transformations in the church as it grapples with authority and freedom provide a model for secular societies. Greater pluralism and the growing need for grass roots acceptance in order for its teachings to be effective indicate the church will offer few if any new dogmatic definitions. In fact this new situation calls into question the very existence of a common creed. Insofar as these new problems (freedom and authority) are the same in the church and in society and share the same general origins, the ways in which the church develops a free, anti-authoritarian, yet effective magisterium could be models for society. Rahner ends this section with a summary (178).

c) The role of the "grass roots." The church can no longer live in confrontation with its members. It can only be the church by deliberately being the church from *below*. Societies share this problem: how to insure the active participation of educated masses which can no longer be treated as minors. Is it so far-fetched to think the church could provide models for this?

17.15   The One Church and the Many Churches
Die eine Kirche und die vielen Kirchen
{1.5}   June 1968 lecture in Münster. *Orientierung* 32 (1968) 155-159.

Abstract: This sociological analysis of the factors separating the churches reveals a new situation and new opportunities for renewed unity based not on the abolition of diversity but on communion in the one church.

Topics: ECUMENISM; CHURCH and the churches.

Subsidiary Discussions: Utopias (189f).

Precis: Although the essence of all churches is Spirit and grace, they are also tangible historical entities. These social realities have significance only insofar as they are signs linking people with Christ and with God.

The present situation as an ecclesiological problem. Different approaches to the problem of the unity of the churches will yield different results. Rahner chooses as his starting-point the sociology of religions rather than dogmatic theology. In an earlier age churches were separated by differing homogeneous denominational consciousnesses. Clerics (sociologically demarcated and institutionally formal groups) were responsible for their particular people. Each group formed a homogeneous denomination.

The situation of the churches from the viewpoint of the sociology of religion. Although separate denominations continue to flourish what distinguishes them is known only by administrators and professional theologians. People belong to churches for historical, cultural, and psychological reasons. Today the key issues which separate us are of little or no consequence to most believers.

Dangers and new opportunities.

–Union without regard for the question of truth? Today's state of affairs gives some the impression that serious theological obstacles to union no longer exist. They have been submerged by the sociological tide of history.

–Actual facts and norms of existence. But facts do not constitute norms. It is always possible that what is the case perhaps should not be the case.

–A secularization of the church? Many very fine people who claim membership in the church do not in fact share the common faith. Often they attempt to co-opt the church to accomplish their own lofty social goals. Such people might quickly give up membership if adherence to strict theological tenets were demanded.

From the established church to the community church. Assuming this will be the church's situation in the future, two important consequences for the unity of the churches might follow from a movement wherein certain people choose to live from the free personal assent of faith to the substance of Christianity.

–Growing consciousness of denominational differences. Old theological division which were once quite important might take on new life and once again become matters of ultimate difference.

–The meaning of the fundamental substance of Christianity. Because the situation of faith is very different than in the 16th century former differences could become quite secondary in comparison with the basic shared substance of Christianity.

–Easier conversation between the churches. If the latter happens the churches might move toward a common Christian profession of faith embracing even secondary, denominational points of controversy. Summary (194).

The Catholic Church of the future and the unity of the church. This sociological analysis casts new light on the question of the truths dividing the churches. It reveals a very new situation with very new possibilities. True Catholics (not mere social members) believe all will be one in Christ, whether in this world or at the end of time. They have hope for the future, that those who now live separated will find a home in the Catholic church of the future where diversity is respected in communion.

17.16   Is Church Union Dogmatically Possible?

Ist Kircheneinigung dogmatisch möglich?

{2.5}   *Theologische Quartalschrift* (1973) 103-118. Revised, cross referenced.

Abstract: An analysis of the theological significance of the gap between the "official" faith of the church and "sense of the faithful" argues there are no longer any outstanding theological obstacles to the unity of the churches.

Topics: FAITH, *sensus fidelium*; ECUMENISM.

Subsidiary Discussions: Faith, simple (199); Faith, *fides implicita* (201); Faith, *fides quae/qua* (202ff); Magisterium (202f); Truths, hierarchy of (204f); Assent (205f); Concupiscence, gnoseological (206); Petrine office (212f).

Precis: The difference between the official doctrine of the church and actual belief. Though it may vary in extent, there is a gap between the official faith of every Christian church and the beliefs of its members. It seldom entails direct contradiction. It is more often implicit differences in stress or significance. Because the Catholic church has a more clearly articulated magisterium its gap is more visible. This well-known phenomenon has occasioned much theological reflection (list, 199). Rahner's analysis of the notion of *fides implicita* warns that the principle should be applied carefully today.

The normative significance of actual faith. Theologians must explore the relevance of people's actual faith more explicitly for *this* and not the official faith is the saving faith of the church. The Catholic notion of *fides implicita* fails to bridge the gap. Theologians must probe more deeply the question of how and why this faith can exist and be saving faith even in its most rudimentary and implicit form. The official faith of the church is normative only insofar as it successfully reflects this faith of the church. The normative, critical authority of this faith is not a power the faithful derive from magisterial teaching or from theology. This does not, however, justify a purely sociological approach to the truth of faith.

Yet theologians disdain this actual faith or dismiss it as superficial. Why is theology such a poor reflection of this existential hierarchy of truths when greater appreciation for the normative power of this sense of faith could lead to rapid ecumenical progress? Serious study of this sense of faith could also reveal important things about the degrees of assent related to individual theological statements. People of today whose intellectual world is marked by an insuperable pluralism are less likely to absolutize theological statements. They see knowledge as provisional and are more open than people of earlier generations. This bears upon ecumenical discussion. In saying this Rahner is not embracing radical relativism. He is simply pointing to this generation's enhanced appreciation for the historical nature of all theological statements.

The consequences for an institutional union of the churches. Rahner concludes, "the *de facto* faith as we find it in the Churches does not today stand in the way of church union on an institutional level" (208). After summarizing his earlier argument (208f) Rahner sharpens his point: "Faith as it is actually experienced is today the same in the different Churches, among average Christians. Has this fact consequences for the possibility and legitimacy of an institutional unity?" (209). He addresses two difficulties:

i) Doctrinal difficulty: How would such a union safeguard the convictions Catholics hold as irrevocable but which other Christians do not share? Rahner argues it is enough if others do not feel compelled in conscience to condemn these Catholic convictions as absolutely contrary to the faith. Catholics would live in hope that someday others would come to see their own faith more fully expressed in these doctrines. Summary (212).

ii) Institutional difficulty: What about the office of pope as a concrete entity which Catholics hold is constitutive of the church? Rahner allays these fears by insisting that although the Petrine office will endure it need not retain the form it has today. In addition, given the urgent pastoral task of preaching the basic gospel to an increasingly atheistic or pagan world there is little fear the pope will endanger ecumenical progress by promulgating new *ex cathedra* statements.

Rahner concludes that today there are no outstanding obstacles to the reunion of the churches. Based on an appeal to the sense of the faithful, church leaders need no longer wait for theologians to smooth out every detail of the official faith before they can act for unity.

17.17   Third Church?

Dritte Konfession? Christen zwischen den Kirchen
{1.5 } October 1972 Reformation Day lecture in Munich.

Abstract: The theological relevance of the "third church" (those who identify more with Christianity than with particular denominations) must be examined more closely for it contains seeds of the oneness Christ promised the church.
Topics: ECUMENISM; CHURCH and the churches.
Subsidiary Discussions: Dialogue (215f); Church, membership (221ff).
Precis: Christians between the churches. Many people today stand *between* the institutionally constituted churches and seem to form a "third church."
New partners. Who constitutes these new partners in dialogue among Christians? In the past, Christian denominations were separated geographically and socially. Boundaries were maintained by a clerical elite. Today conditions are leveling out as all Christians live amidst a growing pagan culture. Civil society no longer supports churches. Church members no longer view the world from within strict confessional stances. They are largely uninterested in the controversies they inherited. Their lives are structured by other concerns. Hence, members of the "third church" find little which distinguishes them from members of other Christian denominations and prefer it that way.
People belonging to the third church. For all their differences, generally members of the "third church" do not see themselves as a sect. They prefer to retain their denominational affiliation even though they find no significant difference among the churches. Many explicitly consider the theological controversies which separate the churches as unimportant and demand recognition of what they consider the already existing full unity of the churches. The existence of this third church is an indisputable fact.
The third church in the life of the church as a whole. How should one view the matter-of-factness of ecumenical activities today, the many ways in which the third church makes itself felt in the churches (list, 220)? What should the churches say to their members who identify with this third church? They should be cautioned that Christian unity will never be realized if the denominational churches are simply by-passed. The official establishment of a third church would lead to greater sectarian division. The "basic elements" of the church are not enough to insure its mission. "[F]aith and its liberating power need to be upheld by a fellowship which is also socially institutionalised—in this sense the Church" (222). Ecumenical progress can only be made by third church members lobbying within their churches for progress on important issues: mixed marriage, intercommunion, more

effective witness to the gospel, etc. Along the road of greater individualism lies the ruin of ecumenism. Summary (224). **The third church and ecclesial authority.** Church authorities too often identify the faith of the church with their own official theologies and conduct ecumenical dialogue on this basis. The shared, saving faith of the third church challenges this assumption and its relevance must be given more serious theological consideration. The third church is right to insist common Christian ground exists and binds us together even now. The importance of this great truth of the third church must neither be hastily overstated nor dismissed. For it is the very "'oneness' which God in Jesus Christ gave to all Christian Churches ... the living seed from which the fulness of unity can flower" (227).

17.18 Religious Feeling Inside and Outside the Church
Kirchliche und außerkichliche Religiosität
{2.5} *Stimmen der Zeit* 191 (1973) 3-13. Based on a working paper for the German Episcopal Synod.

Abstract: Presupposing God's universal salvific will and the fact that no one finds salvation without encountering God, it must be possible to encounter God in primal, non-reflected, extra-ecclesial, transcendental experiences.

Topics: GOD, experience of; TRANSCENDENCE; ANONYMOUS CHRISTIAN.

Subsidiary Discussions: Piety, ecclesial (228ff); God, salvific will of (231f); Nature and grace (234); Mystagogy (235,238ff); God-talk (237f); Mysticism (238, 241); Jesus Christ (239f).

Precis: Piety is the personally adopted and freely accepted relatedness of a person to God in faith, hope, and love. Though Christians experience this in Jesus Christ and express it in communion with the church it is only real when it is "animated by the innermost, free turning of man to God which is sustained by God's grace" (228).

Church piety. Relationship to God and to the church, though connected, are not identical. Church piety takes many forms and can be experienced subjectively as either foundational or merely secondary. Rahner warns against the consequences of attempting to overcome these variations with an overly glib "both-and" solution. Church piety can also occur in mistaken forms when it takes on an independent importance (list, 230). Such forms must be strongly resisted since they seriously block access to understanding the true attachment to the church. In any case attachment to the church is a secondary element in piety. This must be true since saving piety can also be found outside the church. The experience of God and Christ is more primal than the experience of church.

Piety outside the church. Saving piety exists not only reflectedly in non-Catholic Christian churches but also in unreflected forms outside the churches. This should not be seen as merely an attempt at relationship "from below" since this anonymous piety is sustained by the grace of God as much as Christian piety is. Hence, Christians do not indoctrinate from outside, rather their message gives explicit form to a pre-existing human experience. Incorporation in the church is not the beginning but the goal of grace. The ultimate, primal, free and grace-sustained alignment of knowledge and freedom towards God must be distinguished from its material, historical objectifications in space and time, in word and deed.

The experience of God as piety outside the church. The most primal and sustaining ground of all piety outside the church is the experience of God. Rahner distinguishes between primal experience (joy, fear, hope, etc.) and a reflective, verbally objectifying knowledge of God. The latter can always be inadequate to express the former. Here the classical distinction between grace and nature is not of decisive importance. Instead Rahner speaks of the experience of God as "a transcendental necessity" existing unreflectively always and everywhere people exercise their spiritual knowledge and freedom. Were this not the case God would be reduced to one more thing among things.

The experience of transcendence. The foundation for the transcendental experience of God is our own experience of transcendence. Both are expressions of one and the same reality. Rahner sketches this experience of transcendence (235-238). Essentially it is that part of us which reaches beyond every finite reality to the goal of incomprehensible mystery. Ordinary people and not only trained philosophers regularly have this experience, although only trained professionals explicitly reflect on it regularly. After listing numerous examples of such experiences (236f) Rahner concludes, "in all these situations God, as the condition which makes all this possible, is already experienced and accepted, even if this is not expressly and objectively formulated" (236f). The fact that these are not sporadic but generally accessible in no way deprecates explicit doctrines about God. Rahner apologizes for the abstract and general nature of these reflections but warns against overly concrete, graphically descriptive language which he fears localizes God who can only be spoken of indirectly.

The possibility of the transcendental experience of God. Rahner warns against demonstrations about God which appeal to "mystical experiences" which are the province of a chosen few. Real transcendental experience is open to all, even if not everyone has the capacity to reflect on it. A mystagogy of reflection on one's personal experiences of God can, however, be cultivated. Where possible one must be helped to connect these personal experiences with the historical and social understanding of God. They connect with Christ insofar as he is the "fruitful model" *per se* for a committed reliance on the mystery of existence which Christians call God. It is always possible, however, that these attempts will miscarry and lead one into a troubled atheism.

The oneness of piety in the church and outside it. Church piety which reflects on the death and resurrection of Christ fulfills the transcendental experience of God that is given to everyone everywhere. But this historical contingency is a two-edged sword: it makes this reality tangible while opening it to criticism. Hence, church piety must always be referred back to the primal, transcendental experience it means to interpret. This does not do away with the possibility of wordless mysticism but embraces it. To those who object that this analysis is overly theologically abstract Rahner counters that however one expresses it, his is the only approach which avoids recourse to mysticism and does justice to the reality of God's universally salvific will.

17.19   Some Clarifying Remarks about My Own Work
Einfache Klarstellung zum einigen Werk
{0.5}   P. Eicher, *Die anthropologische Wende. Karl Rahners philosophicher Weg vom Wesen des Menschen zur personalen Existenz, Dokimion I* (Fribourg 1970) ix-xiv. Revised.

Abstract: Rahner defends the genre of "theological investigation" by pointing out the impossibility of saying anything of existential importance today in a thoroughly scholarly way.
Topics: PHILOSOPHY, method; THEOLOGY, method; PLURALISM, gnoseological.
Subsidiary Discussions: Reflection, primary/secondary (244ff).
Precis: Since Rahner never claims to be a philosopher how, he wonders, can philosophical books be written about his work? Rahner claims to be writing in an emerging genre which he never names. It is neither theological nor philosophical scholarship, nor literature, nor popularization of scholarship. He makes no excuse for this new genre since the specialized scholarship of the experts is "existentially empty and ineffective" (244). Thus, it is quite legitimate for someone who wants to say something important to say it in a less than completely scholarly way.

This intellectual situation which makes complete mastery even of one's own narrow academic field practically impossible is relatively recent. Thus, the "*haute vulgarisation*, the high-class popularisation of earlier times, is no longer merely a secondary by-product of scholarly theology and philosophy. It is more or less the only way in which someone who wants to write something important in this field can write at all" (246f).

This being so, Rahner hopes all who go hunting for philosophy in his works "will be merciful. A reader should be lenient and remember...to listen more to what I wanted to say than what I actually did say. For in matters of theology and philosophy, he must not forget that today the difference between what is said and what is meant is greater than ever before" (247f).

XVIII. God and Revelation
XIII. *Gott und Offenbarung*

German edition: Einsiedeln, Benziger, 1978
U.S. edition: N.Y., Crossroad, 1983
Edward Quinn, translator

This volume in the English edition comprises the first seventeen essays in *Schriften zur Theologie*, XIII.

18.01 Yesterday's History of Dogma and Theology for Tomorrow

Dogmen- und Theologiegeschichte von gestern für morgen
{2.0}   *Zeitschrift für katholische Theologie* 99 (1977) 1-24.
Abstract: Suggests how theories, principles, and tools used to explain the historical development of doctrine, along with examples taken from the process of historical development, can be enlisted to anticipate future developments.

Topics: DOGMA, development of; STATEMENTS, theological; THE-OLOGY, history of; MAGISTERIUM and development of doctrine.

Subsidiary Discussions: Controversy (7f); Dogma, unity of (16ff); Hermeneutics, biblical (22ff).

Precis: Twentieth century theology has seriously considered the nature of the development of doctrine as a whole and its limits. Various theories attempt to reconcile the permanent identity of the faith with its undeniable historicity. They are perhaps too retrospective. This essay considers methodological and hermeneutical principles which might apply to future developments of doctrine.

The great theologians of mid-century saw Catholic doctrine as practically complete. However, the history of dogma continues and must continue. The task of transposing ancient dogma into a modern idiom is never completed. Rahner argues one can find in theories of development of doctrine useful principles for grasping future development. He bases his ideas not on fine points of theology but on straightforward observations of doctrinal development up to now. The essay is copiously illustrated. Rahner adds that the principles he is about to put forward must be valid since the magisterium itself employs them to authenticate it own developments in doctrine.

I. The development of doctrine always was and will be beset with friction and accompanied by struggles, conflicts, and denunciations. In the past the church characterized its opponents as stupid or malicious. It no longer does so, recognizing that developments in doctrine are never a simple matter of logical progression. Today because the subjectivity of conscience with regard to truth takes precedence over the objective dignity of truth, it is impossible to declare those who question developments in doctrine "subjective" heretics.

II. Since the development of doctrine is not a smooth, progressive unfolding from obscurity to clarity, the future history of doctrine (like the past) will continue to see the magisterium revising its declarations considerably.

III. Reform and development of doctrine is possible because of the distinction between the unchanging truths which comprise the doctrine and the historically contingent forms and modes of thinking in which it is expressed. After listing many examples (11ff) Rahner returns to the necessity of distinguishing content from form in the "amalgam" of doctrine and of eliminating those elements which prove in time to be contrary to the fullness of the gospel. During this process the faithful must be educated, theologians must refrain from being apodictic, and the magisterium must be very patient.

Rahner considers: i) how to evaluate statements against the background of the historical period in which they emerged; ii) how to assess statements today when content and form can be distinguished and the latter can be replaced with more adequate forms. Rahner insists the original formulation may have been true and appropriate at its time insofar as it was the best or only form available to convey the intended truth. Hence, one must not say the old formulation was erroneous but only that within a new intellectual horizon it has *become* erroneous. Rahner confines his analysis to religious statements, all of which struggle to express the ineffable mystery.

IV. Recourse to a statement's origin can also provide a criterion for correctly understanding it and perhaps for eliminating erroneous interpretations. After all, doctrine is not a mere additive sum of statements. They all cohere within the original and unitive center of the reality of faith: God's absolute self-communication in Jesus Christ. This same principle which is employed in interpreting scripture clarifies the meaning and limits of magisterial statements without reducing theology to the teaching of the catechism (examples, 19). A further argument for the validity of appealing to the global and original understanding of the faith is its use in Pius XII's 1950 proclamation of Mary's Assumption (19f). After listing more examples (21) Rahner admits this is all still rather vague and calls for a complete theory of the development of dogma. But until it appears, he cautions the magisterium against basing its arguments for development of dogma primarily on appeals to authority.

V. The now universally accepted rules of biblical hermeneutics could also be applied to interpreting magisterial teachings since the same questions are involved. Rahner suggests the notion of literary genre might be particularly fruitful as it is possible to distinguish in magisterial statements a number of literary forms in addition to purely theological statements (e.g., prayer, directives, counsels, etc.).

VI. Rahner also suggests a closer look at "linguistic usages"—terms which came into being to explain theological truths but which are not themselves a necessary part of revealed doctrine and may be modified or discarded when explaining the faith to a new generation (examples, 26f). To underscore the changeable nature of linguistic usages Rahner points to seemingly promising new terms (Mary mediatrix of all grace) which have been all but abandoned.

VII. Theological disputants should not be painted as winners or losers. Much in the favored doctrinal statement may still need clarification. Much in the discarded statement may later prove to be of great value.

VIII. The history of doctrine remains history: unpredictable and outside the control of people and even of church authority. However organic it may appear, it is always free. It can never be logically deduced, not even after the fact. Hence, prognosis is vain. To say a statement is a truth of faith reveals nothing about how that formulation will fare over time (examples, 31).

IX. Rahner sees the history of theology in three broad periods: the first four centuries which saw the emergence of doctrine in confrontation with a pagan milieu; the period to the Enlightenment which saw the construction of a universal system within a homogeneous cultural milieu; the period from the Enlightenment to today which is similar to the first period and will produce a more pluralistic theology because it addresses an insurmountably pluralistic world. In this new age the magisterium has the new task of proclaiming the gospel in a new voice which must speak to a new, diverse world. Summary (34).

18.02   Pseudo-Problems in Ecumenical Discussions
Scheinprobleme in der ökumenischen Diskussion
{2.0}   August 1977 lecture. Frankfurt am M. 7th Ecumenical Congress of Jesuits.
Abstract: Careful study of the many open questions surrounding Catholic dogma reveals no compelling dogmatic reasons for continued separation of churches.
Topics: ECUMENISM; DOGMA.
Subsidiary Discussions: Sacraments (38f); Orders, sacrament of (39-43); Petrine office (43-45); Infallibility (45-49); Faith, *sensus fidelium* (47f); BVM, Immaculate Conception of (49f); BVM, Assumption of (50f).
Precis: This essay is restricted to certain individual dogmatic questions which the magisterium and traditional textbook theology too quickly assumed it had answered. Although the essay is meant to spur ecumenical unity, question of *sola fide, sola scriptura, sola gratia* are not discussed here (37).

Sacraments. Today the sacraments are generally seen to originate from Christ in the sense that he instituted the church. By seeing each sacrament as a concrete actualization of the one basic sacrament, the church, problems like *opus operatum* can be made intelligible to Protestant and Catholics alike.

Ministry. All we can say with binding force is that a ministry of leadership must exist in some historical and sociological reality with its powers derived from the nature of the church. How it is divided or ordered is not a matter of divine law. Even if it were, the church is competent to divide it further. Thus, union wouldn't need to insist on adopting Rome's division of ministries. Nor does divine law dictate how office holders are chosen.

Recognizing orders of separated churches [cf., *Vorfragen zu einen ökumenischen Amtsverständnis, Questiones Disputate* 65 (Freiburg 1974)]. Vatican II teaches that ministries in the Eastern and Reformation churches have positive importance for salvation. This is because they share in the basic nature of the church as it participates in the victory of Jesus Christ. It does not derive from their compliance with statuary law. (Here Rahner draws an analogy with the individual and with marriage of non-Catholics.)

Papal primacy. Catholic theologians and the pope must do much more to distinguish what is essential to the nature of the Petrine office. Primacy of jurisdiction is not obviously dogmatic. Papal authority is already restricted by moral norms. Protestants need not think of infallibility as a blank check. First because the pope speaks *ex cathedra* only in clarifying the existing faith of the church. He receives no new revelation. Thus, consultation is morally imperative. Second, this exercise of power is historically conditioned to its times. Contemporary needs indicate a greater call to express the basic and ultimate faith of the church in a more compelling way. Thus, the need for future *ex cathedra* pronouncements seems increasingly unlikely.

Marian dogmas. The dogma of Mary's Immaculate Conception will be better appreciated by Protestants when it is contextualized in a more adequate (non-binding) theology of original sin (50). Her Assumption will be received better as all churches continue to demythologize the resurrection of the body (51).

Catholic theologians can rightly assume today there are no absolutely binding theological opinions which necessitate the division of the churches (51). Thus, churches cannot lay the blame for lack of progress in ecumenism at the feet of theologians. But the church has far to go in assimilating its own orthodox theology. Theologians are desperately needed for this task.

18.03   Magisterium and Theology
Lehramt und Theologie

{1.5}   March 1977 lecture in West Berlin to Catholic Academy of Berlin.
Abstract: Theology and magisterium are mutually dependent. Magisterial teaching has a normative authority for theology; theology is an indispensable condition for the existence and success of magisterium. Each has a specific but partial function. Both depend on the Spirit for their connection and unity.
Topics: MAGISTERIUM and theology; THEOLOGY and magisterium.
Subsidiary Discussions: Authority (55ff); Dialogue (64ff); Statements, theological (66ff); Conflict (69f); Pluralism (71f).
Precis: These brief, unsystematic reflections on this important topic should interest professionals and educated laity. It begins with a summary of the absolutely binding doctrines concerning the magisterium's self-understanding (55-59). The one church instituted by Christ has a sociological structure of authority through which it fulfills its divine mandate and mission. This legitimate authority, sustained by the Spirit, is exercised in ordinary and extraordinary ways by the college of bishops in union with its head the pope. It's teaching authority is intrinsic and not simply justified by the strength of its arguments. It invokes this authority in various degrees ranging from absolutely binding dogmas to authentic but provisional and non-binding statements. Though these degrees can easily be distinguished in theory they are hard to distinguish in practice. It is difficult to know how this teaching authority can co-exist with the rights of individual conscience. Although Rahner shies away from applying to it the term "magisterium," theologians have their own proper role in authentic teaching.

Rahner's unsystematic observations are meant to clarify the relationship between theology and the magisterium. Magisterial teaching is always theology insofar as it is formulated in terms and concepts which are not themselves revealed. Every magisterial pronouncements is always an "amalgam" of irreformable truth and contingent elements open to challenge and change. Because theology is an intrinsic element (prior and subsequent) of magisterial teaching, the latter is dependent on the former albeit not in a legal way.

Strictly binding teachings bring truth to the attention of the faithful but do not thereby simply affect what they proclaim. To succeed they rely on theology to find appropriate means to express the unchanging dogmatic truth within ever-changing circumstances (e.g., original sin, 62). After a brief summary (62f) Rahner concludes that theology and magisterium are mutually dependent. Though magisterial teaching has a normative authority for theology, theology is an indispensable condition for the existence and success of the magisterium. Each has a specific but partial function, and both depend on the Spirit to maintain their connection and unity. The two have a continual reciprocal causality which is the history of the truth of the church. As real history it is guided by God and is impossible completely to fathom or control.

Rahner closes with five concrete, practical conclusions.

1) Though they do not have the same function, both the magisterium and theologians must have a genuine will for dialogue.

2) Instead of appealing to its authority the magisterium must show more clearly how its statements have been formed by dialogue with theologians.

3) Distinguishing the true content from the contingent form of dogmatic statements is the most important object of dialogue today between theologians and the magisterium. Although disagreements may distress the faithful they are an intrinsic, unavoidable part of the process of the development of doctrine.

4) The magisterium should indicate clearly the degree of binding force it attaches to its various pronouncements. Theologians could help by producing a meaningful and manageable system of formal qualifications.

5) The task of the magisterium changes in no small degree as the world changes. Today is a time of insurmountable pluralism which touches even theology. In this environment the magisterium cannot concentrate on theological subtleties or in-house disputes. It has the task of proclaiming the basic substance of the faith to the whole world in a recognizable and believable voice. Rahner closes with this analogy: theology and magisterium are related like muscles and bones in the human body. Each has a separate but necessary function. But only the guidance of the Spirit can direct them to work harmoniously together to attain their final goal.

18.04   On Bad Arguments in Moral Theology
Über schlechte Argumentation in der Moraltheologie
{3.0}   H. Boelaars, R. Tremblay, eds., Festschrift for Bernard Häring: *In Libertationem vocavi estis: Miscellanea Bernard Häring, Studia Moralia SV* (*Academia Alfonsiana*, Rome 1977) 245-57.

Abstract: Examining the fact that moral arguments generally assume the conclusion they hope to prove leads Rahner to discuss the criteria for good moral arguments and to reappraise the task of today's moral theologian.
Topics: THEOLOGY, moral (argument).
Subsidiary Discussions: Church, conservatism in (79ff); Conflict (81); Statements, true/false (81).

Precis: These few vague remarks address the fact that arguments in moral theology seem to smuggle into their premises the very conclusions they set out to prove. As a result they convince only those who already hold such conclusions. It is not enough to say every field of human studies similarly begs the question or that these types of arguments are a necessary part of any science of practical behavior. Here Rahner considers i) the right and ii) the limits of this type of appeal by looking at what lies behind it.

   Right. Moralists try to explain theoretically positions they are already committed to in practical life. It is always possible their conclusions remain correct even if their arguments are weak or even false. How can one know the truth of the "conclusion"? Rahner alludes to the possibility of "a global, still implicit, but perhaps entirely correct and effective insight which is prior to theory, to conceptual articulation and objectification, which is itself the inner light of practice as such" (76). Thus, a bad argument in moral theology is not disposed of simply by showing it is not logically conclusive. The critic must still address the fact this conclusion was held by so many people for so many centuries. Without this deeper reflection moral discourse risks being reduced to nihilism or theological positivism.

   Bad arguments can implicitly be indicating a global knowledge of revelation poorly objectified or a natural instinctive human insight which perhaps appears in numerous ways over the course of history. The justifiable respect given the conclusions depends on the special character of the truth which lies behind it. Moral theologians who take exception to magisterial teaching must always allow for the possibility of these deeper truths.

   Limits. The tacitly and implicitly operating prior conviction of the correctness of what is to be proved can also, however, be false or even highly prejudiced. It is unfortunate the church often only recognizes such moral theological arguments to be untenable once their basis has been discredited by other disciplines. The church's natural conservatism makes it especially prone to maintaining problematic preconceptions too long. Rahner calls this the "dark tragedy of the Church's history of ideas" (79), especially because it has imposed such heavy and unfair burdens on so many people.

For all these reasons, the task of moral theology today must be to analyze "much more closely, critically, and courageously the provenance and historico-sociological relativity of those preliminary decisions which are at work behind the arguments of traditional textbook theology and also of the Church's magisterium" (80). This means distinguishing the revealed truth from the historical forms in which it has been expressed. This latter human tradition can be absolutely right in one age and quite wrong in another. Moral theology must both conserve what is good in the past and break down any false preconceptions which obscure the splendor of that truth—a task which seldom meets with gratitude from the magisterium. Since theology has a real history no one can know in advance the outcome of its development. And since friction and conflict are unavoidable, moral theologians must have courage to defend as well as to criticize accepted positions.

Rahner ends (81-85) with some technical suggestions for moving this process forward. He concludes from the Thomistic notion that every concept relies on a contingent, concrete image that the argumentative process in moral theology has no end. Any given theologian can only hope his/her theories will survive the test of time. Rahner also sharpens his distinction between true and false arguments. An argument can be true either of transcendental necessity or based on the representational model. Of this latter variety the model on which the argument is based can either be generally accepted and undisputed (even by those who oppose it) in which case the argument can be called true; or the model used can be imperiled. In this case the argument can be considered provisionally true but threatened.

Moral arguments are false when they cannot be proven by transcendental deduction or when the model on which they rest is unsustainable. This latter happens in one of two ways: either the person making the argument has lost touch with currents in modern society (this often happens in the church), or an appeal is made to a situation which even though it has not yet passed away is patently disintegrating. These two forms of wrong argumentation tend to overlap. Rahner concludes with a summary (85).

18.05   The Human Question of Meaning in the Face of the Absolute Mystery of God

Die menschliche Sinnfrage vor dem absoluten Geheimnis Gottes
{3.5}   November 1977 lecture at University of Bamberg.
Geist und Leben 50 (1977) 436-50.
Abstract: An incomprehensible God can only be the answer to the question of human meaning if reason is understood as our capacity to be seized by the incomprehensible, and if truth and love are seen as mutually interpenetrated.
Topics: GOD, incomprehensibility of; KNOWLEDGE; MEANING.
Subsidiary Discussions: God, attributes of (92ff); Theodicy (95); God as horizon (97f); Virtues, perichoresis (99f); Love (100f); Freedom (103f).

Precis: Every age has its key concerns. This generation's is "meaning." Christian theology must engage its times by taking these key concepts seriously, challenging them and allowing itself to be challenged by them. This essay analyzes the concept of meaning in conjunction with God's incomprehensibility.

God's incomprehensibility in doctrine and theological tradition.
After an overview of the history of the theological term "incomprehensibility" (90f) Rahner notes that except to say this attribute of God is not provisional (i.e., it persists even in the beatific vision) traditional theology generally takes no trouble to explain this concept.

How can the eternally incomprehensible God be the meaning of our life?
Theology too often looks at God's incomprehensibility as one among many divine attributes, a marginal phenomenon. Rahner insists it should be the starting-point always and everywhere determining God's unique character. Without this as a starting-point, when we say God is the meaning of our existence we are in danger of thinking of meaning in our sense: "that which is seen, that which is understood, controlled, that which is justified in *our* sight and is given into our hands, put at our disposal, so that finally the pain of the emptiness of meaning of the unanswered question ceases" (93).

Though God is the fundamental unity of all meaning, it remains unclear how the incomprehensible and nameless can be *our* meaning. Christians cannot be content to say God is the guarantor and content of our meaning insofar as God created a finite something which is comprehensible and amounts to our fulfillment. Furthermore God's incomprehensibility extends beyond his own nature to encompass his attributes relative to us: his decrees, freedom, justice, mercy, fidelity, etc. It is wrong, therefore, to proffer an apologetical theodicy to domesticate God's terrible freedom. All this points to the fact that simply appealing to God as the answer to the question of meaning does not solve all our problems. One thing is certain: any attempts to come to terms with God's incomprehensibility by using the modern ideal of instrumental knowledge dooms us to a sentence of death on the question of meaning.

Two basic questions on the clear/obscure "solution" of the dilemma.
Two closely connected but not identical questions flow from Rahner's assumptions that the question of meaning is legitimate and that God's insurmountable incomprehensibility must govern any approach to the question of meaning.

1) How must knowledge be understood if it is have anything to do with God's incomprehensibility? Knowledge as the power to grasp individual objects and their relatedness can never incorporate divine incomprehensibility. Reason must be thought of as the capacity for the incomprehensible, not as the power to master and subjugate but to be seized by what is insurmountable (Aquinas' *excessus*). In the intellectual grasp of any object, its transcendent and its provisional nature is manifested. The infinite horizon against

which finite objects stand out, the darkness which illumines the object and is co-known in the act of knowing, points to God's incomprehensibility (summary, 98). Even if this explanation is dismissed as idle dialectic, the knower is left with the question of what this horizon indicates: an abysmal meaninglessness or a sheltering incomprehensibility relieving us of ourselves and our questions.

2) How exactly can we understand the human act of allowing for God's incomprehensibility without either being broken by it or dismissing it as completely irrelevant? To say the power of comprehension is the power to come face to face with the incomprehensible does not make us irrationalists. Rather it identifies the condition for the possibility of conceptually elaborating, delimiting, and discriminating knowledge. But in going this far have we already transcended and thus objectified this horizon? Here Rahner calls to mind Aquinas' teaching on the mutual interpenetration of knowledge and will, and the difference between these two powers found in their proper objects (the transcendentals of truth and goodness). Based on these insights we can allow for and accept divine incomprehensibility not in the act of knowledge but "in the act of self-surrendering love trusting entirely in this very incomprehensibility, in which knowledge surpasses itself, rising to its supernature, and is aware of itself only by becoming love" (100). Rahner argues this same point from the other direction, asking what else but love could one call the act of submitting to this incomprehensibility without being broken by it? This love is glimpsed and known analogously in the human experience of love in which we surrender ourselves to one another (101).

Ultimate fulfillment of meaning only in the free and loving acceptance of the incomprehensibility of God. Though it may seem this essay has lost sight of the question of meaning it has not. Human meaning consists in God's gracious offer of self-communication in his most intimate reality. But this means nothing less than coming into immediate contact with God's incomprehensibility— not the limit but the content of beatitude. Unfortunately, the church's proclamation of this fulfillment too often settles for a God who is secretly subject to human selfishness. For Rahner the choice is clear: either an incomprehensible God or an empty and absurd existence. In this question knowledge and freedom/love cannot be separated. Rahner returns to the perichoresis of the transcendentals (unity, truth and goodness) to find an antidote for our tendency to settle for a God who is less. Somewhat rhetorically Rahner asks where the Christian proclamation speaks clearly and firmly today of the eternally incomprehensible ways and decrees of God's freedom. God is the answer to the question of meaning. But our theology becomes an idol if it does not bring us, self-surrendering, into the presence of the incomprehensible God.

18.06 Oneness and Threefoldness of God in Discussion with Islam

Einzigkeit und Dreifaltigkeit Gottes im Gespräch mit dem Islam
{4.0} May 1977 lecture at St. Gabriel's, Mödling bei Wien.

Abstract: The dogma of the Trinity can easily slip into tritheism, especially when it rests on the use of the term "person." Rahner argues Trinitarianism is not a supplement or attenuation of monotheism but its radical realization.
Topics: GOD, monotheism; TRINITY, economic/immanent; NATURE and person.
Subsidiary Discussions: Islam (passim); Hypostesis (112f); Transcendence/history (114ff); Demythology (117); Trinity, processions within (118f).
Precis: This essay aims to contribute to the dialogue between Christianity and Islam by examining monotheism and the threefoldness of God which can easily appear as a thinly veiled but pernicious tritheism. In doing so Rahner realizes he must risk speaking for himself and not for the church. Because he is not a scholar of Islam his work will concentrate more on clarifying the essential questions about monotheism than on the actual dialogue with Islam.

Christianity is a primarily monotheistic religion. The oneness of God, its basic dogma, is not primarily a metaphysical statement. It is a revealed truth with its own history. It refers "to the God experienced concretely in his actions on us, to the God of Abraham, of Isaac, to the God of the prophets, the God of Jesus" (107). Because Christian propositions about God's oneness refer to a concrete absolute, either the object of a radically religious experience is one and unites and authenticates all religious expressions, or this religious intentionality misses the goal and worships an idol.

Polytheism maintains the pluralism of numinous expressions, the ultimate religious data. Metaphysically minded polytheists banish the possibility of any meaningful unity behind these diverse experiences, whereas monotheists claim the one God can reach us "without dissipating its oneness, can as itself penetrate into the pluralism even of this world and be present there, can itself become incarnate" (108). Hence, the monotheism of Christianity, Judaism and Islam must be seen as both concrete and universal, inevitably possessing a radically incarnational character (in book, covenant, person). Rahner's basic thesis is that "the doctrine of the Trinity can and must be understood not as a supplement or attenuation of Christian monotheism, but as its radicalization ..." (109).

Before turning directly to his basic thesis Rahner attempts to clear up some crude but widespread misunderstandings of the doctrine of the Trinity. The term "person" is the most misleading element of the doctrine, the most open to misunderstanding largely because this theological term has subsequently developed its own independent history (110-112). Today the term "three persons" immediately conjures up visions of three personalities, three independent subjects. This heterodox view is latent even at the highest levels of theology and has a long history stretching back to Augustine. It is not enough to draw the veil here and appeal to the mystery of the Trinity, especially not if this "mystery" is merely confusion caused by the indiscriminate use of the term "person." Rahner also warns against using the words "person" and "hypostasis" as if they were synonymous (112-114). They are not. He suggest theologians would avoid more dangers today if instead of the term "three persons" they spoke of "three hypostases" or "three modes of subsistence." Rahner returns to his thesis (114-121) this time from the standpoint that the economic Trinity is the immanent Trinity and vice versa. No Christian can seriously doubt a certain threefoldness revealed in the economy of salvation: Father, Son, and Spirit. "For Christian faith then there are two utterly radical and definitive and unsurpassable factualities, modes of existence, of one God in the world [i.e., history and transcendence], factualities which are the final salvation freely granted by God to the world" (114).

Rahner argues that the historicity and transcendentality of the human being provide an adequate aid to understanding the distinction, unity, and exclusiveness of the two factualities of God. This assumes we are made in God's image, and that our nature as recipients of a revelation must necessarily correspond to the nature of the communication, in this case God's self-communication. The unoriginated and permanently sovereign God is called Father; in his self-communication to history God is called Logos.

Logos and Spirit are not mediating realities. For then they would be like other created, finite realities and only hint at but not truly mediate God's innermost reality. For someone satisfied with an infinite and incomprehensible God who remains utterly remote, this distinction is unimportant. But for those who desire a God who is utterly close, and for those who hear and respond to the New Testament, "it is impossible to avoid the admission that there is a twofold self-communication of God in diversity and unity, the modalities of which in their unity and distinction are again God himself strictly as such" (116). This implies that the trinitarian doctrine (i.e., that Logos and Spirit are God himself) is not an attenuation but a radicalization of monotheism rightly understood.

Rahner returns to the point that if monotheism is not an abstract metaphysical theory about a remote absolute but concerns the God with whom we deal concretely in salvation history, then Christians and other religious monotheists are confronted by three alternatives: demythologizing all mediations of the relationship with God as purely created and reverting to a theoretical monotheism which keep God ever remote; holding to theoretical monotheism while being for all practical purposes polytheistic; having absolute confidence in the absolute God who is also absolutely close, seeing the mediating modes of factuality as themselves divine. Whoever adheres to this third position must affirm the other two statements even if unable to synthesize them within one intelligible viewpoint. "This absolutely comprehensive dual statement is therefore the radicalization of that monotheism which comes within the religious dimension" (118).

All this is merely another way of saying that any form of created mediation renders God absolutely remote, turns concrete monotheism into abstract monotheism, and permits one to be practically polytheistic in the concreteness of one's religious life. Hence, "God must mediate to himself through himself" (118).

Rahner concludes with a note on "internal divine processions" as the theological term which embodies the notion of the historical and transcendental modes of divine factuality. In his humble opinion this language of "modes of subsistence" is superior to the term "persons" in describing the life of the Trinity. Finally, he again cautions against the dangers of misinterpreting the reality of the Trinity when one uses the word "person." This is no less a problem for Christian theologians as for Islamic partners in dialogue.

18.07   Dialogue with God?

Gebet—Zweigespräch mit Gott?

{1.5} J. de Vries, W. Brugger, eds., *Der Mensch vor dem Anspruch der Wahrheit und der Freiheit* (Frankfurt am M. 1973) 229-238.

Abstract: Even when prayer is demythologized, modern people can honestly claim it is dialogue with God by referring to its transcendental dimensions.

Topics: PRAYER; HUMAN NATURE.

Subsidiary Discussions: Word of God (125f); Spirit, discernment of (130f); Ignatian Loyola, *indifferençia* (130).

Precis: Modern people have a problem understanding prayer as dialogue with God. Either prayer seems to be an interior monologue which sparks insights little different from artistic or generally charismatic inspiration (123), or prayer seems to be God's way of breaking into the world from outside as in the case in physical miracles. This essay examines whether there is a demythologized sense of prayer which can still maintain that it is dialogue with God.

Rahner examines and dismisses four approaches to understanding prayer as dialogue with God: the charismatic (124); the scriptural (124f); the illuminist (126); the personalist (126f). Each approach ends in greater confusion because each states the problem incorrectly. They all assume that in dialogue with God, God tells us "something"—imparts categorial information alongside the other bits of categorial information we already possess (127).

Rahner asks, "how would it be if we were to say and could say that in prayer we experience ourselves as those who are spoken by God, who in the concreteness of our existence have our origin in and are at the disposal of God's supreme freedom? What if we say that what God tells us first of all in prayer [is that] we are ourselves in the determinedness of our freedom, in the indeterminability of our future, in the never completely revocable and never functionally rationalizable facticity of our past and present?" (127). Then it becomes clear that prayer is indeed dialogue with God but in a unique way. This is the transcendental aspect of prayer. Summary (128f).

The second aspect of prayer justifies the transcendental aspect and clarifies erroneous mythological or miraculous misattributions. It could be called "the logic of existential knowledge and freedom" (130) and responds to the problem of understanding poetic or charismatic inspiration. Unconditionally accepting one's absolute openness toward God brings what Ignatius Loyola calls "indifference" toward categorial things. This indifference elevates categorial objects into a medium for the experience of God's immediacy, and thus explains the feeling that inspiration is God's breaking into the world.

Rahner knows his attempt to demythologize prayer as dialogue with God is inadequate and unsatisfying. In fact it may even make prayer more difficult initially. But "going through these considerations and this disenchantment, [one] may experience prayer in a kind of fresh naïvety as dialogue with God, simply because that is what it is in truth" (131).

18.08   The Death of Jesus and the Closure of Revelation
Tod Jesu und Abgeschlossenheit der Offenbarung
{3.5}   1975 lecture at Rome to International Congress of Passionists.
Abstract: The "end" of revelation history can come only in the death of one who is revelation bearer and revelation event in one. Though the cross closes revelation history its concrete victory continues to be achieved.
Topics: REVELATION, closure of; JESUS CHRIST, death/resurrection of; CROSS, theology of; ESCHATOLOGY.
Subsidiary Discussions: Word (136ff); Death (139ff) Transcendence/history (141).
Precis: Despite the axiom that binding Christian revelation ceased with the death of the last apostle, Vatican II made no explicit reference to apostles or to the close of the apostolic age. The "close of revelation" is a difficult idea for the modern person who sees him/herself as absolutely open to the future, distinguished by a freedom which is always freshly and surprisingly realized in self-transcendence into the future. "To say that the history of revelation is at an end seems to him to deprive history as a whole of its ultimate depth and dignity" (134). If it is taught that the Spirit continues to lead the church in the history of the acceptance of revelation this notion is more palatable. If it is stressed that with Jesus revelation is not so much complete as unsurpassable, the notion of the closure of revelation becomes even more palatable. What, however, is the content of this unsurpassability?

Vatican II greatly clarified this unsurpassability. First it emphasized revelation is not so much the communication of propositions as the unsurpassability of the Christ event. Second it emphasized that saying "after Jesus nothing more is revealed" does not leave much unsaid but indicates nothing is left to say. "[A]ll is in fact given in the beloved Son in whom God and the world have become one" (135). Though Rahner suggests more ways this unsurpassability can be conceived (list, 135) this is not his chief interest. What interest him is "how the *death* of Jessu as such has significance for the unsurpassability of the revelation event in Jesus Christ, and how in this light it is possible to make a contribution to the reconciliation of the modern mentality of an open future with the dogma of the unsurpassability and 'completedness' of Christian revelation" (135). Rahner maintains the death and resurrection of Jesus *as such* has an essential and irreplaceable significance in establishing this unsurpassability of Christian revelation (thesis, 136).

History can only persist as the history of human freedom and as revelation history if the conclusive or unsurpassable character of the Christ event is seen as the offer and acceptance of God's absolute self-promise as such and as the goal of history. Any other word, being finite, could not be final. At best it could explain but never replace God's promise. Rahner distinguishes these words as *prophetic* (essentially provisional) and *eschatological* (God's absolute irrevocable self-promise). God does not offer this eschatological word as a mere possibility. It is an irreversibly triumphant offer, effective grace, which nevertheless leaves human freedom intact. "In the eschatological word God promises himself to the world, not merely as its final and unsurpassable opportunity, but as his own effective fulfillment of this opportunity" (137). This is also the meaning of Jesus' message.

How are we to think concretely about this one eschatological and unsurpassable word of revelation? Assuming revelation is achieved in a unity of "deeds and words," and assuming the unity and solidarity of the events of human history, Rahner insists the only way this promise can appear historically (and so be a matter of deeds and not mere words) is in a person who has accepted this self-promise freely and definitively. A mere word remains a mere offer. The word must occur through an historical event (138f). This free and definitive acceptance of God's self-offer can only come about by the *death* of the person who freely accepts that offer—a death redeemed as in the resurrection of Jesus. "In this sense the *death* of Jesus is an internal constitutive element of God's eschatological self-promise to the world" (139).

For Rahner death is the self-realization of creaturely human freedom in which one faces God and totally disposes of oneself for or against God. One does this in a state of creaturely powerlessness that reaches its depth at death. The death of Jesus is no less "the act of supreme freedom in absolute powerlessness, centered at the same time on finality" (140). In his death Jesus definitively accepts God's promise. God reveals the success of Jesus' acceptance by the gift of the resurrection. Jesus' death is a necessary constitutive element in the eschatological word of God's self-promise to the world as its absolute future. It alone comprises and reveals the closure of revelation. Hence, the cross is not just one event in the history of salvation. It is its gnoseological axis which reconciles the transcendental and historical dimensions of human life.

Rahner returns to his initial concern: how our absolute will for a boundless future makes us resist the notion of a closed revelation. Yet this will of ours is continually repudiated and foiled by death. The modern person must recognize this fatal contradiction and search history for signs that death is not the nullifying end of history. Christian faith in the cross of Christ is the event in which history is dissolved by God's act into the infinite freedom of God. What Jesus has achieved he promises also to us.

18.09   What Does it Mean Today to Believe in Jesus Christ?

Was heißt heute an Jesus Christus glauben?

{3.0}   May 1976 lecture at Innsbruck to *Katolisches Bildungswerk*, Tyrol.

Abstract: Searching history to find anyone who achieved the destiny we hope for the whole of our own lives (questing christology) we confront the proclamation, "Christ is risen," our hope and the source of classical christology.

Topics: CHRISTOLOGY; FAITH in Jesus Christ.

Subsidiary Discussions: Christology, questing (145ff); Mysticism (145f); Resurrection (147, 151f); Christology, New Testament (149); Jesus Christ, self-awareness (149ff); Saints, communion of (154f).

Precis: Four preliminary observations: the following arbitrary remarks do not exhaust this subject; insofar as the christology offered here addresses the question of our existence, Rahner is concerned here with the whole, mysterious nature of human existence; though christology could be approached in a number of equally valid ways, Rahner tries here to meld a number of different ways; although what follows presumes and does not contradict the official teaching of the church, it suggest a different more modern starting-point.

"Questing christology" points to our concern with ourselves and the meaning of our lives definitively and as a whole. But no finite, particular concern can reveal or insure the meaning of our existence. Even mysticism is irrelevant to the question of our meaning. Hence, we look within human history to see if there is another human being who, by God's free power, ever achieved and made perceptible the salvation for which we long, hoping that in solidarity with that person we too might have a share in that salvation. Rahner calls that person for whom we look "the absolute bringer of salvation." His fate also becomes our salvation if he exists in absolute solidarity with us and we with him. Such definitive solidarity can only occur with the death of "the bringer of salvation" since only then is his history complete, his surrender definitive. For this to be made tangible his death must pass into what Christians refer to as resurrection.

Seen merely as a person this absolute bringer of salvation (whom Rahner has up to this point described a priori) is not himself salvation since our salvation can only be the immediacy and finality of the self-communication of God. "But this person who is sought is the absolute salvation bringer insofar as his consummation occurring through death and resurrection in the power of God in solidarity with us is for us the irrevocable sign that God has promised himself as the consummation of our salvation" (147).

Rahner makes no attempt to prove this questing christology is identical with classical christology. But he does insist that whenever a person sees oneself saved through such an absolute bringer of salvation then one is practicing questing christology implicitly or explicitly. Thus classical christology need not be regarded as an odd and unrealizable myth.

Rahner now comes to the core of Christianity (148): the church's declaration that Jesus Christ is the sought after absolute bringer of salvation. By what right does the church say this? Certainly it is no obvious conviction. It is loaded with difficulties. In addition this conviction is only possible for those who realize all the most important events of concrete existence are historically unique and as such not scientifically verifiable. Yet one cannot take shelter in a superficially skeptical attitude because our historical knowledge of Jesus is inadequate indication that Jesus' "self-understanding implied a peculiar character and unsurpassability which permitted us to say that in him God's self-promise as our salvaton became event historically in a matchless and irreversible way and was then finally sealed by his redeemed death ..."(149). There we see a Jesus who understood himself as unique and unsurpassable, God's promise as our salvation become a matchless and irreversible historical event sealed by his redeemed death. Jesus does more than proclaim a liberating message about God, a proclamation which could be superceded later. The man and his message are inseparable. He not only speaks of the irreversible victory of God's offer of the kingdom of God brought about through God's free self-communication, it becomes historically tangible in him, in his proclamation and redeemed death (even though we grasp this only in hope). After a brief remark on Jesus' self-understanding, Rahner concludes with a summary (150f).

Jesus' resurrection is the historical seal and manifestation of God's victorious promise to humanity. We can grasp in faith the meaning of Jesus' resurrection only if we keep in mind four factors in their indissoluble unity. When these four factors (below) are seen united in faith and hope Christians have the courage to justifiably believe in the resurrection of Jesus without being lost in myth:

—resurrection is a statement about the unique, definitive destiny of the one whole person which does not return one to history but redeems history by elevating it;

–Jesus' resurrection can only be grasped in light of the destiny we hope for ourselves;

–when our hope meets the disciples' claims about the fate of Jesus, what justifies us in withholding our assent?

–when in grace we experience an ultimate freedom over sin and all human relativities, and when we find this experience made tangible in the history of one person and proclaimed first by the disciples and then by the church, in this unity of mental experience and historical event we experience the Risen One in ourselves.

The Risen Jesus is no mere symbol of our relationship to the eternal God. He is the guarantor "that we can reach God himself in the fulness of his life and his freedom, in his blessed light and his love" (154). Christians can have and should cultivate a relationship with this permanent intermediary to the immediacy of God in himself. They should hope, love, and trust this redeemed Jesus in the uniqueness of his human reality. Doesn't the doctrine of the communion of saints urge us to include in our hope for ourselves a hope for the resurrection destiny of all and a subsequent solidarity? Because Jesus lives in himself and for us we can establish a personal relationship with him which Rahner describes in warm detail (155). If we identify with the fate of Jesus in faith, hope, and love even to the point of dying with him then we shall grasp in his Spirit that we really can enter into contact with the living God. If we love Jesus and unconditionally accept his life and death as the pattern of our own then we will find that he is the way, the truth, and the life that leads not to annihilation but to eternal life.

18.10   Following the Crucified
Nachfolge des Gekreuzigten
{2.5}   March 1978 lecture in Mainz.

Abstract: Every Christian at all times follows Jesus by *dying* with him: surrendering to the infinite as if surrendering to infinite love. Following Jesus has its ultimate truth, reality, and universality in the following of the Crucified.

Topics: CHRISTOLOGY; JESUS CHRIST, death/resurrection of; CHRISTIAN LIFE, piety.

Subsidiary Discussions: Jesus Christ, imitation of (158ff); Poor, preferential option (159f); Death, *prolixitas mortis* (160f); Faith (168).

Precis: Preliminary observation: although this topic could be pursued in terms of New Testament exegesis Rahner only offers some tentative, arbitrary reflections drawn from systematic theology. He distinguishes between "imitating" and "following" Jesus. We are not called to reproduce the historical details of Jesus' life in slavish imitation but to complete his historical individual reality by becoming one with him. This is what it means to follow Christ. But Rahner warns against thinking of following Jesus as merely following his example, as if he were a mere concrete instance of a moral universal which would remain valid with or without him. It is for this reason that Christian piety has always contained an element of imitation and was never completely comfortable with a mere interior disposition. Rahner gives the historical examples of martyrdom, monastic life, preferential option for the poor (158f).

After summarizing the dilemma (160) Rahner offers his thesis: "every Christian at all times, follows Jesus by *dying* with him; following Jesus has its ultimate truth and reality and universality in the following of the Crucified" (160). This does not excuse one from following Christ in one's life since as *prolixitas mortis* life is a continual dying. Such a life can take many different forms (list, 161). Furthermore, by death Rahner is not simply referring to its medical sense. The question then becomes in what exactly does the following of the Crucified (by participating in his death) consist, and why is sharing the same fate something in which we not only resemble him but depend upon him? At first it might only seem as if in his death Jesus shares our lot. Here Rahner outlines his theology of death, distinguishing physical death from the spiritual act of deciding for or against God in a definitive way. This we do over the course of a lifetime (161f). Yet the free subject can encounter physical decline and death in either of two ways: culpably refuting its absolute futility in a radical protest; or accepting it with resignation and hope that the infinity into which we venture is not in fact completely empty. In the first case death is the event of perdition, in the second it is the beginning of redeemed finality in God.

Rahner returns to the common feature in Jesus' death and in our own, however greatly their concrete circumstances differ. Jesus surrendered himself to the encircling darkness, in which even the closeness of God's love seemed to fall away, as if surrendering himself to eternal love and not to the hell of futility (summary, 166). Saying Jesus died as we die, we focus on how he follows in our footsteps not we in his. But if we focus on the fact that the eternal Logos died as we die, it brings ineffable dignity and consolation to our death as well. His death becomes a productive model for ours, his death actually changes ours insofar as he died into his resurrection. "His death is the event of gaining the finality of his human reality in the life of God himself" (166).

To this Rahner adds a few points. Jesus' resurrection is no unexpectedly glorious adition to his death. It is the consequence of his death as such, and forms along with it an intrinsic unity. "In his resurrection the very same thing that happened in his death is completed and made effective…. We can really say that…his death is his resurrection and vice versa, since he entered into definitive life precisely in death and in no other way" (167). But since this is true only of him as the Son of the Father, his death is unique and becomes a real determinant of our own death only if he gives us a share in his death. This assumes that his death takes place for us and that we can accept in freedom the opportunity of dying with him as a beginning of life. Since both of these are possible we can really follow the Crucified.

One more thing must be added to the way in which the similarity of death with Jesus and with us becomes a real following of the Crucified in dying. Our death and the death of Jesus are radical acts of faith, as is our following of the Crucified. Furthermore the resurrection of Jesus, even though it took him from our sight, was an event within human history. Though it cannot be empirically verified that with our death we enter his resurrection, the historicity of his death/resurrection does shed some light on our dying with Christ. In the history of the world, before the resurrection of Christ, the victorious irreversibility of God's self-communication to the world was merely possible. After the resurrection things are different. Hope is different. "From the one reality already existing the success of other possibilities can be presumed" (169).

Since death occurs throughout our lives it is appropriate for Christian piety to have sought to realize the following of the Crucified in Christian life in the acceptance of the cross. When we die by installment we are forced to decide how to accept them: in protest and despair or in hopeful resignation. If we choose the second way we are taking up our cross daily, "practising faith and loving hope in which death is accepted as the advent of eternal life and the following of Jesus, the Crucified, reaches its completion" (170).

18.11   Experience and Transcendence from the Standpoint of Christian Dogmatics

Transzendenzerfahrung aus Katolisch-dogmaticher Sicht

{3.0}   November 1977 lecture in Vienna. G. Oberhammer, ed., *Transzendenzerfahrung, Vollzugshorizont des heils. Das Problem in indischer und christlicher Tradition. Arbeitsdokumentation eines Symposiums* (Vienna 1978) 137-149.

Abstract: The experience of human transcendence, however conceptually objectified, is the root of all true mysticism in and outside the church. There are also parapsychological experiences with no absolute theological meaning.

Topics: TRANSCENDENCE; MYSTICISM.
Subsidiary Discussions: Experience/verbalization (176ff); Mediation (179f); Supernatural existential (181ff); Theology, limits of (184ff).
Precis: Preliminary observations: Not being an Indianologist, Rahner confines himself to presenting in an unsystematic way four theses on human transcendence from the viewpoint of Catholic dogmatics he hopes will be helpful. These remarks, while compatible with official teaching, are personal and go beyond what is strictly binding (list, 174).

1) Christianity refuses to recognize a systematic, technically developed mystical experience of transcendence as the sole, necessary way to perfection.

It does, however, recognize mystical experience as a possible stage on the way to perfection and as a paradigmatic elucidation of what happens in faith, hope, and love on the Christian path to the perfection of salvation. The fact Christianity rejects such an elitist interpretation of the spiritual life, along with the theory of the transmigration of souls, does not mean it dismisses the possible constitutive importance of such experiences for the actual process of salvation. It seems to Rahner the task of theology is to show how the real basic phenomenon of the mystical experience of transcendence sustains all Christian living; how systematically practiced mysticism may be of a higher degree psychologically (though not theologically) and thus possesses a paradigmatic character and exemplar function.

2) Christianity insists on the irreversible difference between an original experience of transcendence and the objectifying reflection on it. It maintains that creaturely mediation does not remove the immediacy of God from the graced mind. It actually makes it possible. It follows from the first part of this thesis (177-179) that the existence of contradictory theologies of mysticism does not rule out the possibility they all refer to the same original experience. Differences in objectification can mean either the original experiences were different or the conceptual tools being used to describe the same experience are different. The exact case is discovered through dialogue. For all the differences between experience and objectification, the two form a mutually dependent unity. Hence, Christianity can never regard its own verbalizations as completely superfluous. Similarly this explains why it is possible for one to embrace a particular theory (e.g., theoretical atheism) in such a way as to existentially deny one's transcendence.

The second part of this thesis is even more important (179-181). Rahner maintains the historical reality of Jesus, church, word and sacrament are ways of reaching God in the sense that they are themselves internal and constitutive elements of this salvific relationship. This "sound finiteness" insists that created realities mediate the relationship between the absolute God and the finite recipient of God's self-communication. These realities make an immediate relationship possible, guarantee it, attest to it in our historico-categorial dimension. "Christian faith denies that radical immediacy to God who imparts himself to man as himself in his absolute reality, and creaturely mediation of this self-communication of the absolute are opposed to one another as mutually exclusive alternatives" (179). Rahner develops in detail how this presents problems for some Eastern interpretations of mysticism (180). At the same time Christian theology is also aware of many modes and degrees of creaturely mediation to the immediacy of God. So long as non-Christian mysticism does not insists on its being absolutely formless, Christianity has no reason to oppose it while at the same time pointing out that the fullness of its explicit meaning is made manifest in Jesus Christ.

3) Personal achievement of definitive self-realization (which may or may not take place in mystical experience of transcendence) is always sustained

and radicalized by the Holy Spirit (supernatural grace, self-communication of God) whether or not this becomes the specific object of explicit reflection. Though many theologians think sanctifying grace is intermittent, Rahner see it as God's universally salvific will existing always and everywhere and hence, also even outside institutional Christianity. It follows that the mysticism rightly interpreted by Christian theology as a real experience of grace can and must be found even outside institutional Christianity. Rahner dismisses as false the dilemma that the mystical experience of transcendence must either be interpreted in an explicitly Christian sense or be dismissed as purely natural mysticism. Christian dogmatics does not forbid the philosopher of religion a priori from discovering authentic, grace-inspired mysticism even outside Christianity (183).

4) From all that has been said so far, Christian theologians do not know and cannot judge the graced nature of all mystical experiences of transcendence. They cannot say whether there are also some psychological acts and states (albeit rare) which can be classified as "mysticism" broadly speaking, but which are not actual experiences of theological transcendence. Christianity recognizes such "parapsychological" occurrences (ecstasies, levitations, telepathy, etc.) but considers them secondary and unessential (summary, 186f). Though theologians are self-effacing enough to allow other professionals to research such experiences, there is no reason they cannot apply such findings in the religious field. They do not thereby sanction the terms or concepts in which the other sciences have objectified their research. Theologians must insist such objectivizations of transcendental experience are wrong whenever they deny its grace-inspired character as a free personal relationship to a free, personal absolute; deny a sound finiteness; deny a universal opportunity for salvation for all people even outside an explicit practice of mysticism. But Christianity cannot claim all extra-ecclesial mysticism is a priori guilty of these denials. Nor is there any need for Christianity to do so for it can see even in these other forms of mysticism an implicit "questing christology."

18.12   Experience of the Holy Spirit
Erfahrung des Heiligen Geistes
{2.0}   May 1976 meditation for Pentecost.
Erfahrung des Gesites (Freiburg 1977) 9-63.
Abstract: Because each original experience of transcendence (implicitly or explicitly) is an experience of God, a fundamental experience of the Spirit is possible in the midst of ordinary life. This is "mysticism of ordinary life."
Topics: SPIRIT, experience of; EXPERIENCE, transcendental; TRANSCENDENCE; MYSTICISM.
Subsidiary Discussions: Experience/verbalization (193); Charismatics (193ff); Piety (204); Jesus Christ, death of (206f); Charisms (208f); Spirit, discernment of (209).

Precis: I. This essay addresses scripture's challenge to know the Spirit we experience in ourselves. But this experience of the Spirit is incommensurable with everyday experiences, individual realities, or other finite objects. Among the singular, original, primordial experiences Rahner lists the subject's experience of the self as united and whole. Just because we often overlook such experiences does not mean they do not exist. The danger in relying solely on testimony of scripture for the experience of the Spirit is that we may come to regard this testimony skeptically as ideology or mythology. Is there an experience of Spirit which makes understandable and authenticates the testimony of scripture to the indwelling of the Spirit? After explaining how the necessity of asking this question about the existence of such genuine experience does not immediately invalidate the question, Rahner mentions two such experiences: mysticism (192f) and the charismatic movement (193f).

II. What of those who are neither mystics nor charismatics? Are they forever barred from any experience of the Spirit? Supported by scripture, everyday Christians confess to having such an experience of necessity, even if they often overlook, suppress, or deny it. The remarks that follow cannot avoid theoretical and abstract notions of knowledge and freedom. Here Rahner gives his standard description of human transcendence (195-197) in a very lucid manner. (In knowing particular things the infinite, incomprehensible horizon is co-known though it seldom becomes the explicit object of reflection. This infinite nameless mystery is what Christians call God.) Rahner concludes from this analysis that we can call this fundamental experience of transcendence "mysticism" but only if we allow that it occurs in the midst of ordinary life since it is the condition of the possibility of ordinary experience. For him, "transcendental experience is always also experience of God in the midst of ordinary life" (197). This gift grasped philosophically as a possibility, theologically as a reality, and existentially (explicitly or implicitly) as hope, is a gift (grace) always sustained by God's self-communication. It is always an experience of the Holy Spirit even it if remains unthematic, anonymous, and implicit.

Everyday concrete realities point to this transcendental experience of the Spirit. It can be implied in the positiveness of categorial reality in which their greatness and glory, goodness, beauty and transparency point with promise to eternal life and light. Or it can be found where the definable limits of our everyday realities break down and are dissolved—experiences of absurdity and death. Rahner furnishes four pages of random, concrete, examples (200-203) and ends by urging readers to search their own lives to find such experiences of the Spirit. He suggests this begins to explain the attitudes and actions of the saints: people of the Spirit who live on the frontier between God and the world, time and eternity. Summary (205f).

Rahner concludes this section by answering with a few hints the objection that this mysticism of ordinary life is not related closely enough to Jesus

Christ, the crucified and risen one. First, the fact this mysticism of ordinary life is present and available even outside the church is an expected, concrete embodiment of the church's own teaching concerning God's universally salvific will made available to all in the grace of Christ. "The grace of God … is consequently the grace of Jesus Christ even when it is not yet explicitly and reflectively grasped and interpreted as such" (205f). Furthermore, in the last resort the real experience of transcendence in the Holy Spirit occurs at the point where one's life is made definitive in free abandonment and liberated hope: "in a word, at the point of death where dying is a passing into the incomprehensibility of God" (206). This is the point of identity between experience of the Spirit and participation in the victorious death of Christ. **III.** Rahner closes with two observation on the connection between experience of the Spirit and the ordinary routine of life. First he insists the experience of the Spirit is not elitist. It occurs always and everywhere in the concrete lives of whoever has awakened to personal self-possession and to the act of freedom in which one disposes of onself as a whole. Special forms of meditation and other spiritual exercises are at best rehearsals for more fully accepting or clarifying experiences of the Spirit.

His second observation concerns discernment. Charisms are intrinsically connected to possession and experience of the Spirit, though not identical to them. They are powers or possibilities of Christian action authorized, sustained and animated by the Spirit of God for the building up of the community. Since these possibilities are always more than an individual with limited time and energy can ever fully realize, how is one to choose among them in such a way as to regard one's choice as "God's will"? In light of what has been said Rahner suggests that when a particular choice (in addition to being morally appropriate) does not obstruct or obscure an ultimate openness to the real experience of the Spirit in unlimited freedom, and when one is aware of an ultimate synthesis between the basic experience of the Spirit and one's will for a particular object, then one is acting charismatically. Summary (209f).

18.13   Faith as Courage
Glaube als Mut
{1.5}   September 1975 lecture in Berne.

Abstract: Actual faith in the full sense of the term is possible only in free hope, which is absolute courage. Because hope in the absolute future is a response to the divine offer of self-communication it is properly revelation.
Topics: FAITH; CHRISTIAN LIFE, courage; HOPE.
Subsidiary Discussions: Word, primordial (211ff); Virtues, perichoresis (213f); God as ground of hope (216ff); Salvation (216); Revelation (219ff); Jesus Christ, hope in.

Precis: Christian faith is really a very simple affair. It is only difficult because it is the concreteness of something we describe as courage in all its radical-ness. There are two categories of words: substantive words which refer to empirical experience (e.g., tree, hydrogen, house, etc.) and words whose starting-point is clear but which in their radicalness are open to the totality of human existence and reality as such (e.g., faith, hope, love). These words tend to merge into one another. Elsewhere Rahner calls this latter category *Urworte*. Each generation has its key words. Such a word for today is "hope," a radical realization of its close relative "courage."

"It is difficult to say what courage is. Not because we do not know, but because as a particular realization of the existence of the whole person it cannot be defined as a particular occurrence distinguished from many others" (215). It is an *Urworte*. It has something to do with uncertainty, danger, freedom, decision and risk. Courage is required to bridge the gap between one's precalculation and one's goal, especially when it relates to decisions concerning the totality of human existence—one's salvation (summary, 216f). The distance encountered in such decisions can only be bridged by absolute hope in an absolute future as possible and actually offered. Christians call this God, whom they know originally and properly only *in* this hope. The decision for such hope takes courage grounded not in empirical detail but on the incomprehensibility of God, which we do not master but to which we must entrust ourselves. Examples (218).

Before proving how this hopeful courage is also faith in the strictly theological sense, Rahner distinguishes unthematic acts of courageous hope from those acts which are thematized in explicitly religious language. He insists the former can be salvific acts while the latter, despite their explicit connection to religion, may not issue from the deepest center of the acting subject and thus fail to accomplish what they intend. Rahner insists this truly courageous hope which surrenders itself to the ultimate redeeming mystery we call God is itself faith: an assent to God's personal revelation in a rudimentary form which needs further development. Why? Because such courageous hope is a realization of freedom, a human dynamic which reaches out to one finite reality after another but is never satisfied by anything less than the infinite God, the absolute future of our hope, the innermost dynamism of this boundless movement of hope. "The very fact that God himself thus becomes by grace the dynamism and goal of our hope means that revelation has taken place. Grace, given to spirit as such, the possibility of hope founded on grace, anticipating God himself as its goal, this is revelation" (220). This is really divine personal revelation whether grasped explicitly or anonymously, whether communicated in propositions or a matter of the heart. These expressions of absolute hope are not primarily discreet religious events for exceptional people. They are manifested by ordinary people in the attitudes they assume towards the dull routine of mundane life.

Rahner turns to the courage needed for explicitly Christian faith and hope. The plethora of dogmas which accompany Christianity make it seem as if the courage needed to accept oneself as total and whole, oriented to the incomprehensibility of God, is quite different from the courage needed to cope in faith with the complicated matrix of Christian doctrine. Although the two are not merely identical (one can inculpably express the former without being able to produce the latter) they are simply two forms of the same courage differing as seed from flower. "[T]he courage for Christian faith properly speaking is nothing but the concreteness of the courageous hope of which we have been speaking up to now" (222).

This assumption rests on what Rahner sees as the two parts of the one basic message of Christianity at its deepest level. First, that both forms of courage are really the same thing distinguished only as an unthematic and a considered realization of existence. Second, that in Jesus crucified and risen the absolute hope that was his and is ours was really achieved, became historically tangible and irrevocable. Seen in this light the Christian's courage for faith is relatively simple. "He [the Christian] takes hold of Jesus, crucified and risen...precisely as the historical happening of what he grasps for himself by hope in that courage...as the ultimate achievement of our existence" (223). Summary (223f). All other doctrines can be related to and derived from this ultimate faith in the risen Jesus. When a particular individual cannot sufficiently link doctrines to the reality of the risen Lord, one should not deny those doctrines but leave them aside with the hope they may become more clear in time. Allowing it is possible to fail to achieve the courage needed for salvation, and allowing that we can never know beyond doubt the status of one's own salvation/damnation, whenever one finds the courage for total hope one finds faith in the Christian sense.

18.14 Christian Dying
Das christliche Sterben

{3.0}   J. Feiner, M. Löhrer, eds., *Mysterium Salutis*, 5 (Zurich 1976) 445-446.

Abstract: Examines the nature and experience of Christian death and dying. In particular, the teaching of scripture and the church; dialectical "hiddenness of death"; relationship between death as punishment and death as natural.

Topics: DEATH; FREEDOM and death.

Subsidiary Discussions: Death, *prolixitas mortis* (228ff, 232f); Finitude (230f); Illness (232f); Annointing of sick (234); Fundamental option (236f); Soul, transmigration (237, 243f); Death, hiddenness of (244ff); Death and sin (247ff); Devil (250); Jesus Christ, death of (252ff); Renunciation (254f); Love of God/neighbor (256); Martyrdom (256).

Precis: I. *Prolixitas mortis.*

1) Introductory preliminary remarks. In speaking of Christian death two elements must be coordinated: physical death as such, and the permanence of the eschatological consummation it entails. More than anthropology is needed for this. It involves the two Christian doctrines: human sinfulness and the redeeming death of Christ. Because the theology of death touches every element of anthropology (list, 227f) the following comments will of necessity seem rudimentary and arbitrary.

2) Fundamental option and clinical death. Death is not to be equated with the biological occurrence at the end of life. In principle it is the event that takes place throughout life in which we freely decide for or against God. This view liberates death from fabulous or mythical renderings which are neither probable nor necessary.

3) Experiences of oncoming death. Rahner describes three heralds of death: a) disappointment that comes with the experience of radical finitude; b) suffering and failure; c) serious illness.

4) *Memento mori.* Within life one has to live with death. It cannot and should not be avoided or suppressed. Resigning ourselves daily to our finitude in hope is practice for death.

5) Styles of dying. Each time and culture has its own "rules for dying" and its own models. Though death in our time is rather "shapeless" a Christian remains bound to die in an explicitly Christian way.

6) Advent of death. Rahner does not explore criteria for clinical death.

II. Dying seen in the light of death.

1) Official statements of the church. The following essentials of the Christian tradition on death are somewhat formal and abstract.

   a) Rahner marvels at the gaps in the tradition's treatment of death.

   b) Though the church teaches death is a penalty for sin, this can only be in an analogous sense which must be harmonized with its being a part of human nature.

   c) With death comes the unique finality of our basic option. Though this rules out apocatastasis and transmigration of souls it leaves open when our definitive stance occurs vis-à-vis the moment of physical death.

   d) Death is universal at least in the sense that the freedom of each person will at some point be definitively achieved.

2) Death as close of the history of freedom in the presence of the pardoning God.

   a) In this section Rahner addresses the biblical witness regarding death. He assumes it has a positive content. Stripped of its concrete imagery the Old Testament concept of Sheol is simply the conviction that with death an absolute definitiveness and a real end is reached. Further life in some other realm is not an option, only eternal life is (i.e., the finality of this earthly life and its subject possessing it in freedom). In this light the fate of the individual is seen as a resurrection of the dead, "a resurrection that does not come subsequently as the lot of the body as additional to that of the soul" (240). Judgment, particular or general, indicates merely the setting by death of an internal limit as a consummation of freedom from within. In short, "There is only this one earthly history, which is ended by death as its internal limit, and this history has an irremovable finality and permanency before God (240). The New Testament makes clear God's final sentence is a consequence of our deeds in this world and nothing else, thus ruling out apocatastasis or any other kind of self-disposition made by any other criteria after death.

b) The theological understanding of death as the elevation of the history of freedom into its finality must take into account three factors simultaneously: i) the intrinsic nature of freedom; ii) the unity of the self-realization of the corporeal-historical and spiritual-personal human being; iii) the precise nature of the consummation which is made possible for the freedom required of it. Freedom is not the ability endlessly to do/omit categorial things, but to dispose of oneself with finality. Hence, freedom makes real history and real responsibility possible. This definitive self-disposal happens not in bypassing the categorial but within our spacio-temporal historical life. For the Christian there is one history, the history of freedom before God which for that reason possesses unfathomable depth and absolute radicalness. It occurs in the course of the ordinary routine of life. Yet how can Christians believe a finite yet transcendentally free subject can really and definitively decide for or against this infinity of life (i.e., God) through the meager categorial acts of spacio-temporal history? Rahner concludes this section by showing that transmigration of souls does not answer but merely postpones an answer to this question (243f).

c) The history of freedom ending in death stands in dialectical relationship to our disposability which finds it radical manifestation in death. Only in this dialectic of freedom and disposability is the real nature of "infralapsarian" death present. Only this makes it possible for death to manifest both sin and redemption/liberation. Because infinite freedom is always finite in its concrete realization, its disposability (i.e., its nature as gift, something granted and assigned) is experienced radically and irrepressibly in dying and death. Hence, in freely and hopefully accepting our powerlessness in its face, death becomes "both man's final self-determination *and* final, irrevocable disposability" (246). Because this passive disposability masks the nature of freedom as self-disposal and because the boundless range of freedom can give the impression of absolute autonomy, death has the character of hiddenness.

3) Death as manifestation of sin.

a) How can one rectify the two elements of church teaching: that death is both a punishment due to sin (whether *poena* or *poenalitas*) and at the same time natural? To answer this Rahner must identify what there is in our human nature that ought not to be.

b) The penal character attributed to death can consist only in its hiddenness, a retarding factor which must be overcome during our lives with the aid of grace. Because we know this kind of integration actually does occur gradually over time, albeit asymptotically, we know it is not positively contrary to human nature. Hence, the real punishment of sin consists in this hiddenness of death, our protest against its darkness and its concealing powerlessness. Summary (249).

c) Death in its hiddenness is not merely the expression of Adam's sin it is also the consequence of serious, unremitted personal sins in our total corporeal reality. Rahner relates this to Paul's teaching on the link between death and the law of God.

d) He also comments on the role of the devil.

e) Since death is natural and universal why does it evoke fear? This can only be explained by the Christian insight that we are expected to elevate the history of our freedom into finality through the way we live. But we ought not to have to suffer the darkness of death. The fact that our consummation is not simply assured is not a punishment imposed on us by God from outside. It is an intrinsic manifestation of sin. Our secret dread of death is the extension of our sinful shrinking from the ultimate mystery of emptiness, helplessness, and nothingness which come from being finite creatures.

4) Death as dying with Jesus as event of grace.

a) Traditional textbook theology offers only a sketchy treatment of the relationship between our death and the death of Jesus. Leaving aside the question of when one achieves final consummation of historical freedom, the New Testament insists the death of every graced person is to be regarded as a salvific event.

b) How to conceive of "the dying in Christ" is best answered with a complete theology of Jesus' dying and death. All Rahner can do here is point to the fact that Jesus did not redeem us "on the occasion of his death" by some moral act of obedience, but by accepting death in faith, hope, and love and thus transforming it into the manifestation of the obedient surrender of the whole person to the incomprehensibility of the holy God.

c) Since Rahner is attempting to understand death as dying with Christ in the light of grace he must show how the nature of grace corresponds with Christ's dying and death. Grace is God's gracious self-offer of immediate self-communication. To accept this offer means self-renunciation and self-transcendence. We find ourselves only insofar as we radically submit ourselves to God's disposal. So long as we are alive this invitation to renunciation strikes us as a task. Nowhere is this more clear than in the challenge of accepting death where we are deprived of everything, even our very selves. But facing such a death is also the culmination of the grace of Christ crucified and thus a dying with Christ.

d) We do not die in an abstract mode of renunciation. The self-abandonment of death is one aspect in realizing the grace of faith, hope, and love. Rahner mentions in particular how dying can be an act of faith and an act of love of God and neighbor.

e) Christians rightly see martyrdom, death freely endured and accepted to bear witness to the faith, as the most perfect way of dying with Christ.

18.15   Justification and World Development from a Catholic Viewpoint
Rechtfertigung und Weltgestaltung in katolischer Sicht
{1.5}   April 1977 lecture in Mainz in a series on justification.

Abstract: Justification as event consists in making faith, hope, and love real in the world by contributing to its development. Though the proper object of these virtues is God, world development is a legitimate Christian activity since immediacy to God is always mediated through human action in the world.

Topics: JUSTIFICATION; VIRTUES, theological.

Subsidiary Discussions: Ecumenism (260); Freedom (262ff); Anonymous Christian (263f); Grace (264f); Virtues, moral (265); Mysticism (266ff); Love of God/neighbor (269f); Hope (270f).

Precis: In the Catholic tradition "the event and effect of justification consists in the realization and free acceptance of the three theological virtues of faith, hope, and love" (261). The question then becomes whether the offer and/or free acceptance of these virtues involve a particular relationship of the Christian to the world—a world that is at once finite, distinct from God, and yet presents a task for active human freedom.

God offers these virtues not merely at one point in time and space but always and everywhere as a human existential (262f). It follows that one's relationship to the world and its development is always characterized by justification, i.e., liberatedness for the immediacy of God. This is true whether or not one grasps this in explicitly Christian terms (263f). This offer of virtue is God's gracious self-communication. To accept it is to accept God.

Thus, theological virtues are distinguished from moral virtues. The former are oriented to the immediacy of God whereas moral virtues have finite objects. Immediacy to God (i.e., justification) brings with it freedom over all the powers and authorities of the world. This characterizes the justified person's relationship to the world and its development. Justification turns one toward the world and not away from it, in order to further God's self-communication to the world, not as part of the world but as its proper goal. Thus the justified are never merely servants of the world because they realize their relationship to the world in light of their relationship to God (266).

In short, accepting God by accepting the theological virtues endows one with freedom. This freedom characterizes the justified person's response to the world. At the same time Christianity mistrusts pure mysticism. People normally need the mediation of the world to realize their immediacy to God (267). God is reached in and through routine encounters with the world. "The world is rightly grasped and faced precisely when this happens in virtue of that freedom and superiority over the world which God offers...in his threefold grace and in which he is himself immediately God" (268). Summary (269).

If he had more space Rahner would relate this discussion to his views on the relationship between the love of God and love of neighbor (269f); the theology of hope (270f); sin (272); and a host of other issues he simply mentions here.

18.16 Law and Righteousness in the Catholic Understanding
Gesetz und Gerechtigkeit im katolischen Verständnis
{2.0} July 1978 lecture in Munich to the Society of Christian-Jewish Collaboration.

Abstract: Describes the proper Catholic understanding of law and righteousness: forgoing the faded glory of moral rectitude for God's acceptance of one's self in an utterance of love.

Topics: LAW and justification; JUSTIFICATION.
Subsidiary Discussions: Freedom, law of (276f); Grace (279f); Love (280f); Law, natural (282); Moral development (285f).
Precis: Rahner first describes different laws: natural (275); social (275f); and the internal law of freedom which "if unobserved brings the subject into fatal conflict with itself" (276). Christians interpret the absolute authority of these laws as God's law. "Knowledge of God is nothing but the radical interpretation of the experience of absolute laws, of freedom and its responsibility" (277). This however raises a problem: how can God meaningfully will finite values (loyalty, truthfulness, etc.) absolutely?

At this point Rahner makes a fresh start switching his focus to righteousness. It is not a legal term regulated by an authority superior to both parties but a term that signifies being in the right relation with God. It is an unmerited gift decreed by God's love—the gift of God's own self, established on God's own initiative (279). Thus, for the Christian, law and righteousness are disparate factors. Neither is the precondition or the consequence of the other (280). Even the "command to love God" is in no real sense a law (281).

What then is the proper relationship between law and righteousness? Does it provide the answer to the problem posed earlier of how particular moral laws can be endowed with absolute meaning? Rahner suggests and discards a number of possible solutions: an appeal to theonomy (282f); an appeal to natural law (282); an appeal to the universality of God's free offer of self-bestowal (283); a general appeal which identifies the God who justifies with the God who commands obedience (283). None of these solutions goes the distance.

Rahner next suggests three approaches to the right relationship between law and righteousness which might hold a solution, though he does not develop them here: i) as a personal revelation from God who is a person; ii) as reconciliation between us and God and forgiveness of sin; iii) a closer look at the history of salvation and revelation where this relationship is worked out.

Salvation history reveals Christ's irreversible triumph of righteousness over law. This same irreversible dynamic is often repeated in individuals who first experience the absolute claim of moral law but slowly see its achievement as finite and ambiguous. Absolute fulfillment beyond finite morality becomes one's greatest hope. If this hope is radically accepted by freedom, the law is surpassed "into the inward law of love that the Holy Spirit writes in our hearts...its fulfillment is turned from an achievement of respecting holy law from outside into the utterance of a love which, since it possesses God himself, is not a law and lives in the freedom of God himself" (286).

18.17   On the Importance of the Non-Christian Religions for Salvation
Über die Heilsbedeutung der nichtschristlichen Religionen
{2.0}   October 1975 lecture in Rome to International Congress of Missiology on the theme, Evangelization and Culture.

Abstract: From God's universally salvific will Rahner concludes that non-Christian religions, though incomplete, rudimentary, and partially debased, can be realities *within* a *positive* history of revelation and salvation.

Topics: RELIGIONS, non-Christian; GOD, salvific will of; REVELATION and non-Christian religions.

Subsidiary Discussions: Vatican II, *Nostra aetate* (288ff); Grace, habitual (291f); Supernatural existential (291f); Israel (292f); Mysticism (294).

Precis: At a very abstract and formal level this is an inquiry of systematic theology into whether non-Christian religions (excepting Judaism and Islam) have any importance for salvation. Vatican II's *Nostra aetate* clearly states there is a relationship between the church and non-Christian religions as such (not merely with non-Christian individuals) built on the universal salvific will of a sovereign and benevolent God. "In a word, the council invites us to take seriously the non-Christian religions as such" (289). Nevertheless, the council leaves open how this relationship is possible. Precisely what is the relation of non-Christian religions to salvation (questions, 290f)? How can systematic theology be optimistic not only about the salvation of the non-Christian individual but also about the role of non-Christian religions in the history of salvation?

Rahner offers three theses. He begins with a reappraisal of habitual grace in light of God's universally salvific will. Such grace does not merely occur at isolated points in time. It is a permanent existential of humankind and our history, "always and everywhere present, as permanently present possibility of a salvific relationship of freedom to God" (291). Second, because this fundamental orientation of human transcendence toward its finality is also the most fundamental event of revelation, the history of supernatural revelation and the history of supernatural salvation are co-extensive. This is true even where this history of revelation is not fully or correctly objectified (e.g., the institutional failure of the Old Covenant, 292f). Hence, we are not in the dilemma that non-Christian religions must be seen as either an entire objectification of divine revelation and grace, or merely as a human invention from below, or simply as an evil perversion of divine revelation. Third, if the opportunity for supernatural salvation and a real saving faith in revelation are universally available, then "such a revelation and such a faith ... occur *concretely* and *on the whole* only by the mediation of those categorial, institutional, and verbal realities which we know as non-Christian religions" (293). This is because our transcendent relationship to God, even in formless mysticism, is always mediated through categorial realities. If such salvation is possible even for an atheist, how much more for a non-Christian believer, since moral theology allows that even an objectivity objectively opposed to God can nevertheless mediate a positive moral act? "Non-Christian religions then, even though incomplete, rudimentary, and partially debased, can be realities *within* a *positive* history of salvation and revelation" (294). Rahner challenges historians of religion to see what they can discover a posteriori based on the indications he has given (examples, 295).

XIX. Faith and Ministry
XIII. *Gott und Offenbarung* (1978)
XIV *In Sorge um die Kirche* (1980)

German edition: Einsiedeln, Benziger
U.S. edition: N.Y., Crossroad, 1983
Edward Quinn, translator. Paul Imhof, S.J., editor

This volume in the English language edition comprises essays from *Schriften zur Theologie* XIII, #s 16-18, and *Schriften zur Theologie* XIV, #s 3-11, 13, 14, 16, 26-28.

19.01   Foundations of Christian Faith
Grundkurs des Glaubens

{1.0}   Previously unpublished February 1979 lecture at Freiburg im Breisgau.
Abstract: Introductory comments on the purpose, form, and contents of his 1976 "Foundations of the Christian Faith; An Introduction to the Idea of Christianity."

Topics: CHRISTIANITY, foundations of; FAITH, foundations of; THE-OLOGY, basic course.

Subsidiary Discussions: Reflection, primary (5ff); Transcendental method(8f); Causality, quasi-formal (8f); Supernatural existential (8ff); Christology (10ff); Anonymous Christian (10); Theology, political (14f).

Precis: The book's title causes some confusion. Though it is meant as introductory it is still a scholarly work in the sense that it intends to bring "Christianity as a whole under one *idea* ... [and reflect] on the ultimate unity and the essential coherence of everything that Christianity proclaims" (4).

The distinctive character of the book lies in its determination "to pursue the question of the essence of Christianity on what I would describe as a 'primary plane of reflection'"(4f) vs. scholarly (i.e., secondary) reflection. Modern scholarship is too vast for any one person to comprehend it all. Thus, this book is gives "an account of the meaning and credibility of Catholic belief precisely in the way that is possible for one person" (7). Though scholarly, it does not rely on exhaustive secondary scholarship to prove each of its assertions.

Regarding content, Rahner begins with his method. It is fair to call it transcendental so long as that includes history, since history is the only place the transcendentality of human freedom is actually realized. He views supernatural grace as an actual internal principle, not simply as an efficient cause but as a quasi-formal cause—the a priori dynamism of one's knowledge and freedom toward the immediacy of God.

The free response to God's gracious self-communication reveals how the history of mind is coextensive with the history of revelation (9). Proceeding from a universal pneumatology it is possible to say that salvation is possible even to those who do not know of God or Christ in categorial terms but strive to follow the dictates of conscience (anonymous Christian). This approach in no way denigrates historical christology. Much of the book is given over to the complex formulation of this christology which Rahner summarizes here (11f). Rahner sees some shortcomings in his work: too brief a treatment of the Trinity; too optimistic an approach to the mystery of evil; nothing on angels or devils; a somewhat triumphalist ecclesiology; a weak political theology.

19.02   On the Relationship between Natural Science and Theology

Zum Verhältnis von Naturwissenschaft und Theologie

{1.5}   Previously unpublished July 1979 lecture to Protestant Academy of Tutzing.

Abstract: Due to concupiscence conflicts between science and theology are inevitable. These must be endured with patience and modesty. The open relationship between the two disciplines rules out hegemony on the part of either.
Topics: THEOLOGY and science; SCIENCE and theology; CONCU-PISCENCE, gnoseological; PLURALISM.
Subsidiary Discussions: Truth (17); Dialogue between theology and science (passim); Sin (21f); Death (22f).

Precis: Long-standing mistrust between theology and natural science stems from the tendency of science to speak about the human person as one and whole, something beyond its ken. Yet theologians must recognize the many conflicts that arise are legitimate and ultimately reconcilable in the oneness of truth. Natural science cannot always unambiguously restrict itself at the outset to only those fields of inquiry which do not touch upon theology. Their boundaries do not allow such clarity. Thus, the two disciplines must coexist even if they inevitably threaten and disturb each other.

The relationship between science and theology can best be defined in terms of the theological concept of gnoselogical concupiscence: the pluralism of human faculties and impulses which in practice can never be integrated into an absolute unity surveyable and controllable from a single point. While such concupiscence confronts the asymptotic goal of unity it can always lead to essentially destructive sin. Summary (18).

Christians must learn to allow for irreversible pluralism especially since the sciences and theology among them have different origins and historical developments. They are irreducibly pluralistic. And theology, even though it concerns itself with the one God who unites all things, is simply one science among others and cannot impose theological totalitarianism. This concupiscence which manifests itself in irreducible pluralism must be endured with a prudent restraint and the humility befitting creatures. Hence, theology has the task of unmasking all totalitarian claims and returning itself to a modesty that permits each and every science to be subject to God and not to itself. Its uneasiness with science must never lead it to deny the autonomy or meaningfulness of science. Hence, there is an open relationship between science and theology. Summary (20).

The de facto pluralism of the sciences is not static. It presents an ever-changing task, a moral obligation for each science to enter interdisciplinary dialogue. For only by transcending itself through such dialogue can any discipline understand its own true nature. The university is the palace for such dialogue, even if in the end no all-encompassing universal formula for knowledge is possible. In the end all must surrender "all knowledge in a *docta ignorantia* to the eternally abiding mystery of God and his underivable will" (21). Failure patiently to endure concupiscence leads to sin (examples, 21f). Neither scientists nor theologians are angels. Knowing this should remind them to allow for inevitable conflicts and to strive for as much peace as possible.

Only believing scientists can experience their defeat by the finite realities they study as actually the possibility of their greatest victory. For this is nothing else than their particular share in the dying of Christ. Summary (23).

19.03   The Church's Redemptive Historical Provenance from the Death and Resurrection of Jesus

Heilsgeschichtliche Herkunft der Kirche von Tod und Auferstehung Jesu

{1.0}   November 1976 lecture to Philosophical-Theological College, St. Pölten. J. Reikenstorfer, ed., *Zeit des Geists*. (Vienna 1977) 11-26.

Abstract: The church is "instituted" by Christ in that its provenance lies in his death and resurrection. Without a community of believers Jesus would not be who he claims: the definitive victory of God's self-promise.

Topics: CHURCH, instituted by Christ; JESUS CHRIST, death/resurrection of.

Subsidiary Discussions: Jesus Christ, imminent expectation of (26ff); Law, divine (33ff); Church, future of (36f).

Precis: After a brief preview Rahner asks whether today we can speak of Jesus of Nazareth "instituting" the church. His answer is sensitive to the distinction not often made in traditional textbook theology between the pre-Easter Jesus and the risen Christ. Textbook theology from Bellarmine to Vatican II envisioned the institution of the church as a *societas perfecta* on the juridical/propositional plane. This model sits unreconciled next to the Pauline model of the church as mystical body.

The most serious challenge to this traditional view comes from taking seriously the pre-Easter Jesus' imminent expectation of the end times. Why set up an "institution" if the world is ending? The second problem arises from the fact the church today bears little resemblance to the church of apostolic times. These problems led theologians like Hans Küng to assert Christ did not institute the church. Although he cannot deal with the exegetical problem of Jesus' imminent expectation, Rahner hopes to maintain the teaching of the church by interpreting the term "institution" as "provenance." "The Church comes from the death and resurrection of Jesus as part of the eschatological permanence of the Crucified and Risen One" (29f).

Prior to Jesus' death and resurrection the inner dynamism of the world as oriented to the free offer of God's immediate presence was not clearly known. The fate of mankind, the end of history, remained open. Its concrete outcome remained unclear. With his death and resurrection "this actually ambivalent salvation history in acceptance *or* rejection of God's self-offer does in fact have a definitive *good* outcome" (31). Humanity is victoriously saved by God and loved into God's own glory. This is definitively sealed by Jesus' resurrection. Summary (31f).

The church, the community of faith, is the permanent presence of this self-communication of God in history and now victorious over the world. Without such a community Jesus would not exist as God's self-promise to the world. It is in this sense that the church derives its provenance from the death and resurrection of Christ. Were there no church, Christ would not be who he claims to be.

What of the concrete structures of the Catholic Church (e.g., papacy, episcopate)? How can these later developments be accepted as *jus divinum*? Rahner argues that institutions, like people, have a one-way history. A free historical decision can become irreversible and absolutely binding for later generations. Notwithstanding, the church has an open future. It continues on a course of free, unpredictable development. Summary (37f).

19.04   Brief Theological Observations on the "State of Fallen Nature"

Kleine theologische Bemerkungen zu dem "Status Naturae Lapsae"
{2.0}   Previously unpublished.

Abstract: Maintains the classical Catholic notion of original sin by linking it more closely, clearly, and intrinsically with the notion of concupiscence.
Topics: THEOLOGICAL ANTHROPOLOGY, guilt; SIN, original; JUSTIFICATION; CONCUPISCENCE.
Subsidiary Discussions: Grace (39); Freedom (45f); Adam (49ff).

Precis: This essay can only be understood in relation to Rahner's entire theological project of making theological truths accessible to a modern audience by grounding them in realities verifiable by an appeal to one's lived experience. The essay begins by restating in classical theological terms the Catholic position on the state of human nature after the fall (39-44).

In contrast to Lutheran theology which locates the essence of fallen nature and original sin in the experience of persistent concupiscence (stirrings against the law of God), Catholic theology since Trent never saw concupiscence as sinful in itself. In locating the essence of original sin in the lack of justifying sanctifying grace, Catholic theology transfers the state of fallen nature to a dimension which is not as immediately accessible to existential religious experience (42). Thus, a strange tension creeps into Catholic teaching. Trent would argue that a crucial change takes place in baptism through the restoration of sanctifying grace. But in modern theology this change is "a very abstract trans-existential factor, which cannot be experienced existentially at all and can become known only by theological indoctrination from without" (43). How could such a tremendous ontological change not register existentially?

Rahner insists there is such a thing as an anthropological "state" with a distinct philosophical and theological character. He sets this out in detail (44-49) by defining "state" (44f); by speculating on its original, elevated character in terms of God's free offer of self-bestowal as the dynamism and goal of human freedom (45f). One learns of this true original state primarily through reflection on human history as a whole, and secondarily by encountering and responding to the claims of theology (46f).

From this encounter one "recognizes that he is not God *and* that he respects himself as the recipient of God in himself" (47). Though grasped on the existential level, this basic experience of divine origin and consummation is oddly fragmented. One experiences the contradiction between concupiscence and mortality on the one hand, and one's absolute destiny to the immediacy of God on the other. Not only is this a universal experience, no one experiences this gap between "is and ought" as innocuous. We instinctively feel it should not exist (48).

To deny or overlook the unhappiness which accompanies concupiscence transfers the Catholic doctrine of fallen nature from the realm of experience to the realm of myth (49). In biblical terms this unhappy tension is found in the feeble human response to the call to love God with all one's heart. Though Catholics do not see this failing as sin, it is certainly not innocuous (49).

Rahner completes his essay by applying his understanding of fallen nature to other areas of Catholic theology (49-53). How does this understanding square with the protological and eschatological stories of the Fall? After a long discussion he concludes that the idea of paradise is legitimate insofar as it underscores the unnaturalness of concupiscence, and safeguards the notion that this state was not God's original desire for creation (51).

All that can be said in terms of chronology is that, "Prior to his personal decision in freedom man is *simul justus et pecator*" (52). Justification is experienced in God's ever-renewed offer of self-bestowal; sinfulness is experienced in the human person's never being wholly able to dispose oneself definitively toward this offer. This is not an experience of private inwardness. It also implies a situation of human corporeality and sociability. This has implications for understanding both human history and ethics which Rahner cannot develop here (53).

19.05   Consecration in the Life and Reflection of the Church

Weihe im Leben und in der Reflexion der Kirche
{1.5}   Previously unpublished November 1976 lecture to Catholic Academy in Freiburg im Breisgau.

Abstract: Focusing on the existential consecration that precedes any ecclesial, sacramental consecration makes it possible to rethink the effects of baptism and holy orders, and to expand the pool of candidates for orders.
Topics: SACRAMENTS, theology of; SUPERNATURAL EXISTENTIAL; RELIGIOUS LIFE, consecration; ORDERS, sacrament of.
Subsidiary Discussions: Baptism (58f, 64); Virtues, theological (58f); Revelation history (60f); Penance (64); Church as *Ur-sakrament* (64ff); Parish ministry (68ff); Women, ordination of (69); Orders and women (69).
Precis: There is a sacredness to human existence that not only precedes sacramental consecration but is the condition for its very possibility. Baptism, confirmation, marriage, and holy orders, along with such sacramentals as the consecration of virgins, abbots, etc. do not establish one's consecratedness. They are the ecclesial-cultic manifestation of a sanctity which exists always and everywhere in light of God's universal salvific will. When this insight is applied to baptism (58f), the prior condition for receiving other sacraments of consecration, one is forced to reconsider the "effects" proper to baptism.

Rahner's thesis implies a basic conception of the relationship between God/world, nature/supernature, revelation/salvation-history not widely accepted in traditional theology. The latter tends to view revelation and sanctification as discrete interventions by God which can be linked to form a history. But Rahner sees salvation- and revelation-history taking place "from the innermost center of the world and history where God as imparting his own sacred glory has always already established himself, is already and always in immediacy the dynamism, sanctification, and goal of the world" (61). Sanctification is simply our free acceptance of God's offer of self-communication.

What makes this view not only possible but also necessary today? First, this view reconciles God's self-communication and the history of salvation/revelation. Second, only this view makes sense of Vatican II's insistence that supernatural salvation is possible for all of humanity by a faith sustained by God's grace. If this is true there is no need to think faith, hope, and love are infused only after baptism. Rahner closes this section with notes on the necessary predispositions for valid reception of (adult) baptism and penance which for him are rooted in this prior existential elevation of human nature.

Before listing the implications of his thesis Rahner offers an interim consideration (64-66). The connection between existential consecration and sacramental consecration is ultimately grounded in the fact that the church is the eschatological sign, the basic sacrament, not only of God's self-offering to our freedom but also of its victorious establishment. "[T]he Church as a whole is holy, not only in the dimension of word and sacraments, but also in the existential acceptance of grace by man's freedom" (66).

Consequences (67-72). What really happens in sacraments of consecration is "the historical manifestation and sociologically concretizing specification in the dimension of the visible Church of a holiness and consecratedness which has always existed inescapably in that person in the form of an offer in terms of God's salvific will" (67). Sacraments refer their recipients back to their existential consecratedness which they share in common with all humanity. They charge them to enter it increasingly clearly, existentially and radically. What separates clergy and laity is not a hierarchy of grace but a distinction in tasks. Priestly ministry is not a supplementary task. For those called it is a *the* way of being Christian.

Rahner turns now to the problem surrounding commissioning of pastoral ministers, i.e., those called upon to run parishes in the absence of a priest. History shows that establishing grades and orders of sacramental ordination (below that of pope and bishop) lies within the discretion the church (e.g., priests, deacon/esses, minor orders). An even greater breath of variation is possible in the future (e.g., men/women). Currently pastoral ministers are "commissioned," not sacramentally consecrated. But these pastoral ministers do not function solely on the basis of that commission but on the basis of their prior consecration, baptismal and existential. The fundamental difference between these pastoral ministers and the ordained would not lie in sacramental consecration but in the importance of their task. This is because ordination "does not imply a sacramental consecration as an additional transmission of the powers involved; it is sacramental because and insofar as it confers these powers and promises the grace necessary for their exercise" (70).

Rahner concludes that roles of equal importance should be conferred equally, i.e., sacramentally. Failure to do this in fact degrades the priestly minister to a mere cultic functionary. The church must cease being schizophrenic in its approach to pastoral ministry. If leadership of the community (and this includes presiding at Eucharist) is an intrinsic and essential element in priesthood then those who lead priestless communities should be ordained priests. Nor should celibacy or academic training on the European style abrogate the essential right of faith communities to have access to Eucharist. These issues must be faced boldly to avoid the laicization of the church. Summary (72).

19.06   Pastoral Ministries and Community Leadership
Pastorale Dienste und Gemeindeleitung
{0.5}   *Stimmen der Zeit* 195 (1977) 733-43.

Abstract: We must rethink the obligation of priestly celibacy which has led to commissioning pastoral ministers to lead faith communities without confirming the sacramental powers that flow from the essential nature of their task.

Topics: SACRAMENTS, theology of; ORDERS, sacrament of; PARISH ministry.

Subsidiary Discussions: Priesthood (74ff); Diaconate (76f); Celibacy (83ff).

Precis: "Pastoral ministers" refers to the exigency of commissioning the non-ordained to act as permanent and normal pastors in parishes without priests.

Priesthood and diaconate. Restoring the diaconate and the exigency of appointing the non-ordained as pastors in priestless parishes raises important theological questions about the essential relationship among these groups of ministers (questions, 74f). Analogous to bishops, priests are leaders of their local churches, proclaiming, presiding, fostering unity. Priests are essentially pastors. Deacons are distinguished by the fact they fulfill their proper tasks *alongside* but *under* the supervision of priests. Both ministries are freely designed by the church as legitimate extensions and concretizations in varying forms of the same office.

Pastoral assistants. Pastoral ministries emerged not from prior theological reflection but from practical necessity: the declining number of those willing to embrace celibacy as a condition for ministry. Theologically trained but non-ordained people have been commissioned to lead parishes and care for souls (essentially priestly functions) but without the sacramental powers to preside at Eucharist or absolve. This leads to a dilemma. Reserving these two powers to priests and separating them from parish leadership distorts the nature of priesthood toward the ritualistic; resolving the problem in favor of ordaining more deacons gives priests and deacons the same essential task and again raises the question of why these two sacramental powers are withheld. Putting aside all theological subtleties, why couldn't the conferral of a permanent office of parish leadership on pastoral ministers be regarded as sacramental?

Commission and sacrament. Because the church can freely determine the mode of transmitting office, the fact that commissioning pastoral ministers is not accompanied by laying on of hands does not count against its being sacramental. Is it theologically consistent to commission leaders of local communities and refuse them the sacramental powers demanded by the nature of their task?

Responsibility and office. Bishops are wrong to withhold the two sacramental powers from pastoral ministers out of fear of merging the profiles of priest and parish minister. Those who function as priests should be ordained as priests. The crux of the problem is celibacy. Imposed celibacy led to the

commissioning of pastoral ministers; abrogating the requirement would solve the problem by allowing the ordination of these qualified people.
Celibacy. "The whole question centers then on the problem of celibacy" (85). Rahner insists the right of a faith community to the celebration of the sacraments outweighs the legitimate desire of the church for a celibate priesthood. If this trend goes on it will lead to the de facto establishment of two classes of clergy and continued confusion among the faithful.

19.07   Theology and Spirituality of Pastoral Work in the Parish

Zur Theologie und Spiritualität der Pfarrseelsorge
{0.5}   December 1976 lecture in Vienna to Austrian Pastoral Conference.
J. Wiener, E. Erharter eds., *Pfarrseelsorge*, (Vienna 1977) 11-25.
Abstract: Theology is an integral element of parochial ministry which today must adopt the spirituality of base communities. It is characterized by the courage to sustain a lonely faith decision through fellowship in the Spirit.
Topics: PARISH ministry; SPIRITUALITY, parish.
Subsidiary Discussions: Parish, territorial (87ff); Fellowship (91f); Theology in parish ministry (92ff); Base communities (96ff); Faith, *fides quae/qua* (98); God, experience of (99); Loneliness (98ff); Spirit, experience of (100ff).
Precis: The nature of ministry is more clearly manifested in parish work than in academic reflection. But secondary theoretical reflection contributes to the practical work of parish ministry. These brief considerations on parochial ministry divide into two parts: its theology and its spirituality.
Theology of pastoral work in the parish. Parochial leadership is not merely a sociological function. It has a religious, dogmatic, and spiritual content which can only be understood in the context of faith.
–The parish as a reality of faith. The territorial structure of the church is necessary. It makes concrete and palpable the mystery of the abiding Spirit of God's self-offer made through the death and resurrection of Jesus.
–The territorial character of the church. Nowhere is the participation of the visible church in the mystery of salvation more clearly realized than in its celebration of Eucharist by the parish community united through it's bishop to the Bishop of Rome and thereby to the church throughout the world.
–The parish—a tangible spiritual reality. The spiritual mission of the church is realized concretely when the local community gathers to share and promote human neighborliness among the circle of believers and beyond.
–Advancement of human fellowship in the secular sphere. The parish's mission is to promote genuine human fellowship, a truly human fraternity of mutual trust and assistance. Eucharist is not merely an external cause for assembling the community. It expresses its mission most fully. Summary (92).

The significance of theology in parochial pastoral work. Theology has and must retain its place and importance in parochial pastoral work.

–Priority of pastoral activity to theological reflection. Proclamation is always prior to professional academic theology. Parish work is never simply a way of expressing and transmitting academic theology.

–Reflection as a constitutive element of practice. Effective parochial ministry cannot be sustained without secondary theological reflection.

–Positive approach to theology—for the sake of human beings. Pastors must have a positive attitude toward theology. They are not mere servants of a cult. They must work to produce among believers the existential transformation demanded by the word of God. This is impossible among today's diverse and well educated congregations without recourse to solid, up-to-date theological reflection.

–Contact with theologians, reading new books, keeping up with periodicals. Pastors must have the courage to use the many resources at their disposal to keep abreast of theological developments and avoid sinking back onto the theological and spiritual plane of childish faith.

Spirituality of pastoral work in the parish. A few arbitrary observations.

–A preliminary reflection. The spirituality of parochial work as such must be the spirituality of "base communities" and of the team directing it.

–Core community as basic community of the parish. Although parishes must welcome everyone they can only be sustained from below by the living faith and fellowship of a core community.

–Parochial pastors—all priests and lay people officially active in the parish. Although this thesis admittedly leaves many details obscure, Rahner concentrates on the special characteristics of a parochial ministry rooted in the spirituality of base communities and their representatives. He identifies two characteristics which form a dialectical unity: loneliness of faith, and fraternal fellowship of faith.

–The loneliness of the faith of "parochial pastors." *Fides qua*, the faith to believe, is always a matter of personal responsibility. Such faith is more difficult today in the absence of a homogeneous social milieu which supports such a decision.

–Decision of faith more radical than formerly. Parish ministry today demands the courage for a lonely decision contrary to public opinion.

–Personal experience of God and his Spirit. In order to persevere individual believers need a wholly personal experience of God and his Spirit emerging from the depth of their existence. "The Christian of the future will either be a mystic or he will not be a Christian at all" (99).

–Independence of public opinion. Those engaged in parish work today must themselves be spiritual persons. Easy to say hard to do. If they can manage this everything else is easy.

–Fraternal fellowship and its experience of the Spirit. The spirituality and experience of the Spirit for Rahner's generation was primarily an individual affair. It did not address the radical loneliness of parish ministry.

–From spiritual individualism to common experience of the Spirit. The spiritual experience of the recent past does not foreclose the possibility of a normal, truly common experience of the Spirit. There are many important new possibilities here to be explored.

–Growth of a spiritual team. Without offering any concrete suggestions as to how it could be accomplished, Rahner insists that to do justice to their pastoral work, current teams of professionals entrusted with parish ministry must become truly spiritual fellowships with a communitarian spirituality.

19.08   The Spirituality of the Secular Priest
Zur Spiritualität des Weltpriesters
{0.5}   November 1977 lecture in Munich to Catholic Academy of Bavaria. F. Wulf, ed., *Mitten unter den Menschen* (Düsseldorf 1979) 27-42.

Abstract: It is impossible to identify essential characteristics of secular priests which comprise a unique spirituality. Rahner merely says secular priests must be disciplined, full-time, mystical, and aligned with the poor.
Topics: SPIRITUALITY, priestly; PRIESTHOOD, spirituality of.
Subsidiary Discussions: Celibacy (107f); Mysticism (115f).
Precis: Rahner admits his essay does not set out a straightforward thesis affirming the existence of a spirituality peculiar to the secular priest as distinct from lay persons and members of religious orders. He offers five preliminary observations on the subject to defend this approach.

1) There are as many spiritualities (concrete Christian ways of coping with one's life) as there are people. If one's task in life (vocation) significantly determines one's spirituality then it would seem appropriate to ask for a list of characteristics which distinguish the vocation of secular priests and have an impact on their spirituality.

2) What is the nature of secular priesthood? Does its essence reside in sacramental powers, in proclaiming the gospel, in leading the local community, etc. (list, 105)? And which of these elements significantly shape the spirituality of secular priests? This approach, however, is stymied by the question of how these characteristics of secular priesthood and spirituality compare with priest members of religious orders. Unless one is very careful the best result from this analysis will be a very abstract and therefore unenlightening common denominator. History, however, presents a hugely diverse picture of secular priesthood (examples, 107). Celibacy presents another difficulty in determining which characteristics of ministry are essential to priesthood and hence, to the spirituality of secular clergy (107f).

3) The concrete lives of human beings are never wholly determined by one factor or by one narrow band of factors. Such monomaniacal radicalization

represents a serious danger. Even when we identify certain concrete differences (clothing, external life-style, etc.) we are left with the task of determining how these things influence a person's innermost feelings and spirituality. Needless to say, a priest's physical circumstances (in the curia or in the African bush) could have an even greater impact.

4) Some might suggest the following thesis: the spirituality of secular priests is materially the same as other Christians and is distinguished only formally insofar as priests have a second obligation arising from their office which impels them to pursue their spirituality with special urgency. Although this thesis helps make sense of the diversity within secular priesthood and avoids spiritual elitism, it fails to distinguish secular clergy from religious and does not take seriously enough the actual material differences present in the lives of clergy due to the nature of their vocation (sacramental ministry, proclamation of the word, etc.). Here too it is difficult at times to distinguish their call to preach the word from the universal vocation of the faithful. This deplorable vacillation does not arise from a lack of courage on Rahner's part to take a position but from the very nature of the problem.

5) Rahner concludes with some very brief comments on the content of the spirituality of secular priests in 1970's Germany. The unique spirituality of secular clergy, whatever it is, must be deliberately cultivated, systematized, and exercised in its own proper fashion (i.e., distinct from monks, religious, and laity). Secular priests cannot see their calling as a 9-5 job. Everything they do, including recreation and leisure, must be colored by their calling to preach the gospel and to identify with the poor. If taken seriously this would demand a revision in the lifestyles of most secular clergy. Like every other Christian, secular priests today will either be mystics or they will not be Christians at all (mystics being those who live from an ultimate, internal religious experience of God and God's grace). Without this grounding priests risk becoming little more than "enthusiastic chairmen of local associations for Christian folklore" (116).

19.09 The Spirituality of the Priest in the Light of his Office

Zur Spiritualität des Priesters vom Amt her gesehen

{1.0} July 1976 lecture at Eisenstadt to a conference on "Spirituality of the Priest Today." S. László, ed., *Priesterliche Spiritualität heute*, (Vienna 1977) 101-32, questions 133-42.

Abstract: Priestly spirituality is radical Christian spirituality. This entails commitment to personal prayer, embracing poverty, serving the faith of others as a spiritual leader, and political activism on behalf of the poor.

Topics: PRIESTHOOD, spirituality of; SPIRITUALITY, priestly.

Subsidiary Discussions: Spirit, experience of (120f); Transcendence (121f); Ignatius Loyola (124); Church, office in (123ff); Parish ministry (127);

Sacraments, theology of (127f); Prayer (129f); Mysticism (130f); Poverty (131ff); Renunciation (131ff); Poor, preferential option (137f).
Precis: Preliminary observations: 1) Rahner apologizes in advance for any circumlocution in his informal talk; 2) We all possess a concrete image of priesthood cobbled together from our life experiences. Rahner's image is shaped by his advanced age and a life of work in theology; 3) He agrees completely with the earlier speaker (cf., 118 ftn2). 4) No one has the right to insist that one's own ideal of a priest is *the* one, normative ideal.

I. Priestly spirituality is simply Christian spirituality—Christian life in faith, hope, and love. This is true in light of the practice and nature of priesthood today. In practice the priest feels all the same stresses as his co-religionists living in secular society. There are many ways to name this spirituality (list, 120). But if one's spiritual life is not essentially a living out of a personal experience of the Spirit it is an empty husk, and one's ministry will be a sham. In a more abstract vein Rahner defines spirituality as our absolute transcendentality dying crucified with Jesus into the absolute mystery we call God, the exact nature of which comes into focus in our lives only slowly. Summary (122).

II. The nature of priestly office plays an essential role in shaping the spirituality of a priest. Priestly office does not add an extra task to Christian living. It radicalizes the life of the priest as an official representatives of Christianity and the church. The exact theological nature of the priestly office is highly controverted today. Rahner warns against defining it in terms of its two unique sacramental powers (presiding at Eucharist and absolution). The great historical variability in the official nature of priesthood (e.g., Ignatius of Loyola) teaches that what is unique is not necessarily decisive.

All dogmatic theology can say is that office in the church (i.e., its power to govern) is "one and whole" (125). This power can and must be split up into individual functions. The remarkable historical variability in how this power has been distributed does not deny the oneness and wholeness of the power, nor does it mean the church could not develop a position/insight which would later become irreversible. It underscores the basic point that the priesthood cannot be completely identified with any one task or set of tasks from any one period in time. Nor is it impossible for people who are not ordained priests to grasp and live out the core of priestly existence (e.g., pastoral ministers entrusted with parish leadership). Such people should "in God's name" (127) be sacramentally ordained, a step that means simply ratifying what they already actually are (just as baptism of adults, penance, and marriage ratify an already existing state). Rahner concludes this section with remarks on the full-time nature of the priestly calling [cf. 19.08].

III. Some concrete aspects of the image of priests today.

They must be able to pray in a personal way, not as part of the job but as a basic structure of their existence. They must discover and continually clarify in themselves and also in others a religious, original experience of existence open to the mystery of God, and then speak from this center. In short priests must be mystics.

They must willingly embrace their poverty as something positive. This free renunciation, this "courage to be poor," encompasses economic, cultural, and spiritual poverty (the dark night).

They must be servants of the faith of others. They must be spiritual leaders, mystagogues of faith for others, who continually learn the faith afresh. Only because they are life-long adventurers, risk takers who struggle with temptation in poverty and darkness, can they be companions and guides to others. Based on his experience of "worker priests" Rahner challenges his audience to consider priesthood an invitation to downward social mobility, to nonconformity, and to being continually over-taxed.

They must remain theologically current. Their personal experience of the Spirit must be verbalized in an effective way which builds up the church. Priests today need not be embarrassed if they are not "sacramental enthusiasts," if presiding at Eucharist or administering sacraments is not the existential high-point of their lives. Experience of the Spirit and celebration of the sacraments are not identical.

Priests today must be political. They have no right to claim "glorious neutrality" especially not faced with the plight of the poor and persecuted.

19.10 On the Theology of Worship
Zur Theologie des Gottesdienstes

{0.5}   *Tübinger. theologische Quartalschrift* 159 #3 (1979) 162-169.
Abstract: Assesses the relative merits of two concepts of grace (actual and habitual) to describe worship and the sacraments to the modern world.
Topics: CHRISTIAN LIFE, worship; GRACE; SACRAMENTS.
Subsidiary Discussions: Liturgy of the world (146f); Mystagogy (148f).
Precis: Today's church possesses two models for how God's grace operates in human history. Each is based on a different understanding of how God acts in the world. Rahner calls the first model "actual grace" (142). It regards the world and nature as substantially secular. God intervenes in this world at specific times and places by means of sacraments. In this model infant baptism is the ideal sacramental type, completely producing the grace it signifies.

The second model, habitual grace, assumes the world is from the outset always and everywhere "encompassed and permeated with the grace of the divine self-communication" (142). Sacraments are "outbursts" of God's innermost, ever present, gracious self-endowment in history. Such eruptions are not limited to sacraments but occur whenever people accept and realize in freedom their existence as radically and immediately dependent on God. Summary (144).

The strength of the first model is its emphasis on the unmerited, historically unpredictable nature of grace and the effectiveness of the sacraments. The second model is more intelligible and easier to reconstruct for people today as it distances itself from magic and mythology. The remainder of the article (145-149) elucidates worship in terms of the second model.

In the second model worship is defined as "the explicit and reflex, symbolic presentation of the salvation event which is occurring always and everywhere in the world; the liturgy of the Church is the symbolic presentation of the liturgy of the world" (146). As the history of the world's freedom, this liturgy attains its irreversibility in Jesus Christ, his cross and resurrection. For those who know Christ, accepting and practicing this liturgy is never optional. Ecclesial worship is important not because something happens there which never happens elsewhere in the world. It is important because it makes present and explicit exactly what goes on in the world constantly, and precisely what gives the world its importance (147).

From a pastoral perspective the many people who are imbued with the first model must be nurtured. But for those who find it a stumbling block pastors should develop the second model. Mystagogy along those lines may help them to discover the divine depths of ordinary life. "Then worship will be seen, not as a strange, reserved, special region in secular life, not as divine liturgy *in* the world, but as the divine liturgy *of* the world, as manifestation of the divine liturgy which is identical with salvation history" (149).

19.11   The Sunday Precept in an Industrial Society

Das Sonntagsgebot in der Industriegesellschaft

{0.5}   *Entschluß* (1979) no. 1, 26-32.

Abstract: The Sunday precept, though dispensable, can be retained. Interpreted with Christian freedom it presents no insurmountable pastoral difficulties.

Topics: LITURGICAL YEAR, Sunday obligation; LAW, church; CHURCH, law of.

Subsidiary Discussions: *Amamnesis* (150f); Sin, serious (152ff); Secularization (156ff).

Precis: Memorial of salvation. *First*, Rahner does not discuss Old Testament Sabbath. *Second*, the theological content of the Sabbath precept and the New Testament Sunday precept are completely different, even though both recall a past event (*anamnesis*) with the common anthropological problems that raises.

Precept of the church. *Third*, Because no Old Testament precept as such is binding on Christians the Sunday precept is not a divine precept but a precept of the church. As such it is subject to an elasticity of interpretation in different historical conditions.

Binding under pain of grave sin? *Fourth*, as a human precept open to interpretation compliance with the Sunday precept does not determine one's salvation/damnation status. Though it must be taken seriously it must be implemented with Christian liberty, with magnanimity and freedom. In short, the Sunday precept cannot in every case be considered binding under pain of grave sin.

Analogy with other precepts. The Christian must frequently celebrate the Eucharist whether or not there is a precept to do so. Attempting to regulate its frequency by law is as absurd as attempting to regulate how frequently a child should visit an aged parent. In both cases there is a serious moral obligation the details of which cannot be legislated.

Existential obligation. Fulfilling the Sunday precept is like obeying speed limits. There is a wisdom embodied in both laws and one is foolish to test the absolute limits of either. *Fifth*, some developments in modern industrial society make fulfilling the Sunday precept easier, others make it more difficult. Theoretically the church could completely abolish the Sunday precept and leave it up to the individual when and how frequently to celebrate the Eucharist.

Reasons for maintaining the tradition. Ought the church to do so? Maybe not. Weekends in modern societies are much freer than in the past and lend themselves to gathering for Eucharist. Tradition and stability of practice are a plus. Not everything that is strictly unnecessary is superfluous. Human beings need to express their transcendent nature in very concrete categorial ways. Rahner concludes the Sunday precept could be maintained and interpreted with Christian freedom without presenting any insurmountable pastoral difficulties.

Influence on secular society. The church need not sit passively and accept the cultural changes introduced by secularization and industrialization. It can work to shape these changes in more humane ways. This could include lobbying for a common day of rest which would promote common worship.

19.12 Basic Communities
Basisgemeinden

{0.5} Previously unpublished June 1975 lecture in Frankfurt am Main to Action 365. Originally, *Ökumenische Baisisgemeinden*.

Abstract: Today base communities (Catholic and ecumenical) are necessary and legitimate. They must, however, avoid the danger of becoming a "third church."

Topics: BASE COMMUNITIES; CHURCH, base communities in.

Subsidiary Discussions: Secularization (160); Parish (161f); Ecumenism, Third Church (165).

Precis: "A few aphorisms" on the relationship of base communities and the church delivered to Action 365, an ecumenical base community (cf., 159 ftn1).

Basic communities in the church. Basic communities are necessary for the church today and in the future when increasingly the church will be built up and sustained from below. Hence, these communities should be promoted and not suppressed. The church today is no longer a homogeneous institution which can expect support or encouragement from society. Church membership is and will be a personal faith decision made in a diaspora situation. People will find support in sharing faith with their co-religionists on the local level.

Such communities are not opposed to the church. They represent a new way of being church. If these communities are not accepted as parishes they risk being seen as their illegitimate rivals. Because base communities are strictly speaking experimental their legitimacy and value cannot be predetermined by reference to theories. Their worth will be proved by experience and by their future performance. They are a venture of hope. Base communities have the obligation to stay connected with the diocesan church, to obey legitimate authority, to remain open to criticism, and to make a concrete contribution beyond their own borders. This does not preclude them having unique constitutions or organizing themselves in less authoritarian, more democratic ways.

Ecumenical basic communities. Ecumenical base communities such as Action 365 are also legitimate and necessary. This is especially true today when it has become obvious that Christian unity will not be achieved without action from below. They are also legitimate insofar as they are particularly suited to fulfill the mission of the church to the world. Their special tasks do not preclude but demand common prayer and spiritual discernment (Rahner leaves aside the question of intercommunion). There is, however, one grave danger to be avoided: becoming a "Third Church." Such a development would retard rather than advance the ecumenical cause and only increase the misery of a divided Christendom. Hence, it is essential for members of ecumenical base communities to remain active and committed members of their own churches, acting in them like a leaven. The sad burdens of church history can only be overcome if there are people willing to bear them.

19.13   Eternity from Time
Ewigkeit aus Zeit
{1.0}   *Entschluß* (1979) no. 4, 7-11.
Abstract: Close examination of human experience (unity in experience, mental experience, free decisions) hints at the nature and reality of eternal life as the coming to be of something definitive vs. an infinite duration of time.
Topics: TIME/ETERNITY; ETERNAL LIFE.
Subsidiary Discussions: Skepticism (169f); Freedom (174ff); God, incomprehensibility of (175f); Salvation/damnation (177).

Precis: Skepticism in regard to eternal life. Ours is the first generation to show little interest in eternal life. This is true because even among Christians the idea has been presented in ways that obscure rather than elucidate its real meaning. In the past it was spoken of as if it were simply time without end. Rahner wants to make only one point: a close examination of common experience hints at the true nature and reality of eternal life.

The tyranny of our concept of time. There are problems approaching eternity as if it were nothing more than the unlimited continuation of time. Then heaven dissolves into hell and vice versa. There are also problems approaching eternity with the aid of negation.

Hints of an eternal reality. A close examination of three aspects of our human experience of time reveals something eternal, i.e., something more than the "now," in the mere moment of time which is ceaselessly destroyed and replaced.

The totality of a history. Although we can think of time as an infinite chain of minute occurrences flashing in and fading out, we actually experience events of some duration which indicate substantial existence (e.g., the life cycle of a flower, human history). "Even what is properly temporal contains more than time: at least something that persists and gives a unity to time in historical temporal shapes" (173).

Mental experience. Human beings have an "idea" of time not as the flow of atoms but as unified and truly meaningful. However this idea may correspond to the physical world, it forces us to ask ourselves how we can understand a subject capable of forming such an idea. The thought that thinks time is not simply time's subject.

Free decisions. We are inescapably responsible for our free actions. There is no refuge in the thought of eternal annihilation. Freedom wills and posits finality and irreversibility. This implies the eternal existence of freedom.

Accepting incomprehensibility. From these hints of eternal life Rahner draws some concrete conclusions for life. Even with the aid of concrete images no one can imagine eternal life. It is filled with the incomprehensibility of God. Although nothing said here proves the Christian dogma of eternal life, nothing in our common experience makes illegitimate the decision to embrace eternal life in faith and hope.

Victory of God's love. Eternal life will be the definitiveness of the moral and free act of our life in which, as one and whole, we made ourselves the persons we finally wanted to be. This reveals both the grandeur and horror of everyday choices. This is true for all people and not merely for certain great souls. Our choices can also lead to eternal perdition although this is not an equal possibility alongside salvation. Christians proclaim the victory of God's love "who bestows himself in and through our freedom" (177). This love causes and guarantees that our brief, passing time creates an eternity which is not made up of time.

19.14 Purgatory
Fegfeuer
{2.0}   Previously unpublished. Festschrift for H. Stirnimann's 60th birthday.

Abstract: In the form of a dialogue between two theologians Rahner considers two problems with the doctrine of purgatory: how change can occur in the absence of time; how beatitude is possible without free, human decision.

Topics: ESCHATOLOGY, intermediate state; ETERNAL LIFE; DEATH.
Subsidiary Discussions: Theological anthropology (183ff); Time (183ff); Becoming (185f); Saints, communion of (188f); Freedom (191f); Soul, transmigration (192f).
Precis: An imaginary conversation between two systematic theologians concerning Paul VI's insistence on the traditional doctrine of purgatory. Not only does this doctrine raise many questions (list, 182) it is not clearly stated anywhere, has little scriptural provenance, and took many historical forms.

Theologian One hopes to formulate the teaching "in a way that ... completely accords with the Church's older doctrinal statements and with Rome's exhortations at the present time and yet ... permits us to see in this formulation something that seems 'realizable', intelligible, credible, and compatible with the rest of our anthropology" (183). He begins with assumptions drawn from current theological anthropology. Key among these is the notion that in death a person achieves permanency. He leaves open the possibility that this definitive final state of the one person is not necessarily completely realized. If this is possible then death opens up several possibilities for a post mortem process leading to fuller integration (although here "process" would be used in an analogous sense). Perhaps death itself and its accompanying pain is the process (186f). Whatever the case, people today don't seem overly concerned with the old doctrine. Perhaps it is enough existentially to surrender ourselves to God and pray for those who have gone before. If so, why be actively concerned over purgatory?

Theologian Two views the problem in a wholly different way. Because the Christian position on an intermediate state (between death and final consummation) is very formal and abstract why not supplement it with what is described in almost all religions about post mortem existence and the ongoing relationship of the dead with the living? After all, is it clear that what the church teaches about the intermediate state is true of all human beings, or does it merely address fully functioning human beings? In other words, what of those who because they died young, or never achieved maturity, or due to limited circumstances never made what could reasonably be called a fully free human decision? Why not posit for them some form of post mortem history of freedom (à la Ladislaus Boros)? Theologian Two wonders about a modified Christian version of transmigration of souls (192f).

Finally the essay observes we have very little exact knowledge in the realm of eschatology. The more we examine traditional doctrines the more confusing things seem to become. But what is so bad about obscurity if in the end we are called to surrender ourselves into the merciful hands of the incomprehensible God in faith, hope, and love?

19.15 Why Does God Allow Us to Suffer?
Warum läßt Gott uns leiden?
{2.5}   Previously unpublished.

Abstract: "In our present concrete state, the acceptance of suffering without an answer other than the incomprehensibility of God and his freedom is the concrete form in which we accept God himself and allow him to be God" (207).

Topics: CHRISTIAN LIFE, suffering; GOD, incomprehensibility of; FREEDOM.
Subsidiary Discussions: Sin (196f, 200ff); Creation (197ff); Eternal life (204f).
Precis: Human suffering is a fundamental and most difficult question.

Permissive suffering. According to Rahner, "Why does God allow us to suffer?" is a very acceptable form of the question. Even without having a firm notion of God at the outset, God as the source of all meaning is clearly the one to whom the question should be directed. The term "allow" avoids the secondary question of whether God causes or permits suffering. Yet Rahner warns lumping all suffering under a broad definition does injustice to its complex reality.

Attempts at a theistic answer. Leaving aside gnostic, skeptical, and atheistic approaches, Rahner critiques four major theistic explanations for suffering.

–Suffering as a natural side effect in an evolving world. This theory posits suffering as a practically unavoidable side effect of a pluralistic and evolving world. Evil is good not fully realized. To protest against suffering is a foolish exaggeration of the importance of our own lives and projects. Rahner finds this view unsatisfactory and superficial. Even granting some degree of material co-determination, human freedom itself causes some forms of suffering which this theory does not address. Great evils such as genocide cannot simply be explained as inevitable strains in the material world.

–Suffering as effect of creaturely, sinful freedom. A second theory maintains God created a good world completely without suffering. Human sin is entirely to blame for its existence. This exaggerates human autonomy since human freedom remains in every aspect dependent on God.

–Suffering as a situation of trial and maturing. That God allows us to suffer to test us and bring us to maturity cannot explain the terrible amount of suffering in the world, especially not the suffering of innocent children.

–Suffering as a pointer to another, eternal life. Although eternal life is the conquest of suffering it in no way authorizes or explains it.

–The incomprehensibility of suffering as part of the incomprehensibility of God. Rahner starts his own reflection from the eternally incomprehensible mystery of God which even in beatitude is endurable only if we love God as God is and allow ourselves to be selflessly absorbed into the divine mystery which has no other justification than the mystery itself to which we surrender. To say we love God in his incomprehensibility is to say we love God in his freedom. The incomprehensibility of suffering is part of the incomprehensibility of God. It is the form in which the incomprehensibility of God appears. To accept the one is to accept the other. An answer to the question of suffering can only be heard in loving surrender to the mystery of God in faith and hope.

19.16   Mary and the Christian Image of Woman
Maria und das christliche Bild der Frau
{1.5}   *Stimmen der Zeit* 193 (1975) 795-800.
Abstract: Two factors challenge Mariology to grow: the developing model of christology from below; the ongoing cultural reappraisal of the role of women.
Topics: BVM, Mariology; WOMAN, image of.
Subsidiary Discussions: Dogma, development of (212f); Christology, ascending (214f).
Precis: From the beginning the church has seen Mary as more than a character in the drama of salvation history. She represents the Christian in purity and fulness. She is therefore also the perfect image of woman. The image of Mary has a concrete history which is more than the history of Marian doctrines. Like all real history it is ongoing, unfinished, incomplete, unforeseeable.

Changes in the image of Mary. Beneath the change there are permanent elements: Mary as believer, as immaculate, as possessing final consummation. None of these attributes eclipses Jesus' unique role as mediator of salvation. Where can we expect to see further change? Admitting that developments in doctrine cannot simply be deduced, Rahner does not envision Marian doctrine continuing to develop in a quantitative way as it has in the last century. In addition, Mary's attributes are archtypic: i.e., not prerogatives unique to her but attributes realizable in the whole of humanity taken together.

New view of Jesus Christ. Modern christology hints at how this might happen. Just as there has been a corrective switch in emphasis from a descending christology to an ascending christology which concentrates on the humanity of Jesus, Rahner sees the possibility of a parallel development in Mariology. He sees possibilities for the development of a Mariology "from below." This effort, based on the premise that Mary is not fundamentally a heavenly being but a human being, will be led by the work of exegesis.

Mary as image of woman. Developments in Mariology will also be fueled by the notion that Mary is and will remain for Christians the pure image of woman, just as in a certain way Jesus presents that image for man. What this means more exactly will be modified by our deepening understanding of the concrete descriptions of the concrete religious experience of women. There is always a danger this image of women is forced to carry unnecessary social and cultural baggage. There is also the possibility that many so-called feminine attributes of Mary (receptivity, silence, humility, etc.) are not peculiar to the spirituality of women. As society continues to question and revise its image of women, the image of Mary will necessarily change. Rahner suggests this new image of women can be most authentically produced by women theologians.

19.17   Mary's Virginity
Jungfräulichkeit Marias

{2.5}   July 1976 sub-commission report at Frankfurt am Main to German Bishops' Conference's Commission for Faith.

Abstract: To keep from becoming a museum piece Mariology must undertake the same post-Enlightenment self-transformation other doctrines already have. Till that process is complete bishops should endure the debate and not intervene.

Topics: BVM, virginity of; DOGMA, development of.

Subsidiary Discussions: Miracles (219f); Truths, hierarchy of (220); Scripture, exegesis (224f, 227).

Precis: Of the many questions surrounding Mary's virginity (specifically those raised by R. Pesch on her postpartum virginity, cf., 218 ftn1) this essay concentrates on two: what preliminary questions must be answered if the church intends to speak rightly about this issue today? How can the church speak convincingly today about this dogma?

Preliminary methodological considerations.

1) To treat the essential problem of Mary's virginity correctly one must face the problem of miracles. Today the idea of miracles suspending the "laws of nature" is highly problematic.

2) To effectively convey the meaning of this doctrine recent studies on development of dogma and advances in exegesis must be considered.

a) In keeping with Vatican II's "hierarchy of truths" this doctrine must be located and explained within the one mystery of God's irreversible and eschatological self-donation in the death and resurrection of Jesus Christ.

b) The content of the doctrine of Mary's virginity must not be seen as a single primary datum based on purely empirical observation. It is deduced from previous convictions regarding Mary and her function in salvation history.

c) This question will like others be answered through recourse to the notion of development of doctrine: a "one-way" process which can be better understood by recourse to the original understanding of faith from which it developed. Such an analysis can identify and separate binding element of the dogma from other elements (amalgams) in which the doctrine is expressed but which are not themselves binding (examples, 222ff).

d) Collaboration between exegetes and systematic theologians in a relationship of mutual dependence and reciprocal questioning is necessary today. It has not yet gone far enough in the field of Mariology and could bring further results if it is impartially and seriously attempted.

e) Since the Enlightenment all Christian dogma has undergone a vast transposition from the horizons of understanding of antiquity and the Middle Ages. It is wrong to see this as a demolition or reduction of dogma. The new faith is the old faith made new. To keep Mariology from becoming a museum piece it must undergo the same transformation.

3) If exegetes and historians establish something as highly probable, systematic theologians must avoid maintaining the less probable on arguments drawn primarily from logic.

4) Why must all questions immediately be given unambiguous answers? Doesn't history teach there is great value in leaving some open for further investigation. Impatient intervention can actually weakening the faith.

Conclusions. Should the German bishops respond to the speculations of R. Pesch on Mary's virginity? If so, how?

1) It seems to Rahner wholly inopportune for them to comment expressly, directly, and solely on Pesch's exegesis. It is not their business to judge the greater or lesser exegetical or historical probability of Pesch's position as such. Not only should bishops respect the freedom of theologians, a brief comment would probably do little to dispel insecurity. Until an effective clarification of the church's sense of faith on this doctrine appears, bishops would do well to endure such theological controversies in patience and hope.

2) Rahner rejects the notion of the bishops using the occasion of Pesch's writing to provide a lengthy instruction on the question. After listing the difficulties he suggests bishops could intervene by urging theologians to apply themselves more urgently to the problem and by aiding them materially.

3) If, however, the bishops felt compelled to respond they would not only have to deal with the other question raised at the beginning of this article, they would be well advised to identify a general theme in which to contextualize their teaching. Rahner suggests the theme of development of doctrine (231).

19.18   On Angels
Über Engel
{3.5}   Previously unpublished.

Abstract: Without proving or disproving the existence of angels/demons, by asking how they could be known, what they would have to be like, and how they would have to function, Rahner warns against any naive approach to this topic.

Topics: ANGELS/DEVILS; DEMYTHOLOGY; REVELATION.

Subsidiary Discussions: Mysteries, revelation of (243f); Prophecy, theology of (245); Faith (245ff); Knowledge, natural (249f); Angels as pure spirits (253ff); Evil (255ff); Cosmos, theology of (260ff); Life, extra-terrestrial (263); Evolution of cosmos (264ff); Time (265f); Substance and structure (267ff); Evolution of life (270); History (270ff).

Precis: Taken for granted for centuries, today the existence of non-human, created, personal beings (angels and demons) is an acute problem. Some say despite their appearance in the Old and New Testament the existence of such beings is not an original teaching of Christianity but a non-binding element from that religious milieu. The real purpose of these writings is to insist on Jesus' victory over all principalities and powers. The teaching of IV Lateran simply maintains that human freedom is not the cause of all evil in the world.

There are three alternative positions on this teaching: i) it remains a strictly binding truth of faith which must be unconditionally upheld; ii) an unequivocal denial of the existence of devils which enlists social science to explain the personification of evil in the world; iii) because options i, ii are unconvincing the question remains open. Since it is not clear whether the church absolutely asserts the existences of such beings and having seen mistakes in the history of doctrine, Rahner suggests it is better to wait for greater clarity to emerge. This essay discusses three often overlooked questions which, while not decisive, are important for resolving this issue.

1) The epistemological question. Are angels/demons the kinds of things that in principle and a priori *can* be supernaturally revealed? Perhaps this important question has never been treated fully because people assumed an all-powerful God could reveal any conceivable truth whenever and however God wanted. From this point of view revelations differ only in content not in the event of revelation itself. Rahner, however, insists there is an a priori axiom which limits the possibilities of supernatural revelation: "in a super-natural revelation ... properly and primarily only God himself ... can reveal himself. Everything else (that is, everything as created distinct from God) can as such by no means be the original object of an actual, supernatural revelation and thus an original object of faith" (242). Although this axiom is self-evident (243) it is bound to arouse bewilderment and protest.

After defending this axiom (243-247) Rahner aks whether the existence of angels (and demons) can be revealed at all? He maintains the revelation of angels is at best of a secondary and derived character *if* it can be proved they are known naturally, *and* if they can have a religious significance sythesizable within the proper reality of faith. (After all, not every finite and knowable reality about which a statement of faith can be made or which might be known by faith can ipso facto be regarded as such a secondary and derived object of faith, 247f). In sum, it is a false dilemma to say either angels are an object of revelation or a merely fallible assertion of natural knowledge. Something can be both naturally known *and* within the sphere of derived and secondary objects of faith. Given this third possibility Rahner maintains the question of the existence of angels cannot be answered unambiguously at the present stage of the controversy.

This raises two questions: i) can natural knowledge prove and make intelligible the existence of angels or is this an absolutely mythological notion? ii) If natural knowledge can prove the existence of angels is this an object of faith or merely an object of natural knowledge about which faith makes hypothetical statements without thereby raising them to the level of objects of faith and thus without forbidding their denial? For Rahner the first question is answered, the second question remains open. Often elements in a particular historical milieu have entered a symbiosis with faith, an amalgam, which gives the impression the two are identical (examples, 251). Because it remains unclear whether belief in the existence of angels is another such symbiosis this is an inopportune time for bishops to intervene.

2) The existential-ontological question. Even assuming the existence of angels and their direct or derived attestation in revelation, what are they? How much of what is described in scripture is simply culturally conditioned and how much is binding? Rahner offers two modest suggestions for demythologizing a folkloristic, primitive belief in angels and demons based on accepted theological assumptions. First he challenges the notion they are "pure spirits" (253-255). Without saying precisely how, Rahner assigns to angels "an essential intrinsic relationship to *that* matter which is the sustaining ground of the finiteness of the world, of the unity of the cosmos and its history of personal beings" (255). Second, he applies to demons the generally accepted Christian theory of evil (256-59): i.e., there is no absolute evil; evil lives by the good and always continues to realize it; wickedness freely chosen reaches to the heart of the creature and defines its relationship with God; demons are radically dependent on God for their existence and do not struggle against God as equals, etc.

3) The question of the theology of the cosmos. After summarizing sections 1 and 2 (259), Rahner asks whether accepting the existence of angels is inconsistent with natural reason. Although a negative answer to this question is not conclusive, it does undercut the position that angels simply do not exist. Rahner begins by assuming that if angels exist they are essential constituents of the finite world and exercise cosmic functions. He bemoans the lack of a significant theology of the cosmos (260-263) and asks whether we can say with confidence that humanity is the only subjectivity rooted in matter toward which this world evolution is oriented. Leaving aside extra-terrestrial life which at this point in time has no theological relevance for us (263), Rahner imagines angels as highly complex and differentiated limited regions of subjectivity whose relationship to matter is different from, yet connected to, our own. As higher principles of unity and order they encompass and incorporate human beings without thereby suppressing them. Rahner justifies this "apparent deviation" on the grounds that it allows us to think of angels participating in the same common evolutionary process of subjectivizing and interiorizing the cosmos as we do. This leads to a brief discussion of time and whether angels are protological or eschatological realities (265-266).

So far these discussions simply intended to make the existence and nature of angels conceivable. But does our experience of the world give any indications of their actual existence along these lines? After discounting mythological, miraculous interventions, Rahner focuses on our experiences of greater unities and orders in the world which their constituent parts cannot explain, and which a simple recourse to chance does not illuminate (e.g., the relationship of substance and structure, 267-269). Rahner suggests we see such principles at work in the history of the evolution of life (270); in the history of humanity (270-272); in the unity of nature and culture (272); in the antagonism in which greater ordered unities encounter one another, e.g., the conflict between the "angels of the nations" in Daniel (272-273).

Rahner admits nothing said here provides conclusive evidence for the existence of angels. It simply indicates regions of possible experience in which our natural knowledge might encounter something like angels without giving these experiences an incredible or mythological interpreta-tion. He concludes by warnings those on both sides of the issue against all primitive thinking when it comes to the existence of angels.

XX. Concern for the Church
XIV. *In Sorge um die Kirche*

German edition: Einsiedeln, Benziger, 1980
U.S. edition: N.Y., Crossroad, 1981
Edward Quinn, translator. Paul Imhof, S.J., editor

This volume of the English language edition comprises selected essays from
Schriften zur Theologie XIV, #s 1,2,12,15,17-25.

20.01   Courage for an Ecclesial Christianity
Vom Mut zum kirchlichen Christentum
{1.0}   W. Jens, ed., *Warum ich Christ bin* (Munich 1979) 296-309.
Abstract: In answering "Why I am a Christian?" Rahner offers a concise
overview of his theology in lay terms: belief in God as mystery; in revelation;
in Jesus Christ; in the church; in Christian freedom.
Topics: FAITH in the church; CHRISTIANITY, belief in.
Subsidiary Discussions: God as mystery (3ff); Revelation (5f); Religions,
history of (6f); Christology (7ff); Church (9f); Magisterium, dissent from
(10ff).
Precis: Belief in Christianity is not belief in one thing among many. It is
belief in the meaningfulness of self and the world. Rahner feels encompassed

and permeated by eternal, infinite mystery. This mystery which he calls God is the inescapable ground of all freedom and knowledge. Logical proofs for God's existence are always secondary to the earth-shattering experience that I can approach this mystery. I can address it. I can pray.

Having experienced what Christians call grace we can never be content with finite things. God's promise of self-bestowal penetrates everything. It is love—the world's dynamic goal and inner force. Whenever this truth is known and embraced we have what Christians call revelation. This revelation constitutes the unity within the history of religions. "[A]s long as man is the man of God's infinite mystery, there will also be religion ..." (6).

Rahner's Christianity has an essential historical dimension. For in the death of Jesus the divine offer of self-communication is fully accepted. In his resurrection it is made irreversibly victorious. In this historical person God's unconditional solidarity with humanity is sealed. For Rahner, Jesus is the Word of God's promise, despite the fact this is often expressed in theologically unhelpful and misleading ways. This does not bother Rahner too much since in the long run Christianity is not about intellectual illumination but trust that our death passes into the life of God. For this reason we can never escape historical revelation in Jesus Christ.

"Since I am a human being and a Christian ... I am a Christian in the Church, an ecclesial Christian" (9). Christianity is never a purely private affair. Attachment to the church is the price we pay for our historicity. We know all too well the far-too-human failings of our church. Therefore, we live in the hope of the victory of grace and eschew all false triumphalism.

The church's checkered past confirms the right of each member to criticize elements in it which are not absolutely binding. There are many teachings from which believers can disassociate themselves without being exiled to the fringes of the church. But when believers are suppressed for challenging the church they must bear it patiently. Dissenters need not leave the church which Rahner sees as able to allow extraordinarily wide scope for diverse organizations. Rahner suggests that those who suffer far too much from the church have not properly understood its true nature or their ultimate relationship to it. He concludes by sharing how he deals with the stresses and strains of being a thinking person in the church (12).

20.02   On the Situation of Faith
Zur Situation des Glaubens
{3.0}   Previously unpublished.

Abstract: Even in our age of skeptical relativism an absolute assent of faith can and does occur, not at the level of secondary reflection but as a fundamental option. Thus, people can in good faith remain in the church even if they cannot presently embrace specific truths maintained by the magisterium.

Topics: FAITH, assent of; MAGISTERIUM.

Subsidiary Discussions: Concupiscence, gnoseological (13ff); Faith, *analysis fidei* (22ff); Faith, *fides quae/qua* (25ff); Freedom (27ff); Fundamental option (27f); *Actus honestus/salutaris* (29f); Intellectual honesty (30ff).

Precis: Although today it is impossible to integrate realities in the secular sphere and realities of Christian faith into a homogeneous worldview, it remains a duty arising from faith to seek to do so. When less was known this task was easier. Today the explosion of knowledge and the opportunities for real dialogue among these centers of knowledge make such a positive integration concretely and practically impossible. As a result people today seldom make absolute claims. They make only provisional claims about ultimate realities. Ours is an age of "skeptical relativism" (examples, 17).

This has significant consequences for Christian faith as concretely lived. First, the church's teaching authority in practice and existentially now takes a very secondary place in one's own system of faith (18-20). For most people authority is no longer the beginning or ultimate ground of faith. It is generally a secondary element which must itself be made credible by reference to a more fundamental theology and apologetics. "Today it is the credibility...of the fundamental dogmas of Christianity that makes credible the existence of a supernatural revelation … and not *vice versa*" (21). Today one must honestly admit the church is a burden to faith—one that cannot be thrown off but which can only be redeemed by the cross of Christ.

A new problem for faith arises in this new age of skeptical relativism: how is absolute assent (part of the essence of Christian faith) possible? If divine truth is always conveyed through human knowledge, and if we are rightly skeptical about the absolute truth claims of human knowledge, how can absolute assent of faith be made with intellectual honesty? This presents entirely new problems for the *analysis fidei* (22-26). After suggesting and discarding solutions based on the distinction between *fides quae* and *fides qua*, Rahner switches the focus from human knowledge to human freedom. People necessarily *do* make absolute and free commitments and not merely conditional, provisional ones. Absolute assent remains possible in the realm of free action even if one cannot completely subject one's decision to representational and reflex consciousness and thus remains a skeptical relativist in the realm of knowledge.

Rahner answers two objections arising from traditional theology (28-30): i) the absolute assent of faith must assert a specific something; ii) what is believed in this theory cannot be understood as coming from historical revelation. In the first place Rahner points out that because God's revelation is always and everywhere the precondition of any salvation history, it is false to say revelation must either be a definite historical event or it is unhistorical. Secondly, freely accepting God's offer of self-communication is always an historical act. He concludes with some remarks on the scholastic distinction between *actus honestus* and *actus salutaris* (29f).

Formed as they are by the relative skepticism of this age many Catholics today cannot give absolute assent to individual dogmas of Christianity and wonder whether they are still Catholics. Rahner insists they are because an absolute assent on the practical level is possible even when a particular dogma is rejected on the intellectual level. This being so, many other theological questions could be profitably reexamined (list, 31).

Rahner concludes with suggestions for a pastoral approach to such Catholics. It is one thing to admit one cannot understand or embrace a particular doctrine. It is another to insist the doctrine is therefore false. It is enough to affirm the ultimate basic substance of Christianity and remain open to those aspects of doctrine one cannot now embrace. Intellectual honesty does not demand leaving the church if one cannot at present give absolute assent to every particular of the faith. This approach applies no less to statements about magisterial authority than to any other doctrine. Rahner hopes his essay furnishes pastors with the intellectual underpinnings to justify the pastoral approach many of them currently take in counseling unchurched Christians.

20.03 Women and the Priesthood

Priestertum der Frau?

{1.5}   *Stimmen der Zeit* 195 (1977) 291-301.

Abstract: Because the central argument in the 1976 declaration on women's ordination is defective, theological discussion must continue.

Topics: PRIESTHOOD and women; WOMEN and priesthood; MAGISTERIUM and women's ordination.

Precis: This essay limits itself to the theological arguments contained in the Congregation for the Doctrine of the Faith's (CDF) 1976 "Declaration on the Question of the Admission of Women to the Ministerial Priesthood."

The Declaration of the Congregation for the Doctrine of the Faith of 15 October 1976. A clear summary outline of the six parts of the Declaration.

The theological qualification of the Roman declaration. Because this is an authentic declaration of the Roman authorities on faith it must be given more weight than the arguments of individual theologians. Nonetheless, it is not a definitive statement. It is in principle reformable and may even be erroneous. Although the Declaration appeals to an "uninterrupted tradition" it is unclear whether this tradition is definitive and absolutely binding—whether it is human or divine. Thus, on the one hand theologians must treat this document with respect. On the other hand they have the right and the duty to examine it critically, even if such criticism is not appreciated by the magisterium. If the criticism of theologians reveals the document is defective it can be questioned or impugned as erroneous.

Observations on the argumentation. The central theological argument assumes that in excluding women from the Twelve, Jesus intended something which is not historically or socially conditioned and thus holds for all times. Brief preliminary observations. This argument is defective. It fails to accept the burden of proof. It maintains others would have to disprove it. It uncritically and anachronistically identifies the Twelve with the modern structure of bishops and priests. It fails to appreciate the impact of "immanent expectation" of Jesus and the early church. In reducing priestly ministry to the sacramental powers of consecration and the office of preaching the Word it undervalues the call to community leadership and begs the question of the nature of priestly ministry. It fails to explain how the church can be absolutely bound by an argument which is admittedly less than certain.

Was the attitude of Jesus and the apostles culturally and sociologically conditioned? Preliminary observation. A course of action can be so culturally and socially conditioned that even though it is open to change today it could once have been both socially acceptable and morally binding (e.g., slavery, usury, Old Testament polygamy, and laws of war, 42). Rahner argues it is historically certain that in a milieu marked by male dominance Jesus and the early church could not have considered, more less set up, a leadership structure which included women. Their decision may even have been morally required at that time and through the centuries till today. The burden of proof that this is *not* the case rests with the CDF. The Declaration makes no attempt to do this.

In addition, unless the CDF offers substantial theological reasons why Jesus and the early church intentionally excluded women from church leadership that decision can only appear completely arbitrary. Rahner dismisses arguments which equate maleness with the notion *in persona Christi* and any other arguments drawn from flawed anthropologies. After a word about the status of the historical record (44) Rahner concludes, it "seems inescapable that the attitude of Jesus and his Apostles is sufficiently explained by the cultural and sociological milieu in which they acted and had to act as they did, while their behaviour did not need to have a normative significance for all times... when this cultural and social milieu had been substantially changed" (44-45). Hence, excluding women from orders is a human tradition not a divine command.

The discussion must continue. Because the CDF's arguments are not adequate, serious theological discussion of the issue must continue. Any thorough discussion must encompass many other outstanding questions (list, 45f). Any final answer must be one on which the faithful, the magisterium, and theologians can be in complete agreement in theory and in practice. Insofar as it may take some time to reach such an understanding Rahner urges patience and confidence. But he also warns that stalling may have dire consequences. However true it is that the church must always remain faithful to Christ, the real question is what such fidelity entails. This remains an open question today.

20.04   The Church's Responsibility for the Freedom of the Individual

Die Verantwortung der Kirche für die Freiheit des Einzelnen

{2.0}   Previously unpublished.

Abstract: Because church and society face similar challenges in balancing the rights of free individuals with the duty of authority to maintain order, structural changes in the church could provide models for changes in society.
Topics: CHURCH, change in; FREEDOM and the church; AUTHORITY.
Subsidiary Discussions: Realism, Christian (52ff); Utopias (54f); Future (55); Power, coercive (58f, 62f); Pluralism (60f).
Precis: Rahner begins with a warning and an apology. Freedom and the church's role in safeguarding freedom raise a host of questions (list, 51f). This essay is an arbitrary reflection on one aspect: the importance of structural change in the church for secular society and for the freedom of the individual (57).

I. The church teaches that real, true, total, definitive human freedom consists in the eschatological possession of salvation itself—a sheer gift of God which brings finite history to its end. Although the psychological freedom of choice oriented to finite objects is a precondition of saving freedom, it is always finite, limited, and self-alienated. Restricted by the material on which it works, creaturely freedom always reveals a gap between the subject's infinite claim to freedom and the actual opportunities to possess it. Christianity teaches that to deny or repress this gap is sin.

Forthright Christian realism insists that insofar as our freedom is inalterably finite it can only be liberated by God's act of self-donation. Although Christian realism disenchants us it also has positive significance precisely in the struggle for greater freedom. It protects us against finite, material utopianism (54f) by training our eyes on the eternal kingdom of God. Far from paralyzing us, Christian realism empowers us to take risks, knowing that both success and failure are encompassed within the eschatological victory Christ has irrevocably achieved. "The Church's gospel of Christian realism is and remains the primary service that Christianity performs for the freedom of the individual and society" (56).

II. To say that on some level the church has always enhanced human freedom by preaching its brand of realism in no way denies past abuses of authority (56). Nonetheless, Rahner insists structural change in the church can be important for secular society. He considers two possible consequences, leaving aside any discussion of precisely *whether* and *how* such change would be translated from one arena to the other. He bases his hope on two factors in the modern church: its new minority status, and its ability to change its structures more rapidly than secular society.

–Common convictions in church and society. Both the church and secular society are founded on common convictions respected by all their members. Each society must devise ways to maintain, regenerate, and transform these foundations. The "power" to do this is generally wielded by an institutional elite. Today when the members of society are better educated and cherish individual freedom, new models are needed to insure mutual respect and balance between government and the governed. Here the church might set an example. It is in a better position to do this today for many reasons: it can no longer rely on civil authority to enforce compliance with its teachings; its own theology is irreducibly pluralistic; a universal sense of faith is more difficult to establish or maintain; etc. Rahner's summary (61f) talks in general terms of the need to develop an "ecclesiology of marginality" able to embrace propositions which seem logically inconsistent simply because they exist on existentially and sociologically different planes.

–The church as minority in society. In the church's minority situation groups emerging from the base must and will acquire new importance. This will demand very different structures. An analogous need for new structures to mediate the relationship between ruling elites and the people they serve (in both western democracies and socialist countries) is so important and so similar that the differences between these two kinds of states begin to pale to insignificance. The church, responding to this new reality and renewing its own structures, could model new possibilities for secular society.

20.05 Theological Justification of the Church's Development Work

Theologische Begründung der kirchlichen Entwicklungsarbeit

{2.0} Episcopal Commission for Misereor, ed., *Misereor—Zeichen der Hoffnung*. Festschrift for Gottfried Dossing (Munich 1976) 71-79.

Abstract: Rahner justifies the involvement of the church itself (not merely of its individual members) in social development by appealing to the theological relationship of love of God to love of neighbor, and to eschatological hope.

Topics: CHURCH, development work of; LOVE of God/neighbor; HOPE, eschatological.

Subsidiary Discussions: Renunciation (71f); Freedom (71); Utopias (72).

Precis: Since Vatican II's *Ad gentes* 11-12 forbids using social development for pre-evangelization, how can involvement in social development be an essential task of the church if it takes place wholly within the secular sphere and if it shares this responsibility with other secular agencies and individuals? Such involvement seems to blur the distinction between secular and religious and between the duties of individual Christians and those of the church itself. Rahner justifies church involvement in social development based on its mandate to love one's neighbor (66-70) and on its eschatological hope (70-73).

Rahner questions whether the church has sufficiently reflected on the radical questions raised by the command to love God and neighbor (list, 66f). He is not satisfied with the widely accepted view that love of neighbor is simply subsumed under love of God as a remote conclusion (67). He maintains that finite, material beings can only love God in and through love of neighbor even though that love is very often unthematic. If this is so, then love of neighbor is a universal determinant of human existence and demands social and historical expression not as one isolated area of human life but as a religious attitude towards the world. Religions cannot be indifferent to concrete expressions of love of neighbor. In fact "to some extent love of God must forget itself in love of neighbour in order to reach its own full nature" (68). Two things must be remembered: i) the church itself (not simply as the sum of its individual members) must realize its love for God in the worldliness of the world; ii) Love of neighbor it not a private affair. It has as its proper object changing the structures of society to insure greater freedom and justice for all. Rahner concludes this section with specific comments on *Misereor*, the group he is addressing.

Rahner also justifies the development work of the church by appealing to eschatological hope. According to *Lumen gentium* 35, Christians must be strong in hope. They must express this hope by turning to God in their struggle within the framework of secular life. Although in practice this appeal to hope has often been misinterpreted as opium intended to keep the masses passive, in principle it is a hope that insists on risk and practical action even when the outcome is veiled. "The eschatological hope of the Christian awaits the final consummation dissolving history as sovereign deed and gift of God" (71). At the same time it is an intra-mundane hope. How else could Vatican II urge Catholics to express it in the framework of secular life? Eschatological hope relativizes our goods and deeds, making us free and open to future possibilities without deceiving us with the lure of this-worldly utopias. After a brief word on how *Misereor* does this Rahner concludes with a summary (73).

20.06 Basic Theological Interpretation of the Second Vatican Council

Theologische Grundinterpretation des II. Vatikanischen Konzils
{1.0}   *Zeitschrift für katholische Theologie* 101 (1979) 290-299.
Abstract: In historical terms the theological importance of Vatican II's move to make the church a "world-church" ranks second only to the caesura created when Paul moved the church beyond the synagogue to embrace the gentile world.

Topics: CHURCH, history of; VATICAN II; CHURCH as world-church; ENCULTURATION.

Subsidiary Discussions: Vatican II, decrees (80ff); Latin language (80f, 86); Theology, pluralism in (87f); Law, canon (86, 88); Pastoral Constitution (89); Petrine office (89).

Precis: The basic theological interpretation of Vatican II centers on its effort to discover and officially recognize itself as *world-church*. Although the predominantly western European church always had this potential for which there were historical precedents, before the council this was manifested only very rudimentarily and hesitantly. This new prospect raises important cross-cultural questions (list, 79) for which there are no easy answers.

The consequences of this change to a world-church, the meaning of this qualitative leap, can be seen in an analysis of the conciliar documents (80-82). At a deeper level it reveals to Rahner the fact that the theological history of the church can now be divided into three great epochs (83): 1) Judaeo-Christianity; 2) The church within Hellenism and European culture and civilization; 3) The church whose living space is the whole world. Although these periods can be further subdivided Rahner defends the theological correctness of this basic tripartite division. He draws parallels between the caesura inaugurated by St. Paul and the caesura brought about by Vatican II. If this analysis is correct it raises two questions:

1) In what precisely does the theological and not merely the cultural-historical singularity of such caesurae consist (84-86)? The first interruption in the seeming continuity of salvation- revelation-history is a real caesura. Without a fully articulated theology the early church abolished many previously sacred laws regarding Sabbath, diet, worship (list, 85). Rahner maintains (with reservations, 85) we are today for the first time living in a similar period. If the church fails to see and recognize the essential cultural differences into which it must enter as a world-church, if it fails to accept with Pauline boldness the necessary consequence of this reality and remains a Western church, it betrays the meaning of Vatican II.

2) What follows if we apply the theology of the first transition to the transition we are living today and for which Vatican II was a kind of official ecclesial beginning (86-88)? Today's new Christianity needs a new material content. It remains unclear how legitimate it is for today's church to seize the creative power to reform itself and its message. The council could only hint at the task. How to realize it concretely is veiled by the future. In any case it will call for a new proclamation of the basic message. This will be accomplished by reducing the Christian message to its ultimate basic substance. There would follow real pluralisms of proclamation, liturgy, and canon law suited to the many cultures of the earth. Needless to say this raises serious questions about how to maintain orthodoxy and authority. After a summary (88) Rahner questions the future of the pastoral constitution genre, and the unsolved question of harmonizing papal primacy with collegiality.

20.07 The Abiding Significance of the Second Vatican Council

Die bleibende Bedeutung des II. Vatikanischen Konzils
{0.5}   *Stimmen der Zeit* 197 (1979) 795-804.

Abstract: Vatican II will have lasting significance if the church embraces its call to be a world-church with a pluralistic theology, ecumenically oriented, eschewing coercive power, and optimistic about God's will to save all people.
Topics: VATICAN II; CHURCH of the future.
Subsidiary Discussions: World-church (91f); Latin language (92); Power, coercive (93f); Theology of the future (94ff); Magisterium (95f); Ecumenism (97ff); Dogma, development of (98); God, salvific will of (99ff).

Precis: There is a difference between historical and theological significance. A council could be significant for the church as a whole without being significant for regional churches. Nonetheless, the lasting significance of Vatican II rests in what it mandated for the universal church. If the church embraces these new challenges the council will have lasting meaning.

Council of the world-church. The council was the first act in a history in which the "world-church" began to exist as such in the dimension of doctrine and law. The repercussions of this permanently significant new reality can be seen in the irreversible transposition of the liturgy into the vernacular. It may herald greater liturgical enculturation and overall regional autonomy.

Relationship to the world. In its Pastoral Constitution the church outlined a fundamentally new relationship with the world especially in its renunciation of coercive power. Although the church will always remain tempted to join with secular states to further its own agenda, a frontier has been crossed.

Theology of the council. The council ended the dominance of neo-scholasticism in favor of a more open, biblical, ecumenical, and pluralistic theology. It left theology in a fluid state of transition feared and resisted by the Congregation for the Doctrine of the Faith. The council proved theology is continually self-renewing. A theology of the future will be more pluralistic and less monolithically western. Such a theology redefines the tasks of the magisterium.

Ecumenical change of mind. The council marked a caesura in church relations with non-Catholics and non-Christians. It defended its uniqueness without overstating its difference with other Christians or different religions. It definitively abandoned an older mentality that completely excluded "obdurate" non-Catholic Christians and all non-Christians living in the terrible darkness of paganism from ever experiencing God's saving grace. Rahner insists this is not a victory of liberalism but of Christianity (99).

Optimism of universal salvation. The council definitively rejected the Augustinian pessimism which culminates in the horrible prospect of a *massa damnata*. It was optimistic about the effectiveness of God's universal salvific will extending even to atheists "in a way known only to God" (100). Though it maintains eternal perdition always remains a possibility for human freedom, it does not assume heretics and non-Christians are simply culpable. Summary (102).

20.08   The Future of the Church and the Church of the Future

Die Zukunft der Kirche und die Kirche der Zukunft

{0.5}   Previously unpublished September 1977 lecture in Offenburg.

Abstract: The future of the church is only grasped in faith and hope. The future church will be different from today's and yet the same insofar as God's unalterable promise to be our absolute future can assume many concrete forms.

Topics: CHURCH of the future; CHURCH, future of.

Subsidiary Discussions: World-church (103f, 110f); Faith (106ff, 112f); Hope (106ff, 112f); Base communities (110); Petrine office (111).

Precis: "Church of the future" refers to the world-church as a whole as it finds itself in today's society. It is also the church in its ecumenical dimension. As a result of this focus Rahner's comments may seem broad and vague. After concisely describing the church as *Ur-sakrament* whose essential task demands engagement with the world (104) he argues the nature and function of the church remain independent of its size relative to world population. Although its size will continue to make it an important world force these considerations are essentially provisional and external. The real future of the church can only be grasped within the context of faith and hope (106f).

Since the hope of believers encompasses the affirmation of the church and its eschatological future, it is not troubled by any purely human prognoses for the church. Over and above the assurance which comes from the actual survival of the church for two thousand years, hope for the future of the church is grounded in an ultimate decision of faith rooted in the depth of existence—belief in Father, Son, and Spirit. "In the last resort, the future of the church is not a theme for secular futurology, but an object of the faith that relies unconditionally on God himself" (108).

Can we know anything about the content and essential character of this future? How can we know it? Because the future of the church remains at the disposal of God's freedom and human freedom, less of it can be foreseen than of the future of secular society. Far from being unfortunate, this unforeseeability of the future of the church is the condition for the possibility of true freedom and of self-surrendering faith. Nevertheless, Rahner insists we can make at least two statements about the future of the church: it will be different from the present in many ways; it will be the future of the one and enduring church in which we believe today. "Change and endurance belong equally to the nature of the church" (109) even if we cannot always know in advance which concrete elements constitute its unchanging nature.

As for changes, Rahner sees the voluntary faith of grassroots believers becoming increasingly important. He expects a breakdown in the current symbiosis of church and civil government in European societies. He foresees an increasingly important and autonomous role for the church of Africa and South America which will force a reform of the Petrine office.

As for permanence, the real message of Christianity can never perish not simply because it is based on the essential nature of human beings, but also because it is God's unalterable promise to reach us as the fulfillment of time and history (112). God is our absolute future. The church is the incarnation and sign of that promise for all time. This message can never be superseded. Those who believe in this promise and in this absolute future are obliged to be its heralds to the world. Summary (113f).

20.09   Structural Change in the Church of the Future
Structurwandel der Kirche in der künftigen Gesellschaft
{0.5}   K. Rahner, *Strukturwandel der Kirche als Aufgabe und Chance* (Freiburg 1972).

Abstract: After arguing that structural change of the church is theoretically possible, Rahner maintains future changes in society will make ecumenism and democratization more opportune for a "world-church" in a diaspora setting.

Topics: CHURCH, future of; CHURCH, change in; CHURCH, subsidiarity in; CHURCH of the future.

Subsidiary Discussions: Secularization (117f); Petrine office (119f); Episcopate (120ff); Church, democracy in (122ff, 126); Laity (123ff); Future (125ff); Ecumenism (127f); Church diaspora (128); Base communities (128f); Parish (128f).

Precis: With a dogmatic theologian's eye on the perennially valid elements of revealed ecclesiology, Rahner examines the possibilities for the structural change of the church in a future society. Though the Roman authorities seem hesitant and timid, Rahner sees great opportunities for "structural" change (definition, 115f).

I. In the "Pian epoch" (1789-1962) the church understood itself as unchanging both in its constitution and in natural law. This outlook enshrined by an a-historical neo-scholasticism was a defensive reaction to the changes ushered in by secularism. By challenging this outlook Vatican II revealed a greater range of possibilities for structural change than heretofore admitted.

Chief among these changeable elements is the task and function of the pope in relation to the autonomy of regional churches (119-122). After showing how even under the older dispensation the pope's universal jurisdiction was limited (e.g., by morality and concordats with civil governments) Rahner suggests it is now opportune to negotiate similar arrangements between the Holy See and regional churches. This would strengthen the council's teaching that bishops govern their churches immediately and in the name of Christ and not as branch managers for Rome. Rahner turns next to the possibility of greater democratization in the structures of the church especially at the regional level (122-125). Not only will the laity bear an ever greater responsibility for the effectiveness of the mission of the church, Vatican II teaches they have a real and perceptible right to engage in the decision making of the church. Rahner sees no reason (*jure divino*) why their voice could not be deliberative as well as consultative.

II. All that has been said so far is that despite its enduring nature structural change is theoretically *possible* within the church. But to know which changes would be opportune or desirable takes insight into the future shape of secular society. Admittedly the church is not even in step with the world of today. If it were it would be "a declericalized, serving, caring Church" (126). Nevertheless, what special features of the future can one foresee even now which might be important for a structural change in the church? First, growing interdependence among all elements of society makes the ecumenical task of a world-church more acute. At the same time regional churches (Africa, South America, etc.) must be granted new fields for the actualization of their own natures.

Secondly, since future societies will be more pluralistic it is reasonable to say that churches will find themselves in a "diaspora situation"—one voice within society with no preferential treatment from civil government. In this setting the effectiveness of the church will be determined less by church authorities from above than by "the assent of faith freely given by individuals and the commitment of its members 'from below'" (128). This will entail transforming individual parishes from sacramental filling stations to living communities of faith. Even though there exists the danger that in meeting the needs of its own members these parishes will lose sight of their mission to the world, what is needed now is creativity not timid conservatism which only grudgingly allows for change when there is no alternative. Somewhat rhetorically Rahner asks why church authorities are so fearful.

III. Like every other society the church will always possess conservative and progressive elements reflecting the need for both continuity and change. Although the structures of the church are for the most part "relative realities" which represent the human sphere, the fact they are "sacramentally" linked to the eternal gives them a disproportionately great significance. The danger for both progressives and conservatives lies in absolutizing what is simply relative and historically conditioned, granting it a permanent and eternal validity which must be reserved for God alone. This error radicalizes and poisons discussions which in turn become profoundly un-Christian.

20.10   Dream of the Church
Der Traum von der Kirche

{1.0}   May 1977 radio lecture as, *Vision und Wirklichkeit der Traum von der Kirche*. M. Krauss, ed., *Ich habe einen Traum* (Stutgart 1978) 77-78.

Abstract: In the guise of a "dream" Rahner's future "pope" suggests how a particular understanding and implementation of binding teaching authority could make it acceptable in ecumenical circles.

Topics: PETRINE OFFICE; INFALLIBILITY; ECUMENISM.

Subsidiary Discussions: Faith, *sensus fidelium* (137f).

Precis: Not too fantastic. Rahner relates a hopeful dream of a relaxed working session of ecumenical church leaders and theologians addressed by an imagined future pope on the topic of papal primacy of teaching.

The pope's suggestion. After sharing his conviction that problems surrounding the magisterium cannot be solved by exegetical or historical investigations, the pope suggests a different method: Rahner's ecumenical thesis that if all the churches assume they all stand in a salvific union with God and one another, then they will tolerate one another's beliefs without feeling compelled to condemn or embrace them, or to force their own beliefs on each other (135).

Moving to the topic of the Petrine office, the pope admits in the past the Catholic Church has not sufficiently distinguished between what must be absolutely firmly held as matters of doctrine and practice in its regard and what is simply conditional. The "pope" makes two remarks. First he links absolutely Vatican I's teaching on papal infallibility to the whole church's assent of faith with the assistance of the Holy Spirit. What is lacking today is a clear articulation of how such a consultation prior to any new binding teaching would be conducted. It is not surprising that in its absence non-Catholic Christians continue to fear an arbitrary manipulation of this papal prerogative. He suggests the concrete contents of a new consultative procedure could and should include leaders of non-Catholic churches. Secondly he points to the fact that historical patterns of exercising papal authority do not bind the future. He foresees an exercise of authority that is more democratic, pluralistic, subsidiary, and focused on the fundamentals of the faith.

Spontaneous reactions. When the "pope" excuses himself from the meeting to allow for more candid discussion, three voices are heard: one states that what the pope has just said shows clearly the Petrine office cannot be an obstacle to unity; another voice is more suspicious and calls it a verbal obfuscation of the same basic stance; a third sees it as a hopeful sign of progress although far from definitive. Rahner admits his dream does not point to a glorious future but to a continuation of theological debate. This is only realistic. And isn't it better to pursue a realistic dream with a prospect of rapid success than simply to pursue a glorious one?

20.11   The Spirituality of the Church of the Future
Elemente der Spiritualität in der Kirche der Zukunft

{0.5}   Previously unpublished January 1977 lecture at Münster to the Catholic University Chaplaincy.
Abstract: Five characteristics of future Catholic spirituality.
Topics: SPIRITUALITY; CHURCH of the future.
Subsidiary Discussions: Secularization (147ff); Mysticism (149ff); Fellowship (150ff); Church of sinners (152f).
Precis: Because spirituality is a "mysterious and tender thing" (143) different in every Christian, and because the future of the church is hidden, Rahner can only offer five arbitrarily selected characteristics of a spirituality of the church of the future. His focus is the Catholic church and he is not overly concerned whether or not these characteristics are currently fully present.

1) Because the church is always one, Catholic spirituality of the future will retain a "mysterious identity" with the spirituality of the past. It will be God-centered, Christ-centered, ecclesial, sacramental, political (protesting against the idols of wealth), historically conscious, and charismatic.

2) In an increasingly secular and atheistic environment Christian spirituality will concentrate on the essentials of Christian piety—the ultimate data of revelation rather than on particular devotions (e.g., Jesus Christ and not the Infant of Prague).

3) Because Christianity in the future will lack the homogenous support of its social/political milieu, spirituality will be based on the faith of the individual springing from a deep personal experience of God. The Christian of the future will either be a mystic or no Christian at all.

4) Christian spirituality of the future will find expression in fraternal fellowship even to the point of communal discernment of spirits.

5) Christian spirituality will have a different ecclesial aspect. The individual's relationship to the church will be less childlike; the church itself will be less triumphalistic. Believers will come to see the history of the church in great part as a burden to bear not a triumph in which to glory. Believers will increasingly need more patience with the church.

20.12   Unity of the Church—Unity of Mankind
Einheit der Kirch—Einheit der Menscheit

{3.5}   May 1977 lecture to Protestant and Catholic Theological Faculties at Academy of Hamburg. Same title (Freiburg 1978) 50-76.
Abstract: An analysis of unity (transcendental, human, ecclesial) concludes that working toward the unity of humanity is both a secular necessity and an essential task of Christianity as this aids in its spread through the world.
Topics: UNITY; ECUMENISM; CHURCH unity.
Subsidiary Discussions: God as ultimate unity (154f, 157f); Becoming (155f); Love (157); Monogenism (159f); Salvation, universality of (160f);

Sin (161f, 164); Utopias (161); Atheism (163f); Europe, history of (162ff); Church as *Ur-sakrament* (166f); Truths, hierarchy of (168); Magisterium (169ff).

I. Unity.

1) The concept of "unity." Rahner maintains the scholastic notion that God is the unity which precedes and sustains all plurality. From this ultimate primal unity each individual existent possesses both an essential internal unity and a relationship to everything else that is real.

2) Unity as existing and as a task. Since everything other than God is in the state of becoming we can identify several concepts of unity: the unity of the individual being, and unity as the transcendental goal of individual beings which Rahner calls "unity imposed as a task."

3) Unifying unity. Both forms of unity are sustained by "the unifying unity of the absolute being that we call God" (156) in such a way as to presuppose this ultimate unity. There are also "partial unifying unities." Unity as a task can be related both to one's internal unity and to one's unity with the rest of reality. The two are correlative and mutually dependent. Insofar as unity as a task always remains in the realm of becoming it is only approached asymptotically. This gives the task of unity a real history.

4) Unity through love. Initial unity (unity as task) and unifying unity are analogical concepts realized either through the history of free subjects or through the pure history of nature. In the former this unity is only produced by love: "the consummation of unity in accepting the absolute otherness of *everyone* else (in accepting *this* other as one's very own) and thus the reconciliation between universal unity and enduring plurality, which itself is accepted as good, as its own, by the loving subject" (157).

5) Absolute unifying unity: God. Because in a world of becoming "unity as task" is an unobtainable and asymptotic goal, absolute reconciliation and unity is conceivable only if the absolute unifying unity (God) imparts himself and if this offer is accepted in love. This absolute reconciliation is the innermost dynamism of reality and a goal to be victoriously attained. This love is the faith and hope of Christians.

II. Unity of mankind.

1) A theological theme. Though the unity of humanity is a theological statement (i.e., one made in the light of revelation) it is a theme on which many secular interests are concerned and competent. Theology offers such statements to the secular self-understanding to see whether they agree. If what theology offers is accepted, humanity moves closer to the unity central to its own proclamation. One should not assume this vision of human unity is necessarily embraced by secularism apart from Christianity's insistence on it.

2) Biological unity. Christianity understands the unity of humanity as a datum. Monogenism is one model for this. Rahner points to human biological compatibility as well as to our ability to communicate, surmount differences, and understand and share one another's transcendental striving.

3) One salvation for all. To this Christianity adds that all human beings have the same final destiny and share one history of salvation prior to and separate from any particular history of salvation and religion.

4) Sin. The task of unity can be damaged or destroyed by the selfishness of sin, interior or social. This tragic situation will remain a permanent existential of our history to the very end. Yet simply because utopia is impossible is no reason not to plan and fight for a more united world.

5) Finite unifying unity. In addition to God, the absolute unifying unity (summary 162), there are also particular finite, and regional unifying unties, e.g., Imperial Rome, Byzantium, the Holy Roman Empire. The church seems to find such unities legitimate in principle. Does unity remain a proper task and goal for humanity? If so, in what does it consist? It can be shown empirically that such unity is a growing fact.

6) Unifying atheism? If we can justify this task of uniting humanity because its real progress is concrete and inexorable, can it also be justified as a truly moral and human task? After mentioning the fact that unity breeds its own diversity and that the future remains veiled and unpredictable, Rahner turns to the more theological dimensions of this question. Since the task of unity is always marked by sin, achieved unity will always have the character of oppression. Rahner connects this with the rise of militant atheism, a phenomenon whose theological content has not yet been sufficiently analyzed.

7) Unifying Christian Europe? Rahner finds theological meaning in the fact that the increasing unity of humanity prevailing today began in the technology of Christian Europe--that the church furthered its universal mission by riding the wave of European conquest despite the sinfulness of the latter.

III. Unity of the church—and unity of mankind.

1) Church as basic sacrament. The church is no mere interior conviction. It is indispensably and essentially visible. Only thus does it continue the historical mission of Christ. As basic sacrament it must do its utmost to establish its presence everywhere. Leaving aside the question of numbers, the more united humanity is, the more broadly the church can proclaim its message.

2) Scandal of separation—existing unity. The fractured state of the church, whatever its reasons or degrees, should not be. This sinful state is a terrible scandal contradicting the church's mission. In spite of it an initial unity of faith has been maintained. Today such concepts as the "hierarchy of truths" helps us see and admit the positive, salvific significance of all the churches. Also today we can hope for unity without insisting on uniformity.

3) Unity in the profession of faith. Church leaders must realize the present situation is far different from Reformation times. Unfortunately it is difficult to know today who can speak authoritatively for Protestants. Equally unfortunate is the fact Catholics have not yet attempted to render their own

dogmas comprehensible to those outside its theological culture. Nor have they shown how burgeoning, irreducible theological and cultural pluralism can be made compatible with the exercise of binding magisterial authority.

4) Unity and institution. Church leaders and the faithful must move more boldly (without being irresponsible) to establish institutional unity of the churches. Rome must abandon its culture of Pian monolithism (examples, 171).

5) Unity of the church and unity of mankind. Summary (171f).

20.13   The Inexhaustible Transcendence of God and Our Concern for the Future
Die unverbrauchbare Transzendenz Gottes und unsere Sorge um die Zukunft

{3.0}   September 1978 radio lecture. A contribution to the Salzburg Conference on Humanism: *Hoffnung in der Überlebenskrise?* Published in *Zugänge zur Theologie*. Festschrift for W. Joest (Göttingen 1979) 201-214.

Abstract: Only "useless" love of God for God's own sake (not for any good that may follow) endows individual ethical actions with the dignity of a divine commandment and forestalls the idolization of all particular tasks and goals.

Topics: LOVE of God; FUTURE, hope for.

Subsidiary Discussions: God as mystery (174f); Christianity, message of (177f); Humanism (179); Love of neighbor (180, 184f); Freedom (181ff); Idolatry (185f).

Precis: Rahner contributes one item to this humanist conference "Hope in the Crisis of Survival": the Christian message of God can only be a message beyond earthly hopes and fears, optimism and pessimism, if we do not reduce God to an instrument of our concern for the future but succeed in leaving God's transcendence unexhausted. All that follows attempts to elucidate this point.

Christians assume belief in the existence of God is necessary and helpful for our existence. But in what sense can this be true if God remains absolute, incomprehensible mystery for all eternity? In this light God might equally well appear as the fundamental impossibility of solving our own vital questions. This calls for a restatement of our true relationship with God as acknowledged by authentic Christianity. This relationship is one of love described here by Rahner as mutual, but not simply mutual gratification. "True love is self-abandoning, never returning to itself" (176). We are constantly tempted to reduce love to an instrumental good. In addition we can never be certain whether or to what degree our love has succumbed to this temptation. What Rahner sees at work in this kind of relationship he calls the "principle of the irreversibility of a relationship, of the non-congruence of reciprocal relationships, or … principle of the inexhaustibility of transcendence" (176).

Authentic Christianity insists salvation can only be gained though love of God and neighbor exercised in an irreversible and inexhaustible transcendence which never becomes a mere instrument for one's own self-realization. After summarizing this essential message of Christianity (177f) he asks in what sense Christianity can be considered a consolation since it "cannot and will not relieve us of our deadly terror at this demand involving life and death; it offers no facile optimism ..." (178). The answer lies in the fact that only selfless love which seems to overtax us can produce salvation. Only a God who is greater than our hearts can lead us from the prison of selfishness into redeeming freedom. This incomprehensible love takes many forms (list, 178).

What then is the significance of the Christian message to the question of "Hope in the Crisis of Survival"? First, Christianity is utterly different from humanism. The saving love it preaches far exceeds humanism's goal of harmony through the balance of mutual interests. God must be loved in and for himself and never merely for the advantages that love brings. This love of God is not an optional commitment but the heart of one's whole existence; it is never completely subsumed into love of neighbor. "Christianity would cease to exist if it no longer had the courage to speak of the blessed uselessness of love for God" (180). But where are the prophets to proclaim this today?

Our need for God is not the justification of God. If God were merely the guarantor of our concern for ourselves God would be a mere projection of our needs as Feuerbach thought. Rahner sees loving God for God's own sake as freedom and consolation. Such love alone relativizes all the uncontrollable and incalculable powers and forces threatening our existence. The central question is not whether in this love we have infinite freedom in God but whether we actually manage to love God in this way. Yet only when we have the courage to let the question rest do we find true freedom and consolation—not the security of hikers on solid ground but that of swimmers who manage to keep their heads above the threatening waves. Such selfless love of God comes again and again as a sheer gift.

What impact does this inexhaustible transcendence of humanity to God have on concrete life? Preliminary remarks: 1) no positive answer to this question can actually "justify" this transcendence; 2) though Rahner is uncertain what the growth or decline of such love means for the history of the world, in itself such love never renders the realization of intra-mundane possibilities superfluous.

Only such love of God endows moral action in the present world (love of neighbor) with the practical and effective dignity of a commandment expressing the divine will. In addition, such love relativizes and deprives one's immediate goals and tasks of their idolatrous character. It never allows us to see any individual thing, not even ourselves, as absolute.

XXI. Science and Christian Faith
XV. *Wissenschaft und christlicher Glaube*

German edition: Einsiedeln, Benziger, 1983
U.S. edition: N.Y., Crossroad, 1988
Hugh M. Riley, translator. Paul Imhof, S.J., editor.

This volume in the English language edition comprises the first three parts of *Schriften zur Theologie*, XV.

21.01   Profane History and Salvation History
Profansgeschichte und Heilsgeschichte.
{2.0} *Christlicher Glaube in moderner Gesellschaft*, vol. 23 (Freiburg im Breisgau 1982) 111-123, as, *Weltgeschichte und Heiligeschichte*.
Abstract: These random musings affirm that God, the goal of human freedom, supplies the ultimate meaning of history as a whole. They also explain why a radically hopeful Christianity is both anti-utopian and anti-elitist.
Topics: HISTORY, theology of; MEANING; REVELATION-/SALVA-TION-HISTORY.

Subsidiary Discussions: Eternal life (4); Freedom (4ff); Time (5ff, 9); Hope (6f); God as meaning of history (8f); Christology, Christ-event (10ff); Utopias (13); Poor (15).

Precis: Limitations and presuppositions of the inquiry from the viewpoint of Christian faith. Professional historians are stymied when faced with the question of the meaning of history as a whole. Can Christianity go further? Although it is impossible to present here a complete theology of history Rahner offers a few unsystematic remarks. He presumes faith in "everlasting life" as a culmination of the history of freedom, faith, hope, and love before God. He warns that merely assuming the meaning of history comes from God does not solve the question of human suffering.

The history of humanity as the history of freedom before God. Christianity maintains the history of humanity is a history of freedom tending towards its finality. It realizes freedom cannot easily be distinguished from constraint. Human freedom and absolute divine sovereignty cannot be resolved into a higher synthesis. All that can be said is that categorially free human acts do lead to something definitive: either to blessed completion or to eternal loss. "Human beings as Christians have the right and the sacred obligation to hope that for themselves and for all others...there will be a blessed conclusion to the history of freedom" (6) through surrender before the unfathomable disposition of the Lord of history. Nevertheless, the question of the meaningfulness of history as a whole remains open. It remains for the Christian a matter of hope.

The definitive meaning of history hidden in God. Christians hope the whole of human history will be resolved in luminous brightness and transparency. Yet this resolution only comes about in surrender to God when knowledge dissolves in love and one abandons the quest for an autonomous, individual meaning. This hope leaves unanswered the question of precisely how our perverse human egotism will finally be overcome. Summary (9).

On the dialectic character of the meaning of history. God as the meaning of history lies both within and beyond history, as its dynamism and its goal. This leaves open the question of whether the completion of history occurs within or beyond time.

On the problem of the relationship between the history of revelation and the profane history of humankind. Even though scientific history is unable to supply the ultimate meaning of history proclaimed by Christianity, it can grasp partial complexes of meaning for the individual and for societies. Sadly it seldom succeeds in connecting these fragments. Yet if as Christianity asserts, the coming of Jesus ushered in a new phase of history it is legitimate to expect some empirical evidence for its claim. Rahner believes it is easier to see such evidence if one extends the timeline of salvation- revelation-history back far earlier than Abraham to include the whole history of humanity and the contributions of the other great religions.

The realization of transcendence in history according to the Christian understanding. The historical search for meaning is a search for the eternally valid despite all contingency. Although they may disagree over precisely how to interpret it, all Christians profess the significance of the Christ-event: that in Christ the irrevocable promise of a blessed meaning of history to be revealed at the end has appeared. Hence, even though humanity may be seen to develop, history as such does not. However much human beings and human societies may change, theirs will always be a human history for which God revealed in Christ is the ultimate meaning and fulfillment. Because only God provides the meaning of history Christians remain anti-utopian.

On the relationship between the collective and the individual history of salvation. The meaning of history is not merely the aggregate of the meaning of individual lives. Nations and peoples too seem to have their proper meaning and fulfillment. Although states and individuals condition one another they do not simply combine to yield a single and complete structure of meaning. Precisely how they are related is beyond the power of human comprehension.

The "greats of history" and the "greatest in the kingdom of heaven." Christianity is radically anti-elitist. Although it maintains there is a hierarchy of holiness in the kingdom of heaven, this structure might in no way reflect the existing divisions on earth which separate the great and small.

21.02   Natural Science and Reasonable Faith
Naturwissenschaft und vernünftiger Glaube

{3.5}   A. Battke, ed., *Christlicher Glaube in moderner Gesellschaft*, vol. 3 (Freiburg im Breisgau 1981) 34-78, Part II of *Weltall—Erde—Mensch*.

Abstract: Any theory of evolution that includes the possibility of self-transcendence can be made compatible with Christianity although it may demand that theology rethink some borderline questions such as time and space, death and sin, extraterrestrial life, creation, size of the cosmos, etc.

Topics: SCIENCE and theology; THEOLOGY and science; EVOLUTION; THEOLOGICAL ANTHROPOLOGY, self-transcendence; MATTER and spirit.

Subsidiary Discussions: Epistemology (16ff); Dialogue (17f, 24ff); Science, method (19ff); Theological method (21ff); Agnosticism (23); Angels (29, 51, 55); Substance (30f); Creation (31ff); Time and space (31ff); Self-transcendence (34f, 37ff); Becoming (34f, 37ff); Causality, quasi-formal (36f); Soul, creation of (41ff); Animals, status of (42); Matter and form (44); Death and sin (46ff); Sin and death (43ff); Cosmos, size of (48ff); God, incomprehensibility of (50); Life, extraterrestrial (51f); History of salvation/cosmos (52ff); Resurrection of the body (52ff); Logos (51, 55).

OUTLINE:

Theological perspectives for dialogue with the natural sciences.

Preliminary questions on theological epistemology and the philosophy of science.

Possible coexistence of convictions and elements of knowledge not yet synthesized.

On the fundamental relationship between theology and natural science.
   –Natural Science: the investigation of concrete individual phenomena and their interrelation in a posteriori experience.
   –Theology: the a priori question about the totality of reality and its ground.

The possibility of secondary conflicts between theology and natural science.
   –The mutual trespassing of boundaries: example and background.
   –"Truce" or peace treaty? Presuppositions and possibilities of dialogue.

A general discussion of the basic themes of dialogue.
   –Spirit and matter in traditional metaphysics and in natural science today.
   –Matter and individual singular substance.

Createdness of the finite world as a problem of temporality.

The problem of evolution as seen by theology.
   –The methodological point of departure in the theological formulation of the question.
   –Belief in creation as the transcendental experience of the origination of all being from absolute being.
   –Divine causality: on the ontology of the relationship between God and what is created.
   –On the compatibility of the teachings of evolution and the Christian conception of the world.

The question of the human being in the framework of a general theory of evolution.
   –Empirical-biological anthropology and fundamental propositions of theological anthropology.
   –The transcendentality of the human subject and the conception of a universal evolution.

The problem of death: theological interpretation and the understanding of natural science.
   –Death as consequence of sin?
   –A distinction on theological grounds.

The size of the cosmos as an existentiell and theological problem.
   –Being lost in the cosmos as the expression and mediation of an ultimate experience of contingency.
   –A history of "spirit" on another star?

The History of human salvation and the natural history of the entire cosmos.

Precis: Theological perspectives for dialogue with the natural sciences.
Because theology has long ignored the borderline questions between itself
and science these remarks can only be brief and fragmentary.

**Preliminary questions on theological epistemology and the philosophy of
science.** Though it would be desirable to begin this dialogue with agreement
on certain epistemological questions, scientist are less conversant with
epistemology than theologians even regarding the foundations of science
itself. Theologians on the other hand have not achieved consensus among
themselves on this issue. In any case it is more often differences in history, culture,
and outlook rather than in epistemology which scuttle productive dialogue.

**Possible coexistence of convictions and elements of knowledge not yet
synthesized.** When a positive synthesis between contradicting possibilities
has not been achieved theologians should admit it is legitimate to hold both. Real
ongoing dialogue occurs in the open area between such contradictory positions.

On the fundamental relationship between theology and natural science.
Theology and natural science cannot in principle contradict one another
since they are distinct in content and method.

–Natural science: the investigation of concrete individual phenomena and
their interrelation in a posteriori experience. Natural science investigates a
posteriori individual phenomenon and their relation to one another. Theology concerns itself with the a priori question of the meaning and ground
of the whole of reality. Hence, one need not fear conflict between them
unless one discipline encroaches on the other. It flows from the nature of
natural science that it can never encompass the whole because: 1) however
many objects it may grow to encompass these are merely an aggregate and
never constitute the whole; 2) every bit of newly acquired knowledge
demands a reappraisal of what was formerly known.

–Theology: the a priori question about the totality of reality and its
ground. Theology makes affirmations about God as the one and absolute
ground of all realities. These are not proper questions for natural science
which is and should be methodologically atheistic. Theologians must avoid
temptations to explain natural phenomenon by positing God as simply one
more in a chain of empirical causes. The questions and methods of
metaphysics and theology need not and cannot be legitimized at the bar of
natural science. They proceed it logically and existentially whenever one
turns transcendental reflection onto oneself. For as difficult as it is clearly to
set out the point of departure for theology as the science of revelation (22f)
scientists must beware the danger of positivism that restricts reality to the
empirical. Such positivist agnosticism is itself a metaphysical system beyond
scientific proof.

**The possibility of secondary conflicts between theology and natural
science.** The secondary conflicts that regularly arise between theology and
natural science can and have been solved regularly once both disciplines
realize their conflicting statements are not absolutely contradictory.

–The mutual trespassing of boundaries: example and background. The reason for secondary conflicts is the trespassing of boundaries which is only noted when the aggrieved party brings it to the attention of the trespasser. Painful as this process may be, without it dialogue is impossible. Rahner lists illicit incursions by theology into science many of which occured in the long Enlightenment transition from the medieval to the modern mind (24f). Although today the church pursues a more humble and tolerant course it remains unclear whether all the conflicts which can be settled have been settled.

–"Truce" or peace treaty? Presuppositions and possibilities of dialogue. Most attempts at dialogue between theology and science break down because theologians and scientists know so little about one another. The situation today, which includes the inaccessibility of modern science to most people, leads at best to an uneasy truce between science and theology. Nonetheless, Rahner will attempt to say something about a few important scientific themes.

A general discussion of the basic themes of dialogue.

–Spirit and matter in traditional metaphysics and in natural science today. Because of the widely held theory of evolution theologians today can no longer be satisfied with the traditional textbook treatment of the relationship between matter and spirit (28). Rahner prefers the older scholastic approach which sees matter as basically spiritual based on its origin, destiny and capacities. Although there is a legitimate distinction between matter and spirit within the individual, nothing in theology prohibits this approach.

–Matter and individual singular substance. Much in modern science makes the application of the scholastic notion of individual substance problematic. This is a legitimate question as long as scientists do not deny the individual substantiality of the human subject.

Createdness of the finite world as a problem of temporality. Science's understanding of finite time and space have an impact on the Christian notion of creation—a notion less clear than some theologians admit. Because the affirmation that the world has been created is a theological and not scientific statement there can be no quarrel between them. Creation is not one act at the beginning of time by a first cause, but the continuing relationship of the world to its transcendent ground. Statements about the finiteness of the world are statements that distinguish the world from its ground. Natural time is an analogical extension of the free subject's inner experience of time pointing to the irreversibility of free choices and their orientation to finality.

The problem of evolution as seen by theology.

–The methodological point of departure in the theological formulation of the question. After equating the two evolutionary questions (development of the cosmos and of life) Rahner asserts there is no theological objection to affirming either. He proceeds to link the position of science with the hypothetical position of the theologian: "if sciences says this, then ...."

–Belief in creation as the transcendental experience of the origination of all being from absolute being. Since everything was created by an incomprehensible God all things, however diverse, share an ultimate unity. Matter is merely the lowest stage of spirit, all of which is ultimately intended, planned, and oriented to finality however difficult it may be to discern this in all its particulars.

–Divine causality: on the ontology of the relationship between God and what is created. The relationship of finite things to God is the single act of creation and preservation. This leads into a refutation of pantheism in favor of Rahner's notion of quasi-formal causality. The important conclusion he draws from this distinction is the existence of a divine pressure on things which makes them capable of becoming more than themselves.

–On the compatibility of the teachings of evolution and the Christian conception of the world. Rahner sees no reason theologians cannot embrace a radical notion of scientific evolution (38) which allows for the possibility of self-transcendence (that the greater can come from the smaller) provided: i) knowledge of the transcendental relationship of God to the world is seen as prior to scientific knowledge based on causality; ii) the capacity to become more is seen as a divine gift, not a necessary determinant of finite being (conclusion and summary, 39). In short, wherever natural science concedes in its theory of evolution the possibility of self-transcendence, theology need not postulate the intervention of a special divine causality to explain or safeguard the unique character of life or of animal consciousness.

The question of the human being in the framework of a general theory of evolution.

–Empirical-biological anthropology and fundamental propositions of theological anthropology. Since Pius XII, evolution has been an acceptable theory so long as it provides for the immediate creation by God of the spiritual soul (not a self-evident theological proposition). In lieu of a universal theological anthropology Rahner offers the following observation. Theologians need only insist on an essential distinction between people and animals based on what we know to be the person's fundamentally unlimited transcendentality and openness to being as such in knowledge and freedom (42).

–The transcendentality of the human subject and the conception of a universal evolution. Since human transcendence is always mediated through empirically sensory consciousness the human being is a unity of matter and spirit, however difficult it may be to bring this truth to reflexive clarity. What the scholastics said about matter and form remains valid even if today these terms are not the most apt. But even if human corporality can be explained within the context of evolution, what does it mean to reserve the creation of the soul to a creative act of God? If this theological proposition is meant to emphasize that human transcendence cannot be completely derived from material presuppositions then science already says as much in admitting self-transcendence. Great caution must be exerted if this proposition is linked to the idea that God intervenes in every human act of reproduction. Rahner contends that assuming divine causality is the dynamic ground and bearer of evolution is enough to describe "the creation of the soul." Summary (45f).

The problem of death: theological interpretation and the understanding of natural science.

–Death as consequence of sin? It is difficult to separate mythological from theological elements in scripture's paradisaical protology, especially in its claim that death is somehow the result of sin.

–A distinction on theological grounds. Rahner suggests theology can hold the scientific view that death is a normal part of life present from the beginning, even before the sin of Adam. It can also reserve the right to consider that death is now experienced existentially in a way quite different than it would have been experienced before the introduction of sin.

The size of the cosmos as an existentiell and theological problem.

–Being lost in the cosmos as the expression and mediation of an ultimate experience of contingency. The move from a geo-centric to a solar-centric to a gallacto-centric view of the cosmos fills people with existential dizziness. Rahner, however, finds this new scientific view "more theological" than the older one. The immeasurability of the cosmos is the spacial counterpart to the theological datum of God's incomprehensibility. We must learn to accept and live with both insights.

–A history of "spirit" on another star? Theologians need not resist the scientific speculation that there may well be intelligent consciousness elsewhere in the cosmos. Because a multiple incarnation of the Divine Logos in different histories of salvation is not absolutely unthinkable, theologians need not veto the very idea of extraterrestrial life.

The history of human salvation and the natural history of the entire cosmos. The fact that the evolutionary history of the cosmos contains the history of human freedom is not a problem for theologians who maintain that matter is ultimately spiritual and oriented toward spirit. From this vantage point human salvation is seen as the apex of the history of the cosmos located both outside the cosmos yet within it ("resurrection of the body"). The fact that these affirmations are currently unsynthesizable does not make it illegitimate to hold both simultaneously (cf., 18). Nor are these eschatological problems solved merely by labeling them future realities since the glorified Jesus and Mary exist in some relationship to the cosmos even now.

At the same time, evolutionists must allow room in their theories for the empirical fact of the existence of human freedom and self-transcendence in the evolutionary process. In such an evolutionary world, matter cannot be seen as purely provisional. This insight is preserved in the doctrine of the resurrection of the body. Even though it is impossible to form a concrete notion of this new reality, theologians need not resist this scientific conclusion. Finally, although the freedom Christians posit within the evolutionary process can help explain defective developments, dead ends, faltering progress, etc., Christians remain optimistic about its outcome. This is based on their faith in the irreversible totality of the history of freedom announced and achieved by the incarnate Logos, Jesus Christ.

21.03   Theology Today
Theologie heute

{1.5}   1980 lecture in Münster, Westphalia. H. Dollinger, ed., *Akademische Festreden zum Jubiläum 1980. Schriftenreihe der Westfälischen Wilhelms-Universität Münster*, No. 1 (Münster 1980) 43-54.

Abstract: When pursued properly theology is the gadfly to university sciences (historical, natural, social) by insisting as it does on their relativity.
Topics: GOD; THEOLOGY and science; SCIENCE and theology.
Subsidiary Discussions: God-talk (59f, 68f).
Precis: By what right does theology claim to be a science and deserve a place in the university? Tolerant indifference is not reason enough to include it and lack of popular interest is not reason enough to exclude it.
The history of theology in the university. If theology were dismissed from the university would it not have to be admitted in another guise (history of culture, etc.)? How can an institution based on neutrality dismiss the study of theology on anti-clerical bias? After all, modern theology attempts to embrace all religions and produces as much scholarship as other disciplines.
The task of theology in the university. Rahner now turns to the task theology accomplishes in particular without claiming this task is unique to theology.

–The concern of theology is God. If the essential concern of theology is not God but merely talk about God, then it is simply funeral orations for God. This God is the unutterable, ineffable mystery whom Christians believe draws near in the person of Jesus Christ. This primordial ground of reality is the only proper object of theology whereas the proper object of the other sciences are particular, concrete realities. Thus, theology addresses all people whether or not they want to be addressed. It speaks to everyone of the death of Jesus precisely to address their own concerns over death.

–Theology and the natural sciences. Although other university sciences may accept theology as one like themselves (the science of religion) they grow hostile when theology addresses each of them and the world outside the temple of science. Theology is threatened with expulsion when its proper object cannot be identified as simply another object within the scope of other sciences. No wonder theology becomes timid. Nevertheless, Rahner insists theology should not withdraw from the university because it alone speaks of that to which the person belongs and not simply of that which belongs to the person. It radically opposes absolutizing any immanent reality studied by other sciences. The God it proclaims makes all else provisional. All sciences risk absolutizing themselves. When they transgress their limits they cease to be themselves and begin to pursue theology. Rahner shows how this is true for the historical sciences (65), natural sciences (65f), and social sciences (66f).

–Theology and *universitas*. Though it is subject to all the pettiness of any other discipline, at its best theology is the gad fly of the university. Too often it keeps its place because it does not practice what it preaches: the holy relativism and silent openness to the ineffable mystery. When theologians discuss "God-talk" instead of the mystery of God they betray their ultimate task and become mere philosophers or scientists of religion. They should not then be surprised if their remarks sound jaded and go unheeded.

21.04 The Present Situation of Catholic Theology
Zur momentanen Situation der katolischen Theologie
{1.0} Previously unpublished. September 1979 radio lecture, *Stand der katholischen Theologie heute.*
Abstract: Rahner's overview of the last hundred years of Catholic theology awards current theology a "C." To improve, theology needs more human and financial resources and must commit itself to the theology of proclamation.
Topics: THEOLOGY, modern.
Subsidiary Discussions: Theology, history of (71ff); Theology, neo-scholastic (71f).
Precis: Theology today is no longer a European affair. It is as pluralistic as the geographic locations in which faith thrives. Its contact with other sciences has led to the development of many new problems and new approaches. This pluralism makes it impossible to give an exact account of theology today.
The change in Catholic theology. Theology in the first half of this century was dominated by neo-scholasticism. Ecclesial theology was static, defensive, self-absorbed, and middle class.
The new theology. The theology of the second half of the century was deeply influenced by modern trends in biblical exegesis. It was less dogmatic, more conversant with modern philosophy, and more open to the milieu in which contemporary Christians had to live their faith. As a result it was more attuned to the concrete questions of everyday people. This brought with it a great pluralism in theology and led to finding new answers in the realms of morality, ecumenism, exegesis, etc. This new theology has definitively replaced neo-scholasticism without thereby annulling its great value.
Theology today. What can be said of post-Vatican II theology? From his 1979 vantage point Rahner saw no significant threat to the new theology despite certain curial tendencies. There was nothing on the horizon to challenge it.

A patient continuation. Since Vatican II the vibrant enthusiasm of new theology has waned. We are in a pallid phase of "patient continuation" with no clear successors to the brilliant theologians of the recent past (list, 74f).

The advancement of theology. Since the quality of theology is also influenced by its environment it is fair to ask whether theologians have been sufficiently encouraged (verbally or financially) by church officials.

The tasks of theology. What should systematic theologians do today? Rahner insists their theology must serve the proclamation of the gospel. They must consider non-believers as well as believers. Only the radical unity they forge by word and deed between fundamental and dogmatic theology will reveal the credibility of living the faith today in a genuine way. Theologians must be faithful without reverting to pietism; authoritative without relying merely on appeals to Roman authority; relevant without becoming slaves of novelty.

21.05   Aspects of European Theology
   Aspekte europäischer Theologie
{1.5}   K.-H. Neufeld, ed., *Problemi e prospettive di teologia dogmatica* (Brescia 1983).

Abstract: Though Roman teaching authority will continue to enjoy a place of special privilege and duty, it can learn much by accommodating itself to the emerging, non-European theologies as it already has from Eastern religions.

Topics: THEOLOGY, European; FAITH, unity of; MAGISTERIUM.
Subsidiary Discussions: Theology, pluralism in (79ff); Mystery (84f); Church, subsidiarity in (88f); Theology, political (93); Dialogue, inter-theological (94).
Precis: **General preliminary considerations.** Today the science of theology must include self-reflection on its historical, social, and cultural circumstances. This will reveal the hidden factors which shaped and limited it. This task can only be done by theologians since the critic must be a person of faith.

   –Different forms of theology. There is an underlying unity to the diverse forms theology takes in diverse circumstances. Pluralism in theology cannot be a harmful aberration since the magisterium itself has sanctioned competing theologies. But precisely how can the unity of faith be maintained in a situation of theological pluralism? It is only possible with a strong eschatological hope and with faith in the presence within the church of the divine grace of truth (summary, 81). Unity of faith cannot be achieved by minimizing differences between theologies or resolving them in a false Hegelian synthesis.

   –Theology in a worldwide church. So long as European theology held sway theological pluralism was not as acute a problem as it is today within a "world-church." But without minimizing the differences among theologies how can a concrete religion be universally present in all civilizations without forfeiting its historical identity? How can these theologies coexist without simply being homogenized? Rahner briefly suggests their unity can be found in the fact they are all related to "the unity and immediacy of the absolute God ...related to Jesus, crucified and risen ..." (84). Their unity is founded on the assumption that human beings are able to reach mutual understanding both on the level of sign and on the level of truth, both of which are filled with the grace of God, "God himself" (85), the ineffable mystery.

European theology. Because of its complexity one cannot show the particular task of European theology within the church by first describing its unique character.

–The theology of *Rome* and the theology of the worldwide church. Here "European church" refers to the Roman teaching office. Without denying its authority, Rahner insists it too has a distinctive theology without which it cannot fulfill its mandate from the Holy Spirit. Up to now that theology has been European neo-scholasticism. Not only has this theology made mistakes and will continue to do so, with the rise of non-European theologies the danger of errors and misunderstandings will only increase. How can these dangers be countered? Certainly not by Rome forfeiting its duty to teach authoritatively. Nor is the internationalization of the curia a sufficient counterweight to these dangers (87f). Rahner ends this discussion with a call for greater local subsidiarity and greater circumspection on the part of Rome in involving itself in local problems.

–European theology as the guardian of tradition. Due to God's mysterious disposition, European theology will always be elder sister to emerging theologies. This "favoritism" implies both a privilege and an inescapable obligation to guard and preserve the tradition of the faith of the first two millennia. It does this not only in its teaching and research but more especially by the way it lives the faith and witnesses to it in new and credible ways. By taking a critical view of itself it can help emerging theologies to see which of the elements it contains are binding and which are merely European. European theology with its Enlightenment heritage is uniquely able to engage in this process of self-reflection.

–European theology and today's world civilization. Assuming cultural pluralism is good, European theology can perhaps discern for itself the new task of preserving cultural pluralism from the threatening onslaught of European "rational-technical" civilization which some say was fostered by Christianity and seems at least partially responsible for the loss of the numinous in today's world. Perhaps European political theology could assist emerging theologies to avoid the pitfalls of past European theology.

–European theology as mediator among the other theologies. At the purely technical level European theology will continue to be the broadest, most intensive, most scientific, and best financed school of theology. For this reason and because other theologies have their roots in European theology it is in the best position to mediate among various emerging theologies. Intercommunication must be cultivated to overcome any tendencies the emerging theologies may have to isolate themselves. But European theology can only mediate authentically if it gives up its own tendency to dominate.

–European theology as a safeguard against the dangers threatening the other theologies. Rahner cites two such dangers: identifying elements within their native, non-Christian cultures as compatible with the Christian message when they are not, or dismissing essential elements of European theology as unnecessary simply because they are European. "It is often easier for an outsider [read European theology] to discern the elements in a culture which correspond internally to the Christian message" (95).

–European theology in the process of learning. Although the non-European theologies Rahner anticipates do not yet exist, they are inevitable. By anticipating and accommodating the problems these new theologies will bring, European theology can pave their way and in the process could learn a great deal. Rahner cites two examples of European theology learning from non-Western spirituality: transmigration of souls and meditation. He also sees a positive result of taking Eastern religions more seriously in the way European theology today accords a higher priority to pneumatology and to the doctrine of grace over christology (97f). If European theology has already benefitted so much by taking non-Christian religions more seriously, how much more could it gain from the emerging Christian theologies?

21.06 A Theology That We Can Live With
Einen Theologie, mit der wir leben können

{1.5} Previously unpublished July 1982 lecture to theology faculty at the University of Würzburg.

Abstract: Rahner touches various topics: the nature of theology; why theologians must possess faith; the basic course in theology; why theology must be both ecclesial and intellectually rigorous; the place of mystery in theology.

Topics: THEOLOGY, education.

Subsidiary Discussions: Faith and theology (100ff); Truths, hierarchy of (105ff); Theology, fundamental (110f); Theology and magisterium (107f); Revelation (110f); Mystery (111f).

Precis: Theology for life—but for what life? It is wrong to approach this question as if one already possesses a fully formed life apart from theology into which one must see to it theology can be fit. Furthermore if one equates modern life with a culture that disallows non-empirical sciences from the outset then obviously theology has no place.

Theology and the reality of faith. Rahner does not mean by theology what a few researchers are paid to do, however legitimate such academic theology may be. The claim that theology is worthwhile for life "presupposes an existentiell relationship to the reality of faith.... Theology is a science of faith in the bosom of the Church, and this is the only way it can be pursued, pursued, that is, in a way that one can live with it" (101). Though it is legitimate for young theologians to turn to academic theology to ground their faith, reflexive argumentation neither must nor can catch up with naive faith.

Theology as a special discipline. What concrete form must theology take today for people to be able to live with it? Without denigrating specialized fields of academic theology (e.g., Christian archeology, medieval exegesis) young theologians today are looking for a theology that can orient them among the conflicting theological claims and help them lead more religious lives. In comparison, scientific theology can seem to be of secondary importance. Though their legitimate concerns do not absolve young theologians from the rigors of academic theology, such academic endeavors are clearly not ends in themselves.

Suprascientific theology. Theology must reach beyond the confines of "science" and concentrate on the core: the really fundamental, life and death problems for Christianity (list, 104f)—"suprascientific theology."

A hierarchy of truths. Rahner distinguishes a three-fold hierarchy of truths: an objective hierarchy; a socially subjective hierarchy based on the cultural/social moment; a personal hierarchy which each person, especially young theologians, must work out for themselves.

A course in the fundamentals of faith. Although Vatican II envisioned a "sufficiently long introductory course into the mystery of salvation" (105) it has not yet materialized. Rahner sees it as a blend of fundamental and systematic theologies. In its absence young theologians must assume the responsibility of hammering it out for themselves...developing their own hierarchy of truths, "so that they can really live with their theology" (107).

Ecclesial theology. Any basic course in theology must be "ecclesial." Although there is a legitimate place for dissent in the church, it is not enough for young theologians to fasten on areas of conflict with the magisterium. Their theologies must help them to live and work within the church.

A thinking theology. Theology can never dispense with rigorous, sharp, logical, precise philosophical thinking. Though theology always involves a recourse to mystery it does not demand a *sacrificium intellectus* at the outset. Rahner details what this means for theologians today (109f).

A theology of revelation. This special section underscores the fact that no theologian today can bypass the central question of revelation.

A theology of mystery. Theology today must be a theology of mystery not of mere propositions. Recourse to mystery is not the admission of an embarrassing remnant. It is actually what is meant by God. It is the core of theology and comes even before the beginning of academic theology. Summary (112).

21.07   The Mature Christian
Die mündige Christ
{1.5}   *Stimmen der Zeit* 200 (1982) 3-13.

Abstract: Because mature Christians today are more free and responsible than believers in previous generations they find greater challenges in faith, morality, and church law. Therefore they need greater courage and wisdom.
Topics: CHRISTIAN LIFE, maturity; CONSCIENCE; CHRISTIAN LIFE, courage.
Subsidiary Discussions: Moral norms (universal) (118f); Magisterium, binding (122ff); Truths, hierarchy of (122f); Theology, moral (123ff); Law, church (126ff); Law, marriage (128); Freedom and maturity (128f).
Precis: Rahner analyzes a catchword of post-Vatican II Christianity: maturity. The church has always recognized various levels of maturity among its members who are all continually challenged to become more mature.

The situation today. Human maturity has entered an essentially new phase marked by a huge increase in the number of issues presented to the individual for responsible decision. In this vastly more complex secular world people have actually become more immature. Because they find it increasingly difficult to apply universal norms to these complex problems people today also feel more helpless. Summary (119).

The essence of maturity. At its core maturity is the courage to make decisions in the absence of universally accepted norms. Such maturity presumes the willingness to inform onself, the readiness to be self-critical, and a host of other virtues and attributes.

The maturity of the Christian in the church. Christian maturity cannot be divorced from secular maturity. In the church too the present situation is more highly complex than ever before. Church members are better educated and live in much more pluralistic cultures.

Maturity in questions of faith. Educated believers must weigh the church's teachings on complex moral issues against their own knowledge and experience. To do this they must be able to distinguish the binding force of church pronouncements. They also need a sense of the hierarchy of truths. In this way they can reduce potential areas of conflict with the church. When mature people, both in the church and in secular society, come to a kind of personal truce they bear the remaining conflicts calmly and with patience.

Maturity in questions of morality. Tensions are prevalent in the area of Christian morality, especially concerning sexual morality where the church's magisterium can issue erroneous statements. Rahner quotes at length from a 1967 letter of the German bishops (123ff). The magisterium has the twofold responsibility of advancing binding teachings *and* leaving Christians alone, respecting their proper responsibility for the ultimate decision in cases where it feels incapable of rendering a binding decision. Summary (126).

Maturity and church law. Although church law has a dogmatic core of a binding nature, its concrete form, its concrete norms, and its mode of implementation are human traditions and by no means binding. Whereas the conflicts that arise over church teachings on faith and morality concern borderline areas of divine revelation, the conflicts over church law are essentially human realities and hence in this area Christian conscience has a broader kind of leeway. Examples (127f).

Courage for greater freedom. "Maturity means courage for greater freedom and this freedom means greater responsibility" (128). Maturity entrusts us with our own problems and makes us more lonely. Though the church today offers guidelines it cannot provide concrete solutions in advance. Summary (129).

21.08 Justifying Faith in an Agnostic World
Glaubensbegründung in einer agnostischen Welt
{2.0} March 1983. *Frankfurter Allgemeine Zeitung*, Saturday Supplement no. 84, as, *Der brennender Schmerz unserer Existenz.*
Abstract: By identifying the inescapable core of life's incomprehensibility as the personal God of Jesus Christ, Rahner argues that the only radical agnosticism is actually Christian faith.
Topics: FAITH, agnosticism; GOD, incomprehensibility of; GOD, experience of; HOPE.
Subsidiary Discussions: Jesus Christ, eternal validity of (135f).
Precis: **The roots of agnosticism**. Many today despair of finding certainty. They fear their ideas are little more than a nebulous haze disconnected from true reality. Faced with the incomprehensibility of things they feel uncertain.
On the situation of agnosticism. Rahner outlines three possible responses to incomprehensibility. Many try to repress life's unfathomable dimension, though even a staunch denial could be interpreted as anonymous belief. But how to face this "burning pain of our existence" (132) is today's unique, original experience of God. Contemporary theism is impossible without an open encounter with this kind of agnosticism
Agnosticism and the experience of God. Agnosticism is not today's only experience of God.
The incomprehensibility of God. The essence of faith is to interpret life's uncertainty as saving mystery, not despite but *because* of its incomprehensibility. We can never be sure whether or not our commitment is really a desperate act of self-assertion. We can only hope. Accepting the incomprehensible is accepting a personal God and not merely an impersonal "it." This is because incomprehensibility is the very core of personhood.
Jesus of Nazareth. Christ is the eternally valid, ultimate witness of the trustworthiness of God. In solidarity with him we dare to hope in God.

True agnosticism. Unconditional self-surrender to God is the only radical agnosticism because every other position views agnosticism as innocuous. Philosophical agnosticism is the unsuccessful attempt at the true agnosticism demanded of Christians who adore in hope and love the Incomprehensibility which is called God.

21.09   The Church and Atheism
Kirche und Atheismus
{1.5}   October 1980 lecture at Rome to Pontifical Urban University. *Stimmen der Zeit* 199 (1981) 3-13.

Abstract: From the rise of modern atheism Rahner concludes: Catholic theology is not yet ready for serious dialogue; the church is the sacrament of salvation even for atheists; atheism must be resisted with intelligent courage.

Topics: ATHEISM; GOD, belief in.

Subsidiary Discussions: God, incomprehensibility of (140ff, 148); Church as *sacramentum salutis mundi* (142ff); Anonymous Christian (144ff); Theology, ecumenical (148f).

Precis: For all its variations, world-wide, post-Enlightenment atheism (the result of social, rational, and technological developments) enjoys universal recognition and shares common assumptions and characteristics. Christianity is still not sufficiently prepared to meet its challenge.

Readiness for dialogue. Despite Vatican II's call for dialogue with atheism little has happened. Both atheists and believers are responsible for this impasse. Atheists are split into various camps. The church is hobbled by its Enlightenment-era theism. It tends to see God as one object among others and fails to appreciate God's radical incomprehensibility and the alarming and agonizing way people experience the question of God today. By and large the modern theology of God fails to grapple with the human existential dilemma and hence, its arguments end up convincing only those who already believe.

The church as universal sign of salvation. Vatican II insisted the church is the sacrament of salvation for atheists also. Since the church is the concrete sign of the promise and the efficacious grace of salvation even for those who are not visibly incorporated as its members, it is such for atheists as well. This assumes people can be atheists and remain inculpable. Rahner refers to such persons as anonymous Christians. Summary (146).

The struggle against atheism. Since modern atheism is not innocuous, Christians must struggle against it courageously with all legitimate means. It radically contradicts the central Christian belief (either explicitly or by indifference) and can lead people to disregard even the dictates of their own consciences. Nevertheless, the struggle against atheism is always primarily the struggle against a primitive picture of God which by denying God's incomprehensibility makes God into an idol. It is a struggle with the adequacy of our own theism.

Rahner suggests the value of an alliance of believers ("theistic ecumenists") to counter modern atheism. Such an alliance might have the further result of easing strife among various religions and teaching the church things about itself and how it is seen by other believers. Rahner also suggests combating atheism by rearranging our proclamation, emphasizing the central tenet of belief in God and downplaying lesser truths (e.g., indulgences). He also suggests this theme could be the subject of a papal encyclical, although it would have to be written in a radically new way.

21.10 The Act of Faith and the Content of Faith
Glaubenakt und Glaubensinhalt.
{3.5} E. Hultsch, K. Lüthi, eds., *Bekennendes Bekenntnis. Form und Formulierung christlichen Glaubens* (Gütersloh 1982) 63-71, as, *Fides qua—Fides quae.*

Abstract: Rahner distinguishes *fides quae* from *fides qua* without falling into modernism by insisting that although the content of saving faith is universal (radicalized human transcendentality) it depends on historical revelation.

Topics: FAITH, *fides quae/qua*; GRACE; REVELATION; SUPERNATURAL EXISTENTIAL.

Subsidiary Discussions: Knowledge, co-natural (152f, 154f); Virtues, theological (155f); History (157ff); Dogma, development of (159f); Faith, absolute assent of (160f); Magisterium (159ff).

Precis: Faith is reality in the human being. In everyday thinking the distinction between the act of faith and the content of the act of faith seems to present no problem. But it cannot be explained without a theory of their precise relationship which is obscure and difficult. How can it be explained theologically without either making the precise content of faith completely dispensable, or making the act of faith completely neutral? Today's ecumenical and inter-religious dialogue makes this enquiry essential. It also presents serious challenges to New Testament scholarship since scripture seems to insist that to be saved one must believe certain things about Jesus, whereas Vatican II teaches that even atheists can be saved (i.e., have a saving *fides qua* without many seemingly essential elements of the Christian *fides quae*).

Rahner proposes a tightly worded thesis to address this problem (153f) maintaining that the *fides qua* available to all people possesses essentially the same revelation content as New Testament revelation, although for the non-Christian it remains unobjectified. After insisting that this thesis in no way bypasses the unique place of Jesus Christ, Rahner adds a few observations.

Revelation: radicalizing transcendentality. Everyone accepts co-natural knowledge: our capacity to be conscious of something without being able to objectify it verbally. For Rahner the grace of the theological virtues is one such type of co-natural knowledge. It is God's free gift which bestows on all people a permanent capacity, the condition for the possibility of any salutary act (believing, hoping, or loving). The theological virtues present to consciousness a new formal object (i.e., God) which cannot otherwise be known. This is what Rahner means by the gift of grace which radicalizes human transcendentality to the immediacy of God. Rahner connects three notions to this concept: that grace is always and everywhere present at least in the mode of divine offer of self-communication; that revelation is gratuitous, oriented to a new formal object which is personal, and fundamentally historical; that because revelation is a kind of co-natural knowledge one need not insist every dimension of revelation be mediated in a concrete event in the strict sense.

History: the place where revelation occurs. Grounding the theological content of the *fides qua* in this way in no way diminishes its content. Here Rahner distinguishes his understanding from that of modernism (G. Tyrell) by drawing out the ramifications of the historicity of revelation (158). Rahner ends this section by comparing the *fides quae* of an individual with that of the church itself. For him it is obvious the two are not simply identical. The content of the church's faith, covering as it does a great expanse of time, is necessarily fuller and more variated. But the content of an individual's faith may be richer because it is lived at a deeper and more personal level. In many important ways the faith of the church relies on that of the individual for its dynamic development. It is often the individual who first grasps a truth which only becomes clear to the wider community, including the teaching magisterium, at a later time.

Justifying faith on its "grounds." Rahner concludes with remarks on the "absolute assent of faith" (160) individual Christians are expected to make to the content of the church's faith. Rarely is this assent grounded in the individual's belief in the church's teaching authority. More likely it is grounded in the objective and existentiell structure of one's *fides quae*—in a Christian's experience of God and of Jesus Christ rather than in the teaching authority of the church. However regrettable it may be, the assent of faith of people today is more often "provisional" than absolute, and it is difficult to say which statements in particular are held with absolute assent. Most likely the answer to this question changes over time. Today neither the authority of scripture nor of the magisterium grounds the faith of most believers. As a result it is not sufficient for the Catholic Church to assume that merely proclaiming a truth will convince believers to give it their assent. It must be argued on its own merits.

21.11   A Hierarchy of Truths
Hierarchie der Warheiten
{1.0}   *Diakonia* 13 (1982) 376-382.

Abstract: Rahner suggests Vatican II's teaching on the hierarchy of truths leaves many important unresolved questions with significant theological and pastoral implications.
Topics: TRUTHS, hierarchy of.
Subsidiary Discussions: Faith, *fides quae/qua* (163); Creed (164); Dogma, development of (164f).
Precis: Central truths and remote truths. Though it is not the most important teaching of Vatican II, the hierarchy of truths will continue to have a significant effect on theology and pastoral practice.
The Second Vatican Council's Decree on Ecumenism. The basic conciliar notion that truths are of greater or lesser importance based on their proximity to the foundations of faith leaves many significant problems unresolved.
The fundamental truths. What is the foundation of faith? In addition to the New Testament (itself problematic) Rahner considers whether one might find the foundations of faith in traditional creeds. But however venerable they may be, these creeds do not say all that is needed about faith in every age.
The "existentiell" hierarchy of truths. Rahner identifies both an "objective" hierarchy of truths and an "existentiell" hierarchy of truths based on the importance of the particular truths to the faith of the individual. Realizing these two are bound to be somewhat different, one still hopes to find them closely approximated. What is true in the life of the individual is also true of history. Only this can explain and justify the fact of the development of doctrine as well as the legitimate diversity found in different schools of spirituality. It is absolutely and unavoidably clear that truths advance and recede in importance over time.
Changing plausibilities. From a pastoral point of view we ought to become more aware and analyze more profoundly this existentiell hierarchy of truths.
Questions to those engaged in pastoral work. Although this notion of a hierarchy of truths may at first sound foreign, whoever has tried to summarize the faith of the church in fifteen minutes to any non-Christian understands what this terminology signifies.

21.12   Christianity's Absolute Claim
Über den Absolutheitsanspruch des Christentums
{3.0}   *Informationszentrum Berufe der Kirche, Antwort des Glaubens*, no. 21
(Freiburg im Breisgau 1981), as, *Stribt das Christentum aus?*

Abstract: Despite changes in how it is expressed, essential Christianity will
never pass away because the God revealed in Jesus Christ answers the deepest,
unsurpassable longings of the human person.
Topics: CHRISTIANITY, essential; GOD, Christian concept of; JESUS
CHRIST.
Subsidiary Discussions: Image and reality (172f); History, goal of (175f);
Hope, Christian (178f).
Precis: How can one respond to those who wonder whether Christianity,
like so many other religions, will someday come to an end?

Changing forms and views. Admittedly much of Christianity is of human
making, is conditioned by time and circumstances, and hence, is destined to
die out. This is true of many religious practices and theological views because
truths are always clothed in time bound images and conceptions. Christian
faith must always separate what it means from how it conveys these truths.
Summary (173).

Has Christianity's time passed? No one knows how many Christians there
will be in the future. The real question is whether what Christianity actually
means (its permanent validity) will one day be cast aside. Granting the
existence of eternally valid concepts (e.g., the principle of non-contradiction, historical statements, certain moral demands) Rahner underscores the
possibility that particular historical actions can possess irrevocable finality.

What does "Christianity" actually mean? In its ultimate essence Christianity teaches that the finite world has an absolute, infinite, primordial ground:
God. Hence, God is not merely one object among others. Nor is God an
eternally distant mystery beyond the world. Rather God is the innermost
principle of the world's movement. In the history of free personal spirit God
becomes our immediately present goal and makes possible both faith in and
self-surrender to the incomprehensible mystery of our existence. In this way
God is the completion of human history.

Does history have a goal? Christianity also makes the unique assertion that
the world has a history. It is experienced as the history of freedom in
individual human beings themselves. This history is a mix of triumph and
tragedy, the culpable and the innocent. Honest self-reflection can never fully
decide whether history will achieve its goal. That is why human beings are
always searching history for an answer to this question which cannot be
evaded.

Jesus—God's definitive promise of himself in history. Our encounter with
Jesus Christ, crucified and risen, convinces Christians that in him we meet
the concrete form of God's promise to bestow himself on human history so
that it actually achieves its goal. The church is the historical continuance, the

fellowship of faith in God's self-promise and palpable presence. To know this is what is meant by "God" and "Jesus" is to know the core of Christianity. **Christian faith cannot become obsolete.** Proponents of skeptical resignation can never be refuted. Christian hope on the other hand is convinced there will always be people who hope and believe in the unsurpassable completion of their own history and that of the world. No other religion can replace this hope since it is the ultimate human hope. Skeptical relativism is the only alternative. Christians themselves must never reduce the content of their faith in the full completion of human history. There is no greater human destiny than the incomprehensible God. "In the act of unconditional surrender to the incomprehensibility of God who is loved the fear that this might one day be obsolete is dissolved. And this is Christianity" (179).

The abiding significance of Jesus for us. Does this render Jesus ultimately superfluous? After recalling that even a "mystical-universal religion of an abstract idea of God" (179-180) requires a concrete historical embodiment, Rahner insists that belief in Jesus does not nullify belief in the incomprehensible God but rather realizes this faith more precisely. Jesus' life, death, and resurrection is God's definitive invitation to surrender ourselves to his irrevocable promise which alone saves us. Jesus is the imperishable testimony to the effective possibility of arriving at immediacy to the true God. No previous prophet or religious leader ever gave such testimony. No future prophet can ever promise more. Jesus has already promised "everything" in an unsurpassable way. Summary (181).

Is Christianity's existence threatened from within? Yes. Rahner warns that the legalism and ritualism, thirst for power, and worldliness within the church threaten to obscure and distort the Christian's authentic relationship to God. It jeopardizes the future of the church and must constantly be resisted.

Courage for the future of faith. Although one can only speculate at the future size and influence of the church, nothing proves the essence of the church will ever be superseded. Although its institutional structures will continue to change as they always have (e.g., 182f) there will always be people who go forward to an infinite promise, gazing on Jesus in faith, hope, and love. Because this future is already present in faith, today's believers are responsible for the future of Christianity. Rahner ends on an autobiographical note. He insists one must not abandon the faith s/he has been bequeathed except for the gravest reasons. He has never found such grave reasons.

21.13   The Specific Character of the Christian Concept of God

Über die Eigenart des christlichen Gottesbegriffs
{3.0}   December 1981 lecture to *Club Pro Wien*. *Diakonia* 13 (1982) 150-159.

Abstract: Christianity makes two unique claims about God based not on natural metaphysics but on positive revelation. God who is distinct from the world is also its innermost dynamism and goal; in the incarnation of Jesus the world has irrevocably entered the phase of its blessed conclusion.

Topics: GOD, Christian concept of; CHRISTIANITY; REVELATION.
Subsidiary Discussions: Reason, natural (185f); Freedom, divine/human (191f).
Precis: Whether or not Christianity has its own specific concept of God is more difficult to answer than most people might think.

The ability to know God by natural reason. Catholic theologians must maintain with Vatican I that the existence of the true God can be known with certainty by the light of natural reason *and* that divine revelation by word is a moral necessity for pure and complete knowledge. Because such knowledge can occur outside Christian revelation this becomes a complex problem.

The efficacy of revelation even outside of Israelite and Christian history of religion. Other factors which further complicate this issue are the distinction between divine revelation (from above) and human attempts to know God (from below); Vatican II's insistence on the universal salvific will of God; hermeneutic problems surrounding biblical revelation.

The ancient biblical concept of God and the Near Eastern history of religion. For example, one need not insist the God of the Old Testament is unique simply because Israel's God alone was a God of history and covenant.

Historical development of the Christian concept of God. The Christian concept of God has a history. We can assume it will have a future subject to numerous transformations and unexpected turns. Since that future concept may well be influenced by non-Christian theologies we must be careful not to insist that what seems particular to the Christian God today will always seem so.

Positive statements on the specific character of the Christian concept of God. Rahner offers a positive statement about the distinctly Christian concept of God, realizing it is not the only statement that could be made.

The relationship between God and the world. This is a twofold relationship.

–The God who dwells beyond the world. In this non-Christian view God dwells beyond the world and communicates to it by means of mediators which are not God. Salvation consists in recognizing this unbridgeable distance.

–God's self-communication. Christianity, however, maintains that God in his own reality is the fulfillment of finite existence. Despite the fact that average Christians do not perceive this, because creatures are able to receive God's life as their own perfection, creatures really are *capax infiniti*. God is both giver and gift. Rahner calls this a paradox (191).

The reciprocal relationship of freedom. However problematic the concept of freedom may be today (list, 191f) Christianity can only be thought of as a reciprocal relationship of freedom between God and personal, spiritual creatures. Far from canceling each other out, it is only the existence of mutual freedom which makes anything unique or definitive in salvation- revelation-history possible. In principle it is legitimate to ask what phase this history has reached.

The history of revelation and the history of salvation. Within its own strict confines human history cannot determine whether salvation will be gained or lost. But with the historical event of Jesus' incarnation, history entered a phase of the irrevocable assurance of salvation. God's eternal plan succeeds without abrogating human freedom. In the incarnation God offers human freedom more than a mere possibility of salvation. God transforms this offer into an irreversible reality. God demands a free response without determining it.

The Christian concept of God. As opposed to atheism, pantheism, deism, polytheism, and panentheism, Christianity lets God be God (according to Vatican I: one, almighty creator, incomprehensible, and essentially different from the world). Since historical Christianity never claims to be able to attain a pure concept of God, everything it says about God is derived from actual revelation (not limited to Old and New Testament) and not from metaphysical knowledge deduced from the created world as such. Rahner offers a dense summary of the two characteristics positive revelation makes known about God and God's relationship to the world: i) that God is the inner dynamic of the world; ii) its history has been definitively achieved in Jesus (195). If at a later point it can be shown that these characteristics are also present in non-Christian religions, theologians would most likely speculate that due to God's universally salvific will, faith and salvation are possible everywhere.

21.14 The Question of Meaning as a Question of God
Die Sinnfrage als Gottesfrage

{2.5} June 1982 lecture at Freiburg im Breisgau to *Reinhold-Schneider-Stiftung. Reinhold-Schneider-Stiftung Hamburg*, no. 20 (1982) 21-28.

Abstract: "Absolute meaning" and "God" explain one another. The question of total meaning, if it is not denied and if it is permitted full articulation, contains its own answer. It is what Christians call "God" [cf., 21.15].

Topics: GOD as absolute meaning; MEANING, absolute.

Subsidiary Discussions: Agnosticism (197ff); Skepticism (197ff); Reason (198ff); Freedom (198ff); Mystery (203f); God, proofs for (205); Revelation (206); Anonymous Christian (206f).

Precis: People today seem more interested in the question of meaning than in the question of truth. Whatever this may mean, Rahner does not explore it here because for him God is both absolute meaning and absolute truth.

Understanding meaning in its totality. "[T]he meaning of human life" refers to the one, total, universal, and definitive meaning of the whole of human existence which reveals itself as something good and beatific. Rahner hopes to prove this notion is identical with God. To prove it one must presume the existence, meaningfulness, and answerability of such a question. This is not self-evident. Agnostics and skeptics admit there are moments of meaning, but their failure to experience over-arching meaning and the seeming senselessness of finitude keep them from believing in any absolute meaning.

Exerting reason and freedom. Affirming absolute meaning requires the utmost effort of reason and freedom. It takes a complete, free commitment in a reciprocal interpenetration of knowledge and freedom, theory and practice, insight and love. Even though it does not compel a particular answer, the simple act of being responsible to our own reason and freedom confronts us with the question of absolute meaning (list, 199). Attempts at evasion point to the unique nature of this particular question: that total meaning is not simply one object or idea among others. It brings us face to face with the infinite, with the obscure and the unmasterable.

The human being confronted with the question of meaning. This unavoidable question of total meaning Rahner calls "a question of conscience," one which makes neutral abstention impossible. Total meaning cannot be pieced together from things that yield partial meaning. It is conceivable only "outside" the course of history. The comprehensive meaning of history can never be a mere fragment of history, even though there is an open transcendence toward (a prehension of) complete meaning in the act of grasping any historical fact. Affirming absolute meaning frees people from those individual realities that would otherwise enslave them. Rahner counters the argument that even people with no hope in absolute meaning bear up as well as believers by suggesting the former have not yet really comes to grips with the void.

Before turning to the relation between God and absolute meaning Rahner further clarifies his notion of meaning (203f): that it is unencompassable mystery. When we speak of this mystery we are in fact referring to our own existence. To admit and surrender to it in love is nothing other than accepting our own true nature. This raises an odd crisis: total meaning, far from being the penetrating light of reason we are used to in daily affairs, turns out to be unencompassable mystery.

From the question of meaning to the question of God. Everything said about meaning can be said of God (summary, 204). Rahner realizes many cannot embrace this notion of absolute meaning (205). He also admits his inquiry into meaning is not the only or even the best way to approach the question of God (although he thinks the question of God will always involve an analysis of human transcendentality). Even though the affirmation of absolute meaning is also the affirmation of God, without Christian revelation the relationship between God and definitive human freedom would remain an open question. Summary (206).

The unavoidable question of absolute meaning is not answered simply by importing some concept of God. Rather, accepting the question fully yields the existence of absolute meaning and thus of the existence of God. Therefore, a knowledge of God is already present in the question of meaning, even for those who can make no sense out of the traditional term "God" or "absolute meaning" (i.e., anonymous Christians). One's response to the question of meaning is one's ultimate position on the question of God. This does not make explicit faith superfluous since those who can verbalize the object of their faith, hope, and love can structure their lives on the basis of that conviction.

21.15   Jesus Christ—The Meaning of Life

Jesus Christus–Sinn des Lebens
{3.0}   1980 lecture in Bad Ischl. to a convention of Austrian physicians.
   Geist und Leben 53 (1980) 406-416.
Abstract: If the absolute meaning of life is God and if Jesus is God, then Jesus is the absolute meaning of life. This essay examines the sense in which Jesus is God and concludes that ascending christology "from below" is completely orthodox. It coincides with classical descending christology.
Topics: MEANING, absolute; GOD as absolute meaning; CHRISTO-LOGY, ascending; HYPOSTATIC UNION.
Subsidiary Discussions: Mystery (210f); Christology, Chalcedonian (213ff); Christology, communication of idioms (213f); Jesus Christ, faith in (218f).
Precis: The formal answer Rahner offers to the question of how Jesus can be the total meaning of human existence in no way spares us the trouble of seeking answers to partial and individual questions of meaning in daily life.
The question of meaning [cf., 21.14]. Here meaning refers to the one, total, definitive and universal meaning of the whole of human existence, the possibility of which is not self-evident. Christians call such meaning "God." This meaning cannot be pieced together from partial instances of meaning. It is transcendent and unavailable within daily experience. It is and will always be incomprehensible mystery calling for surrender in silent, adoring love.
The question of Jesus. How is Jesus the answer to this question of meaning? It is not enough to say Jesus is the eternal Logos of God, God is total meaning,

therefore .... Such an answer fails to address the significance of Jesus' concrete human history for the meaning of our lives. The answer to the urgent question, how Jesus is identical with God, is expressed in many ways by scripture and tradition (list, 212f). These explanations fall into two groups: pure Chalcedonian and neo-Chalcedonian. After distinguishing the views of these two schools of descending christology on the hypostatic union and "communication of idioms" (213-215) Rahner suggests an approach from below: ascending christology. He attempts to understand the hypostatic union beginning with the saving significance for us of Jesus and his fate. "The way suggested leads, then, 'from Christ for us' to 'Christ in himself'" (215, summary).

Jesus Christ, meaning and salvation of humankind. Rahner argues Jesus' significance for us is definitive and unsurpassable based on the outcome of his twofold unconditional solidarity with God and humanity. That outcome, his death and resurrection, shows that his fate and person have a significance far surpassing their usual humanness. They definitively establish God's self-communication to the world. Accepting the irrevocability of this divine self-communication is the same as confessing Jesus as the consubstantial Son of God. Summary (218).

Faith in Jesus Christ. After another concluding summary Rahner turns to those for whom such academic speculation is too strenuous. He insists that whoever with unreserved faith trustingly says that in Jesus' death and resurrection God has pledged his life to us in a definitive, unconditional, unsurpassable, and irreversible way is an orthodox Christian who finds salvation in Christ.

21.16 Christology Today
Christologie heute

{2.0}   *Concilium* 18 (1982) 212-216.

Abstract: These fragmentary remarks about modern christology insist it cannot ignore classical formulations. It must be a christology of ascent which sees Jesus as God's irreversible pledge, sealed by Jesus' death and resurrection.

Topics: CHRISTOLOGY, modern; CHRISTOLOGY, ascending.

Subsidiary Discussions: Dogma, formula (220ff); Creed, "Word became flesh" (222f); Death of Jesus (226).

Precis: Catholic theologians today who ignore the classical christological formulations risk their own impoverishment.

The christological tradition. Theologians must be willing continually to learn from classical theology. This is true even though the most sacrosanct formulations still need to be expressed and expanded for new generations of believers. Profound reflection on ancient formulations can yield astonishing, even upsetting new truths. Hence, theologians must bring classical christological formulations into a positive relationship with today's ways of thinking. There is no reason to think the history of christological dogma has reached its end (e.g., Jn 1). Even if some modern formulations are found wanting they must be examined with respect.

A christology of ascent. Christology today must begin with the concrete, historical Jesus of Nazareth. This "precedes convictions about the Church and its teaching office and the inspiration of the New Testament" (223). The controlling question of such a "Christology of ascent" is the significance of Jesus "for us" which leads to the question, "who must he be if he has this significance for us?" (224) One should not be surprised or alarmed to find modern answers to these questions vary greatly in their approach or completeness.

Two aspects of an orthodox christology. Any christology of ascent will inevitably yield two fundamental insights:

–Jesus Christ, God's irreversible pledge. One will have to see Jesus as "the unsurpassable access to the immediacy of God in himself" (224) not merely as a promise but as realization. Although such an offer of immediacy is God's gift, because of the inviolability of human freedom it remains an offer until it becomes irrevocable in Jesus. To be definitive it must be identical to God's very self and explode the model we generally have of God's relationship to the world. Rahner maintains this christology of ascent contains all the important elements of classical orthodox christology.

–Jesus' death and resurrection. At this point in history we see the irrevocable acceptance of God's self-offer in Jesus. His death "is of fundamental importance to salvation history because it makes definitive the acceptance of God's offer of himself to Jesus" (226).

These are only a few fragmentary suggestions about modern christology. Rahner is convinced any future christology must pay much more serious attention to the highly personal loving relationship of the individual human being to Jesus of Nazareth. Such an approach might build a bridge to other world religions.

21.17   Brief Observations on Systematic Christology Today
Kleine Anmerkungen zur systematischen Christologie heute
{2.0}   J. Blank, G. Hasenhüttl, eds., *Glaube an Jesus Christus* (Düsseldorf 1980) 134-144.
Abstract: Rahner offers five observations on the status of christology today.
Topics: CHRISTOLOGY, modern; JESUS CHRIST.
Subsidiary Discussions: Magisterium (229); Mysteries (232); Salvation, theology of (233f); Christology, transcendental (235ff).
Precis: [This essay concludes with an excellent summary in five points. Those points are inserted verbatim in italics under their proper headings along with other highlights of the discussion.]

The permanence of faith. *"First, traditional, classical Christology still has a normative significance."* The past is still a vital reality and will always remain such. Theologians have a responsibility toward it. Without denying the binding force of authoritative teaching each generation must work hard to make the reality signified by the classic formulations its own.

A new formulation of faith. *"Second, an ignorant and superficial parroting of these traditional Christological formulations, coupled with the perhaps highly questionable feeling of having understood what they mean, does no service to the Church, to the faith, or to Christianity.*

"Third, there are in fact other ways of formulating the same Christology. This difference in formulation will perforce cause the object being treated to emerge in a somewhat different light." Rahner hopes his approach to christology (summary, 231f) clears up many problems inherited from traditional christology (e.g., the virgin birth).

The unity of christology and soteriology. *"Fourth, in traditional Catholic Christology there should be a closer unity between Christology and soteriology because statements of function and statements of essence condition and imply one another, and it is absolutely impossible to conceive them apart from this reciprocal interaction."*

Transcendental christology. *"Fifth, a much clearer Christology of ascent could be developed and a transcendental Christology as well because if I were not in reality already a crypto-Christian thanks to the grace of God I receive from the Spirit of Jesus, I could not make any sense of what is being said about this Jesus as the Christ."*

Theology and faith. Five summary points (cf., Precis).

21.18   The Christian Understanding of Redemption
Das christliche Verständnis der Erlösung

{3.0}   February 1981 lecture to *Institut für Indologie*, University of Vienna. G. Oberhammer, ed., *Epiphanie des Heils. Zur Heilsgegenwart in indischer und christlicher Religion* (Vienna 1982) 149-160.

Abstract: Rahner offers five central propositions of Catholic theology concerning redemption—"a few fragmentary notions chosen at random."
Topics: REDEMPTION; FREEDOM; GRACE and nature.
Subsidiary Discussions: Eschatology, intermediate state (limbo) (239f, 253f); Pelagianism (240ff); Virtues, infused (241); Sin (244ff); Jesus Christ as redeemer (247ff); Redemption, vicarious (248f); Symbol, real (250f) Hypostatic union (251); Resurrection of body (252f); Dogma, development of (252f); Demythology (253).
Precis: Redemption takes place in the realization of freedom. Prescinding from the difficult marginal question of how those who seem incapable of exercising freedom are saved (239f), the final salvation of the ordinary human is bound up with freedom: our unique capacity to achieve definitive validity. The remainder of this section argues "it is simply wrong to maintain

that self-redemption and redemption from the outside are … mutually exclusive" (241). Redemption never happens without human collaboration. Summary (241f).

Redemption implies the salvation of human beings in all their dimensions. We are not redeemed *from* concrete, historical realities, rather we come to the perfection of these realities themselves, a perfection which transforms them. Non-Christian views of redemption hold that *either* we are liberated from history *or* history perfects itself. Christianity insists that history is perfected in human freedom when that freedom reaches its definitive goal: God. Redemption only occurs in and through concrete history.

Redemption occurs in God's definitive communication of himself. This is true because Christians view the person as *capax infiniti*: a finite creature who cannot reach its completion short of the infinite, incomprehensible God. The redeemed person does not disappear into the infinite but finds true completion with the gift of God's self-donation.

Redemption precedes sinfulness. Redemption does not spring from our need to have sinfulness removed. Our need for redemption precedes sinfulness. This is simply another way of saying salvation is grace. "Human beings even prior to their sinfulness … can find their perfection only through an absolutely gratuitous self-communication of God which originates from God's free love" (245). It is subsequently true that we also need to be redeemed from the guilt of sin. But these two redemptions are not identical. This section closes with a discussion of those "naive innocents" who find sin innocuous today (246f).

Redemption originates from Jesus Christ. Although this truth is central to Christian faith it is not easy to say precisely what it means. For Rahner the key questions are how redemption (God's self-communication) can depend on the historical event of Jesus Christ when this event "is itself the result and historical manifestation of a salvific and redemptive will of God that has always existed and therefore which is both cause of this event of the cross itself as well as the effect which flows from it" (248). After voicing dissatisfaction with some elements of the concept of "vicarious redemption" (248f), Rahner suggests Scotus' position that God would never have permitted sin in the world if in his love he had not already determined to overcome it with the death and resurrection of Jesus (249). Although human freedom always makes damnation a possibility, Christians are never forbidden to hope for universal redemption.

Rahner turns next to the specific character of the redemptive causality of Christ's cross. He imports a term from sacramental theology to describe the cross as "*signum efficax*" in which sign and cause have a reciprocal relationship. [He means by it the same reality indicated by "real symbol."] In the cross the possibility of God's self-donation achieves irreversible historical definitiveness. In this sense it is like human freedom which achieves its definitiveness in particular actions. This notion presents no insuperable difficulty in light of the doctrine of the hypostatic union (250-251). None of what is said here argues that one should eliminate or ignore older ways the church has interpreted the reality of the redemption.

The resurrection of the body. The proven legitimacy of the notion of doctrinal development leads to the hope that future reflection on such elements as the body and the cosmos will uncover new dimensions of christology.

Against an abridgement of the doctrine of redemption. Rahner concludes with a warning against abridging the doctrine of redemption through misdirected "demythologizing." When theologians forget the abstract and formal character of their concepts they lose sight of the huge distance between what they mean and what their concepts can actually convey. They forget that these gaps can be filled in many different ways. When "demythologizers" remove certain crude concepts from an earlier age without replacing them with anything more adequate they do a great disservice. Because we cannot say everything about a particular concept with complete explicitness (e.g., the life of the soul after death) does not mean we are bound to remain completely silent.

21.19   Reconciliation and Vicarious Representation
Versöhnung und Stellvertretung

{3.5}   November 1982 lecture in Stuttgart to the Academy of the Diocese of Rottenburg-Stuttgart as, *Maximilian Kolbe und die Kraft der Versöhnung. Geist und Leben* 56 (1982) 98-110.

Abstract: Guilt, although it is not absolute, remains serious. Since we cannot forgive our own guilt, salvation comes as a gift from God. It is mediated through Jesus' solidarity with humanity and with the Father culminating in his cross and resurrection. It is vicarious representation in a restricted sense.

Topics: CHRISTOLOGY, reconciliation in Christ; JESUS CHRIST, solidarity with; SIN and forgiveness.

Subsidiary Discussions: Sin (255ff); Guilt and its remission (257ff); Freedom (258ff); Hope (260f); Jesus Christ, death of (262f); Love of God/ neighbor (263f).

Precis: Rahner sets out to explore the relationship between our reconciliation with God and with one another.

Minimizing or exaggerating the idea of sin. Today it is no longer obvious that the spiritual situation in the world presupposes the need for reconciliation or redemption. This is because many fail to grasp the full peril of sin while others view sin as absolute, irreversible, and irrevocable.

The hopelessness of guilt. The Christian position lies between these two extremes: people can use their freedom in radically sinful ways *and* God can forgive their guilt. Why are people incapable of forgiving their own guilt?

–The dialogical structure of becoming guilty. Human guilt and its remission cannot be understood with the model of civil law. The hopelessness of guilt arises from the dialogical character of human existence in reference to God—a two-sided relationship which cannot be restored by the act of only one party in the relationship.

–The ultimate validity of free human decision. Human freedom is not the capacity to choose endlessly. It is inherently ordered to establishing our ultimate validity before God. For this reason past events, even those for which we have repented, are never simply over and done. God is the name Christians give to the hope that their eternal acts of betrayal will be forgiven—a mystery which utterly transcends their own freedom. Summary (260).

The incomprehensibility of God's forgiveness. Christianity proclaims its hope that God is always eager to reconcile, to overcome our guilt which we must neither minimize nor absolutize. This forgiving and reconciling love of God which ultimately encourages us to forget our sins is incomprehensible. God only permits guilt in this world because from the beginning the world has been irrevocably encompassed by God's forgiving and reconciling love.

–Reconciliation through Jesus Christ. Christians find the truth of this love in the cross where Christ's unconditional solidarity with sinners meets his unconditional love of the Father in a consummate and irrevocable way.

–Forgiveness through God's grace. This forgiveness cannot be expressed in terms of a juridical act. It takes place through divine grace, God's very self-communication. God makes himself part of the offense of guilt to eradicate it and to reconcile us.

–The objective nature of what happens in Christ's death on the cross. What was said above describes the "subjective" nature of reconciliation. But what of the "objective" way? This invites a discussion of "vicarious satisfaction." Rahner warns that the cross in no way can be seen to *cause* God's gracious reconciliation. It is always/only the *effect* of God's unmerited love.

–Reconciliation with God as the source of reconciliation with one another. Just as love of neighbor is impossible apart from love of God, so human reconciliation is impossible apart from reconciliation with God. Human wisdom demands we forgive one another, but only God's self-communication in love can wipe away the guilt which separates and isolates us. To hope with all our might for such reconciliation is already to hope in God.

Vicarious reconciliation.

–The inadequacy of the juridical interpretation. This concept cannot be grasped in juridical terms. The real question is whether another person can relieve me of a moral debt which I myself owe to God. Rahner says no.

–The action of another cannot be substituted for a free human action. Vicarious representation cannot be thought to absolve me from fulfilling my responsibilities before God. Although none of us is bound to do more than we can, none of us is exempted from doing whatever we actually can. But redemption through our own efforts and redemption from outside (by Jesus Christ) are not mutually exclusive concepts. Through God's grace the cross of Jesus makes possible our radical self-surrender in faith, hope, and love. Leaving aside those incapable of making fully free choices, we can say, "[R]edemption from outside is the gratuitous bestowal of our own self-redemption" (266). Hence, Rahner suggests it is better to avoid the concept vicarious representation.

–The solidarity of human beings extends to their free acts. The element within the concept of vicarious representation which is valid and true is solidarity—solidarity among human beings in Christ which is relevant to our salvation. This is not simply a physical solidarity. It is spiritual as well. It extends to where the ultimate decisions of our salvation are made. All people of all times and places stand in solidarity with one another: "the situation and the possibilities of the freedom of all are jointly conditioned by all for all" (268). In short, there is a single field of human existence.

Solidarity in Jesus Christ. This single field is constituted/consolidated by the solidarity between humanity and Jesus, and between the Father and Jesus who, by accepting death on the cross, made our own salvation a gift. "[T]he entire history of humankind and the history of salvation is one great symphony of praise to the love of the God who moves the sun and the stars" (269).

XXII. Humane Society and the Church of Tomorrow
XVI. *Humane Gesellschaft und Kirche von Morgen*

German edition: Einsiedeln, Benziger, 1984
U.S. edition: N.Y., Crossroad, 1991
Joseph Donceel, S.J., translator, Paul Imhof, S.J., editor

This volume of the English language edition comprises the first three parts of *Schriften zur Theologie*, XVI.

22.01 Conscience

Vom irrenden Gewissen

{2.0}   March 1983 lecture in Vienna. *Orientierung* 47 (1983) 246-250

Abstract: Rahner explores the relationship between conscience and God starting from Vatican II's teaching that even "erroneous" dictates of conscience are absolutely binding.

Main Topics: CONSCIENCE.

Subsidiary Discussions: Transcendence (9-10); Vatican II, freedom of conscience (10-12); Conscience, freedom of (11ff) Freedom of conscience (11ff).

Precis: Freedom and the dignity of human decision. Theological statements about conscience unavoidably assume the obscurity of religious language.

–The many questions that may and should be asked. No objective ethics can dismiss subjective human consciousness because it is the objective relationship between God and human freedom which renders individual norms absolute. Only through a personal decision of conscience do norms present themselves as binding. Human judgment is the highest court of moral appeal.

Starting from the erroneous conscience.

–The absolutely binding character of the dictates of conscience. Where a choice has to be made, a decision is a dictate of conscience only if it looks absolutely binding to the subject. Such judgments can be objectively erroneous but still remain binding (5-8).

–Erroneous conscience. Conscience, which frequently errs from invincible ignorance, retains its dignity in both right and erroneous decisions because the same basic moral reality is at work in both. Error refers only to the concrete data to which the decision is applied.

–The dignity of a dictate of conscience. The dignity and binding character of any dictate of conscience come from the nature and structure of the decision of conscience itself. They do not derive solely from its agreement with any categorial object or value.

–The transcendental ground of the absolute claim. Every dictate of conscience affirms human transcendentality insofar as all free actions assert the necessity of the permanent and fundamental distinction between good and evil. Conscience is an unconditional appeal addressed to me as a responsible subject. The response is up to my freedom. Certain implications follow:

–Conscience as God's voice. Conscience is theonomic in this sense: it points to the existence of an absolute obligation and responsibility of freedom which subjects can reject only by destroying themselves. The infinite, unfathomable Mystery implicitly, yet often anonymously, offered to us as we reach out to accept human freedom and responsibility is the transcendental reality called God.

–The freedom of conscience. Through conscience, human beings are real subjects compelling respect from all social and religious institutions. Though one's freedom of conscience must not infringe on another's, this does not mean church and society must not teach, exhort, and defend objective norms of morality. The church particularly should stress the theonomic nature of conscience: that in striving to know and do the good we are striving for God.

–Dictates of conscience that err about concrete morality are superior to those which are objectively correct but which never affirm in freedom the transcendent dimension that refers to God.

–By presuming the presence of a real dictate of conscience in others we stress what we hold in common before God, even though a contradiction in the material content of those decisions might render one or both positions false. Such an approach fosters genuine tolerance.

22.02 Dialogue and Tolerance as the Foundation of a Humane Society

Dialog und Toleranz als Grundlage einer humanen Gesellschaft
{1.5} June 1983 lecture in Pforzheim. *Stimmen der Zeit* 201 (1983) 579-589.

Abstract: Rahner explores the limits of tolerance and dialogue imposed by the state's
demand for the common good and the Christian demand for freedom.
Topics: CHRISTIAN LIFE, tolerance; FREEDOM and coercion; DIALOGUE; SOCIETY and common good.
Subsidiary Discussions: Vatican II (15f); Freedom of conscience (21ff); Conscience, freedom of (21ff); Power, coercive (24f).
Precis: The role of tolerance and dialogue in constituting a humane society is problematic. Any society's appeal to the common good would seem able to set appropriate limits to toleration and dialogue. But this is not clearly the case. And the more pluralistic the society is, the harder it becomes to make such an appeal. Nor is it obvious that the more tolerant and free a society is, the more humane that society necessarily becomes.
Limits of dialogue and tolerance—the common good. Tolerance as required by Christianity. The Christian demand for tolerance is rooted in its understanding of human freedom (even though the church itself has been slow to appreciate and enunciate this insight).
The erroneous conscience. Stated most radically the church holds that, "[w]hen in a given situation persons have to act, and when, to the extent of their possibilities, they reach a decision which they consider true and morally right, and preferable to another available one, this judgment is binding for them; it is a dictate of conscience that is absolutely obliging .... One's judgment concerning one's concrete moral attitude and decision my be wrong and still be a real, radical decision of conscience that obliges one absolutely in an inescapable responsibility" (20).

Acknowledging the dignity of freedom. Thus, for Christians tolerance is more than a rule of the game, more than a maxim for peaceful coexistence. It is the respect we pay to the freedom of the other person. Though it is true that "error has no rights," erring people do have rights and an inviolable dignity. In this light, tolerance is seen to derive both from Western humanism and from genuine Christianity.

Tolerance and intolerance. Yet even in this Christian context it remains unavoidable that there can be no tolerance without some intolerance. Nor is there any clear, handy criterion to determine the allowable limits to human freedom in society. To say as much freedom as possible should be allowed leaves the question unanswered.

Pre-eminence of freedom. In these ongoing debates Christianity takes the side of freedom. "There can exist unavoidable necessities, coercions, and restrictions of freedom. But in the final analysis they have to justify themselves before the bench of freedom, and not the other way around" (24). How predisposed I am to tolerance and dialogue can be gauged by responding to these questions: "Are you really willing to grant freedom to the other person, insofar as it can be done without harming others, even when you hold a different opinion and have the power to prevent others from doing what they want? Are you willing and patient enough, as far as possible, to find out and to try to feel what others (or another group) want to be and how they want to understand themselves?" (24). These are questions the theologian will insist we will one day be asked by God.

22.03 Utopia and Reality: The Shape of Christian Existence Caught between the Ideal and the Real
Utopie und Realität

{1.0} February 1983 lecture in Bad Camberg, as, *Christliche Welt- und Lebensgestaltung zwischen Anspruch und Wirklichkeit.*

Geist und Leben 56 (1983) 422-32.

Abstract: Rahner explores the proper Christian response to existence in the world, which is neither idealistic utopianism nor meaninglessness.

Topics: HOPE.

Subsidiary Discussions: Utopias (26ff); Perplexity (34ff); Death (36f).

Precis: The dualism of utopia and reality. The words "utopia" and "reality" point to a basic dualism in human experience. Their juxtaposition reminds us of the gap between what we can and ought to strive for, and the actual shape the world is in despite our efforts.

The idealistic and the realistic solution of the conflict. There are two principle responses to the mess of the world: 1) false idealism which recoils and takes refuge in other-worldly ideals; 2) realism which looks soberly on the shabbiness of human life and expects little more. The proper Christian response lies between and ultimately redefines these alternatives.

Fragments of a Christian answer. Taking the utopia of God seriously. For Christians what seems utopian is true reality based on the fact that an infinite, absolute, eternal God is the reality "that suffuses everything, orders everything, attracts everything towards himself.... And precisely as this incomprehensible reality God renders all other realities around us questionable, relative, and imbued with their own incomprehensibility" (30).

Enduring the lasting tension between fulfillment and lack of it. Affirming the existence of this tension between utopia and reality theoretically does not resolve it. Christians must react to it properly. Throughout their lives they must exercise their deepest freedom whole-heartedly, discharging their political responsibility to love their neighbors even without the absolute assurance of how they actually stand with God. All the while two temptations remain open to them: to lose themselves to an idealistic dream of heaven, or to a godless love of the earth.

Living with hope in God. To accept the challenge to walk the right path between the dualism of utopia and reality is called hope. Christians aim for the incomprehensible God—their true utopia. Christian hope does not leave the reality of the world in its wake but brings it mysteriously transformed to perfection in God.

Patiently waiting for the dawning of God's mystery amid the growing perplexity. Walking in this hope tries our patience for Christian reality remains always incomprehensible, forever unfinished, forever resisting harmonious synthesis. Bewilderment keeps growing. Christians bear their perplexity because it is nothing less than the concrete dawning of the sacred mystery called God. The only alternative is to interpret perplexity as the unveiling of the basic absurdity of life.

The test of death. Christian life calls for courage not moderation. Christians should not try to avoid failure or disappointment by recourse to ideology, for even these point to the nearing of the incomprehensible, unmanipulable God. Only our deaths will reveal how well we mediated the tension between the ideal and the real.

22.04   The Theological Dimension of Peace
Die theologische Dimension des Friedens
{0.5}   *Entschluß* 38 (3/1983) 11-13, as, *Die Offenheit auf Gott hin.*
Abstract: Rahner explores the conditions for the possibility of resolving conflicts: a belief in God as infinitely greater than any finite compromise made in pursuit of peace.
Topics: CHRISTIAN LIFE, peace.
Subsidiary Discussions: Conflict resolution.
Precis: Peace is a complex reality Rahner defines as the absence of conflict.
Reasonable adjustments and compromises. Conflict is inevitable because the multiplicity of finite realities encountered in human existence cannot be

made to fit harmoniously together. Each person defends the particular nature of a certain reality and hesitates to yield to any claim that contradicts it.

The realm of unconditioned freedom. Equilibrium can often be restored between competing claims by reasonable adjustments and compromises. Yet at times peace can only be restored if one or both parties give up a claim with no hope of compensation, reward, or thanks. Such generosity is only possible in the context of faith in God, "the real, universal and all-encompassing possibility of that peace, the possibility and meaningfulness of which can no longer be shown by means of the individual elements that constitute human reality" (40).

Not putting up with everything. But not every conflict can be solved even by such trusting submission. In fact, many unscrupulous rulers invoke such holy submission to further their unjust ends. Trust in God does not mean putting up with everything. Though the concrete decision to submit or to resist cannot be made from general principles, either decision can equally well be motivated by the love of peace found in openness to God.

22.05   The Problem of Europe's Future
Die Frage nach der Zukunft Europas
{3.0}   F. König, K. Rahner, eds., *Europa—Horizonte der Hoffnung* (Graz 1983) 11-34.

Abstract: a rambling exploration of the possibility that even in the future Europe may have a culturally distinct yet eternally valid contribution to make to the universal human culture which is rapidly approaching.

Topics: EUROPE, role in salvation; PHILOSOPHY of history; THEOLOGY of history.

Subsidiary Discussions: Israel as chosen people (48ff); Church, future of (60); Freedom and determinism (54f); Hope (56); Futurology (56ff).

Precis: The future and the problem of the whole. Skeptics find the question of the future of Europe invalid because: 1) upon close inspection the concept of "Europe" dissolves; 2) "the future" in any meaningful sense is radically unknowable; 3) "meaning" is undiscoverable; 4) history reveals no norms, ideals, or directions that could guide choices about Europe's future. But to Rahner it remains a valid metaphysical question because by extension it concerns the totality of individuals and their world.

About the reality of Europe. Can we take for granted that Europe has a reality about which anything important can be said? Yes, if by analogy one extends to a human collective the absolute significance philosophers since the Enlightenment have predicated to individuals. The analogy does not, however, imply that all collectives, like all individuals, will somehow exist eternally.

The significance of collective realities. Philosophy regards persons in one of two ways: 1) as absolute individuals; 2) as radically social. Yet these two dimensions are inseparable, irreducible, and co-conditioning, just as God is irreducibly one and many. As eternal significance attaches to one's individual and social dimensions, so by analogy human collectives as the locus of human activities have eternal significance. The Old Testament seems to affirm the significance of a people, whereas the New Testament emphasizes the call of the individual (48f). Both are valid.

Europe as part of the definitive consummation of history. Is Europe that kind of collective to which one may attribute absolute eternal significance, such that the question of its future is equally significant? Yes, because of: 1) the importance of its "profane" history to humankind; 2) its special role in salvation history as the concrete locus of the church. In this way Europe's place in salvation history is analogous to the place of Israel in Christian theology. If salvation history really exists, then Europe has a universal significance (51) even though we cannot concretely know its potential significance in the future. Summary (53).

God's salvific will for Europe. Although it is not obvious from a rational appraisal that Europe's contribution has been positive, European Christians have a right to hope that just as God judged Israel's contribution to be positive God will judge Europe's likewise. Thus, Europeans should not lose heart.

Europe as the outcome of a free history. Unpredictability of the future. Europe's history was formed in part by the free choices of its people. Its future will be also. Still, that future remains in principle unknowable due to the continuing interplay of freedom and necessity (54f).

Futurology. The courage to risk and to plan. Though the future is a journey into the dark, it calls for sober planning. It also demands certain virtues: courageous risk taking which combats lazy conservatism, and hope (56) which allows risk taking.

Historical and future identity of Europe in a worldwide society. Harmonizing these two mandates is not easy. Among other things it raises the question of what kind of body should be empowered to plot Europe's future (58).

Downfall or future of Europe? Should Europe work to safeguard its identity or, sensing its being subsumed into a more universal human culture, should it have the good sense and courage to call it quits? Just as Christians hold that not every particularity of Christian history will be made irrelevant, Europeans can rightly hope that since Europe has been the locus of much of Christian history, much of its particularity will also survive into the future.

Values and norms of Europe. In the future Europe may be absorbed into a more universal culture, or it may retain its identity in all essential respects. Since either is possible Europeans may freely choose their course and not despair. Just as people are not forced to abandon all their particularities when they participate in society, regional cultures need not abandon their particularities when participating in a more universal culture. A further complication is the difficulty of separating any particular cultural value from its distinctive cultural stamp. In cultural change either or both can be lost.

22.06   Realistic Possibility of a Unification in Faith?
Realistiche Möglichkeit der Glaubenseinigung?
{1.0}   January 1982 lecture in Basel. H. Fries, ed., *Das Ringen um die Einheit der Christen: Zum Stand des evangelisch-katholischen Dialogs* (Dusseldorf 1983) 176-192, as, *Was kann realistischerweise Ziel der ökumenischen Bemühungen um die Einheit im Glauben sein?*
Abstract: Rahner's personal suggestion for moving toward unity of the churches by extending to all Christian churches the same epistemological latitude they offer their own believers.
Topics: ECUMENISM; UNITY.
Subsidiary Discussions: Theology, pluralism in (68); Knowledge, profusion of (68ff); Tolerance (72f); Petrine office (78).
Precis: Since Christ commands that all Christians be one there must be a means to that unity. If the church seeks to move from rapprochement to real unity, a bold, almost utopian, and perhaps seemingly heretical suggestion should be considered. Rahner offers a dogmatic suggestion, realizing that it leaves unresolved many other juridical, canonical, and pastoral issues.
The fundamental thesis of the dogmatic side of the ecumenical problem. The present spiritual climate. The mentality of people today on spiritual matters is quite different than in former times. Formerly, scholars inhabited a commonly understood world of discourse which some of them could claim to have thoroughly mastered. In this environment even inter-denominational disputes took place "in house." Today the world of knowledge is much more complex. No one can claim mastery in any field, not even in one sub-specialization of theology. It is almost impossible for theologians to clearly understand one another. Even simple synthesis is impossible. Today everyone is educated in some respect and ignorant in others.
Consequences for the ecumenical question. When confronted with a proposition or area of knowledge about which one is inadequately informed, one does not err by simply refraining from affirming that proposition. What is true of individuals applies to the larger group as well. What is true of general statements applies to creedal statements. To be a legitimate member of the Christian community it is enough for the baptized to lead a Christian life. The church does not inquire too closely into exactly what propositions are believed or in what sense. "This epistemological, somewhat minimalistic tolerance is quite unavoidable, and it is also legitimate in the churches" (73).
The unity of the churches. Other ways of conceiving unity. Rahner suggests that, "From the dogmatic point of view and with respect to the faith of the Church, unity of the separated churches is conceivable, if no Church declares

that a statement held to be binding by another Church is absolutely irreconcilable with her own understanding of the faith" (73). Under such a rubric church unity seems possible immediately.

Further unsolved questions. Importance of the Ecumenical Movement. If one holds out for the full realization of the conditions of an ideal unity, then unity becomes unreachable and ecumenism becomes lip service. But if one accepts the existing unity among the churches as sufficient, then progress becomes possible. In this atmosphere all grass roots ecumenical action is important insofar as it clarifies the broad extent of our existing unity.

22.07   Concrete Official Steps toward Unification

Konkrete offizielle Schritte auf eine Einigung hin?
{0.5}   K. Froehlich, ed., *Ökumene Möglichkeiten und Grenzen heute* (Tübingen 1982) 80-85.

Abstract: a challenge to the official organs of the churches to do what is clearly already within their power to promote Christian unity.

Topics: ECUMENISM.
Subsidiary Discussions: Petrine office (82).

Precis: Such great progress toward church unity has been made by dogmatic theologians that church officials can do much more than utter friendly words about ecumenical good will. What could the Catholic Church do tangibly today?

First, it should re-examine and courageously resolve concrete pastoral problems of an inter-confessional nature, e.g., intercommunion, Sunday obligations for partners in a mixed marriage joint religious education for children of mixed marriages. Clearly in these areas we have not yet reached the limits of implementing agreements already embraced by theologians.

Second, the church should clarify its self-understanding, take advantage of every opportunity to declare officially the progress that has been made towards unity: that unity does not mean completely subsuming the Protestant churches; that bishops could be appointed and serve in ways different from those outlined in canon law; that the Petrine office could be exercised in a more collegial way even in matters *ex cathedra*; that the Mass is not a repetition of Calvary; how the sacraments are not magic, etc.

The magisterium can do more than condemn error. By officially stating the conclusions of ecumenical dialogue as its own, the Congregation for the Doctrine of the Faith could greatly add to the momentum of ecumenical initiatives. There is much along these same lines which the Protestants could do, but here one runs into the problem of who can speak authoritatively for them.

22.08   Ecumenical Togetherness Today
Ökumenisches Miteinander heute
{0.5}   *Quartember* 44 (1980) 3-12.

Abstract: Five maxims for Christians and their churches to achieve unity and overcome the stagnation, resignation, and listlessness hampering ecumenical work today.

Topics: ECUMENISM; UNITY.

Subsidiary Discussions: Creed (85ff); Truths, hierarchy of (89f).

Precis: Radicalization in the direction of Jesus Christ. All Christians in all churches must become more intensely and radically Christian. Christianity is not a theory to be handed down but a challenge to be lived. If everyone were more radically Christian many points which now separate Christians would fade to obscurity. We must be as concerned about orthopraxis are we are orthodoxy.

No third confession. It is meaningless and often harmful to ecumenism to implement practical ecumenical projects so quickly that something like a third confession is created. Real unity must be realized within the churches and not against them. This may mean moving more slowly than some might like.

Against confessionalism. Admit that some obstacles to unity are creations of a narrow confessionalism. Unity must not be envisioned as absorption. Unity does not demand uniformity. A model for such juridical, canonical, and liturgical pluralism already exists in Rome's dealings with the Uniate churches. Think creatively!

Getting to know the other confessions. All Christians must really get to know each other very well. This takes bravery and impartiality and dispels distrust and indifference.

The present unity. Christians must always celebrate with joy and anticipation the broad unity which already exists among all the baptized.

22.09   Forgotten Dogmatic Initiatives of the Second Vatican Council
Vergessene Anstöße dogmatischer Art des II. Vatikanischen Konzils
{0.5}   Previously unpublished. November 1982 lecture in Freiburg.

Abstract: There are three pastoral initiatives of Vatican II which in Rahner's view have not yet received sufficient dogmatic reflection or elaboration: dialogue with atheism; collegiality; universality of the offer of salvation.

Topics: VATICAN II; THEOLOGY, fundamental.

Subsidiary Discussions: Atheism (98f); Petrine office and collegiality (100ff); Episcopate, synod (101f); Salvation, universality of (103f).

Precis: Atheism and personal guilt. Regarding atheism the council taught that divine providence does not deny the help necessary for salvation to those who, without blame on their part, have not yet arrived at an explicit knowledge of God. It also taught that we ought to believe the Holy Spirit in an unseen manner known only to God offers to every human being the possibility of being associated with the paschal mystery. The questions for dogmatic theology remain, how is this possible? Is this anonymous theism? What is the nature of human consciousness that can explicitly deny something so important yet affirm it in some other way?

Relation of the teaching and jurisdictional primacy of the pope to the fulness of power of the college of bishops. The council taught that the college of bishops bears the highest fullness of all sacramental and canonical power in the church. And following Vatican I it taught that the pope also has supreme and universal primacy of jurisdiction. The questions for dogmatic theology remain. How is this possible? In one society how can two subjects be invested with fulness of power? What is or could be the power of an episcopal synod or regional bishops' conference?

The universality of salvation. The council teaches Christians to hope for universal salvation: of the whole world, of all other churches, and even of non-Christian world religions. The questions for dogmatic theology remain whether and how grace can be thought of as circumscribed in space or time? How is salvation possible where nothing of the Old or New Testament has penetrated? How can we square the absolute character of Christianity with a positive salvific significance of non-Christian religions? What does it mean when the council says the church of Jesus Christ *subsistit* in Roman Catholicism?

Tasks for systematic theology. Rahner concludes with a paragraph listing other unsolved questions raised by most of the major conciliar documents. Whatever weariness or resignation exists among systematic theologians today it cannot be because the council left them with nothing to do. These questions must be tackled bravely so that God's word may be heard clearly and God's grace may be active and glorified.

22.10   Perspectives for Pastoral Theology in the Future
Perspektiven der Pastoral in der Zukunft
{1.0}   *Diakonia* 12 (1981) 221-35.
Abstract: Rahner raises the awareness that the church has a duty to develop an explicit strategy for meeting its pastoral tasks as a "world-church."
Topics: CHURCH of the future.
Subsidiary Discussions: Episcopate, synod (107f); World-church (109f); Future, planning (and human freedom) (110ff).
Precis: A pastoral strategy for the world-church. The church must develop a new global pastoral strategy for its new status as "world-church."
Pastoral strategy and the Synod of Bishops. Perhaps the Synod of Bishops is the most appropriate and promising organ to foster this development because the curia seems inadequate to the task.

Pastoral strategy and Roman central government. Two facts undergird this discussion and together make clear the possibility, nature, and necessity of a pastoral plan for a world-church, along with who should execute it: 1) a world-church already exists today; 2) humanity has already begun to plan its unity. Though the mission of the church has always been universal, only with the globalization of social intercourse and the decline of Western hegemonies has it really become a world-church. Only recently has the future as such become a serious object of study and a subject of rational, albeit limited, planning. These developments are irreversible.

Plan and freedom. In this new context the church must plan in a new way, fully realizing that given the nature of human freedom, planning always comes up against something radically incomprehensible and thus uncontrollable.

Duties of the world-church. Pastoral planners face five challenges:

–Building a new awareness of the faith. A huge gap exists between what the church teaches and the faith people actually believe and live. There is a great need for assessment and instruction, perhaps also for a new brief creedal statement. Without denying its particular origins, Christianity must become more historically neutral.

–Universal church and particular churches. The church is faced with a problem of retaining its unity within a context of geographical, cultural, theological, and ecumenical pluralism.

–The world responsibility of the church. Vatican II insisted on the importance of the church's mission for world peace and justice. Does the church need a new agency to think seriously, plan, and speak authoritatively about these matters?

–The disapora situation of Christians. An intact homogeneous Catholic Christianity is dead. Most Catholics live in a diaspora, speaking the language of their environment. How can the church speak to them and make itself believable? Is the church naively taking for granted that its principles regarding marriage, the economy, the arms race, etc., actually make sense to the vast majority of its people?

–Turning away from a bourgeois church. The future of the church cannot be "bourgeois" business as usual. Cultural relativism, clerical celibacy, the role of lay ministry must all be examined if the church is not to become a mere vestige of its ancient self. The question is not what will happen to the future church, but what is the church's plan is to meet the unknown future.

22.11   The Future of Christian Communities
Über die Zukunft der Gemeinden
{1.0}   *Entschluß* 37 (12/82) 11, 16-20, as, *Warum die Christen einer Minderheit bleiben.*

Abstract: How today's parish and its ministries might be transformed into a new oasis-type Christian community in the rapidly dechristianizing West.
Topics: CHURCH of the future.
Subsidiary Discussions: Church as *sacramentum salutis mundi* (123f); Anonymous Christian (124); Church, mission activity of (124f); Priesthhood of the future (125ff); Base communities (126f); Women, ordination of (130f).
Precis: To envision the future of parishes one needs to ask the meaning of the fact that after 2,000 years the world is still not completely Christian, and yet God's salvific will remains effective even for the non-baptized.
A Christian world? One must also realize that even if the world were all nominally Christian, it would still be a place where human freedom contended with choices for good and evil. Zealous, faithful Christian would still be a minority in this universal church (15%) and would find themselves opposed. These would constitute local oases of faith.
Oases in a non-Christian world. Since in much of Europe this "ideal scenario" is the real situation, one can say the future is now! Rather than mope over the 85% only nominally connected to the church, efforts should focus on sustaining the zeal of the 15%.
So that God's salvation may become visible. Vatican II taught that the universal church is a sacrament of universal salvation. It is the sign of the world's salvation, though actual salvation extends far beyond church membership. By analogy the parish community is such a sign within its neighborhood, though more are saved than are on parish registers. Why then remain explicitly Christian? Because those who already know salvation in Christ risk losing it if they opt to move away from the church.
Made free for a missionary task. The primary task of an oasis church is missionary. First it must see that as a sign it continues to exist. Then, continuing its mission of love, it must gain new members, initiating others into explicit knowledge of Christ.
The task of the priest. In such an oasis community the priest through his existence, deeds, and words is the living, believing, hoping, loving witness to God's message. He shares his faith with others primarily through celebrating the Eucharist with a "base community" where everyone has a special function (**Base Christian communities and changes. The example of a chess club**).
New functions in the church. Though the church of the future will have deacons, priests, and bishops, they might function quite differently. Many other specialized ministries (teaching, psychotherapy, social criticism, etc.) might be added. After all, holiness has never been the exclusive preserve of

church leaders. There might be temporary priests (**Temporary pastors**) or women priests (**The ordination of women**). **The farthest become the nearest.** We have become today a global community. Every Christian can and must do something to alleviate suffering wherever it arises in the world. **A community of prayer.** The Christian community is not a service station where people simply satisfy their individual needs for piety and salvation. Both prayer and social action will always be essential characteristics of any truly Christian community.

22.12   Rites Controversy: New Tasks for the Church
Ritenstreit—Neue Aufgaben für die Kirche
{1.0}   *Entschluß* 7/8/1983, 28, 30f, as, *Austausch statt Einbahn?*
Abstract: The path to successful enculturation in the church is tolerance.
Topics: ENCULTURATION; CHURCH unity.
Subsidiary Discussions: Ecumenism (136f); Tolerance (137).

Precis: Today's rites controversy is driven by two facts: 1) that the Catholic Church has truly become a world-church; 2) that Western European/North American cultural hegemony has waned. Though the task of enculturation may seem a simple matter of adjustment or adaption it is in fact very difficult.
No synthesis. The root question is whether one and the same church can exist in different cultural milieux. Though Christians are convinced it can, the problem is how. Though the church must have a visible unity in worship, law, and faith, how can unity be achieved while respecting profound differences among cultures especially where trust seems lacking?

The first steps have already been taken by Vatican II's decrees on the Eastern Church which acknowledge its positive autonomous character. Thus, absolute uniformity is not required for unity. But how does the church keep lawful pluralism from becoming anarchistic? (**New tasks**).
Unity in Christ. In canon law, liturgy, and theology the law of tolerance should prevail. Presently the rule seems to be whatever does not positively agree with the church's position is unacceptable. But knowing we profess one creed, couldn't Rome tolerate theologies, etc., that it did not fully understand how to integrate within its own? Isn't this analogous to how people actually learn to accept one another? We never demand absolute conformity.
Limits of tolerance. Still there would be limits to tolerance. The church can never say yes to everything. A rule of thumb in judging among conflicting systems might be to ask which system is most open to learning from the other. In such a style of discernment each culture has much to offer and receive from all others.
The role of the Europeans. Mission activity is no longer a one-way street. Each culture in the church has much to teach and much to learn.

22.13   The Relation between Theology and Popular Religion

Zum Verhältnis von Theologie und Volksreligion

{1.5}   K. Rahner, et al., eds., *Volksreligion—Religion des Volkes* (Stuttgart 1979) 9-16, as, *Einleitende Überlegungen zum Verhältnis von Theologie und Volksreligion.*

Abstract: Rahner explains how popular religion is in some ways superior to theology itself, having its own creative and normative significance.

Topics: THEOLOGY and popular religion; RELIGION, popular.

Subsidiary Discussions: Church as People of God (142f); Revelation, original (144f); Faith, *sensus fidelium* (145f).

Precis: Popular religion has something to say to learned theology "not only because popular religion is the popular application of an official proclamation of the Church ..., but also because the people themselves (within the whole Church) are an addressee of primitive revelation" (147).

Theory and practice. It is not enough to say theology and popular religion are related like theory and practice because the practice of religion is itself a source of theology.

Theology and popular faith. To see the relationship between theology and popular religion one must first define theology (141f). But even the simple statement, "theology has an essential relation to the faith of the Church" is easily misunderstood. It must not be taken to mean that revelation exists somehow as the pure Word of God and that the faith of popular religion is the human response the People of God make to it.

Religion of the people. The "people" of popular religion and in the church's self-description by Vatican II as "The People of God" (144ff) consist of all men and women addressed by God's universally salvific will, and as such invited to accept divinization through grace. Theologians reflect on this invitation and the people's response.

Revelation and people. Insofar as this secondary theological reflection is more historically limited than the living address itself, popular religion is primary and superior to theology.

Church and people. Though the church possesses the most developed theology in its dogma and scriptures, it is built and carried on by people who received God's gracious self-communication in a more primitive, original, or primordial way: "the 'unction of the Spirit' by which every individual is taught by God" (146). Thus, Vatican II affirms the laity's own proper "*sensus fidelium.*"

Popular religion in the church. There is a history of faith and revelation both within and outside the church. It is determined and kept alive by all that occurs in human history. Today's theologians must pay more attention to this complex reality and to its source in popular religion.

22.14   South American Base Communities in a European Church

Südamerikanische Basisgemeinden in einer europäischen Kirche?
{0.5}   *Entschluß* 36 (1/81) 4-8.

Abstract: South American-inspired "base communities" offer an attractive model for today's changing European and U.S. parish communities.

Topics: BASE COMMUNITIES; PARISH LIFE.

Subsidiary Discussions: Christianity, sects (152f).

Precis: What is properly meant by base communities? Ideally every Christian community should be a "base community": i.e., Christians coming together to build one another up in Christ through prayer, praise, and service.

Contact and unity with the parishes. Such communities are not alternatives to traditional parishes. In fact every parish should be a base community rather than a mere geographical, administrative unit. The existence of traditional groups (Holy Name, Legion of Mary, etc.) shows the church has never lost sight of the need for base communities in some form.

No blind imitation of South American communities. However valuable South American base communities may be, they cannot be slavishly copied in developed nations. For one thing Europe and North America already have a parochial infrastructure. To ignore it would invite the proliferation of short-lived sects. In addition, governments in developed countries already provide many services unavailable in the developing world. There is no need to turn back the clock and have the church provide basic education, hospital care, or social services in Europe or North America.

Difference from a sect. Should base communities in developed countries do more than pray, worship, receive the sacraments, and spread the gospel? Yes, although this does not mean becoming self sufficient for all personal needs, wishes, aspirations, and activities...the very definition of a sect (152f).

More than a prayer group. The precise nature and scope of services to be provided by base communities in developed countries demand creative thought. Surely base communities seem perfectly suited to addressing the widespread isolation felt by many in the post-industrial world.

22.15   Christian Pessimism

Christlicher Pessimismus?
{0.5}   Previously unpublished, November 1983 lecture in Frankfurt.

Abstract: How the ineradicable perplexity in every Christian life which leads to pessimism is at the same time enveloped and saved by Christian hope.

Topics: CHRISTIAN LIFE, perplexity; CHRISTIAN LIFE, pessimism; HOPE.

Subsidiary Discussions: Death (160f); Human nature (156f); Existential/Existentiell (155 ftn1).

Precis: Christians are "ever perplexed but never despair" (II Cor 4:8).
Humanity's fundamental situation. Rahner begins his meditation on this paradox with a long description of humanity's fundamental situation. "Our existence is one of radical perplexity" (156). No human attempt to overcome evil succeeds completely. Our solutions often generate greater problems. This is not a transitory phenomenon, but a permanent human existential which leads Christians to embrace a "realistic pessimism."
Task of Christian preaching. The main task of Christian preaching is to uphold Christian pessimism and defeat any facile belief in the inevitability of human progress. Likewise the scholars of Catholic academies must make concerted attempts to infuse all secular discussions with this realistic pessimism.
Tasks for an academy. St. Paul urges Christians to trust in God and thus be "freed and consoled in all our needs and fears by the Holy Spirit" (160). But how can perplexed pessimists admit to being irretrievably lost in existence and not be driven to despair? For Rahner the answer lies in the fact that each of these realities (the experience that leads to perplexity and the other which staves off despair) has its sources in a different way of knowing. The former arises from experiencing the limits of our own powers. The latter comes from the knowledge believers receive from God and God's grace.
The solution of the Apostle Paul. This alone explains how these two incompatible truths may coexist in human life, how "Christians may feel the hopelessness of their existence, accept it without illusion, and for these very reasons be free, cheerful, and (in a certain sense) persons who have already arrived" (160); how Christians can admit the futility of every human scheme for development and at the same time commit themselves to bringing about the kingdom of God. This paradoxical resolution finds its counterpart in the Christian's attitude towards death and in his/her belief that final fulfillment lies in surrendering oneself to God in love (161).

22.16   What the Church Officially Teaches and What the People Actually Believe

Offizielle Glaubenslehre der Kirche und faktische Gläubigkeit des Volkes

{1.0}   K. Rahner, H. Fries, eds., *Theologie in Freiheit und Verantwortung* (Munich 1981) 15-29.

Abstract: Examining the difference between what the church teaches and the actual salutary faith of average believers has significant ramifications both for church teaching and for ecumenism.
Topics: FAITH; MAGISTERIUM.
Subsidiary Discussions: Theology, pluralism in (166); Faith, *sensus fidelium* (169ff); Dogma, development of (171ff); Ecumenism (173f).

Precis: Average Catholics believe both less and more than is explicitly presented by the magisterium.

A preliminary remark. Although this gap has always existed it is more acute today because: 1) Christians live in cultures awash with elements positively contradictory to the faith; 2) the complexity of theological data is almost impossible even for most scholars to harmonize.

The refusal to acknowledge this. It is not enough to say that explicit faith in the church implies faith in all the church teaches. Many of the faithful positively withhold assent from specific teachings or from the very notion of the absolute authority of the magisterium. To a great degree the church refuses to recognize this situation and still speaks, writes, and teaches as if all Catholics had a harmonious shared grasp of the faith.

Positive theological evaluation of the difference. To Rahner this gap is not merely negative. It has a positive value as well. Sophisticated knowledge of theology does not insure personal assimilation. It can in fact be an obstacle. "Moreover, it is the faith in the Church that actually exists in heads and hearts...that immediately and in itself is *the faith* that constitutes the Church.... The faith of the average Christian is not just a pitiable sketch of the official faith. It is a salutary faith borne by God's self-communication. It is really the faith that God's grace wishes to bring forth and keep alive in the Church" (169).

The normative significance of popular faith for the magisterium. This faith of the people has a normative significance for the magisterium. The two are mutually (albeit not equally) co-conditioning in that dogma develops out of the lived faith of the people (who include in their ranks theologians).

Why the accent should shift. Since lived faith is the source and norm for official faith, it would be a good thing for the magisterium somehow to poll the faithful to understand better what aspects of faith need to be stressed, corrected, or elaborated.

Acknowledging popular faith and its consequences for church and theology. This line of thought has great significance for ecumenism. Given the completely salvific nature of the very partial faith of most believers, how much doctrinal uniformity should the churches insist on achieving before reunion? Finally, keeping in mind that any salutary faith must contain a moment of absolute assent, by studying the actual empirical moment of that assent in the lives of the faithful the magisterium could shape and direct its efforts at evangelization in the modern world more effectively.

22.17   Theology and the Roman Magisterium
Die Theologie und das Römische Lehramt
{0.5}   *Stimmen der Zeit* 198 (1980) 363-375, as, *Theologie und Lehramt.*
Abstract: What each side must grant to the other for the magisterium and working theologians to establish their proper relationship.

Topics: MAGISTERIUM and theology; THEOLOGY and magisterium.
Subsidiary Discussions: Church, Congregation for the Doctrine of the Faith (184f); Tolerance (188f).
Precis: The relationship between magisterium and theologians remains obscure. Even with good will misunderstandings will remain. Rahner paints with very broad strokes the views each party has of the other. Although it is difficult to see how these positions can be reconciled, he maintains their demands are not contradictory. He includes what each side must grant the other to move towards reconciliation. Part 1 is written in the first person voice of the magisterium (178-185). Part 2 is written in the theologian's voice (185-190).
Magisterium:
–Self-understanding and praxis. We admit to being human and, hence, capable of error. Still we have a legitimate function in the church which theologians cannot dismiss. We should modify our praxis and expressly indicate in the texts we promulgate how binding our declarations are.
–Reactions of theologians to measures taken by the magisterium. Though it is unclear how far theologians can challenge a reformable declaration, we are willing to learn. This does not mean we lack the right to impose silence for a time or even to remove a theologian from office. There are serious consequences to public actions. That's life.
–Strictly binding decisions. Those who openly deny binding decrees of the pope or council have no right to be called church theologians. The magisterium must intervene. Where theologians believe their formulations agree with binding decrees but the magisterium does not, the church has the right to ask for a declaration of belief. When theologians are asked to withdraw their positions the matter becomes very complex.
–Reinterpretation of the dogmas. Though dogma is irreformable, its fallible inter-pretation demands reformulation in every age. Here theologians have much work left to do. Here the magisterium has great need of theologians.
–About the Procedure of the Congregation of the Doctrine of the Faith. Definitely needs reform.
Theology:
–Self-understanding and praxis. We are not a mafia. Still, our collective declarations (which should be more carefully crafted) deserve serious consideration by the magisterium.
–Acknowledging the magisterium. Although we have an autonomous function in the church we recognize the authority of the magisterium. It remains unclear exactly what this recognition requires of us.
–To what do official declarations oblige? We must frame all our comments on church teachings with prudence and courage. Silence and docility are not always the right response. The magisterium should react with tolerance and let history decide many non-binding issues.

–Tolerance of the magisterium with regard to theology. The magisterium should not restrict the pursuit of truth even for praiseworthy goals or motives. The burden of proof rests of necessity on those who would limit freedom.

22.18 The Perennial Actuality of the Papacy
Die unvergängliche Aktualität des Papsttums
{0.5}   B. Moser, ed., *Das Papsttum: Epochen und Gesalten* (Munich 1983) 277-292, as, *Paul VII. an Peppino—Ein Papstbrief aus dem 21. Jahrhundert.*
Abstract: An ideal picture of the future papacy. Rahner's dream in the form of a letter from the newly elected Paul VII to his best friend Peppino.
Topics: PETRINE OFFICE.
Subsidiary Discussions: Ecumenism (197f); Infallibility (198); Futurology (198f); Enculturation (199f).
Precis: "Paul VII" sees no reason to be "an ambitious pope." As prone to flattery as anyone, he will continue to need honest criticism from friends. Though he accepts Vatican I's claim that his office possesses the fullness of power, he will continue to "demythologize" the office (190ff).
The bureaucracy might be simplified. Administratively he will shrink the Vatican bureaucracy since he no longer envisions the world-church being "ruled" from the center. He will be more self-critical than his recent predecessors since the office is strengthened by admitting limitations and even mistakes. He will listen and learn (193ff).
A modest pontificate as counterbalance. He will not strive to be a "great" pope since that has often unnecessarily exaggerated the office. He does not see himself as the font of every initiative. The fullness of juridical authority alone has never made a pope a saint. There are many charisms in the church and the pope does not possess them all, nor can he alone evaluate all that goes on in the church (195ff).
Progress on ecumenism is an urgent necessity. He is not convinced the church has done everything possible up to now. The courage of "ecumenical probabilism" (definition, 197) holds the key to ecumenical progress.
Intelligent experts instead of solemn dignitaries. He will move slowly and will plan for the future with the help of the secular discipline of futurology (198f). A world-church needs a plan. It also needs more deeply to enculturate the gospel message more deeply (199f).
Three facts must be kept in mind. He hopes always to remember three things (200ff): i) the provisional nature of the papacy; ii) that belief in the papacy is not essential for salvation; iii) although he ceaselessly preaches Christ, the savior of the world, he does not have the answers to the most practical needs of particular human beings. As pope he will be open to dialogue with the secular world (203). He will shun triumphalism and learn when to speak and when to keep silent.

The Christian message and secular knowledge complete each other. He knows there is a difference between the substance of revealed truth and its historical accretions. But he is not sure exactly how this truth plays out in understanding the role of the papacy in the modern world (202ff). He closes by wondering whether he will die in office or whether he will have the grace to resign should that prove necessary (207).

22.19   Understanding the Priestly Office
Zur Frage des Amtsverständnisses
{2.0}   P. Neuner, F. Wolfinger, eds., *Auf Wegen der Versöhnung: Beiträge zum ökumenischen Gespräch* (Frankfurt 1982) 215-219, as, *Kleine Randbemerkungen zur Frage des Amstverständnisses*. This essay clarifies a previous discussion of validity of orders, 18.02, "Pseudo-Problems in Ecumenical Discussions."

Abstract: Sacraments are efficacious due to what they signify (Christ irrevocably offered as the salvation of the world) and not from what they effect. Thus, insofar as the rites of separated churches actually make this salvation concrete in the world, they too can be seen as valid.

Topics: SACRAMENTS, efficacy of; ORDERS, sacrament of; ECUMENISM.

Subsidiary Discussions: Church as *sacramentum salutis mundi* (210f).

Precis: The sacraments as signifying and as effective. The traditional Catholic understanding of sacraments which maintains that orders in separated churches are invalid is defective. It forgets that "sacraments signify grace and bring it about" insisting instead that "sacraments bring about grace by signifying it" (209). The grace which sacraments signify in time and space has its origins in Christ and has been irrevocably and victoriously introduced into the world (210). The real sacramentality of sacraments only makes sense if they are seen as basic activities of a church that itself derives from Christ, and which is the real sacrament of the world's salvation. This ecclesial reality confers upon sacraments their nature and effectiveness. This is the reality the sacraments originally signify.

How the church becomes manifest as basic sacrament. This eschatological reality can be made tangible in degrees. Some such manifestations are called sacraments while other efficacious manifestations (e.g., common prayer) Catholics call sacramentals. However such sacramentals are classified, they should be considered legitimate whenever their content refers properly to the fundamental sacrament, they appeal to it, and are performed with Christian faith. More cannot be required for legitimacy (211). Validity does not require a priori that they be used expressly within the juridical sphere of the Roman Catholic Church (hence the validity of baptism even by heretics).

What then distinguishes a valid sacrament performed within the normal Roman sacramental order from one performed outside of it? To insist that the latter is invalid because it does not conform to the Catholic norm would place the rules of the normal Catholic order above God and his salvific will. How could one explain or justify the right of the Catholic Church to impose such apodictic norms for the validity of the sacramental signs that it excludes even the possibility of exception?

22.20 Book of God—Book of Human Beings
Buch Gottes—Buch der Menschen
{1.5} *Stimmen der Zeit* 202 (1984) 35-44, as, *Die Heilige Schrift—Buch Gottes und Buch der Menschen.*
Abstract: How scripture is at once authored by God and produced by human freedom and contingency can only be understood in the context of revelation, i.e., how God meets human beings and the world in history.
Topics: SCRIPTURE; REVELATION, biblical.
Subsidiary Discussions: Theological anthropology (214f); History (216f); Church (218f); Scripture, Old Testament (221f).
Precis: Humankind in the universe. Human life and history seem inconsequential to the cosmos. But faith insists this is not so because 1) the vast power that posits the cosmos is one God; 2) this God communicates himself to humans. To do this God instills in us an infinite openness and receptivity, a capacity with which we can objectively represent ourselves to ourselves along with the universe as a whole. (Other beings may also have this capacity, angels or extraterrestrials, 216.) Thus, the overwhelming power which made us seem so insignificant actually reveals our importance, uniqueness, and the definitiveness of humans and human history (216).
Meeting of God and world. Thus, secular history is the history of God's unfolding self-revelation. Obscure as progress is, faith is convinced the final, definitive stage of history has arrived with Jesus Christ: the appearance of God in the world. This pledge of the world's salvation in its eschatological irrevocability remains present in the church: the indestructible community of believers (216f).
Holy scripture as constitutive of a primitive community. The unique, unrepeatable and absolute event of the God-man and his continuing presence in the church remain forever the norm. This church is constituted within a particular cultural situation, one constitutive element of which is the book—a norm for all time to come. Only in such a context can scripture be: 1) understood without an appeal to the miraculous; 2) shown as absolutely unique from the writings of other religions (218).
Holy scripture—word of God and word of human beings. Vatican II teaches that humans wrote scripture. In what sense is God its author? First, God caused both the Christ-event and the church. Second, God wills these always to be the norms of faith. Insofar as the primitive community could not be such a norm over time without objectifying itself in writing, God

authored the scriptures in authoring the church (219f). This leaves completely open the question of the role of human freedom both in composing the scriptures and in determining the canon. The "Old Testament" is scripture for Christians insofar as: 1) it was the scripture of Jesus; 2) it is about Christ, albeit without the explicit knowledge of its own fulfillment. It must always be read with an eye toward the events which complete it (221).

Holy scripture as a book. Scripture is a human word insofar as in it human beings bear witness that God hastens to meet human history. As God's word it bears witness to God as infinite gift to the world. This is only possible if God's self-communication here is unique, beyond God's usual creative activity. Thus scripture is not only words about God, and thus only human words having diverse dimensions and degrees of binding force. It is indeed also words of God. Though scripture was essentially present and normative in the primitive church, its proper nature as the book of everyone was only achieved with the advent of printing. Summary (223f).

XXIII. FINAL WRITINGS
XV. *Wissenschaft und christlicher Glaube,* 1983
XVI. *Humane Gesellschaft und Kirche von Morgen,* 1984

German edition: Einsiedeln, Benziger
U.S. edition: N.Y., Crossroad, 1992.
Paul Imhof, S.J., editor
Essays 1-7 translated by Hugh M. Riley from
Schriften zur Theologie (SzT) XV
Essays 8-19 translated by Joseph Donceel, S.J., from
Schriften zur Theologie XVI

23.01   Anxiety and Christian Trust in Theological Perspective

Angst und christliches Vertrauen in theologischer Perspective
{1.5}   *Christlicher Glaube in moderner Gesellschaft*, vol. 9 (Freiburg im Briesgau 1981) 86-98. Part II of *Angst und christliches Vertrauen*.

Abstract: A certain "anxiety before God" is a relevant and indispensable dimension of Christian faith and theology.

Topics: HOPE; CHRISTIAN LIFE, fear/anxiety.
Subsidiary Discussions: God, fear of (3ff); Transcendent/Categorial (5) Sin, forgiveness of (6); Contingency, experience of (7f); Virtues, theological (9); Freedom (10); Despair and trust (10f); Salvation/damnation status (11f); Salvation (12); Psychotherapy (13f); Spiritual direction (13f).

Precis: The theological connection between anxiety and fear. Since fear is the relationship between a conscious subject and a particular object it is linguistically but not technically correct to speak of "fear of God." God is not one object among many. "Anxiety of God" would be a more apt if less elegant description. Is this still a relevant dimension of Christian faith today?

–Necessary distinctions between fear and anxiety. Although it is possible to distinguish "categorial" fear and "objectless transcendental" anxiety, in fact due to the nature of human consciousness the two always exist in a synthesis. One can be more or less conscious of either dimension.

–Anxiety concerning salvation or the ultimate security of existence before God? Many people today maintain Christian faith should dispel all anxiety. Others insist on the importance of a holy fear of God. Who is right?

Existentiell insecurity and the experience of contingency as the reason for the existential anxiety of human beings. Rahner assumes we all experience an ultimate insecurity about our existence due to our contingent nature. Human freedom always retains the power to repress this experience in sinful or in inculpable ways. But it can never be completely exorcized.

Existence in anxiety and existential fundamentals of Christian trust. This being so (summary, 9) embracing our contingency and its accompanying anxiety in a fundamentally salvific way "can develop into three fundamental Christian existential components: faith, hope, and love" (9). Here Rahner concentrates on hope as trust, not in a single element in our existence but our act of self-abandonment to existence itself as Jesus abandoned himself to the Father.

Trust and despair as acts of human freedom. Though radically different, our two possible free responses to contingency are either trust or despair. Because either choice can easily look like the other we are never sure of our salvation/damnation status. Real trust can only be determined indirectly. This is why it is experienced as grace, salvation, the peace surpassing all understanding. Such inner security cannot be manufactured. In fact willingness to forego such reassurance is the condition for the possibility of finding it.

Clinical psychology and theological pastoral care. This existential anxiety remains different from psychological anxiety. The two can as easily be found together as apart. Therefore, psychotherapeutic intervention and spiritual direction remain valid but distinctly different helping activities.

23.02 Nuclear Weapons and the Christian
Die Atomwaffen und der Christ

{1.0}   Co-authored with T. Cremer. A. Battke, ed., *Atomrüstung—christlich zu verantworten?* (Dusseldorf 1982) 98-115.

Abstract: Argues for a complete rejection of nuclear armaments and immediate steps towards unilateral disarmament by appealing to reason and to the cross.

Topics: SOCIETY and nuclear weapons; CHRISTIAN LIFE, morality.
Subsidiary Discussions: Just war theory (17f); Cross, theology of (25ff).
Precis: Though Christians always had the responsibility to work for peace, the advent of nuclear arms has introduced a qualitative distinction.

Just war teaching. In this qualitatively different nuclear age we must have the courage and will to reconsider the traditional just war theory. Each Christian has this obligation. The discussion cannot be left to experts.

Rejection of nuclear armament.

–Epistemological uncertainties. Even though absolute decisions must be made about nuclear weapons, one cannot deduce with absolute theoretical certainty what to do. Such decisions lie in the area of human prudence and discretion. In this situation one must avoid the temptation to canonize one's own decisions and motives or to demonize those of one's opponents.

–Preventing war. We must all work to prevent war. But intelligent people of good will can reasonably disagree on the best steps towards this goal.

Reasons for a position of pacifism.

–Rational-humane objection. Rahner presents what he believes are cogent challenges to the prevailing nuclear strategy in the form of open questions.

–The message of God's kingdom. In addition to strictly rational arguments there is for Christians a second set of arguments based on the theology of the cross of Christ set forth as evangelical counsels (the Beatitudes and Paul's "folly of the cross") for those who can take it. This appeal to conscience is not, however, limited to Christians. These counsels are not simply personal. They are also political. To say these appeals are not relevant to the nuclear weapons debate it to say they lack any meaning at all.

–Nuclear disarmament. It follows that nations have the duty to disarm unilaterally—not as a calculated strategy to see how the "other side" will respond, but as the only morally defensible course of action. Clearly this involves dangers. But so does the current strategy. This demand is necessarily and inseparably bound up with the demand for a change in attitudes. It must begin with "our side." Our obsession with security must be replaced by concern for the misery of millions of poor.

The burden of proof lies with the powerful. After a brief summary of his position and an appeal to tolerance toward those who disagree, Rahner adds two considerations: 1) opponents of the current nuclear strategy cannot be dismissed as well-intentioned folk who have misguidedly strayed from the realm of personal to political morality; 2) the powerful must defend before God their reliance on a strategy of "mutually assured destruction" rather than the powerless who challenge it.

23.03   Plea for a Nameless Virtue
Plädoyer für einen namenlose Tugend
{0.5} K. Rahner, B. Welte, eds., *Mut zur Tugend: Von der Fähigkeit, menschlicher zu leben*. Festschrift for R. Scherer (Freiburg 1980) 11-18, as, *Die Spannung austragen zwischen Leben und Denken*.

Abstract: Faced with the need to act without having complete theoretical certainty people can become weary relativists or obstinate fanatics. There is an important virtue midway between these two options. It has yet to be named.

Topics: VIRTUE; CERTAINTY.
Subsidiary Discussions: Skepticism (35); Fanaticism (36).

Precis: People have always recognized and named virtues they saw and admired in others. Is it possible certain virtues have gone unnamed? Yes. Time and circumstances can clarify and reveal the existence of new virtues.

Anonymous virtue. Identifying and naming these new virtues can be difficult. Rahner suggests one unnamed virtue resides in our response to situations today when "the moral reflection antecedent to the action itself cannot provide that unambiguousness and unquestionable certainty with which, whether we want it or not, we nonetheless perform the action itself" (35).

Skeptical relativism. Some people respond to this lack of certainty in the face of the need to make moral decisions with skeptical relativism. They deny the complexity of the situation or permit themselves to act arbitrarily.

Ideological fanaticism. Christians have all too often responded to this situation with ideological fanaticism. They act as if theirs is the only position for intelligent people of good will.

The middle way between the two extremes. The nameless virtue lies between these two responses. Humbly admitting the limits of one's theoretical knowledge, people with this virtue bravely and serenely decide and act. They respect the mutual relationship and the dissonance between theory and practice, knowledge and freedom. What name should one give to such a necessary virtue?

23.04   Intellectual Patience with Ourselves
Über die intellektuelle Geduld sich Selbest

{0.5}   Previously unpublished. May 1983 lecture delivered in Tübingen.

Abstract: The knowledge explosion has made us more stupid. We know less of what there is to know than our ancestors did. This invites us to experience God as incomprehensible mystery, to be more tolerant, and to act more bravely.

Topics: CHRISTIAN LIFE, patience; CONCUPISCENCE, gnoseological.
Subsidiary Discussions: Despair (38f); God, incomprehensibity of (40, 45f); Concepts, clarity of (43f); Future, *docta ignorantia futuri* (45f); Tolerance (46f); Freedom and knowledge (48f); Knowledge and freedom (48f).

Precis: Is patience something obvious? When "the person inside us that we really are greets painfully the person that we want to be" (38) then we need patience with ourselves. Historically conditioned, sociologically conditioned, biologically threatened, we are all in the process of becoming and we know it. We need the courage to embrace our disquiet rather than repress, manipulate, or stoically endure it.

The patient person is serene. "People who are truly patient, however, really endure their disquietude" (39) even when they cannot know whether they are in fact patient or despairing. They are patient with their own impatience. They are serene, hopeful, and free. Such people are not bowing to inevitably overpowering nothingness. They are responding to God as incomprehensible mystery.

The mental climate of our times: boundless knowledge. Because knowledge today increases at such a rapid pace we actually know less of what there is to know than our ancestors did. Although we can profit from the knowledge of others (we can use a radio without being able to fix one), no one today can know everything. Today the great problem is how we fool ourselves into thinking we know more than we do.

The fundamental lack of conceptual clarity. All knowledge is interrelated. Therefore, as knowledge becomes increasingly complex the ideas we use (e.g., time, space, substance) become increasingly unclear. It is the price we pay.

The intellectual virtue of patience. In the face of our own ignorance we must be patient with ourselves and others. This is not easy. We must struggle to avoid skeptical relativism and ideological fanaticism as well as complacency.

   –Patience as a way to God. Patience is akin to the Eastern *docta ignorantia*. Experiencing the infinite ocean of nameless mystery surrounding our pitifully small island of knowledge and submerging ourselves in it with courage can be what Christians call surrender to God—the blessed mystery.

   –Patience and tolerance. This new situation also demands genuine tolerance. Those who oppose us are not necessarily ignorant and/or malicious.

–Knowledge and freedom. This new situation increasingly demands that we make absolute practical decisions without absolute theoretical certainty. **In wintry times: Patience.** There is great danger in today's situation which has almost completely uncoupled knowledge and virtue. Summary (49).

23.05   A Basic Theological and Anthropological Understanding of Old Age

Zum theologischen und anthropologischen Grundverständnis des Alters

{0.5}   M. Schmid, W. Kirchschläger, eds., *Nochmals glauben lernen: Sinn und Chancen des Alters; Lebensstationen im 20. Jahrhundert* (Innsbruck 1982) 9-21.

Abstract: The elderly live on the borderline between time and eternity where they have their most sacred task: reshaping their lives and bridging the generations by living life with courageous hope despite their waning powers.

Topics: CHRISTIAN LIFE, old age; ETERNAL LIFE.
Subsidiary Discussions: Freedom (53ff); Conversion (54f).
Precis: A thorough study of old age starting from a review of current literature or from scripture or church tradition would take more time and energy than this 80-year-old theologian has left.

Old age as a historical and social phenomenon. The human process of aging, affecting as it does our essential unity as matter and spirit, defies total analysis even by the natural and social sciences. Although death may have the same physical causes today as in the past, it is always experienced in ever new culturally and individually unique ways.

Old age and the past. In the eyes of the world the old have most of their lives behind them. To Christians the old have most of their lives yet to live. Although through their free choices the old have already become somewhat definitive, their history of freedom is not yet over. This is true even if their faculties and energies are reduced. In any case, the elderly have the opportunity to reshape their past and its meaning through the choices still available to them. They can let go of past injuries and become more tolerant of others. Rahner adds (55f) that in God's eyes serious loss of faculties is accompanied by reduced culpability. God binds no one to impossible standards.

Old age as a bridge between generations. The elderly have the special task of bridging the generations. Rahner describes the "ascesis" of attending difficult meetings, parties, and church functions and trying to participate fully.

Faith in eternal life. The elderly are inescapably close to the border between this life and the next. For the Christian this fact calls forth more than mere resignation. It demands the courage of lively hope in the midst of diminution. It is wrong to "let oneself go" and become unkempt. It is wrong to dwell on one's own aches and pains, inflicting them on others in our conversations.

Faith in eternal life is not an escape, it is a sacred task. Old age demands no less prayer or devotion than any other stage of life. Perhaps it demands more. In the end each person will continue to be spiritual in his/her unique way. Each will become a definitive self and each will meet death in a unique way as well.

23.06 Authority
Autorität
{3.5} *Christlicher Glaube in moderner Gesellschaft*, vol.14 (Freiburg im Breisgau 1982) 5-36.
Abstract: Applying his long, theoretical analysis of authority in society (in particular the relationship between authority and coercive power) to the magisterium, Rahner argues Rome should show much greater self-restraint. It has no legitimate authority to police the faith of its individual members.
Topics: AUTHORITY; SOCIETY; POWER, coercive; MAGISTERIUM and power.
Subsidiary Discussions: Utopias (65f); Word, primordial (69); Church, charism and office in (74); Justice, punitive (75); Church as society (77f); Apostolic succession (78ff); Dogma, development of (80ff); Church and power (82f).
Precis: Authority in general. Etymology offers little insight on this matter.
–Preliminary remarks on conceptual methodology and limitation of the inquiry. An analysis of *auctoritas* yields little useful toward a definition of authority. God's authority over creation is so radically different from human authority that it is a poor starting-point.
–Possible "frictions" among free subjects as a starting-point for a general concept of authority. Human beings are at once free and determined. This manifests itself in society through "friction"—people holding out for their own interests.
–Authority as the mandatory power to regulate "frictions." Since these frictions cannot be eliminated and a permanent state of war is unthinkable, mandatory regulation in the form of authority is established.
–Human freedom presupposes the necessity of social regulations. Rahner limits his investigation to social authority. He dismisses utopian ideologies (65f). As to precisely how such authority is established and what is its legitimate scope, Rahner is content to say it is all temporary and provisional. Given the nature of human beings and human societies justice will always have to be dispensed on a case by case basis. Freedom will always present more than one morally legitimate possibility.
The intrinsic nature of authority.
–The general concept and the concrete manifestation of authority. Rahner maintains his working analysis of authority supplies an adequate definition.
–An attempt to describe briefly the reality of authority. Although it cannot be exhaustively defined (*Urwort*) it is adequate to call it "the morally justified

capacity of a human being to regulate and determine social relations among members of society in a way that is binding on these members" (69). A person in authority always remains a finite human being answerable to God.

–Individual and collective bearers of authority. Presuming the existence of necessary and freely established governments, these of necessity have authority and bearers of authority who remain individual human beings however they may be constituted.

–Basic elements concerning the appointment of bearers of authority. Individual bearers of authority are generally chosen by some kind of pre-existing body with more original authority. However that body is constituted and whatever its mechanism for conveying authority to an individual (it need not be universal suffrage) it is always individuals who bear real authority.

–The theory of delegation and the theory of designation. To Rahner these two scholastic modes of transferring authority amount to the same thing.

–The dignity of authority and the order of precedence among its bearers. The individual with the most authority in society does not necessarily occupy the highest position. That place is reserved to those who contribute most to society realizing its essential nature. Hence, in the church those who are holy rank above those who merely govern. Charism is superior to office.

–The relationship between authority and coercive power. These two concepts are completely separate in theory. Those with authority may lack power (definition, 75). Those with power may lack authority. Nothing about authority precludes its using coercive power (punitive justice).

Summary and conclusions. A dense and not entirely clear reprise of the above.

Authority in the church. The necessity of church authority as a result of the socialization of a common faith. Since the church is by nature a society it necessarily possesses structures of authority. Rahner limits his few disparate, unsystematic observations on this matter to the Catholic Church.

The origin of authority in the church.

–Church authority and the problem of the church's foundation. The Catholic Church holds as dogma that its authority comes not from its members (from below) but from Jesus Christ (from above) to present day office holders through an unbroken apostolic succession. This is a more hotly discussed position today than in the past (79).

–The historical margin of freedom for shaping official church office and its authority. Structures of authority in the church can be both *juris divini* and subject to historical development. A free historical development (one that cannot be simply deduced from prior conditions) can become irreformable.

On the relationship of authority and coercive power in the church. Because "the concrete exercise of authority always implies a change in the freedom possessed by a member of this society prior to his or her consent" (82) church authority includes coercive power. The question is whether the church has exercised more such power than it was legitimately authorized to use. Clearly this was so in former times. Given the church's self-understanding today any attempt to exercise such coercive power again would be either a sad holdover from former times or simply illegitimate. Rahner concludes, "the church should nowhere respond to a conflict between itself and one of its members with civil and material consequences" (83).

Teaching authority in the church. Rahner limits the nature of the authority of the magisterium (whose authority is always derived from the truth of revelation in Christ) to bear witness to the truth. As a consequence the Church "is not in a position to supervise the conformity of the individual's specific faith with the Church's doctrine" (85). At most it can give negative certification, a *nihil obstat*, that nothing in one's views is contrary to the universal faith of the church.

23.07   The Situation of the Society of Jesus Since its Difficulties with the Vatican

Zur Situation des Jesuitenordens nach den Schwierigkeiten mit dem Vatikan

{0.5} April 1982 lecture in Freising at a symposium of the South German Province of the Society of Jesus.

Abstract: This blunt criticism of papal delegate Fr. Dezza's instructions to Jesuits concludes that in the advancement of justice, obedience to legitimate hierarchical authority cannot simply be blind nor can it be the sole norm.

Topics: RELIGIOUS LIFE, evangelical counsels (obedience); SOCIETY OF JESUS; MAGISTERIUM.

Subsidiary Discussions: Society, modern era (92f); Church, charism and office in (92ff); Assent (94f); Dogma, formula (97); Error (97ff); Theology, task of (100f); Vatican II (101f); Faith and justice (102ff); Love of God/neighbor (102ff).

Precis: The following remarks in three parts are not comprehensive or systematic. They are respectful but honest and do not pretend to answer all the outstanding questions concerning Jesuits and church teaching authority.

The conditions of our times as a cause of the difficulties of the Society of Jesus. The Jesuits' current difficulties in the church mirror the radical, momentous changes taking place in society as a whole (list, 92f). This should be no surprise. Remedies must be part of a more universal analysis of the times. Good answers cannot be found in a naive return to past practices. Ignatius' Constitutions require as much modern interpretation as scripture.

–Obedience. The phrase in the Jesuit Constitution, "total obedience to the Holy See" needs careful interpretation. For example, obedience can never override conscience nor can it require us to sin.

–The notion of church. Rahner finds Rome's notion of church "false from a dogmatic, human, and realistic standpoint" (93). Valid initiatives do not need to originate in Rome. There can and must be a plurality of theologies. Rome has made many errors in the past (list, 94). The obedience owed to the church is not submission to ecclesiastical totalitarianism.

The Jesuit Order and the teaching office.

Magisterial teachings deserve respect in proportion to the degree of truth they contain. Many past statements have been false (list, 95). Catholics in general and Jesuits in particular must make a serious effort to evaluate positively and to appropriate even a provisional doctrinal statement. Nevertheless, they can and must dissent from such teachings when they contain error. Anything less is dishonesty and they would be discredited.

On the theology of the Jesuits. 1) Fr. Dezza's paper is too imprecise, 2) too simplistic, and 3) too one-sided to be any real help to theologians. If implemented it would mean the death of theology. He gives examples of past errors which needed vigorous refutation (98). One can never promise "complete agreement" with error. 4) Although not all theological speculation is appropriate for all the faithful, Dezza never makes clear where theologians can voice dissent. 5) Dezza's instructions lack a fully realistic understanding of the task of theology. He makes it seems as if magisterial statements were free from theological speculation when in fact they are based on it. 6) Fr. Dezza confuses the authority of encyclical letters with solemn definitions. 7) Dezza needs to confer with serious theologians before promulgating his instructions. 8) How can the pope encourage Jesuits to uphold Vatican II *and* at the same time pledge allegiance to this style of obedience? They seem incompatible.

The apostolate of the Society of Jesus.

–Faith and justice. Like love of God and neighbor, serving faith by advancing justice can neither be divorced nor merely conflated. Although the actual practice will look different in different locales, excesses should always be avoided. The "faith" being advanced is not merely Roman teaching but the absolute totality of Christian life.

–An order of priests. No one can do everything. Each institution in society has its proper function. Jesuits are primarily an order of priests. This limit is appropriate. But there can be cases which legitimately call for or even demand a fuller scope of action (e.g., direct political action). Serving the church in "accordance with the directives of the local hierarchy" is important (105). But it cannot be the sole principle governing the apostolate. Nor can blind obedience be the sole norm for advancing justice.

23.08 Dimensions of Martyrdom

Dimensionen des Martyriums

{0.5} *Concilium* 18 (1983) 174-176.

Abstract: Expanding the category of martyr to include both those who passively endure death for their faith and those who meet death with active resistance (e.g., Oscar Romero) might encourage others to struggle for peace and justice.

Topics: CHRISTIAN LIFE, martyrdom; SAINTS, martyrs.

Subsidiary Discussions: Jesus Christ, death of (110f); Aquinas on mysticism (111f).

Precis: Traditionally the category of martyr was reserved for those who freely endured death for the sake of their faith or some element of their faith. It did not include those who died in active combat. By including fallen fighters the church could strongly recommend their imitation. Rahner argues the historical concept "martyr" is theoretically open for expansion. Though the two ways of accepting death really differ, they have essential similarities. Jesus' own death was not completely passive. His life and death cannot be separated. He was condemned to death *because* he fought. Clearly not everyone who dies in the struggle against injustice is de facto a martyr. But some could be (e.g., Oscar Romero). In addition, the ways in which they "professed" their faith can differ greatly from the proto-martyrs (e.g., Maximilian Kolbe). In the end the differences between these two ways of dying are too subtle and their similarities too great to keep them forever separate (summary, 111). Finally, Aquinas' theology would seem to find this grouping congenial and it could inspire others to commit themselves to work more courageously for peace and justice.

23.09   Eucharistic Worship
Eucharistiche Anbetung
{0.5}   *Geist und Leben* 54 (1981) 188-191.

Abstract: A plea to continue private devotion before the Blessed Sacrament.

Topics: EUCHARIST, devotion to; CHRISTIAN LIFE, piety.

Subsidiary Discussions: God, presence of (114ff).

Precis: Because there is a real history of Christian piety, long-discarded elements can someday enjoy new life. Like the church itself, devotions change while retaining their ancient nature. This is especially true of Eucharistic devotions. Many such devotions have waned in recent years. Some should perish irretrievably. Others perhaps not. Rahner pleads for retaining the practice of private prayer in church before the reserved sacrament. Those who know best that God is everywhere and can be worshiped everywhere appreciate most deeply God's special and unsurpassable nearness to us in the tabernacle. It is not necessary for one to be false for the other to be true.

23.10   Devotion to the Sacred Heart Today
Herz-Jesu-Verehrung heute
{0.5}   *Korrespondenzblatt des Canisianums* 116 (1/1982/83) 2-8.

Abstract: Despite its current state of crisis, Rahner argues Sacred Heart devotion retains a special meaning for modern times and should be promoted.
Topics: JESUS CHRIST, Sacred Heart of; CHRISTIAN LIFE, piety.
Subsidiary Discussions: Church, change in (117ff); Law, divine (120f); God, salvific will of (123ff); Hope for universal salvation (123ff); Truths, hierarchy of (126); Word, primordial (126); Heart (126f).
Precis: The church is subject to change. Because the church and its piety have a real history particular devotions wax and wane. In our dark times some may find devotion to the Sacred Heart bland, individualistic, and introspective.

The church needs people with mystical-charismatic experience. Rahner is convinced Sacred Heart Devotion can and must play an important role in the church universal. Though this role may be limited to a humble and unselfish elite of saints, it should contain as many priests as possible. It will retain its distinctive character even if it is realized in a very new style. Rahner recommends devotion to the Sacred Heart on two counts: from the history of theology and from the new historical situation in which the church exists today.

The church—a unity that keeps its identity in history. The church has a real history. Although its form changes in surprising ways it always remains itself. Some of its historical developments in fact become irreversible. "The church always brings her history with her into the present and in this way carries it on" (121). Rahner cites numerous examples (121f). He ends with a summary.

The devotion to the Sacred Heart belongs to the worship of the church. Despite historical foreshadowing, devotion to the Sacred Heart is essentially modern. After so great a flourishing it should not simply be forgotten. Just because we *can* forget it does not mean we *should*. We have a responsibility to continue the church's history. The future might never forgive our laziness.

The church harbors a universal hope for all humanity. The church has been deeply affected by Enlightenment optimism. Today, instead of insisting on God's righteous condemnation the church proclaims its hope for the salvation of all. Having faced the limits of progress in many areas (list, 124f) humanity is losing its naive optimism. In this seemingly dark abyss Christ shines even more brilliantly as the true hope of the world. This hope is not a narcotic. It is the modern form of the folly of the cross—hope against all hope. Such demanding hope fills us with courage and determination.

The heart as the innermost center. How is devotion to the Sacred Heart connected to this frightfully new world situation? In the welter of religious truths there is a hierarchy made up of certain fundamental words (*Urworte*).

"Heart" is one such word. It refers to the mystery of God. Those who find this a mere verbal duplication of "Jesus Christ" have not yet launched out into the depth of Mystery or sensed the immensity of God's mercy revealed in the heart of Christ. Rahner closes this essay in prayer (128).

23.11 Courage for Devotion to Mary

Mut zur Marienverehrung
{1.0}   *Geist und Leben* 56 (1983) 163-173.

Abstract: Rahner encourages veneration of Mary and the saints who show us that God's salvation actually comes near us in our historical particularity.

Topics: BVM, devotion to; CHRISTIAN LIFE, piety; SAINTS, veneration of.

Subsidiary Discussions: Saints, communion of (131ff); Women, equality of (136f).

Precis: Despite official pronouncements and the great fervor of the past, devotion to Mary has clearly waned since Vatican II. This should be revisited.

An anthropological approach. We should not disparage the human motivation which undoubtedly influenced the traditional cult of Mary in the past.

Christian roots of the veneration of Mary.

–Solidarity with the deceased. Do we really believe in the "communion of saints"—our living solidarity with those embraced by God's love after death?

–Living relation to the deceased. Today it is hard not to think of the dead as completely swallowed up in the incomprehensibility of God. But the church teaches union with God completes us. It does not annihilate us.

–Veneration of the saints. The communion of saints shows that salvation, our consummation in God, actually has and does come near us. Veneration of saints tells us something about the history of God's self-donation through which God actually becomes the innermost dynamism of our life. If it is possible to find and venerate such holy people, how much more true is this of Mary?

Mary's importance in the history of salvation. Each saint achieved salvation in his/her unique way. Mary is unique in her humility and sovereign freedom. "She is not grace, she is not the one mediator, but she is the free acceptance of grace and of the one mediator, that in the history of salvation occurred once for all of us" (135). It is unimportant whether or not her role is described as co-mediatrix.

About the equality of men and women. Modern anthropology forces us to reconsider thoroughly the role of the "maleness" of the savior, and to extend to all women the dignity the church has historically attributed to Mary and her role in salvation.

Veneration of the saints and veneration of Mary on the basis of final salvation in God. Summary (137). We see God come near us in the glory of the saints (especially Mary) who even in death retain their unique history of grace.

Concrete veneration of Mary. Not everyone has the charism to venerate Mary or the saints. In some it is only present as good will. One must not judge those who are suspicious of some dimensions of Marian devotion. Rahner suggests it is better to remain open than aloof. Each individual will concretize the church's veneration of Mary in his/her own style. The church has honored Mary in many different ways throughout its past, most recently under the title "Mother of the Church," and will continue to do so.

23.12 Understanding Christmas

Zum Verständnis des Weihnachtsfestes

{0.5}   Forward to K. Gröning, "*Fürchtet euch nicht": Das Weihnachtsgeschehen in Zeugnissen der abendländischen Kultur* (Munich 1983) 11-19. Largely derived from K. Rahner, *Die Gabe der Weihnacht* (Freiburg i Br., 1980) and *Gott ist Mensch geworden* (Freiburg i Br., 1975).

Abstract: Christmas marks the dawn of the redemptive life, death, and resurrection of Jesus—the divine answer to the question of our life's meaning.

Topics: LITURGICAL YEAR, Christmas; SALVATION; CHRISTOLOGY, incarnation.

Subsidiary Discussions: Death (140f); God, incomprehensibility of (141); Meaning, historical (142f); Creed "Word became flesh" (144f).

Precis: The message of faith. To understand Christmas we must remember it celebrates the birth of a man who died and rose from the dead. This feast marks the beginning of his redemptive death—his total loving surrender to the incomprehensible God in complete obedience.

The central difficulty. Two factors make it difficult for people today to celebrate Christmas: its remoteness in time and its contingent historicity.

Remoteness in time. The strain people feel today in trying to grasp the meaning of Jesus' birth stems in large part from their tenuous grasp and appreciation of history.

A single event in history with a universal significance? For the past three hundred years theologians have been struggling with how a contingent historical event can have irreversible universal importance.

The descent of the Word of God into the world. Rahner begins his analysis with the central christological claim: "the Word was made flesh." God not only created the world, God also entered the world. His coming was prepared by a pre-history all during which time the Spirit moved as the innermost dynamism of the world.

Jesus, the beginning of the realization of all human hope. Christmas is the point where the human question and the divine answer to the question of meaning are given in the saving life, death, and resurrection of the historical Jesus. Christmas is the dawn of the eternal meaning of life. In Jesus divine intimacy and divine incomprehensibility are united.

The child—born like us. Like us, like any newborn, the child in the manger finds himself thrown into an existing world too late to protest. But unlike us this child experiences his existence not as thrownness but as the effect of love. This fundamental act of this child accompanies him to the cross.

Accepting our existence. It remains an open question whether we whole-heartedly accept our existence this way in all its dimensions. It is easier to think of God being everywhere than being in a particular, narrow place like we are.

Saved and liberated by the child. This child wants to and perhaps will save us from our desperate flight from ourselves—unbidden. Perhaps even in spite of ourselves.

God is near us. Rahner concludes with a very poetic invitation to journey into the "innermost unreachable chamber in our heart" (148) because there we will find the word has become flesh, and God is near.

23.13   The Theology of the Religious Meaning of Images
Zur Theologie der religiösen Bedeutung des Bildes
{1.0}   November 1983 lecture in Munich. *German Society for Christian Art*, (5/1983) 2-8.

Abstract: Because all human concepts are necessarily accompanied by sense experience, and because the five senses are incommensurable and irreplaceable, art plays a unique and legitimate role in religious knowledge.

Topics: EXPERIENCE, sense; ARTS, visual.

Subsidiary Discussions: Knowledge (149f); Resurrection of the body (151f); Knowledge, *vorgriff* (158); Transcendence (158f); Icons, veneration of (160f).

Precis: Christian anthropology. Ordinary Catholic anthropology is convinced that all conceptual knowledge, even spiritual knowledge, is necessarily reached by an intuition that depends on sensory, historical experience.

Religious experience—sense intuition. Even so, knowledge of God is possible. However abstract the concepts we use to understand God may become, they remain essentially tied to sensory experience.

Religious activities involve the body, refer to the nameless God. The doctrine of the resurrection of the flesh insists the body and its sensory way of knowing are not simply provisional.

Sense powers—a complex reality. Senses are an irreducibly complex reality.

Incommensurable plurality of sense experience. The five senses share an incommensurable pluralism. Human beings perform best when all of our senses are fully engaged.

The eyes of faith—the eternal logos as God's eternal image. Although the ears which hear God's word have a place of honor they cannot replace other sense organs. We also speak of the "eyes of faith" and the "beatific vision."

Why religious images are important in Christianity. Despite some iconoclastic impulses, Christianity generally accepts religious images. The East sees them participating in the divine; the West sees them as the poor man's bible.

Our own starting-point. With a nod to the long history of writing on this topic Rahner offers his own starting-point.

Theology of religious seeing. Images have their proper religious significance that cannot be replaced by the word. Word can never substitute for image (or movement, aroma, taste, or touch) in the fundamental religious act.

Reaching God with the earth. To know how the senses work we must use them. Artists must use images, not words! Art justifies itself in the doing.

Events of salvation history must also be contemplated. Just as a portrait conveys something a biography cannot convey, images convey something about the events of salvation history which words cannot express.

Viewing a properly religious phenomenon. A reality is religious only when it helps refer us directly to the absolute God. This happens only through grace.

Religious image—its mediating function to the absolute God. Peak experiences of any sense domain may be the basis of a religious act. Because every act of the senses takes place against an infinite backdrop, any act of sensing particular things has the potential to reveal transcendence.

Seeing too implies a sensory experience of transcendence. This transcendental pre-apprehension is possible in every act of seeing.

Religious images without immediate religious themes. Even reflection on non-religious images can achieve this transcendent effect, just as any moral act (it need not be overtly religious) can be conducive to salvation.

Images that point to salvation history. This does not deny the need for and the legitimacy of explicitly religious art (crucifixes, statues, etc.).

Image and word have complementary functions. Images do not do away with the need for commentary. The two complement one another.

The collective function of the cultic image. Icons, cultic images in the strict sense, are venerated with official approbation. How can this be justified? These images are venerated for their shared, lasting religious meaning, and for the way they function in the community. One need not insist that icons are only venerated for the reality they represent.

23.14   Art Against the Horizon of Theology and Piety
Die Kunst im Horizont von Theologie und Frömmigkeit
{1.0}   *Entschluß* 37 (1/1982) 4-7, as, *Nicht jeder Künstler ist ein Heiliger: Zur Theologie der Kunst.*

Abstract: Good theology expresses one's personal relationship with God. Insofar as any wordless art form (music, sculpture, architecture) concentrates one's whole being on questions of ultimate meaning it too is theological.

Topics: ARTS, visual; THEOLOGY and art.

Subsidiary Discussions: Mystagogy (163f); Symbol (164f); Being, analogy of (164f).

Precis: Are the wordless arts (music, architecture, sculpture, etc.) inferior to arts which employ words? No. They too are irreducible, autonomous modes of human expression.

Art—active element of theology. What is the precise relationship between these wordless arts and theology? If theology is thought of as the total human self-expression insofar as it is backed up by God's self-communication, then these wordless arts are a constituent element of theology. To reduce theology to words impoverishes both theology and the arts.

A road to the original experience. Word-dependent art is theological to the extent it recalls people to their own original religious experience. Today we lack such poetic theology. Perhaps future theology will be more mystagogical, i.e., it will direct people beyond concepts to their own religious experience.

Difficulty of a new symbolization. The analogy of being enables poets to use concrete words, even if they are not explicitly religious, to help us understand a certain human experience as mysteriously pointing to God. In this sense the whole of Christian theology should be "subjective," i.e., it should speak of faith, hope, and love—our personal relationship to God. When theology fails to do this and it becomes "objective" it becomes bad theology.

The eternal in historical peculiarity. Art and theology exist only because analogy opens to transcendentality. Artists announce what is eternal concretely and historically.

The whole person listens. Eyes and ears cannot see or hear God. But when the eyes and ears focus the attention of the whole person this can lead to a powerful religious experience. Art is not theological because of its subject matter. It is theological because it has the power to bring us to complete attention in such a way that we encounter questions of ultimate meaning.

Being holy and human. Cretans in the realm of art can be exceptionally holy. Gifted artists can be scoundrels. Rahner poses but leaves unanswered the question of the relationship between artistic talent and holiness.

23.15 Against the Witch Hysteria
Wider Hexenwahn
{0.5}   *Geist und Leben* 56 (1983) 284-291.

Abstract: Friedrich Spee, S.J. (1591-1635) is worthy of emulation by both gifted and ordinary people. He was not only the courageous author of the *Cautio criminalis* and the tender author of poetry, he was an ordinary priest active in schools, jails, village pulpits, and chairs of theology.

Topics: CHRISTIAN LIFE, holiness; SAINTS; SOCIETY OF JESUS.

Subsidiary Discussions: Love of God/neighbor (172); Religious life, obedience, (174ff); Conscience (174ff).

Precis: What can Friedrich Spee tell us today? Rahner is reassured because modern Jesuit life is not so different from Spee's outer life 300 years ago.

Imitating the crucified one: dying in order to live. Like any good Jesuit, Spee's inner life also conformed to the crucified Christ. His sufferings were occasioned both by the outward rigors of Jesuit religious life and by the chaos of his times. His life forces us to ask how brave and hopeful we are.

A fearless fighter against the inhumanity of his time. Many people today find Spee's poetry insufferably saccharine. But is the strangeness we find in it not perhaps a product of our own lukewarm piety? After all Spee's devotion continually showed itself in actions more courageous than our own.

Out of an unconditional, worshipful love of God. Spee's poetry forces us to ask ourselves how wholeheartedly we love God. Since clearly Spee's love of God supported his courageous love of neighbor we cannot simply shrug off as "baroque" the rapturous love of God he extols in his poetry.

Mass hysteria—formerly, yesterday, and today. Spee's *Cautio criminalis*, a courageous rebuke to the mass hysteria of witch hunts in his day, deserves to be reread. Do we confront the mass hysteria of our age as courageously? How do we treat today's prophetic voices? Too often the institutional church defends only that which is already generally accepted. Perhaps we need a new *Cautio*.

Between the voice of conscience and religious obedience. The degree to which Spee acted against the will of his superiors in writing and publishing the *Cautio* remains an open question. But if he obeyed the dictates of his conscience he remained a good and loyal Jesuit even if his actions contradicted the conscience of his legitimate religious superiors. In any case his untimely death of plague kept the issue from ever being fully aired.

Example for both high and low. Spee's life can inspire both the highly gifted and mundane laborers in the vineyard. Spee found greatness in the ordinariness of his life and ministry.

A saint? Like many others, Spee is worthy of emulation even if he has never been officially declared holy by the church.

23.16   Faith and Sacrament
Glaube und Sakrament

{3.5}   H. J. Auf der Mauer, et al., eds., *Fides Sacramenti: Sacramentum Fidei.* Festschrift for P. Smulders (Assen 1981) 245-252, as, *Kleine theologische Reflexion über die gegenseitige Beziehung von Glaube und Sakrament.*

Abstract: Christianity wants to be both universal and sacramental/historical. But the universal availability of saving faith seems to divorce it from sacrament. Rahner solves this dilemma with his supernatural existential to which he adds the historical unity of revelation which is necessarily categorial.

Topics: FAITH, universality of; SACRAMENTS; REVELATION and historical development; SALVATION, universal.

Subsidiary Discussions: Baptism (181f); Word as sacrament (182f); Vatican II (183f); Supernatural existential (184); Transcendent/categorial (185f); Revelation, original (186); Jesus Christ, summit of freedom (187); Mysteries (188).

Precis: The relationship between faith and sacraments is unclear. For example, the church teaches baptism is needed for salvation *and* salvation is available through faith alone. This seems to make the sacraments secondary. But faith is itself sacramental. God's self-revealing word is not a word about God. It is God whose self-donation accomplishes faith in us. The sacraments are not additions to this sacramental word of faith. They are peak moments in the realization of this faith. This is the sacramental character of faith in light of which the other sacraments are made intelligible.

Faith and revelation. The salvation of pagans makes it more difficult to understand the relationship of faith and sacrament. For Rahner salvation is possible through the supernatural gift of faith even for those who have never been baptized or heard of Jesus. Although Rahner's "supernatural existential" (definition, 184) can be deduced transcendentally in such a way that faith remains a divine gift, he admits his explanation seems to reduce the historical and fully sacramental character of both faith and revelation.

History and grace. Universality and sacramentality seem difficult to reconcile. The big problem is not that faith exists apart from explicit sacraments. The problem is how this universal faith possesses an incarnational character which refers it to the church. Rahner asks whether universal grace becomes sacramental, incarnational, and historical simply through the fact that human beings always and only express their transcendence (spirit and freedom) categorially. Before answering this question he adds a note on how to understand primordial revelation and the first human beings (186).

Grace and revelation. Solving this problem means admitting two things: grace is always transmitted through historical concreteness; the grace of revelation is always historical revelation. History and history of revelation are not identical, but revelation always takes place in history. Potentially, revelation can occur anywhere in human life. In fact it occurs only where the voice of moral conscience is heard. This is the transcendental proffer of grace, the self-realization of God which constitutes the historical revelation of God despite its seemingly "natural" character. Because human history is a unity, every moment in the human history of freedom is objectively referred to its totality, its summit: Jesus Christ. In addition, whenever we make an absolute, free commitment we tacitly accept the unexpressed implications behind that free decision: Christ. Summary (187f).

Any solution beyond this (which Rahner insists is sufficient and necessary) ends in a dilemma: either too many people are excluded from the possibility of salvation, or salvation becomes possible apart from Christ. Rahner concludes by maintaining his approach is also able to explain and safeguard the unity of the mystery of faith.

23.17　Questions on the Theology of Sacraments

Fragen der Sakramententheologie

{1.0}　*Entschluß* 38 (11/1983) 6, 8-9, as, *Das endgültige und siegreiche Zusagewort für die Welt.*

Abstract: This essay situates sacraments among other human signs which effect what they signify. It also considers the sense in which they are "instituted by Christ" and how their legitimate celebration changes over time.

Topics: SACRAMENTS, efficacy of.

Subsidiary Discussions: Church as founded by Christ (189ff); Symbol (189f); Sacraments instituted by Christ (190f); Church as *sacramentum salutis mundi* (191f); Sacraments, *opus operatum* (192ff).

Precis: Sacraments belong to the larger group of human signs which bring about what they signify (e.g., a slap in the face).

Expression and effect. The church has solemnly identified seven gestures which it calls official sacraments.

Deriving from Jesus. Each sacrament blends words and actions to produce its effect. The church maintains all sacraments exist in virtue of the authority of Jesus, even though some are not explicitly mentioned in scripture. Not only can the sacraments be traced back to Jesus in different ways, they can all be traced back to him insofar as his action is sacramental: Jesus is God's definitive and irreversible pledge of himself to the world, the sign of God's gift whereby that which the sign intends is irrevocably given to the world.

The permanent acceptance. The church is the human community which accepts and keeps alive this pledge God made to the world in Jesus. As such it is the sacrament of salvation for the world. When the church utters itself at specific points in history the sacraments appear. These are unfailingly effective for those who receive them in faith. Their irrevocable significance is indicated by the term *opus operatum*.

History is not finished. The sacraments have had a long history of legitimate change. They will continue to change in new and unexpected ways. It is even possible the church today may be conferring sacraments without yet being consciously aware of doing so (e.g., the commissioning of pastoral ministers may in fact be a new division of holy orders the church does not yet recognize).

A greater latitude. Sacraments remain ineffective unless their reception is accompanied with the appropriate faith of the recipient. Proper disposition is needed for true and faithful reception. Rahner ends with an inconclusive note on the relationship between confession of sin and reception of Eucharist.

23.18 Baptism and the Renewal of Baptism
Taufe und Tauferneuerung
{1.0}   *Entschluß* 37 (9/10/1982) 6-11, as, *Das göttliche Feuer in sich lebendig halten.*

Abstract: Baptism retains its value and effect even if salvation is available without baptism or visible incorporation in the church. Rahner also examines sacramental causality, infant baptism, and frequent renewal of baptismal vows.

Topics: BAPTISM.

Subsidiary Discussions: Mission mandate (195f); Symbol (196); God, self-donation (196f); Causality, sacramental (198ff); Baptism of infants (200f); Baptism, renewal of (202ff).

Precis: A complete theology of baptism would demand a complete analysis of Christianity. This essay simply asks why baptism even exists if salvation is available to heathens and atheists who follow the dictates of conscience.

Disposition and gesture. In human beings disposition and gesture form a unity. An external gesture can often produce or intensify one's inner experience.

Irrevocable offer. God loves each individual from the first moment of existence. God is each person's inner strength, dynamism, and final goal. Though we remain free to accept or reject this offer, the offer itself can never be withdrawn. This reality is essentially Christian whether one knows it or not. The proper external response to this offer is baptism and incorporation in the church. Yet whoever responds even implicitly to this offer is justified.

Body of grace. Those who understand clearly what God's self-offer invites by way of baptism and explicit incorporation but refuse it are culpable. The individual who sees the legitimacy of God's invitation cannot ignore or refuse the particular concrete way it is expressed in the church. What causality is operative in baptism? How are we to understand the practice of infant baptism?

Action of God himself. It is not enough to portray baptism as the disclosure of a reality that is already given without it. Baptism also effects something. Using the model of adult baptism Rahner shows how the fruitful reception of baptism depends on the prior existence of faith, hope, and love in the adult. Since other theological explanations of how graces are "intensified" in baptism seem to Rahner artificial, he suggests employing the notion of gesture and disposition. Hence, baptism as the sign of grace is the cause of grace.

The baptism of children. Why is the baptism of children meaningful? Insofar as God's self-offer and invitation always precede our response, parents gain nothing in waiting to baptize their children until they are of age to decide for themselves. Infant baptism is never an insult to justice or freedom. Those who say the incorporation into the visible church which attends infant baptism unfairly limits the child's future freedom have not noticed the church's decree on religious liberty and freedom of conscience that holds both inside and outside the church. Baptism "is not an anticipation of a decision that depends only on human freedom" (201). Finally, regardless of the age at which we were baptized, the ultimate and decisive acceptance of baptism in personal freedom takes place throughout the length and breadth of our lives.

Renewal of baptism. Because the whole of Christian life is a deepening of the invitation accepted initially at baptism, Rahner encourages frequent even daily renewal of our baptismal vows to reject the lure of evil and to remain in the grace of solidarity with the church.

23.19   The Status of the Sacrament of Reconciliation
Zur Situation des Bußsakramentes
{1.0}   *Entschluß* 35 (9/10/1980) 4-12, as, *Warum man Trotzdem beichten soll.*

Abstract: Rahner is "optimistic" about the decline in confession if it results from the penitent's greater appreciation of the subjective element in serious sin. He ends with suggestions for strengthening "confessions of devotion."
Topics: PENANCE, sacrament of; SIN, serious; SIN and forgiveness; SYMBOL.
Subsidiary Discussions: God, salvific will of (208f); Hylomorphism, embodiment (214f); Sin, social (215f).
Precis: It is unclear whether the modern decline in the practice of sacramental confession is a healthy or an unhealthy development.

Confession and serious sin. Divine law only obliges us to confess objectively and subjectively serious sins promptly (within a year) privately to a priest.

Subjectively and objectively grave sin. In the past the church emphasized the objective gravity of sin. Today there is a deeper appreciation on the part of the faithful for subjective gravity. People today are more skeptical about the possibility of committing objectively *and* subjectively serious sin. They are more optimistic about the wideness of God's mercy.

Decrease in the frequency of confession. Rahner attributes the decline in confessions to the actual decline in what people rightly consider their need to confess according to divine law. Along with the church they see no need to confess sins that are not subjectively grave.

Confession—not put off until death. There are, however, many good things which are not commanded by divine law. One such thing is the practice of confessing even those sins which are not objectively *and* subjectively serious. If confession were once again reserved for serious sin Rahner envisions a return of the practice of deathbed confessions. The following considerations make frequent confessions of devotion more meaningful.

Sacramental and existentiell forgiveness. It is not immediately obvious why Christians find added confidence in the remission of their sins when they receive sacramental absolution. For Rahner this added assurance arises from our human nature in which inner and outer penetrate and intensify one another.

Sacramental activity as embodiment. Our innermost religious experiences tend spontaneously to embody themselves in degrees. Sacramental reconciliation expresses and intensifies our inner attitude of repentance. Inner and outer are mutually related. Penance expresses and induces feelings of repentance.

Social dimension of sin and forgiveness. Sacramental reconciliation underscores the public, social nature of sin and forgiveness. Reconciliation is always to some degree reconciliation with the church. Good Christians should use the many opportunities available to them (including sacramental reconciliation) to review their lives often and turn to God for forgiveness.

Frequency of confession. The recommended frequency of sacramental confession depends greatly on the individual and the events of his/her life. Without the proper inner attitude there is absolutely no value in the simple repetition of absolutions. To optimize its value those who choose frequent confessions of devotion should look for a confessor/spiritual director. Although advice giving can accompany the sacramental encounter between priest and penitent, extremes should be avoided: confession is not the time for psychotherapy. But neither should the priest be turned into an absolution dispensing machine.

INDEX of TOPICS

PROPER NAMES

SUBJECTS

INDEX of
SUBSIDIARY
DISCUSSIONS

Marquette Studies in Theology
Andrew Tallon, editor

Frederick M. Bliss. *Understanding Reception*

Martin Albl, Paul Eddy, and Rene Mirkes, OSF, editors. *Directions in New Testament Methods*

Robert M. Doran. *Subject and Psyche*

Kenneth Hagen, editor. *The Bible in the Churches. How Various Christians Interpret the Scriptures*

Jamie T. Phelps, O.P., editor. *Black and Catholic: The Challenge and Gift of Black Folk. Contributions of African American Experience and Thought to Catholic Theology*

Karl Rahner. *Spirit in the World.* CD

Karl Rahner. *Hearer of the Word.* CD

Robert M. Doran. *Theological Foundations. Vol. 1 Intentionality and Psyche*

Robert M. Doran. *Theological Foundations. Vol. 2 Theology and Culture.*

Patrick W. Carey. *Orestes A. Brownson: A Bibliography, 1826-1876*

Patrick W. Carey, editor. *The Early Works of Orestes A. Brownson.* Volume I: *The Universalist Years, 1826-29*

Patrick W. Carey, editor. *The Early Works of Orestes A. Brownson.* Volume II: *The Free and Unitarian Years, 1830-35*

Patrick W. Carey, editor. *The Early Works of Orestes A. Brownson.* Volume III: *The Transendentalist Years, 1836-38*

John Martinetti, S.J. *Reason to Believe Today*

George H. Tavard. *Trina Deitas: The Controversy between Hincmar and Gottschalk*

Jeanne Cover, IBVM. *Love: The Driving Force. Mary Ward's Spirituality. Its Significance for Moral Theology*

David A. Boileau, editor. *Principles of Catholic Social Teaching*

Michael Purcell. *Mystery and Method: The Other in Rahner and Levinas*

W.W. Meissner, S.J., M.D. *To the Greater Glory: A Psychological Study of Ignatian Spirituality*

Virginia M. Shaddy, editor. *Catholic Theology in the University: Source of Wholeness*

Thomas M. Bredohl. *Class and Religious Identity: The Rhenish Center Party in Wilhelmine Germany*

William M. Thompson and David L. Morse, editors. *Voegelin's **Israel and Revelation**: An Interdisciplinary Debate and Anthology*

Donald L. Gelpi, S.J. *The Firstborn of Many: A Christology for Converting Christians.* Volume 1: *To Hope in Jesus Christ*

Donald L. Gelpi, S.J. *The Firstborn of Many: A Christology for Converting Christians.* Volume 2: *Synoptic Narrative Christology*

Donald L. Gelpi, S.J. *The Firstborn of Many: A Christology for Converting Christians.* Volume 3: *Doctrinal and Practical Christology*

Stephen A. Werner. *Prophet of the Christian Social Manifesto. Joseph Husslein, S.J.: His Life, Work, & Social Thought*

Gregory Sobolewski. *Martin Luther: Roman Catholic Prophet*

Matthew C. Ogilvie. *Faith Seeking Understanding: The Functional Specialty, "Systematics" in Bernard Lonergan's* **Method in Theology**

Timothy Maschke, Franz Posset, and Joan Skocir, editors. *Ad fontes Lutheri: Toward the Recovery of the Real Luther: Essays in Honor of Kenneth Hagen's Sixty-Fifth Birthday*

William Thorn, Phillip Runkel, and Susan Mountin, editors. *Dorothy Day and The Catholic Worker Movement: Centenary Esssays*